MACRO SECOND EDITION

ECONOMICS

ADDISON-WESLEY PUBLISHING COMPANY

**Reading, Massachusetts · Menlo Park, California · New York
Don Mills, Ontario · Wokingham, England · Amsterdam · Bonn
Sydney · Singapore · Tokyo · Madrid · Bogotá · Santiago · San Juan**

MACRO ECONOMICS

SECOND EDITION

ALLEN R. THOMPSON
UNIVERSITY OF NEW HAMPSHIRE

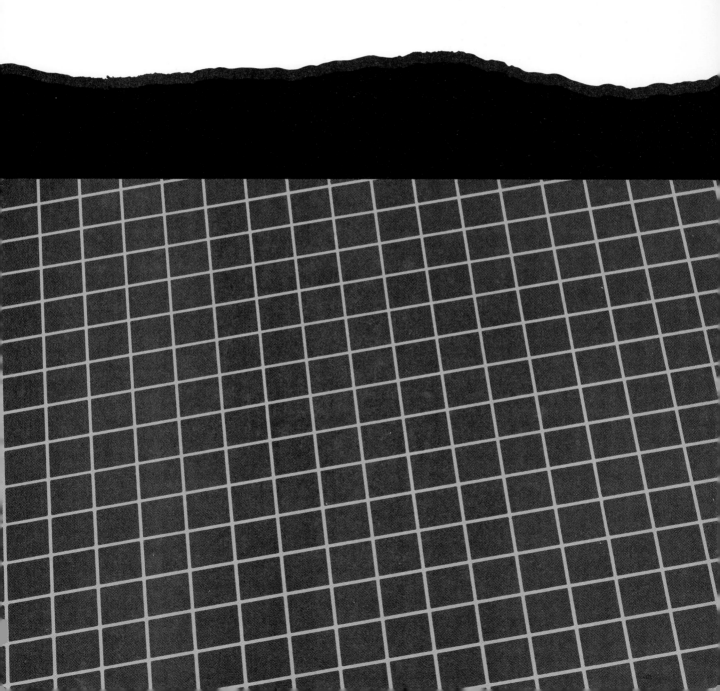

Sponsoring Editor:	Stephen Mautner
Developmental Editor:	Linda J. Bedell
Production Management:	Sherry Berg
Production Supervisor:	Nancy Behler
Copy Editor:	Jerrold A. Moore
Art Director:	Marshall Henrichs
Art Development:	Dick Morton; Meredith Nightingale
Text Design:	Margaret Ong Tsao
Layout Artist:	Lorraine Hodsdon
Illustrators:	Long Associates; George Nichols
Manufacturing Supervisor:	Roy Logan

Reprinted with corrections, May 1988

Library of Congress Cataloging-in-Publication Data

Thompson, Allen R.
  Macroeconomics.

  Includes index.
  1. Macroeconomics.   I. Title.
HB172.5.T48   1988   339   87-916
ISBN 0-201-09684-6

BCDEFGHIJ-RN-898

P R E F A C E

Although only a few beginning students go on to become professional economists, everyone faces situations in which economic reasoning is very important. For example, economic reasoning can help you identify the benefits and costs of choosing between taking a job immediately after graduation or continuing your education. Businesses rely on economic reasoning in deciding whether to build a new plant or produce a new product. And, as citizens, we make political choices that are based in part on economic policies proposed by politicians. An understanding of economics can help you make more informed choices.

The aim of this textbook is to teach you economic reasoning. But even a casual reading of the newspapers reveals wide disagreements among professional economists. You may ask yourself, "How can I learn to use economic reasoning when economists themselves can't seem to agree on what is reasonable?" Despite the impression created by the media, economists do agree on many points. In particular, economists share some important and fundamental principles that constitute the economic way of thinking. These principles are the major focus of this book and the key to understanding a wide variety of economic issues.

As you approach your study of economics, try to focus on the practical applications of economic principles and economic reasoning. For example, when you encounter a new concept, ask yourself "How can I use this principle to answer economic questions in my own life?" Students who take this approach are not only the most successful students, but they come away from the course knowing how to apply what they have learned to their own lives.

Second, as you can see by flipping through the pages of this textbook, economic analysis relies heavily on graphs to clarify abstract concepts. I urge you to study the introduction to graphs in the appendix following Chapter 1. Since graphs are important both to learning and applying economic principles, I have carefully explained each new type of graph when it is introduced. (The *Workbook* that accompanies this text contains an introductory chapter appendix devoted to graphs. In addition, the *Workbook* contains a special section on each new type of graph introduced in the text as well as considerable applications that allow you to practice reading and drawing graphs.)

Almost all graphs in this textbook have a numerical scale and all are color-coded: Demand-related curves are blue, while supply-related curves appear in red. In some exhibits the same information appears in both tabular and graphical form to facilitate understanding the graphs and the economic principles they illustrate. Be sure you understand how to read each type of graph and how to draw graphs yourself.

At first you may be perplexed by the new terms you encounter in introductory economics. However, this vocabulary was not developed to confuse you, but to enable economists and students to speak precisely. Learning this vocabulary is critical to learning economics. Each time a key economic term is introduced, it appears in bold print with a definition in the margin. For easy review, there is a glossary of key terms in the back of the textbook.

One final note: Economics may not be the easiest subject you ever tackle, but it is one of the most exciting and useful. In fact, I make a standing offer to my students. If they can find elements of my course that have no practical use, I promise to delete that material from the course and award them bonus points on their next exam. I can't offer the same bonus to you, but I will promise to delete material with no practical use from subsequent editions of this textbook. I don't, of course, expect that you will find any nonpractical concepts. But I believe that if you always look for the practical use of the concepts you encounter, your exam grades will be satisfactory even without those extra bonus points.

TO THE
INSTRUCTOR

The challenge in writing about or teaching principles of economics is to demonstrate the power of economics as a tool for understanding our world. I can think of no better way to convey that power than by proceeding with two parallel goals in mind. First, show the broad spectrum of problems that economics can help us solve, from increasing U.S. competitiveness to budget-balancing. At the same time, teach students economic analysis. Enable them to put this powerful tool to work for themselves.

My objective is not to prepare students for careers as professional economists but to teach them how to think like economists. One strategy for achieving this goal is to teach the basics very well, so that certain economic principles become more than ideas—they become actual perspectives on the world. In the text, I focus the students' attention on the most fundamental principles of economics and return to and extend these principles again and again. Concepts such as demand, supply, opportunity cost, rational choice, and the role of expectations are introduced early, explained carefully, and then constantly applied to new situations. Students quickly get into the habit of looking for opportunities to put economic analysis to work.

In preparing this revision, I drew on the advice and experience of many readers of the first edition of *Macroeconomics*. The book you are now reading benefitted not only from a thorough review of every draft of the manuscript, but also from a comprehensive evaluation by users of the previous edition. Many students and instructors who were using the first edition agreed to submit critiques on a regular basis, assessing the effectiveness of the presentation, the graphs, and the other pedagogical features. Their valuable input has allowed me to pinpoint features to retain and strengthen and others to add or revise.

Class-Tested Features

Several highly praised qualities of the first edition still distinguish this text. These features include careful step-by-step explanations of important concepts and the frequent *application* of these concepts, clear and readable graphs, abundant real-world examples to illustrate theory, built-in flexibility, and a distinctive, un-cluttered design.

A focus on core principles.   As a teacher of economics, I have successfully used a unifying, step-by-step approach to help students grasp fundamental principles. Whenever I introduce a new concept, I carefully explain the logic behind it and its connection to previously learned material. For example, I introduce the role of expectations early and apply it to aggregate supply, the determination of interest rates, and the Phillips Curve. And by carefully developing and then returning to basic themes like efficiency, price stability, and economic growth, the text enables students to see the common logic underlying apparently different economic decisions.

Graphs as analytical tools.   A graph is the economist's shorthand for depicting an economic relationship. No single element in this textbook has received more attention than the treatment of the graphs. Several features in the text help students overcome the problems they commonly have with graphs. An appendix after Chapter 1 provides a simple introduction to the use of graphs. Throughout the book, the exhibits themselves are color-coded: Demand-related curves are blue, supply-related curves are red. This device helps students build on previously learned material. Almost all graphs contain background grids and display numbers on both axes. Students generally find such graphs more accessible than the type displaying only abstract symbols. Finally, any graph used to present a new economic concept is accompanied by a related table, enabling students to see that both the graph and table contain the same basic information.

The *Workbook,* available with *Macroeconomics, Second Edition,* also contains an appendix on graphs, a guide to each new type of graph introduced, and a host of exercises that ask the student to read, interpret, and utilize graphs to answer economic questions.

Applications and other pedagogy.   I rely on applications and examples to illustrate how economic concepts help us understand the real world. Many are woven right into the text. We examine the impact of the 1986 tax reform on saving and investment behavior or the effects of monetary policy actions in the 1980s.

We have two kinds of boxes in this text. "Cases in Point," a feature retained from the first edition, are brief case studies that illustrate a specific economic concept. One case compares sources of growth between the United States and other countries. Another looks at historical examples of expansionary gaps. The "Cases in Point" are always extensions, or clarifications through example, of topics covered in the text. Many new "Cases in Point" have been added to the second edition. An exciting new feature of the second edition is a series of brief articles called "Economic Encounters." These explore the economic aspects of trends and happenings in our world.

The textbook is full of useful pedagogical features. Chapters open with a series of "Questions to Consider" that alert students to the relevance of the material in the chapter. Definitions of new terms and recaps of important points are found in the margins. Figure captions fully explain each graph and diagram. The illustration program alone serves as a visual digest of the analytical content of each chapter. Coming at the end of the chapter are numbered summaries and a large variety of questions and problems designed to get students to apply the economic concepts presented in the text.

Flexibility.   Since no two instructors teach the principles course in exactly the same way, I consider it important to maintain the text's great flexibility. *Economics* is available in a hardcover version covering both macroeconomics and microeconomics and in separate paperback volumes. I have taken great care to make sure that no discussion in *Macroeconomics* depends upon material covered in the parent text's microeconomics chapters. Therefore, the book can as easily be used in a class in which macro is treated first. Furthermore, while the text contains core chapters that are central to all principles courses, there are several optional chapters from which instructors can pick and choose.

Chapter-end appendixes offer the reader a more detailed look at topics covered in the main text. The use of price indexes, the algebra of the multiplier effect, and joint equilibrium in goods and money markets are all covered in these optional sections, providing the instructor and student with additional means of approaching key economic principles. Boxes and end-of-chapter problems offer still other opportunities to explore economic topics in greater detail. This textbook was designed so that a variety of paths could be taken through it. Its flexibility allows it to suit many different course syllabi. Just as significant, however, is the capability of this textbook, through appendixes, boxes, and problems, to challenge the more motivated student.

What's New in This Edition

Macroeconomics, Second Edition offers several exciting new features, including a restructured treatment of macroeconomics, a new approach to economic policy issues, the addition of "Economic Encounters," and a special emphasis on international economics.

Presenting macroeconomics.   To offer a contemporary and cohesive approach to macroeconomics at the principles level is a particular challenge. My objective in restructuring this half of the textbook was to simplify and condense the presentation while retaining full coverage of all important macroeconomic concepts. As a result, there are fewer chapters than in the previous edition. Yet there are more examples, both historical and current, of macroeconomics in action.

I have maintained a contemporary approach to macroeconomics, emphasizing the role of expectations and providing a full discussion of the aggregate demand

and aggregate supply model. I introduce the AD/AS model early, actually in the first chapter of the macroeconomics section, but I fully develop it in a new, separate chapter only after all the elements of the model are fully explained. I then apply the AD/AS model to macroeconomic policies.

A new approach to economic policy issues.   This text takes a major stride toward offering a more balanced and unified approach to economic policy than one typically finds in principles textbooks. Rather than devoting entire chapters to single policy issues such as the federal budget deficit, or at the other extreme, touching on a wide variety of issues only briefly as examples in the text, I have developed a new chapter that contains several short essays on macroeconomic policies. This chapter begins with an introduction that explains how economists analyze policy issues and provides a general framework for policy analysis. The introduction is followed by a series of individual policy cases, averaging four to five pages each, that then apply that analytical framework. The chapter includes sections on the budget deficit and international competitiveness, to name just two.

Naturally, the discussion of policy has not been confined to these chapters. The rationales and practical limits on government fiscal and monetary policy and many examples of government policy in action are discussed throughout the text.

Economic Encounters.   We have added a series of short pieces to the textbook that further illustrate the economic content of the world around us. These two-page articles focus on economic aspects of our political, social, and commercial lives. They ask us to consider the workings of the underground economy and the troublesome debt of Third-World nations, always emphasizing that there are more sides to an economic story than might at first be apparent. Why does unemployment persist in a nation where almost any newspaper contains numerous help-wanted advertisements? What must it be like to live in a country experiencing hyperinflation? "Economic Encounters" bring us face to face with the economic forces that shape people's lives.

A spotlight on international economics.   International trade and finance is a crucial component of today's economy. It has been said that there are no closed economies in the world, only closed economists. If students are to leave the principles course with a proper understanding of the workings of the U.S. economy, then they must be aware that the United States is only one part of an increasingly interrelated world economy.

In this edition, international economics is not just a topic relegated to the back of the textbook; rather it is integrated throughout. I apply the principles of exchange to international trade in the introductory chapters. A simple circular-flow model in Chapter 6 shows both trade and capital flows. Examples drawn from the international economy abound. Throughout the text, students see that foreign firms compete with U.S. firms, that foreign individuals, businesses, and governments play a major role in U.S. financial markets and purchase U.S. goods and services, and that it is no longer possible to dissociate economic events in other countries from events in our own. Additionally, three chapters at the end of the book offer more in-depth discussions of international trade, finance, comparative economic systems, and economic development.

Supplements Available to Accompany This Textbook

Workbook.   This supplement, written by Neil Niman of the University of New Hampshire and myself, is designed to enhance student comprehension. Like many study guides, it contains a list of learning objectives, fill-in questions covering key terms, and multiple-choice questions to test the student's understanding of the basic concepts in each chapter. A unique feature is a guide to each new graph encountered by the student, explaining what it shows and how to read and interpret the economic principles illustrated. Other features are "Avoid These Common Mistakes" and "Some Useful Tips." But the wealth of applications contained in this volume makes it more than a study guide. Students are given practice reading and drawing graphs, using data to make economic decisions, and solving numerical problems. The emphasis is not just on developing mechanical skills; students are asked to interpret data, make decisions, or otherwise show an understanding of the economic principles.

Instructor's Manual.   Prepared by Richard Burdekin of the University of Miami and myself, this supplement contains answers to the Questions for Discussion, points of special emphasis, teaching hints and current applications, and other useful information.

Test Item File.   A test item file containing over 2,000 multiple-choice questions has been prepared by Susan McHargue of Southern Methodist University, Kari Battaglia of North Texas State University, Teri Riley of Youngstown State University, and Jeffrey Wrase of Arizona State University. The file is available on hard copy and computer disk for ease of test preparation.

Transparencies.   Approximately 100 color acetates developed from graphs in the text are available to adopters.

Graphecon II.   An interactive computer tutorial written by Lee D. Olvey and James R. Golden of the U.S. Military Academy of West Point makes full use of computer graphics capabilities. This powerful program fully complements the text and offers students valuable practice in graphing and in putting economic concepts to work. Four instructional disks prompt the student to analyze problems in supply and demand, microeconomics, macroeconomics, and international trade. This enhanced version of *Graphecon* strongly reinforces correct answers and offers careful explanations in response to incorrect answers. Also, users have extensive control over the graphics on the screen, enabling them to see immediately the effect of new information on economic relationships.

A Note on Pagination

We often see both the hardcover, single-volume and paperback, two-volume versions of *Economics* used in the same principles classroom, or alternatively, know of many instructors who teach out of the hardcover while having their students buy the paperback. We therefore have deliberately chosen to keep the pagination consistent between the two versions of this text in order to achieve a maximum ease of cross-referencing.

ACKNOWLEDGMENTS

This book owes a great deal to other people. I would like to thank the students in my classes and my colleagues at the Whittemore School of Business and Economics—especially Manly Irwin, Neil Niman, Robert Puth, and Dwayne Wrightsman. I have learned much from each of them and they may well find some of their favorite examples included in the text. In addition, a former colleague, Michael Conti, along with the many reviewers of the first and second editions, provided many helpful suggestions.

I certainly owe a good deal to the professional assistance provided by the editorial and production staff at Addison-Wesley, including Debra Hunter and Steve Mautner who provided overall editorial direction; to Linda Bedell and Darlene Bordwell, whose development assistance was invaluable; to Dick Morton and Meredith Nightingale, who developed and produced the artwork; and to Sherry Berg, who skillfully guided the production of the manuscript. Working with such a professional and personable group was both a pleasure and an education.

Last, but certainly not least, I must acknowledge the contributions of my family—Dianne, Chris, Jen, and Lindsay. My wife Dianne not only assisted in word-processing, but read the manuscript in every phase, providing many useful suggestions. I cannot imagine completing this project without their support, encouragement, and patience.

REVIEWERS

CARLOS AGIULAR
El Paso County Community College

TED AMATO
University of North Carolina, Charlotte

KARI BATTAGLIA
North Texas State University

CARSON BAYS
East Carolina University

RONALD G. BRANDOLINI
Valencia Community College

NEIL BROWNE
Bowling Green State University

RICHARD BURDEKIN
University of Miami

RAYMOND L. COHN
Illinois State University

WILLIAM J. FIELD
DePauw University

DAVID GAY
University of Arkansas

JANET J. GLOCKER
Monroe Community College

TIMOTHY J. GRONBERG
Texas A&M University

RALPH L. GUNDERSON
University of Wisconsin, Oshkosh

CHRISTINE HAGER
University of Georgia

R. S. HANNA
Eastern Michigan University

ROBERT HORN
James Madison University

R. JACK INCH
Oakland Community College

E. JAMES JENNINGS
Purdue University, Calumet

ZIAD KEILANY
University of Tennessee, Chattanooga

ROBERT M. KENNEY
Miami-Dade C. C., South Campus

ARJO KLAMER
University of Iowa

SUSAN N. KOENIGSBERG
San Francisco State University

LEONARD LARDARO
University of Rhode Island

JULES LAROCQUE
Lawrence University

BOZENA LEVEN
Long Island University, C. W. Post

WADE E. MARTIN
University of Michigan, Flint

SUSAN MCHARGUE
Southern Methodist University

LEE R. MCPHETERS
Arizona State University

JOSEPH MESKEY
East Carolina University

DAVID J. MOLINA
North Texas State University

PANOS MOURDOUKOUTAS
Long Island University, C. W. Post

ARTHUR PETERSON
Middlesex County College

JOHN PETRAKIS
Long Island University, C. W. Post

JOHN PISCIOTTA
Baylor University

PHILIP ROBINS
University of Miami

REYBURN ROULSTON
Broward C. C., Central Campus

GEOFFREY P. RYAN
McHenry County College

JOHN SAPINSLEY
Rhode Island College

ROBERT F. SEVERSON
Central Michigan University

STEVE SHAPIRO
University of North Florida

STEVE SHEFFRIN
University of California, Davis

RONALD J. SKOCKI
Weber State College

GARY W. SORENSEN
Oregon State University

HELEN TAUCHEN
University of North Carolina, Chapel Hill

JENNIFER L. WARLICK
University of Notre Dame

WALTER WESSELS
North Carolina State University

NANCY A. WILLIAMS
University of Alaska, Fairbanks

RICHARD WINKELMAN
Arizona State University

JEFFREY WRASE
Arizona State University

ECONOMICS

B R I E F   C O N T E N T S

Macroeconomics is a split volume from Allen Thompson's *Economics.*

MACROECONOMICS
B R I E F   C O N T E N T S

CONTENTS

P A R T
SIX   Macroeconomic Measures and Models

P A R T
SEVEN   Money, Banking, and Economic Activity

P A R T
EIGHT   Macroeconomic Role of Government

P A R T
NINE   International Economics

SECOND EDITION

MACRO

ECONOMICS

PART ONE

Introduction to Economics

CHAPTER 1

The Economic Way
of Thinking

QUESTIONS TO CONSIDER

☐ Why is the study of economics important to an understanding of our world?

☐ What is the basis of all economic activity?

☐ In what ways do the economic meanings of resources and costs differ from their everyday meanings?

☐ How do economists study economic activity?

☐ Why do economists sometimes disagree about solutions to economic problems?

As you begin to study economics, you may be curious about what we will be discussing. Ask yourself the following questions: What determines the price of automobiles, TV sets, food, and other items you buy? What determines whether the economy next year will grow and prosper or experience problems such as unemployment and inflation? What determines the amount of income you can earn and the total income earned by all individuals in the economy? Should you spend your time tomorrow studying economics or in another way?

These and similar questions are what economics and this textbook are all about. Of course, to be able to answer them, you will have to learn something about the principles of economics and how to think like an economist. Economics has been jokingly described as "what economists do," which, although true, is not very revealing. In this chapter we will expand this definition and you will learn a great deal about what economists do and how they do it. You will also learn how the study of economics can be of value to you even if you do not plan to become a professional economist. But keep in mind that economics is, above all, a subject devoted to understanding how the economy works. For that reason, you should find economics interesting and exciting.

WHAT IS ECONOMICS?

No simple definition of economics can fully explain all that economists do. However, we can say that economists study how the economy works and why—as evidenced by such problems as poverty, unemployment, and inflation—it sometimes works poorly. In fact, economics can be characterized by the questions it seeks to answer.

Economics is also a way of thinking. Economists approach the study of real-world problems from the standpoint of certain basic economic principles. They assume that individuals choose those options that best help them achieve their goals. Economists also believe that a business seeks to maximize profits and that it will produce more goods when it can earn greater profits.

Economics may also be viewed as a collection of concepts about and perspectives on some of the problems societies face. These concepts and perspectives are derived from the economic way of thinking. In later chapters, you will learn many principles to help you understand and predict economic events. First, however, we need to look at what economists study and to see how these studies have led to some basic economic principles and ways of thinking.

Economics Is a Study of the Real World

First and foremost the study of economics is motivated by a desire to understand the real world. Although economists sometimes find it useful to consider how the economy might operate under hypothetical situations, they do so in order to help them understand how an economy in the real world operates. In the final analysis, *economics is a study of the real world.*

In this textbook our principal focus is on the economy of the United States—the individuals who work, manage businesses and households, and run the government. We want to understand why they engage in economic activities such as working, producing, saving, investing, and consuming. We want to know how they react to changes in economic circumstances that have occurred or might occur. For example, in the 1970s, certain events caused a significant rise in the world price of oil. Economists studied this unprecedented change and what happened as a result. And, when Congress was debating the tax reform measures passed in 1986, economists helped by predicting the results of various proposals.

When economists study real-world problems, they ask—and try to answer—many questions. Why is the unemployment rate so high and what, if anything, can be done to lower it? What causes inflation and what can be done to minimize it? What are the causes and consequences of the large federal budget deficit? Why does the United States have a large trade imbalance? What caused the Great Depression in the 1930s and the recession in the early 1980s? Should a business build a new plant, or produce a new product? What are the economic advantages and costs of buying a new house, or attending college? Without an understanding of economic principles you cannot answer such questions.

Economics Is a Study of Scarcity

One of the economic facts of life is that each of us has wants: food to eat, clothing to wear, cars to drive, and, of course, a college degree. Economists recognize, however, that individuals and societies must face the fundamental problem of **scarcity**: Although individual and collective wants are unlimited, the resources available to satisfy those wants are limited. Scarcity is one of the most important economic concepts, and you should understand what it means at the outset.

Economists agree that the individual and collective wants of society are unlimited. No matter how much we have, we always seem to want something else. Of course, we might have enough of some specific thing at some particular time—all the turkey we want during Thanksgiving dinner, for example. But history suggests that no matter how hard we work and how prosperous we become, we are unlikely to be able to satisfy *all* our wants.

Scarcity. The fundamental conflict between unlimited human desires and limited availability of resources.

At the same time the ability to satisfy wants is limited. Scarcity is most evident to each of us as the limited income we have and the limited amount of time in each day and week. We must decide how to spend our income and time. Society's ability to satisfy wants is also limited. At any one time, only so many natural resources, only so many factories, and only so many workers are available. Scarcity—the inability to have all that we want—is a fundamental fact of life. *Economics is a study of how society addresses the fundamental problem of scarcity.* We consider what economics has to say about the meaning and implications of scarcity in Chapter 2.

Economics Is a Study of Choices

Scarcity is important because it requires individuals and society to make choices. But how do individuals decide what to buy, how do businesses decide what to produce, and how does government decide what activities to undertake? Economists are very much interested in these questions, and many of the principles of economics that you will encounter are ideas about how choices are made and the factors that influence choices. All choices are related to the implications of scarcity. Since we cannot satisfy all wants no matter how hard we try, we have to choose among them. *Economics is a study of how individuals and society choose which wants to satisfy and how to satisfy them.* We begin to look at economic choices in Chapter 2.

Economics Is a Study of Trade or Exchange

Although scarcity means that we cannot have *everything* we want, we can obtain some of the things we want through trade or exchange. Trade or exchange between individuals and economies is an extremely important economic activity. Trade occurs in all types of societies and in all kinds of ways. Individuals in positions of authority may trade favors: "Help me with this, and I'll put in a good word for you" or "You vote for my bill and I'll vote for yours." Trade occurs between individuals, individuals and businesses, businesses and businesses, and economies. *Economics is a study of how trade or exchange is carried on.*

One very important economic principle is that trade can benefit both parties; that is, both parties to a trade may be better off as a result. For example, you want to eat at a nice restaurant this weekend but are short of funds. Your roommate has $20 and is in danger of flunking the upcoming economics quiz. By trading your tutoring services for the $20, you both gain: Your roommate passes the economics quiz, and you enjoy a nice meal.

Trade results from different preferences, different resources, and different capabilities. In each case, trade can lead to mutual gains. For example, you and I may have different musical preferences. I love opera but consider rock music to be noise. Your musical tastes are the opposite. If I trade you three tapes of rock music my teenaged children bought me for my birthday for three tapes of opera your parents bought you to improve your musical tastes, we will both be better off. Different preferences make trade desirable.

Countries often trade because they possess different resources. Saudi Arabia, for example, has a lot of oil but little land suitable for growing wheat. The United States, on the other hand, uses more oil than it produces but has a lot of land suitable for growing wheat. By trading wheat for oil, both countries can get more of what they want. Differences in resources make it possible for both parties to gain from trade.

Finally, trade allows individuals and countries to specialize, that is, to concentrate their efforts and resources, supplying goods that they can produce most efficiently. For example, suppose that we are neighbors, each with two jobs to do this week: paint our houses and build sheds in our backyards. I am a good carpenter but a lousy painter; your skills are just the reverse. If I build both sheds and you concentrate on painting both houses, we can both finish sooner and have more free time. Specialization offers many advantages to individuals, businesses, and countries. The increased efficiency of specialization offers the possibility of mutual gain from trade.

In the United States and similar economic systems, most exchanges take place in *markets*. A market is the economist's way of referring to the arrangements that bring together the buyers and sellers of some particular resource, good, or service. Because of their importance in the United States, we will devote a significant amount of time to understanding how markets work.

Economics Is a Study of Organization

In the United States, trade occurs most often between different components of the economy, which we can generally class as households (and the individuals within them), businesses, and government. These components interact in a variety of ways. Individuals work for businesses and government. Businesses produce goods and services for households, government, and other businesses. Government taxes households and businesses and provides roads, national defense, and laws regulating economic and noneconomic behavior. Viewed as a whole, economic interactions constitute an **economic system**, or the way society is organized to address the economic problem of scarcity. *Economics is a study of how different economic systems address the fundamental problem of scarcity*.

There are many types of economic systems. The economic system of the United States, for example, is known as **market capitalism**. It has two principal characteristics: (1) most resources are owned by private individuals; and (2) most economic interactions occur in markets, where resources, goods, and services are bought and sold. But there are other types of economic systems. The system in the Soviet Union is **planned socialism**. In this type of system most resources are owned and their use is controlled by the government. While both the United States and the Soviet Union face the problem of scarcity, their economic systems— how they address scarcity—are very different. *Economics is a study of the implications of different forms of economic organization*.

In this textbook we consider primarily market capitalism, the system used by the United States, Canada, Japan, and the countries of Western Europe. However, within the basic framework of market capitalism, alternatives and choices affect how each economic system operates. In the United States, for example, we constantly face the question of whether more or less of the basic economic choices should be made or controlled by government. While economists do not always agree about whether more or less government is better, they do agree that it is important to study how a change may affect the economy.

Economic system. The institutions and mechanisms used to determine what and how to produce and who will receive the goods and services produced.

Market capitalism. An economic system in which most resources are privately owned by individuals and most economic interactions occur in markets.

Planned socialism. An economic system in which most resources are owned by government and their use is controlled by a government plan.

Microeconomics. That level of economic analysis concerned with the activity of individual units of the economy and their interrelationships.

Macroeconomics. That level of economic analysis concerned with the activity of the entire economy and the interactions between large sectors of it.

Economics. The study of how individuals and societies, faced with the problem of scarcity, choose how to produce, exchange, and consume goods and services.

✓ Regardless of the type of economic system, certain economic principles always apply. For example, trade or exchange plays a role in every society. In addition, all societies face the problem of scarcity; thus all are forced to make choices. And regardless of how a society is organized, all decisions are ultimately made by individuals. In the United States, where private ownership prevails, individuals decide how to use the resources and goods they own. In the Soviet Union, with its system of public ownership and centralized control, more decisions are made by individuals in government agencies. You can better understand either system by learning more about how choices are made.

Microeconomic and Macroeconomic Perspectives

Economic interactions take place on many levels: from trading clothes with your roommate to complex trade agreements among dozens of nations. Thus economists have to study economic activity from both the microeconomic and macroeconomic perspectives.

Microeconomics focuses on the activities of individual units within the economy. For example, at the microeconomic level an economist might explore how U.S. automakers have responded to the increased competition from Japanese and other foreign automobile producers, or how U.S. consumers are likely to react if automobile prices fall by 10 percent.

Macroeconomics, on the other hand, concentrates on the activities of the entire economy and the interactions among its major sectors—households, businesses, and government, both domestic and foreign. For example, at the macroeconomic level an economist might study why the average price of all goods in the United States increased by more than 10 percent per year from 1979 to 1981, or why 1.5 million more people were unemployed in 1980 than in 1979.

✓ Consider how economists might study the impact of a proposed cut in income taxes. A microeconomic analysis would ask questions such as: "How will a tax cut affect house prices?" "How will it affect the behavior of producers of personal computers?" A macroeconomic analysis of the same policy would ask: "How will a tax cut affect the total amount spent by all households in the economy?" "What effects will it have on the general price level and unemployment?"

Although we make a distinction between them here (and generally throughout this textbook), a complete economic analysis of a government policy must consider both macro and micro implications. That is, the effects on individual units of the economy (the microeconomic level) *and* on the economy as a whole (the macroeconomic level) should be considered. In fact, a significant amount of research in economics over the past decade has been aimed at improving our understanding of the microeconomic foundations of macroeconomics, that is, to merging the two branches of the economic discipline.

In this brief overview we have identified what economists do. The broad range of topics mentioned may help you understand why it is difficult to give a simple yet comprehensive definition of economics. At the risk of oversimplification, however, we may define **economics** as the study of how individuals and societies, faced with the problem of scarcity, choose how to produce, exchange, and consume goods and services.

THE LANGUAGE OF ECONOMICS

Economists seek to understand how the real world operates and to address real-world problems such as unemployment, inflation, and scarcity. In order to describe the economic world and possible solutions to its problems, economists have developed an economics vocabulary. At times, the terms used in economics may seem like a foreign language. Worse, economists often have special meanings for common words. You may be tempted to ask, "Why don't economists just use plain, ordinary language?" Unfortunately, ordinary language is imprecise. For example, consider the word "competition." In everyday use the word is used to mean rivalry, as between two athletic teams. But the economic concept of competition has a special and technical meaning: the presence of sufficient numbers of buyers and sellers so that no one of them can influence the market price.

For now, you do not have to worry about remembering the special meaning of competition. But the technical precision of economic terms means that you must carefully note the *economic* meaning of terms like competition, demand, costs, unemployment, and inflation when we introduce them. To help you in your mastery of economic terms, such words appear in bold type in the text when first explained, and their definitions appear in the margin. A glossary of all these terms appears at the end of the book. To illustrate this method and how economic terms are a part of the economic way of thinking, let's consider how economists define and use the concepts of resources and opportunity cost.

Resources

A major part of economic activity is devoted to producing goods and services that satisfy wants. To provide goods and services businesses combine **resources**. You probably think you know what resources are, but the economic meaning of this term is somewhat broader than its common, everyday meaning.

Economists identify three types of resources that can be used to produce goods and services. Minerals, water, air, and land are **natural resources**. Buildings, factories, schools, machinery, computers, ships, railroads, and trucks—long-lasting goods—are **capital resources**.

As important as natural and capital resources are, they cannot produce goods and services by themselves. Society also relies on **human resources**—the skills, talents, and time of individuals. Human resources are required to operate machinery, extract minerals from the ground, make and assemble products, and provide services. Human resources are also required to organize, plan, and direct the use of resources. And human resources are used to develop improved machinery, better methods of organizing production, and new products.

Resources are one of the economy's fundamental building blocks. They enable goods to be produced and wants to be satisfied. By increasing the quantity and quality of resources or the efficiency of their use, society can satisfy more wants. The study of economics is largely the study of resources and resource use.

Opportunity Cost

Any business interested in earning a profit must consider the cost of the resources used to produce its product or service. But what is the cost? In everyday language, the cost of resources is the price businesses pay to acquire them. If

Resources. The human, capital, and natural resources that can be used to produce goods and services.

Natural resources. The land, water, minerals, climate, and other products of nature that can be used to produce goods and services.

Capital resources. The buildings, machinery, roads, transportation equipment, and other long-lasting items that can be used to produce goods and services. Also called *capital goods*.

Human resources. The strength, skills, training, and talents of society's population that can be used to produce goods and services.

Opportunity cost. The value of the next best option that must be sacrificed when a choice is made.

Economic model. A simplified verbal, tabular, graphic, or mathematical representation of a real economy that is used to analyze and predict how the economy would work under the specified conditions.

workers are hired for $10 per hour, a product requiring three hours of labor has a labor cost of $30 per hour.

But in the economic way of thinking, **opportunity cost** is a more precise measure of the cost. Because of the fundamental economic problem of scarcity, every time a resource is used in one way, it cannot be used to produce other goods. For example, if a business uses materials to produce blue suede sneakers, it cannot use those same materials to produce other types of shoes. If you faithfully attend your economics class, the hours you spend in that way cannot be used for another purpose. If the government chooses to spend tax dollars to provide subsidized housing, those same tax dollars are not available for other government expenditures or for private individuals to spend as they please.

Economists use the concept of opportunity cost to measure the sacrifice involved in a given choice. In particular, the opportunity cost is the value of the next best option. For example, if you choose to attend your economics class at eight o'clock in the morning, the opportunity cost of that decision might be the value to you of sleeping late (although some individuals have demonstrated an ability to combine these two activities). For a business, the opportunity cost of producing one product may be best measured by the profit it could have earned if it had produced a different product. For government expenditures, the opportunity cost is the value of other government expenditures that could have been made or the value to taxpayers of goods and services they otherwise could have consumed.

Because we live in a world characterized by scarcity, we face a sacrifice or opportunity cost for every choice we make. We explore choice and opportunity cost in Chapter 2. For now, though, you should note that thinking in economic terms requires an explicit recognition of sacrifice—that is, the opportunity cost—involved with every choice we make.

METHODS OF ECONOMIC ANALYSIS

In addition to defining terms precisely, economists construct models or theories of economic behavior. An **economic model** or theory is a simplified representation of how the economy, or parts of the economy, behave under particular conditions. In building a model, economists do not try to explain every detail of the real world. Rather, they focus on the most important influences on behavior because the real world is so complex.

For example, consider an economic model of consumer behavior, which seeks to understand what causes individuals to buy more or less of some particular product. This model focuses on only a few of the many possible influences, such as the benefits that consumers receive from the product, the income of consumers, the price of the product, and prices of other products. Economists assume that other factors—the smile of a salesclerk, the weather, and the whims of particular buyers—are irrelevant. By simplifying, the economist is able to concentrate on the most important variables and predict the behavior of consumers as a group.

You might ask, "Why don't economists just stick to the facts?" Facts are descriptions of the past, but economists are primarily interested in predicting the future. Facts are very important, however, in helping economists understand the past and present. Economists use facts in developing and testing their economic models and theories. Those that do not explain the facts of the past accurately or predict reasonably well what will occur in the future are worthless.

In addition, facts do not always tell a clear, unambiguous story. For example, suppose that you were given facts showing prices and quantities sold of a given product over a period of time. You might find that sometimes prices rose and quantities sold fell. But you will no doubt find that at other times both prices and quantities sold rose. What do these facts tell you? They appear to tell two different stories, not allowing you to easily predict prices and quantities. Economists combine a model of consumer behavior with a model of seller behavior to explain such apparently confusing facts. You will encounter this model of demand and supply in Chapter 3.

Many beginning students in economics (and other disciplines) ask, "Are we going to learn something practical and useful or just a bunch of theories?" Economics does offer a number of theories and models describing how the economy operates (and you will no doubt be asked to recall them on exams). Some people believe that theory belongs only in the classroom and is useless in the real world—definitely a false impression.

There is no major gap between well-developed theories and models and the real world. A good theory helps us to understand the real world. Moreover, a model allows us to predict the effects of a possible or proposed event, such as increased tuition at the state university, decreased federal income taxes, or improved production methods. That is, we can predict what is likely to happen, who is likely to benefit, and what policies to use to increase or lessen the event's effects.

Well-constructed models are not guesses or wishful thinking. Economists subject their models to a stern test: How well do they explain the past and predict future real-world events? Models or theories that do not pass this test are discarded or revised—an ongoing process in economics.

Graphic Models

Economic models are sometimes presented as verbal descriptions but more often as tables, mathematical equations, or graphs. The graph in Exhibit 1.1, for example, is a model that describes the relationship between the amount of household income and spending each year. The model indicates that if its income is $20,000 per year, the household will spend $20,000; if its income is $60,000, it will spend $40,000. To be useful, of course, the model must accurately reflect how the household's decisions are influenced by its income. Because graphs are so much a part of economics, we included a special appendix at the end of this chapter to explain more about how to construct and read graphs. In addition, the study guide that accompanies this textbook has an entire chapter on the use of graphs, including exercises to let you practice using the types of graphs you will encounter later in the text.

Using Models to Predict
Economic Outcomes

Whatever their form, economic models are useful because they can help economists make predictions of economic outcomes. Using models, economists can consider the relationship between two economic variables. For example, when

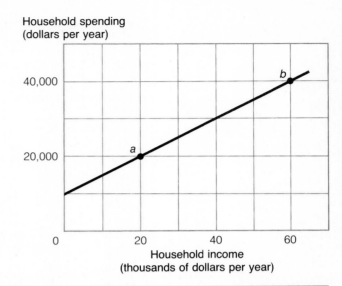

Household spending
(dollars per year)

Exhibit 1.1
A Model of Houshold Spending
This graph shows a model that relates household spending to household income. The model indicates that the household will spend $20,000 per year, if its annual income is $20,000 (point *a*). If annual income is $60,000 per year, the household will spend $40,000 per year (point *b*).

Household income
(thousands of dollars per year)

studying the U.S. economy we are interested in the relationship between the price of a product and the quantity that consumers seek to buy. As you will see in Chapter 3, focusing on these two variables allows us to make the following statements: (1) if the price of a product falls, consumers will buy more; and (2) if the price rises, consumers will buy less.

A series of "if A, then B" propositions and assumptions about behavior comprise a model of how two economic variables—price and the quantity consumers seek to buy—are related. Using this model we can predict the economic outcome of a price change. For example, if producers lower prices, we can expect consumers to buy more. Of course, the outcome predicted reflects both the model used and the prediction of how prices will change. Economists who use the same model but expect different changes in price will predict different amounts of consumer purchases.

Models can also help economists understand the effects of a proposed government policy. Suppose that Congress is considering a law requiring foreign producers to raise their prices (thus making goods produced in this country relatively less expensive). The model of consumer behavior predicts that the law will cause consumers to buy fewer foreign goods. By helping economists forecast the results of a change in economic conditions or government policies, such models provide an important and useful tool for those who have to make far-reaching decisions.

Building, testing, and using economic models is an important part of the economic way of thinking. The objective of economics and economic models is to help you and others understand the real world. Without theories, economics would be neither useful nor practical. In fact, a good way to learn economics is to ask yourself continually what questions a given theory can help you answer. This method will not only test your understanding of the theory but also will help you put economic theory to work for you.

Avoiding Logical Errors

Because models are so important to our understanding of the economic world, they must be as accurate as possible. Thus in building and using models, economists must be aware of certain logical errors, most notably errors of causation and correlation, the fallacy of composition, and the fallacy of division. An understanding of these possible errors will help you detect the mistakes of others and avoid them yourself.

Causation and correlation. A model describes the relationships among the various factors selected as important to a particular economic activity. However, in building a model we must be careful not to confuse correlation with causation.

Correlation is a statistical term that measures the degree to which two variables tend to move together. For example, if the number of tickets sold to a football game increases each time the price of tickets rises, ticket sales are *positively* correlated with ticket prices. If unemployment in the U.S. economy decreases whenever the number of kangaroos born in Australia falls, unemployment is *negatively* correlated with the birthrate of kangaroos.

Serious mistakes can be made in model building if economists who find a high degree of positive or negative correlation between two factors assume that one factor *causes* the other. There may be no justification to assume **causation** and no proof of its validity. Correlation is a measure of a statistical relationship, *not* proof of cause and effect.

While correlation may suggest a relationship between two variables, a result may actually be caused by a factor not included in the analysis. For example, the positive correlation between ticket prices and ticket sales may be explained by the fact that ticket prices rise only when a team is highly successful. Correlation may even be merely a coincidence, such as the correlation between unemployment in the United States and the birthrate of Australian kangaroos.

Economic history is littered with stories of errors in causation and correlation. W. S. Jevons, a nineteenth-century economist, observed a correlation between sunspot activity and economic prosperity. From this correlation he derived a theory of how the economy operated. Later analysis found other economic factors that better explained the variations in economic activity and discredited the sunspot theory. Remember: Causation cannot be proved from correlation; it must be demonstrated in more direct and different ways.

Fallacy of composition. Another form of model-building error can arise as economists examine the facts of the real world and attempt to sort them into meaningful patterns. For example, some economists study how businesses that produce automobiles react to and are affected by increases in the price of their products. Economists may observe that profits rise when prices rise and that automakers produce more cars when prices increase. But can we conclude that businesses will be affected in the same way if *all* prices in the economy rise? No, and as a matter of fact that would not be true. Higher prices for automobiles are good for automakers when they rise relative to other prices. But if all prices in the economy increase, the cost of producing cars also rises, and automakers will not earn more profits or produce more cars.

Correlation. The statistical relationship between two factors and the extent to which changes in one factor are accompanied by changes in the other.

Causation. The presumption that a change in one factor causes a change in another factor with which it is statistically correlated.

Fallacy of composition. Incorrectly concluding that what is true of the part is also true of the whole.

Fallacy of division. Incorrectly concluding that what is true of the whole is also true of every part.

Positive statement. A statement limited to a factual description of what is or what will be.

Normative statement. A statement involving value judgments of what ought to be.

The preceding example illustrates the **fallacy of composition**. A change that affects only one individual or one business may not have the same effect if all individuals or businesses in an economy are affected. When economists try to predict what will happen to large groups of individuals and businesses, or the economy as a whole, they must be careful to avoid the fallacy of composition.

Fallacy of division.   Another common mistake may occur when economists try to predict the effect on an individual from a prediction of an effect on a group. For example, when the economy goes into a recession, sales of goods and services in total, and the income of consumers as a group, will fall. However, this decline does not mean that sales by all firms will decline or that incomes of all individuals will be lower. The **fallacy of division** states that what is true for the economy as a whole is not always true of each part.

Maintaining Objectivity: Facts versus Opinion

One of the most important elements in model building is maintaining an objective attitude toward the subject being studied and the conclusions that emerge. Economists have feelings, beliefs, and opinions, just like everyone else. But in applying the tools of economics, they must make a distinction between facts and opinions and remain emotionally neutral.

Because their models can help predict what will happen, economists are often asked to give advice on the effects of proposed governmental policies. They may give one of two types of response. They may supply a factual answer, a projection of what they believe *will* happen if the policy is enacted. They might, for example, predict that a government policy will cause an increase in the price of some particular product or service. A statement of facts or a projection of what is likely to happen is a **positive statement**. Sometimes, however, economists may give an opinion on what the government *ought* to do about a problem. If this opinion is influenced by the values of the individual, it is called a **normative statement**.

It is difficult but necessary to distinguish facts from value judgments. But as some economists note, it is almost impossible to make a purely objective statement of fact, especially to a question such as "Is it in the best interest of the country to implement this policy?" The choice of models and the weighing of evidence are often influenced by personal biases. Still, to apply the economic way of thinking, we must distinguish between statements of objective fact (positive statements) and statements influenced by political and philosophical biases (normative statements).

RECAP

Economists must be careful not to confuse correlation and causation and must learn to avoid common fallacies such as those of composition and division.

Economists must try to maintain objectivity and not confuse fact and opinion.

Economists make a distinction between positive statements—factual descriptions or predictions of what is likely to happen—and normative statements—personal opinions of what should be done.

WHY DO ECONOMISTS DISAGREE?

If models have been checked for logic errors and philosophical bias, then why are they not perfect? Why do economists seem—at least in the news media—to disagree so much about what effects a given action will have and what economic policies should be followed? First, as we noted earlier, models are an attempt to simplify a complex world. Economists have yet to devise a model that explains or even attempts to account for *all* aspects of economic interaction in the real world. Sometimes economists disagree about the facts and what economic models are most appropriate. Moreover, value judgments are often required to choose the "best" solution to economic problems. Thus economic disagreements occur because economists have differing personal values.

What Are the "Facts"?

Even if they use the same models, economists may reach different conclusions if they cannot agree on the facts. It is difficult to measure economic activities precisely and accurately. Economists therefore must sometimes rely on imperfect and incomplete information when making predictions or policy suggestions. Naturally, interpretations of imperfect information may differ.

Economists also disagree about some fundamental aspects of the economy. Do individuals have the ability to make choices on their own, or are they dominated by powerful organizations? Are individuals able to acquire the goods and services they demand by their own efforts, or is government needed to provide many of the goods and services required in a modern economy? Strong arguments have been made for each position. Although many of the arguments are based more on philosophy than facts, it is not always easy to know which "fact" is the more accurate description of reality.

Which Theory Is Best?

Economists also disagree about how the economy will react to various changes in conditions. Because they are unable to conduct controlled experiments, economists sometimes cannot agree on the precise theoretical model that best describes the outcomes of economic policies. Thus at any one time, there are often several different, competing theories about how the economy operates and which policies will yield the desired results.

What Are the Benefits and Costs?

Even if economists could agree on the facts and on the best theory, they might still disagree on which policy is best. With the same theory and the same facts, economists would, of course, be able to agree on the predicted outcomes. But they may give very different opinions about whether such outcomes are desirable. The degree to which these differences are related to unclear aspects of *positive* economic factors and to *normative* economic factors is very hard to determine.

For example, economists strongly disagree about whether the government should intervene in economic activity. Part of the disagreement is over the relative importance of economic goals. Some economists emphasize the importance of maintaining individual freedom of choice. Others believe that government must occasionally step in to offset uncontrolled attempts by large organizations to alter individual behavior. Thus those who are concerned about freedom of choice may view advertising primarily as a means of providing information for individuals to use in making decisions. But those concerned about the power of large organizations may view advertising more as an attempt to manipulate the individual's decision-making process, thereby reducing the individual's autonomy.

Economists disagree about the relative benefits and costs of inflation and unemployment. Some believe that the effects of inflation are so damaging that it is preferable to accept high rates of unemployment for short periods, if doing so would eliminate inflation. Other economists suggest that a reduction in unemployment is worth some cost to the economy in terms of inflation. Behind this controversy are major disagreements over the relative costs of unemployment and inflation and over how much unemployment must fall to reduce significantly the rate of inflation.

Some economists believe that our major national goal should be maximum production. Others place more emphasis on a more equitable distribution of whatever is produced; some of these economists would accept a smaller economic pie in return for a fairer distribution of its pieces. This difference, of course, reflects opinions, not facts.

As you can see, individual economists are not likely to reach identical conclusions about what the future holds or about the effects of different economic policies. As individuals, they have different values and sometimes observe economic events in different ways. Although there are differences, there is also clearly an "economic way of thinking." It represents a common basis for economic analysis and a way of testing the validity of economic ideas. In this textbook we focus on the areas of agreement but point out where and why important differences exist.

CONCLUSION

In later chapters you will learn much more about what economists do and how they do it. Those chapters build on the foundation we laid in this chapter. Economics is a way of thinking that uses certain concepts (scarcity and opportunity cost, for example) to build models (like the model of consumer behavior). In all cases, the purpose of economic analysis is to learn to understand and predict real-world outcomes. Thus you should try to apply the concepts and models you learn. Remember: The test of economic theories—and your understanding of them—is how well they answer real-world questions.

SUMMARY

1. In this chapter we introduced you to the study of economics, what economists do, and the methods economists use.

2. Economics is the study of interactions in the real world that are related to the concept of scarcity: limited resources but unlimited human wants. Scarcity forces individuals and societies to make choices. Economics is also a study of how choices are made. Many choices involve trade among different sectors of an economy or among economies. And economics is a study of the implications of different forms of economic organization.

3. Economic activity can be studied on two levels: macro and micro. Microeconomics involves studies of the activities of individual units within the economy, such as

the market for a single product. Macroeconomics covers studies of the activities of the economy as a whole or major sectors of the economy. Sound economic analysis requires consideration of both.

4. Economists use a special language, and economic concepts enable economists to communicate their ideas clearly. Resources are the minerals, land, buildings, machinery, and human talents used to produce goods and services. Opportunity cost is a measure of the sacrifice involved with any specific choice and, in particular, is the value of the next best option.

5. In order to describe economic behavior, economists build theories and models. Economic models are simplifications of the real world but can help the economist to predict the outcome of real-world economic events

or changes in government policy. Economic models may be expressed as verbal descriptions, tabular data, graphs, or mathematical equations.

6. Builders of economic models must be careful not to confuse correlation and causation and must learn to avoid common fallacies, such as those of composition and division. They must try to maintain an objective attitude toward the subject being studied and the conclusions reached. Economists distinguish between positive statements—those limited to factual descriptions or predictions of what is likely to happen—and normative statements—those involving personal opinions and values or suggestions of what should be done.

7. Economists share many common principles and theories, but they also disagree from time to time. Disagreements exist because unambiguous facts are not always available, because it is not always clear which model is best, and because economists have different values and stress different goals.

KEY TERMS

QUESTIONS FOR REVIEW AND DISCUSSION

1. What facts of life underlie the study of economics?
2. What are the basic objectives of economic study?
3. Why do economists, applying the principles of economics, sometimes reach different conclusions? Can you always prove one group of economists to be wrong? If so, how?

4. What implication does scarcity have for a society? What implication does it have for a society if a resource becomes more scarce? Less scarce?

5. What do you believe is the appropriate role of economists in formulating economic policy? Can you think of situations in which there is no "correct" economic policy? What is the appropriate role of politicians in formulating policies to deal with economic problems?

6. The government is considering whether to raise or lower income taxes. What kinds of questions would you raise from a microeconomic perspective? From a macroeconomic focus?

7. Which of the following are *positive* statements and which are *normative* statements?
   a) "An increase in prices will reduce the quantity purchased."
   b) "The government shouldn't raise taxes because some groups in the economy will be worse off."
   c) "Businesses will produce more of their products when they expect to sell more."
   d) "Businesses should be more careful not to spoil the environment."

8. What is the purpose of theory? What kinds of questions do economists hope to answer by developing theories and models? Can you explain what causes inflation without a theory? If you were developing a theory of inflation, explain why it would be important to (a) identify which economic factors were related to inflation (and which were unrelated); (b) know whether the identified factor was directly or indirectly related to inflation; (c) test your theory against historical facts; (d) not let your philosophical ideas influence the choice of variables to include.

9. Explain why each of the following conclusions is incorrect.
   a) "Whenever there's a large snowfall, sales of snow shovels increase. Therefore, if we want it to snow, everyone has to buy more snow shovels."
   b) "The government reported today that the income of households in the United States increased by 6 percent last year. This implies that everyone in the nation is better off this year than last."
   c) "If a farmer can earn a greater income by producing a larger crop, the income of all farmers will increase when they're able to increase production."

10. Use the appendix to this chapter and the graph on the following page to answer questions (a)–(f).

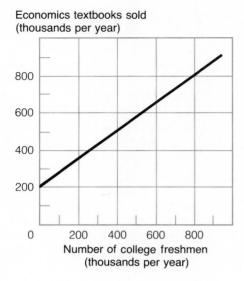

Economics textbooks sold
(thousands per year)

Number of college freshmen
(thousands per year)

a) Are the two variables shown in the graph—number of economics textbooks sold and number of college freshmen—directly or indirectly related?

b) Is the slope of the line shown in the graph positive or negative?

c) According to the graph, how many copies of economics textbooks will be sold next year if there are 400,000 college freshmen? If 800,000 copies of economics textbooks were sold last year, how many college freshmen were there?

d) What is the slope of the line? What is the intercept of the line?

e) According to the slope, how many more economics textbooks will be sold if the number of college freshmen increases by 100,000?

f) Write an algebraic expression to show the relationship between textbooks sold (T) and the number of college freshmen (F). Let textbooks sold be the dependent variable and college freshmen be the independent variable.

Appendix to Chapter 1

Use of Graphs

In Chapter 1 we noted that economists use graphs and mathematical models to depict economic data or to describe economic relationships. Because you will encounter graphs frequently in this textbook and in economic analyses, the ability to read a graph is an important skill for you to develop. The purpose of this appendix is to explain how to read a graph and how either real or hypothetical data can be plotted to form a graph. Data can be displayed in graphic form in many different ways. In this appendix we concentrate on only one: the simple arithmetic line graph. This form of graph is the one we use most often in this textbook and is a good one with which to begin.

In everyday experience, we often observe that one thing depends on another. For example, the time it takes to read a chapter of this textbook will depend on the number of pages in the chapter. Mathematicians speak of such dependencies as "functional relationships." How well you perform on your first economics exam will depend on—is a function of—the number of hours you have spent studying. In a dependent relationship, one variable (in this case, your exam grade) is said to be the **dependent variable**, whereas the other—the one that is free to fluctuate

Dependent variable. In any given relationship, an element that is affected by a change in the value of an independent variable.

Independent variable. In any given relationship, an element that is subject to independent change. A change in the value of an independent variable affects the value of the dependent variable.

Origin. The point on a graph representing a zero value for both variables; the intersection of the horizontal and vertical axes, generally the lower left corner of a graph.

or that can be directly controlled (in this case the number of hours you study)—is called the **independent variable**.

Much of what you study in economics can be expressed in terms of such dependent relationships. In fact, much of the work of economists consists of learning how, and to what extent, some variables, such as unemployment or product prices, depend on others. When we have only two variables, we can show their relationship on a two-dimensional graph. In mathematical terms, a graph is a pictorial display of the relationship that exists between two (or more) variables.

PLOTTING A GRAPH

To illustrate how a graph is plotted, we will use the hypothetical data in Exhibit 1A.1, which shows the relationship between the prices charged by Paulo's Pizza Parlor and the number of pizzas that people in Collegetown will buy from Paulo's in a given week. As the data in the table indicate, the number of pizzas Paulo can sell *increases* as the price charged *decreases*. Because the two variables move in opposite directions, they are said to be *inversely* related. (When two variables move in the same direction, they are said to be *directly* related.)

The graph accompanying the data indicates how a simple line graph is plotted. This particular graph shows the number of pizzas sold per week (the dependent variable) on the *horizontal axis* (along the bottom of the graph) and the price charged (the independent variable) on the *vertical axis*. At the bottom left, where the two axes intersect, is the **origin**.

Exhibit 1A.1
Paulo's Pizza Parlor: Prices Charged and Quantities Sold

(a)

Price (dollars per pizza)	Quantity sold (pizzas per week)
8.00	25
7.50	50
7.00	100
6.50	175

(b)

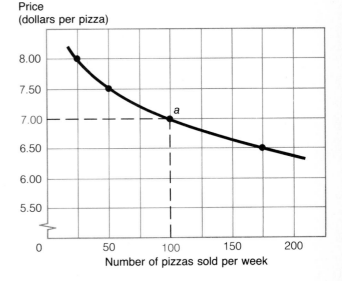

Moving to the right along the horizontal axis corresponds to an increase in the number of pizzas people will buy. The interval between each vertical grid line represents 25 additional pizzas. Moving up from the origin along the vertical axis represents an increase in price. The interval between horizontal grid lines represents $0.50. Note, however, that the first price shown is $5.50. The jagged line that interrupts the vertical axis between the origin and this price simply indicates that some of the dollar amounts have not been labeled.

Each point on the graph represents a combination of price and quantity (a price and the quantity that will be bought at that price). To plot a point, locate a price on the vertical axis and a quantity on the horizontal axis. Extend a line to the right from the price axis and up from the quantity axis. The point where the two lines intersect is the price and quantity combination for the two values you selected. (You should test your understanding of the connection between the data in the table and the points on the graph. Try your hand at plotting points on the graph.)

For example, the table shows that Paulo's customers will buy 100 pizzas each week if Paulo charges $7.00 per pizza; the corresponding point on the graph has been labeled *a*. (Be sure that you can see how point *a* represents this combination. Note that by following the dashed line down, you arrive at a quantity of 100; by following the other dashed line to the left, you arrive at a price of $7.00.) Typically,

Exhibit 1A.2
Unemployment Rate in the United States, 1960–1986

(a)

Year	Unemployment rate	Year	Unemployment rate
1960	5.4%	1975	8.3%
1961	6.5	1976	7.6
1962	5.4	1977	6.9
1963	5.5	1978	6.0
1964	5.0	1979	5.8
1965	4.4	1980	7.0
1966	3.7	1981	7.5
1967	3.7	1982	9.5
1968	3.5	1983	9.5
1969	3.4	1984	7.4
1970	4.8	1985	7.1
1971	5.8	1986	6.9
1972	5.5		
1973	4.8		
1974	5.5		

Source: Economic Report of the President, 1987, Table B-31.

when known points are plotted, a smooth line is drawn between them. In drawing the line, we assume that any intermediate point is both possible and a realistic approximation of the relationship.

On a two-dimensional graph we can show the relationship between two— and only two—variables. If we listed the variables that would influence the purchase of pizzas in this example, we would include the number of college students in Collegetown and the number of other places to eat and the prices they charge, among others. It is important to recognize that for any two-dimensional graph, the values of all variables other than the two that we are considering are held constant. In this case we see only the influence of price on the number of pizzas sold.

READING A GRAPH

Reading a graph is simply the reverse of plotting a graph. Consider the graph and table in Exhibit 1A.2, which shows the unemployment rate in the United States for the years 1960–1986. The two variables are the rate of unemployment (the dependent variable) and time (the independent variable).

To read the graph, first choose a year, say, 1980. Locate the year on the horizontal axis, then move vertically up from the horizontal axis to the line of the

(b)

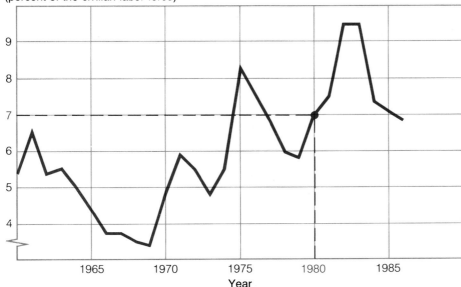

Unemployment rate
(percent of the civilian labor force)

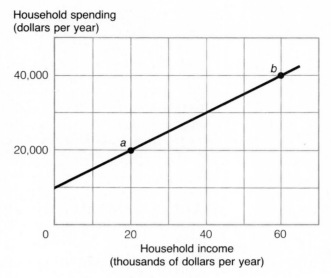

Exhibit 1A.3
A Model of Household Spending

graph. At that point, move horizontally across to the vertical axis. You should find that in 1980 the unemployment rate was 7.0 percent.

Unlike Exhibit 1A.1, this is a graph of real data. The source of the data is given so that you can see where these numbers came from. The data on which the graph was based are also given, so you can practice reading the graph. Many of the graphs that you will encounter in this textbook are accompanied by data, but some are not. You must become thoroughly familiar with graphs and be able to read them if you are to understand many of the economic concepts presented. (Check your understanding by reading other points on the graph and verifying them against the data in the table. Some points lie between grid lines, so you will have to approximate some unemployment rates.)

SLOPE OF A LINE

A simple line graph shows how two variables are related. In Exhibit 1A.3 the graph shows that household spending is directly related to household income. When studying this relationship, economists will want to know how fast household spending increases when income increases. The answer to this important question is indicated by the **slope** of the line. The slope is the ratio of the change in the vertical direction to the change in the horizontal direction between two points on a straight line. For example, we can measure the slope of the line in Exhibit 1A.3 between points *a* and *b* by dividing the change in household spending—the change in the vertical direction—by the change in household income—the change

Slope. The ratio of the change in the vertical direction to the change in the horizontal direction between two points along a graph of a straight line.

in the horizontal direction. Thus

$$\text{Slope} = \frac{\text{Vertical change}}{\text{Horizontal change}}$$

$$= \frac{\text{Change in household spending (point } b - \text{ point } a)}{\text{Change in household income (point } b - \text{ point } a)}$$

$$= \frac{(\$40,000 - \$20,000)}{(\$60,000 - \$20,000)} = \frac{\$20,000}{\$40,000} = 0.50$$

The numerical value of the slope of a line is significant. A *positive slope* (as in this case) indicates that the two variables are directly related. On a graph, a positive slope is shown by a line that slopes upward and to the right (as in Exhibit 1A.3). A *negative slope* indicates that the two variables are inversely related and is shown on a graph as a line that slopes downward and to the right (as in Exhibit 1A.1).

The magnitude of the slope—a measure of the rate of change—also has economic significance. In this example, the slope measures how fast household spending increases as income increases. The value ($+0.50$) indicates the direct relationship between the two variables (more income results in more spending) and the magnitude of the relationship ($100 of additional income increases household spending by $50).

INTERCEPT OF A LINE

In a graph the point at which the line touches one of the axes is called the **intercept**. Often the intercept has economic significance. In Exhibit 1A.3 you can see that the intercept on the vertical axis shows that when household income is zero, household spending is predicted to be $10,000.

MATHEMATICAL MODELS

In addition to graphs, economists also use mathematical models to depict economic relationships. For example, an economist might describe the relationship between household spending and household income shown in Exhibit 1A.3 by the following equation.

$$C = 10 + 0.50Y$$

where the symbol C stands for household spending (in $000s) and Y for household income. In fact, this equation describes the relationship depicted in the graph. The constant term (10) is the amount of household spending when income is zero. This term represents the intercept (where the spending line touches the vertical axis). The coefficient of Y (income) is the slope of the household spending line; it says that spending increases by $0.50 for each $1 increase in income. Using the equation we predict that household spending will be $40,000 when household income is $60,000. That is,

Intercept. The point at which a line on a graph touches one of the axes.

$$C = 10 + 0.50(60) = 10 + 30 = 40 \quad \text{or} \quad \$40,000$$

Although the use of mathematical models in this textbook is limited to the mathematical appendices, you may find it useful to learn to use mathematical as well as graphic models in studying economics. To test your understanding of this equation and its relationship to the graph, determine (a) the level of household spending when income is $30,000 and (b) the level of income when household spending is $35,000. (The answers, which you can find from both the equation and the graph, should be (a) $25,000 of spending and (b) $50,000 of income.)

CONCLUSION

The ability to read and interpret graphs is essential to learning economics. You will have many occasions to use graphic skills. However, economics is not about graphs (or mathematical models) but about the economic relationships depicted by graphs. In addition to learning how to read graphs—and determining the value of the slope of a line—pay close attention to the economic significance of the relationships. Graphs (and mathematical models) are only tools for learning and expressing economic ideas.

KEY TERMS

Dependent variable, 18   **Slope, 22**
Independent variable, 19   **Intercept, 23**
Origin, 19

Scarcity and Economic Choice

QUESTIONS TO CONSIDER

☐ What are the economic goals of every society and how are they interrelated?

☐ Why can we achieve allocative efficiency but not eliminate scarcity?

☐ What does the production possibilities curve mean to our goal of economic growth?

☐ What underlying principles do economists assume govern all economic decisions?

☐ Why do economists care more about marginal costs and benefits than absolute costs and benefits?

In Chapter 1 you learned that economics is, in part, a study of scarcity. In this chapter we take a closer look at the meaning and implications of scarcity. All societies face scarcity and, as a result, are forced to address certain basic economic questions. As we noted in Chapter 1, an important implication of scarcity is that individuals and societies are forced to make choices. In this chapter, we will look at what economists assume about how choices are made.

IMPLICATIONS OF SCARCITY

Scarcity exists because human wants are unlimited and economic resources are limited. Consequently, the individual and collective wants of a society exceed its capacity to produce goods and services. Since we can't have everything we want, we must make choices. Which wants will we satisfy and how will we use our resources?

Competition and Rationing

The limits imposed by scarcity mean that there will always be competition and rationing. Because society cannot produce all the new housing that individuals want, they have to compete for the new houses that are built. Because the amount of oil that can be produced in a specific period of time is limited, distributors and retailers must compete for the amounts that they receive. Such competition exists in every society. We are familiar with competition in market economies like that of the United States. But competition for scarce resources and products also exists in planned socialist economies like that of the Soviet Union. *Competition is inevitable and exists in all societies because of scarcity.*

Scarcity also means rationing. Rationing is the determination of how resources will be used—to produce education or new cars or national defense—and how goods and services will be distributed. But society needs criteria and mechanisms to determine how to ration resources. Scarce seats in medical schools may be rationed on the basis of college grades by an admissions committee. Distribution of new cars is rationed in the market by who will pay the highest price. Congress and the president ration the amount of national defense produced. Tickets to rock concerts are rationed partly by price, but also by a first-come, first-served process. There are many options, but *society must have some criteria and mechanism to ration every scarce resource and product*.

A study of scarcity is, in large part, a study of how competition operates and how rationing is performed. But we also want to be able to evaluate how well any rationing process operates. Economists approach the study of scarcity by assuming that a society would seek to do the best it can with its available resources. But just what is best?

In order to decide what is "best," every society must answer three questions: (1) What goods and services should be produced and in what quantities? (2) How should the goods and services be produced? (3) To whom will the goods and services be distributed? Obviously, these *fundamental economic questions* (as we shall refer to them) have many possible answers. Moreover, obtaining answers from individuals about what is best for them would be relatively easy. (You probably have a ready answer to the first and third questions, for example.) What is best from a society's perspective, however, depends on collective as well as individual values and requires recognition of certain goals.

Economic Goals

Each fundamental economic question is related to an economic goal that defines what is generally meant by the "best" answer. These goals are allocative efficiency, technical efficiency, and equity.

Allocative efficiency. Let's begin with the question of what goods and services will be produced, or put another way: Which wants will society decide to satisfy? In seeking to answer this question in the best way, society must be careful not to waste resources on one product when another would better meet its wants. For example, we must choose between cleaner air and more autos and between more autos and more missiles. Economists define the "best" social choice by the term **allocative efficiency**. Allocative efficiency results when no other mix of goods and services that could be produced with the available resources would better satisfy society's wants. Thus the best answer to the question "What goods and services should be produced?" is the allocatively efficient mix of goods.

Defining allocative efficiency in terms of a society's wants means that different societies may choose to use their resources differently. In studying the U.S. economy, we generally define society's economic goals in terms of the wants and satisfactions of individuals. Thus allocative efficiency is achieved when no other mix of goods and services would give individuals greater total satisfaction. The economic goals of the Soviet Union, however, appear to be quite different. The concerns of Soviet leaders appear to be maximum growth of output and military strength. This choice leads to a different allocation of resources and a different mix of goods and services.

In addition, societies may use very different mechanisms for determining the goods and services to be produced. Under the U.S. economic system (market capitalism), markets are the primary mechanism for deciding what to produce. As a result, individual consumer wants greatly influence what is produced. Under the Soviet economic system (planned socialism), government officials decide what

Allocative efficiency. Producing the combination of goods and services that satisfies society's wants to the greatest degree.

Technical efficiency. Producing goods and services for the least possible cost while maintaining full utilization of resources.

Equity. Distributing goods and services in a manner considered by society to be fair.

will be produced. However, no real-world economic system is completely capitalistic or socialistic; all economies are mixed. Markets guide production of some goods and services in the Soviet Union and other socialist countries. Government determines the quantity of national defense, public education, and other public goods and services in the United States and other countries that have market economies.

Technical efficiency.   A society must also decide how to produce the goods and services it wants. Because scarcity limits what can be produced, the full and effective use of available resources is important. To produce in any other way involves waste. Economists define this goal as **technical efficiency**. When a society is technically efficient, it is not possible to increase the total output of the economy for a given quantity of resources and technology. To be technically efficient, a society must produce each good and service at the lowest possible cost and maintain full utilization of resources. Technical inefficiency results when more resources than necessary are used to produce a product, when highly skilled workers perform tasks that fail to utilize their skills fully, and when resources—workers and/or machines—are allowed to remain idle.

Equity.   In addition to deciding what to produce and how to produce, society must determine how goods and services are to be distributed. Since scarcity means that every want cannot be satisfied, a society must determine which wants (and whose wants) will be satisfied and which will not be satisfied. The question of distribution can also be expressed as society's desire for **equity**, that is, finding a fair or just way to distribute goods and services among its members.

Of course, deciding what is "fair" or "just" is not easy. In fact, the manner of distribution—and by implication the definition of equity—is fundamentally different in different types of economic systems. In market-oriented systems, such as the U.S. economy, equity is often associated with individual effort and productivity: The more productive you are, the greater your income will be and the more goods and services you can buy. Note that equity is not the same as equality (although a society can choose to distribute goods equally). In fact, in the United States, equality is clearly not the rule. Karl Marx defined equity as "to each according to his need," believing that the distribution system in market-oriented economies was unjust. However, productivity is still an important basis for the distribution of goods in the Soviet Union.

More so than the other questions of what and how to produce, the question of distribution is a normative one. Determining what is "fair" and "just" always involves value judgments. Positive economic theories and models can predict how goods and services are likely to be distributed, given certain economic events and government policies. But economic theories cannot decide whether the distribution is equitable. They cannot help us make those normative judgments about which manner of distribution is best.

Interrelatedness of economic goals.   As with most economic choices, we often make trade-offs among economic goals. Achieving all three economic goals simultaneously can be difficult or even impossible.

Let's consider a single economic resource: soft coal. This resource has the following characteristics: (1) when mined and burned, it causes some damage to the environment; (2) in many industries it is less expensive to use than alternative fuels; and (3) it is a major, inexpensive source of heat for a large number of people.

Because clean air, clean water, and beautiful scenery are among the wants of society, the first characteristic of coal—causing environmental damage—creates a dilemma. The more soft coal we use, the fewer environmental wants we can satisfy. In seeking allocative efficiency we must ask whether our society will be better off enjoying more clean air or using more soft coal. At the same time, soft coal is less expensive for some industrial purposes than other fuels. Thus if we use less soft coal, technical efficiency will tend to decrease and our society will have to sacrifice the production of other goods. Finally, if we reduce the use of soft coal, some families will face increased heating costs and consequently a lower standard of living. Should those individuals be penalized in order to protect the environment? Is this type of trade-off equitable?

This example is typical of most economic choices facing our society and clearly shows how we are forced to make difficult trade-offs. Technical efficiency, and perhaps equity, may be improved when soft coal is used. But the costs associated with the resulting environmental damage may mean that the economy is worse off from the perspective of allocative efficiency. We can illustrate other trade-offs by examining the limits imposed on production.

Production Possibilities

We can express the limits faced by a society as a **production possibilities curve**. The economic model represented by this curve shows the various combinations of goods that an economy *can* produce during some period of time if it is technically efficient. This curve also reflects the fact that even if a nation succeeds in achieving technical efficiency, what it can produce is still limited by available resources and technology.

As with all economic models, the production possibilities curve is based on several assumptions. First, we assume that regardless of what goods society chooses to produce, it will always utilize its resources at maximum technical efficiency. Second, we assume that the supply of all resources is fixed—both in quantity and in quality—and that technology also remains constant. Finally, in order to easily depict the production possibilities, we assume that the economy produces only two goods. Like all models, the production possibilities curve cannot accurately represent a real-world economy. Economies produce more than two goods and do not always produce efficiently. However, despite these assumptions, we can use this model to illustrate some fundamental economic principles.

Production possibilities curve. A curve showing the various combinations of output that an economy can produce with its existing resources when operating at maximum technical efficiency.

For the sake of discussion, let's consider the production possibilities for a hypothetical economy that produces only TV sets and ice cream. The table in Exhibit 2.1 summarizes the various combinations of TV sets and gallons of ice cream that can be produced in a year with the resources and technology available. For example, the society could produce 3 million TV sets and 15 million gallons of ice cream (combination D), or 4 million TV sets and 11 million gallons of ice cream (combination E). By transferring these data to a graph, we can illustrate the production possibilities model. We can let the horizontal axis represent the output of TV sets and the vertical axis the output of ice cream. By plotting each combination (A–G) and connecting the points with a smooth line, we get the production possibilities curve shown in Exhibit 2.1. Each point on the curve is a possible option for society; that is, it can be obtained if production is technically efficient.

(a) Production possibilities schedule

Possible combination	TV sets produced (millions)	Ice cream produced (millions of gallons)
A	0	21
B	1	20
C	2	18
D	3	15
E	4	11
F	5	6
G	6	0

(b) Production possibilities curve (PPC)

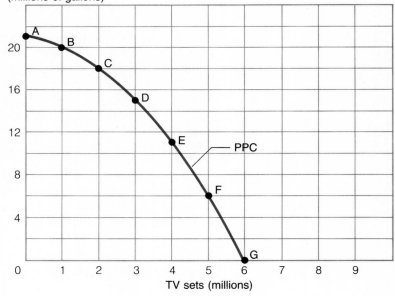

Exhibit 2.1
Production Possibilities Curve for TV Sets and Ice Cream
Each point on the production possibilities curve represents a possible combination of TV sets and ice cream that could be produced, with current resources and technology. However, these points can be reached only if the economy operates at maximum technical efficiency. The curve indicates only possibilities. It does not show what combination is best from the standpoint of allocative efficiency.

Note that the curve does not indicate which of the possible points is best. The answer to that question relates to allocative efficiency and depends on the relative values society places on the two goods. The production possibilities curve merely indicates the *possible* choices.[*]

Production possibilities and opportunity cost. The production possibilities curve illustrates the relationship between scarcity and opportunity cost. The curve itself reflects the limits of scarcity. For any point on the curve, we cannot produce more of one good (say, TV sets) without having to sacrifice producing some of the other good (ice cream). The magnitude of the sacrifice is the opportunity cost.

Suppose, for example, that the economy is currently producing 3 million TV sets and 15 million gallons of ice cream (combination D). What is the opportunity

---

[*] As you can tell by flipping through the pages of this textbook, we use many numerical examples like this one. If you are having difficulty with the graph used in this example, you should review the appendix to Chapter 1. The study guide that accompanies this textbook also contains helpful information and practice exercises on how to read and use graphs.

cost of increasing the production of TV sets to 4 million? If we move to combination E, in which 4 million TV sets are produced, the production of ice cream declines to 11 million gallons, a reduction of 4 million. In other words, to produce the extra 1 million TV sets the society must sacrifice the opportunity to have 4 million more gallons of ice cream. Thus the curve illustrates the following economic principle: *To increase the quantity of one product requires a sacrifice, or opportunity cost.*

Opportunity cost is a natural result of scarcity. Recall that for any one production possibilities curve, we assume that technology and the quantity of resources available remain unchanged. Thus by choosing to produce more of one good, the society also chooses to produce less of another. To test your understanding, calculate the opportunity cost of producing the third million TV sets, moving from point C to D. (The answer is an opportunity cost of 3 million gallons of ice cream.)

Increasing costs.   The production possibilities relationship we are using as an example also illustrates another economic principle: *The more the quantity of one product increases, the greater is the opportunity cost involved.* Exhibit 2.1 indicates that the opportunity cost of producing the first million TV sets (moving from point A to point B) is 1 million gallons of ice-cream. The opportunity cost rises as more and more TV sets are produced. In moving from point D to point E, for example, the opportunity cost of 1 million more TV sets is 4 million gallons of ice cream.

Why do opportunity costs increase? First, most workers, either by nature or by training, are better at one job than another. For example, a person trained to assemble TV sets is not likely to be as skilled an ice-cream maker as one with training in that field. In order to expand the production of TV sets, the society must (at full employment) move some workers (and other resources) from making ice cream to making TV sets. Workers better suited to assembling TV sets will be moved first. But continued expansion of TV-set production will mean moving workers who are less skilled in making TV sets and more skilled in making ice cream, resulting in higher costs. The cost of TV sets will rise both because more workers will be needed to make another 1 million TV sets and because the last workers switched to making TV sets could have produced more ice cream than the first workers moved. The same reasoning applies to other resources. Machines used to make ice cream cannot be used to manufacture TV sets, for example. As you will find, increasing cost characterizes many economic activities.

Technical inefficiency.   Although we have focused only on those combinations that lie on the production possibilities curve, every combination of TV sets and gallons of ice cream in the shaded area of Exhibit 2.2 (the area inside—to the left of—the production possibilities curve) can be produced. The combinations on the curve are *maximum* production levels that can be reached only if the society achieves technical efficiency. Whenever production is technically inefficient, the society will find that it cannot reach these limits.

For example, suppose that the actual output of the society is 11 million gallons of ice cream and 2 million TV sets (shown in Exhibit 2.2 as point U). This combination means that the society is not producing all its potential output. In fact, the economy could produce more TV sets and the same amount of ice cream (that is, a move to point E) or more ice cream and the same number of TV sets (a move to point C). It is even possible to produce more of both items (point D).

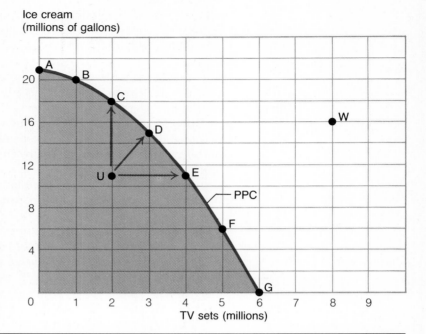

Ice cream
(millions of gallons)

TV sets (millions)

Exhibit 2.2
Production Possibilities
and Inefficiency
The production possibilities curve (PPC) represents the maximum limits of production, assuming maximum technical efficiency. If society is inefficient, less than the maximum will be produced (point U). Society can produce more TV sets or ice cream or both, if technical efficiency is increased. Points outside the curve (point W) are beyond society's production possibilities for the current state of technology and the current supply of resources.

In short, the society is not achieving technical efficiency (the maximum output attainable from a given quantity of resources) whenever actual production is within the limits of the production possibilities curve (in the shaded area of the graph).

Technical inefficiency can occur if some workers are unemployed or if production of one or both goods unnecessarily wastes resources. By eliminating inefficiency, a society can increase its output of one or both of the goods.

Production possibilities and economic growth. For any particular production possibilities curve, production is limited because we assume that the society has a fixed supply of resources and a certain level of technology. This means that at any one time, points beyond the production possibilities curve (points to the right of the curve) cannot be obtained. For example, point W in Exhibit 2.2, representing 8 million TV sets and 16 million gallons of ice cream, is currently unattainable. This is not to say that the society can never achieve that level of production, but rather that it cannot do so currently, owing to the constraints of existing technology and resources.

What happens, however, if the quantity of resources increases, the quality of resources improves, or technology progresses? For example, what happens if the number of workers in the society increases, the current workers receive additional training, or someone discovers a more efficient way to make TV sets or ice cream? As illustrated in Exhibit 2.3, these changes would expand the production possibilities of the society and result in an outward (to the right) shift in the production possibilities curve (from PPC_1 to PPC_2). If the society had been producing at point E_1 on the original curve (4 million TV sets and 11 million gallons of ice cream), it would now be possible to expand ice-cream production to 20 million gallons without reducing the quantity of TV sets produced (point C_2), or to expand

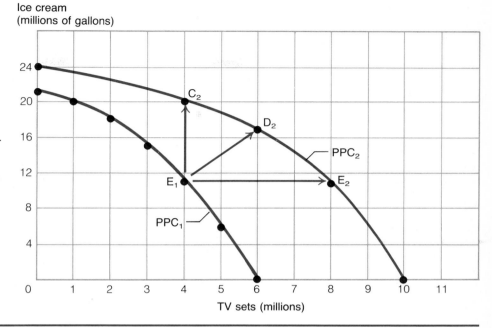

Exhibit 2.3
Production Possibilities and Economic Growth
Any production possibilities curve (PPC) is based on the assumption that the level of technology and the supply of resources are fixed. When either technology improves or the supply of resources increases, society can produce more. This change is illustrated as an outward shift in the production possibilities curve (from PPC_1 to PPC_2). When economic growth occurs, society can produce more of one product without sacrificing any amount of the other product, or it can have more of both products.

production to 8 million TV sets while producing the same quantity of ice cream (point E_2). Either of these combinations—or any other combination on the new production possibilities curve—is a possible option. The changes in technology or availability of resources results in **economic growth**. Economic growth increases society's production possibilities, that is, the ability to satisfy more of society's wants.

Economic growth: Capital resources versus consumer products.
Economic growth may result from obtaining more natural resources, more highly skilled labor, or better technology. In addition, economic growth may result if a society produces more capital resources in the form of factories and equipment. An increase in the quantity of capital resources increases the capacity to produce. By investing more in capital resources today, society can produce more consumer goods and services in the future.

However, as with all economic choices, this trade-off means sacrifice. We cannot produce more capital resources without sacrificing some **consumer products**—food, cars, movies, and health care, for example—that are produced to satisfy society's current wants. Scarcity forces a trade-off between satisfying wants now or in the future. We can have more consumer products tomorrow if we produce more capital resources today. The effect of today's choice on tomorrow's production possibilities is illustrated in Exhibit 2.4.

The possibilities shown on this graph are consumer products (on the vertical axis) and capital resources (on the horizontal axis). The current production possibilities curve is labeled PPC_1. Two current options for the economy are labeled A and B on PPC_1. If society chooses option A, it will produce more consumer products and fewer capital resources than if it chooses option B. The results of

Economic growth. An increase in society's production possibilities.

Consumer products. Goods such as autos, food, appliances, and movies, and services such as health care that directly satisfy consumer wants.

Quantity of
consumer products

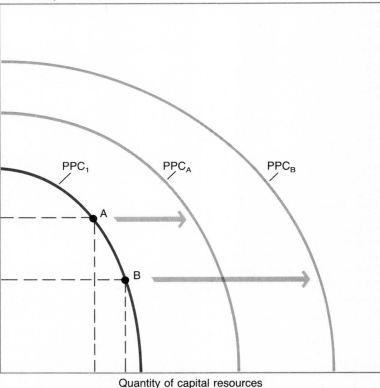

Exhibit 2.4
Capital Resources and
Economic Growth
The economy's current production possibility is shown as PPC₁. Today, society
must choose between two options: producing more consumer products (option
A) or more capital resources (option B).
The selection of either option will determine future production possibilities,
shown as PPCₐ or PPCᵦ. For example,
society will experience greater economic
growth if it chooses to produce more
capital resources. But there is a price:
The opportunity cost of more growth is
less production of consumer products
today.

Quantity of capital resources

this choice are shown as PPCₐ, or the future production possibilities of the
economy. However, if society chooses option B, it can further increase its production possibilities (to PPCᵦ) in the future; it will have produced more capital
resources and thus increased its production potential.

Is society better off choosing option B? Not necessarily. Society must sacrifice
consumer goods and services today in order to achieve greater production potential tomorrow. We can say only that the economy will be better off in the future
but worse off today if option B is selected. Producing more capital resources today
requires a willingness to sacrifice temporarily the production of some quantity of
consumer products that would increase satisfaction today. The current wants that
could have been satisfied represent the opportunity cost associated with the
decision to increase capital spending.

All societies face this dilemma: To increase society's capital resources requires
a sacrifice; to be able to produce more goods next year, we must consume less
today. But all societies do not make the same choices. Production of capital
resources accounts for about 16 percent of all output in the United States but
about 35 percent in the Soviet Union. The higher output of capital resources in
the Soviet Union has helped the Soviet economy achieve a relatively high rate of
growth. This growth has come at the expense of satisfaction of individual wants
because the production of consumer products is relatively low in the Soviet Union.

A production possibilities curve indicates the various combinations of goods that can be produced with the available resources and technology, assuming that society operates at maximum technical efficiency.

Points inside the curve (to the left) represent technical inefficiency. Points outside the curve (to the right) cannot be obtained with the resources and technology available.

The opportunity cost of increasing output of one good or service is measured as the amount of the other good or service that must be sacrificed.

Economic growth results from increasing the quantity or quality of resources, the production of capital resources, and development of better technology. Economic growth causes the production possibilities curve to shift outward (to the right).

If we assume that these differences reflect the preferences of the two societies, it would seem that growth has a higher priority in the Soviet Union and satisfying current consumer wants has a higher priority in the United States.

Production possibilities: To work or not to work?   At any one time society's production possibilities reflect levels of technology and resources. One of the important resources is labor—the skills, talents, physical effort, and time of individuals. We could increase the total output of the economy if everyone were willing to devote 10 percent more time to producing goods and services. In Japan, for example, the typical employee works 2250 hours per year compared to only 1900 hours in the United States. Increasing the number of hours worked would involve a cost: We would have to sacrifice other uses of our time. This sacrifice might include leisure activities, such as going to the beach, skiing, or reading a book for pleasure. It might also affect other activities—gardening, studying economics, or painting your house—that are not exactly leisure but clearly have value. Should we spend more time working? Would the extra benefits from the increase in output be worth the sacrifice? We cannot easily answer such questions but should be alert for economic events that may affect such personal decisions. Some economists, for example, believe that very high tax rates, such as those in Sweden and Great Britain, reduce the amount people work and thus affect not only current output but also future economic growth.

ECONOMIC CHOICE

Because production possibilities are limited, individuals and society must make choices. Economists want to understand how choices are made so they can predict the economy's response to economic events. Economists believe that decision making can be best understood and predicted by assuming that individuals apply the principles of **rational choice**, as discussed in this section.

Self-Interest

As we mentioned earlier, all decisions are ultimately made by individuals. Individual consumers decide what goods and services to buy. Individual business managers decide what goods and services to produce and how to produce them. Individual government officials decide what government goods and services to provide and what laws and regulations will govern economic and noneconomic actions. Economists believe that individual choices can be best understood by assuming that *individuals act in their own self-interest to gain what they see as the maximum advantage from the resources they control.*

It is easy to misunderstand what economists mean by rational choice. Some people wrongly interpret it as the economist's belief that individuals are selfish and greedy. No doubt some are, but self-interest does not exclude actions by individuals to make gifts or serve the "public interest." Even in those activities, economists see self-interest at work. Individuals give gifts because they get satisfaction from doing so. They may volunteer time and money to worthy causes because of the emotional benefits they receive. The idea of self-interest is important in developing a model of choice because it helps us to understand how individuals react to changes in economic conditions.

Rational choice. Selecting among economic alternatives by comparing extra benefits expected to be received with extra costs expected to be incurred; an economic model used to explain the choices made by individuals, businesses, and government.

Minimizing Costs and Maximizing Benefits

In assuming that individuals make rational choices, economists mean that decision makers choose deliberately, intending to "economize." That is, *people seek to minimize the costs of attaining any objective and to maximize the benefits of any expenditure.*

If individuals act rationally in their own self-interest, we can predict how they will react to changes in economic conditions. An increase in benefits or a decrease in costs will result in more activity; a decrease in benefits or an increase in costs will mean less activity. Thus rational choice theory allows economists to understand economic behavior and to predict the effect of changes in economic circumstances, including government policies.

For example, we predict that more individuals will attend college when expected salaries of college graduates increase. We expect members of Congress to be more likely to vote in favor of a particular bill if it is changed to increase their chances of reelection. We expect a business to produce more computers when the profits they expect to earn are greater.

At the same time, we can expect predictable responses to changes in costs. If your instructor announces a major exam for the next class period, the cost of skipping class will rise, and we can predict fewer absences. A decrease in personal computer prices will spur a major growth in sales. Government imposition of a new tax on imported automobiles will cause consumers to buy fewer foreign cars.

Rational Expectations

Because we live in an uncertain world, individuals cannot always know exactly what benefits and costs are associated with a choice. Thus *decisions are made on the basis of expectations.*

When you decide to pay $5 to see a new movie, economists say that you expect to receive at least $5 of benefits. Of course, you can be disappointed and believe after you saw the movie that it wasn't worth $5, but like most decisions, this one was made based on expectations. Similarly, when a business decides to produce a new product, it does so because it expects consumers to buy enough of the product at a high enough price to earn the firm a reasonable profit. A firm cannot be sure that it will earn a profit. Future prices and costs are uncertain. But a decision to produce is based on *expected* benefits and *expected* costs. You will find many occasions to note the effect of expectations on economic choices.

Marginal Costs and Benefits

Economists suggest that individuals making rational choices select those options for which the expected *extra* benefits outweigh the expected *extra* costs. Economists use the term **marginal** (meaning extra) because they recognize that few decisions require an all-or-nothing choice. You do not have to choose between eating 10 pizzas or none, for example. You can choose to eat 1, 2, or more. Moreover, you can choose incrementally, that is, you can eat one pizza before ordering a second one. When deciding whether to buy a second pizza, you would, following the principles of rational choice, consider how much additional satisfaction the second pizza would provide.

Marginal. A term used by economists to denote *extra* or *additional.*

The principles of rational choice also imply that economic choice involves considering only those factors that are likely to change as a result of a particular decision. For example, in deciding whether to attend your next economics class, the tuition payment you made at the beginning of the term is irrelevant because it will not change. In deciding whether to come to class, you would weigh the extra benefits of attending against the extra costs, and would not be concerned with anything not affected by the decision.

Economic Approach to Decision Making

Economists use this model of rational choice in two ways. First, by assuming that decision makers use this model, economists can derive other economic principles. In Chapter 5 we show how this model implies that smoothly functioning markets tend to result in allocative efficiency, for example. But the model of rational choice can also be used by individuals, business managers, and government officials to improve their economic choices.

The economic approach to decision making recognizes that each decision involves at least two possible options. The first step in making a rational choice is to list and evaluate the available options. For example, if you are hungry you may satisfy your hunger in several ways. Before deciding which is the best way, you consider your options.

Economists also recognize that options are mutually exclusive. That is, if one option is chosen, another one is precluded. If you choose to spend $5 on a movie, you cannot spend that same $5 to buy a book. In other words, each option chosen has an associated opportunity cost—an option that must be sacrificed. Thus the value of any one option must be compared to that of other options. Most importantly, considering opportunity cost reminds us that we cannot simply have cleaner air or more national defense or more clothes or more vacations. Every time we choose to have more of any one item, we have to accept less of another. Most of the time, those who argue that "there's no substitute for ..." fail to recognize opportunity cost and fail to apply the principles of rational choice.

Economists also assume that decision makers have a particular goal or goals in mind. For example, economists most often assume that businesses seek to earn maximum profits. The goal of profits helps the business manager to determine how to value benefits and costs.

Finally, the model of rational choice suggests that decision makers collect information on the expected extra benefits and the expected extra costs of each option. This notion implies that they focus on those benefits and costs that *change* as a result of the decision they make. That is, the costs that remain constant are irrelevant. If a business uses the same machines and the same building regardless of the product made, there are no relevant costs for the building or machines. If we calculate marginal costs and compare them with marginal benefits, we can determine what information is relevant to a decision. Those who argue that "we can't forget what we've already spent on this project ..." fail to focus on expected extra benefits and costs and, as a result, may make serious errors.

When collecting information, we must apply the same basic principles, weighing both benefits and costs. Typically, the potential benefits of collecting information are greater when there is more uncertainty initially. For example, we spend more time collecting information on the price and availability of new cars than we do for a newspaper. Acquiring information can also be expensive. For example, how much time and money would you have to spend to personally obtain information on the safety of a new prescription drug? In some cases, we consult individuals—such as stock brokers—who specialize in information. In other cases—such as finding the best buy in a new car—we tend to rely on our own efforts. The important point is that information is expensive. We collect only as much information as we can justify on the basis of extra benefits and extra costs.

In summary, the following steps represent an economic model of decision making.

1. Identify the several alternatives, or possible choices.

2. For each alternative, estimate the expected extra benefits and the expected extra costs, remembering to use the concept of opportunity cost and applying benefit–cost judgment to the collection of information.

3. Whenever the extra benefits of an alternative are expected to outweigh the extra costs—and this difference exceeds that for other options—that alternative has an advantage over the other options and should be accepted.

As you study economics, you will come across many applications of rational choice principles. Economists apply these principles in describing consumer choice, producer choice, and public choice. Although the circumstances differ, the principles remain a constant guide for making choices. Of course, when developing this model of rational choice, economists had to depart from reality to some extent. The model cannot predict the behavior of an individual consumer, who may act on whim and who is probably unable to obtain all the information available about all possible options. However, the model of rational choice does a good job of predicting behavior of consumers as a group. The purpose of any model is to predict, and evidence indicates that this model—and others based on rational choice principles—are good predictors. The use of rational choice principles is illustrated in A Case in Point: How Many Prisons to Build?

Rational Public Choice

Consumers and businesses and are not the only ones faced with economic choices. Even in the United States, where most economic decisions are made by individuals acting in their own private interests, political decisions have important effects on the economy. The federal, state, and local governments purchase about 20 percent of the nation's goods and services and employ about 25 percent of the labor force. Government laws and regulation limit many individual choices. We must understand public choice, as well as private choice, if we are to understand how our economy operates.

From the perspective of the economy as a whole, a socially desirable law or government decision would increase society's benefits more than its costs. But economists recognize that such decisions are made by individuals—politicians and government officials. In fact, a whole body of theory called **public choice theory** relates to how decisions are made in the public (government) sector. Public choice theory assumes that all individuals act in their own self-interest and uses this assumption to predict the behavior of voters and the choices of government officials.

Public choice theory. An economic theory based on rational choice principles that attempts to explain how choices are made in the public (government) sector.

A Case in Point
How Many Prisons to Build?

To illustrate the application of the principles of rational choice, consider the following situation. A state is considering building one or two additional prisons and has collected accurate information on the total benefits and costs to society. The cost of building one prison is $50 million; the cost of two, $120 million. This information is presented in the table below. Stop reading for a minute, consider the information and the options available, and decide what you think the state should do. Refer if necessary to the discussion on rational choice.

Benefits and Costs of Building More Prisons in the State

Number of new prisons	Total social benefits	Total social costs
0	—	—
1	$100 million	$ 50 million
2	150 million	120 million

How many prisons do you think the state should build? If you understood the principles of rational choice and are beginning to think like an economist, you decided that the state should build only one additional

prison. Let's examine each option separately, weighing the extra benefits and extra costs.

Consider first the choice of building one additional prison. When the first new prison is built, the social benefits increase by $100 million, whereas the social costs rise by only $50 million. (Note that there are neither costs nor benefits if no new prisons are built.) By building the first prison, society gains $50 million, or $100 million of extra benefits less $50 million of extra costs. (Note that this conclusion is based on the fact that *all* costs and benefits have been included in the table.)

If two prisons were built, total benefits are still greater than total costs. But focusing on *extra* benefits and costs, you can see why it does not make economic sense to build the second prison. The extra benefits of the second prison are only $50 million (total benefits increase from $100 million to $150 million). However, society has to incur an extra cost of $70 million ($120 million for two prisons versus $50 million for one). Thus the second prison adds $50 million in extra benefits but $70 million in extra costs. Seen in this light, the second prison is clearly not a good idea. This example, although simple, is very important. The principles of rational choice that it illustrates are central to the study of economics.

Public choice theory suggests that the public choices made are not always those that are best for society as a whole. For example, a special interest group, such as the owners of a local sports team, will benefit greatly if the city builds a new sports arena with public funds. Individual taxpayers bear the costs, but no single taxpayer pays much more. Public choice theory predicts the owners (who will gain a lot) will lobby strongly. Taxpayers (who each lose a little) have less incentive to make their opinions known. The result, according to public choice theory, is predictable—there are many such public facilities.

Ultimately, politicians—elected officials, not professional economists—determine economic policy. As we have already stated, economic analysis often does not lead to a single conclusion. In Chapter 1 we noted some of the reasons why economists disagree on policy issues. The tendency of economists to note both benefits and costs led President Harry Truman to wish for a one-armed economist because he got tired of hearing economists say "on the one hand ..., but on the other, ..." Even if economists agreed on the facts and used the same economic models, the normative, equity issues of any policy choice always raise issues of benefits and costs that cannot be decided by economic theory. Under our form of government, decisions about which segments of society to favor are left to the political process.

For example, in 1986 Congress passed a tax "reform" bill, seeking to raise the same total amount of tax revenues in a simpler, "fairer" manner. But in order to raise the same total amount of funds, it was necessary for every decrease in taxes paid by one group to be balanced by an increase in taxes paid by another group. If the poor were to pay less, other groups would have to pay more. Economic models were used to predict the effects of various policy changes. That is, the models enabled economists to make some positive statements about the "facts." But decisions about the normative aspects of the legislation—whether such changes were "good"—were necessarily political judgments.

Unfortunately, the political decision-making process adds a new set of goals and potential conflicts. These conflicts sometimes cause politicians and government officials to make choices that meet their personal objectives but not society's economic goals. Policies that make good economic sense may not meet political objectives such as attempting to ensure reelection, rewarding political friends, or penalizing political opponents. One of the most important aspects of this economics course is to enable you to understand the differences between economic theory and political reality. Politicians will be more willing to implement sound economic policy if they believe that the voters understand and accept economic realities.

Although economists cannot always determine which policies are best, sound application of economic principles can be a useful guide to policy making. If politicians focus on the expected extra benefits and costs of policies they are considering, they can avoid many mistakes. Economic reasoning tells politicians not to ignore the costs of policies (although some critics of government argue that this occurs frequently). Economic analysis can be used to predict whether a policy is likely to have the desired effects. Clearly, a policy that fails to achieve its purpose is undesirable. In addition, economic models can be used to forecast the results of several policy options, helping politicians find the one that achieves their objective at minimum cost and thus helping society achieve allocative efficiency.

RATIONAL CHOICE IN ACTION

As you have seen, rational choice requires recognition of scarcity and opportunity cost. In the following examples, we note the presence of scarcity, some of the options that may be considered, and the opportunity cost involved.

Example 1: A personal decision.   When you plan the expenditures you will make during the next month, you personally face the problem of scarcity. Your expenditures are limited by your income and by any savings you have. (We should add, of course, that the possibility of borrowing may exist, but for this example, we assume that the bank will consider you to be a poor credit risk.) You would very much like to have a stereo system that costs $450. Obviously obtaining the stereo will require a sacrifice.

While considering this option, you will, of course, want to consider how much it will cost. "That's easy," you say, "because I know the price is $450." But is $450 the *real* cost? An economist would recognize it as the monetary cost but suggest that you also think of the cost in terms of the satisfaction you might gain from spending the money in another way (on a skiing trip during winter vacation, for example). That is, the real sacrifice, or opportunity cost involved in buying the stereo is the value of the next best opportunity, or the most important alternative use of the scarce resources you have. Be careful not to confuse monetary cost with opportunity cost. Although these costs are sometimes related, they are not the same. Rational choice requires that you examine the opportunity cost.

Example 2: A public decision. A second example of the concepts of scarcity and opportunity cost is the dilemma faced by Congress when trying to decide whether to spend an additional $3 billion on a particular public-works program. Consider, for example, the arguments of Senator Porkbarrel, a distinguished (but economically illiterate) member of Congress: "We must go ahead with this project, there *are* no substitutes. We've sunk too much money in the program to quit now. The benefits of the project to this great nation are incalculable."

In his statement, Senator Porkbarrel violated the principles of rational choice in three ways. First, his argument that there are no options ignores the fact that there are alternative ways to meet the objectives of virtually any program. Moreover, the Senator is acting as though scarcity is not a problem. Whether Congress explicitly recognizes it or not, scarcity means that the resources used by this program cannot be used for another public program or by the private sector.

Second, in his zeal to have Congress approve the project, the Senator wants his colleagues to consider the money already spent. The money already spent, however, cannot be recovered and used for another purpose. The Senate should focus its attention on the expected *extra* benefits and costs, according to the principles of rational choice. Because the money spent in the past cannot be recovered, it is neither an extra benefit nor an extra cost associated with the program.

Finally, Senator Porkbarrel engages in an old trick. Because he favors the program, he emphasizes the benefits of the program but ignores the costs. Rational decision makers must learn to be skeptical of such one-sided statements. Before making any decision the Senate needs to know both the expected extra benefits *and* the expected extra costs. Every expenditure has an opportunity cost.

In measuring the cost of this program, an economist would not really be interested in the monetary cost, the $3 billion. Instead, an economist would ask: "What will be sacrificed?" If Congress spends the additional $3 billion on this project, what other government projects may have to be delayed or scrapped? What is the value to individuals of the goods and services they could obtain with lower taxes? Because of scarcity, Congress should think of the sacrifice required to make any particular choice, that is, in terms of its opportunity cost.

CONCLUSION

In later chapters, we continue the discussion of the principles of rational choice in analyzing how economic systems function, because the choices made by consumers, business managers, and government officials are the driving forces of the economy. By better understanding how rational choices are made, we can better determine the effects on the economy of changes in economic conditions. Scarcity, we have seen, forces society to make choices. If society is to achieve the economic goals of allocative efficiency, technical efficiency, and equity, it must have some mechanism for determining wants and the relative scarcity of resources and for ensuring efficient production. One such mechanism, the use of markets, is the primary choice of the United States and most Western European nations, although there are other options. We devote the next three chapters principally to discussing how markets work.

SUMMARY

1. In this chapter we discussed the implications of scarcity and introduced the principles of rational choice.

2. Because of scarcity, three fundamental economic questions face all societies: (a) what goods and services to produce, (b) how to produce them, and (c) to whom they should be distributed. Related to these questions are the goals of allocative efficiency, technical efficiency, and equity.

3. Allocative efficiency is achieved when society obtains the greatest possible satisfaction from the available resources. Technical efficiency requires that each product be produced with the least sacrifice of resources and that all resources be fully utilized. Equity requires that goods and services be distributed fairly and justly but not necessarily equally. Achieving all three goals simultaneously may be difficult or even impossible.

4. A production possibilities curve shows the limits imposed by scarcity as the maximum combination of goods and services that can be produced with a particular quantity and quality of resources and the best technology available. Each point on the curve shows the economy operating at maximum technical efficiency.

5. The production possibilities model indicates that even if society achieves technical efficiency, all wants cannot be satisfied; that increased production of one good or service requires a sacrifice or opportunity cost of less production of another good or service; that failure to achieve technical efficiency imposes costs; and that economic growth—attainable by increasing the quantity or quality of resources, producing capital resources instead of consumer products, or developing new technology—can ease but not eliminate the problem of scarcity.

6. Economists believe that economic behavior can be best understood by assuming that individuals apply the principles of rational choice. According to this model, individuals act in their own self-interest. They respond predictably to changes in benefits and costs: Increases in benefits and/or reductions in costs will cause individuals to undertake more of any activity. The model is also based on the assumption that individuals react to expected benefits and costs. They make one-time or incremental decisions by focusing on these extra, or marginal, benefits and costs.

7. In order to make a rational economic choice, a decision maker must consider the most important alternative. For each option, the expected extra (marginal) benefits and expected extra (marginal) costs must be calculated and compared. Cost must be defined as opportunity cost. An option should be selected only when marginal benefits exceed marginal costs.

8. Economic analysis cannot always indicate which government policy is best because equity issues are normative and not subject to objective theorizing. Thus government officials—both elected and appointed—make many decisions about national economic policy. In keeping with the principles of rational choice, we can expect politicians to act in their self-interest in making public choices. Rational economic analysis can help guide public decision making by indicating the effects of current and proposed policies and by helping public decision makers avoid mistakes, such as failing to consider only extra costs or ignoring either benefits or costs.

KEY TERMS

Allocative efficiency, 27
Technical efficiency, 28
Equity, 28
Production possibilities curve, 29
Economic growth, 33
Consumer products, 33
Rational choice, 35
Marginal, 36
Public choice theory, 38

QUESTIONS FOR REVIEW AND DISCUSSION

1. Economists assume that economic resources are limited and that human wants are unlimited. Explain how the following statements indicate a misunderstanding of these assumptions.
   a) The development of technology offers a solution to the problem of scarcity.
   b) Economists are wrong to assume that wants are unlimited, because I have all the food I want to eat at each meal.
   c) Not all resources are scarce; consider the unlimited nature of the universe.

2. How do the three economic goals discussed in this chapter provide ideal answers to the three fundamental economic questions?

3. If all producers have achieved maximum technical efficiency, does allocative efficiency exist? If society has attained both allocative efficiency and technical efficiency, has the goal of equity also been reached?

4. Consider the statement: "The best things in life are free—air, a beautiful sunset, libraries, free speech. Moreover, other things ought to be free—such as medical care."
   a) Some goods are available at a zero price (you do not have to give anyone money to obtain them). Does this mean that the goods are free? Why or why not?
   b) What are the costs of libraries, free speech, and air? Who pays these costs?
   c) Can the government make medical care available at no cost to the user? Can the government make medical care free to society? Explain the difference between these two questions.

5. Consider the oportunity costs of going to college. What are some of the important expenditures you must make? What are some of the other costs involved? (Be sure to carefully note where and why the list of opportunity costs and the list of expenditures differ.)

6. If economists can so easily define the goals of a society, why is it so difficult to achieve them? If you and I agree that allocative efficiency is a desirable social goal, do we necessarily agree on what mix of goods and services should be produced?

7. In which (if any) of the following situations would you say that resources are not fully employed?
   a) A college student chooses to study full time rather than combine school and work.
   b) A parent of a preschool-age child chooses to work only at home.
   c) A 70-year-old couple retires from a lifetime of work in order to enjoy leisure.
   d) A worker trades an opportunity to work overtime on Saturday for a chance to go on a family camping trip.

8. Based on the following data, draw a production possibilities curve. Label the horizontal axis "guns" and the vertical axis "butter." Using the curve, answer the following questions.

Butter (millions of pounds)	Guns (millions)
0	30
1	25
2	15
3	0

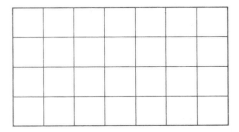

   a) Can the economy produce 35 million guns? Can it produce 4 million pounds of butter? Can it produce 25 million guns and 1 million pounds of butter?
   b) What is the opportunity cost of producing 3 million pounds of butter instead of 2 million? Of producing 25 million guns instead of 15 million?
   c) How does the cost of butter change as more is produced?
   d) Which, if any, of the points on the curve are "best" for society? (Consider the question from the perspective of each of the three economic goals presented in this chapter.)
   e) Label the point on the graph where society is producing 1 million pounds of butter and 10 million guns as U. What does this point tell you about technical efficiency?
   f) How would the production possibilities curve change if new technology increased the productive potential of the economy? (Draw a new curve on the graph to indicate this new possibilities curve.) What other factors could cause this shift?

9. For each of the following social choices, note how two (or more) economic goals are in conflict.
   a) A choice between spending more for national defense or social welfare programs.
   b) A choice between protecting fishing grounds in New England and the Gulf of Mexico and developing offshore oil wells to provide more energy.
   c) A choice between higher taxes to build highways and bridges and lower taxes. (*Note:* Lower taxes mean that households would have additional income.)
   d) In what way(s) are such conflicts resolved?

10. Explain how, if at all, each of the following will affect a society's production possibilities. Also, indicate some of the opportunity costs involved, if any.
    a) Owing to increased exploration efforts, new supplies of natural resources are discovered.
    b) Society devotes more production to capital goods.
    c) Businesses devote fewer resources to research and development.
    d) The federal government increases expenditures on education and training.
    e) The economy fails to maintain full employment.

11. Applying the principles of rational choice to each of the following situations, what extra benefits and extra costs would need to be measured and compared?
    a) Whether to increase taxes in order to increase financial support for the state university.
    b) Whether (from a firm's perspective) to produce and sell a new product.
    c) Whether (from a family's perspective) to spend $500 for a vacation this year or to put that money in the bank to help pay for the future college education of two of its members.

12. Based on the following data and the principles of rational choice, how many miles of highway should the state build next year? (Assume that the data accurately measure *all* social costs and benefits.)

Number of miles	*Total social costs*	*Total social benefits*
1000	$100,000,000	$500,000,000
2000	250,000,000	700,000,000
3000	450,000,000	850,000,000

13. Explain how each of the following statements fails to apply the principles of rational choice correctly. (*Hint:* Rational choice requires a comparison of extra benefits *and* extra costs.)
    a) The more capital goods we have, the more goods we can produce in the future; therefore we should devote most of our current production to capital goods.
    b) We shouldn't build the proposed dam because there'll be some environmental costs.
    c) The city council mustn't cut the budgets of the police and fire departments. Those services are absolutely essential.

14. When discussing rational choice, we noted that individuals respond in predictable ways to changes in benefits and costs. Try using this simple proposition to analyze the actions that you would expect to occur if the price of oil is expected to rise significantly in the near future.
    a) What actions would you take? Would you expect other individuals to take similar actions?
    b) What actions would you expect businesses to take? (Consider the actions of oil producers separately from those of other businesses.)
    c) Why would economists say that all these actions are the results of efforts to "economize"? What does this word mean to you?

CHAPTER 3

Laws of Demand
and Supply

QUESTIONS TO CONSIDER

☐ How does demand differ from wants?

☐ What factors affect quantity demanded? Demand?

☐ What factors affect quantity supplied? Supply?

☐ Why is equilibrium important in a market economy?

☐ How do government price ceilings and supports affect equilibrium price and quantity supplied?

Because we live in a world of scarcity, we must choose among alternative uses of scarce resources. We must decide how best to use our own resources to meet our individual goals. Society must decide what to produce, how to produce it, and to whom to distribute the goods and services produced. But how are these decisions made? In the United States and many other nations, households and businesses make most of the production, consumption, and resource allocation decisions by exchanging—or trading—in a **market**.

Markets do not always work perfectly. Nor is a **market economy** the only mechanism for answering economic questions. The economic systems of the Soviet Union and China, for example, rely heavily on central economic planning. Government authorities fix wages and prices, establish production levels, and ration products. Moreover, even in the United States, government is involved to some extent in setting prices and determining quantities produced. Nevertheless, we stress the operation of a market system in this textbook because a knowledge of markets is basic to understanding how our economy functions.

Trading, the core of any market economy, is a fundamental economic activity. You may agree to trade an hour of your time to help a friend with mathematics in exchange for an hour of help in studying for your economics exam. You may give the local grocery store $20 in exchange for a small bag of groceries. In any economy, millions and millions of such trades occur each day.

When trading, the parties involved must agree on a **price**, which is the amount of one item that an individual is willing to sacrifice to obtain another item. For example, if you are willing to sacrifice one hour of your time in exchange for one hour of help with your economics studies, the price of the exchange is one hour. An item has a price attached to its use because of scarcity; that is, an item such as time is not unlimited, so some sacrifice must be made if the item is used. The price reflects the *opportunity cost* of the sacrifice being made.

Of course, many exchanges take place in markets larger than two persons. Indeed, people often think of geographical places when they think of markets— the local grocery market, a flea market, or the stock market. Economists use the concept of a market to represent the trading that occurs between potential buyers and sellers. There are markets for resources—such as materials, labor time, and machinery—and for products—such as autos, haircuts, and restaurant meals. The markets for many products—autos, video cassette recorders, and wheat, for example—are international in scope. They represent trading between buyers and sellers in many countries.

Market. The interaction of buyers (market demand) and sellers (market supply) which determines a price and quantity exchanged.

Market economy. An economy in which households and businesses interact in markets to determine prices and thus answer the fundamental economic questions of what and how much to produce, how to produce it, and to whom to distribute goods and services.

Price. The amount of one item that an individual will sacrifice in order to obtain another item and often stated in terms of the quantity of money that must be sacrificed.

When describing a market, economists use the concept of demand to represent the behavior of buyers and the concept of supply to represent the behavior of sellers. Each participant in the market seeks to gain from exchange. Buyers, of course, want the lowest price possible; sellers, the highest price. The interaction of buyers and sellers in markets establishes a market price, generally stated in terms of a unit of money—dollars and cents in the United States. Markets also determine how much of each product is produced.

Consider a few economic questions. Why have prices of computers and video recorders fallen in the past few years? Why do hotels and airlines raise their prices during peak travel seasons? How do rent controls affect the quantity and quality of rental housing available? To answer these questions you must understand the concepts of demand and supply and how they interact to determine market prices.

DEMAND

Like other economic terms, demand has a specific and technical meaning. To an economist, **demand** means *the quantities* of a product that buyers are both *willing and able to buy* at *every possible price* during a *specified period of time*, with *all other things unchanged*. Each phrase in this definition is important to understanding how economists define and use the concept of demand.

Noneconomists often use the term *demand* to refer to a specific quantity. A sales representative, for example, may say that local customers demand 300 new cars per month. To an economist, demand is not a single, specific quantity but a *series* of price and quantity combinations. Can you say how many new automobiles you will buy next year or how many all U.S. consumers will buy without knowing the price? Would you expect different answers if the average price of a new car were $50,000 rather than $5000?

Economists recognize that the number of new cars bought during a specific period of time depends on price. In fact, because economists are especially interested in how quantity purchased changes with price, they define demand as a relationship between price and quantity. Thus the term **quantity demanded** refers to a particular quantity that consumers will buy at a particular price during a particular time. The distinction between demand and quantity demanded is important, and we explain it further later in this section.

It is also important to recognize that in the definition of demand we refer to quantities that buyers are "willing and able to buy." Consumers buy products to satisfy some want, but wanting is not the same as demanding. To demand a product, a buyer must not only want it, but must be willing and able to make the necessary sacrifice to obtain the product. For example, it matters little that you want a private yacht or an expensive automobile if you are unable or unwilling to make the sacrifice necessary to buy it. Economists stress the importance of distinguishing between demand and wants. (So do economics professors in making up exam questions, a fact that might increase your willingness to make the sacrifice necessary to learn the difference.)

Automakers in the United States discovered the difference between wants and demand the hard way. In the 1970s, while U.S. buyers were purchasing large numbers of small foreign cars, U.S. automakers were publicly stating, "Americans want large cars, and we're going to give them what they want." Although it may

Demand. All the quantities of a product that individuals are both willing and able to buy at every possible price during a specified period of time.

Quantity demanded. The amount of a product that consumers are both willing and able to buy at a specified price.

have been true that Americans still *wanted* large cars, they were no longer *buying* many of them. If automakers had been willing to *give* cars away (and that is the literal meaning of their words), it would have been appropriate to find out what consumers wanted. However, since the automakers wanted to *sell* cars, it was more important to focus on demand, or the willingness and ability of consumers to buy at various prices.

In addition, it is important to keep in mind that our definition of demand applies to quantities demanded within a certain period of time. Obviously, we would expect people to demand more cars in a year than in a month.

Law of Demand

The nature of demand has led economists to formulate the **law of demand**: When prices of products decrease, the quantities that buyers are willing and able to purchase increase; when prices rise, the quantity demanded falls. That is, there is an *inverse* relationship between price and quantities that consumers will buy. You can see this relationship at work in everyday life. We all tend to buy more when products are offered at a special price and to buy less when prices rise relative to those of similar products.

The law of demand follows directly from the principles of rational choice introduced in Chapter 2. An increase in price raises the extra cost to the buyer. Thus we would expect the willingness and ability to consume to diminish. Note that higher prices do *not* make consumers want fewer goods. You might get as much satisfaction from going to a movie if the ticket costs $10 or $5. But you will probably go to fewer movies each month if ticket prices are higher. Again, wants and demand should not be confused. Higher prices reduce quantity demanded, but not quantity wanted.

Demand Schedules and Demand Curves

Economists most often present information about demand either as a demand schedule or as a demand curve, both of which are illustrated in Exhibit 3.1. The table in Exhibit 3.1(a) is an example of a **demand schedule**. It shows quantities of doughnuts that consumers are willing and able to buy per week at different prices. You can see that consumers will buy 400 dozen doughnuts per week if the price is $3.00 per dozen. If the price is $3.50, quantity demanded drops to 350 dozen per week. This demand schedule supports the law of demand: Higher prices reduce quantity demanded.

The same information is shown by the graph in Exhibit 3.1(b), which is an example of a **demand curve**. We obtain a demand curve by plotting each combination of price and quantity demanded from a demand schedule and connecting the points with a smooth curve. Any one point on the graph shows a particular quantity demanded at a particular price. Point *a*, for example, indicates that at a price of $3.00 per dozen, consumers will buy 400 dozen per week.

Like a demand schedule, a demand curve shows a *relationship* between price and quantity demanded, that is, a *series* of price and quantity combinations. By convention, economists put price on the vertical axis and quantity on the horizontal

Law of demand. The principle that as the price of any product decreases (increases), the quantity of the product demanded will increase (decrease).

Demand schedule. A table showing quantities of a product that consumers are willing and able to buy at various prices during a specified period of time.

Demand curve. A graphic representation of the demand schedule; the demand curve always slopes downward and to the right.

(a) Demand schedule

Price (dollars per dozen)	Quantity demanded (dozens per week)
4.00	325
3.50	350
3.00	400
2.50	475
2.00	575

(b) Demand curve

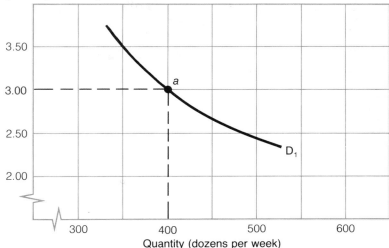

Exhibit 3.1
Demand for Doughnuts
The demand curve slopes downward and to the right, showing an inverse relationship between price and quantity demanded. Lower prices cause an increase in quantity demanded. Thus the demand curve reflects the law of demand. For any particular demand relationship, the all-other-things-unchanged assumption holds. That is, we observe the response of consumers to a change in the product's price. All other influences are assumed to remain constant.

axis. A demand curve thus slopes downward and to the right, reflecting the inverse relationship between price and quantity demanded, or the law of demand.*

We can read a demand curve in either of two ways. For a specific price, demand indicates the *maximum quantity* that buyers are willing and able to purchase at that price. For a specific quantity, demand indicates the *maximum price* that sellers could charge and sell that quantity. However, a demand curve (or a demand schedule) cannot tell us the "best" price or predict the actual price. Demand simply shows a range of possible outcomes for the relationship between price and quantity. At each price level, buyers acting rationally will compare the extra benefits of consuming additional units of the product with the extra costs they will have to pay.

The "all-other-things-unchanged" assumption. Price is not the only factor determining the quantities that buyers will purchase. In constructing demand curves and schedules, however, economists make the **"all-other-things-unchanged" assumption**. That is, they isolate the effect of price on quantity

"All-other-things-unchanged" assumption. The assumption commonly made in demand-and-supply analysis that all determinants of quantity demanded and quantity supplied, except price, are held constant.

* As noted in Chapter 1, graphs are a convenient and often used economic tool. If you are still having some difficulty with graphs, reread the appendix to Chapter 1. Although economics is not about graphs, economic analysis is often presented in graphic form.

from the effects of all other factors that influence buying decisions. Why? Because price is the major source of information about the relative scarcity of resources, changes in wants, and other important economic events in a market economy.

Because of the all-other-things-unchanged assumption, along any given demand curve all influences other than the price of the product are assumed to remain constant. If, as quite often happens, one of the other factors changes, the demand curve will shift. A new demand curve is then required to describe the new relationship between price and quantity.

Changes in Demand and Quantity Demanded

When some factor other than price causes us to construct a new demand curve, we say that that demand curve has *shifted*, reflecting a *change in demand*. Noneconomists often fail to distinguish between changes in demand and changes in quantity demanded, but it is an important difference.

Exhibit 3.2 illustrates this difference for our doughnut example. In part (a), curve D_1 represents the original demand relationship shown in Exhibit 3.1. If the price of doughnuts falls from \$3.50 to \$3.00 per dozen, buyers will increase quantity demanded (purchased) from 350 to 400 dozen doughnuts per week. This change shows up as a movement along D_1 from point *a* to point *b*. Along any demand curve, quantity demanded changes in response to a change in the product's price, assuming that all other factors affecting demand remain unchanged.

Contrast this response to what might happen if scientists discovered that doughnuts prevent cancer. We would expect consumers to buy more doughnuts than before *at the current price*. In Exhibit 3.2(b), this change in demand for doughnuts is represented by a shift in the demand curve from D_1 to D_2. Note that along D_2, consumers are willing to buy 425 dozen doughnuts per week at a price of \$3.50 per dozen, or 75 dozen more than when D_1 represented demand. (Compare point *a* on D_1 with point *c* on D_2.)

Any change in a nonprice factor will lead to a new demand relationship between price and quantity demanded. In this example, unless new evidence emerges or some other factor affecting demand changes, D_2 describes demand for doughnuts. Of course, if scientists reported instead that doughnuts *cause* cancer, demand would decrease, moving in the opposite direction. This change in demand is shown in Exhibit 3.2(b) as a shift from D_1 to D_0. *An increase in demand shifts the demand curve to the right; a decrease in demand shifts the demand curve to the left.*

Note that in describing a change in demand, we said nothing about a change in the price of doughnuts, as we did when discussing a change in quantity demanded. When a product's price falls, buyers will increase *quantity demanded* at the *new price*. On the other hand, a change in a factor such as a preference for doughnuts creates an entirely new demand relationship, not just a new quantity demanded. When demand increases, buyers will be willing to purchase more at each price or to pay more for any quantity bought.

If buyers purchase more only because the price of the product has fallen, economists say that there has been an increase in quantity demanded. If buyers purchase more at every possible price, economists say that there has been an increase in demand.

(a) Change in quantity demanded

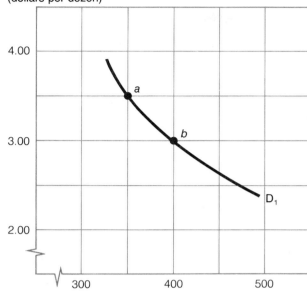

(b) Change in demand

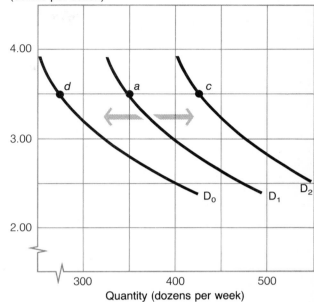

Exhibit 3.2
Changes in Demand and Quantity Demanded
In part (a) the curve D_1, representing demand, indicates that a decrease in price from $3.50 to $3.00 per dozen will cause an increase in the quantity demanded from 350 to 400 dozen per week (compare point *a* with point *b* on D_1). Buyers are responding only to a change in the product's price. If one of the other factors changes, as in part (b), a change in demand occurs and the entire demand curve shifts. For example, an increase in demand is shown by the shift to the right in the demand curve from D_1 to D_2. When there is an increase in demand, buyers will purchase a larger quantity at the same price (compare point *a* on D_1 with point *c* on D_2). A decrease in demand is shown as the shift to the left from D_1 to D_0 (compare point *a* on D_1 with point *d* on D_0).

Determinants of Product Demand

What other factors influence demand? Economists have identified five factors, or determinants of product demand: preferences, income, complements and substitutes, expectations, and number of buyers. Whenever one of these factors changes, demand shifts, creating a new relationship between price and quantity demanded. Be sure that you know the way in which each factor changes demand because later you will have to know whether a particular event will increase or decrease demand.

Tastes and preferences. In choosing which products to buy, consumers consider the satisfaction they expect to receive. The value to you (and thus the price you are willing to pay) to attend a concert will depend on your preference in music. You may especially like classical music and be willing to pay $10 to hear the Collegetown Symphony Orchestra; if you like hard rock music less, you may be willing to pay only $3 to see Rocky Stone and the Rockettes. Economists refer to this influence as *tastes and preferences.*

Tastes and preferences are influenced by improvements in the quality of a product, successful advertising and marketing campaigns, fads, or the introduction of new products. We noted previously, for example, that the preference for doughnuts might increase because of evidence that doughnuts prevent cancer. *Whenever the taste or preference for a product increases, demand for the product will increase; a decline in taste or preference brings a decrease in demand.*

Using the principles of rational choice we can say that an increased taste for doughnuts increases the extra benefits consumers receive. As a result, consumers are willing to pay more for the same quantity than before, an indication that demand has increased. The increase in demand also means that consumers are willing to purchase more doughnuts at any given price.

Income.

Because consumers must be able to pay in order to demand products, it is not surprising to find that income is a determinant of demand. An increase in income will usually—although not always—cause consumers to buy more of most products. This effect is the reason for suggesting an income tax cut as a way to stimulate the economy. Lower taxes give consumers more spendable income; more income means greater demand for products. (Note that this simplified analysis ignores other economic variables. A complete analysis would consider both microeconomic and macroeconomic changes.)

Changes in income are also important in determining international trade. Consumers in the United States, for example, will buy more foreign imports if their incomes rise. Consumers in Europe or South America will buy fewer U.S. exports if their incomes fall.

Finally, changes in income cause people to change the *types* of goods they buy. Economists recognize two types of goods based on the response of demand to a change in income. For **normal goods** demand varies directly with income; that is, an increase in income increases demand and vice versa. For **inferior goods** demand varies inversely with income; that is, demand decreases when income increases. Margarine is an inferior good; when incomes rise, less margarine is demanded. Steak, on the other hand, is a normal good; more is demanded when incomes rise. One study indicated that skiing in New England is an inferior good. When the economy is booming and incomes are rising, more East Coast skiers go to Europe or Colorado. When the economy is slumping and incomes are falling, demand for New England skiing rises.

Prices of substitutes and complements.

In making rational choices, consumers recognize that some goods are related to others. Hot dogs and hamburgers, for example, are **substitutes**. They can be used in place of each other; consumers can satisfy a desire for food by purchasing either of them. Hot dogs and hot-dog rolls are **complements**. They are used together, and consumers who buy one will typically buy the other as well.

For example, suppose that you go to the local grocery store planning to buy hamburger for dinner. A sign in the meat department indicates that hot dogs are on sale at 20 percent below the regular price. Confronted with an unexpected change in price you may revise the dinner menu: Hamburgers are out; hot dogs

Normal goods. Goods for which demand varies directly with income, rising as income rises and decreasing as income decreases—for example, steak.

Inferior goods. Goods for which demand varies inversely with income, decreasing as income rises and increasing as income falls—for example, margarine.

Substitutes. Goods that satisfy similar desires and therefore compete for the consumer's dollar. When two goods are substitutes, an increase in the price of one leads to an increase in demand for the other.

Complements. Goods that can be used with other goods, such as hot dogs and hot-dog rolls. When two goods are complements, an increase in the price of one leads to a decrease in demand for the other.

will be served instead. The change in the price of hot dogs caused a change in the *quantity* of hot dogs demanded. (Demand for hot dogs does not change; the response is due solely to a change in the product's price.) That is, you buy more hot dogs only because the price is lower.

The change in the price of hot dogs has two other effects. First, it causes you to demand less hamburger. Even though the price of hamburger has not changed in absolute terms, hamburger is relatively more expensive than hot dogs because the price of hot dogs has dropped. Demand for hamburger decreases because one of the factors affecting demand has changed. The price of hot dogs, a substitute product, has fallen.

In addition, you will probably buy hot dog rolls to go with the hot dogs. Because you will buy more rolls even though their price has not changed, demand for them has increased. You demand more hot-dog rolls because a nonprice factor affecting demand has changed. The price of hot dogs, a complement, has fallen.

A change in the price of a good directly affects demand for its substitutes. If a good's price increases, demand for its substitutes will increase. For complements, price and demand are inversely related. When a good's price increases, demand for its complements will decrease.

At this point, you should be aware of a good technique to use when studying economics. You have just read how changes in the price of one good affect demand for substitutes and complements—two of many relationships you will be asked to learn in this course. You may be tempted to try to memorize these relationships. If you are able to do so, fine. But if your memory has a way of fading at the most inopportune time—as in the middle of an exam—it is best to remember a simple example. You can then use the example—such as hamburgers, hot dogs, and hot-dog rolls—to reason out the relationships.

To illustrate this point let's suppose that you were asked how demand for good A is affected by an increase in the price of substitute good B. Hamburgers and hot dogs are substitutes and you can reason out how demand for hot dogs is affected by a change in the price of hamburgers: Higher prices for hamburgers will increase demand for hot dogs. In this way, you can rely on your reasoning and not just your memory. Using this technique not only will help you make better grades on exams, you will also be more likely to remember the useful tools of economic analysis after completing your economics course.

Expectations of buyers. Buyers are also influenced by expectations, especially anticipated changes in income and prices. For example, individuals tend to increase their spending immediately when they anticipate higher incomes in the near future. (How many college graduates wait until they receive their first paycheck to begin to spend their increased income?) In this way, *expectations* of higher incomes and actual increases in income have the same result: They increase demand for normal goods and decrease demand for inferior goods.

The converse is also true. When people fear that incomes will drop and unemployment will spread, they become less willing to buy those items that can easily be postponed, such as a new car. This reaction is why President Reagan was upset in 1982 when Wall Street analysts predicted that his economic program would not solve the nation's problems. His plans to increase demand by cutting taxes could not succeed if people expected that economic conditions would not improve, an expectation that decreases demand.

Expected price changes also affect consumer demand. Purchasing a product now or purchasing it in the future are alternative (substitute) choices. Therefore, if consumers expect a product's price to be higher in the future, they tend to increase their current demand for it. If they expect lower prices, they decrease current demand.

Similarly, expectations of a shortage can, by changing demand, actually create a shortage. In the early 1970s, rumors spread that toilet paper would become scarce. Consumers increased their demand for toilet paper in response, causing a toilet-paper shortage.

Number of consumers.   The final factor affecting product demand is the number of consumers. Economists are mostly interested in market demand for products because it (together with market supply) determines the relative price of products. Market demand represents the sum of individual consumer demand. In other words, if you are willing to buy 10 rolls of film and your friend is willing to buy 15 at a price of $5, the market demand curve would reflect the fact that together you will buy 25 rolls at that price. Because market demand represents the sum of individual consumer demands, *an increase in the number of consumers will tend to increase demand, and a decrease in the number of consumers will tend to decrease demand.*

Thus an increase or decrease in population—whether because of births and deaths or migration—affects demand. Shifts in the age distribution of the population are also important for particular products. For example, a nationwide decline in the number of school-aged children will decrease demand for schools and teachers. The growing elderly population in the United States has increased demand for nursing-home care.

Demand and Quantity Demanded Reconsidered

The five determinants of product demand are the ones to which the all-other-things-unchanged assumption refers. For any demand curve, we assume that these factors remain unchanged and focus on the influence of price on quantity demanded. When any of these factors changes, we have a new demand relationship—an increase or decrease in demand—which is reflected by a shift in the demand curve.

In economic terms, a change in a product's price does not alter the demand relationship. However, a change in one of the other factors results in a new demand relationship, or a shift in demand. Thus an economist would not say, "Demand for cars rose this month because car prices fell," but rather, "Quantity of cars demanded increased as a result of the fall in car prices." This phrasing identifies the effect of a change in quantity demanded caused by a change in product price. It is not a change in demand, which results only from a change in some other factor affecting demand. This distinction is central to understanding demand.

Changes in Relative Prices

Relative price. The price of one good in comparison to the prices of other goods.

When the price of a good increases, quantity demanded falls. When the price of a substitute good increases or the price of a complement good falls, demand increases. In each case, however, we are talking about a change in **relative price**, that is, the price of one good in comparison to the prices of other goods.

In the real world, the prices of many goods rise or fall at the same time. Thus we must ask whether the price of a good has increased faster (increased relatively) or slower (decreased relatively) than other goods. For example, from 1974 to 1978, gasoline prices rose an average of 5.2 percent per year. However, because the average price of all goods rose an average of 7.3 percent per year, the *relative* price of gasoline decreased. The fall in the relative price of gasoline helps to explain why gasoline consumption increased during that period.

Price changes must also be considered in relation to income. Higher prices reduce quantity demanded if income is unchanged. However, in the real world prices and income often rise at the same time. Thus we must ask whether price increases more than income (which should decrease demand) or less than income (which should increase demand). For example, if the price of new cars increases by 5 percent while income increases by 10 percent, we might expect increased demand for new cars. On the other hand, if the price of new cars decreases by 5 percent while income decreases by 10 percent, we might expect decreased demand for new cars. In such a case, price has actually increased *relative to* income.

These examples show that changes in relative prices—not in absolute prices—cause changes in demand and economic decisions. Relative prices determine what consumers will buy, what producers will sell, and where individuals will choose to work.

SUPPLY

Buyers are not the only ones who must make choices. Sellers must decide how much to produce. **Supply** means the quantities of a product that sellers are both willing and able to offer for sale at every possible price during a specified period of time, with all other things unchanged. Economists use the concept of supply, like the concept of demand, in a precise and technical way. Like demand, supply refers to a *relationship* between price and quantity. And just as economists distinguish demand from quantity demanded, they also distinguish supply from **quantity supplied**.

Law of Supply

The nature of supply led economists to formulate the **law of supply**: Sellers will offer a larger quantity for sale when price rises. That is, there is a *direct* relationship between quantity supplied and price. The law of supply follows directly from the principles of rational choice. To a supplier, the extra benefit gained from supplying a product is the price received. The extra costs are the costs of supplying more of a product. Thus we can relate price and extra costs in the case of supply in the same way we related price and extra satisfaction in the case of demand. This result is helpful in understanding how supply is affected by various changes and how a market economy operates.

Supply Schedules and Supply Curves

Exhibit 3.3 shows the supply side of our doughnut example. Note that supply, like demand, refers to a quantity for a specified period of time, or in this case, doughnuts per week. We can express the supply relationship as a **supply schedule**, as we did for demand. The supply schedule supports the law of supply: As

Supply. All the quantities of a product that suppliers are both willing and able to offer for sale at every possible price during a specified period of time.

Quantity supplied. The quantity of a product that suppliers are both willing and able to offer for sale at a specified price.

Law of supply. The principle that as the selling price of any product increases (decreases), the quantity of the product supplied also increases (decreases).

Supply schedule. A table showing quantities of a product that suppliers are willing and able to offer for sale at various prices during a specified period of time.

(a) Supply schedule

(b) Supply curve

Price (dollars per dozen)	Quantity supplied (dozens per week)
4.00	475
3.50	450
3.00	400
2.50	325
2.00	225

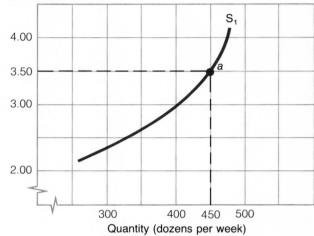

Exhibit 3.3
The Supply of Doughnuts
The supply curve slopes upward and to the right, showing a direct relationship between price and quantity supplied. Higher prices cause sellers to offer greater quantities of their product. Lower prices reduce quantity supplied. Thus the supply curve
reflects the law of supply. For any particular supply relationship, the all-other-things-
equal assumption holds. That is, we observe the response of sellers to a change in
the price of the product. All other influences are assumed to remain constant.

Supply curve. A graphic representation of the supply schedule;
the typical supply curve slopes upward and to the right.

RECAP

Supply refers to the quantities of
a product that sellers are willing
and able to offer for sale at every
possible price during a specified
period of time.

The law of supply states that
prices and quantities supplied
are directly related.

Supply indicates how sellers balance the extra costs of producing
additional quantities of a product
against the extra benefits of selling as reflected by the market
price.

price increases, so do quantities offered for sale. In this case, the quantity of
doughnuts offered for sale increases from 400 to 450 dozen per week as price
increases from $3.00 to $3.50 per dozen.

We can also plot this information graphically as a **supply curve**, as we did
for demand. We put price on the vertical axis and quantity on the horizontal axis.
The positive slope (upward and to the right) of the supply curve reflects the direct
relationship between price and quantity (following the law of supply) and the
relationship between extra cost and price. In Chapter 2 we noted that production
is subject to increasing costs. That is, the extra cost of producing additional
quantities rises as quantities produced increase. Supply expresses a direct relationship between price and quantity because extra costs rise as quantity increases.
Sellers must receive higher prices for the product to cover higher extra costs.

We can read the supply curve in either of two ways. For a specific price,
supply indicates the *maximum quantity* that sellers are willing and able to sell at
that price. For a specific quantity, supply shows the *minimum price* that sellers
will accept for that quantity. (We can assume that they would gladly take a higher
price.)

Finally, as we did for demand, we make an all-other-things-equal assumption
when referring to a supply relationship. That is, along a particular supply curve
all factors except the price of the product are assumed to remain constant. When
any of these factors changes, a new supply relationship occurs.

Changes in Supply and Quantity Supplied

As for demand, economists distinguish between a change in quantity supplied—which causes movement along a supply curve—and a change in supply—which causes a shift in the supply curve. Exhibit 3.4 illustrates this difference, again using our doughnut example. The original supply curve is labeled S_1. If price decreases from $3.50 to $3.00 per dozen, the sellers will reduce quantity supplied from 450 to 400 dozen per week. In part (a), this change shows up as a movement along S_1 from point a to point b. Since only the price has changed, this change represents a decrease in quantity supplied.

Suppose, however, that the cost of flour increases. This change raises the cost of making doughnuts. Because it costs more to produce each dozen, doughnut sellers will charge higher prices for each quantity they offer for sale. This change in the relationship between price and quantity supplied represents a decrease in

Exhibit 3.4
Changes in Supply and in Quantity Supplied
In part (a) where supply is S_1, a decrease in price from $3.50 to $3.00 per dozen results in a decrease in quantity supplied from 450 to 400 dozen per week (compare point a to point b on S_1). Sellers are responding only to a change in the product's price. If a factor other than price changes, as in part (b), a change in supply occurs. On the graph, a decrease in supply is shown by the shift to the left in the supply curve from S_1 to S_0. A decrease in supply results in sellers offering less for sale at each price (compare point a on S_1 with point c on S_0). An increase in supply is shown as the shift to the right from S_1 to S_2 (compare point a on S_1 with point d on S_2).

(a) Change in quantity supplied

(b) Change in supply

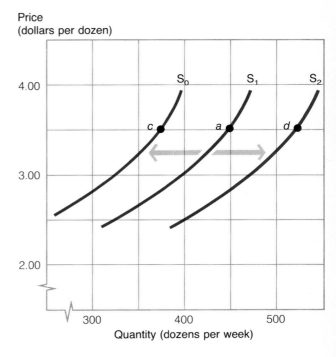

supply (from S_1 to S_0 in Exhibit 3.4b). This change also reflects the principles of rational choice, as sellers balance price (representing extra benefits to them) with the extra costs required to produce the product. A decrease in supply also means that sellers offer less for sale at each price. For example, at a price of $3.50, sellers now offer only 375 dozen doughnuts per week (point c on S_0) instead of 450 dozen (point a on S_1).

An increase in supply has the opposite effect. If supply increases from S_1 to S_2 in Exhibit 3.4(b), sellers will supply 525 dozen doughnuts per week (point d on S_2) at a price of $3.50 compared with 450 dozen (point a on S_1) before. *An increase in supply shifts the supply curve to the right; a decrease in supply shifts the supply curve to the left.*

Note that in describing a change in supply, we said nothing about a change in the price of doughnuts, as we did when discussing a change in quantity supplied. When a product's price falls, sellers will reduce *quantity supplied* at the *new price*. On the other hand, a change in a factor such as the ingredients used in doughnuts creates an entirely new supply relationship, not just a new quantity supplied. When supply decreases, sellers will sell less at each price or charge more for any quantity supplied.

If sellers offer more only because the price of the product has risen, economists say that there has been an increase in quantity supplied. If sellers offer more at every possible price, economists say that there has been an increase in supply.

Determinants of Supply

What other factors influence supply? Economists have identified five major factors, or determinants, of product supply: prices of resources, available technology, prices of alternative goods, expectations, and number of sellers. Whenever one of these factors changes, supply shifts, creating a new relationship between price and quantity supplied.

Prices of resources. Before a product can be offered for sale, it must be produced from various resources. Steel, labor, and rubber are some of the resources used to make a car, for example. To supply medical services requires the labor time of the doctor and support staff, rent on the office building, supplies, malpractice insurance, and other resources. Resource prices affect the cost of a product and hence are a determinant of supply. *An increase in the price of resources increases costs and decreases supply; lower resource prices decrease cost and increase supply.*

Available technology. Technology generally refers to the process by which a product or products are made. An improvement in technology implies that the product can be produced more efficiently, that is, at a lower cost. Thus *an improvement in technology lowers the cost of the product and results in an increase in supply.*

Prices of alternative goods. Like all rational decision makers, sellers consider alternatives when making a supply decision. A farmer may choose between planting corn or soybeans or between raising a crop or livestock. Makers of TV sets must choose between producing color or black-and-white models and between consoles or portables. Both the farmer and the maker of TV sets could produce some of each, but the capacity to produce is limited at any one time. If more of one good is produced, fewer alternative goods can be made. Thus one cost of producing color TV sets is the opportunity cost of not producing (and not selling) black-and-white models.

When the price of color TV sets rises relative to the price of black-and-white TV sets, the opportunity cost of producing black-and-white models increases. Sellers will produce the same quantity of black-and-white sets only if their price increases. But setting higher prices for each quantity supplied is a decrease in supply. Thus *supply of a good will decrease when prices of alternative goods that sellers could offer for sale rise. Supply will increase when prices of alternative goods fall*. Note, however, that a rise in *relative* prices is what causes seller decisions to change.

Expectations of sellers. You have seen how buyers take anticipated events into account in making demand decisions; sellers do the same when making supply decisions. For example, suppose that shoemakers expect demand for shoes to rise in the near future. They may react by increasing current shoe production so that they will have more shoes available to meet the higher sales expected.

More production by itself does not mean an increase in supply, however. Supply increases only if sellers are willing to offer more goods for sale at each price or to accept a lower price for each quantity offered for sale. We would not expect shoemakers to sell for a lower price today if they can sell for a higher price next week. An expected increase in prices raises the opportunity cost of selling today instead of next week. Like any other increase in costs, the higher opportunity cost decreases supply. Thus *when prices are expected to increase, current supply will tend to decrease; if prices are expected to decrease, current supply will tend to increase.*

Number of sellers. So far, we have discussed factors that relate supply to changes in direct costs (resource prices and available technology) or indirect or opportunity costs (expectations and prices of alternatives). Each of these changes affects the supply decisions of individual producers. Economists are mostly interested in the market supply, that is, in the total quantities supplied by all sellers in the market at each price. An increase in the number of sellers means that more goods will be offered for sale at each price. Thus, *an increase in the number of sellers increases market supply; a decrease in the number of sellers decreases market supply.*

Supply and Quantity Supplied Reconsidered

To derive a specific supply curve we make an all-other-things-unchanged assumption, holding constant the five determinants of product supply. When we consider the response of sellers to a change in the product's price, we move along the supply curve and observe only a change in quantity supplied. When one of the five other determinants of supply changes, however, sellers' responses will change, a new supply relationship will result, and the supply curve will shift.

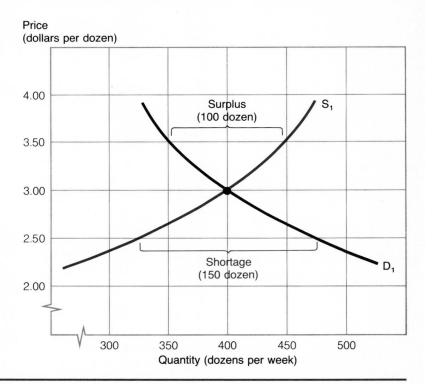

Price
(dollars per dozen)

Exhibit 3.5
Market for Doughnuts
For demand D_1 and supply S_1 in this market, the equilibrium price is $3.00 per dozen and the equilibrium quantity is 400 dozen, located at the intersection of the two curves. If the price were $3.50 per dozen, a surplus of 100 dozen would result (the difference between 450 dozen offered for sale and 350 dozen bought). If the price were $2.50 per dozen, a shortage of 150 dozen would result (the difference between 475 dozen demanded and 325 dozen offered for sale).

MARKET EQUILIBRIUM

At the beginning of this chapter, we noted that decisions in a market economy are made through the interaction of buyers and sellers. Thus far we have discussed demand and supply—the actions of buyers and sellers—separately. To see how a market works to determine prices, we need to put the two together.

In examining this interaction, we return to the principles of rational choice. That is, we assume that buyers and sellers make decisions by comparing extra benefits and extra costs. Each strives to get more (in terms of extra benefits) for less (in terms of extra costs) out of the exchange. Thus, in a fundamental sense, the interests of buyers and sellers clash. Sellers would like to receive the highest possible price; buyers want to pay the lowest possible price.

Given the conflicting interests of buyers and sellers, how is market price determined? The market's solution is what economists refer to as the **equilibrium price**—a price at which quantity demanded and quantity supplied are equal. Exhibit 3.5 shows the market for doughnuts by combining the demand curve from Exhibit 3.1 and the supply curve from Exhibit 3.3. The demand and supply curves intersect at a price of $3.00 per dozen, where both quantity demanded and quantity supplied are 400 dozen doughnuts per week. Thus $3.00 per dozen is the equilibrium price in this particular market as represented by its demand and supply conditions.

Equilibrium price. The price at which quantity supplied equals quantity demanded; graphically, the point of intersection of the demand and supply curves.

The equilibrium price is a compromise between the interests of sellers and buyers and thus is not necessarily ideal for either. Equilibrium means that all of

Market equilibrium. A state in which neither buyers nor sellers have any reason to change quantity demanded or supplied; the market in balance, with quantity demanded equal to quantity supplied at the existing market price.

Shortage. A situation in which quantity demanded exceeds quantity supplied at the existing market price; excess demand.

a product that sellers offer for sale is purchased and that all of a product that buyers will buy is supplied. Because there are many buyers and sellers acting independently, no individual buyer or seller has the ability to influence the market price.

Market equilibrium is similar to physical equilibrium, meaning at rest or in balance. When a market reaches equilibrium price, the forces of demand and supply are in balance. Moreover, markets tend automatically to adjust to equilibrium whenever the forces of demand and supply are out of balance.

Shortage

Let's look at how markets achieve equilibrium by considering what happens if the market is unbalanced. Suppose, for example, that doughnuts sell for $2.50 per dozen, or below the equilibrium price. The demand curve in Exhibit 3.5 indicates that consumers are willing and able to buy 475 dozen per week at $2.50. The supply curve, however, shows that sellers will offer only 325 dozen for sale. That is, quantity demanded exceeds quantity supplied by 150 dozen per week at $2.50. Economists call excess quantity demanded a **shortage**. *Whenever the current market price is below the equilibrium price, quantity demanded will exceed quantity supplied, creating a shortage*.

When a shortage exists, we can predict market prices will rise to the equilibrium price. For example, some people who cannot buy as many doughnuts as they want at the current price are willing to pay more. Moreover, a shortage allows sellers to sell more at higher prices. Pressures from both sellers and buyers thus force prices up. As price rises, quantity supplied increases (a movement along the supply curve). At the same time, quantity demanded falls (a movement along the demand curve). These two changes reduce the size of the shortage. As long as the market price is less than $3.00 per dozen (the equilibrium price) the shortage will continue to put upward pressure on price. But once the price reaches $3.00 per dozen, the market is balanced: Quantity demanded equals quantity supplied at the equilibrium price; there is no shortage and no pressure on the market price.

Scarcity versus shortage. As we have mentioned, economists use some words in technical and precise ways to avoid confusion. Two such words are *scarcity* and *shortage*. Consider the following statement: "Scarcity is an unavoidable feature of the human condition, but shortages can be easily eliminated." This assertion may sound like nonsense to a noneconomist, but it makes perfect sense in economics.

As we noted in Chapter 2, scarcity reflects the fact that resources are limited, while wants are unlimited. It is true therefore that "scarcity is an unavoidable feature of the human condition." But a shortage is a market condition in which, at the prevailing market price, quantity demanded exceeds quantity supplied. Shortages can always be eliminated by allowing market prices to rise to equilibrium levels. When you mean that all wants of society are not being met, use the term "scarcity." When you mean that the current market price is too low (that is, below the equilibrium price) and thus quantity demanded exceeds quantity supplied, use the term "shortage."

Surplus

What if the current market price is too high, that is, above the equilibrium price? Exhibit 3.5 shows that at $3.50 per dozen, sellers will offer 450 dozen doughnuts for sale but buyers will purchase only 350 dozen. Once again, the market is out of balance: Quantity demanded is less than quantity supplied at the current price. Economists call excess quantity supplied a **surplus**. In our doughnut example, a surplus of 100 dozen per week occurs when the price is $3.50. *Whenever the current market price is above the equilibrium price, quantity supplied will exceed quantity demanded, creating a surplus.*

A surplus usually causes market prices to fall to the equilibrium price. Faced with a surplus, doughnut sellers have two choices: to eat the leftover doughnuts, or to cut prices to increase sales. A surplus also allows consumers to buy more at a lower price. Thus pressures from both the demand and supply sides of the market push market prices lower. The decline in prices decreases quantity supplied (a movement along the supply curve) and increases quantity demanded (a movement along the demand curve). Downward pressure on prices continues until the price reaches $3.00 per dozen. At this equilibrium price, the market is balanced: Sellers offer and buyers purchase 400 dozen doughnuts per week; there is no surplus and no remaining pressure on prices.

Changes in Market Conditions and Equilibrium Prices

The market's tendency to move to equilibrium allows us to predict how markets will respond to changes in demand or supply. We can expect prices to adjust to eliminate any shortage or surplus that may be created initially.

Changes in demand. Exhibit 3.6 provides an example of the market's response to changes in demand. As before, when D_1 represents demand and S_1 represents supply, the market is in equilibrium at $3.00 per dozen and 400 dozen doughnuts per week bought and sold (point *a*). What if some factor other than price changes? For example, what if income increases and doughnuts are a normal good? What if the price of blueberry muffins (a substitute for doughnuts) increases? In either case, the all-other-things-unchanged assumption is no longer valid. Demand for doughnuts would increase, and buyers would demand more doughnuts at each possible price.

As shown in Exhibit 3.6(b), an increase in demand causes the demand curve to shift to the right—from D_1 to D_2. Consumers will now buy 500 dozen (instead of 400 dozen) doughnuts per week at the old equilibrium price of $3.00. However, suppliers will continue to supply only 400 dozen, so the increase in demand creates a shortage of 100 dozen doughnuts per week at the old equilibrium price. Because a shortage puts upward pressure on the market price, the shortage is eliminated and upward pressure disappears when the market price rises to a new equilibrium level. The new equilibrium price lies where the new demand (D_2) and old supply (S_1) intersect—at $3.50 per dozen. The market price rises to $3.50, and the quantity demanded and supplied is 450 dozen per week (point *b*).

Surplus. A situation in which quantity supplied exceeds quantity demanded at the existing market price; excess supply.

(a) Demand schedules

(b) Demand curves

Price (dollars per dozen)	Quantity demanded (dozens per week)		
	D_0	D_1	D_2
4.00	175	325	425
3.50	200	350	450
3.00	250	400	500
2.50	325	475	575
2.00	425	575	675

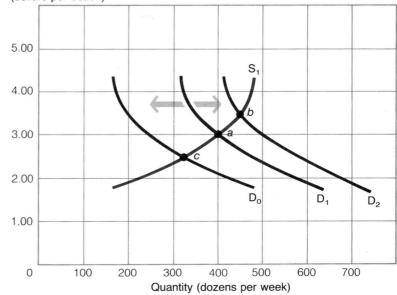

Exhibit 3.6
Changes in Demand for Doughnuts
An increase in demand results in a shift of the demand curve to the right from D_1 to D_2. It causes the equilibrium price to rise from $3.00 to $3.50 per dozen and the equilibrium output to rise from 400 to 450 dozen per week. A decrease in demand results in a shift to the left from D_1 to D_0. As a result, the equilibrium price drops to $2.50 per dozen and the equilibrium output falls to 325 dozen per week.

Conversely, an increase in the price of coffee (a complement to doughnuts) or a decline in income will cause demand for doughnuts to decrease. This effect is shown in the graph in Exhibit 3.6 as a shift to the left in the demand curve (from D_1 to D_0). Demand will fall from 400 dozen doughnuts at the old equilibrium price of $3.00 per dozen to only 250 dozen, creating a surplus of 150 dozen doughnuts per week. A surplus puts downward pressure on the market price until a new equilibrium price is reached—at the intersection of the new demand (D_0) and old supply (S_1). Thus when the price falls to $2.50 per dozen, 325 dozen doughnuts per week will be both bought and sold (point *c*), and the market will once again be in equilibrium.

In both cases, the final results reflect the market's automatic response. An increase in demand causes a shortage to develop, which automatically raises prices. A decrease in demand causes a surplus to develop, which automatically decreases prices. As long as the market is allowed to adjust, we can predict its response. *An increase in demand causes both market price and quantity sold to increase. A decrease in demand causes a decrease in both market price and quantity sold.*

(a) Supply schedules

Price (dollars per dozen)	Quantity supplied (dozens per week)		
	S_0	S_1	S_2
4.00	375	475	625
3.50	350	450	600
3.00	300	400	550
2.50	225	325	475
2.00	125	225	375

(b) Supply curves

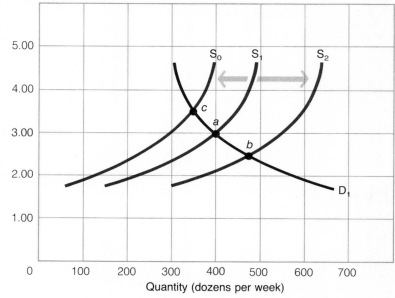

Exhibit 3.7
Changes in the Supply of Doughnuts
An increase in supply results in a shift of the supply curve to the right from S_1 to S_2. It causes the equilibrium price to fall from $3.00 to $2.50 per dozen and the equilibrium output to rise from 400 to 475 per week. A decrease in supply results in a shift to the left from S_1 to S_0. As a result, the equilibrium price rises to $3.50 per dozen and the equilibrium output falls to 350 dozen per week.

Changes in supply. Changes in supply also affect equilibrium. We expect a change in supply when any determinant of supply other than the price of the product changes. For example, the cost of flour (a resource) might fall; a more efficient machine for producing doughnuts (available technology) may be invented; or the price of blueberry muffins (which doughnut producers can make instead) may fall. In each case, the supply of doughnuts will increase and sellers will offer a larger quantity for sale at each possible price.

Exhibit 3.7 shows the effects of changes in supply. An increase in supply appears as a shift of the supply curve to the right (from S_1 to S_2). At the old equilibrium price of $3.00, sellers now offer 550 dozen doughnuts per week instead of 400 dozen. That is, an increase in supply means that a particular quantity will be offered for sale at a lower price. For example, sellers required a price of $4.00 per dozen to justify selling 475 dozen doughnuts per week before (on S_1). After the supply increases, they will sell 475 dozen per week for only $2.50 per dozen.

used a variety of means, including direct purchase of farm products, in attempts to prevent surpluses from pushing farm prices down.*

Economists are generally skeptical about imposing ceiling and support prices because of two major problems. First, by sending out false price signals, such policies distort the allocation of resources. If the price falls because of a ceiling price, sellers receive a signal identical to that caused by a decrease in demand. The signal suggests they are producing too much; they respond by reducing the quantity supplied. The signal to buyers is identical to that caused by a fall in product cost. They respond by increasing the quantity demanded. The result of this false signal is a shortage, meaning that too little is produced relative to allocative efficiency. A support price is also a false signal to buyers and sellers. In this case a surplus is created, meaning that too much is produced relative to allocative efficiency.

Second, in most cases ceiling and support prices do not achieve their stated objectives. A ceiling price benefits some consumers, but quantity supplied decreases, so fewer consumer demands can be met. Some consumers gain and others lose, but because the results are allocatively inefficient, society as a whole stands to lose. In addition, other policy options may address a problem more directly (see A Case in Point: Effects of Price Ceilings and Price Supports). Most economists do not claim that ceiling and price supports are never justified; however, they do suggest that such policies are very often inferior solutions to economic problems.

CONCLUSION

In this chapter we laid the foundation for the study of markets and the operation of a market economy. The true test of your understanding of demand and supply will come as you use these concepts to understand, describe, and predict the effects of economic changes on relative prices. As you do so, you should first identify whether the economic change affects demand or supply. Although in the real world many changes often occur at the same time, you will find it helpful to consider them separately, recognizing that the final result depends on putting them all together. Next, determine whether the identified change will increase or decrease demand or supply. Finally, graph the market effect as a shift in demand or supply, so that you can predict the effect on equilibrium price and quantity.

In this chapter we explained the factors that change demand and supply. But *how much* do demand and supply change in response to changing expectations, for example? The degree of change that we can expect is the topic of Chapter 4. Although we have described the individual market—a market for one particular product—we still need to consider how a market economy as a whole operates. In Chapter 5 we will look at how a system of markets interrelates to provide answers to the fundamental economic questions of what, how, and for whom to produce.

---

*The first issue in Chapter 19 is a study of agricultural price supports in the United States, which presents an in-depth description of price supports in action.

A Case in Point
Effects of Price Ceilings and Price Supports

The mayor of Collegetown has been presented with a petition from students at State University urging the mayor to do something about the lack of affordable local housing. Currently, the housing market is in equilibrium. All 800 apartments available are rented at an average price of $500 a month.

The students propose a ceiling price of $400 per month, a price most of them can afford. But the mayor explains that a ceiling price below the equilibrium price will not solve the problem, but will instead cause a shortage of apartments. As shown in the graph below, at $400 per month, quantity demanded (1200 units) exceeds quantity supplied (400 units). At the lower price, local landlords will rent fewer apartments to students. Students who succeeded in locating apartments would benefit from the lower price, but many students would have no place to live.

The head of the city council suggests a support price of $600 per month to encourage local builders to construct more apartments. The mayor noted that this policy will create a surplus. The graph at right shows that a support price would increase the number of apartments supplied to 1000 per month. But the number demanded would fall to 600 units because many students could not afford the $600 rent. The result would be a surplus of 400 apartments.

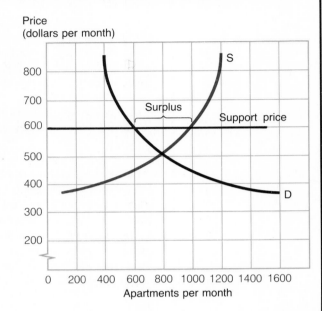

Price
(dollars per month)

Price
(dollars per month)

As this example illustrates, neither a support price nor a ceiling price will give students more housing at lower prices. In fact, each policy creates a new problem: what to do with the surplus in the case of the support price and what to do about the shortage in the case of the ceiling price. If the objective is to increase the quantity of apartments offered and rented, regulated prices will not help.

Two other options—an increase in supply and an increase in demand—offer some potential benefits. Lowering property taxes on apartments would increase the supply *and* lower the price of apartments. Alternatively, increasing the incomes of students who cannot afford existing housing would increase demand. Student income could be increased indirectly through training or employment programs, or directly through financial aid (loans and/or grants). Both solutions have costs, but unlike price ceilings and price supports they would at least address the problem of scarce, affordable housing.

What should the mayor do? Most economists would advise the mayor to reject regulated prices because they do not solve the problem. Other policies have both benefits and costs so a trade-off will have to be made. Ultimately, the decision will depend on whether the mayor feels that the extra benefits (more satisfied students) outweigh the extra costs (lost property taxes, for example).

SUMMARY

1. In this chapter we discussed the operation of a market, that is, how the forces of demand and supply, representing the interactions of buyers and sellers, determine market price.

2. Demand represents the quantities of a particular product that buyers are willing and able to purchase at every possible price during a specified period of time. Consumer wants and their desire to buy products do not represent demand if they are not willing and able to pay.

3. The law of demand states that price and quantity demanded are inversely related: A higher price will reduce the quantity consumers will demand; a lower price will raise the quantity they will buy. Demand shows how consumers balance the extra satisfaction received from a product against its extra cost (reflected by price).

4. For any particular demand relationship, economists assume that factors other than the price of the product are held constant; this is the *all-other-things-unchanged* assumption. A change in any factor other than price results in a new demand relationship, that is, a change in demand and a shift in the demand curve. A change in the product's price results in movement along a demand curve, representing only a change in quantity demanded.

5. Nonprice determinants of demand include tastes and preferences, income, prices of substitutes and complements, expectations of buyers, and the number of consumers. Demand for normal goods varies directly with income; demand for inferior goods varies indirectly with income. Substitutes can be used in place of each other, whereas complements are used together. When the price of a product rises, demand for its substitutes increases and demand for its complements decreases.

6. Supply represents to the quantities of a particular product that sellers are willing and able to offer for sale at every possible price during a specified period of time. The law of supply states that price and quantity supplied are directly related. Supply shows how sellers balance the extra costs of making a product against the extra benefits of selling it (reflected by price).

7. A change in the price of a product results in movement along a supply curve, representing only a change in quantity supplied. A change in any nonprice factor results in a new supply relationship, that is, a change in supply and a shift in the supply curve. Nonprice determinants of supply include prices of resources, available technology, prices of alternative goods, expectations, and the number of sellers.

8. A market is in equilibrium when at the current (equilibrium) price, quantity demanded equals quantity supplied. If the market price is below the equilibrium price, quantity demanded exceeds quantity supplied, resulting in a shortage. If the market price is above the equilibrium price, quantity supplied exceeds quantity demanded, resulting in a surplus. Market forces work to eliminate shortages and surpluses by causing the market price to adjust to the equilibrium price.

9. Changes in demand and supply affect equilibrium prices and output. An increase in demand shifts the demand curve to the right, resulting in higher prices and output. A decrease in demand shifts the demand curve to the left, resulting in lower prices and output. An increase in supply shifts the supply curve to the right, resulting in lower prices but higher output. A decrease in supply shifts the supply curve to the left, resulting in higher prices but lower output.

10. Government may intervene to establish a controlled price that is different from the equilibrium price. A ceiling price below equilibrium causes a shortage; a support price above equilibrium causes a surplus. Controlled prices may sometimes be justified, but can also cause inefficiency. They send false price signals to the market.

KEY TERMS

Market, 46
Market economy, 46
Price, 46
Demand, 47
Quantity demanded, 47
Law of demand, 48
Demand schedule, 48
Demand curve, 48
"All-other-things-unchanged" assumption, 49
Normal goods, 52
Inferior goods, 52
Substitutes, 52
Complements, 52
Relative price, 54
Supply, 55
Quantity supplied, 55
Law of supply, 55
Supply schedule, 55
Supply curve, 56

QUESTIONS FOR REVIEW AND DISCUSSION

1. Recalling the definition of demand, comment on the statement: "Most people would prefer a Rolls Royce to a Toyota, but more people buy Toyotas. This choice indicates that people are irrational."

2. If the price of ice cream rises 5 percent while prices of all other goods rise 10 percent, in what sense has the price of ice cream actually fallen? How might this price change be expected to influence the market for ice cream?

3. Recognizing the difference between changes in demand and changes in quantity demanded, comment on the statement: "Increasing the tax on gasoline may cause the price of gasoline to fall because consumers will respond by reducing demand, and when demand falls prices tend to fall."

4. An appliance store owner scoffs at the law of demand: "Economists say that price and quantity sold are inversely related, but I raised my prices this year and I'm selling more." Explain how price and quantity sold can both increase.

5. Recalling the difference between scarcity and shortage, comment on the statement: "If the price of feed grains goes up again this year, there'll be a shortage of Thanksgiving turkeys, and everyone who wants one won't be able to buy one."

6. Comment on the following: "A shortage is simply another way of indicating that the current price is too low; a surplus just means that the current price is too high."

7. If you were the manager of a small retail store, how would you know which items were priced too high and which ones too low? Could you tell the difference if you were a customer?

8. There are two parties to a market exchange: buyer and seller. Do both parties to the exchange necessarily gain? Will they gain equally?

9. Markets for some items are seasonal. Explain why the price of fresh strawberries falls during their peak season, whereas the price of Christmas cards rises during their peak season.

10. When the price of beef goes up, the price of chicken also tends to rise. Give two reasons for this reaction, considering both demand and supply. Can you think of other products that react similarly?

11. What change in demand and/or supply best explains the following statements? (Be sure to note which specific factors cause the change in demand and/or supply.)
    a) Prices of personal computers have fallen in recent years, while quantities sold have increased.
    b) Airlines sell more tickets during the peak travel season at higher prices than at other times.

12. Use demand and supply analysis to explain the effect of each of the following changes on equilibrium price and quantity exchanged in the market for college textbooks (consider each case independently).
    a) An increase in the price of paper.
    b) An increase in tuition and other fees.
    c) An increase in the expected income of individuals with college degrees.

13. Over time the prices of some goods (such as home appliances) are fairly steady, but those of other goods (such as farm products) change constantly. How do you account for these differences? Can you think of other examples in each category?

14. Suppose that the Collegeville city council decides to help hold down the cost of rental housing for college students and passes an ordinance limiting the rent that can be charged (a ceiling price). Explain its effect on:
    a) The quantity of rental property available.
    b) The quantity and/or quality of new rental property being constructed in Collegeville.
    c) The welfare of the student population as a whole (or of subgroups that may gain or lose).
    Can you think of other effects (such as demand for bus service from neighboring communities and the amount of property taxes collected by the city)?

15. Use the appendix to this chapter and the following equations relating demand and supply in a market to answer questions (a) and (b).

$$Qd = 300 - 3P$$

and

$$Qs = 50 + 2P$$

a) What are the equilibrium price and quantity in the market?
b) If a support price of 60 is established by the government, how big will the resulting surplus or shortage be?

Appendix to Chapter 3

Algebra of Market Equilibrium

In this chapter, you saw how demand and supply interact to achieve an equilibrium price and quantity, how a market responds to a change in demand and/or supply, and how a market reacts when the government imposes a ceiling price or support price. The same concepts can be examined using algebraic expressions for demand and supply relationships.

EQUATIONS FOR DEMAND AND SUPPLY

We can use the following equation to represent the original market demand for a hypothetical product:

$$Qd_1 = 100 - 2P$$

where Qd_1 = quantity demanded and P = market price. The equation is a **demand function**, that is, an algebraic expression for the relationship between quantity demanded and market price. This equation reflects the all-other-things-unchanged assumption, as indicated by the single variable—the product's price—on the right-hand side. The influence of other factors is represented by the constant term, 100. This equation supports the law of demand: the higher the price, the smaller the quantity demanded. To be sure that you understand why this is true, find quantity demanded at a price of 5 and at a price of 10. (Your answers should be 90 and 80.)

Likewise, we can express the original market supply for a hypothetical product as

$$Qs_1 = 10 + 4P$$

Demand function. An algebraic expression showing how quantity demanded is affected by market price and other factors influencing demand.

Supply function. An algebraic expression showing how quantity supplied is affected by market price and other factors influencing supply.

where Qs_1 = quantity supplied and P = market price. This equation is a **supply function**, that is, an algebraic expression for the relationship between quantity supplied and market price. As we did for demand, we make the all-other-things-unchanged assumption, with market price being the only variable affecting quantity supplied. The influence of other factors is represented by the constant term, 10. This equation supports the law of supply: Market price and quantity supplied are directly related. Test this statement by calculating quantity supplied at a price of 5 and at a price of 10. (Your answers should be 30 and 50.)

DETERMINATION OF EQUILIBRIUM

Using the equations for demand and supply, we can determine the equilibrium price by finding the price at which quantity demanded (Qd) equals quantity supplied (Qs). For the expressions given in the preceding section,

$$Qd_1 = Qs_1$$
$$100 - 2P = 10 + 4P$$
$$6P = 90$$
$$P = 15$$

Thus the equilibrium price in this example is 15, a price at which quantity demanded equals quantity supplied. To find quantity sold, therefore, we need only to find how much will be supplied (or demanded) at a price of 15. Using the equation for quantity supplied, we get

$$Qs_1 = 10 + 4P$$
$$= 10 + 4(15)$$
$$= 10 + 60 \quad \text{or} \quad 70$$

Because the price of 15 is the equilibrium price, we know that quantity supplied equals quantity demanded equals quantity sold. To verify this statement, substitute the price of 15 into the demand equation. (You should obtain a quantity demanded of 70.) Thus in this example, the market will reach equilibrium at a price of 15, at which the quantity exchanged equals 70.

AN INCREASE IN DEMAND

So far we have considered only changes in quantity demanded and supplied. In contrast, an increase in market demand means that quantity demanded will be greater at each possible price. We can express an increase in demand using a new demand function for our hypothetical product:

$$Qd_2 = 130 - 2P$$

You can verify that this equation represents an increase in demand by examining quantity demanded at a market price of 15; that is,

$$Qd_2 = 130 - 2P$$
$$= 130 - 2(15) \quad \text{or} \quad 100$$

Note that the constant term (130) in this new demand function is greater than the constant term (100) in the original demand function. Thus at each price buyers will demand 30 units more than before. You can verify this answer by determining quantity demanded at a price of 15 under the new demand conditions. Instead of the 70 units demanded before, 100 units will be demanded now, indicating an increase in demand. (You should also prove to yourself that this result holds at other prices by calculating quantity demanded under both demand functions at a price of 10.)

To examine the effect of an increase in demand, we can determine the equilibrium price and quantity exchanged for the new demand function and the original supply function. To do so, we equate quantity demanded and quantity supplied as follows:

$$Qd_2 = Qs_1$$
$$30 - 2P = 10 + 4P$$
$$6P = 120$$
$$P = 20$$

To find quantity exchanged, we substitute the equilibrium price into the demand function.

$$Qd_2 = 130 - 2P$$
$$= 130 - 2(20) \quad \text{or} \quad 90$$

As you saw in the graphs in this chapter, the increase in demand increased both the equilibrium price and quantity sold. To check your understanding of this point, find the equilibrium price and quantity under the following demand and supply conditions:

$$Qd_1 = 100 - 2P \quad \text{and} \quad Qs_2 = 40 + 4P$$

You might first ask whether the new supply function represents an increase or a decrease in supply compared to the original relationship. (Your answer should be "an increase" because the constant term 40 is greater than the constant term 10.) Then you should ask whether the equilibrium price and quantity sold would be higher or lower. (Your answers should be $P = 10$, or "lower," and $Qs_2 = 80$, or "higher.")

EFFECTS OF A CEILING PRICE

What would happen if, under the original demand and supply functions (Qd_1 and Qs_1) the government imposed a ceiling price of 12, which is lower than the equilibrium price of 15? To answer this question, you have to substitute the ceiling price into both the demand and supply functions to find quantities demanded and supplied. Thus

$$Qd_1 = 100 - 2P \qquad Qs_1 = 10 + 4P$$
$$= 100 - 2(12) \quad \text{or} \quad 76 \qquad = 10 + 4(12) \quad \text{or} \quad 58$$

As noted in this chapter, a ceiling price below the equilibrium price results in a shortage. A price of 12 causes a shortage of 18, or the difference between quantity demanded (76) and quantity supplied (58). This shortage would normally cause prices to rise, but government imposition of a maximum price of 12 means the shortage will continue.

To test your understanding of the operation of ceiling and support prices, try to answer the following questions (assuming the original conditions for demand and supply): (1) What surplus would be created if the government established a support price of 18? (2) What would be the effect on the market if the government imposes a ceiling price of 18? [Your answers should be (1) a surplus of 18; and (2) equilibrium at $P = 15$ and $Q = 70$, because a ceiling price above equilibrium would not keep the market from reaching equilibrium.]

CONCLUSION

When you have identified demand and supply functions that indicate the algebraic relationships among quantity demanded, quantity supplied, and market price, determining equilibrium algebraically is a two-step process. First, find the equilibrium price from Qd = Qs; that is, find the one price that will equate quantity demanded and quantity supplied. Second, calculate quantity exchanged by substituting the equilibrium price into either the demand function or the supply function.

In both economic theory and real-world economics, algebraic representation of demand and supply—and other economic concepts—is extremely useful. Therefore, throughout this textbook, you will find a series of appendixes designed to give you a better mathematical understanding of economics.

KEY TERMS

Demand function, 71
Supply function, 71

Elasticity of Demand
and Supply

QUESTIONS TO CONSIDER

☐ Why is the concept of elasticity important in analyzing economic activity?

☐ How do goods with price-elastic demands differ from goods with price-inelastic demands?

☐ What factors determine the price elasticity of demand? The price elasticity of supply?

☐ Why is income elasticity an important factor in business decisions?

☐ When would you use the formula for cross elasticity of demand?

We discussed the laws of demand and supply in Chapter 3, and how demand and supply together determine an equilibrium price and quantity. We showed that a decrease in supply will cause an increase in price and a decrease in quantity. But our analysis did not tell us *how much* price and quantity would change. This chapter expands on the concepts of demand and supply and introduces the concept of *elasticity*.

The concept of elasticity allows us to predict how much price and quantity respond to changes in demand and supply. It also helps us answer a number of economic questions. For example, why do wheat farmers generally earn less when the weather has been exceptionally good than when poor weather wipes out part of the wheat crop? Why is New York State better off taxing tobacco products than wines produced in the state? Why does a rapid population increase in an already crowded metropolitan area often cause a relatively large increase in housing prices in a short period of time? Why does a general increase in income lead to a greater increase in the profits of motel owners than in those of farmers?

PRICE ELASTICITY OF DEMAND

We can use the concept of price elasticity of demand to help Mr. H. B. O'Neil, owner of the Showcase Theater. Showcase's ticket prices are currently $5 per person. On average, 1000 people attend movies at the Showcase each week, earning Mr. O'Neil $5000 per week from ticket sales. To finance his son's tuba lessons, Mr. O'Neil is considering raising ticket prices to $6. But will this change increase his income?

The law of demand tells us that if ticket prices are raised, fewer people will come to the Showcase Theater, but each person attending will pay more. (Conversely, attendance would increase if the price were lowered, but each customer would pay less.) We cannot predict whether increasing (or decreasing) ticket prices will increase Mr. O'Neil's income unless we know *how responsive* attendance will be to a price change.

To answer questions such as this, economists use one of several elasticity concepts. In this case, we want to apply the concept of **price elasticity of**

Price elasticity of demand. A measure of the response of buyers to a change in price, usually expressed as the percentage change in quantity demanded divided by the percentage change in price.

Price elastic. A situation in which the percentage change in quantity is larger than the percentage change in price, giving an elasticity coefficient greater than 1 (ignoring the sign).

Price inelastic. A situation in which the percentage change in quantity is smaller than the percentage change in price, giving an elasticity coefficient less than 1 (ignoring the sign).

demand, that is, the responsiveness of quantity demanded to changes in the product's price. If consumers are very responsive to changes in the product's price, we say that demand is **price elastic**; if they are not very responsive, we say that demand is **price inelastic**.

Exhibit 4.1 shows two possible demand relationships. In the first case (D_1), a $1 change in ticket price will gain (or lose) Showcase Theater 100 customers per week. In the second case (D_2), the change in ticket sales is much larger: 400 customers per week. Because quantity demanded responds more to price changes in the second case than in the first, economists say that demand is more price elastic in the second case and more price inelastic in the first.

Why does Mr. O'Neil care whether demand for more tickets is price elastic or price inelastic? The cost of showing a movie for 10 or 200 people is about the same. Thus Mr. O'Neil's profit depends largely on ticket sales. Suppose that he raises the ticket price from $5 to $6. If he loses only 100 customers, he will earn $5400 ($6 per ticket × 900 tickets), or $400 more than he currently earns. But if he loses 400 customers, he will earn only $3600 ($6 per ticket × 600 tickets), or $1400 less than he currently earns. In other words, he gains from an increase in ticket price if his customers are not very responsive to price (if demand is price

---

Exhibit 4.1
Two Possible Demand Relationships for Showcase Theater
The demand curve (D_1) in part (a) is price inelastic because consumers are relatively unresponsive to a change in price. The demand curve (D_2) in part (b) is price elastic because consumers are relatively responsive to a change in price. Along D_1, only 100 fewer tickets will be sold when the ticket price increases from $5 to $6 each. As a result, the increase in price will increase total revenue from $5000 to $5400 per week. Along D_2, 400 fewer tickets will be sold if ticket prices are raised from $5 to $6. In this case, total revenue will fall from $5000 to $3600 per week.

(a) Price-inelastic demand

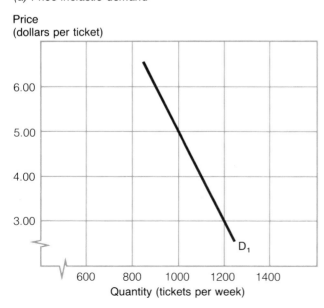

(b) Price-elastic demand

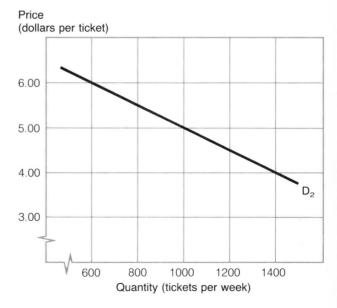

inelastic), but loses if they are quite responsive (if demand is price elastic). In fact, if demand is price elastic, Mr. O'Neil would earn more by *lowering* the ticket price to $4. (To check your understanding, verify this statement by calculating total receipts for both cases.)

This example clearly indicates the importance of price elasticity of demand. To apply this concept, however, you must learn how to recognize the circumstances under which demand is likely to be price elastic or inelastic and how to measure elasticity.

Price Elasticity as a Relative Concept

In the preceding example, a change of 400 in ticket sales was clearly larger than a change of 100. However, absolute changes in quantity sold are not always a good measure of response to price changes. If customers will buy 2000 more units of a product when its price is lowered, is that a small or a large response? We cannot answer that question unless we know how large current sales are. In the wheat market, where millions of bushels are exchanged each year, an increase of 2000 bushels per year is insignificant. But for a small-town shoe store, the sale of 2000 more pairs of shoes per month would be a very significant increase.

Percentage changes in quantity and price. We can tell whether demand is price elastic or not if we know the *relative* size of a change in quantity. For this reason, economists measure elasticity as a percentage change. To calculate the percentage change in quantity we divide the difference in quantities demanded $(Q_2 - Q_1)$ by the *average* of the two quantities:

$$\text{Percentage change in quantity} = \frac{\text{Difference in quantities}}{\text{Average of quantities}} \times 100$$

$$= \frac{(Q_2 - Q_1)}{(Q_2 + Q_1)/2} \times 100$$

As we have mentioned before, memorizing formulas is not easy. To help you remember the principles involved, let's consider an example. Exhibit 4.2 shows the demand for tennis rackets at C&J Sports Center. If the price decreases from $90 to $80 per racket, the quantity of tennis rackets demanded increases from 1200 to 1300 per year. Substituting into the formula for percentage change in quantity, we find that

$$\text{Percentage change in quantity} = \frac{(1300 - 1200)}{(1300 + 1200)/2} \times 100$$

$$= \frac{100}{1250} \times 100$$

$$= 0.08 \times 100 \quad \text{or} \quad 8\%$$

You may be wondering why in the formula we divide by the average of the two quantities. If we did not use the average, we would have to divide by either the original quantity or the new quantity. As a result, we could get two different answers. In our example, if we divided by Q_1 (1200), we would get an answer of 8.3 percent. But if we divided by Q_2 (1300), we would get an answer of 7.7 percent.

Price (dollars per racket)	Quantity demanded (rackets per year)	Price elasticity of demand coefficient[a]
140	700	
		1.80
130	800	
		1.47
120	900	
		1.21
110	1000	
		1.00
100	1100	
		0.83
90	1200	
		0.68
80	1300	
		0.56
70	1400	

[a]The price elasticity of demand coefficient shown is the absolute value of the number obtained using the elasticity formula. Price elasticity is always negative; economists are interested in its magnitude, not the sign.

Exhibit 4.2
The Demand for Tennis Rackets at C&J Sports Center

By averaging the quantities, we get a divisor of 1250, and a constant answer of 8 percent change. This difference may seem trivial, but it can be significant. To prove this point to yourself, calculate the percentage change for quantities of 50 and 100, dividing by 50, 100, and 75 (the average of the quantities). (You should get answers of 100, 50, and 66.7 percent.)

We also measure the size of price changes in relative terms. Using a similar formula, we divide the differences in price ($P_2 - P_1$) by the average of the two prices. That is,

$$\text{Percentage change in price} = \frac{\text{Difference in prices}}{\text{Average of prices}} \times 100$$

$$= \frac{(P_2 - P_1)}{(P_2 + P_1)/2} \times 100$$

Substituting the prices $90 and $80 from Exhibit 4.2, we obtain

$$\text{Percentage change in price} = \frac{(\$80 - \$90)}{(\$80 + \$90)/2} \times 100$$

$$= \frac{-\$10}{\$85} \times 100$$

$$= -0.117 \times 100 \quad \text{or} \quad -11.7\%$$

Formula for price elasticity of demand.   Elasticity is a relative concept in a second sense as well. We want to measure the size of the consumer response *relative to* the size of the price change. We cannot tell whether a 10 percent change in quantity demanded is large or small unless we know whether price changed by 5 percent or 50 percent. To measure price elasticity of demand (the responsiveness of quantity demanded relative to changes in price) we combine the formulas for percentage changes in quantity and price as follows:

$$\text{Price elasticity of demand} = \frac{\text{Percentage change in quantity demanded}}{\text{Percentage change in price}}$$

$$= \frac{\text{Difference in quantities/Average of quantities}}{\text{Difference in prices/Average of prices}}$$

$$= \frac{(Q_2 - Q_1)}{(Q_2 + Q_1)/2} \div \frac{(P_2 - P_1)}{(P_2 + P_1)/2}$$

Again using the data from Exhibit 4.2, we can calculate elasticity of demand for a price change from $80 to $90:

$$\text{Price elasticity of demand} = \frac{(1300 - 1200)}{(1300 + 1200)/2} \div \frac{(\$80 - \$90)}{(\$80 + \$90)/2}$$

$$= \frac{100}{2500/2} \div \frac{-\$10}{170/2}$$

$$= \frac{0.08}{-0.117}$$

$$= -0.68$$

Mathematically, price elasticity of demand is *always* negative because price and quantity demanded are inversely related. For convenience, therefore, *economists generally ignore the sign* and express price elasticity of demand in *absolute-value* terms—in this case a value of 0.68. (Note that all the elasticity figures in Exhibit 4.2 are shown as positive values.)

Elasticity coefficients.   The value obtained from the formula (0.68 in this case) is what economists call a **price-elasticity coefficient**. If the price-elasticity coefficient is greater than 1, demand is price elastic; if the coefficient is less than 1, demand is price inelastic. In our example the elasticity coefficient was 0.68, meaning that the demand for tennis rackets at C&J Sports Center is—for this particular price change—*price inelastic*.

Why does this method of expressing elasticity work? Recall that price elasticity compares the percentage change in quantity to the percentage change in price. If the percentage change in quantity is smaller than the percentage change in price, buyers are not responding strongly to a price change. If the relative change in quantity is less than the relative change in price, the elasticity coefficient will always be less than one. Conversely, if the percentage change in quantity is larger than the percentage change in price, buyers are responding strongly to price changes. And when the relative change in quantity is greater than the relative change in price, the elasticity coefficient will always be greater than 1. Finally, in some cases, the percentage change in quantity is the same as the percentage change in price, making the elasticity coefficient equal to 1.

Price-elasticity coefficient. The number obtained by using the price elasticity formula. When its absolute value (ignoring the sign) is greater than 1, the demand (or supply) is price elastic; when it is less than 1, the demand (or supply) is price inelastic; when it equals 1, the demand (or supply) has unitary elasticity.

Unitary price elasticity. A situation in which the percentage change in quantity demanded (or supplied) equals the percentage change in price; the absolute value of the elasticity coefficient is 1.

Exhibit 4.2 indicates that price elasticity of demand is not constant. For a price change from $120 to $130 per racket, the coefficient is 1.47. Thus for this price range, demand for tennis rackets is *price elastic*. When the price of tennis rackets changes from $100 to $110, the coefficient equals 1. In this case, the price and quantity changes are identical in percentage terms. Economists use the term **unitary price elasticity** to refer to this type of situation. (As you will no doubt be asked to calculate price elasticities soon, you should use the price elasticity formula to verify some of the coefficients shown in Exhibit 4.2.)

Because price elasticity of demand is an important concept, the characteristics of the elasticity formula and the steps involved in its use are worth repeating. First, we obtain the percentage changes in quantity and price. Second, we calculate the percentage changes in quantity relative to the percentage changes in price. Third, we ignore all signs and express the price elasticity coefficient as a positive number. And finally, we compare the coefficient to 1 to determine whether demand is elastic, inelastic, or has unitary elasticity for a given price range.

Slope of demand curve versus price elasticity. Exhibit 4.3 shows the demand curve for tennis rackets. As you can see, at the upper end of the price range, demand is price elastic ($E_D > 1$), and at the lower end, it is price inelastic

Exhibit 4.3
Price Elasticity of Demand for Tennis Rackets
The price elasticity of demand for tennis rackets varies along the demand curve. The demand is price elastic at the higher range of prices ($E_D > 1$) and price inelastic at the lower range of prices ($E_D < 1$). Between $100 and $110, the demand has unitary elasticity ($E_D = 1$).

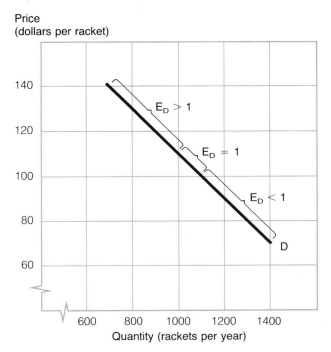

($E_D < 1$). This pattern is characteristic of price elasticity of demand because a small change in quantity represents a much larger percentage change when the original quantity demanded is small than when it is large. For example, a 10-unit change in quantity is a 100 percent change if the original quantity demanded was 10 units, but only a 1 percent change if the original quantity demanded was 1000 units.

Be careful not to confuse elasticity with the slope of the demand curve. The demand curve for tennis rackets in Exhibit 4.3 is a straight line and thus has a constant slope, but elasticity is not constant. Slope is the ratio of *absolute* changes in quantity and price between two points on the curve. Elasticity is the ratio of *percentage* changes in quantity and price. In Exhibit 4.3, for example, each $10 drop in price raises the quantity of tennis rackets demanded by 100. But the percentage change in price represented by a $10 drop in price and the percentage change in quantity demanded represented by an increase of 100 rackets are not the same. Thus elasticity changes as we move along the curve.

Price Elasticity of Demand and Total Revenue

Earlier we indicated that Mr. O'Neil would want to know price elasticity of demand before deciding whether to raise or lower ticket prices at his theater. We showed that if his customers were very responsive to a price change, he would lose money by raising the price of tickets; if they were relatively unresponsive, he would gain. In other words, the best price change in terms of total revenue for Mr. O'Neil's theater depends on the price elasticity of demand.

In fact, there is a general relationship between price elasticity and **total revenue (TR)**. Total revenue is simply the product of price (P) and quantity (Q) sold, or TR = P × Q. Exhibit 4.4 shows the relationship between total revenue and price elasticity of demand for C&J Sports Center. Note that as the price of tennis rackets falls from $130 to $120 each, total revenue rises from $104,000 to $108,000 per year. In this price range, the price-elasticity coefficient is greater than 1; that is, demand is price elastic. This relationship is true: *When demand is price elastic, a decrease in price will increase total revenue.*

The change in total revenue reflects two changes that occur when price is lowered. First, C&J can sell 100 more rackets at the new price of $120, a gain of $12,000. However, each of the 800 rackets it could have sold for $130 now sells for $10 less, a loss of $8000. Because the gain from increasing sales (reflecting the response of quantity) is more important than the loss from lowering the price, C&J has a net gain of $4000. Intuitively, this result also makes sense, because when demand is price elastic, the quantity response affects total revenue more than the price change does. In other words, the increased number of customers outweighs the fact that each customer pays a lower price.

In the lower price ranges, demand is price inelastic (the elasticity coefficient is less than 1). Thus a decrease in price from $100 to $90 will decrease revenue from $110,000 to $108,000. This relationship between elasticity and revenue is also true: *When demand is price inelastic, a price decrease will decrease total revenues.* Again, the net result reflects two changes. When the price is lowered, C&J sells 100 more rackets, a gain of $9000. But each of the 1100 rackets it could have sold at $100 now sells for $10 less, a loss of $11,000. The net effect—a loss of $2000—indicates that the increase in quantity sold is less important than the fact that each racket is sold for less. This is the expected result when demand is

Total revenue (TR). The total number of dollars received from sales, calculated as the product of price and quantity sold, or TR = P × Q.

Price (dollars per racket)	Quantity demanded (rackets per year)	Total revenues (dollars per year)	Change in total revenue (dollars per year)	Price elasticity of demand coefficient[a]
140	700	98,000		
			+6,000	1.80
130	800	104,000		
			+4,000	1.47
120	900	108,000		
			+2,000	1.21
110	1000	110,000		
			0	1.00
100	1100	110,000		
			−2,000	0.83
90	1200	108,000		
			−4,000	0.68
80	1300	104,000		
			−6,000	0.56
70	1400	98,000		

Exhibit 4.4
Demand for Tennis Rackets: Elasticity and Total Revenue

[a]The price elasticity of demand coefficient shown is the absolute value of the number obtained using the elasticity formula. Price elasticity is always negative; economists are interested in its magnitude, not the sign.

price inelastic; the effect of the quantity response is small, and the effect of the price change is large.

Note that the price-elasticity coefficient is 1 for a price change from $100 to $110. This relationship is also true: *When demand has unitary price elasticity, a change in price has no effect on total revenues.* In this case, the price and quantity changes, in percentage terms, are equal. Thus the effect on total revenue of having fewer customers as the price is increased is exactly balanced by the effect of each paying a higher price.

So far we have assumed that changes in price are relatively small. However, if price were doubled, we could move from a price-inelastic portion of the demand curve to a price-elastic portion of the curve. However, measurements of price elasticity tend to be meaningful only for relatively small price changes. Even so, elasticity is a useful concept in the real world. When trying to decide whether to raise prices, most business managers consider the effect of relatively small increases, not a doubling of prices overnight.

To remember the important relationship between percentage changes in quantity and price, focus on the law of demand, the meaning of price elasticity of demand, and the calculation of total revenue. The law of demand means that a price increase causes the quantity demanded to fall. The increase in price will tend to raise total revenue; the fall in quantity will tend to reduce total revenue.

To determine the net effect on total revenue, we must know by *how much* quantity demanded falls. If demand is price elastic and price increases, the percentage drop in the quantity demanded will exceed the percentage increase in price; hence a price increase will reduce total revenue. Try the other possibilities, using the law of demand to determine the *direction* of change in price and quantity, and price elasticity to indicate *how much* quantity demanded changes relative to price. See if you can verify that the following statement is true: *A price increase will result in higher total revenue if demand is price inelastic; total revenue will fall, however, if demand is price elastic.* See A Case in Point: Who Pays a Sales Tax? for another example of the relationship between revenue and price elasticity of demand.

Two Extreme Cases

Thus far we have assumed that the usual demand relationship and curve exist: an inverse relationship between market price and quantity demanded, and a curve that slopes downward and to the right. In two extreme cases, however, demand does not fit the usual pattern. Exhibit 4.5(a) shows a perfectly price-elastic demand curve, and Exhibit 4.5(b) shows a perfectly price-inelastic demand curve.

The perfectly price-elastic demand curve, shown in Exhibit 4.5(a), suggests that consumers are willing to buy an infinite amount of the product at or below a price of $3. Demand is said to be perfectly price elastic because if price increases by even a small amount above P_1, quantity demanded falls to zero—an infinitely large response. You may think that such a demand relationship could not exist. It is unusual, but not unheard of. Most often, this type of relationship exists when each individual seller is a very small part of a market. A common example is the wheat farmer who sells thousands of bushels of wheat in a market in which millions of bushels are·exchanged. Individual farmers can sell all they want at the going price, but nothing at a higher price. Of course, a single farmer cannot really sell an infinite amount. By expanding sales enough (say, to 1 million bushels), the farmer would become a significant part of the market and could influence market price. Thus demand for the farmer's wheat is perfectly price elastic only over a rather small range of quantity.

The second extreme, shown in Exhibit 4.5(b), is perfectly price-inelastic demand. In this case, the vertical demand curve means that quantity purchased does not vary with price. Regardless of price or how much of their income it would take to buy a small quantity, buyers will purchase a total of 1500 units per week. Situations in which demand is completely insensitive to price are rare, and in most cases apply only to a reasonably small range of prices. Medicines are the most common example. Many diabetics must take a certain amount of insulin each day; taking more or less than the necessary dose can prove fatal. Because medical insurance and government health programs cover the insulin expenses of many diabetics, demand for insulin is probably perfectly price inelastic, at least across the usual range of prices. Even so, at some point price would become too high and quantity demanded would decrease.

Market demand for most products is far from being either perfectly price elastic or perfectly price inelastic and usually follows the law of demand. As a beginning student in economics, you should be careful to distinguish between price-inelastic demand and perfectly price-inelastic demand. When demand is price inelastic, the quantity response to a price change is small; when demand is perfectly price inelastic, the quantity response is zero.

(a) Perfectly price-elastic demand (E$_D$ = ∞)

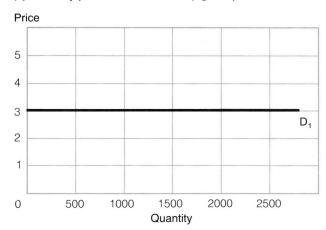

(b) Perfectly price-inelastic demand (E$_D$ = 0)

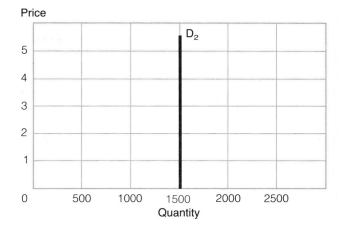

Exhibit 4.5
Elasticity Extremes
Part (a) shows a perfectly price-elastic demand curve. Consumers will buy infinite amounts of this product, if the price is $3 or less. If price were to rise above $3, quantity demanded would fall to zero. Consumers make an infinite response in terms of quantity demanded (reducing purchases from an infinite amount to zero) to a price increase. Part (b) shows a perfectly price-inelastic demand curve. Consumers will buy the same quantity of this product, 1500 units per month, no matter how high or low the price is.

Determinants of Price Elasticity of Demand

Although price elasticity of demand is important, in the real world, data defining the demand relationship usually are not available. Without such data, we cannot apply the price elasticity of demand formula. How, then, can Mr. O'Neil and C&J Sports Center set their prices? By applying economic logic, they can identify some factors affecting price elasticity of demand and make an educated guess about whether demand is price elastic or price inelastic.

Availability of good substitutes. Consumers are usually more responsive to price changes when they have a number of options from which to choose. When good substitutes for a product exist, consumers can get much the same satisfaction from any of them. Thus we expect a significant response when the price of one of these products changes. For example, if you walk into the local supermarket and find that the price of one brand of cereal has risen, you have only to check the shelves to find many close substitutes. You can make a significant response to the price change if you stop buying one brand and switch to another. *Demand becomes more price elastic as the number of close substitutes increases.*

Note that we are talking about *good* substitutes, where there is little difference in the satisfaction received. Using the telephone to call your mother who lives 1500 miles away and driving over to her house for a quick chat are substitutes,

A Case in Point
Who Pays a Sales Tax?

State and local governments often use sales taxes to raise revenue. We can use the concept of elasticity to help determine how much revenue a sales tax will raise and who pays the sales tax.

The city council of Collegetown is considering placing a $1.50 tax on a six-pack of beer and a $1.50 tax on SuperSub sandwiches. To explore the importance of elasticity, let's assume that demand for beer is price inelastic and demand for SuperSub sandwiches is price elastic. The two graphs in Exhibit 4C.1 show the current market conditions and the changes that would occur with the sales tax. For ease of comparison, we assume that in both cases the market price without a tax is $3.00 and that the quantity sold of each product is 400 per week.

What is the impact of a sales tax? As the two graphs indicate, the sales tax shifts the supply curve (from the perspective of the buyer) up by the amount of the tax. Note that at each quantity, the price paid by the consumer will be $1.50 more. Because the tax raises the price paid by the consumer, we can expect quantity demanded to fall. In both graphs, the new equilibrium (where D intersects S_1 + tax) shows a higher price and lower quantity sold.

We are now ready to estimate revenue and identify who pays the tax. First, how much revenue will the sales tax raise? Because we have assumed the same supply relationship for each product, the answer depends on the price elasticity of demand. The tax to be paid in each case is the amount of tax ($1.50 per unit) times quantity sold. For beer, the tax revenue would be $525 per week, or 350 six-packs sold at $1.50 tax per six-pack. For SuperSubs, the city would receive $450 per week, or 300 sandwiches at $1.50 tax per sandwich. (On the graphs in Exhibit 4C.1, the shaded areas identify total taxes to be paid.)

The tax revenue from the sale of beer would be more than that from the sale of sandwiches because demand for beer is more price inelastic. (The absolute value of the price-elasticity coefficients for the change in price is 0.47 for beer and a 1.86 for sandwiches.) Because they are less responsive to the price increase, buyers of beer reduce quantity demanded less, but the city still collects more from the tax on beer.

You may think that the question of who pays the sales tax is silly. Perhaps you assumed that buyers pay the entire amount of the sales taxes. However, the taxes actually are paid partly by the buyer and partly by the seller. The buyer pays more because of the tax but the seller earns less. For beer the price (including tax) is $1.00 more than it was before. But the seller receives only $2.50 per six-pack instead of $3.00, given market demand. Of the total $1.50 per unit tax, two-thirds ($1.00) is paid by the buyer and one-third ($0.50) is paid by the seller. For sandwiches, the burden shifts. The seller pays two-thirds of the tax (receiving $1.00 less per sandwich); the buyer pays one-third ($0.50 more per sandwich).

too. Either choice allows you to talk with your mother, but they are hardly good substitutes. The availability of an alternative (driving 1500 miles) does not make the demand for telephone service price elastic. Only when good substitutes are available will consumers make a significant response to a relatively small price change.

This distinction is especially important to sellers. When a firm produces a product that is a good substitute for those of its competitors, demand for its product is always more price elastic than the market demand for all such products. For example, demand for gasoline (over a short period of time) is price inelastic, but demand for gas at Fred's Friendly Filling Station is likely to be quite price elastic if Fred is one of four stations in a two-block area. Price elasticity of demand also changes when new competitors enter the market. For example, in the 1970s demand for automobiles made in the United States became much more price elastic because of new competition from Japanese and Western European firms.

Who pays the sales tax depends on the price elasticity of demand. When demand is price inelastic (as for beer), buyers pay more of the tax because they are less sensitive to price changes. But when demand is price elastic (as for sandwiches), suppliers pay more of the tax.

(a) Demand for SuperSubs
   (demand is price elastic)

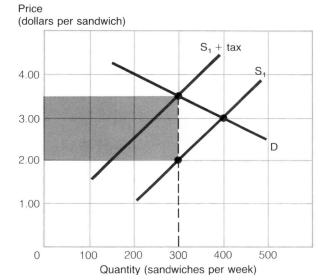

(b) Demand for beer
   (demand is price inelastic)

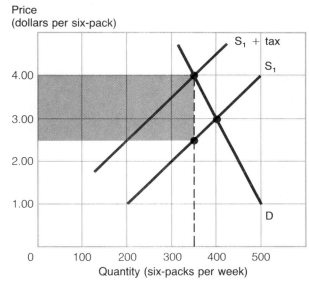

Exhibit 4C.1

Product price relative to income. When a product has a price that represents a large share of the consumer's income, demand is often quite price elastic. For example, a 10 percent increase in the price of cars gets a greater consumer response than a 10 percent increase in the price of toothpaste. However, to a child with a $0.50 weekly allowance (income), a $0.05 increase in the price of a $0.40 candy bar *is* significant. In general, we say that *demand is more price elastic when a product's price is a large portion of the consumer's income; demand is more price inelastic when the price is a small portion of income.*

The relevant time period. The relevant time period for the demand relationship also affects elasticity. As we noted in Chapter 3, a demand or supply schedule refers to a specific time period—the number of tennis rackets demanded per year or the number of movie tickets sold per week. Given a longer time period in which to respond, consumers can find more alternatives. Thus, in general, *when the relevant time period is short, demand is price inelastic; when the relevant time period is long, demand is price elastic.*

For example, demand for oil tends to be quite price inelastic over a short period of time. Individuals who heat their homes with oil and drive their cars to work have few easy options and tend to make only small adjustments in quantity demanded. However, as the response of U.S. consumers to the sharp price increases in the 1970s indicated, demand for oil is price elastic over a long period of time. Better insulation for homes, smaller and more fuel efficient automobiles, and car pooling may take time to develop, but they permit significant changes in consumption.

Consider the following situation. It is an extremely hot day; you have been outside working up a thirst. You walk into the only grocery store in a small town (the next town is 20 miles away). You go to the cooler for a cold drink, only to discover that prices at this store are unusually high. What is your response? Under the conditions outlined, you probably pay the price, grumbling all the time. Your demand at the moment is price inelastic because you are thirsty, and a drink 30 minutes from now is not a good substitute for one right now.

Necessity or luxury?   Some believe that price elasticity depends on whether a product is viewed by consumers as a necessity or a luxury. They define necessities to include not only goods essential to physical survival (such as food and medical care) but also goods perceived as minimum requirements for a decent standard of living. As you might expect, they predict that demand for necessities will be price inelastic and demand for luxuries will be price elastic.

Be aware, however, that this distinction is not always clear-cut and is not always an accurate predictor of price elasticity. For example, demand for the best seats for a symphony orchestra concert is often rather price inelastic, although it is hardly a necessity. Moreover, many necessities have a number of relatively close substitutes and therefore have price elastic demand. Demand for food in general is certainly price inelastic, but no one eats "food in general"; we eat steak or chicken or spinach. Demand for some specific food items is price elastic. (Interestingly, the elasticity coefficient for beer is estimated to be 0.80, making demand price inelastic. Whether this condition makes beer a necessity depends on your point of view.)

Price Elasticity of Demand in Action

Now that you know something about price elasticity of demand, you should be able to answer some of the questions posed at the beginning of this chapter. For example, why are wheat farmers as a group likely to profit from a generally poor crop? Demand for wheat, like many agricultural products, is price inelastic. (How much more bread would you buy if the price of a loaf drops even by as much as 25 percent?) A poor crop decreases the supply of wheat, raising the market price. Since demand is price inelastic, quantity response will be relatively small and price response relatively large. Thus a poor crop means considerably higher prices and, consequently, higher farm incomes. (Recall that a price increase raises total revenue when demand is price inelastic.)

Why would New York State raise more tax revenue by taxing tobacco products instead of wines produced in the state? Consider the determinants of price elas-

Price elasticity of demand reflects the responsiveness of quantity demanded to a change in the price of a product. It is measured by the elasticity coefficient, calculated as the percentage change in quantity demanded divided by the percentage change in price.

When the elasticity coefficient is less than 1, demand is price inelastic; when the coefficient is greater than 1, demand is price elastic; when the coefficient equals 1, demand has unitary price elasticity.

Determinants of price elasticity of demand include the availability of close substitutes, the product's price relative to the consumer's income, and the length of the relevant time period.

ticity. To those who smoke (and chew) there are few good substitutes for tobacco products, so demand for tobacco is price inelastic. A tax on tobacco therefore would tend to raise a considerable amount of revenue for the state. Smokers would pay the higher price for nearly the same quantity demanded. Wines produced in New York State, on the other hand, have many good substitutes—wines produced in California or imported from other countries, for example. As a result, demand is price elastic, and consumers could easily avoid the tax by buying substitute products. Thus the tax would reduce the quantity of New York wines sold more than it would raise money for the state government.

OTHER TYPES OF ELASTICITY

We can also use the concept of elasticity to describe other responses that buyers and sellers will make to various changes. In this section, we discuss three other types of elasticity commonly used in economic studies: price elasticity of supply, income elasticity of demand, and cross elasticity of demand. Each has much in common with price elasticity of demand. In particular, we use variations of the formula for price elasticity of demand to calculate elasticity coefficients. And each type of elasticity refers to the responsiveness of quantity. The similarities should help you remember what these types of elasticity mean and, more importantly, how to use them.

Price Elasticity of Supply

Price elasticity of demand is the response of buyers to a price change; **price elasticity of supply** is the response of sellers to a price change. If sellers respond strongly to a price change, we say that supply is *price elastic*. If sellers do not respond much, we say that supply is *price inelastic*.

To measure the price elasticity of supply, we use a formula similar to that for price elasticity of demand. Here, however, the change in quantity refers to the change in quantity *supplied*.

$$\text{Price elasticity of supply} = \frac{\text{Percentage change in quantity supplied}}{\text{Percentage change in price}}$$

$$= \frac{(Q_2 - Q_1)}{(Q_2 + Q_1)/2} \div \frac{(P_2 - P_1)}{(P_2 + P_1)/2}$$

This formula expresses responsiveness of quantity supplied *relative* to a change in price (that is, in percentage terms), as does the formula used to measure price elasticity of demand.

Like that for the price elasticity of demand, this formula produces a coefficient, and again we ignore the sign. As with the demand coefficient, we compare the price elasticity of supply coefficient to 1 to determine whether supply is price elastic or price inelastic, or has unitary price elasticity. When the coefficient is greater than 1, supply is price elastic, since the percentage change in quantity supplied is greater than the percentage change in price, indicating sellers are very responsive to a change in price. When the coefficient is less than 1, supply is price inelastic, since the percentage change in quantity is less than the percentage change

Price elasticity of supply. A measure of the response of sellers to a change in price, usually expressed as the percentage change in quantity supplied divided by the percentage change in price.

in price. And when the supply elasticity coefficient equals 1, the percentage change in quantity equals the percentage change in price, and supply has unitary price elasticity.

Price elasticity of supply depends on the willingness and ability of sellers to respond to a change in price. Several factors affect seller responsiveness and thus how price elastic supply will be.

Cost and economic feasibility of storage. Some products are quite durable and can be easily and inexpensively stored. Oil producers, for example, can respond to a price drop by storing the oil they have on hand (or in the ground), while waiting for a better price. The ability to respond to a price change in this way makes supply price elastic. Other products—fresh vegetables, for example—are perishable or expensive to store. Sellers cannot pull large quantities of such goods off the market and store them economically. Supply of these products thus is often price inelastic. *The lower the cost of storage and the more practical storage is, the more price elastic the supply will be.*

Flexibility of the production process. For some goods, the production process does not allow a quick and easy response to price changes. For example, the high retooling and setup costs involved in making new car models limit the sellers' ability to make easy or quick responses. Similarly, construction of high-rise buildings cannot be changed much, once begun. For some chemical products, however, switching from one product mix to another is relatively easy. *When sellers can make quick and inexpensive responses to relatively small price changes, supply is usually very price elastic.*

The supply of by-products, such as kerosene, which is produced whenever gasoline is refined from oil, or sawdust produced by sawmills is typically price inelastic. Supply of these by-products depends primarily on demand for the primary product; seller response just to the price of kerosene or sawdust is not economically practical.

Cost and availability of resources. As we noted in Chapter 3, supply reflects the extra cost of producing an additional unit. Whenever this extra cost is high and rises quickly, supply tends to be price inelastic. If extra units can be produced for nearly the same cost as previous units, supply tends to be price elastic. *When increasing production requires the purchase of increasingly expensive resources, supply tends to be price inelastic.*

Relevant time period. As with demand, each supply curve measures quantity supplied over some specified period of time—a day, a month, a year. Given more time, sellers have greater flexibility and more options for supply. *The longer the time period, the greater the response suppliers can make to a change in price, and hence the more price elastic supply will be.*

Income Elasticity of Demand

In Chapter 3 we also noted that demand and supply, unlike quantity demanded and supplied, are affected by factors other than the price of the product. In discussing the effect of income on demand, we explained how demand for normal goods varies directly with income, and demand for inferior goods varies inversely with demand. That is, for normal goods increased income means increased demand. For inferior goods increased income means decreased demand. **Income elasticity of demand** measures responsiveness of demand to changes in income and is expressed as

$$\text{Income elasticity of demand} = \frac{\text{Percentage change in quantity demanded}}{\text{Percentage change in income}}$$

$$= \frac{(Q_2 - Q_1)}{(Q_2 + Q_1)/2} \div \frac{(Y_2 - Y_1)}{(Y_2 + Y_1)/2}$$

where Y represents income.

Price elasticity of demand and supply expresses the response of the quantity demanded and supplied to a change in price *along a particular demand or supply curve*. However, income elasticity of demand expresses the extent to which a change in income causes a change in the quantity demanded at the *current* price, or the extent to which the demand curve shifts. This difference is reflected in the way we treat the coefficient for income elasticity of demand. Recall that we ignore the sign of the coefficients for price elasticity of demand and supply because we assume that demand follows the law of demand and that supply follows the law of supply. The sign of the coefficient for income elasticity, however, has special significance. *A positive income-elasticity coefficient means that income and demand are directly related; thus the product is a normal good. A negative sign means that income and demand are inversely related; thus the product is an inferior good.*

Because the sign of the income-elasticity coefficient is so important, you must pay careful attention to the order of the quantity and income data when using the formula. If you do not associate Q_1 with Y_1 and Q_2 with Y_2, you will get the wrong sign and confuse normal goods with inferior goods. However, you still ignore the sign of the coefficient when comparing it to 1 to determine elasticity or inelasticity. When the percentage change in quantity is greater than the percentage change in income, the income-elasticity coefficient is greater than 1, and the demand is income elastic. An income-elasticity coefficient less than 1 indicates income-inelastic demand.

Income elasticity is a particularly important concept for business planning. The more income elastic the demand, the more sales will fluctuate with changes in national economic conditions. For example, income elasticity of demand for automobiles is estimated to be 4.0. Thus a recession causing a 10 percent drop in national income will cause auto sales to drop 40 percent (unless automakers respond by lowering price). On the other hand, brewers are less affected by changes in general economic conditions. Income elasticity of beer is estimated to be 0.4.

Cross Elasticity of Demand

The response of demand to changes in the prices of substitutes (such as hamburgers and hot dogs) and complements (such as hot dogs and rolls) can also be measured. When the price of a product rises, consumers increase their demand for substitutes. The demand for a product increases, however, when the price of a complement falls. The **cross elasticity of demand** measures responsiveness of consumer demand for product A to a change in the price of related

Income elasticity of demand. A measure of responsiveness of quantity demanded to a change in income; usually expressed as percentage change in quantity demanded divided by percentage change in income.

Cross elasticity of demand. A measure of the responsiveness of quantity demanded for one product to a change in the price of another product, usually expressed as the percentage change in quantity demanded for one product divided by the percentage change in the price of another product.

product B. The formula is

$$\text{Cross elasticity of demand} = \frac{\text{Percentage change in quantity demanded of product A}}{\text{Percentage change in price of product B}}$$

$$= \frac{(Q_2 - Q_1)_A}{(Q_2 + Q_1)_A/2} \div \frac{(P_2 - P_1)_B}{(P_2 + P_1)_B/2}$$

For example, you might use this formula to measure the change in quantity of large gas-guzzling automobiles demanded in response to a change in price of gasoline (a complement).

The sign of the cross-elasticity coefficient also is significant. A positive coefficient means that buyers will purchase more of one product when the price of a related product increases. A negative sign indicates that buyers will purchase more of one product when the price of a related product falls. Thus *a positive cross-elasticity coefficient means that the two products are substitutes; a negative cross elasticity of demand coefficient means that the two products are complements.*

As with the income-elasticity formula, be careful how you enter data into the cross-elasticity formula. If you are not consistent—matching initial and final values of both price and quantity—you will get the wrong sign and confuse substitutes and complements.

Again, the size of the coefficient, regardless of its sign, indicates the degree of responsiveness. When the cross-elasticity coefficient is greater than 1, the two products are closely related; thus a change in the price of one will greatly affect demand for the other. When the coefficient is less than 1, the two products are not closely related; thus a change in the price of one will have only a small effect on demand for the other. A coefficient of zero indicates that the products are unrelated (as we would expect to find, for example, if we asked how a change in the price of telephone service affects demand for pecans).

Supply and Income Elasticity in Action

Now that you are familiar with supply and income elasticity, you should be able to answer some of the other questions posed at the beginning of this chapter. For example, why would a rapid increase in the population of an already crowded metropolitan area cause a large increase in housing prices over a short period of time? The key here is to recognize that the supply of housing is price inelastic in the short run. That is, it is both difficult and expensive to expand the housing supply in a short period of time. An increase in demand, caused by a rapid population increase, will have a relatively greater effect on the price of housing than on the quantity of housing supplied. Of course, over a longer period of time, the construction industry will respond, and supply will become more price elastic.

This difference between short-run and long-run responses is also evident when government imposes rent controls that establish a ceiling price lower than the equilibrium price, as in New York City, for example. When controls are first implemented (or when the ceiling price is lowered), landlords have few reasonable options. Thus in the short run, supply does not respond much to the change in price. Over time, however, builders find it unattractive to construct new rental housing, and many landlords find it uneconomical to maintain existing structures. If permitted by law, some existing buildings will be converted to other uses—

RECAP

Price elasticity of supply refers to responsiveness of quantity supplied to a change in price. Determinants of price elasticity of supply include cost and economic feasibility of storage, method of production, cost and availability of resources, and length of the relevant time period.

Income elasticity of demand refers to the responsiveness of demand to a change in income. Normal goods have a positive income-elasticity coefficient; inferior goods have a negative coefficient. The greater the absolute value of the coefficient, the more demand will change when income changes.

Cross elasticity of demand refers to the responsiveness of demand for one product to changes in the price of another product. Substitutes have a positive cross-elasticity coefficient; complements have a negative coefficient. The larger the absolute value of the coefficient, the closer the relationship between the two products.

condominiums, for example—not subject to rent controls. Thus in the long run, supply can become price elastic.

Finally, why does a general increase in consumer income lead to a greater increase in the profits of motel owners than in those of farmers? The key is income elasticity. Demand for food in general is income inelastic, while demand for vacation travel is income elastic. This pattern makes sense if you recognize that the quantity of food you eat is unlikely to increase substantially if your income rises (although the type of food you eat may change). On the other hand, if your income falls, you may cut back on vacation travel expenses, even to the point of eliminating them. Therefore, taking the nation as a whole, increased income will tend to result in a relatively greater increase in demand for vacation travel than for food. Consequently, incomes of motel owners are affected more than incomes of farmers.

CONCLUSION

The concept of elasticity is essential to the study of economics and extends our discussion of demand and supply presented in Chapter 3. Knowing the determinants of demand and supply, we can predict shifts in relationships and determine whether price and quantity exchanged will rise or fall. Knowing about elasticity, however, we can go on to predict *how much* quantity will rise or fall and whether a demand or supply shift will have a greater effect on price or on quantity. We can also predict *how much* demand will shift in response to changes in the price of other goods (cross elasticity) or income (income elasticity).

Thus far, however, our discussion has focused on the operation of a single market. In Chapter 5 you will learn how individual markets are interrelated in a market economy. Changing conditions in many markets are linked by price. In seeking to understand how a market economy may help to achieve the fundamental economic goals, we will use most of the tools discussed so far. Indeed, demand and supply analysis and the concept of elasticity are used continuously from here on to illustrate the effects of changing economic circumstances.

SUMMARY

1. In this chapter we discussed the meaning and implications of elasticity, a concept that measures responsiveness of buyers' and sellers' decisions to various changes in economic conditions. The more elasticity there is, the larger the quantity response will be; the more inelasticity there is, the smaller the quantity response will be.

2. Price elasticity of demand measures buyer response to a change in price. If buyers are very responsive to a price change, demand is price elastic; if buyers are not very responsive, demand is price inelastic.

3. The coefficient for the price elasticity of demand is the percentage change in quantity demanded divided by the percentage change in price. In calculating this coefficient, economists divide the change in quantity and price by the average quantity and price and ignore the sign.

4. When the coefficient is less than 1, demand is price inelastic (the percentage change in quantity demanded is less than the percentage change in price). When the coefficient is greater than 1, demand is price elastic. When the coefficient equals 1, the percentage changes in price and quantity are identical, and unitary price elasticity exists.

5. Total revenue is the product of quantity sold and price. A decrease in price will increase total revenue when demand is price elastic. A decrease in price will decrease total revenue when the demand is price inelastic. Total revenue is unaffected when demand has unitary price elasticity.

6. In extreme cases, a demand may be perfectly price elastic—shown graphically as a horizontal demand curve—or perfectly price inelastic—shown graphically as a vertical demand curve. When demand is perfectly

price elastic, consumers respond to any increase in price by reducing quantity purchased to zero. When demand is perfectly price inelastic, consumers buy the same quantity regardless of price.

7. Demand is more price elastic when many close substitutes exist, when product price is a large portion of the consumer's income, and when a long period of time is allowed for response.

8. Price elasticity of supply measures seller response to a change in price. If sellers are not very responsive to price, supply is price inelastic. If sellers are very responsive to price, supply is price elastic.

9. The coefficient for price elasticity of supply is the percentage change in quantity supplied divided by the percentage change in price. Supply is price elastic when the elasticity coefficient is greater than 1, price inelastic when it is less than 1, and has unitary elasticity when it equals 1.

10. Supply is more price elastic when storage of a product is easy and inexpensive, when the production process allows for quick responses to price changes, when there is little or no change in the extra cost for additional units, and when suppliers have a long period of time to respond to a price change.

11. Income elasticity of demand measures responsiveness of demand to income and is expressed as the percentage change in quantity demanded divided by the percentage change in income. If demand shifts only a little when income changes, it is income inelastic and the elasticity coefficient (ignoring the sign) will be less than 1. If demand shifts a great deal, it is income elastic and the coefficient (ignoring the sign) will be greater than 1. For normal goods the income-elasticity coefficient is positive; for inferior goods, it is negative.

12. Cross elasticity of demand indicates responsiveness of demand for one product to changes in the price of a related product. It is the percentage change in quantity demanded for one product divided by the percentage change in price of another product. The larger the coefficient (ignoring the sign), the more closely the two goods are related. Substitutes have a positive cross elasticity coefficient; complements, a negative coefficient.

KEY TERMS

Price elasticity of demand, 76
Price elastic, 77
Price inelastic, 77
Price-elasticity coefficient, 80
Unitary price elasticity, 81
Total revenue (TR), 82
Price elasticity of supply, 89

Income elasticity of demand, 91
Cross elasticity of demand, 91

QUESTIONS FOR REVIEW AND DISCUSSION

1. Why is the concept of elasticity important to the study of economics? Why would business managers want to know the price elasticity of demand for their product? The income elasticity of demand?

2. For which of the following products would you expect demand to be price elastic? Price inelastic? Why?
   a) A microwave oven.
   b) A degree from a private college.
   c) A piece of sculpture.
   d) Postage stamps used to mail letters.
   e) Cigarettes.
   f) Record albums.

3. A company currently sells 3200 candlesticks each month at a price of $8 each. The sales manager estimates that a $2 per candlestick increase in price would cause sales to drop by 400 candlesticks per month. What is the price elasticity of demand if the sales manager is correct?

4. Which of the following statements is true? False? Why?
   a) When demand is price elastic, total revenue will fall if price is decreased.
   b) The more price inelastic the demand for a good, the greater is the price increase caused by a decrease in supply.
   c) When demand is price inelastic, it's unlikely to shift, but if it does, the shift is likely to be smaller than it would be if demand were price elastic.
   d) If an increase in market supply causes a decrease in total revenue, demand is price inelastic.
   e) If a normal good has an income-elastic demand, there will be only a small decrease in demand if the economy goes into a recession and income falls.
   f) If a seller of a product having many substitutes raises the product's price, total revenue will increase.
   g) When demand is price inelastic, a price change will not affect quantity demanded because buyers have no choice but to pay the higher price.

5. Evidence shows that both the demand for and the supply of agricultural products are quite price inelastic. Moreover, records indicate that supply is subject to relatively large shifts from year to year. Given these facts, explain why the income of farmers often changes dramatically from year to year.

6. A state university facing a budgetary crisis is considering a tuition increase. Use the concepts in this chapter to answer questions (a) and (b).
   a) What will happen to tuition revenue if demand for education at the state university is price elastic?

b) Suppose that the price-elasticity coefficient is 1.50, current enrollment is 10,000 students, and the trustees are considering a $500 increase in the current tuition of $2000, or a 25 percent increase. By approximately how much would total tuition payments change as a result? (*Hint:* calculate the expected percentage change in enrollment, apply this percentage to the current number of students, and note the change in total tuition.)

7. Explain whether the following is true, false, or uncertain: "Over the past 3 years both the market price and total revenue have increased. This proves demand is price inelastic."

8. A nineteenth-century statistician, Ernst Engel, observed that households spend a smaller percentage of their income on food as their income increases, a result known as Engel's law. Does Engel's law suggest that demand for farm products in the United States would grow rapidly or slowly over time? Does it help explain why the number of farmers has declined?

9. Information on three related goods is shown in the following table. Is either X or Y a substitute for Z? A complement? Are the sales of Z greatly affected by a change in the price of X? By a change in the price of Y?

Quantity of Z demanded	Price of Y	Price of X
9,500	$1.45	$5.50
10,500	1.50	4.50

10. The following table shows price elasticity of demand for three products. (*Note:* Following convention, the signs of the coefficients have been eliminated.) For which products is demand price elastic? Price inelastic? Why?

Product	Price elasticity of demand
Furniture	3.04
Restaurant food	1.50
Beef	0.50

11. Answer questions (a)–(c), assuming that the price elasticity of demand for bicycles is 2.0.
   a) If sellers raised bicycle prices by 5 percent, what percentage change in quantity demanded would you predict?
   b) Would you expect sales at Tony's Bike Shop, one of many in town, to respond by the same percentage change if Tony were the only seller to raise prices? Why or why not?
   c) How would your answer to (a) be affected if, during the same time period, all prices rose by 4 percent? (No numerical answer is required here.)

12. If sales of goldfish rise from 12,000 to 20,000 fish per month when per capita consumer income increases from $4000 to $5000 per year, what is the income elasticity of demand? Are goldfish a normal or an inferior good? Will sales by goldfish suppliers be greatly affected if the economy slumps and incomes fall?

Market Economies and Resource Allocation

QUESTIONS TO CONSIDER

☐ What are the conditions that allow a market economy to function smoothly?

☐ How does the circular-flow model depict the interaction of households and businesses in resource and product markets?

☐ How are allocative and technical efficiency encouraged in a market system when individuals act in their own self-interest?

☐ How does a market economy decide what to produce, how to produce, and for whom to produce?

☐ What types of market failures cause allocative inefficiency? Technical inefficiency?

E very society faces the fundamental problem of scarcity—unlimited wants but limited resources—and the fundamental question of how best to use those resources. This question is not easy to answer because each individual has different wants and each resource has different uses.

Gathering the information necessary to decide what to produce, how to produce, and for whom to produce is an enormous and complex task. To organize, coordinate, and direct the use of its limited resources, society must have some basic mechanism or economic system. As you saw in Chapter 1, various societies use considerably different mechanisms in making choices about resource allocation.

Different economic systems reflect different answers to key questions. For example, which decisions should be made by markets and which by government planners? To what extent should property be privately owned and publicly owned? To what extent should goods and services be produced by private industry operating for profits, by private industry on a not-for-profit basis, and by government?

In this textbook, we focus primarily on how market economies answer these questions. (Nearly all market economies are capitalistic—Yugoslavia is a rare exception—so for simplicity, we use the term market economy rather than market capitalist economy.) In market economies the economic role of government is generally limited. Government assists the market economy by issuing money and protecting private property rights through its legal system. But government regulation or planning is typically considered a second choice—something to be used if a market fails for some reason.

CIRCULAR FLOW OF ECONOMIC ACTIVITY

We have much more to say about the role of government in this and following chapters. But first we want to see how a pure market system would operate. In previous chapters, we have discussed the operation of individual markets. Now we want to consider how a system of markets can work to meet economic goals.

You may wonder what keeps the economy moving if individuals in it are free to do as they please. Certainly the U.S. economy does not always work smoothly. However, in order to look at a purer form, we can make some simplifying assumptions. In doing so we want to ensure that demand and supply—the market mechanisms—will work smoothly in moving the economy toward the goals of allocative and technical efficiency. These assumptions are as follows:

1. All resources are owned by private individuals, and private property rights are well-defined.

2. In every market, there are enough buyers and sellers to keep any single buyer or seller from influencing the market.

3. There are no restrictions on the mobility of resources.

4. Buyers and sellers have adequate information about the price and quality of products and resources they can buy and sell.

5. The basic economic activities—buying and selling—are carried out by households and businesses. Government plays no active role in deciding how resources will be used and neither produces nor buys goods. Nor is there any exchange with foreign nations.

Although these assumptions allow us to examine the basic forces underlying a market economy, they do not describe a real-world economy. Having seen the market system's best side, however, we can later examine the consequences when these conditions are not met.

In exploring the operation of this simple economy, we want to answer several questions. First, why and how do individual market exchanges occur? Second, how are markets connected into a system that responds to changes in tastes or scarcity of resources? And finally, how does a market economy answer the fundamental questions of what and how to produce and who receives the goods that are produced? That is, how can it achieve the goals of allocative and technical efficiency and equity?

Circular-Flow Model

In order to understand how a simple market economy works, you must understand something about its two elements—households and businesses—and how they interact. We refer here to households and businesses in an economic sense. No doubt you are familiar with the operation of at least one household, your own, though you may not think of it as an economic unit. When economists look at a household, they focus on its economic rather than its social activities. For this reason, the **household** in economic analysis is not necessarily the same as a family group. It is defined as any person or group of people living together and functioning as a single economic unit.

Similarly, from an economic standpoint, a **business firm** is an organization that produces goods and services for sale. The major function of business firms is to organize production, taking into account both household demand and the relative scarcity of resources.

Exhibit 5.1 shows the interaction of households and businesses in a pure market economy as a **circular-flow model**. In it, households own all economic resources and businesses produce all goods and services; that is, households are

Household. Any person or group of people living together and functioning as a single economic unit.

Business firm. An organization that produces goods and services for sale.

Circular-flow model. A model of a market economy that shows the interaction of households and businesses in product and resource markets.

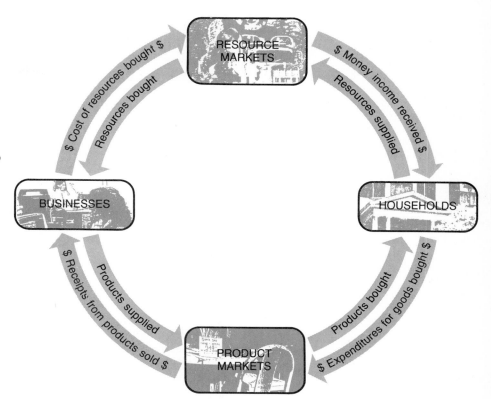

Exhibit 5.1
Circular-Flow Model of Economic Activity
The circular-flow model shows two flows of economic activity. The inner loop is a real flow—the movement of resources from households to businesses, and the movement of goods and services from businesses to households. The outer loop is a money flow—the movement of money from households to businesses in payment for goods and services received, and the movement of money from businesses to households as payment for resources received. The exchange of goods and services for dollars takes place in product markets; the exchange of resources for money takes place in resource markets.

RECAP

The two most common economic systems are the planned socialist economy and the market capitalist economy. While there are no pure types in the real world, the Soviet Union is primarily a planned socialist economy, and the United States is primarily a market capitalist economy.

In a market economy, households and businesses are connected by two circular flows—the real flow and the money flow—that move in opposite directions.

In the real flow, resources move from households to businesses and economic goods and services flow from businesses to households. In the money flow, money moves from households to businesses and back to households.

the only consumers and businesses are the only producers of goods and services. (For simplicity, we ignore goods and services that households produce for themselves and those bought by businesses because they do not affect the basic principles involved.) Individuals in both groups continually make economic choices and engage in market exchanges. As shown in Exhibit 5.1, there are actually two circular flows. The inner (red) loop is the flow of resources and goods and services. The outer (blue) loop is the flow of money.

Starting with the box representing households and the inner loop, we see that resources—land, labor, and capital—flow from households to businesses. Businesses use the resources to make products—such as automobiles, medical care, and food—that then flow to households. Thus the inner loop shows that households indirectly exchange what they have—resources—for what they want—products. Economists distinguish flows of resources and products—*real* flows—from *money* flows.

In contrast the outer loop shows that the money households spend to purchase goods returns to them when businesses spend the money they receive to buy resources. Money flows in the opposite direction from goods and resources. Together the two flows represent the fact that every market exchange involves the trade of something real—labor time or a haircut—for money.

Role of Money

What is **money** and what is its purpose in a market economy? We implied the existence of money in Chapter 3 when we defined market prices in monetary terms. When we say that the price of fancy sunglasses is $10, we mean that the seller is willing to exchange the sunglasses for $10 of money. All economies have some form of money. You probably know money as coins and paper bills. But the funds in your checking account are also accepted in market exchanges and thus are money. Many items have served the functions of money—cattle, gold, whiskey, beads, woodpecker scalps and, as discussed in A Case in Point: The Economic Organization of a POW Camp, cigarettes. In most modern economies only the government has the power to issue and regulate money.

Money is useful in a market economy because it increases the number and efficiency of exchanges. Without money, we would have to **barter** for everything. In fact, we barter for many items. You might ask a friend to help you study biology and offer, in exchange, to help him study economics. But barter can occur only if two parties can find a mutually satisfactory set of items to exchange. Imagine the difficulty of finding products or services to exchange with the local grocery or clothing store for every purchase you wanted to make. Every exchange involves a **transaction cost**, but the time and effort required to arrange barters can be excessive.

Money allows us to avoid some of the complications and transaction costs of bartering. Money allows each of us to specialize in producing what we can make best. In exchange for our services, we receive something everyone else in the economy will accept in trade: money. By reducing the time and effort it takes to trade, money can increase society's production possibilities.

Money. Items such as coins, paper bills, and checking account deposits that are widely accepted in market exchanges.

Barter. An exchange of one product or service for another; an exchange not involving money.

Transaction cost. The time, effort, and other costs of arranging and negotiating an exchange.

A Case in Point
The Economic Organization of a POW Camp

This case, which illustrates many of the basic features of a market economy discussed in this chapter, is based on the experiences of R. A. Radford,* who spent several years during World War II as a prisoner of war (POW). As he observed, the prisoners rather quickly developed economic organizations paralleling those in the outside world.

In the camps, each prisoner was provided with Red Cross food packets containing various foods, including margarine, jam, canned meat, chocolate, cheese, and cigarettes. "Very soon after capture people realized that it was both undesirable and unnecessary, in view of the limited size and the equality of supplies, to give away or to accept gifts of cigarettes or food. Goodwill devel-

oped into trading as a more equitable means of maximizing individual satisfaction." As trading became involved and more sophisticated, cigarettes took on the characteristics of money, and prices of various items were quoted in terms of' cigarettes. Markets spontaneously developed, with prices determined by the forces of demand and supply.

The markets were better organized in some POW camps than in others. In nearly every new camp, as well as the "transit camps," individual desires and hence the equilibrium prices of commodities were not well known. In one new camp, Radford relates, "stories circulated of a padre who started off round the camp with a tin of cheese and five cigarettes and returned to his bed with a complete [Red Cross] parcel in addition to his original cheese and cigarettes; the market was not yet perfect." As the economic organization progressed, however, relative values of commodities in terms of cigarettes be-

*R. A. Radford, "The Economic Organization of a P.O.W. Camp," *Economica*, XII (November 1945), pp. 189–201.

Resource Markets and Product Markets

Money is exchanged in markets, and the circular-flow model in Exhibit 5.1 shows households and businesses connected by exchanges that occur in two types of economic markets: resource markets and product markets. It also indicates how these markets are connected.

Resource markets are markets in which households sell and businesses buy resources—such as labor and raw materials. Businesses enter resource markets on the demand side. They make monetary payments to households in exchange for resources. They use the resources to produce goods and services, which they sell in product markets. Households supply the resources they own in return for monetary payments that represent wages, rent, and other forms of income. *The forces of demand and supply in resource markets determine what resources are bought by which businesses and for what price.*

Product markets are markets in which businesses sell and households buy products—such as automobiles and medical care. As you can see in the circular-flow model, households enter product markets on the demand side. They make monetary payments to businesses in exchange for goods and services that they use to satisfy their wants. Businesses supply goods in exchange for monetary payments that represent revenue. These exchanges show as two flows: a real flow of economic goods from businesses to households and a money flow from households to business. *The forces of demand and supply in product markets determine what goods and services are bought and sold and at what prices.*

The circular-flow model clearly shows the connection between exchanges in resource markets and product markets. As we pointed out in Chapter 3, in order

Resource markets. Markets in which households sell and businesses buy resources used to produce goods and services.

Product markets. Markets in which businesses sell and households buy goods and services.

came well established, and were posted at convenient locations.

Prisoners were segregated by nationality, so that free trade between various segments of the camp was difficult. However, with appropriate bribes, some British and U.S. prisoners were able to visit other sectors. As a result, "the people who first visited the highly organized French trading center, with its stalls and known prices, found coffee extract—relatively cheap among the tea-drinking English—commanding a fancy price in biscuits or cigarettes, and some enterprising people made small fortunes that way."

Radford also observed how relative prices changed: "Changes in the supply of a commodity, in the German ration scale or in the makeup of Red Cross parcels, would raise the price of one commodity relative to others. Tins of oatmeal, once a rare and much sought after luxury in the parcels, became commonplace in

1943, and the price fell. In hot weather the demand for cocoa fell, and that for soap rose. A new recipe would be reflected in the price level: the discovery that raisins and sugar could be turned into an alcoholic liquor of remarkable potency reacted permanently on the dried fruit market."

Public opinion on trading "was vocal if confused and changeable. A tiny minority held that all trading was undesirable as it engendered an unsavory atmosphere; occasional frauds and sharp practices were cited as proof. Certain forms of trading were more generally condemned; trade with the Germans was criticized by many. Red Cross toilet articles, which were in short supply and only issued in cases of actual need, were excluded from trade by law and opinion working in unshakable harmony. But while certain activities were condemned as antisocial, trade itself was practiced, and its utility appreciated, by almost everyone in the camp."

to demand products, households must have the means to purchase those products. The circular-flow model shows that households obtain money—wages, salaries, and other forms of income—from exchanges they make in resource markets. The more money any household receives, the greater is its ability to demand and the greater is the quantity of goods and services it can consume. *Thus a household receives more goods when the resources it owns and sells are more valuable to businesses.*

Similarly, we know that businesses must have money if they are to demand resources. The monetary flow indicates that businesses obtain money by selling the goods and services they produce to households. The more successful a business is in meeting the demands of households, the more money it receives and the more resources it can demand. *Thus resources tend to flow to those businesses that supply the products households value most.*

The circular-flow model confirms that connections between demand and resource markets can help a market system decide what to produce, how to produce, and for whom the goods and services are produced. But within both product and resource markets, households and businesses must make many individual decisions. In the next section, we consider how they make these decisions and how their decision making helps markets direct the flow of products and resources.

MARKETS: SELF-INTEREST AND RATIONAL CHOICE

In a pure market system, no one tells households what products to buy or where to work. No one tells businesses how to produce or what products to supply. Households and businesses are free to make those choices. This description may sound like a recipe for chaos. If individuals do what they want, how will anything ever get done? More to the point, how can such an economy ever hope to achieve allocative or technical efficiency?

Self-Interest: The Invisible Hand

In fact, when markets function smoothly, we can show that self-interest can help the economy achieve its basic economic goals. Adam Smith first mentioned this tendency in his book *The Wealth of Nations*, describing the mechanism as an "invisible hand"; that is, an individual who acts to maximize personal gain

> Neither intends to promote the public interest, nor knows how much he is promoting it. . . . [H]e intends only his own gain, and he is in this, as in many other cases, led by an invisible hand to promote an end which was no part of his intention. . . . By pursuing his own interest he frequently promotes that of society more effectually than when he really intends to promote it.[*]

To understand how a market economy works, we must understand how households and businesses act to maximize personal gain.

[*] Adam Smith, *An Inquiry into the Nature and Causes of the Wealth of Nations.* New York: Random House, 1937, p, 423. Smith's book was originally published in 1776.

Households and Rational Choice

To predict behavior, economists typically assume that households seek to maximize satisfaction and that they apply the principles of rational choice discussed in Chapter 2. To satisfy wants, households make two kinds of market exchanges. They exchange resources they own for money, and they exchange money for goods and services. If they act rationally they will choose options that increase their satisfaction.

When choosing what to buy—another car this year or a vacation, for example—a household will compare the extra satisfaction from a new car with the extra satisfaction of a vacation trip. As we stated in Chapter 3, these decisions determine product demand. Products that give households the greatest satisfaction—within the limits of scarcity—are those in greatest demand. Thus if the economy responds to the demands of households, it will produce the goods and services that give households the greatest total satisfaction.

Households also have to decide what resources to sell and which businesses to sell them to. Generally, when individuals work outside the home, they choose to work where they earn the highest possible income. More income enables households to buy more goods and thus to satisfy more material wants. Thus *acting out of self-interest, households sell their resources to those businesses that pay the highest prices.*

However, obtaining maximum satisfaction is not necessarily the same as earning maximum income. Individuals may rationally take lower-paying jobs when they find the work especially desirable. In addition, in deciding how many hours to work, if any, members of the household have to trade the benefits of greater income for the opportunity cost of time. A household may decide it is more important for a teenager in the household to finish college than to seek employment. You may rationally choose to sacrifice the income you could earn from working on Saturdays for the value of the leisure time you can enjoy instead. By assuming rational behavior, economic theory concludes that such decisions contribute to maximum satisfaction in terms of the household's limited resources.

Businesses and Rational Choice

To predict the decisions of firms, economists typically assume that business managers seek to earn maximum profits. **Profits** equal total revenues less total costs. Following the principles of rational choice, firms will produce those goods and services that add more revenue than cost. Thus if revenues increase more than costs, profits will increase. If firms can buy resources for less or produce more efficiently, they can lower their costs. If firms produce the products most in demand, they can increase their revenues. Thus, *acting out of self-interest, firms will purchase resources at the least cost and will efficiently produce those goods and services that most satisfy households' demand.*

Market Prices and Opportunity Costs

Profits. The difference between the total of all revenues received from the sales of goods and the total of all costs of producing those goods.

We know that households and businesses are guided by market prices. Households use relative prices when they determine what to buy and where to sell their resources. Businesses consider relative prices when they decide what to sell and which resources to use in production. Market prices are a major source of information in a market economy. Indeed, in a smoothly functioning market system equilibrium prices are signals reflecting opportunity costs.

Suppose, for example, that lobsters are selling for $4.00 per pound. If this is an equilibrium price, lobsters are worth no less than $4.00 per pound. In fact, this price would be a good measure of value to the last buyer, who would buy a lobster at $4.00 a pound but not at a higher price. Equilibrium price also means that other products that could have been purchased are worth no more than the value of the lobster. Thus the price reflects the opportunity cost to the last buyer. In addition, equilibrium price reflects the lobsterman's opportunity cost. If the price were lower, the last lobster sold would have remained in the ocean. The price reflects the opportunity cost of the resources—time, boat, traps, and other resources—used to find and bring lobsters to market.

Prices also adjust as opportunity costs change. If demand for U.S. automobiles increases, U.S. automakers will demand more steel. As a result, steel prices will rise. Building construction costs will also rise, reflecting the increased opportunity cost of using steel in buildings instead of in automobiles.

Resource Allocation in Action

Price changes are market signals of changes in demand and supply; self-interest is the "invisible hand" that guides the decisions of businesses and households. As the following examples show, businesses and households are not forced to respond to price signals. They respond because it is in their best interest to do so. And as you will see, their self-interested responses to price changes help the economy achieve its goals of allocative and technical efficiency.

Response to increased scarcity. How would we want households and businesses to react if some economic resource became more scarce? From society's perspective, both should recognize this change and try to use less of the resource. That is, they should switch to other resources, eliminating the least valuable uses of the resource. In fact, this is the exact response they make by acting in their own best interest.

In 1972, a worldwide shortage of anchovies occurred when the anchovies failed to run off the coast of South America. Although few people were aware of it, nearly everyone responded to this economic event. Anchovies, in addition to being a topping for pizza, are a rich source of protein. Therefore they are often used in animal feed as a protein supplement.

The poor harvest of anchovies caused supply to decrease. As a consequence, anchovy prices increased. This price increase was the market's signal that anchovies were more scarce. Anchovy buyers, especially those producing animal feed, responded to higher prices by using fewer anchovies (that is, reduced quantity demanded). In place of anchovies, they substituted soybeans as a protein supplement. Although soybeans had previously been more expensive than anchovies, after the price change they were relatively less expensive. This change in relative prices caused increased demand for soybeans as shown in Exhibit 5.2.

Despite the switch to soybeans, the cost of animal feed increased, which in turn raised the cost to cattle ranchers and caused a reduction in the beef supply. The fall in the supply of beef caused higher beef prices in supermarkets and butcher shops. It was at this point that most households felt the effect of the

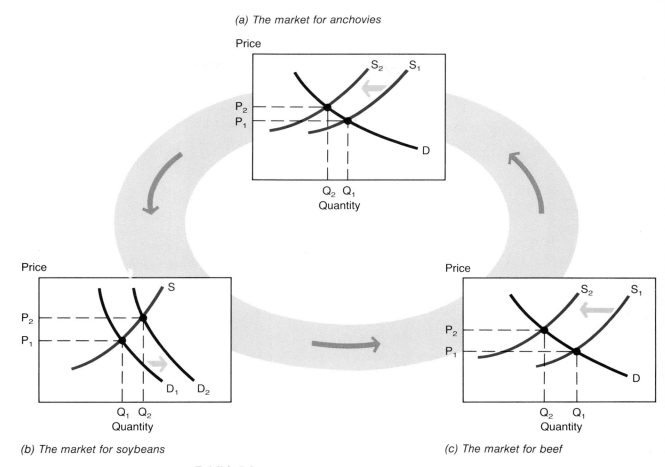

(a) The market for anchovies

(b) The market for soybeans

(c) The market for beef

Exhibit 5.2

Increased Scarcity of Anchovies: Effects on the Soybean and Beef Markets
As shown in part (a), increased scarcity of anchovies caused decreased supply (from S_1 to S_2), and thus higher prices and reduced quantities exchanged. Higher prices for anchovies caused increased demand for soybeans (a substitute), resulting in higher prices and increased quantities of soybeans exchanged [part (b)]. Higher prices of anchovies (and soybeans) increased the cost of producing beef, resulting in decreased supply, higher prices, and lower quantities exchanged [part (c)]. Increased use of soybeans and decreased consumption of beef were the market's response to increased scarcity of anchovies.

scarcity of anchovies. Acting in their own best interests, households responded by buying less beef. In effect, although they may well have been unaware of the cause, households helped the economy conserve on the use of anchovies. In Exhibit 5.2, you can see that the response of households resulted in decreased demand for beef.

Businesses and households responded to the increased scarcity of anchovies, but not because they read about it in the newspapers or heard about it on TV, or because the government informed them. As is typical of a market economy, their source of information was a change in relative prices. This information worked its way through the economy—through the market for anchovies, the market for animal feed, the market for beef, and finally the local supermarket.

Changes in relative prices give households and businesses an incentive to make appropriate responses. It was in the profit-seeking interest of feed manufacturers to substitute soybeans, helping to conserve anchovies. It was in the profit-seeking interest of cattle ranchers to use fewer protein supplements and thus conserve anchovies. And it was in the satisfaction-seeking interest of households to cut back on beef consumption—indirectly reducing the use of anchovies. To be sure that you understand this example, trace the effect of the increased scarcity of anchovies on the markets for soybeans and beef in Exhibit 5.2.

Response to change in demand.   In contrast, how would we want the economy to react if households increased demand for some product? From society's standpoint, businesses should offer more of that product for sale, using more resources for that product and fewer for products that are now less valuable. As you learned in Chapter 3, an increase in demand raises price. As businesses and households react to this price signal, we can expect a shift in resources that will help the economy meet the change in demand.

Suppose, for example, that households become more health conscious and, as a result, increase their demand for aerobics classes while reducing the demand for bowling. Exhibit 5.3 shows the effects of these changes as higher prices for aerobics classes and lower prices for bowling. We would expect businesses to

Exhibit 5.3
Change in Preferences: The Market Response
A change in preference from bowling to aerobics classes will increase demand and price for aerobics classes and decrease demand and price for bowling, as shown. Bowling alley owners respond by closing some businesses. Fitness clubs respond with increased aerobics classes. In a smoothly functioning economy, resources will move from production of bowling alleys, where they are no longer demanded, to production of aerobics classes.

(a) The market for aerobics classes

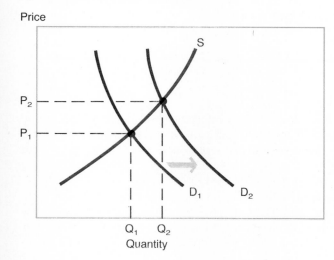

(b) The market for bowling

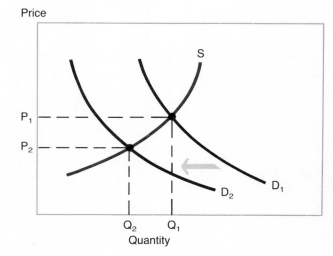

RECAP

To function smoothly, a market economy must have well-defined property rights, competition, adequate information, and mobile resources.

A market system relies on the invisible hand of self-interest. Households seek maximum satisfaction; businesses seek maximum profits. Changes in market price will cause changes in economic decisions.

Equilibrium market price reflects opportunity cost. Demand expresses the opportunity cost of other goods households could buy. Supply reflects the opportunity cost of resources used in production.

Changes in relative demand or relative scarcity of resources will be reflected in changing prices, providing information and incentives for households and businesses to adjust to the changing circumstances.

respond by increasing the number of aerobics classes offered (an increase in quantity supplied along the supply curve) and decreasing the number of bowling alleys operated.

Since changes in product demand also affect resource markets, demand for resources used by bowling alleys falls. Some resources formerly used in bowling are released to the economy. At the same time, demand for resources used by aerobics classes rises. As a result of changes in resource demand, some bowling alleys may be converted into fitness centers offering aerobics classes. Firms that made bowling shirts and shoes may now make exercise shoes and clothing. Individuals who used to work in bowling alleys may find jobs in fitness centers.

As in the anchovy example, all these changes happen automatically. No one has to survey households to discover that tastes have changed. Bowling alleys will notice the falloff in demand when fewer bowlers sign up for league play. Fitness centers will observe the increase in demand when more people sign up for aerobics.

These signals—together with the expected change in prices—will cause the market system to respond. Profit-seeking businesses will be happy to increase the number of aerobics classes because higher prices enable them to earn greater profits. Resources will begin to move so that the economy can adjust to the shift in demand. (Of course, not all these adjustments happen at once or without cost. But the direction of change is correct and more or less automatic.)

MARKETS, ECONOMIC QUESTIONS, AND GOALS

So far, we have only hinted at how market prices and the self-interested actions of households and businesses help the economy achieve its goals of allocative and technical efficiency. In this section we look more closely at why smoothly functioning markets are efficient. We also consider how a market system determines distribution of income and output. With a better understanding of these basic operations, we can find out whether a market economy can achieve not only allocative and technical efficiency, but also equitable distribution of goods and services.

What to Produce and the Goal of Allocative Efficiency

Who determines what goods and services will be produced in a market system? Noneconomists often assume that businesses make these decisions. Economists believe that in a more fundamental sense, households—the buyers of goods and services—determine what is to be produced. Product demand reflects the relative value of goods and services to households. Businesses seeking profits find it in their best interest to respond to changes in demand. Of course, what is produced also depends on supplies of resources and technology, that is, the limits of society's production possibilities.

This pattern suggests that household demand determines what is produced. But is this outcome the "best" product mix, that is, the mix consistent with the goal of allocative efficiency? In Chapter 2 we said that an economy achieves allocative efficiency by producing the mix of goods and services that best meets society's wants. To meet this goal, we must determine what society demands. In most market economies, satisfying the demands of individuals is considered a major economic goal. Thus allocative efficiency produces the mix of goods and services that best meets the demands of individuals.

In this and previous chapters, you have seen how market demand—the guiding force in a market economy—reflects the demands of individuals in a society. That is, it reflects individual decisions about how to spend the income received from selling resources. Demand indicates the relative value to households of different goods and services that could be produced. The limits of scarcity and the relative wants of households cause a smoothly functioning market economy to produce a mix of goods and services that is allocatively efficient.

Note, however, that achieving allocative efficiency does not mean overcoming scarcity. To eliminate scarcity, resources would have to be virtually unlimited, and wants would have to be limited. In contrast, the goal of allocative efficiency requires learning to live with scarcity and making the best use of available resources.

How to Produce and the Goal of Technical Efficiency

The dynamics of markets—the competitive forces of demand and supply—also work to answer the second basic economic question: how to produce. Society seeks technical efficiency, that is, the full employment of resources and production of goods and services at minimum cost. In other words, we want the economy to operate along its production possibilities curve, since points inside the curve represent wasted resources, or technical inefficiency.

How does a market economy provide incentives for households and businesses to be technically efficient? In our simple model of the economy, households own all resources and must decide whether or not to put them to work. The major objective of the household is to satisfy its wants. The quantity of wants that it can satisfy, however, depends on the income it earns from the sale of resources. This connection between employment of resources and satisfaction of wants gives households an incentive to fully employ resources. The more fully resources are employed, the greater the household's income and the more wants it can satisfy.

Although households own all resources, the circular-flow model indicates that businesses purchase resources from households and must then decide how to use these resources. These choices are guided by resource prices and the firms' desire to earn maximum profits. Maximum profits result when businesses fully utilize the resources they control. Idle resources earn no profits.

Businesses also decide which resources to buy and what technology to use to produce goods and services. For example, a firm may have to choose between skilled and unskilled labor to produce its products. It will weigh the extra benefits of skilled labor (more output per unit of time and less waste, for example) against the extra cost (higher wages). The technology that uses the least amount of material may not be the most efficient if it uses the greatest amount of labor. The relative price of resources helps businesses to select the mix of resources and the technology that allows them to minimize cost. This choice is not only best for the firm (maximum profits) but also for society, since it is the technically efficient choice.

Technical efficiency is particularly important in an economy that changes constantly, as ours tends to do. Resource prices and technology change frequently, putting constant pressure on businesses to be technically efficient. Because firms in a pure market economy compete for household dollars, standards of technical efficiency are usually high and businesses are quick to adjust to changes in produce demand and resource supplies.

We cannot conclude that the economy will achieve both allocative and technical efficiency all the time. However, we do know that a market system provides strong incentives for firms to be efficient. Businesses that are not allocatively or technically efficient will not survive. They will be pushed out of the marketplace by more efficient competitors, as in the following example.

Business instability: A sign of success or failure? Each year thousands of businesses fail, and thousands of new ones spring up. One result is considerable economic instability. Is this instability a sign of failure, an indication that a market system has problems? Why do some businesses fail, and why are there so many new businesses? By relating the answers to these questions to the goals of allocative and technical efficiency, we can assess whether the number of firms entering and leaving the market indicate success or failure of the market system.

New businesses spring up in response to either new or unmet demand. Thus the development of new firms is allocatively efficient. In some cases, new firms succeed because they introduce or can take advantage of technological improvements. In such situations, the development of new firms is technically efficient.

If new or existing firms do not respond to household demand—that is, if they do not produce the products households want at prices households will pay—they will fail. In weeding out these failures, the market system improves allocative efficiency. Businesses also fail when their costs are higher than those of their competitors. Unless they use the best technology and the best mix of resources, price will not cover the opportunity cost of producing other goods. Indeed, *to survive in a market economy, a firm must respond to household demand in both an allocatively and technically efficient manner.*

Firms can survive, however, only if they earn adequate profits. Profits are the difference between revenues generated by sales and opportunity costs of production. Inadequate profits and business failures thus result for two basic reasons: Revenues are too low and/or costs are too high. In terms of the economic goals, this indicates either technical or allocative inefficiency. Thus business failures often are a sign of success in meeting the economic goals.

For Whom to Produce and the Goal of Equity

Clearly, market prices guide the economy toward its goals of allocative and technical efficiency. But does the market system also work to achieve equity—the distribution of goods produced in a manner society considers fair? Before we can ask whether distribution in a market economy is equitable, we must know how distribution is determined.

In a pure market economy, no single individual or government agency determines how goods are distributed. Like other decisions, distribution is determined in markets. The exchanges that occur in product markets determine which households receive which goods. Every good is produced for and distributed to any household that is willing and able to pay the equilibrium price.

Because ability to pay is important to market demand, the total market value of goods and services received by a household depends on the income it earns

RECAP

A market economy improves allocative efficiency by producing those goods and services having the greatest market demand. In a smoothly functioning market, demand and supply reflect the relative scarcity of resources and the opportunity costs of producing alternative products.

A market economy improves technical efficiency in two ways. The link between household demand and income obtained from the sale of resources provides an incentive to maintain full employment. Competition forces businesses to maintain low-cost production.

A pure market economy does not directly address equity. Distribution of goods and services depends solely on income, with households that own and sell more valuable resources able to demand more goods. Attempts to change distribution to improve equity often involve sacrificing some efficiency.

by selling its resources. Households with higher incomes can buy more in product markets. Thus the distribution of products, therefore, depends heavily on the distribution of income. However, in a pure market economy, income is not really "distributed." It is determined by the forces of demand and supply. You can increase your income by working more, by acquiring more valuable skills, and by working for employers who will pay you the highest wage. The more resources you supply, the larger your income; the greater the demand for the resources you own, the greater will be your income.

But is the distribution determined by market forces fair or equitable? As we noted in Chapter 2, answers to equity issues depend on personal values, that is, on normative judgments. Whether any distribution is equitable is a subject of much debate. Although a pure market system automatically weeds out allocative and technical inefficiency, it does not directly address the goal of equity. No automatic adjustment mechanism exists to change an unfair distribution to one that is more equitable.

Distribution of income is an emotional issue, but we can identify some important economic issues involved. First, changing income distribution means changing product distribution. If society is operating on its production possibilities curve, it cannot produce more. If more is given to one group, less will be received by another; there will be both winners and losers. Only by growing—increasing the production possibilities—can society increase total output and improve the standard of living of all individuals.

Second, in a market system, income and efficiency are connected. Because income results from selling resources, households have strong incentives to fully utilize their resources. Moreover, the possibility of earning higher wages encourages individuals to increase their skills.

A distribution mechanism that is not connected to employment may create inefficiency as it tries to improve equity. For example, consider the effects of a welfare system. In order to provide income to those deserving of support (equity), society has to accept a potential weakening of the work incentive (efficiency).

We continue to raise the issue of equity because it is one of society's goals. However, as we noted before, economists have no scientific way to determine whether any decision improves equity. Debates over equity occur because individuals have different values and different perceptions of how well the economy is functioning. As you will see in the next section, when individual hardships result from problems in a market, concerns over the equity of income distribution often surface.

CAN THE INVISIBLE HAND FAIL?

In discussing how a market system operates, we have assumed that markets function smoothly. In fact, we deliberately made certain assumptions that show the market system in the best possible light. These assumptions were critical to our finding that markets generate allocative and technical efficiency. In this section we examine these assumptions and consider what happens when they do not accurately describe the real world. That is, we will consider the effects of **market failure**.

Market failure. A condition that causes a market to fail to reach allocative or technical efficiency; for example, poorly defined property rights or lack of competition.

Private Property Rights

When you sell something, the presumption is that you have a legal right to the property in question. Markets work on the basis of an exchange of property rights. For example, if you agree to sell your labor services to an employer, you obtain a property right to a paycheck. The business obtains a property right to determine (within limits) how you spend part of your time. If a business sells you a product, you obtain a property right to use that product as you see fit. The business obtains part of your income, which it can use to obtain property rights to additional resources.

Property rights help markets to function efficiently. When you sell something to which you have a property right, you will insist on receiving a payment equal to its opportunity cost. For example, would an oil company spend time and effort to discover new supplies of oil if it were required to give the oil to anyone who asked for it? Would you be willing to sacrifice your income to buy an automobile if you had to lend it to anyone who asked? When property rights are difficult or impossible to establish, exchange becomes difficult and markets do not work effectively.

You probably think of property rights as a legal mechanism, enforced by police and the legal system. But resources also exist for which property rights are difficult, if not impossible, to establish. Clean air, for example, is an economic good because we generally prefer more than less of it and because we must sacrifice to keep it free of pollution. However, there is no market for clean air. Where do you go to buy more of it? Moreover, air is owned by everyone in common. No one has any clear property right to it. Thus we can use this scarce resource without making any payment to its owners. Air has opportunity costs but a zero market price. With a zero price, no individual or business has an incentive to use air in an efficient way.

Property rights are important because otherwise we cannot be sure that market prices reflect opportunity costs. When market prices do not accurately reflect opportunity costs, the market fails, and society suffers. One of the interesting questions economists are currently exploring is whether property rights to such goods as clean air and clean water can be established. If such rights can be established, it may be possible to rely on the market system to determine how clean our air and water should be.

Throughout this textbook and in the real world, you will encounter other areas in which property rights are poorly defined or impossible to establish. As you will see, the tendency for markets not to work efficiently in such cases has often led to government intervention.

Competition

We have also assumed that there are sufficient buyers and sellers in each market to prevent any one of them from having a significant influence on the market. This situation, which economists call *competition*, is important because it prevents any buyer or seller from establishing a market price that favors one or the other. Competition also helps to ensure that market price reflects opportunity cost. In a competitive market, a seller has many opportunities to sell. As a result, no buyer can expect to pay less than the equilibrium price. Likewise, no seller can sell at a price above equilibrium, because buyers would turn to other sellers.

Competition pressures markets to quickly respond to market signals, as we see in A Case in Point: The Ballpoint Pen Industry. It forces businesses to utilize the best mix of resources and the best technology, that is, to be technically efficient. Otherwise, their competitors can sell for less. Competition also requires businesses to respond to the demands of households, that is, to be allocatively efficient. If they do not respond, they will not earn even the minimum profit necessary to survive.

In the real world, few markets are perfectly competitive. Many large industries—oil, steel, and soap, for example—are dominated by a small number of large firms. In such cases, the market may not operate smoothly. When firms have some control over market prices, these prices may not reflect opportunity costs, and allocative efficiency may suffer. Moreover, there is less pressure on these firms to adjust quickly to changes in tastes or relative resource scarcity, thus jeopardizing technical efficiency.

Information

Decisions made by households and businesses reflect the information they have about the prices of alternative products and resources, about the opportunity costs associated with alternative uses of resources, and so on. As you have seen, in a pure market economy each household or business need not gather information about all possible alternatives. Changes in market prices generally provide sufficient information about changes in resource supply and household demand.

However, information can be inadequate or incorrect. For example, even in a pure market economy, households might not automatically get sufficient information about workplace safety or dangers of new medicines. Moreover, while much information is available from market prices, demand and supply schedules sometimes inaccurately reflect relative scarcity of resources and relative wants. In such cases, the market system may not achieve allocative or technical efficiency.

In the real world, then, we are confronted with the possibility of imperfect or inadequate information. But since information, like any other product, is scarce, the cost to any decision maker for gathering all possible information is prohibitive. The market system does address the demand for information to some degree through businesses that specialize in selling information. Such businesses include employment agencies, real-estate brokers, and the publishers of *Consumer Reports*. These "middlemen" help markets achieve efficiency by supplying information at a price reflecting the value of that information. Nevertheless, beyond a certain point, the extra cost of acquiring more information exceeds any extra benefit.

Resource Mobility

If the economy is to operate efficiently, resources must be mobile. A change in household demand also means a change in demand for resources. To respond to the new demand, resources must move out of industries where demand is falling and into industries where demand is increasing. These adjustments take time and have costs. During the adjustment process, some resources will be underutilized or unutilized. Adjusting to a long-run change in demand may cause some firms to go out of business and others to enter business; it may require retraining and relocating workers. When resources are very mobile, the economy can adjust quickly, smoothly, and at low cost. If resources cannot adjust, or if the costs of adjusting are large, resources will not be fully utilized.

A Case in Point
The Ballpoint Pen Industry

The dynamics of competition can be illustrated by a short history of the ballpoint pen industry. The year 1945 marked the production of the first ballpoint pen in the United States. Its manufacturer, Milton Reynolds, sold it for $12.50, although it cost only $0.80 to produce. Still, the seemingly high price did not deter buyers, who responded eagerly to the new product, and Reynolds profited greatly. The high profits, however, attracted the attention of other firms, who saw an opportunity to profit themselves. As a result of the competition for ballpoint pen sales, by 1948 prices had fallen to $0.39 and production costs to only $0.10 per pen.

The results demonstrate how competition can help achieve economic goals. Households expressed a desire for the new product by their willingness and ability to pay a high price for it. Guided by buyer demand, businesses shifted resources to alter the mix of products in order to satisfy the new tastes of society—thereby moving toward allocative efficiency.

Prices in the industry fell as a result of competition. Reynolds could not continue to charge his original high price, because competitors were willing to sell the product for less. The desire for profits and the intensity of competition led manufacturers to outdo themselves in lowering costs. They developed new technologies and technical efficiency was stimulated. Although forces other than competition—such as a willingness to accept less profit on Reynolds's part—might also have led to lower costs, in this case competition clearly worked to further society's goals.

Resource mobility is important because it increases the economy's flexibility and lowers the costs of adjustment. Resources are seldom perfectly mobile in the real world, especially over a very short period of time. But the greater the mobility, the better is the economy's overall performance. Indeed, rapid adjustment and movement of resources are a sign of a successful economy.

Some resources are not very mobile, however. For example, specialized machinery that is useful in one industry may be worthless—or at least worth much less—to another industry. Human resources may not be mobile, either because the skills of individual workers are not easily transferable or because individuals are unwilling to make changes. This situation is particularly true for highly trained or skilled personnel.

For example, a fall in demand for textiles and a rise in demand for computers would cause demand for textile workers to decline and demand for computer technicians to increase. To become computer technicians, however, unemployed textile workers would have to receive significant new training. And if unemployed textile workers live in North Carolina and computer technician jobs are in California, relocation costs would be significant—if, in fact, the workers were willing to move.

In the case of human resources, the loss to society is not limited to the loss of production or to efficiency. Because unemployment means less income, households affected by unemployment are also likely to suffer personal loss, a matter that raises questions of inequity as well as inefficiency.

Macroeconomic Instability

An important, though controversial issue, is whether a market system can avoid major problems of macroeconomic instability. That is, can the market system avoid serious fluctuations in the overall level of employment, output, and prices? The U.S. economy has gone through periods of macroeconomic instability. Since 1970, for example, total output actually decreased on four occasions; rapid and erratic increases in overall prices occurred in the 1970s and early 1980s. Macroeconomic instability makes it difficult for the economy to achieve efficiency and equity. The causes and consequences of macroeconomic instability are a major topic in the macroeconomic portion of this book.

Different Economic Goals and Economic Views

Thus far we have implied that a smoothly functioning market economy is highly desirable from the standpoint of allocative and technical efficiency. But not everyone agrees. Critics of the market system believe that the invisible hand fails because the economic goals are wrong or because the market mechanisms—private property and competition—have undesirable consequences.

For example, in discussing market systems we defined allocative efficiency as the production of the mix of goods and services that best satisfies individual demand. However, not all economists agree that the goal of an economy should be to produce to meet individual wants. Some critics argue that social wants should take precedence. Others believe that market systems tend to divide the population into haves and havenots; to stress material wants instead of human values.

Another feature of the market economy that contributes to efficiency—the link between income and ability to buy goods and services—has also drawn fire. Critics argue that because of this link, market economies often overproduce luxury goods and services for the rich while underproducing essential goods and services for the poor.

Certainly, in the real world, market systems are not the perfect solution to all economic problems. We noted, for example, that the goal of equity is not directly addressed by a market economy. Also, some economists suggest that insufficient competition and information will always cause problems in market systems. But in the United States and other market economies there is a widespread belief that market systems provide the best way to organize most economic activities. At the same time, most economists believe that there are situations in which government activity may improve an economy's performance.

CONCLUSION

In this chapter we considered how a simple, smoothly functioning market economy addresses the questions of what to produce, how to produce, and to whom to distribute the goods and services produced. You learned how market forces provide strong incentives for households and businesses to act in a manner consistent with allocative and technical efficiency.

Achieving efficiency requires smoothly functioning markets. In the real world, not all markets have the conditions necessary, and maximum efficiency is not achieved. The important questions, however, are these: Are conditions in the real world close enough to the ideal world of smoothly functioning markets for us to conclude that efficiency is achieved? If there are market problems, what is the best approach to their solution? What, if anything, do we want to do about the distribution of income from the market system?

In the rest of this textbook, we focus on how the U.S. economy has answered these questions and how the answers have changed over time. As you will see, when real-world markets are perceived to be imperfect or to have failed to meet society's goal of equity, government has often intervened. In the course of your lifetime, you can certainly expect to see economic situations in which government action is proposed. Decisions about government's role in the economy are heavily influenced by political considerations. But by learning the principles of economics, and studying the strengths and weaknesses of our economy and past policies, you will be able to intelligently consider the issues as they arise in the future.

SUMMARY

1. In this chapter we discussed the operation of a market system and considered how it can help a society meet the economic goals of allocative and technical efficiency and equity.

2. All economies must have some means of organizing economic activity. In planned socialist economies, resources are owned collectively and allocated according to government plans. In market capitalist economies, most economic resources are privately owned and markets are the principal mechanism determining what, how, and for whom to produce. No real-world system is pure, however.

3. In a pure market economy (a) all resources are privately owned and property rights are well-defined; (b) all markets have enough buyers and sellers to prevent anyone from influencing the market; (c) resources are highly mobile; (d) buyers and sellers have adequate information on which to base decisions; and (e) households and businesses are the only buyers and sellers.

4. There are two circular flows in a simplified economy: one of money and one of products and resources. Money flows from households to businesses in exchange for products and returns to households as businesses exchange money for resources. Money is useful in a market economy because it makes exchange and specialization easier.

5. There are two types of markets: (a) resource markets, in which households sell to businesses the resources used to produce economic goods; and (b) product markets, in which businesses sell to households the goods and services used to satisfy wants.

6. Economists assume that households and businesses are guided by self-interest. Households seek maximum satisfaction, so they will sell their resources to the business offering the highest price and buy those products having the highest value per dollar of sacrifice. Businesses seek maximum profits, so they will choose to produce those goods and services that offer the greatest increase of revenue over cost.

7. In a pure market system, market price reflects opportunity cost. Market demand reflects the opportunity cost to households of other goods they could buy. Market supply reflects the opportunity cost to businesses of resources they must buy and other goods they could produce.

8. A change in market price is a signal that changes in resource use are desirable. If a resource becomes relatively scarce, its supply decreases and its price rises, motivating households and businesses to conserve. Shifts in relative demand cause demand for resources and market prices to change, motivating businesses and households to shift resources to meet changing tastes.

9. Within the limits of scarcity, market demand—the willingness and ability of households to buy—determines what is produced. Profit-seeking businesses must respond to changes in household demand if they are to survive. Thus a market economy encourages allocative efficiency.

10. A market economy encourages technical efficiency in two ways: (a) by linking household demand to income (thus providing an incentive to maintain full employment); and (b) by requiring businesses to keep resources fully employed and to produce at minimum cost (in order to earn sufficient profits to survive).

11. In a market economy the distribution of goods depends on the distribution of income. Equity, a normative issue, is not directly addressed by the market system, and the tie between income and distribution creates potential trade-offs between equity and efficiency.

12. A market system may fail to achieve efficiency when property rights are poorly defined, if competition is insufficient, if information is poor, or if resources are not sufficiently mobile. Macroeconomic instability is also a potential problem for a market system.

KEY TERMS

Household, 98
Business firm, 98
Circular-flow model, 98
Money, 100
Barter, 100
Transaction cost, 100
Resource markets, 101
Product markets, 101
Profits, 103
Market failure, 110

QUESTIONS FOR
REVIEW AND DISCUSSION

1. What is the circular-flow model, and what connections between resource and product markets does it illustrate?

2. Economists typically assume that a business firm seeks maximum profits. In fact, some economists have said that the most socially responsible businesses are those that diligently do so. Do you agree or disagree with this statement? (Before answering, consider what the economists are saying, focusing especially on efficiency.)

3. What are the basic economic activities of households? In what ways do household decisions affect allocative and technical efficiency? (Consider how changes in the choices households make as consumers and resource owners affect the economy.)

4. Assuming a smoothly functioning market economy, answer questions (a) and (b).
    a) Drought wipes out a large portion of the wheat crop in the Soviet Union. How would the price of bread and the income of U.S. wheat farmers be affected?
    b) How did the increased popularity of video games affect the profits of firms specializing in pinball games and the price of rubber flippers used in pinball machines?

5. Steel is a resource that can be put to many uses. In a market economy, what factors would determine which firms producing which products would get the greatest quantity of steel? In what way is your answer to this question related to the relative values households place on various products?

6. What assumptions are associated with smoothly functioning markets? How does the absence of any of these assumptions show that market prices may not reflect opportunity costs? In achieving the goals of allocative and technical efficiency, why is it important for market prices to reflect opportunity costs? (Give examples in each case.)

7. In a pure market economy, how is the relative scarcity of two resources reflected in market prices? How is the opportunity cost of not producing a certain product reflected in the market for another, unrelated product?

8. Adam Smith's doctrine of the "invisible hand" suggests that if individuals act so as to maximize their own welfare, the welfare of society is also maximized. Explain how this is true and what conditions are required to make it true.

9. Comment on the statement: "A reasonable price for a gallon of gasoline is what the average person can afford." In what sense are equilibrium prices always reasonable in a smoothly functioning market? If some of the conditions required for a smoothly functioning market were not present, would you still conclude that the price is reasonable?

10. Consider the statement: "Prices for eyeglasses are lower in states that allow advertising because those states tend to attract cheap, low-quality businesses." What other explanation can you give for lower prices if the market is smoothly functioning?

11. Recall the principles of rational choice explained in Chapter 2 and discuss the statement: "Because more information will help me make a better decision, I should postpone making a decision until I've gathered all relevant information." (*Hint:* Consider the difference in the amount of information you would typically gather before buying a new car and the amount you gather before buying a new pencil.)

12. Consider the statement: "If a product or resource is exchanged at other than its true value, one party to the exchange loses, and the other gains."
    a) Using the concepts of this chapter, what do you think a product's "true value" is?
    b) What arguments could you use to equate equilibrium price in a smoothly functioning market with a product's "true value"?
    c) Does market price reflect "true value" if the market is not smoothly functioning? Why or why not?
    d) In what way do government price supports or ceilings disturb the market's ability to signal a product's "true value"?
    e) What does an increase in a firm's profits signal about the "true value" of its products?
    f) Suppose that a firm enlists the government's help to make it the sole manufacturer of a product. It can then successfully raise the price and increase its profits. How does the firm gain and how do buyers lose?

g) In a pure market economy, does an increase in price mean that households lose and businesses gain? Does a decrease in price mean that households gain and businesses lose?

13. Changes in market prices not only imply shifts in resource use but also changes in income distribution. What groups would tend to be better off and which worse off as a result of the following?
    a) Foreign oil producers successfully raise the price of oil.
    b) U.S. textile mills get Congress to impose a tariff (a tax) on imported fabrics.
    c) Households decide to eat more fish and chicken and less beef and pork.

14. Consider the statement: "Information's nice, but it's certainly never worth paying for."
    a) Does information have any value?
    b) What does a real-estate broker sell? Do you think that sellers of houses would be better off if they did not use the services of real-estate brokers? Would buyers of houses?
    c) Why are individuals often willing to pay more for a used car they buy from a reputable car dealer than the same make and model of car from an individual who runs a newspaper ad?

Economic Encounters
Labor Mismatch: Balancing Demand and Supply

As we explained in the first few chapters of this textbook, for a market system to operate efficiently, resources such as machinery, raw materials, and people must be mobile. The mid-1980s saw dramatic shifts in U.S. labor markets, leading experts to ask, "How do we retrain workers, decrease unemployment, and make the economy run more efficiently?"

Baby Bust Blues After World War II, the population of the United States boomed because of, among other things, a healthy economy and medical advances. The teenage "baby boomers" found jobs quite easily in the blossoming economy of the 1960s. However, baby boomers decided to have fewer children, or to have children later in life, than did their parents.

The resulting "baby bust" of the decade spanning 1965 to 1975 caused a sudden drop in youth labor in the 1980s, a trend that experts predict will continue into the 1990s. In fact, the Bureau of Labor Statistics claims that by 1995 the United States will have 3.8 million fewer workers in the 16–24 age bracket (the traditional source of entry-level employees) than there are today.

To compound the problem, the U.S. economy began to grow vigorously during the 1980s. As business ac-

> **Shifting demand and supply created labor market imbalances in the mid-1980s.**

tivity increased, demand for labor increased. The result was a labor shortage, particularly in entry-level positions in the service sector. Assuming moderate growth, the Bureau of Labor Statistics projects that between 1984 and 1990, the creation of new jobs will outnumber new entrants in the work force by a million.

The Right People for the Right Jobs Finding the right people to fill the right jobs became a severe dilemma in the 1980s. In the early part of the decade, experts detected a shift in hiring demands. Demand increased for skilled employees in high-tech industries, such as electrical engineering and computers. At the same time, decreasing demand for labor in slumping industries such as farming and auto-making drove workers with specialized skills into unemployment lines. Even more importantly, low-wage jobs in service industries, such as restaurants, increased dramatically.

Unfortunately, most blue-collar workers were reluctant or unable to make the transition to white-collar or service jobs. Take the story of Doris, mother of four living in a depressed area of Detroit, who lost her job as an autoworker due to layoffs. Unable to find work that put her skills to use, she faced a dilemma: Should she remain in Detroit, join the unemployment rolls, and possibly go on welfare? Should she accept a job as a waitress or clerk at a fraction of her former salary, just to keep her family at subsistence level? Or should she uproot her family, moving them across the country to search for retraining and employment as a computer programmer in Boston or Atlanta?

In the 1980s, auto workers found themselves on the unemployment lines, often unable to apply their skills to other types of jobs. (Donald Dietz/Stock, Boston)

Frank's story was similar. Born on a farm in Iowa, Frank inherited his father's property—and career—in turn grooming his three kids to take over when they reached adulthood. In the 1970s Frank's farm began to fail; he took out more bank loans for equipment and supplies, but couldn't make the payments when his crops were ruined by drought. He mortgaged his home, getting deeper into debt; his sons and wife took part-time jobs to help out, but eventually the family faced the inevitable. After bank foreclosures on their property, Frank and his family watched their possessions go up on the auction block. Left bankrupt, with few skills to apply to the modern world, Frank was a poor candidate for most jobs he applied for. Job retraining was too expensive for Frank; he finally took a job as a janitor in a local high school.

Labor mismatch (a situation in which workers like Doris and Frank are in the wrong place with the wrong skills and unable to meet the increased demand for skilled labor in other industries) was a common scenario all around the country. Certain industries, such as computer technology, suffered severe setbacks because of those labor shortages, and some businesses failed altogether.

> **When dealing with people as a resource, experts must recognize that human emotions come into play.**

Often the people searching for jobs and the jobs that were available were incompatible. Businesses in affluent areas outside cities lacked a worker pool from which to hire word processing specialists and computer programmers. On the other hand, many inner-city youths, living in neighborhoods where the unemployment rate sometimes hit 50 percent, were unable to find work, turning instead to drugs and street gangs. Some businesses tried to tap the concentrated youth

To compensate for the lack of young people looking for entry-level jobs in the 1980s, McDonalds began hiring older, semiretired workers who needed extra money or who found staying at home too dull. (Darlene Bordwell)

population by setting up training programs in inner-city communities. However, the cost of maintaining such programs proved more than many businesses were willing, or able, to bear.

Service with a Smile? Rapid increases in demand coupled with falling supplies of teenage workers forced service industry employers to try innovative ways of luring new workers. For example, fast-food franchises like McDonalds and Burger King had long provided summer jobs for high school students before they moved on to college or other careers. However, the baby bust of the late 1960s left the fast-food eateries in a labor crunch in the 1980s. In an unusual move, Burger King—employer of more than 160,000 people nationwide—advertised for management trainees on MTV, the cable rock channel, offering educational grants to crew members to attend college or vocational school. Faced with the same youth shortage, McDonalds launched a program aimed at hiring older or semiretired workers (called "McMasters") in positions previously held by teenagers.

Other service industries expanded day-care facilities in hopes of attracting young mothers back into the work force. Increasing salaries, another incentive, caused some restaurant owners to stretch the $3.35-an-hour minimum wage to as much as $8 an hour. Experts predict that a growing number of employers will turn to immigrants to fill jobs previously held by teenagers or young adults.

Learning New Skills The quality of public education was questioned as labor experts explored the problem of labor mismatch. One report revealed that 40 percent of 17-year-olds cannot adequately understand written material, while almost 70 percent cannot solve two- or three-step math problems. With American youth poorly prepared for entering the labor markets, employers faced the choice of lowering their hiring standards or spending more time and money in their search for capable employees. Poor career preparation also meant that there were a disproportionate number of employees available for lower-skilled service jobs than in more challenging positions.

For many businesses, job retraining has become a major goal. Because training and education are expensive, some labor experts called for reinstatement of government training programs such as those slashed by the Reagan Administration in the early 1980s. Other experts pointed to the public education system as a potential source of retraining for jobless workers.

As in any other market, the labor market possesses mechanisms to adjust supply to demand. But for many workers, this adjustment means lower incomes. Moreover, it is not as easy to pack up and move people as it is to transport coal or fruit to areas where demand is greater. When dealing with people as a resource, experts must recognize that human emotions, preferences, attitudes, and abilities come into play. In the service-oriented economy of the 1980s and 1990s, balancing supply and demand in the labor market will not be an easy task.

CHAPTER 6

Overview of the
U.S. Economy

QUESTIONS TO CONSIDER

☐ Why are business firms useful to the economy?

☐ What are the advantages and disadvantages of the three legal forms of business?

☐ Which sources of household income are the most important?

☐ In what ways can government potentially improve the economy's performance?

☐ How does the foreign sector affect the domestic economy?

R ecall that in Chapter 5 we presented a simple model of a market economy consisting of only two groups: households and businesses, which comprise the **private sector**. In the real world, of course, economic systems are more complex. To complete an overview of the domestic economy, we must also examine the **public sector**, that is, federal, state, and local government. And finally, we must consider the **foreign sector**, or the foreign individuals, governments, and businesses that participate in a nation's product, resource, and financial markets. We discuss how these sectors affect and are affected by the economy in later chapters. In this chapter, however, we lay the groundwork for that discussion by presenting some basic facts about the sectors of the U.S. economy.

THE PRIVATE SECTOR: BUSINESS

In primitive economies, households produce a large portion of the economic goods they consume. But in all modern economies business firms produce the vast majority of goods and services. This rule holds true regardless of the economic system. The difference is that in market economies businesses are privately owned, whereas in planned socialist economies firms are government owned.

The simple circular-flow model in Chapter 5 shows that business firms are the only producers of goods and services. In the real world, government also provides goods and services, such as roads, schools, and national defense. Moreover, the United States gets an increasingly large proportion of goods and resources from the foreign sector. Nevertheless, the business portion of the private sector, which consists of all U.S. firms, is extremely important.

Role of Business Firms

To understand how the economy operates, you must understand the role played by businesses and why it is useful. Economists stress that businesses exist because they offer four advantages to society: (1) organizing and monitoring team production; (2) reducing the number and costs of market exchanges; (3) lowering costs through economies of scale; and (4) accepting risks. Economists also generally agree that businesses enable a society to be technically efficient.

Private sector. The part of a nation's economy made up of households and businesses.

Public sector. The part of a nation's economy made up of federal, state, and local governments.

Foreign sector. The part of a nation's economy made up of foreign individuals, businesses, and governments that participate in the nation's product, resource, and financial markets.

121

Organizing and monitoring team production. Economists have long recognized that two or more individuals working together can produce more efficiently than if they worked alone. For example, a single individual could build an entire house working alone, but a team of carpenters can build the same house in fewer total hours of work. Another example of teamwork is the assembly line. Henry Ford used the assembly line to great advantage in producing automobiles. Before introduction of this method of production in 1914, one worker could produce a car in 728 minutes; the assembly line reduced the time required to 93 minutes.

Teamwork requires organizing and monitoring individual performance. Someone must spend time deciding what tasks need to be done, who is to perform them, how each task contributes to total output, and how well each individual performs the tasks assigned. The business firm performs these functions, and society gains the advantages of team production.

Reducing the number and costs of market exchanges. In Chapter 5 we described the advantages of market exchanges and noted that transaction costs are associated with exchanges. These costs include, for example, the time required to search for information and the costs of negotiating contracts.

A large corporation is in business on a long-term basis and can therefore offer jobs on a long-term basis. This allows the firm to avoid the costs of locating and hiring suitable employees every time it wants another task performed. Having a long-term relationship also enables the firm to acquire better and less costly information about employee skills and performance.

Similarly, a textile firm can manufacture many or all of the items it uses to make a finished product. The firm can dye its own thread, weave its own cloth, make its own patterns, cut the cloth, and stitch the final product. Using internal coordination, it can save the cost of negotiating contracts with other firms to do some of those tasks. Of course, substituting managerial for market coordination has costs as well. But when the savings outweigh the costs, technical efficiency increases.

Taking advantage of economies of large-scale production. Economists also recognize that production on a large scale can be more efficient. For example, the publisher of a large daily newspaper can use larger, more efficient presses that would not be economical for a local weekly newspaper. Large-scale production allows specialization of labor, which also offers significant cost advantages. Ford's assembly line, for example, enabled individual workers to concentrate on only a few tasks, at which they became proficient. Because of their size, large firms can afford more specialized machinery, production workers, and managers. Increased size does not always make a firm more efficient, but small firms are often at a competitive disadvantage.

Accepting risks. A final role of businesses is that of accepting risk. Many risks are associated with producing goods and services. If demand drops, for example, a firm may be stuck with products it cannot profitably sell. Firms invest large sums in plant and equipment, accepting the risk that these investments will enable them to produce profitably in the future. The owners of the firm enjoy the benefits of success (profits) but also suffer the costs of failure (losses).

Not all individuals view risks in the same way. Some are willing to accept the high risks of ownership. Others prefer the lower risks of being an employee.

Workers have to bear some risks—the possibility of losing a job, for example—but they generally agree to work for a specified wage or salary. They receive their pay as long as the business continues and regardless of profit levels. By pooling the resources of those willing to accept high risks, the firm can offer the advantages of lower risks to others.

Size of Business Organizations

Business firms vary in size from the small corner drugstore—owned and operated by a single individual—to the huge corporation—owned by thousands of shareholders and operated by thousands of employees. The largest corporations are indeed mammoth in size, as Exhibit 6.1 indicates. Sales by General Motors, for example, are larger than the total value of goods produced in Sweden. Sales by the five largest U.S. corporations exceed Canada's total output. The combined sales of the top 25 U.S. coporations represent 22 percent of the total output of goods in the United States.

Despite the advantages of size, we must recognize that costs become more important as the size of the business increases. First, as the business grows, its

**Exhibit 6.1
The 25 Largest U.S.
Industrial Corporations—
Ranked by Sales**

Rank	Name	Sales (millions)	Assets (millions)	Net income (millions)	Employees (number)
1	General Motors	$ 96,371.7	$ 63,832.8	$ 3,999.0	811,000
2	Exxon	86,673.0	69,160.0	4,870.0	146,000
3	Mobil	55,960.0	41,752.0	1,040.0	163,600
4	Ford Motor Company	52,774.4	31,603.6	2,515.4	369,300
5	IBM	50,056.0	52,634.0	6,555.0	405,535
6	Texaco	46,297.0	37,703.0	1,233.0	54,481
7	Chevron	41,741.9	38,899.5	1,547.4	60,845
8	AT&T	34,909.5	40,462.5	1,556.8	337,600
9	E. I. du Pont de Nemours	29,483.0	25,140.0	1,118.0	146,017
10	General Electric	28,285.0	26,432.0	2,336.0	304,000
11	Amoco	27,215.0	25,198.0	1,953.0	49,545
12	Atlantic Richfield	22,357.0	20,279.0	−202.0	31,300
13	Chrysler	21,255.5	12,605.3	1,635.2	107,850
14	Shell Oil	20,309.0	26,528.0	1,650.0	35,167
15	U.S. Steel	18,429.0	18,446.0	409.0	79,649
16	United Technologies	15,748.7	10,528.1	312.7	184,800
17	Phillips Petroleum	15,676.0	14,045.0	418.0	25,300
18	Tenneco	15,400.0	20,437.0	172.0	111,000
19	Occidental Petroleum	14,534.4	11,585.9	696.0	42,353
20	Sun Oil	13,769.0	12,923.0	527.0	37,818
21	Boeing	13,636.0	9,246.0	566.0	104,000
22	Procter & Gamble	13,552.0	9,683.0	635.0	62,200
23	R. J. Reynolds	13,533.0	16,930.0	1,001.0	147,513
24	Standard Oil	13,002.0	18,330.0	308.0	42,100
25	ITT	12,714.3	14,272.5	293.5	232,000
	Top 25	$773,682.4	$668,656.2	$37,145.0	4,090,973
	Top 10	549,766.5	452,817.4	28,723.6	2,847,923

Source: Fortune, April 28, 1986, pp. 182–183.

management costs grow. Beyond some point, there may be few additional advantages in relying on internal managerial coordination. Second, advantages of economies of scale are also limited. When a firm is large enough to take advantage of the best technology and the best level of specialization, becoming even larger will not lower its costs.

Finally, some economists fear that very large businesses may have too much economic and political power. A gain in economic power means a decline in competition, which (as we said in Chapter 5) is extremely important to society. A gain in political power may enable a firm to obtain political favors not in society's best interests. Whether current firms are too large and have too much power is a subject of much debate but little general agreement.

Types of Business Organizations

In Chapter 5 we defined the goal of businesses in a market economy as earning maximum profits. However, in the real world, some business firms—hospitals and educational institutions, for example—are classified as not-for-profit institutions. Although such firms do not seek profits, they are still interested in responding to consumer preferences and reducing costs. By being more efficient, they can provide more and better services to their customers. Recent research, however, suggests that such organizations do not always operate in an efficient manner. To some extent this result may reflect the absence of the incentives provided by profits. Although the not-for-profit portion of the private sector is growing in importance in the U.S. economy, we will generally assume as we develop economic principles that business firms operate with a profit motive.

Even though all business firms have similar goals, they can have one of three legal forms in the United States: proprietorship, partnership, or corporation. The legal structure is important because it determines who receives the profits, who has control, and who bears the risks.

Proprietorship. The simplest legal form of business is the **proprietorship**. A proprietor is the sole owner of the business, or the individual who receives all the profits and bears all the risks of the business. Many small retailers—clothing and hardware stores, service stations—and professionals—doctors, lawyers, dentists—operate their businesses as proprietorships.

Proprietorships are easy to form, requiring no extensive legal arrangements and, except for licenses in some cases, no government permission. In addition, the proprietor does not have to share decision-making authority with anyone else. A proprietor may hire employees and delegate some responsibility to a hired manager. But the proprietor is ultimately responsible for decisions and for the success or failure of the business.

Proprietorships also have disadvantages. The financial resources of the firm are the savings of the proprietor, the proprietor's ability to borrow is often quite limited and, as a result, most proprietorships are small. A small firm may not be able to take advantage of economies of scale in buying equipment or hiring specialized workers. This drawback helps to explain the lack of proprietorships in the automotive and steel industries. In addition, small firms often cannot offer the job security that many workers desire. Finally, a proprietor has unlimited liability for the firm's debts. This characteristic is not a problem if the business is a success, but if it fails, the owner must personally cover the debts, if necessary selling personal property to pay off creditors.

Proprietorship. A firm in which one person owns all the productive property, receives all the profits, and is personally responsible for all the liabilities.

Type of enterprise	Number of businesses		Sales		Net income	
	(thousands)	(%)	(billions)	(%)	(billions)	(%)
Proprietorship	11,262	70.1	$ 516.0	6.1	$ 70.8	24.4
Partnership	1,644	10.2	375.2	4.4	−3.5	−1.2
Corporation	3,171	19.7	7604.2	89.5	223.0	76.8
Total	16,077	100.0	$8495.4	100.0	$290.3	100.0

Exhibit 6.2
Distribution of Business Firms, Sales, and Profits by Type of Enterprise, 1984

Source: U.S. Department of the Treasury, Internal Revenue Service, *Statistics of Income Bulletin* (Winter, 1986–1987).

Partnership. A business firm with two or more co-owners who share the control and profits of the firm is called a **partnership**. Like a proprietorship, a partnership is relatively easy to form, although the partners must agree on the contributions each will make and how they will share profits and control. Partnerships are the least common form of business organization, accounting for only 5 percent of the total number of firms in the United States. They are most commonly found in firms of lawyers, doctors, and accountants.

Partnerships can have an advantage over proprietorships because they pool the talents and financial resources of more than one person. They offer a greater potential to take advantage of specialization and other economies of scale. On the other hand, decision making can be complicated because the partners share control. Partnerships can also be unstable because, legally, a partnership is dissolved when any one of the partners withdraws or dies. Moreover, each partner is personally liable for all the debts of the business if it fails, even if those debts and the failure resulted from the poor decisions of only one of the partners.

Corporation. By most measures the **corporation** is the major legal form of business organization in the U.S. economy. Exhibit 6.2 shows the sales and profits of the three forms of business. As you can see, less than 20 percent of all businesses are organized as corporations, but they accounted for almost 90 percent of all sales and three-fourths of all business profits in 1984. Corporations dominate the manufacturing, transportation, public utilities, and finance industries and account for slightly more than one-half of all business in the trade and construction industries. Some economists suggest that encouragement of the corporate form of business was an important factor in the growth and development of the U.S. economy.

In order to understand the advantages of the corporation, we can consider how one is formed and operates. First, a group of investors decides to form a corporation. To do so, they must obtain a charter from a state government. The charter establishes the corporation, in the eyes of the law, as a "legal person" separate and apart from the owners. After receiving a charter, the investors contribute to the firm's financial resources in return for shares of **stock**. Shares of stock are ownership claims entitling the holder to a share of the firm's assets and income. Usually, these shares also give the holders some control over the business's operations. In fact, however, large corporations often have thousands or even millions of individual shareholders. Thus most shareholders (owners) do not personally work in the business. The shareholders elect a board of directors

Partnership. A form of business organization in which two or more individuals share the ownership, profits, and liabilities of the firm.

Corporation. A firm created as a legal entity separate from the persons who established it. It is usually owned by many individuals, whose liability is limited to their investment in the firm.

Stock. Shares of ownership in a corporation.

to represent their interests. The board of directors hires managers, who actually make the business decisions under the board's control.

The most important legal characteristic of the corporation is that of *limited liability*. The owners (shareholders) are not personally liable for any debts of the corporation. If the business fails, they may lose whatever they have invested, but no more. Limited liability makes it easier for a corporation to raise funds by selling additional shares of stock, drawing on the resources of a large number of individuals. This would not be practical if all the investors had to be partners and were responsible for the corporation's total debts. (Would you risk investing in IBM if it meant that you were personally liable for all the firm's debts?)

The ability to attract funds is very important. It allows the corporation to grow large enough to take advantages of economies of large-scale production and specialization. The corporation can spend more for research and development and can hire professional managers and experts to help it produce more efficiently and respond more quickly to consumer demands.

The corporation also has a "permanent" life. That is, it continues as long as the business is solvent, regardless of what happens to individual shareholders. This permanency also enables shareholders to sell their stock to other individuals, generally without having any effect on the business.

However, corporations also have disadvantages. First, the separation of ownership and management may create conflict. Managers may be more interested in preserving their jobs than in seeking maximum profits. In Chapter 5 we described the importance of profit-seeking to allocative and technical efficiency. If managers do not seek to increase profits, corporations may not produce desirable results for society.

Second, corporations can grow quite large, as shown in Exhibit 6.1. If their size gives them too much economic or political power, we would have reason to be concerned. Before reaching any final conclusion about the desirability of corporations we must weigh their benefits against their possible costs to society.

Classification and Grouping of Businesses

All businesses, of course, are not alike. Economists find it useful to classify firms by **industry**, that is, a group of firms producing the same or similar products, such as the automotive industry. Using this definition, we can associate industries with product markets. In the automotive industry, for example, U.S. automakers compete both with each other and with foreign automakers. Often, a business firm is involved in more than one industry. For example, Ford Motor Company is also in the home appliance and television industries.

Economists also group industries into broader categories, as shown in Exhibit 6.3. Note that agriculture (including farms, fishing, and forestry) employs a relatively small percentage of the work force. In terms of total employment, the most important industries are manufacturing, financial services, and other services. Other services include hotels, education, health care, auto repair, and entertainment and employ the largest and fastest growing proportion of the private-sector work force. Employment in services increased by 80 percent from 1969 to 1984, compared with a less than 33 percent gain for all private-sector employment. Services and retail trade together accounted for over 70 percent of the new jobs

Industry. A group of firms producing the same or similar products.

Industry	Percentage of total employment		
	1969	*1984*	*1995*
Agriculture	4.4	3.1	2.5
Mining	0.6	0.6	0.5
Construction	5.4	5.5	5.4
Manufacturing	25.1	18.5	17.2
Transportation, utilities	5.7	5.1	5.1
Trade	20.5	22.7	23.0
Financial services	4.7	5.9	6.0
Other services	18.6	23.6	26.2
Federal government	3.4	2.6	2.3
State and local government	11.6	12.3	11.7
Total	100.0	100.0	100.0
Total employment (thousands)	81,508	106,841	122,760

**Exhibit 6.3
Employment by Industry,
1969 to 1995**

Source: Monthly Labor Review, November, 1985, p. 28.

created during this period and almost 80 percent of the expected increase between 1984 and 1995. Although manufacturing accounts for a declining proportion of all jobs, employment in manufacturing is expected to remain virtually constant.

Business Finances

You will be able to understand business activities better, if you know something about business finances. Consider Exhibit 6.4, which shows two reports for a fictitious firm, Longview Binoculars Corporation (LBC). The *income statement* shows that the firm sold $3 million worth of goods and that its net income after all costs and taxes was $240,000. Like most manufacturers, LBC's major production expenses were for the resources it bought from other firms (such as leather for straps and binocular cases) and for labor resources (wages of production workers and salaries of management). The firm also had a small amount of interest expense on loans it took out to finance its operations and to purchase machinery. In addition, the firm had to pay sales, property, and income taxes.

One expense, **depreciation**, requires further explanation. Most other expenses represent actual costs of resources—such as materials and labor—purchased and used during the year. Depreciation, however, is an estimate of that part of the original cost of plant (factory buildings) and equipment that has been used up or worn out during the year. For example, LBC bought a machine last year for $50,000. This machine is expected to be useful to LBC for 5 years. Thus LBC estimated $10,000 (one-fifth of the original cost) as the fraction of the machine used up in each of the 5 years. This $10,000, along with similar figures for other plant and equipment, represent the $500,000 of depreciation shown on the income statement. In effect, depreciation represents the amount of profit the firm would have to earn to be able to replace capital resources as they wear out or become obsolete.

Depreciation. An estimate of that part of the original cost of capital goods, such as machinery and buildings, that has been used up or worn out during a specific period of time.

Income Statement

Total revenues		$3,000,000
Less: Expenses		
Materials	$750,000	
Wages and salaries	950,000	
Interest	200,000	
Sales and property taxes	50,000	
Rent	150,000	
Depreciation, plant and equipment	500,000	
Total expenses		2,600,000
Net income before income taxes		$ 400,000
Less: Income taxes		160,000
Net income after income taxes		$ 240,000
Distribution of net income		
Dividends paid to shareholders	$ 40,000	
Retained earnings	200,000	
	$240,000	

Balance Sheet

Assets		
Inventory	$300,000	
Plant and equipment	900,000	
Other assets	400,000	
Total Assets		$1,600,000
Liabilities		
Bank loans	$200,000	
Bonds	400,000	
Other liabilities	100,000	
Total Liabilities		$ 700,000
Equity		
Common stock	$300,000	
Retained earnings	600,000	
Total Equity		900,000
		$1,600,000

**Exhibit 6.4
Income Statement and
Balance Sheet for the
Longview Binocular
Corporation for the Year
Ending December 31, 1987**

Depreciation is special in another way. The costs of other resources were amounts LBC had to pay its suppliers. But depreciated goods have already been paid for. Rather than being a cost to the firm, depreciation can actually add to the funds LBC can spend, since it reduces the firm's tax obligation. For example, LBC had to pay $160,000 in income taxes last year, or 40 percent of its income before taxes. Without depreciation, its pre-tax earnings would have been $900,000 and its tax bill $360,000 (40 percent of $900,000). Thus depreciation added $200,000 to LBC's available funds. However, in 1986 Congress decreased the rate at which

Dividends. The portion of a corporation's profits paid out to its shareholders.

Retained earnings. The portion of a corporation's profits not paid out to its shareholders but retained by the corporation to finance future production.

Bonds. IOUs of a business or government representing a promise to pay a specified sum of interest at regular intervals (usually every four or six months) for a specified period of time. At the end of the loan period, the borrower is obligated to repay the original amount loaned.

Transfer payments. Payments, usually made by government, to individuals for the purpose of redistributing income.

RECAP

The roles of business firms are to organize and monitor team performance, to reduce the costs and number of market exchanges, to take advantage of economies of scale, and to accept risks. If they grow too large, however, costs of managing may rise and economic power may become too concentrated.

The three principal legal forms of business organization are the proprietorship, the partnership, and the corporation. Most goods and services are produced by corporations.

Business income is the difference between revenues (dollar sales) and costs (including materials, wages and salaries, rent, interest, and taxes). Income can be distributed as dividends to shareholders or reinvested in the firm as retained earnings.

All business assets—inventory and plant and equipment, for example—must be financed. Liabilities are funds borrowed by a business from nonowners such as banks; equity represents funds invested by owners.

firms could charge depreciation expenses against income, forcing firms to borrow more money to have the same amount of available funds.

The lower part of the income statement shows what LBC did with its income from last year. First, it paid out a total of $40,000 as **dividends** to its shareholders. The remaining $200,000, shown as **retained earnings**, represents the portion of its income that LBC reinvested in the business.

Exhibit 6.4 also contains a second statement, called a *balance sheet*. This statement is called a balance sheet because it always shows the total value of assets as exactly equal to the total value of liabilities and equities. *Assets* are items of value, including a firm's inventory (resource materials on hand and goods ready for sale) and its capital resources (plant and equipment). As of December 31, 1987, LBC's assets were $1.6 million. In contrast, *liabilities* represent future payments the firm must make to nonowners, usually for money it has borrowed. The financial contributions made by owners are called *equities*.

The balance sheet also reflects the fact that every dollar spent by the firm to acquire assets has been obtained from one or more sources of financing. Bank loans and **bonds** are forms of liability financing. Both obligate the firm to make regular and specified interest payments and, at a specified time, to return the funds borrowed. There are two principal sources of equity financing. By selling new shares of stock, the firm acquires new owners and new financing. The firm also obtains funds from shareholders indirectly, by retaining a portion of its net income. In fact, about 75 percent of the funds firms use to buy new capital resources and expand operations are obtained from retained earnings and the tax savings from depreciation.

THE PRIVATE SECTOR: HOUSEHOLDS

As we discussed in Chapter 5, the household is a major decision-making unit in a market economy. Households own economic resources and household demand heavily influences the production of goods and services.

Size and Characteristics of the U.S. Population

Exhibit 6.5 presents some basic facts about the U.S. population. As you can see, the population is expected to increase from nearly 240 million individuals in 1985 to a projected 260 million in 1995. Some 117 million, just less than half of the population, are officially classified as members of the labor force—either working or looking for work. Most of the rest depend on income earned by other household members, accumulated wealth or savings, or government **transfer payments**. Among those not in the labor force are many of the 26 percent of the population under the age of 18 and the 12 percent over the age of 65. Many of these not officially part of the labor force—homemakers, for example—perform valuable economic services, although they are not paid wages.

Recent population statistics show several trends that have important economic implications. First, both the number and the proportion of the population over the age of 65 are growing rapidly. Although some of these individuals continue to work, a large number are retired. Many of those who are retired obtain a significant

	1965	*1975*	*1985*	*1995*[a]
Population (millions)	194.3	216.0	238.8	259.6
Under 18 years of age (percent)	35.9	31.1	26.3	25.9
Ages 65 and over (percent)	9.5	10.5	12.0	13.1
Labor force (millions)	76.4	95.5	117.2	129.2
Women (percent)	35.2	40.0	44.2	46.4
Teenagers (percent)	7.9	9.5	6.8	5.5

Exhibit 6.5
Selected Characteristics of the U.S. Population and Labor Force, 1965 to 1995

[a]Data for 1995 are projections.

Sources: U.S. Department of Commerce, Bureau of the Census, *Projections of the Population of the United States by Age, Sex, and Race: 1983 to 2080,* Current Population Reports, Series P-25, No. 952; U.S. Department of Labor, *Monthly Labor Review,* November 1985.

proportion of their income from government transfer payments, such as Social Security. Medicare, another government program, pays a substantial portion of the large medical bills of this group.

However, many people over the age of 65 have accumulated wealth in the form of land, buildings (especially homes), savings accounts, corporate stocks, and bonds. Should they be required to sell some of these assets instead of receiving government transfer payments? Should society support this growing group with transfer payments or encourage more employment and reliance on private means? As the older population expands, these policy issues will become increasingly important.

A second trend is the increasing proportion of women who work outside the home. In 1965 only one-third of all women were in the labor force. By 1985 over one-half of all women worked and by 1995 the proportion is projected to be almost 60 percent. This trend, in part, is caused by economic factors. Families are increasingly relying on the income of more than one person to satisfy household demands for goods and services. In many cases, the income of two working adults is necessary to keep the family income above the poverty level. In addition, the growing proportion of single-parent families (most headed by women) has further increased the percentage of women who work. The number of women entering the labor force has increased demand for many goods and services, especially child care.

Sources of Personal Income

When discussing the circular-flow model in Chapter 5, we noted that households receive income from the sale of economic resources they possess. **Personal income** represents the total income received by all households in the economy from all sources. There are six basic sources of personal income: wages, proprietor income, rent, corporate dividends, interest, and transfer payments. Exhibit 6.6 shows the absolute and relative sizes of these sources.

Labor income. The largest single source of income for U.S. households is the wages and salaries paid by producers in exchange for labor. In fact, labor is the only resource that most households have to offer for sale. In 1986, wages and

Personal income. The total amount of income, before taxes, received by all households from all sources.

salaries made up about two-thirds of total personal income, a proportion that has changed very little over the years.

An additional 8 percent of total personal income was derived from proprietor income. This figure includes the businesses of professionals (doctors and lawyers, for example), beauticians, farmers, and the owners of small retail stores—any proprietorship. Proprietor income once accounted for a much larger share of total personal income—19 percent in 1947, for example. Some of that change reflects the choice by many former proprietors to incorporate essentially owner-operated business in order to reduce their personal liability.

Part of proprietor income represents returns on owners' investments in land, buildings, and equipment and on accumulated wealth. But in most nonfarm proprietorships, the owner's labor is the firm's principal resource; therefore most proprietor income is really a payment for labor. If we add proprietor income to wages and salaries, we find that almost three-fourths of all personal income derives from the sale of labor resources.

Income from other sources.   Although labor is the chief resource of households, it is not the only one. Money saved or inherited may be used to buy stocks and bonds or maintain a savings account from which households receive interest income. In 1986, households received $475 billion in interest income, representing 14 percent of total personal income; transfer payments accounted for $353 billion of household income, or some 10 percent of total personal income. Although a relatively small part of total personal income, transfer payments are a very important source of income for the elderly and for the poorest households.

In addition, some households receive dividends on corporate stock that they own. However, stock dividends presently account for only 2 percent of total personal income. Finally, a few households own land, capital resources (such as buildings), and natural resources that they rent or sell, but rental income accounted for less than 1 percent of total personal income in 1986.

Exhibit 6.6
Sources of Personal Income, 1986

Source	Amount (billions)	(%)
Wages and salaries	$2282.6	65.5
Proprietor income	278.9	8.0
Rental income	15.6	0.5
Dividend income	81.2	2.3
Interest income	475.4	13.6
Total	$3133.7	89.9
Plus transfers[a]	353.3	10.1
Total personal income	$3487.0	100.0

[a] Total transfers less personal contributions to social insurance.
Source: U.S. Department of Commerce, *Survey of Current Business,* January 1987, Table 2.1.

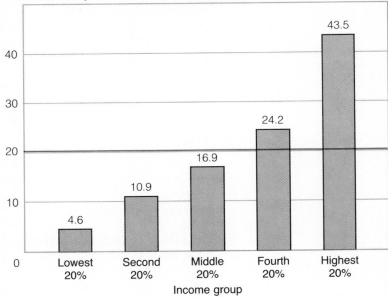

Percent of total personal income received

Exhibit 6.7
Income Distribution for U.S. Families, 1985

Source: U.S. Bureau of the Census, *Money Income and Poverty Status of Families and Persons in the United States: 1985,* Current Population Reports, Series 60, No. 154.

Distribution of Personal Income

These facts about personal income reveal nothing about the distribution of that income. Because income is required to demand goods and services in a market economy, the distribution of income largely dictates their distribution.

If families are grouped by income, as in Exhibit 6.7, we can see that income is unequally distributed. The data indicate that the poorest 20 percent of families received less than 5 percent of the total income, or only one-fourth of what this group would have received if income were equally distributed. By contrast, the richest 20 percent of families received more than twice their proportionate share.

Note, however, that the income proportions shown include cash transfer payments received but not taxes paid or value of medical care, housing, food stamp, and other public services provided to the poor. Although this definition of income closely matches the definition of personal income, it does make the income distribution appear somewhat more unequal than it actually is.

A household's income in a market economy depends on the value of its resources. Thus you might think that unequal resource distribution would explain the unequal distribution of income. In fact, however, relatively few households own any significant amount of land or capital resources; most depend largely on wages and salaries for income. Thus when studying income inequality, we must consider how labor markets operate. This topic is covered in detail in Chapter 15. While the data suggest that income is unequally distributed, they do not indicate whether the distribution is fair or equitable. That depends, of course, on personal values. But you should bear in mind that most economists do not associate equity with an equal distribution of income.

RECAP

Households and businesses together make up the private sector of the economy. Households own most resources and household demand significantly influences what is produced.

Personal (household) income includes wages, rent, interest, proprietor income, stock dividends, and transfer payments.

Income in the United States is distributed unequally. Most economists, however, do not associate equity with an equal distribution of income.

THE PUBLIC SECTOR

Our original simplified model of a market economy included only the two parts of the private sector: businesses and households. There is, however, another important part: the public sector, or government. Government plays an important role in all economic systems. The nature of this role depends on the type of economic system. In planned socialist economies, like that of the Soviet Union, government owns or directly controls the use of most economic resources. Government enterprises produce most goods and services. In market capitalist economies, like that of the United States, the public sector owns few economic resources. Nevertheless, it is a major influence in the economy.

Exhibit 6.8 shows a circular-flow model that includes the public sector. Government enters the real flow by purchasing from the private sector resources, goods, and services such as labor and missiles and provides goods and services such as education and national defense. Government also affects the circular flow by collecting taxes and making transfer payments.

In 1986, the public sector in the United States—federal, state, and local government—spent $1.5 trillion dollars and purchased some 20 percent of the

Exhibit 6.8
The Circular Flow of Government Activity
The government enters the circular flow to purchase goods (computers and police cars) and resources (labor and paper) from the private sector. Matching this real flow is a money flow of government payments. Government also provides goods and services (national defense and education) to the private sector. In return, the private sector provides monetary payments in the form of taxes and other charges (license fees and parking fines).

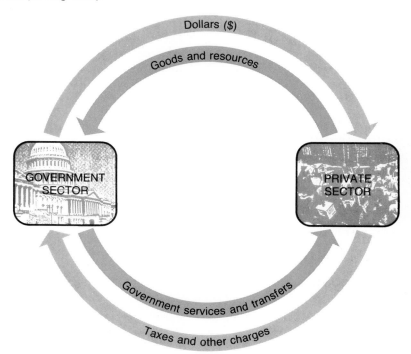

economy's total output. Many goods and services are produced by and for the public sector. National defense is a government service, although most weapons systems are produced by private firms. An agency of the federal government, the U.S. Postal Service, provides mail service. State governments provide college education and highways; local governments provide schools, libraries, and police and fire protection.

In addition, government regulations and taxes have far-ranging effects on the economic decisions of businesses and households. For example, the Environmental Protection Agency regulates air and water pollution. Taxes raise the prices of gasoline, entertainment, and other goods. Government tariffs and quotas restrict purchases of goods and services from other countries. Price supports encourage agricultural production. Government loans encourage more young people to attend college. Tax deductions for interest paid on mortgages increase demand for single-family housing.

Role of Government

Economists typically define the proper role of government as helping society achieve the economic goals of allocative efficiency, technical efficiency, equity, price stability, full employment, and growth. Most economists agree that the private sector sometimes fails to produce results consistent with those overall economic goals. These failures suggest that the performance of the economy *might* be improved through government action. (The stress on the word might is a reminder that government's role is controversial.)

Most economists agree that government can play an important economic role by: (1) facilitating market activity; (2) correcting for market failures; (3) redistributing income and economic opportunity; and (4) fostering economic stability and growth. In this section, we want to see *why* government is involved, *what* economists agree government should do, and *how* government should determine the limits of its activities with respect to the economy.

Facilitating market activity.   You saw in Chapter 5 the importance of property rights to a market economy and how market transactions can be viewed as exchanges of property rights. Well-defined property rights promote allocative efficiency because they provide a strong incentive for resource owners to sell those resources to the highest bidder. For this reason, government often acts to establish, protect, and regulate property rights. Examples include laws protecting and defending ownership claims and making sure that individuals and businesses uphold contractual agreements involving the exchange of property rights. Indeed, most economists believe that government's help in establishing property rights is essential in a market system.

Protecting buyers and sellers promotes equity. For instance, the law states that sellers must deliver the merchandise selected by buyers. Sellers cannot substitute less valuable goods at the same price. Likewise, buyers must pay the full price agreed on with sellers. Buyers cannot pay for purchases in counterfeit bills, shoplift, ride an airplane without buying a ticket, or leave town without paying the landlord.

In addition, government facilitates market activity by establishing and protecting the integrity of money. As we noted in Chapter 5, money helps to simplify the exchange process by allowing individuals to sell resources—labor, for example—in one market and use the income they receive to buy goods and services in other markets. If many individuals or businesses in an economy question the value of the nation's money, exchanges become much more complex.

Correcting for market failures.

Facilitating market activity is important but does not account for much of the economic activity of government, especially on state and federal levels. A more common role for government is correcting for market failures that cause allocative and technical inefficiency. Why do markets fail? What, if anything, can government policy do to correct failures? What does our analysis suggest about desirable and undesirable policy solutions?

Failures due to lack of competition. We noted in Chapter 5 that competition is essential in a market economy. Government helps to maintain competition in a variety of ways. Federal and state laws prohibit many anticompetitive practices, such as collusion among firms to restrict supply and raise prices. When the technically efficient number of firms in an industry is very small—for example, electric power companies in the utilities industry—government regulations substitute for competition.

Failures due to public goods and services. A market system is geared to respond primarily to the household demand for **private goods**. Private goods include all the products and services that people buy from businesses, such as milk, clothing, and cars. Only those who are willing and able to pay the market price receive the benefits of a private good. Movies shown in theaters are private goods because only those who pay the price of admission are able to enjoy them; those who are unwilling or unable to pay are excluded. Because market demand reflects the value of private goods to households, allocative efficiency results as businesses seek to produce the mix of goods and services that best matches demand.

In contrast, markets fail to reflect demand for **public goods** like national defense and clean air. Public goods are collectively consumed. Generally, there is no practical way to exclude anyone from using public goods, even if they are unwilling to pay for them. Consider, for example, national defense. When a certain defense capability is established, you and your neighbors are equally protected. It is not practical to provide more national defense for you and less for your neighbor, regardless of how much you as an individual want or how much you as a taxpayer contribute to pay for the protection.

Private goods. Goods and services that benefit only those people who purchase them. People who are unwilling or unable to pay for them can be prevented from receiving their benefits.

Public goods. Goods and services that cannot benefit one person without benefiting all. People who cannot or will not pay for them cannot be prevented from receiving their benefits.

The characteristics of public goods make establishing a market for them difficult or impossible. If you know that others will pay for their production, there is little incentive for you to pay. Thus, private producers find it difficult to supply public goods profitably. Some public goods could be produced and sold in markets, but market demand always understates the value of public goods and services to society. Thus too little would be produced from the perspective of allocative efficiency.

To correct for this market failure, government provides many public goods and services by acting either as a collective producer or, more often, as a collective purchasing agent. The major problem is to find a substitute for markets that answers the questions of how much to provide and how to pay for what is

Externalities. Benefits and costs from any product that affect individuals other than those who demand and supply the product.

Social benefits. Benefits measured from the perspective of society; include both private benefits and external benefits.

Social costs. Costs measured from the perspective of society; include both private costs and external costs.

External costs. Costs of a product that are borne by individuals other than those who demand and supply it.

External benefits. Benefits from a product received by individuals other than those who demand and supply it.

provided. Typically, government uses a political decision-making process. But there are questions about whether this process functions well enough to meet the goals of efficiency and equity.

Failures due to external costs and benefits. For a market to function efficiently, market price must reflect not only demand for a product but also the value of the resource used to produce it. Some products, however, involve **externalities** that either increase the true cost of producing the product or the product's true benefit to society.

For example, when mills produce steel, they also create air pollution. When your neighbors play loud music while you are trying to study for your economics exam, they create study problems for you. When some families in your community get inoculations against a communicable disease, they also reduce your chances of getting the disease.

But who pays for the air pollution, your lost concentration, your decreased chance of illness? Not the automaker who buys the steel, or the party-goers who enjoy the music, or you, who paid for no medicine. Rather, residents of the area around the steel mill pay in terms of a reduced quality of life. You pay with a C on the exam. Families pay with the pain and cost of inoculation. Hence those who cause externalities are not charged for the costs they impose on others, and they do not receive compensation for any external benefits they create.

The market fails because of the difference between goods and services that involve externalities and those that do not. In making rational economic decisions, consumers and producers always weigh the extra *private* benefits and extra *private* costs. This behavior results in allocative efficiency when externalities do not exist, since producers pay for every resource they use and consumers pay for every product they receive. Firms will stop producing and consumers will stop buying when the next unit adds more to the costs than to benefits. But making rational social choices also requires weighing extra **social benefits** and extra **social costs**. If externalities do not exist, private benefits equal social benefits and private costs equal social costs. Thus consumer and producer decisions that balance private costs and benefits also balance social costs and benefits. When externalities exist, however, a balance of private costs and benefits does not yield a balance of social costs and benefits.

Externalities can arise when property rights are nonexistent or poorly defined. For example, the steel mill that produces pollution uses up one of society's scarce resources—clean air. However, because no one in particular owns the air, the mill pays nothing for the use of the resource. The clean air used up has real social costs, but they are **external costs** to steel producers because the clean air costs them nothing. When there are external costs, the social costs—the costs of all the resources used—exceed the private costs reflected in supply. Because supply does not reflect the full social costs, the output produced is not allocatively efficient. The market provides too much steel and too little clean air.

When there are **external benefits**, as in the case of public health services, some individuals receive benefits for which they pay nothing. The social benefits—the benefits to all members of society—exceed the private benefits to those who decide to buy inoculations. In such cases, market demand tends to undervalue the goods and services, and too little will be bought and sold.

In some cases, allocative efficiency may be achieved through private transactions despite external costs and benefits. If you have an apple orchard that benefits from the bees I keep next door, we might agree that you will pay me to keep more beehives. If your smoking in the dorm room or office we share is offensive to me, I may be able to bribe you to quit, compensating you for the benefits you lose.

But in most cases—public health services and the air pollution created by a steel mill, for example—too many people are involved and the transaction costs of negotiating an agreement are too high to make private arrangements practical. In such cases, the government may act to correct for the market failure and restore the balance between social benefits and social costs. For example, federal and state laws restrict the quantity of air pollution that steel mills can create. Communities regulate the amount of noise you and your neighbors can make. Government provision of public health services increases their use. Although government actions may lead to an improvement in conditions, the principles of rational choice remind us that we must also consider the costs of government action when deciding whether it is appropriate.

Failures due to imperfect information. Market failure also occurs when information available to private decision makers is imperfect. For example, if the potentially harmful effects of a new prescription drug are not known to buyers, those who buy it may be subject to unrecognized risks. Government may help the market to achieve efficiency by providing information that might not otherwise exist about potential benefits and costs. Warning labels on pesticides, studies of potential hazards of drugs, and listings of job opportunities are all examples of information provided by government in an effort to assist the market system.

Redistributing income and economic opportunities.

In addition to outcomes that are allocatively and technically efficient, society wants outcomes that are equitable, that is, determined by rules that it believes are fair and just. We noted earlier in this chapter that income in the United States is unequally distributed: The richest 5 percent of U.S. families receive more than three times their proportionate share of income, whereas the poorest 20 percent receive less than one-fourth of their proportionate share. Equity, especially in a market economy, is not, however, generally defined to require equal incomes.

Economists and politicians agree that income is unequally distributed. However, they disagree strongly about the causes of this inequality. Some argue that inequities in the system—racial, sex, or age discrimination, for example—are responsible. Others believe that unequal incomes merely reflect individual choices about how much to work and how much education to obtain. But when the goal of equity is not being met by the market system, many economists believe the government should seek to improve equity by redistributing income and economic opportunity.

In the United States, transfer payments such as welfare and Social Security are the primary means by which government redistributes income. In addition, government laws and policies against discrimination and programs such as student loans seek to promote equal opportunity. Defining equity, however, requires personal value judgments. Moreover, it is difficult to determine the exact causes of inequalities. Because of these difficulties, government programs that seek to improve equity are controversial.

Fostering economic stability and growth. We also hope that the economy can grow and avoid major swings in economic activity that can lead to high unemployment and/or rapid inflation. By altering its levels of spending and taxation and by regulating credit, the government can affect the level and stability of total economic activity. Government can also affect the rate at which the economy grows over time.

Although most economists agree that government *can* affect the economy's stability and growth, not all agree that government can do so effectively. In the 1970s, in particular, the U.S. government was not very successful in maintaining price stability and avoiding high unemployment. The role of government in such activities is both complex and controversial and is a major topic in the macroeconomics portion of this textbook.

Government and Rational Choice

Economists generally agree that the government roles discussed above are appropriate *in theory*. But many disagree with particular government actions *in practice*. One point on which there is a strong consensus, however, is that when government makes economic decisions, it should do so using economic analysis and the principles of rational choice. That is, it should weigh the costs and benefits of potential actions and act only when the extra social benefits outweigh the extra social costs.

Size and Nature of the Public Sector

The preceding discussion indicated some of the reasons why government is involved in the economy. Let's now consider the degree to which government is involved by looking at the size and distribution of government expenditures. As Exhibit 6.9(a) illustrates, the size of the public sector has increased greatly. In absolute terms, public sector—federal, state, and local government—expenditures increased from $13.4 billion in 1935 to $98.5 billion in 1955 to $1.5 trillion in 1986. Absolute increases, however, are potentially misleading because the size of the economy has also grown. However, government expenditures have also increased in relative terms as well, from 18 percent of total output in 1935 to 24 percent in 1955 and 35 percent in 1986.

Exhibit 6.9(b) divides government expenditures into purchases of goods and services and transfer payments. Government purchases—national defense, public education, roads, and the judicial system, for example—represent a transfer of resources from private sector to public sector use. After rising from 14 percent of total output in 1935 to almost 19 percent in 1955, government purchases have remained a fairly constant 20 percent of total economic output.

Unlike government purchases, transfer payments do not represent a reduction in the quantity of private goods and services consumed. (Although, as we point out in Chapter 18, transfer payments may slightly decrease work effort and hence output.) Instead, they represent a transfer of income from one part of the private sector to another and a substitution of public for private decision making. The growth of transfer payments is the major cause of public sector growth. For

(a) As a percent of total output

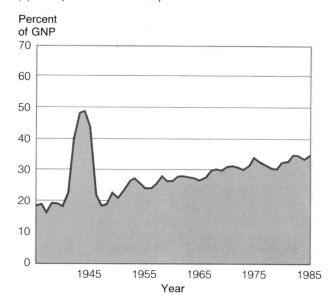

(b) By type

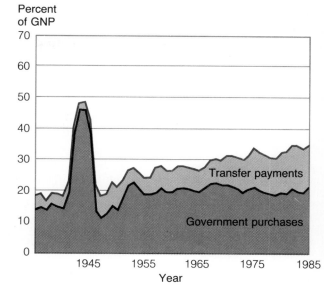

Exhibit 6.9
Government Expenditures
The graph in part (a) shows that government expenditures have steadily climbed from about 20 percent of GNP after World War II to over 30 percent in recent years. The graph in part (b) shows the distribution of expenditures. The lower area of the graph shows that government purchases of goods and services as a percent of GNP has remained relatively constant at about 20 percent of total output since 1955. The upper area of the graph shows transfer payment expenditures. It indicates that the growth in transfer payments accounts for the increased size of government spending, especially since the mid-1960s.

example, transfer payments grew from 4 percent of total output in 1935 to 6 percent in 1955 and 12 percent in 1986. Transfer payments in 1986 represented 34 percent of total expenditures and almost 40 percent of expenditures by the federal government.

Government purchases, however, are only one part of the economic impact of government because they do not include the costs of laws and regulations. The costs to businesses and individuals of complying with government laws are a cost of government, even though they are not government expenditures. For example, government regulations on air pollution force businesses to purchase, install, and operate pollution control devices. Tax laws encourage individuals to spend for health insurance, education, and home ownership, while discouraging other activities. Indeed, whether you receive Medicare or a tax deduction for health costs, you are in effect receiving a government subsidy. Such indirect government expenditures accounted for an estimated $388.4 billion in 1984. If they had been counted with direct expenditures, federal spending as a percentage of total output would have been 34, not 24, percent.[*]

---

[*]See Joseph Stiglitz, *Economics of the Public Sector*, New York: W. W. Norton, 1986, p. 30.

Economists define the proper economic role of government (the public sector) as helping society to achieve its economic goals of allocative efficiency, technical efficiency, equity, price stability, full employment, and growth.

Economic activities of government include facilitating market activity, correcting for market failures, redistributing income and economic opportunity, and fostering economic stability and growth. The exact role government should play and how well it has performed are much debated.

The size of the public sector has increased in the last 30 years, largely because of the growth in government transfer payments.

Imports. The value of goods and services produced in foreign economies bought by U.S. individuals, businesses, and governments.

Exports. The value of U.S. resources, goods and services bought by foreign individuals, businesses, and governments.

Size of Government: International Comparisons

As Exhibit 6.10 shows, government plays a larger role in other market-oriented economies than in that of the United States. Government expenditures account for over two-thirds of total output in Sweden, and one-half of total output in Italy, France, West Germany, and the United Kingdom. By contrast, government represents only a bit over one-third of the total economy in the United States and Japan. In addition, the government's share of the economy grew more rapidly in other countries between 1960 and 1982, almost doubling in Sweden, Italy, and Japan. Exhibit 6.10 does not include countries such as the Soviet Union, Hungary, or China because in planned socialist economies, virtually all economic activity is controlled by government.

Although such comparisons do not suggest that government in the United States is too small (or too large), they do show that government activity is greater in other countries. Nevertheless, government has a major impact on the U.S. economy, both in aiding the market system and in attempting to correct for market failures. In later chapters we will consider further the impact of government and whether its future role should be different.

THE FOREIGN SECTOR

To complete our overview of the U.S. economy, we must recognize the impact of foreign individuals, businesses, and governments—collectively known as the foreign sector. International trade between the United States and foreign economies is certainly important. **Imports**—including platinum, oil, industrial diamonds, coffee, bananas, automobiles, video cassette recorders, and textiles—account for a sizeable portion of the resources used and goods consumed in the United States. At the same time, **exports**—such as wheat, coal, beef, and computers—provide jobs and profits to many individuals and businesses in the United States. Our lives

Exhibit 6.10
International Comparisons of the Size of Government

Country	Expenditures as a percent of total output	
	1960	1982
Sweden	31.1	67.3
Italy	30.1	53.7
France	34.6	50.7
West Germany	32.5	49.4
United Kingdom	32.6	47.4
Canada	28.9	45.8
United States	27.6	37.6
Japan	18.3	34.2

Source: OECD "The Role of the Public Sector," *Economic Studies,* Spring 1985, p. 29.

Category	Exports (billions)	Imports (billions)	Net exports (billions)
Foods and feeds	$ 22.6	$ 24.0	$ − 1.4
Industrial supplies	63.4	103.1	− 39.7
Energy products	8.2	38.1	− 29.9
Capital goods	79.2	75.7	3.5
Automobiles	23.9	78.1	− 54.2
Consumer goods	14.5	78.0	− 63.5
Other goods	18.2	10.6	7.6
Total merchandise trade	221.8	369.5	− 147.7
Services	148.9	126.6	22.3
Trade of goods and services	$370.7	$496.1	$ − 125.4

**Exhibit 6.11
U.S. International Trade by
Category, 1986**

Source: U.S. Department of Commerce, *Survey of Current Business,* March 1987, Tables 2 and 3.

would certainly be different, in some cases difficult, without this international trade. In this section we examine some of the basic features of the foreign sector, reserving a full discussion of international economics to later chapters.

Imports and Exports

Exhibit 6.11 shows some of the major items imported into or exported from the United States in 1986. Agricultural products, industrial supplies, and capital goods were the major items exported. However, except for agricultural products and capital goods, more goods and services in each category were imported than exported.

In 1986, U.S. exports to the rest of the world totalled $371 billion, but imports totalled $496 billion of foreign goods and services. We discuss the complex causes and consequences of these flows in later chapters.

International Trade and Capital Flows

We can show how the U.S. economy relates to the economies in the rest of the world using a circular-flow model as in Exhibit 6.12. The foreign sector participates in both resource and product markets in the United States. The top half of Exhibit 6.12 shows these international trade flows. Like the circular-flow model in Chapter 5, dollars move in the direction opposite the real flow of goods and services.

In addition to trade flows, there are substantial international financial flows. The bottom half of Exhibit 6.12 shows these international financial, or capital, flows as the exchange of money for investments. Residents of the United States, for example, exchange money for foreign physical assets, such as factories, or financial assets, such as shares of stock in foreign companies or bonds of foreign companies and governments.

International capital flows have a major impact on an economy. In 1986, U.S. residents invested a total of $100 billion in foreign economies, while foreigners

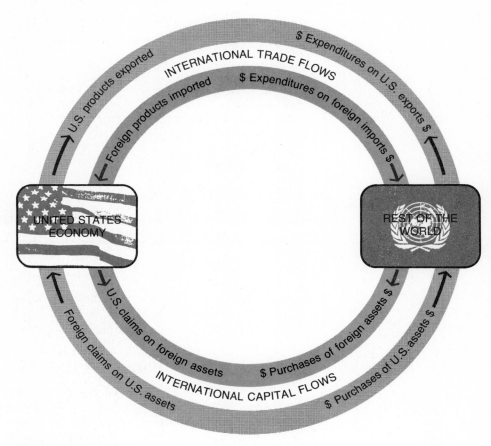

Exhibit 6.12
The Flows of International Exchange
The exhibit shows the international exchanges between the U.S. economy and the rest of the world. The top of the exhibit shows trade flows; exports and imports of goods and services are matched by an equal but opposite flow of dollars. The bottom part shows international financial or capital flows representing financial investments in foreign assets by U.S. residents and financial investments by foreigners in U.S. assets.

invested $213 billion in the U.S. economy. In fact, because interest rates in the United States have been relatively high in recent years, foreigners have supplied large amounts of funds to U.S. financial markets, much of which helped to finance the large U.S. government budget deficits.

As you can see, the foreign sector is an increasingly important part of the U.S. economy. Foreign businesses have increased the level of competition in many U.S. product and resource markets. Foreign products have added much to the variety and quality of products offered for sale in this country. Foreign investment has helped fuel recent growth in the U.S. economy. Although we do not discuss details of the foreign sector's activities until the last chapters, we mention the foreign sector throughout the text, as appropriate.

CONCLUSION

In this chapter we focused specifically on the U.S. economy, although the features discussed—such as the role of the public sector—are characteristic of most market economies. This material completes your introduction to the study of economics. At this point you will go on to study the economy from one of two perspectives: microeconomics or macroeconomics. In the study of *microeconomics*, the focus is on activities of individual economic units and markets. In the study of *macroeconomics*, the focus is on activity of the economy as a whole or on major sectors of the economy. In either case you will have to draw on the principles you have learned so far to further understand how the economy operates.

SUMMARY

1. In this chapter we examined the roles of businesses and households (the private sector), of federal, state, and local government (the public sector), and of foreign individuals, businesses, and governments (the foreign sector) as economic units in a market economy.

2. The role of business firms in a market economy is to organize and monitor team performance, to reduce the costs and number of market exchanges, to take advantage of economies of scale, and to accept risks. If businesses grow too large, however, management costs rise and economic power may become too concentrated.

3. The three principal legal forms of business organization are the proprietorship, the partnership, and the corporation. Proprietorships are the simplest and most common form of business organization; partnerships are the least common. Corporations are the most important form of business organization because they produce most of the goods and services, employ most of the labor and other economic resources, and receive most of the profits.

4. Among the advantages of the corporate form of business organization are that (a) it limits the liability of its owners to their original investment; (b) it can raise more funds than can a proprietorship or partnership; (c) it is a more stable form of organization than the other kinds of business enterprise, which contributes to greater long-range certainty; and (d) it can expand to take advantage of the benefits of size.

5. Firms can either distribute profits to their shareholders in the form of dividends or reinvest them. Business assets—inventory and plant and equipment, for example—must be financed. Liabilities are the funds that a business borrows from nonowners, such as banks; equity represents the funds invested by owners, including the undistributed profits or retained earnings.

6. Households own most of the productive resources (land, labor, and capital), and their demand is significant in determining what is produced. Total personal income is derived from six basic sources: wages and salaries (the most significant source of income for most households), rent, interest, proprietor income, dividends, and transfer payments.

7. Economists define the economic role of government as helping the economy to achieve allocative efficiency, technical efficiency, equity, price stability, full employment, and growth. Specific economic activities of government include: (a) facilitating market activity; (b) correcting market failures; (c) redistributing income and opportunity; and (d) fostering economic stability and growth. The exact role government should play is controversial, and every government action involves both benefits and costs.

8. The size of the public sector has increased in the last 30 years. Government expenditures as a percent of total output increased from 24 percent in 1955 to 35 percent in 1986. Most of the increase represents growth in government transfer payments. The size of the public sector in the United States is smaller than in many European countries, but not as small as in Japan.

9. Foreign individuals, businesses, and governments—the foreign sector—have a growing influence on the U.S. economy. International trade—imports and exports—provides resources, goods and services, jobs, and income to residents of the United States. International capital flows—foreign investment in the United States and U.S. investment in foreign countries—are sizeable. The impact of foreign competition for U.S. businesses is growing. In important ways, the United States is but one part of the world economy.

KEY TERMS

Private sector, 121
Public sector, 121
Foreign sector, 121
Proprietorship, 124

QUESTIONS FOR REVIEW AND DISCUSSION

1. The structure of U.S. business has changed in recent years. Manufacturing accounts for a declining percentage of employment and income, whereas service industries have expanded. What reasons can you give for this change?

2. A corporation is owned by shareholders, controlled by a board of directors, and operated by management. What keeps managers interested in making profits for shareholders? Why might the interests of management and shareholders conflict? What are the consequences of such conflicts for the goals of allocative and technical efficiency?

3. In this chapter we noted that households receive most of their income from wages and salaries. Explain the following statement in light of the link between income and the distribution of goods and services: "Society's distribution system will continue to keep most individuals interested in working, even if productivity gains greatly increase society's production possibilities."

4. How would you define the proper role of government in a market economy? How do economists tend to evaluate government? What criteria for evaluating government can you see in the principles of rational choice? Since economists believe that government should apply the principles of rational choice, why do

they sometimes disagree about whether government should undertake a particular project?

5. Evaluate the following statements using economic principles. (*Note:* Avoid the temptation to simply give your opinion. Give an economic critique of the statements; that is, are they logical?)
   a) Increases in taxes clearly make households and businesses worse off since they have less to spend.
   b) Public goods should be produced by the government even if their benefits are lower than their costs because they will tend to be ignored or underproduced by the private sector.

6. Consider the statement: "Government must assume the responsibility for goods and services that are too vital to be left to the whim of the marketplace. Thus government must provide for national defense, libraries, education, food, clothing, public health, and clean air and water." Which of these, if any, are what economists call public goods? Which of these, if any, involve externalities? Why do economists believe markets can be trusted to provide many vital goods, such as clothing? What economic criteria would determine whether government action will improve allocative efficiency?

7. How does the federal government intervene to correct inequities resulting from the market system? Is this an appropriate area for government action? Why do you suppose this is an extremely controversial area?

8. In evaluating government policies, economists are concerned with the effects on allocative and technical efficiency and on equity. Explain the possible effects each of the following policies might have on each of the three goals. (For equity, consider which groups will gain and which will lose.)
   a) A policy to increase the incomes of farmers that will also raise and maintain farm prices above market equilibrium levels.
   b) A policy that requires all soft drinks and beer to be sold in returnable bottles or cans.

9. If, as is true of almost all government policies, some groups will gain and others will lose, how can an issue be settled? How does your answer to this question help you to understand that what economists believe government *should* do is often different from what government *actually* does?

10. What are some of the benefits and costs from international trade? Do you think the U.S. economy would be better off if international trade were restricted? Why do you suppose that some industries—such as automobile, steel, shoes, and textiles—have asked for and received protection from foreign competition? Is it generally desirable for an economy to restrict trade?

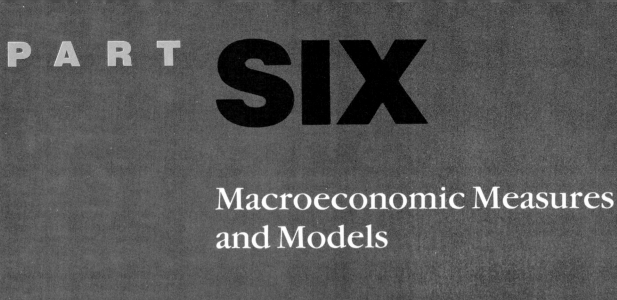

PART SIX

Macroeconomic Measures and Models

C H A P T E R 20

Introduction to
Macroeconomics

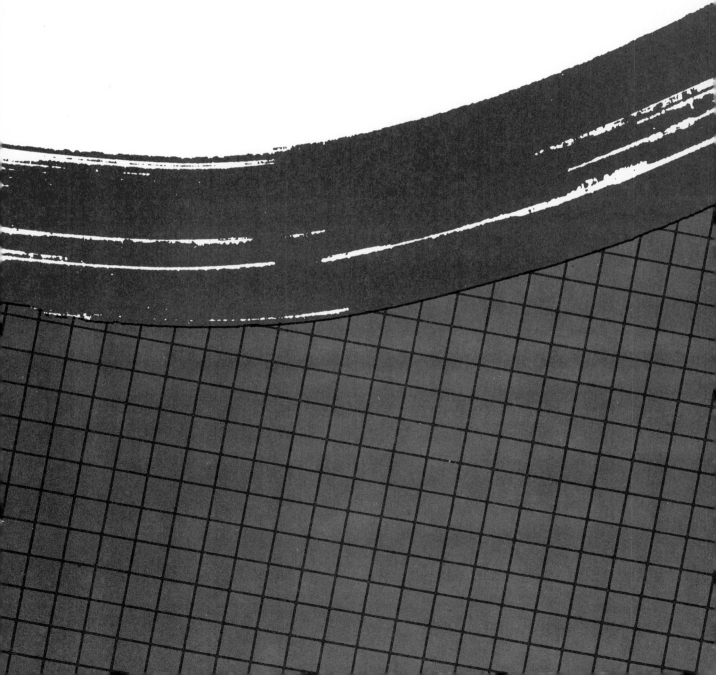

QUESTIONS TO CONSIDER

☐ How do microeconomics and macroeconomics differ?

☐ What do economists mean by *full employment,* and why is it an important macroeconomic goal?

☐ What do economists mean by *price stability,* and why is it an important macroeconomic goal?

☐ How well has the United States met its goals of full employment and price stability since 1900?

☐ Why do macroeconomists focus on changes in aggregate demand and aggregate supply?

We discussed some of the basic principles of economics in Chapters 1–6, noting how individual markets operate and what the basic overall economic goals of the economy are. With this chapter we begin to explore the economy from a macroeconomic viewpoint.

Macroeconomic topics—unemployment, inflation, interest rates, and economic growth—are constantly in the news. If you are a typical college student, however, your experience in the job market and with the general price level has probably been limited. As you will discover in this chapter—and in the world of work after college—unemployment and inflation can severely affect the way people live. Consider how you and your family would have to change your lifestyles if one or both of your parents were out of work for a year. Or if you are trying to live on last summer's income but prices jump 10 percent, you may wonder what caused the inflation that has curtailed your social life.

Macroeconomics is concerned with describing, understanding, and predicting the performance of an entire economy. Economists judge an economy's performance in terms of three basic macroeconomic goals: price stability, full employment, and economic growth. In this chapter we consider some measures of how well the U.S. economy has met these goals. As you will see, it has fallen far short of them at times, and we have experienced high inflation and/or unemployment.

The problems that develop when macroeconomic goals are not met are extremely complex. Thus this chapter is just a first look at them. We return to these problems again and again in later chapters, as you learn more about macroeconomics.

MACROECONOMIC CONCEPTS AND GOALS

As you begin your study of macroeconomics, you should understand what macroeconomics is and how it differs from microeconomics. You will also have to learn some new concepts, which are useful in viewing the economy from the macroeconomic perspective.

Microeconomics versus Macroeconomics

Both microeconomists and macroeconomists study the actions of individuals, firms, and governments in both domestic and foreign economies. But the questions they ask and the perspectives they take differ. The terms *micro* and *macro* come from words meaning *small* and *large*. The terms refer to perspective, not to size. Thus we use the tools and concepts of microeconomics to study the behavior of a firm, regardless of whether the firm is as small as a local grocery store or as large as General Motors. We use macroeconomic concepts and analyses to study output, unemployment, and inflation in an economy as a whole, whether the economy is as small as that of Grenada or as large as that of the United States.

We use microeconomics to explain changes in the mix of goods and services produced—why we are producing more personal computers and fewer large automobiles, for example. We use macroeconomics to explain changes in the total level (quantity) of all goods and services produced. Economists measure this level, called **aggregate output**, as **gross national product (GNP)**. Macroeconomics thus may explain why GNP in 1982 was $83 billion less than in 1981 and why GNP increased at a faster rate in the 1960s than it has since.

Using microeconomics we also explore the distribution of jobs across industries and occupations—why there are more jobs in medical care and fewer in steel production, for example. Macroeconomics explores the total level (quantity) of employment (and unemployment). Why were 1.5 million more people unemployed in 1980 than in 1979? Why were over 9 percent of the workers in the United States unemployed in 1982–1983?

Finally, we use microeconomics to study relative prices of products and resources in an economy—why prices of compact disk players have fallen while college tuitions have risen, for example. But we use macroeconomics to study changes in the **general price level**, that is, the average price of all goods and services produced. Why did the general price level increase by over 10 percent per year from 1979 to 1981 but by under 4 percent per year from 1982 to 1986?

Microeconomic–macroeconomic interrelationships. Although it is convenient (and traditional) to study microeconomic and macroeconomic principles separately, such a division is artificial when we analyze real-world situations. After all, an economy's macroeconomic performance reflects choices in individual product markets. In exploring the effect of microeconomic decisions on macroeconomic results, however, we must avoid the *fallacy of composition*: What is true for an individual consumer or an individual market may not be true for the economy as a whole. For example, if you decide to spend more of your current income, prices and output in the economy will not be affected. But if all households in the economy do the same thing, prices will rise and total output will increase.

We must also avoid the *fallacy of division*: What is true for the economy as a whole may not be true for its each and every part. When unemployment increases, for example, only some individuals lose their jobs. When the average level of prices increases, some prices will rise, but some may stay the same and others may fall.

Nevertheless, you should always keep in mind that microeconomics and macroeconomics are two halves of the complete picture. Thus when economists

Aggregate output. The total quantity of all goods and services produced in the economy in a given period of time.

Gross national product (GNP). A measure of the total market value of all final goods and services produced in the economy during a given period of time.

General price level. The average price of all goods and services in the economy.

were exploring the potential effects of changes in the income tax law enacted in 1986, they considered the effects on macroeconomic factors, such as economic growth and inflation. But they also considered the effects on microeconomic factors, such as demand for U.S. exports and distribution of income. Both economic perspectives are important; they complement rather than substitute for each other.

In the rest of this chapter we turn our attention to the basic macroeconomic goals of full employment, economic growth, and price stability. You will learn how economists describe the ideal macroeconomic performance of the economy. Is it desirable, for example, to eliminate all unemployment? Does price stability mean that all prices remain constant? Economists would say the answer to both of these questions is no.

FULL EMPLOYMENT, UNEMPLOYMENT, AND ECONOMIC GOALS

Full employment is an important macroeconomic goal. The production possibilities curves presented in Chapter 2 show that at any particular time the economy has a certain potential to produce goods and services. This potential can only be realized if resources are fully employed. When they are not, aggregate output falls below the potential level and fewer wants can be satisfied.

Ideally, then, an economy should achieve full employment. But is all unemployment bad for the economy? What causes different types of unemployment? What policies should be used to address them? In this section, we answer these questions and explore government measures of unemployment and a practical goal for full employment.

Official Definition of Unemployment

Calvin Coolidge once remarked that when people are out of work, unemployment results. While not incorrect, this observation is not sufficient for our purposes. We must have a clearer definition and a better explanation of causes of unemployment. Although any resource can be employed or unemployed, the term *unemployment* is most often used to refer to the number of individuals out of work. But we certainly would not consider all idleness to be an economic problem. After all, no human being can work 24 hours a day, seven days a week.

If we want to know the extent to which unemployment is an economic problem, we have to make a distinction between voluntary and involuntary idleness. For example, a retired person who does not want to work should not be considered unemployed. We want to limit the definition to those who are actively seeking work but are unable to find jobs. However, it is not always easy to distinguish voluntary from involuntary choices statistically. In fact, defining and measuring unemployment (and its opposite, full employment) is partly a matter of judgment.

Despite the difficulties, we must be able to measure the magnitude of unemployment in order to evaluate the economy's performance. The Bureau of Labor Statistics, an agency of the federal government, officially measures employment and unemployment. The Bureau conducts the Current Population Survey, which is the basis for the labor-force statistics that are reported monthly in the

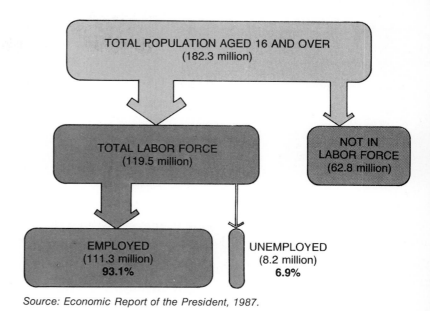

Exhibit 20.1
Population and Labor Force, 1986

Source: *Economic Report of the President, 1987.*

news media. Each month interviewers survey some 60,000 households that have been chosen statistically to represent the total U.S. population.* Interviewers ask about the activities of each household member during a given week, seeking to learn whether the individual was working, going to school, looking for a job, or retired.

Based on the responses, the bureau assigns individuals to one of three categories: (1) *employed* individuals—those who worked for one hour or more for pay during the survey week (or 15 hours or more without pay in a family-owned enterprise); (2) *unemployed* individuals—those who are without work but are actively looking for market work; and (3) individuals *not in the labor force*—those who are out of work but are not looking for work. The total number of people who are either employed or unemployed constitutes the **labor force**. Exhibit 20.1 shows the population aged 16 and over divided into these three categories for 1986. (Because individuals below the age of 16 are typically in school, labor force statistics are based only on those who are 16 and over.)

The labor-force statistic that gets the most public attention is the **unemployment rate**, or the percentage of the labor force that is unemployed. In 1986 the unemployment rate of 6.9 percent was calculated as follows:

$$\text{Unemployment rate} = \frac{\text{Number of unemployed}}{\text{Total labor force}} \times 100$$

$$= \frac{8.2 \text{ million}}{119.5 \text{ million}} \times 100 \quad \text{or} \quad 6.9\%$$

Labor force. The total number of individuals classified by government statistics as either employed or unemployed.

Unemployment rate. The number of individuals unemployed, expressed as a percentage of the labor force.

Interpreting changes in the unemployment rate is not always easy. Some reflect

_____

* Despite the relatively small number of households surveyed, statisticians believe the overall unemployment rate generated from the sample is accurate to within 0.1 percent.

Discouraged workers. Individuals who are out of work and who currently are not looking for work because they believe that they cannot find it. They are not officially classified as unemployed.

Underemployed. Individuals who have jobs but either work part-time when they would prefer full-time work or work at jobs below their capabilities and skills.

seasonal factors. For example, in the summer many young people are out of school and seeking summer jobs. Because such jobs are very hard to find (as all who have tried to find one will testify), the level of unemployment is somewhat exaggerated during the summer. The government therefore adjusts for seasonal factors in its published statistics. Other seasonal adjustments are made in September to reflect students' return to school and in December and January to reflect employment activity during the holiday season.

Who Is unemployed?

In order to understand better the official measure of unemployment, let's consider how government statistics classify several representative individuals. Hal Lerner goes to school full-time; he has no job and no time for one at present. Rita Tyre retired last year at age 65; she has no further interest in working. Most people would agree with the official government definition in these cases: Neither Hal nor Rita is unemployed because neither wants a job. They have chosen to spend their time in other ways and are considered—in official government statistics—to be "not in the labor force."

The government measure of unemployment also excludes Chris Kerr. Chris is raising six children and caring for the family's home. Certainly Chris is working, but he is not considered part of the official labor force because he is not exchanging his services in any market—nor is he seeking to.

What about individuals who are out of work and want jobs? Should all of them be counted as unemployed, or should they have to demonstrate that they are job hunting before being counted? Consider the case of Craig Eisweil, a freezer salesman in Nome, Alaska. Craig is a **discouraged worker**. He would like to have a job, but has given up looking because he does not think he can find one. Because the official definition requires that an unemployed individual be actively seeking work, Craig is not classified as unemployed.

Not all economists agree that discouraged workers should be excluded from government unemployment statistics. Critics argue that many discouraged workers do return to the job market when economic conditions improve. Thus their exclusion from the statistics may cause the official rate to understate unemployment when the economy slumps. Even though the government does not classify discouraged workers as part of the labor force, it does collect statistics on them. In the fourth quarter of 1986, the official unemployment rate was 6.8 percent; if discouraged workers had been included as unemployed, the rate would have been 7.6 percent.

And what about Amy Kau? Amy has a Ph.D. in agriculture, but after a long search could only find a part-time job in a local florist's shop. Amy would be considered **underemployed** because she is not working as much as she wants to or fully utilizing her skills. But Amy does have a job and is therefore considered employed in the official statistics. Some economists challenge this classification, arguing that it, too, understates the unemployment problem.

In other cases, official statistics may overstate the unemployment problem. For example, consider Russell Hack, the teenage son of a successful surgeon. In the past year, Russ has been looking off and on for a job. He has turned down a number of jobs as not "meaningful" enough. His older sister, Lena, graduated from college last month with a degree in philosophy. She has made it clear to potential employers that her minimum salary requirement is $100,000 per year. Should Russ and Lena be counted as unemployed?

Many people say no, but government statistics will count both as unemployed as long as they actively search for work. But should we include those who have rejected job offers, have a low labor-market commitment, or could be employed if they would accept the market wage? Obviously, the official government definition is, in some respects, a compromise.

Types of Unemployment and Economic Goals

Defining, measuring, and interpreting unemployment is difficult in part because individuals are unemployed for different reasons. Some are unemployed because they have been fired or laid off. Others have just begun looking for a job for the first time or after being out of the labor force for several years. Some are unemployed because they are searching for a better job. Others may lack the skills that employers are seeking or might be the victims of racial, sexual, or religious discrimination. Sometimes there may not be enough jobs in the economy as a whole.

Economists have developed several classifications of unemployment based on the reasons for unemployment. Each type of unemployment has a different effect on the goals of efficiency and equity and a different meaning for the goal of full employment. In fact, some unemployment actually benefits the economy as a whole (even though affected individuals are still harmed). Despite the definitions of these different types of unemployment, dividing the measured unemployment rate into separate parts is not possible.

Frictional unemployment. When interpreting government statistics, we must recognize that even in the best of times there is some unemployment. In fact, what economists call **frictional unemployment** is a natural and beneficial part of a market economy. When consumer demand changes, resources should move. For example, if demand for video cassette recorders increases and demand for paperback novels declines, resources (including labor) should shift from producing paperback novels to producing video cassette recorders.

But labor resources cannot move instantaneously, and information about job opportunities does not reach unemployed workers immediately. Thus we can expect some individuals to be unemployed for a short time when demand shifts. In addition, some workers, especially those for whom unemployment is not a terrible hardship, may be very particular about the type of work they will accept. As a result, they may choose an extended job search over any of the currently available jobs.

Because it is temporary and society receives benefits from resource mobility, frictional unemployment is not a major target of unemployment policy. A match between a frictionally unemployed worker and a job is simply a matter of time and job-search effort. Nevertheless, there are benefits to lowering even frictional unemployment. Improved labor-market information or efforts to speed job and geographic mobility may reduce frictional unemployment. Although *some* frictional unemployment serves a useful social purpose, unemployment beyond a certain level—whatever its cause—is a problem. The challenge to policy makers is to determine when unemployment is too high, that is, when higher unemployment involves extra social costs that exceed extra social benefits.

Structural unemployment. Unlike frictional unemployment, structural unemployment may persist over long periods of time. **Structural unemployment** results when unemployed individuals lack the necessary skills to fill available

Frictional unemployment. Unemployment resulting from normal job-search activities, or from imperfect knowledge and imperfect mobility. Although a permanent feature of a dynamic economy, frictional unemployment is temporary for any individual.

Structural unemployment. Unemployment resulting from a mismatch in the labor market between the location and skills of unemployed workers, the location and skill requirements of available jobs; may also reflect discrimination. Unlike with frictional unemployment, unemployment for individuals may be prolonged.

Cyclical unemployment. Unemployment resulting from decreases in aggregate economic output. Cyclical unemployment increases during recessions and decreases during recoveries.

Business cycle. The recurring but irregular swings in aggregate economic activity. A complete cycle has four phases: recession, trough, recovery, and peak.

Recession. The phase of the business cycle in which real aggregate output of the economy is decreasing.

jobs or live far away from areas where job vacancies exist. Discrimination may also cause structural unemployment. Structural unemployment has no real social benefits. But it cannot be easily or efficiently attacked by macroeconomic policies that are aimed simply at creating additional jobs. The only solutions involve relocating and/or retraining individuals, relocating or restructuring jobs, and reducing discriminatory barriers. Whether structural unemployment should be a social responsibility and whether efficient policies to reduce it can be found are strongly debated.

Business cycles and cyclical unemployment. The existence of frictional and structural unemployment means that even in the best of times we cannot expect the measured unemployment rate to be zero. However, changes in the level of GNP and in the rate of unemployment are indirectly related. For example, when GNP fell by 2.5 percent in 1982, the unemployment rate increased from 7.5 percent to 9.5 percent. The increase in unemployment associated with a decrease in GNP is what economists call **cyclical unemployment**.

Changes in cyclical unemployment are generally related to overall fluctuations in aggregate output called the **business cycle**. As shown in Exhibit 20.2, a business cycle has four phases: (1) during a **recession** the economy slows down and GNP

Exhibit 20.2
Phases of the Business Cycle
This graph shows a representative cycle for the U.S. economy. The *peak* of the business cycle corresponds to the maximum level of economic activity. As shown here, peaks occurred in the U.S. economy in 1973 and 1980. Note that the second peak is higher, indicating that the economy has grown. Following a peak, economic activity declines during the *recession* phase (1973–1975). At the *trough* (1975), economic activity reaches its lowest point. Following the trough, economic activity increases during the *recovery* phase of the cycle (1975–1980), culminating again in a peak.

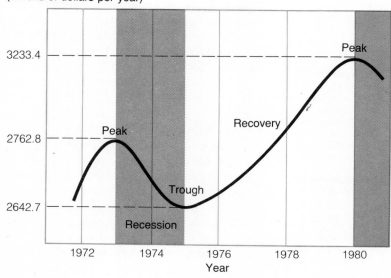

**Exhibit 20.3
Business Cycles Since
World War II**

Length of previous recovery (months)	Dates of recessions			Length of preceding recession (months)
	Peak	to	Trough	
37	November 1948	–	October 1949	11
45	July 1953	–	May 1954	10
41	August 1957	–	April 1958	8
24	April 1960	–	February 1961	10
104	December 1969	–	November 1970	11
36	November 1973	–	March 1975	16
58	January 1980	–	July 1980	6
12	July 1981	–	November 1982	16

drops; (2) at the **trough** GNP stops declining; (3) a **recovery** begins when GNP starts to rise; and (4) at the **peak** GNP stops rising. These fluctuations in aggregate activity have recurred in all market economies throughout history. Some economists, however, find the term *cycle* a bit misleading because it gives the impression that the fluctuations occur regularly. In fact, both their length and size are very irregular.

The National Bureau of Economic Research (NBER) unofficially designates recessions. Many economists define a recession as two consecutive quarters in which aggregate output declines. But the NBER, using a more complicated method, has identified eight recessions since the end of World War II. Exhibit 20.3 shows the dates of official recessions and associated peaks in business activity. Note that periods of recession are typically much shorter than periods of expansion or recovery.

We can view cyclical unemployment—too few jobs available at the current market rate for the number of individuals seeking employment—from at least two perspectives. First, we might conclude that the current market wage is too high; that is, it is above an equilibrium rate. If so, the obvious solution would be to lower wages to allow the labor market to reach equilibrium. When this occurs, everyone who seeks a job at the market wage will be able to find work. (There will still be frictional and structural unemployment, but no cyclical unemployment.)

Or, second, we can view cyclical unemployment as a result of a declining GNP. From this perspective cyclical unemployment represents too few jobs at the current wage. The obvious solution is to increase GNP and thus the number of jobs.

Most economists agree that, unlike frictional unemployment, cyclical unemployment is a problem, offering few benefits to balance against its costs. However, as the two possible views of cyclical unemployment suggest, economists do not agree on whether government should intervene or allow the economy to correct itself.

Unemployment and equity. Regardless of its causes, unemployment always has costs for those who are unemployed and face lower income. Equity concerns led to the federal government's unemployment insurance program. This program reduces the cost of unemployment to individuals by paying those who

Trough. The end of the recession phase; the point at which real aggregate output reaches its lowest level.

Recovery. The phase of the business cycle in which real aggregate output of the economy is increasing.

Peak. The end of the recovery phase; the point at which real aggregate output reaches its highest level.

have lost a job a portion of the wage they would otherwise have received. However, as with many programs, there is a trade-off between equity and efficiency. To some extent, paying individuals to look for jobs may prolong their job search and thus lead to higher unemployment.

Equity issues are also raised because different groups are affected differently by unemployment. For example, the unemployment rate for blacks has consistently been twice that for whites. The unemployment rate for women has consistently been higher than that for men. The reasons behind these differentials are complex and not easily measured.

To the extent that such differentials reflect discrimination, they are an equity concern. However, they may also reflect differences in education, experience, and intensity of job search. Because value judgments are required, economists cannot scientifically calculate the equity costs of unemployment. Nevertheless, concern about equity is a major reason why unemployment is perceived as an economic and a political problem.

Natural, or "Full-Employment," Unemployment Rate

Just as the definition of unemployment is a compromise, so too is the definition and measurement of its opposite: full employment. In Chapter 2, we associated full employment with operating on the production possibilities frontier. That is, full employment is achieved when the economy produces at its full potential.

But does the economy reach full employment only when the measured unemployment rate is zero? Economists generally answer *no*. In fact, as we noted earlier, some frictional unemployment is useful and efficient because it is a response to changes in consumer demand and worker preferences. But what about structural and cyclical unemployment? As we defined it, structural unemployment reflects a mismatch between unemployed workers and job vacancies. It is not a temporary condition and is not easily reduced by macroeconomic policies. For this reason, economists generally agree that some structural unemployment is also consistent with the concept of production possibilities and thus with full employment. In contrast, economists generally agree that cyclical unemployment is inconsistent with full employment.

The unemployment that remains when all cyclical unemployment has been eliminated is known as the **natural rate of unemployment**. In theory, this rate is the expected level of frictional and structural unemployment when the economy is producing at its full potential. Thus the natural rate of unemployment could also be called the *full-employment* unemployment rate. As with many economic variables, measurements of the natural rate are debatable. Current estimates range from 5 to 7 percent.

Defining the full-employment unemployment rate as "natural" does not mean that it represents some law of nature. Rather, it reflects the typical or normal functioning of the market economy. Moreover, defining full employment to include some frictional and structural unemployment does not mean that economists believe that all such unemployment cannot and should not be attacked. If remedies that provide greater extra benefits than extra costs can be found, they should be used to lower frictional or structural unemployment.

Natural rate of unemployment. The unemployment rate achieved when the economy has eliminated all cyclical unemployment; sometimes referred to as the *full-employment* unemployment rate.

Potential GNP. The aggregate output that could be produced with the available technology if labor and other economic resources were fully employed.

GNP gap. The difference between real GNP and potential GNP for a specific period of time. When positive, it measures the output lost as a result of unemployment.

Inflation. A sustained upward movement in the general level of prices.

Price index. A measure of price level in a given year as a percentage of the price level in some specified base, or reference, year.

Consumer price index (CPI). A price index reflecting changes in the prices of consumer goods; involves the use of a constant market-basket approach.

RECAP

The official definition of the unemployed is an individual without a job who is actively looking for a job. Retired individuals, full-time students, and full-time homemakers are excluded.

There are three types of unemployment: frictional, structural, and cyclical. Frictional unemployment occurs when individuals first enter or leave the job market or move from industry to industry. Structural unemployment occurs when the skills of the unemployed do not match the skills required by vacant jobs. Cyclical unemployment occurs when the number of unemployed exceeds the number of jobs available.

Full employment—the natural rate of unemployment—is the level of unemployment that would occur if the economy were producing at its potential GNP level. Full employment is consistent with some frictional and structural unemployment but not with any cyclical unemployment.

The GNP gap is the difference between potential and actual GNP. A positive gap indicates that potential GNP is more than actual GNP. A negative gap indicates that potential GNP is less than actual GNP.

Full Employment and Potential GNP

We can use the concept of the natural rate of unemployment to define and measure full employment. It is the employment level in an economy that has fully adjusted to all existing macroeconomic conditions. Thus **potential GNP** is the level of aggregate output that would be produced if the economy eliminated cyclical unemployment (where actual and natural unemployment rates are equal). By comparing actual GNP in any year to potential GNP, we can measure the amount of output lost when the economy fails to maintain full employment.

The difference between actual and potential GNP, called the **GNP gap**, is often expressed as a percentage of potential GNP. For example, in the fourth quarter of 1986 the GNP gap was estimated to be $176.4 billion, or 4.6 percent of potential. That is, the economy lost $176.4 billion of aggregate output because it failed to attain full employment. In other words, the economy produced only 95.4 percent of the output it could have produced if cyclical unemployment had been zero.

Potential GNP and the natural rate of unemployment give economists a framework for defining and measuring the admittedly ambiguous term *full employment*. But as with almost all economic measures, we are unable to precisely measure potential GNP and the natural rate of unemployment. Thus although economists generally find these concepts useful, they often disagree about the accuracy of any particular measure. Despite this difficulty, we will use the concepts of potential GNP and the natural rate of unemployment as a standard against which to judge the economy's performance.

PRICE STABILITY, INFLATION, AND ECONOMIC GOALS

Another macroeconomic goal, price stability, refers to stability in the general price level. Macroeconomists want to know the significance of changes in the price level for the economy as a whole and for particular groups within the economy. Since World War II, the general price level has consistently moved upward. Such a sustained upward movement is what economists call **inflation**. Inflation was especially high in the United States in the 1970s. Although recent experience has been good (by comparison), inflation is still a potential concern.

Measuring the General Price Level

Economists measure the general price level by constructing a **price index**. A price index measures the price level in a given period of time as a percentage of the price level in a selected *base* (reference) *year*. The most publicized price index is the **consumer price index (CPI)**. As its name implies, this index reflects changes in the prices of a wide range of consumer goods and services. The index is calculated and published monthly by the Bureau of Labor Statistics.

To construct the index the Bureau first identifies a "market basket," reflecting what a "typical" urban family might buy. Currently the CPI market basket is based on a 1982–1984 survey of consumer buying habits. Each month, surveyors shop 85 urban areas to see how much it would currently cost a family to buy the designated items. The limited nature of the items in the market basket means that

Year	CPI (1967 = 100)	Inflation rate (% change in CPI)	Year	CPI (1967 = 100)	Inflation rate (% change in CPI)
1960	88.1	1.6	1974	147.1	11.0
1961	89.6	1.0	1975	161.2	9.1
1962	90.6	1.1	1976	170.5	5.8
1963	91.7	1.2	1977	181.5	6.5
1964	92.9	1.3	1978	195.4	7.7
1965	94.5	1.7	1979	217.4	11.3
1966	97.2	2.9	1980	246.8	13.5
1967	100.0	2.9	1981	272.4	10.5
1968	104.2	4.2	1982	289.1	6.1
1969	109.8	5.4	1983	298.4	3.2
1970	116.3	5.9	1984	311.1	4.3
1971	121.3	4.3	1985	322.2	3.6
1972	125.3	3.3	1986	328.4	1.9
1973	133.1	6.2			

Exhibit 20.4
Consumer Price Index and Annual Inflation Rates

Source: Economic Report of the President, 1987.

the CPI does not measure all price changes. (We illustrate the calculation of price indexes in the appendix to this chapter.)

Price-level changes and the rate of inflation. Exhibit 20.4 shows the CPI from 1960 to 1986. The rate "1967 = 100" indicates that the base year for CPI is 1967. Thus the CPI in any year indicates how much more or less it cost to buy the same items than it would have cost in 1967, the base year. For example, the 1985 CPI value was 322.2. Thus the average price of the items in the CPI market basket in 1985 was 322.2 percent of the average price in 1967. In other words, an item that cost $100 in 1967 would have cost $322.20 in 1985, if its price had increased at the average rate of the CPI.

Economists are concerned mainly with *changes* in the CPI, not in its actual value. The percentage change in the CPI can be used to measure the percentage change in the general price level. Technically, a one-year increase in the general price level is not inflation—economists use the term *inflation* to refer to *sustained increases* in the general price level. However, following normal terminology, Exhibit 20.4 shows inflation rates calculated as the percentage change in the price level from one year to the next. For example, between 1984 and 1985 the CPI increased from 311.1 to 322.2, a 3.6 percent increase or inflation rate. We calculate this figure as follows:

$$\text{Inflation rate, 1984–1985} = \frac{\text{CPI}_{1985} - \text{CPI}_{1984}}{\text{CPI}_{1984}} \times 100$$

$$= \frac{322.2 - 311.1}{311.1} \times 100 \quad \text{or} \quad 3.6\%$$

We multiply the ratio by 100 to change the decimal fraction to a percent. Each of the inflation rates shown in Exhibit 20.4 was calculated the same way. To check your understanding of this formula and this concept, calculate some of the other rates shown.

Price-level changes and the value of money.   The data in Exhibit 20.4 clearly indicate that the general price level has increased rather significantly over the period shown. In order to understand why inflation is bad, you must first understand the implications of a change in the price level. Economists recognize that a change in the price level means a change in the value of money. We have not said much about money so far other than using a monetary unit—the dollar— to express price and to measure other economic variables such as income and government expenditures. But what is a dollar worth? In economic terms, the value of a dollar is measured by the amount of economic goods and services that it will buy. For this reason, an increase in the general price level will lower the value of a dollar.

For example, in 1975 a single-dip ice cream cone cost about 25 cents; in 1985 one cost about 50 cents. Thus a dollar was worth 4 ice cream cones in 1975 but only 2 cones in 1985. The same was true for prices in general. Between 1975 and 1985 the general price level (CPI) also doubled, indicating that a dollar bought about half as much in 1985 as in 1975. *An increase in the general price level decreases the purchasing power of money, that is, the amount of economic goods and services or resources that you can buy with a given number of dollars.*

Economic Facts and Changes in the General Price Level

Changes in the purchasing power of money create a problem in measuring economic variables. When the value of the dollar changes, we have to translate values into constant units to obtain a valid measurement. The following example may help you see the problem.

You want to know how much your nephew has grown in the last two years. You know that two years ago, he was one-half as tall as the small pine tree in your sister's front yard. If you learn that he is now only one-fourth as tall as the tree, would you believe that he has shrunk? Probably not. After all, you have been comparing the height of your nephew with a measure—the pine tree—that is not a constant size. In order to learn how much he has grown, you must compare his height with something that has remained a constant size, such as the height of the rock wall in the back yard.

We cannot use the height of a rock wall to measure economic variables, such as income or expenditures. It is important, however, to have a method of express- ing value in constant terms. When variables are measured in **nominal** terms, they refer to actual dollars and actual prices. To adjust from nominal to **real** terms, economists remove the effects of changes in the price level and express the variables in terms of dollars of constant purchasing power. Economists call this translation or adjustment "deflating" nominal values.

Imagine a very simple economy in which the only product offered for sale is postcards. Suppose that in 1987 you had $200 of income and postcards cost $1 each. In real terms—the maximum number of postcards you can buy—is 200. Suppose that in 1988 your income increases to $300. However, because the price of a postcard increases to $2.00, you can now buy only 150 postcards. The increase in the price of a postcard caused a decline in the value of a dollar. A dollar in 1987 was worth one postcard; in 1988 it was worth only one-half a postcard.

We can express your income in 1988 in two ways. Your **nominal income** (the number of actual dollars) increased by $100, or 50 percent. However, because

Nominal. A term used to identify economic variables measured in terms of current prices.

Real. A term used to identify economic variables measured in terms of constant prices of some base year.

Nominal income. The actual number of dollars of income earned, expressed in terms of current dollars unadjusted for changes in the general price level.

Real income. Income expressed in terms of its purchasing power; nominal income adjusted to remove the effects of changes in the general price level.

the price of a postcard increased by 100 percent, your **real income** (the number of postcards you can buy) fell. If nominal income (or any other nominal value) increases more slowly than the average price of goods and services, its real value will fall. On the other hand, if prices and nominal income rise at the same rate, real income will be unchanged.

In a more complex economy, we use price indexes to translate from nominal to real terms. When we use the CPI, we are in effect translating nominal income or expenditures into "market-basket" equivalents. That is, if the CPI increases by 25 percent, it will take 25 percent more real dollars to purchase the same market

A Case in Point
Using Price Indexes

When the general price level changes, so does the real dollar value of economic variables. Price indexes can be used in two ways: (1) to translate values from nominal into real terms; and (2) to adjust nominal values of pensions or wages in order to preserve their purchasing power.

Using the CPI to Deflate Nominal Values

The data in Exhibit 20C.1 illustrate how the income of the Frieze household can be deflated (translated from nominal into real terms) using the consumer price index. The second column shows the family's nominal income in each of three years. The third column shows the corresponding values of the CPI index (from Exhibit 20.4). The fourth column shows the family's real income, that is, their income after correcting for changes in the purchasing power of the dollar. Because 1967 is used as the base year for the CPI, the family's real income is expressed in terms of the purchasing power of 1967 dollars.

Exhibit 20C.1
Deflating Nominal Income

Year	Nominal income (current dollars)	CPI (1967 = 100)	Real income (constant dollars)
1983	30,000	298.4	10,054
1984	30,600	311.1	9,836
1985	33,660	322.2	10,447

To deflate the Frieze's income, we want to remove the influence of changes in prices. The CPI tells us how much we have to change nominal income to put all figures on a price-adjusted basis. The value of the CPI in 1983 was 298.4. That is, it took $298.40 in 1983 to buy what $100 would have bought in 1967, or in equation form,

$$\frac{\$298.40 \text{ of income}}{\text{at 1983 prices}} = \frac{\$100.00 \text{ of income}}{\text{at 1967 prices}}$$

Dividing both sides by $298.40, the value of the CPI in 1983, we have

$$\frac{\$1.00 \text{ of income}}{\text{at 1983 prices}} = \frac{\$0.3351 \text{ of income}}{\text{at 1967 prices}}$$

In other words, the purchasing power of a dollar in 1983 was only 33.51 percent of that in 1967. Thus to translate the family's income in 1983 into the equivalent purchasing power in 1967 dollars, we can use the following relationship:

$$\begin{array}{c}\text{Real income} \\ \text{in 1967} \\ \text{dollars}\end{array} = \frac{\text{Nominal income in 1983 dollars}}{\text{CPI in 1983}} \times 100$$

$$= \frac{\$30,000}{298.4}(100) \quad \text{or} \quad \$10,054$$

We used a similar procedure to translate the Frieze's income in each of the other two years into real terms. The family's nominal income increased by 2 percent from 1983 to 1984; however, prices increased by 4.3 percent. Because the price level increased faster than nominal income, the family's real income fell. Between 1984 and 1985, prices rose by 3.6 percent; the family's

Nominal GNP. The value of the gross national product measured by current quantities and current prices.

Real GNP. The value of the gross national product measured by current quantities and constant prices.

basket of goods contained in the CPI. Any nominal value that increases by less than 25 percent will fall in real terms. (See A Case in Point: Using Price Indexes, which indicates how such adjustments are made.)

Similarly, we make a distinction between **nominal GNP** and **real GNP**. Only by adjusting nominal GNP for changes in the general price level can we know how much of any change reflects increased production and how much reflects changes in the general price level. (We discuss the specific index used to adjust from nominal to real GNP in Chapter 21, but all indexes remove the distorting effect of price-level changes.)

nominal income increased by 10 percent. Because nominal income increased faster than the price level, the family's real income increased. To check your understanding of the deflation process, apply the same procedure to the other two years.

Using the CPI to Index Nominal Values

To prevent the real value of wages from falling, some labor unions have negotiated indexing clauses in their contracts. Some government transfers, such as Social Security, and some private pensions are also indexed. A price index such as the CPI can be used to determine how much the nominal values of wages, transfers, or pensions must increase to maintain their real values.

The data in Exhibit 20C.2 show how indexing affects the finances of John Elderidge. John retired on December 31, 1982. He was entitled to a monthly, fully

Exhibit 20C.2
Indexing a Pension

Year	CPI as of December	Percentage change in CPI	Real value of pension	Nominal value of pension in January
1982	292.4	—	$171.00	$500.00
1983	303.5	3.80	171.00	519.00
1984	315.5	3.95	171.00	539.50
1985	327.4	3.77	171.00	559.85

Note: The nominal pensions are as of January of the following year. That is, $519.00 is the nominal pension as of January 1984, which reflects the inflation that occurred in 1983.

indexed pension that in January 1983 had a nominal value of $500. Using the December 1982 value of the CPI, his pension had a real value of $171. According to the terms of his pension plan, John's nominal pension changes each January by the same percentage as the CPI in the previous year.

We can calculate the nominal pension values in January in one of two ways. First, we can calculate the percentage increase in the CPI and apply this percentage increase to the previous nominal value. For example, between December 1982 and December 1983, the CPI increased by 3.8 percent. Thus his nominal pension will increase to $519 per month as of January 1984. Second, the increase can be calculated as

$$\begin{array}{c}\text{Real pension} \\ \text{in base year} \\ \text{dollars}\end{array} = \frac{\text{Nominal pension in January}}{\text{CPI in previous December}} \times 100$$

$$\$171.00 = \frac{\text{Nominal pension in January 1984}}{\text{CPI in December 1983}} \times 100$$

Thus,

$$\begin{array}{c}\text{Nominal pension} \\ \text{in January 1984}\end{array} = \$171 \times \frac{\text{CPI in}}{\text{December 1983}} \times 100$$

$$= \$519$$

The other values in Exhibit 20C.2 can be calculated in the same way. Note that this type of indexing (a common form) will not prevent John's real monthly income from falling *during* the year. The lag in the adjustment will cause some erosion of purchasing power during the year. To check your understanding of indexing, verify the nominal pension that John received in January 1985 and January 1986.

Standard of living. The quantity of wants that can be satisfied, or the quantity of goods and services that can be purchased, with current income.

The important point here is that values expressed in terms of actual dollars, that is, in nominal terms, are potentially misleading whenever the general price level has changed. Throughout your study of macroeconomics you must be careful to distinguish between nominal and real values and between higher dollar prices and higher relative prices. Otherwise, you will find it impossible to correctly interpret economic "facts."

Inflation and the Standard of Living

Having seen how a change in the price level affects the interpretation of economic measurements, you are now ready to consider an important question: Is inflation necessarily a problem? Many people believe that inflation is a problem because they think that it automatically means a decline in their **standard of living**. But in economic terms, a decline in the standard of living occurs only when most households (or an identifiable group of households) cannot satisfy as many of their wants as before. Thus the standard of living depends on the quantity of economic goods and services that households can consume. Changes in the price level and changes in the standard of living are not necessarily connected.

Similarly, people often believe that inflation increases their cost of living. This is true only if we define cost in nominal terms, that is, as the average *dollar* cost of purchasing the goods and services required to maintain a certain standard of living. If a higher dollar cost is matched by an equal change in nominal (dollar) income, the *average* standard of living remains unchanged.

It is important to distinguish between a change in the purchasing power of money and the standard of living. A decline in purchasing power occurs whenever the general level of prices increases. A decline in the standard of living occurs only to the extent that nominal income does not rise enough to offset the change in prices.

Sometimes, however, price levels and income do not move at the same rate. For example, between 1929 and 1933, average prices fell by nearly 25 percent, but nominal income fell by over 50 percent. In this case lower prices did not improve the standard of living. Individuals who *had the same income* could purchase more because of lower prices. However, most people suffered a decline in real income and thus could afford to buy less. And between 1970 and 1979, the general price level increased by 80 percent, while nominal income increased by 147 percent. Although prices increased, nominal income rose faster. As a result, real income and the real standard of living went up. These examples indicate that the average standard of living for the economy as a whole is not affected in any consistent manner by changes in the general price level. What is important is whether real income and real output in the economy are increasing.

Inflation and Equity

If inflation does not necessarily mean that the average standard of living is lower, why are government officials, economists, and consumers so concerned about inflation? In the first place, inflation is always a problem for those whose income does not rise as fast as the general price level rises. It is also a problem when the prices of some goods rise more than others, as is often the case. In both situations, inflation raises equity issues.

For example, suppose that you lease an apartment for one year at a fixed rent of $500 per month. If the general level of prices increases during the year, the

Indexation. Adjusting the nominal values of wages, transfer payments, income tax brackets, or other economic variables in direct proportion to changes in the general price level.

real cost of your rent will decrease. You will gain but your landlord will lose. Of course, your landlord is likely to be aware of the potential effect of inflation and has probably considered it when determining your rent. If so, your landlord will lose only if prices rise more than anticipated.

Who wins and who loses from inflation is especially important to borrowers and lenders. In the 1950s and early 1960s, for example, home mortgage loans were available at interest rates of 3–4 percent. But inflation in the late 1960s rose to over 5 percent and averaged 7 percent from 1968 to 1982. With interest payments less than the rate of inflation, borrowers paid for their homes with "cheaper" dollars. Borrowers were pleased, but banks were not. However, inflation in the mid-1980s fell more rapidly than expected. Some people who had borrowed in the late 1970s and early 1980s were forced to pay the banks more, in real terms, than they had planned. Repayment became a very large problem for many farmers, whose real income was falling at the same time their real debt payments were increasing.

Finally, inflation raises equity questions because the nominal incomes of some individuals may not increase as fast as prices. For example, if retired individuals depend on fixed pensions, they will be hurt by inflation. Congress has *indexed* many federal benefit programs, raising payments as the CPI rises. **Indexation** refers to the procedure of adjusting the nominal value of something in order to maintain its real value. It has had a major impact on government transfer payments. Each 1 percent increase in the CPI causes an estimated $4.6 billion increase in federal transfers to Social Security, military, and civil service retirees and food stamp recipients.

Some politicians defend indexation as protecting the real value of government transfers for the recipients. Others oppose automatic spending increases, pointing to the already enormous federal budget deficit and the possibility that the CPI may overstate inflation. To the extent that the CPI overstates inflation, using it to index government transfers and pensions increases their real cost to the economy and the real income of those receiving payments.

Inflation and Efficiency

Rapid and unpredictable changes in the general price level may also decrease efficiency in the economy. For example, if your boss gives you a 10 percent raise at the same time the general price level increases 15 percent, you have actually received a wage cut. In hindsight, you can easily see whether you have gained or lost, but you may not have been able to when you got the raise. If you misunderstand the real economic meaning of your raise, you may not respond appropriately. Decreased real wages signal resources (including you) to seek other employment. If they do not, efficiency suffers (and your real income will fall).

In addition, when virtually all prices in the economy are changing, a business manager may not be sure whether a price rise signals increased demand or merely a rise in the general price level. A manager who mistakes changed demand for simple price inflation will respond inappropriately, and efficiency will suffer. Inefficiency is most likely when the rate of inflation is high and fluctuating, since such inflation creates considerable uncertainty.

Many costs of inflation stem from uncertainty. However, inflation imposes costs on the economy even when it is correctly anticipated. For example, many individuals buy gold, real estate, or works of art in expectation of inflation. If, as buyers hope, the prices of these products rise at rates equal to or above that of inflation,

RECAP

Economists measure the general price level using price indexes, such as the Consumer Price Index. The percentage change in the price index from one year to the next is called the inflation rate.

Increases in the general price level decrease the purchasing power of money. Economic variables such as income or GNP measured in dollar terms must be translated from nominal terms (actual dollars) to real terms (purchasing power). Changes in real income or real GNP change the standard of living.

Inflation redistributes wealth and raises questions of equity. Inflation also distorts price signals and causes individuals to spend time and energy seeking to avoid its effects, raising questions of efficiency.

Price stability requires a relatively stable general price level but allows changes in relative prices to signal changes in resource scarcity and in personal preferences.

the buyers' wealth is protected. Although these purchases are not necessarily harmful, they may direct attention away from more productive uses of time, human energy, and financial assets. To the extent that they do, efficiency suffers. When inflation is both high and uncertain, individuals and businesses spend considerable amounts of time and energy seeking ways to "beat inflation." Although it may pay for individuals to do this, such activities rarely add to the country's overall productivity.

Businesses may also be misled by actual increased consumer demand during inflationary periods. Since inflation reduces the purchasing power of money, individuals who anticipate inflation may try to beat it by spending before the purchasing power of their money declines. That is, they may reduce current saving in order to buy products today that they will not consume until much later. This change in buying habits is not necessarily bad, but it may give businesses false signals about demand for certain products and may lower efficiency.

Price Stability: What Should Be the Goal?

If you are a typical college freshman, you probably have not lived in a year without inflation. Almost every political leader in recent times has worried about inflation and has wanted (or at least stated a desire) to control it. When we speak of achieving price stability, however, we do not mean that all prices should remain constant. Because changes in the prices of individual products and resources are the sources of the market system's information, we expect and even desire changes in relative prices. The goal of price stability is stable *average* prices. To accomplish this goal, prices of goods for which demand is decreasing must fall to offset the rising prices of goods for which demand is increasing.

However, some economists believe that the cost of absolute price stability may be too high. The connection between inflation and unemployment is that an increasing demand for goods results in more jobs and less employment, but greater demand also puts upward pressure on prices. Some economists argue that, in the short run, it may be preferable to trade somewhat higher rates of inflation for somewhat lower rates of unemployment. Politicians who set policy seem to prefer this option, fearing the wrath of an unemployed electorate. As you will discover in your study of macroeconomics, it is rarely possible to work on all of the macroeconomic goals at once. Trade-offs—whether between price stability and unemployment or between price stability and economic growth—may be inevitable.

MACROECONOMIC PERFORMANCE: THE U.S. ECONOMY

We would not expect any real-world economy to perform perfectly. But we are interested in knowing how closely the U.S. economy has come to meeting the goals of price stability, full employment, and economic growth. As you will see in this section, the historical record shows both successes and failures.

Exhibit 20.5
The Level of Aggregate Output: 1909–1986
The graph shows aggregate output (measured as real GNP) from 1909–1986. Data is plotted on a ratio or log scale in which the intervals represent equal percentage changes. Over the period shown, aggregate output has generally increased: The average growth rate has been 3.2 percent per year. There are also periodic fluctuations, the most severe of which occurred in the pre–World War II era.

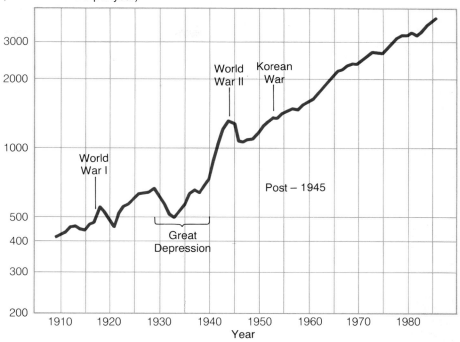

Aggregate output (real GNP)
(billions of dollars per year)

Economic Stability and Economic Growth

Exhibit 20.5 shows the level of aggregate output from 1909 to 1986. Typically, aggregate output is shown as real GNP. We get several general impressions from Exhibit 20.5. First, despite a generally upward trend, the graph shows clear and persistent fluctuations (both upward and downward). These fluctuations are more frequent and more severe in the years before World War II (1909–1941) than after the war. Nevertheless, aggregate output has generally risen. In fact, we could approximate growth in aggregate output from 1950 to the present by a straight line. Over that period the average rate of increase has been about 3.2 percent per year.

Full Employment

Exhibit 20.6 shows that the unemployment rate fluctuated greatly prior to World War II. At the peak of the Great Depression in the 1930s, one of every four workers was unemployed. While this represented the worst case of unemployment in the United States in this century, unemployment has been a fairly constant source of concern.

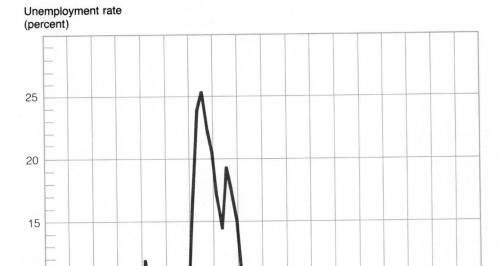

Unemployment rate
(percent)

Year

Exhibit 20.6
The Aggregate
Unemployment Rate:
1900–1986
This graph indicates that the
unemployment rate in the
U.S. economy has fluctuated
widely. The fluctuations are
more pronounced in the pre–
World War II era. In the post–
World War II era, the rate has
shown an upward trend.

Sources: Historical Statistics of the United States; Economic Report of the President, 1987.

Unemployment during recent business cycles. Exhibit 20.7 shows
changes in both real GNP and the overall unemployment rate from 1955 to 1986
and the peaks in the business cycles during this period. From this information we
can make two observations: First, changes in real GNP seem to be inversely related
to changes in unemployment; when GNP grows, unemployment falls. Second, the
unemployment rates associated with peaks in the business cycle have increased
(except for the peak in 1969). Indeed, as the economy recovered following the
recession in 1982, unemployment fell—but remained above 7 percent for almost
4 years.

What does this second observation mean in terms of macroeconomic performance? You might expect that full employment accompanies peaks in business
activity. Do the data then imply that we have been less and less successful in
reaching full employment? Do they mean that the natural rate of unemployment
has changed over the years? Economists disagree strongly about the meaning of
these data. Some believe that the natural rate of unemployment has increased
greatly since the 1960s and may now be as high as 6–7 percent. Others, even
those who accept some increase in the natural rate, believe that the economy has
failed to reach its full employment potential in the 1980s.

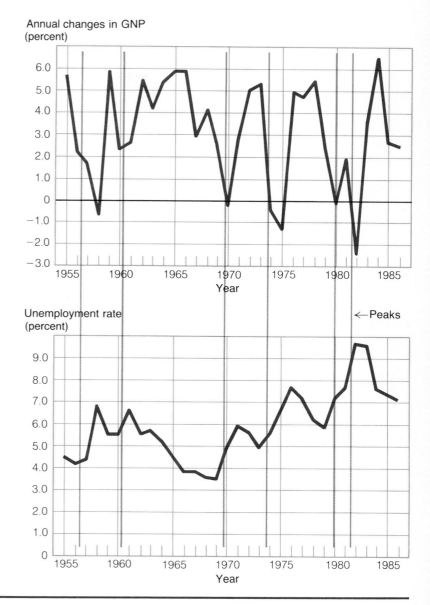

Exhibit 20.7
Changes in GNP and the
Unemployment Rate: 1955–1986
The two graphs indicate that the unemployment rate is inversely associated with changes in real GNP: When real GNP increases, the unemployment rate falls. However, the unemployment rate associated with *peaks* in the business cycle appears to have increased over time. Many economists associate at least part of this phenomenon to increases in the natural rate of unemployment.

GNP gaps as measures of full employment.   Exhibit 20.8 shows one estimate of the GNP gap, both in dollars and as a percentage of potential output, for the years 1955–1986. As you can see, in most years the GNP gap was positive, indicating that actual GNP was below potential GNP. For much of the last two decades, the GNP gap has been substantial. In 1982, for example, the GNP gap was estimated to be $290.4 billion, or 8.4 percent below potential output.

For a few years, however, especially in the late 1960s, the GNP gap was negative. That is, actual GNP exceeded potential GNP. That actual output could exceed potential output may sound strange. However, potential output and the natural rate of unemployment both reflect the behavior of the labor force under

Year	Gap in billions of 1982 dollars	As a percent of potential GNP	Year	Gap in billions of 1982 dollars	As a percent of potential GNP
1957	4.9	0.3	1972	−22.5	−0.9
1958	66.8	4.2	1973	−69.1	−2.6
1959	29.2	1.8	1974	35.1	1.3
1960	46.9	2.7	1975	151.5	5.3
1961	59.3	3.4	1976	103.4	3.5
1962	26.2	1.4	1977	57.6	1.9
1963	12.1	0.6	1978	−10.5	−0.3
1964	−47.8	−2.5	1979	2.9	0.1
1965	−64.4	−3.2	1980	94.2	2.9
1966	−111.8	−5.3	1981	118.9	3.5
1967	−98.9	−4.6	1982	290.4	8.4
1968	−114.4	−5.1	1983	268.4	7.6
1969	−90.5	−3.9	1984	151.0	4.1
1970	0.3	0.0	1985	151.6	4.1
1971	15.2	0.6	1986	160.3	4.2

Exhibit 20.8
GNP Gap: 1957–1986

Sources: Natural GNP data excerpted from Robert J. Gordon, *Macroeconomics,* 4th ed., Table A-1. Copyright © 1987 by Robert J. Gordon. Reprinted by permission of Little, Brown; actual GNP obtained from *Economic Report of the President, 1987,* Table B-2.

"normal" conditions. That is, individuals normally engage in a certain amount of job searching and are willing to trade only a certain amount of leisure for market work.

But such constraints are not absolute. Individuals may be induced to work a few more hours a week for a period of time, or employers may accept workers they might otherwise reject if demand is temporarily high. Potential GNP can be exceeded temporarily since it does not represent a *physical* or *technological* maximum.

Price Stability

Exhibit 20.9 shows how the general price level has fluctuated during the period 1909–1986. (The specific price index graphed, called the GNP deflator, functions much like the CPI; we explain it in Chapter 21.) However, since World War II (1946–1986), prices have consistently moved upward, accelerating rapidly in the 1970s. Thus inflation has been a major fact of economic life for some time.

Two Periods in Recent Macroeconomic History

Looking more closely at the data, we can divide the post–World War II years into two periods. Between 1945 and 1970, policy makers saw a straightforward trade-off between high prices and high economic growth. When the economy grew rapidly and unemployment was low, as in the late 1960s, inflation increased. When unemployment was high and economic growth low, as in the late 1950s, inflation was low. Thus policy makers generally opted for moderate growth in aggregate output and slowly rising prices.

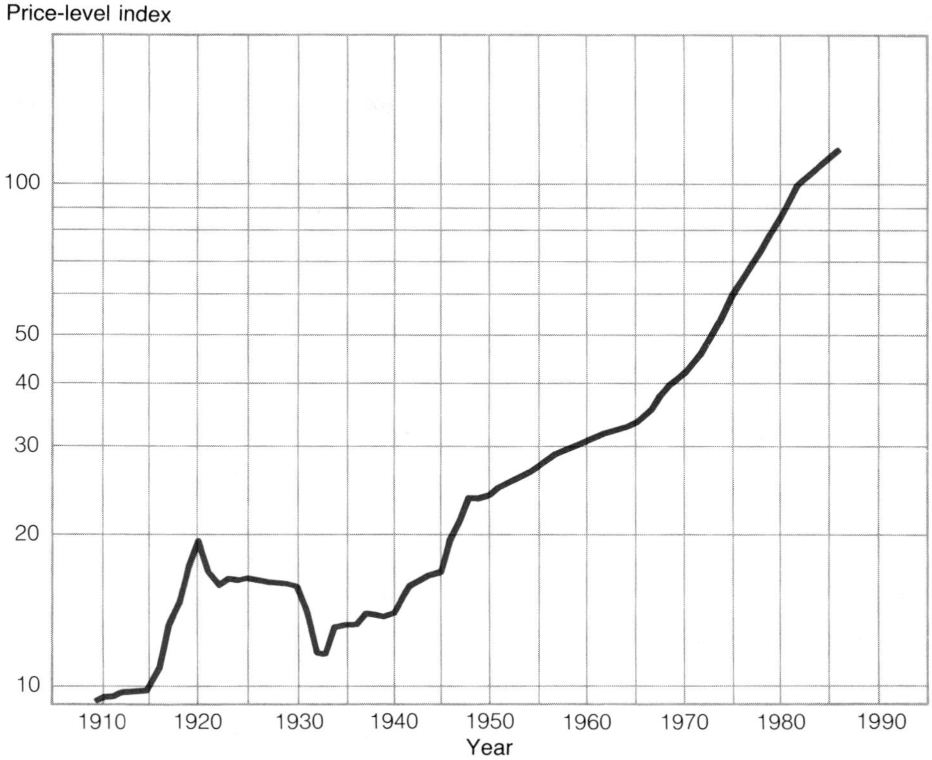

Price-level index

Sources: U.S. Department of Commerce, Bureau of Economic Analysis; *Economic Report of the President, 1987.*

Exhibit 20.9
The General Level of Prices: 1909–1986
This graph indicates how the general price level of the U.S. economy has fluctuated. In the pre–World War II period, prices sometimes rose and sometimes fell. However, since World War II, there has been a consistent upward trend in prices, with an acceleration in the 1970s. The graph is drawn on a ratio scale in which the units on the vertical axis represent equal percentage changes in prices, not equal absolute changes. *Note:* This is a plot of the GNP deflator, a particular measure of the general price level. We discuss the meaning and construction of this measure in Chapter 21.

Stagflation. A period of time during which the total output of the economy falls, while the levels of general prices and unemployment rise.

In the 1970s, however, the economy experienced both rising unemployment and increased inflation. Twice in the decade—in 1970–71 and in 1974–75—aggregate output decreased while inflation accelerated. Unemployment averaged 30–40 percent higher than in the 1950s or 1960s. The average rate of inflation was more than twice as high. Economists termed this double whammy **stagflation**, indicating the combination of stagnation (or recession) and inflation. In dealing with stagflation, the macroeconomic policies chosen in the 1970s appear to have failed. But the economy's performance does not depend solely on such policies. Twice during the 1970s (1973–1974 and 1979–1980), energy prices skyrocketed. The macroeconomic consequences of these events must also be considered when judging the policies used.

Controversy over interpretation of macroeconomic data is typical. As you have seen, some economists even question whether measures such as the unemployment rate and the CPI are accurate. What causes macroeconomic outcomes is even more controversial. In the following chapters, we identify and describe the basic factors that, we believe, determine macroeconomic outcomes. Only with this background will you be able to rationally consider the likely results of different macroeconomic policies.

A PREVIEW OF AGGREGATE DEMAND AND AGGREGATE SUPPLY

Economists generally agree that demand and supply are useful tools for exploring both microeconomic and macroeconomic issues. Recall that microeconomists use demand and supply to analyze changes in price and output for individual goods. Macroeconomists use **aggregate demand (AD)** and **aggregate supply (AS)** to study changes in the general price level and aggregate output.

Aggregate demand in the U.S. economy is the relationship between price level and quantity of all goods and services demanded. It reflects the spending plans of all U.S. households, businesses, and governments, as well as those of foreign households, businesses, and governments for U.S. goods and services. Aggregate supply is the relationship between U.S. price level and total output supplied by all U.S. businesses. The interaction of these two forces determines the level of aggregate output and the general price level.

Graphic Representation

Exhibit 20.10(a) shows demand and supply of doughnuts (see Chapter 3), and Exhibit 20.10(b) shows aggregate demand and aggregate supply for an economy. The two graphs are alike in several ways. Both demand for doughnuts and aggregate demand have a negative slope (downward and to the right). Both supply of doughnuts and aggregate supply have a positive slope (upward and to the right). In both graphs, the vertical axis represents price, and the horizontal axis represents quantity; both graphs show quantity demanded and supplied in a particular period of time.

The two graphs are different in important respects, as well. The microeconomic graph (Exhibit 20.10a) shows the output of a single good. The macroeconomic graph (Exhibit 20.10b) shows general price level as measured by a price index (vertical axis) and aggregate output for the economy (horizontal axis). Of course, no one actually buys a unit of aggregate output. (If you add 2 doughnuts and 3 cups of coffee, what would you call the sum—breakfast?) As we describe more completely in Chapter 21, economists measure aggregate output by adding the market values of all goods and services produced in the economy. For the United States, this amount is rather large. Note that aggregate output in Exhibit 20.10(b) is measured in billions of dollars.

Shapes of aggregate demand and aggregate supply curves. The reasons for the shapes of the aggregate demand and aggregate supply curves also differ from the reasons for the shapes of microeconomic curves. The negative slope of demand for doughnuts reflects the law of demand: A higher price will cause consumers to buy substitutes. The positive slope of supply of doughnuts reflects the law of supply: As prices fall, producers will supply fewer doughnuts

Aggregate demand (AD). Demand for all goods and services in the economy; relationship between total quantity of goods and services demanded and general price level.

Aggregate supply (AS). Supply of all goods and services in the economy; relationship between total quantity of goods and services supplied and general price level.

(a) Microeconomic view

(b) Macroeconomic view

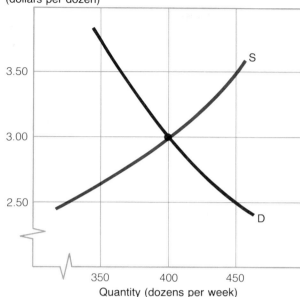

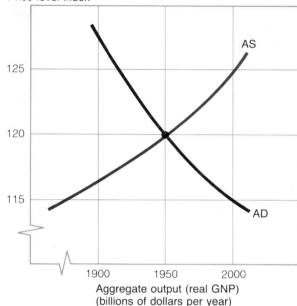

Exhibit 20.10
Two Views of Demand and Supply
The graph in part (a) is a microeconomic view of demand and supply of a single product: doughnuts. The graph in part (b) is a macroeconomic view of aggregate demand and supply of all goods and services produced in the economy. In both graphs, price appears on the vertical axis and quantity on the horizontal axis. While the microeconomic view shows the output of a single good, the macroeconomic view shows the general price level (the average price of all goods and services) and aggregate output (the value of all goods and services produced). Demand and supply curves have similar shapes in both graphs, but the explanation behind the shape and the factors that shift the curves are very different.

and more substitutes. But if the price of all goods (that is, aggregate output) changes, there may be no cheaper substitutes.

The shape of the aggregate demand curve reflects the operation of three forces. First, a decrease in price level will increase the wealth of households. For example, suppose that you have $2000 in the bank that you are saving to pay some of next year's college expenses. If prices of all goods (including college expenses) drop by 10 percent, the purchasing power of your $2000 will have increased. You can spend some of this money and still be able to pay as much of next year's expenses as before. As price level decreases, real wealth of households increases and quantity of aggregate output demanded increases.

Second, a drop in the price level in the United States causes a change in the relative price of U.S. and foreign products. Foreigners will buy more U.S. products and U.S. residents will buy fewer foreign products (and more U.S. products) as

U.S. price level falls. Finally, a fall in the price level tends to reduce the rate of interest, that is, the cost of borrowing. As a result, households will borrow more to finance house and automobile purchases. Businesses will borrow more to invest in machinery and buildings.

The positive slope of the aggregate supply curve suggests that businesses will increase total quantity of goods produced when the general price level increases. As we discuss more completely in Chapter 26, this change often occurs because some costs (wages, for example) may increase more slowly than product prices as price level rises. Thus an increase in the general price level will raise business profits and induce businesses to offer more for sale.

Interactions

The concept of equilibrium is also used in both microeconomics and macroeconomics, but in somewhat different ways. We have already described how individual product markets reach equilibrium where quantity demanded equals quantity supplied, that is, where the demand and supply curves intersect. Similarly, macroeconomic equilibrium lies at the intersection of the aggregate demand and aggregate supply curves. In Exhibit 20.10(b), equilibrium output is $1950 billion per year. The equilibrium price level is 120, which means that prices are (on the average) 120 percent of those in the base year. This equilibrium point tells us the level of aggregate output and the current price level. But in macroeconomics, we are also interested in understanding why price level, aggregate output, and unemployment *change*. Macroeconomists associate these changes with shifts in aggregate demand and supply.

Consider, for example, Exhibit 20.11(a), which shows an increase in aggregate demand (from AD_1 to AD_2). It predicts that both aggregate output and price level will rise. This increase is exactly what happened in the U.S. economy between 1964 and 1966. Aggregate output increased at the rate of 4 percent per year—a very high rate by historical standards. Unemployment fell from over 5 percent to under 3 percent—the lowest level since World War II. At the same time, price level increased at twice its rate of the preceeding five years.

Exhibit 20.11(b) shows a decrease in aggregate supply (from AS_1 to AS_2). It predicts that aggregate output will fall and price level will rise. This pattern describes the performance of the U.S. economy from 1973 to 1975. Aggregate output fell by 0.5 percent in 1974 and 1.3 percent in 1975. Unemployment increased by almost 3 percent. The general price level increased by over 12 percent in 1974 and 7 percent in 1975.

CONCLUSION

We showed how the performance of the economy has certainly been less than ideal, with regard to the goals of full employment, price stability, and economic growth. But the more important (and very controversial) question is what, if anything, the government can do to improve economic performance? Economists disagree sharply on whether such *stabilization policies* are possible and desirable or unnecessary and impractical.

(a) An increase in aggregate demand

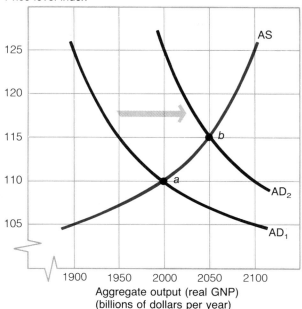

(b) A decrease in aggregate supply

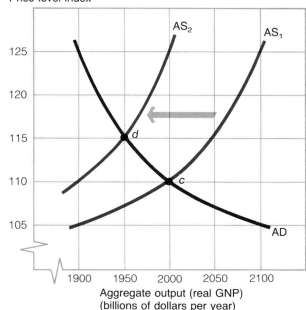

Exhibit 20.11
Changes in Aggregate Demand and Aggregate Supply
Part (a) shows the effects of an increase in aggregate demand from AD₁ to AD₂. Note that at each price level, quantity of aggregate output demanded is greater. As a result, the general price level increases and quantity of aggregate output bought and sold increases. (Compare point *a* with point *b*.) Part (b) shows the changes that occur when aggregate supply decreases. Note that at each price level, quantity of aggregate output supplied is less. As a result, the general price level increases and quantity of aggregate output bought and sold decreases. (Compare point *c* with point *d*.)

In addition, economists do not agree on the conclusions to be drawn from the historical record. The period from 1945 to the present, in which the government became an active participant in efforts to stabilize the economy, is particularly controversial. Some economists believe that this experience indicates how little faith can be placed in macroeconomic policies. Others see benefits from using macroeconomic policies and believe that the economy's recent performance compares favorably with that of earlier periods.

Although macroeconomics involves a lot of controversy, economists generally agree on the validity and usefulness of some basic tools of macroeconomic analysis. In Chapters 26–31 we use the tools of aggregate demand and supply introduced in this chapter and expand on them. As you will see, interactions between aggregate demand and supply help us to see how the macroeconomy functions. And different interpretations of how they interact help explain why economists have reached such different conclusions.

SUMMARY

1. In this chapter we explored macroeconomic perspectives on unemployment, inflation, and aggregate demand and supply.

2. Microeconomics focuses on the relative prices of individual products and resources. Macroeconomics focuses on the economy as a whole: aggregate output and the general price level. Both macroeconomic and microeconomic perspectives are important when considering any economic policy.

3. Full employment is a macroeconomic goal, but definitions of unemployment and full employment are controversial. The official definition of an unemployed person is someone without a job who is actively engaged in looking for work. Official statistics may underestimate the true unemployment rate by ignoring discouraged individuals who have stopped looking for a job and underemployed workers. Official statistics may overestimate the true unemployment rate by counting workers who are voluntarily unemployed.

4. Economists identify three types of unemployment. Frictional unemployment occurs when individuals move into or out of the job market or from industry to industry. Such unemployment is a normal part of the economy and promotes efficiency but at some cost to the temporarily jobless. Structural unemployment occurs when unemployed individuals do not qualify for jobs that are vacant or perhaps because of discrimination. This mismatch serves no useful social purpose but is difficult to overcome. Cyclical unemployment is associated with declines in GNP. Additional jobs are required to reduce cyclical unemployment.

5. Economists define full employment—the natural rate of unemployment—as the level of unemployment that would exist if the economy were producing at the level of its potential GNP. It is the level of unemployment consistent with frictional and structural unemployment, but reflecting zero cyclical unemployment.

6. Potential GNP is the maximum level of output that an economy can produce without putting upward or downward pressure on the general price level. The difference between potential and actual GNP is called the GNP gap. A positive gap occurs when actual GNP is less than potential GNP. A negative gap occurs when actual GNP is more than potential GNP.

7. Economists measure the general price level using price indexes, such as the Consumer Price Index. The CPI is calculated by comparing the cost of a market basket of certain goods with the cost in a specified base or reference year. The percentage change in the price index from one year to the next is called the inflation rate.

8. When the general price level rises, the purchasing power of money falls. To correctly interpret changes in economic variables (such as income or GNP) that are measured in dollar terms requires translation from nominal terms (actual dollars) to real terms (purchasing power). Changes in real income or real GNP represent changes in the standard of living.

9. Inflation represents a sustained increase in the general price level. It erodes the purchasing power of income and some forms of wealth and, especially when unanticipated, redistributes wealth. Inflation may lower efficiency by distorting price signals and causing individuals to spend time and energy trying to offset its effects.

10. Economists define the goal of price stability in terms of a relatively stable general price level because relative price changes are important signals for the economy.

11. The U.S. economy has had varying rates of growth, unemployment, and inflation. Since 1950, the growth rate has fluctuated less than before. But since 1960, the unemployment rate has risen, possibly as a result of a higher natural rate of unemployment. And since 1950, the general price level has generally risen.

12. Aggregate demand and aggregate supply reflect the relationship between aggregate output demanded and supplied and the general price level. Aggregate demand has a negative slope because lower prices raise the real wealth of households, increase the relative price of foreign goods and services, and lower interest rates. Aggregate supply has a positive slope because some resource prices (costs) rise more slowly than product prices. Increases in aggregate demand raise the general price level, increase aggregate output, and lower unemployment. Decreases in aggregate supply raise the general price level, decrease aggregate output, and raise unemployment.

KEY TERMS

Aggregate output, 501
Gross national product (GNP), 501
General price level, 501
Labor force, 503
Unemployment rate, 503
Discouraged worker, 504
Underemployed, 504
Frictional unemployment, 505
Structural unemployment, 505
Cyclical unemployment, 506
Business cycle, 506
Recession, 506
Trough, 507
Recovery, 507

QUESTIONS FOR REVIEW AND DISCUSSION

1. Comment on the statement: "*Micro* means small, and microeconomics is what economists use to study the operations of a small grocery store or the aggregate activity of a small economy such as New Zealand's. *Macro* means large, and macroeconomics is what economists use to study the aggregate economic activity of a large country such as the United States or the operations of a large corporation such as IBM."

2. If the price of an average restaurant meal rises by 5 percent during a period when the general price level rises by 8 percent, are restaurant meals really more expensive? Would you expect more or fewer restaurant meals to be purchased? Why is it important to adjust prices, incomes, and other economic variables for changes in the general price level?

3. Do you believe that inflation or unemployment is the more serious problem today? Why?

4. Between 1982 and 1986, the after-tax income of John Adams, proprietor of the Yankee Doodle Company, increased from $37,500 to $40,000. (Note that in Exhibit 20.4 the consumer price index increased from 289.1 in 1982 to 328.4 in 1986.)
   a) Did John's income increase in real terms?
   b) If John's income was fully indexed to the consumer price index (that is, a 1 percent increase in the CPI meant a 1 percent increase in his income), what would his income have been in 1986?
   c) If John's income rises by exactly the same rate the CPI, does this necessarily mean that his standard of living is unchanged? Why or why not?

5. Based on the official definitions of unemployment would the following individuals be classified as employed, unemployed, or not in the labor force?
   a) John Youngblood, age 15, worked 20 hours last week in a local grocery store.
   b) Mildred Elderberry, a retiree, worked 20 hours last week without pay in her son's paint store.
   c) Robert Pickney, a recent college graduate, was offered three different jobs last week but continued to look for a better job.
   d) Hilda Kraft, a former elementary school art teacher, was laid off last spring because of budget cuts, would like a similar job, but is not currently looking for work.
   e) Bill Bluestone, a factory worker, is not working this week because of illness but will return to work next week.

6. The government publishes indexes showing industrial production for the economy as a whole and for individual product groups. The following table shows some index numbers for July 1981 and November 1982, the start and end of the most recent recession.

	Indexes of industrial production for				
Date	All final products	All consumer products	Autos	Consumer staples	Business equipment
7/81	153.9	150.7	147.6	151.6	184.8
11/82	134.9	141.3	120.7	152.0	146.4

   a) Calculate the percentage change in each index.
   b) Why do you suppose that the index for autos changed more than the index for consumer staples? (*Hint:* Consider a recession as a change in national income and use the concept of income elasticity from Chapter 4.)
   c) What do these data suggest about the distribution of unemployment across industries during a recession?
   d) What do these data suggest about the effect of a recession on consumption spending and fixed investment?

7. What changes in aggregate demand or aggregate supply would explain the following conditions?
   a) An increase in aggregate output.
   b) A decrease in the general price level.
   c) An increase in the general price level and a decrease in aggregate output.
   d) Lower unemployment and a higher general price level.

527

...formation presented in the appendix to this
...and the following data, which show prices and
...ies consumed of three products over two years,
...p you find the answers to (a)–(d).

...duct	1988		1989	
	Quantity consumed	Price per unit	Quantity consumed	Price per unit
Bananas	100 lb	$0.50/lb	110 lb	$0.55/lb
Cloth	200 yd	3.00/yd	250 yd	3.10/yd
Books	10	2.00/book	20	2.50/book

a) Use the constant market-basket approach and calculate an index of the price level for each year, using
1988 as the base year.
b) Use the current market-basket approach and calculate an index of the price level for each year, using
1988 as the base year.
c) Calculate the percentage change in the price level
using each index. Explain the difference.
d) What can you say about the change in the relative
prices of the three items?

Appendix to Chapter 20

Measuring Price Levels

As we noted in this chapter, economists measure average prices by constructing
a *price index* that measures the price level as a percentage of the price level in a
selected base, or reference, year. There are two basic approaches to constructing
a price index: the *constant market-basket* approach and the *current market-basket*
approach. Each is used to calculate average prices; each results in a common
measure of the general price level.

We can contrast the two approaches using a simple economy with only two
products—apples and wooden spoons—and limiting our discussion to two years—
1988 and 1987. Exhibit 20A.1 shows this economy. How should we calculate the
average price in each year? We could, of course, simply take the average of the
two prices. But doing so would not recognize the relative importance of the two
goods. The market value of apples in 1987 was $80 (40 pounds × $2 per pound).
The market value of spoons was $40 (40 spoons × $1 per spoon).

To recognize the greater importance of apples in the economy, we want the
average price to be a *weighted average*. The market value of the goods consumed
weights the prices by the quantity consumed. But we cannot compare the total
market values in the two years. The increased market value in 1988 is only partly
the result of higher prices. Quantities produced and consumed are also greater.

To calculate how much average price has changed, we want to compare the
cost of buying a certain number of apples and wooden spoons. If quantities are
fixed, then all changes in market value must be caused by changes in price. The
constant market-basket approach tells us how much more (or less) it costs to buy

(a) Basic information on prices and quantities

Product	1987		1988	
	Quantity	Price	Quantity	Price
Apples	40 lb	$2.00/lb	60 lb	$2.20/lb
Wooden spoons	40 spoons	$1.00/spoon	80 spoons	$1.25/spoon

(b) Constant market basket (Consumer Price Index)

Product	Market value of 1987 quantities	
	In 1987 prices	In 1988 prices
Apples	$ 80	$ 88
Wooden spoons	40	50
Total	$120	$138

$$\text{Price index, 1988} = \frac{\text{Cost of 1987 quantities in 1988 prices}}{\text{Cost of 1987 quanities in 1987 prices}} \times 100$$

$$= \frac{\$138}{\$120}(100) \quad \text{or} \quad 115$$

(c) Current market basket (GNP deflator)

Product	Market value of 1988 quantities	
	In 1987 prices	In 1988 prices
Apples	$120	$132
Wooden spoons	80	100
Total	$200	$232

$$\text{Price index, 1988} = \frac{\text{Cost of 1988 quantities in 1988 prices}}{\text{Cost of 1988 quanities in 1987 prices}} \times 100$$

$$= \frac{\$232}{\$200}(100) \quad \text{or} \quad 116$$

Exhibit 20A.1
Calculating Price Indexes

the same quantities in the current year as in the base year. The current market-basket approach tells us how much more (or less) it would have cost to buy today's quantities at base-year prices.

CONSTRUCTING A PRICE INDEX: THE CONSTANT MARKET-BASKET APPROACH

The constant market-basket approach is the one used for the Consumer Price Index. The first step is to select a base, or reference, year. The base year for the CPI is 1967. In this example we use 1987 as the base year. The second step is to determine quantities for the market basket using quantities consumed in the base year. In this case, the quantities are the 40 pounds of apples and 40 wooden spoons purchased in 1987. Using 1987 prices, it would have cost $120 to buy this market basket. In 1988, the price of apples went up by 10 percent (from $2.00 to $2.20 per pound). The price of wooden spoons increased by 25 percent (from $1.00 to $1.25 per spoon). But what was the average increase?

In using this approach, we calculate the increase in average price as the percentage increase in the cost of the constant market basket. To determine this increase, we calculate the cost of the market basket—40 pounds of apples and 40 spoons—using 1988 prices. As shown in Exhibit 20A.1, we would have paid $138 in 1988 to buy the market basket. That is, the cost of the constant market basket (average price) increased by 15 percent.

As we also noted in this chapter, economists generally use a price index to indicate the general price level. They construct a constant market-basket price index by dividing the current cost of the market-basket price level by the cost for the base year (then multiply the ratio by 100 to express the index as a *percentage*). Expressed as a formula, the current-year price index is

$$\text{Current-year price index} = \frac{\substack{\text{Cost of base-year market basket} \\ \text{in current-year prices}}}{\substack{\text{Cost of base-year market basket} \\ \text{in base-year prices}}} \times 100$$

The price index will always have a value of 100 in the base year because the numerator and the denominator in the formula are identical. In our example, the constant market-basket price index for 1988 has a value of 115, calculated as

$$\text{1988 price index} = \frac{\text{Cost of 1987 market basket in 1988 prices}}{\text{Cost of 1987 market basket in 1987 prices}} \times 100$$

$$= \frac{\$138}{\$120}(100) \quad \text{or} \quad 115$$

The 1988 price index of 115 means that the price level in 1988 is 115 percent of the price level in 1987. In other words the price level, a measure of average price, increased by 15 percent. To check your understanding of this formula, find the price index for 1986 if 35 apples were bought at $1.80 per pound and 30 wooden spoons were bought at $0.75 each. Keep 1987 as your base year. (Your answer should be 85.)

CONSTRUCTING A PRICE INDEX: THE CURRENT MARKET-BASKET APPROACH

The second method of calculating a price index is based on the current cost of the market-basket quantities. We calculate the price index by comparing the market-basket cost in current and base-year prices. As shown in Exhibit 20A.1, this constant-price approach results in an index for 1988 that is based on 1988 prices. We can state this relationship in a formula as

$$\text{Current-year price index} = \frac{\substack{\text{Cost of current market basket} \\ \text{in current-year prices}}}{\substack{\text{Cost of current market basket} \\ \text{in base-year prices}}} \times 100$$

Using the data from our example, we calculate the current market-basket index for 1988 as 116. That is,

$$1988 \text{ price index} = \frac{\text{Cost of 1988 market basket in 1988 prices}}{\text{Cost of 1988 market basket in 1987 prices}} \times 100$$

$$= \frac{\$232}{\$200}(100) \quad \text{or} \quad 116$$

Again, the 1988 price index of 116 means that the price level in 1988 is 116 percent of the price level in 1987. That is, the price level (average price) increased by 16 percent. To check your understanding of this formula, find the price index for 1986 if 35 apples were bought at $1.80 per pound and 50 wooden spoons were bought at $0.90 each. Keep 1987 as your base year. (Your answer should be 90.)

Economists use the current market-basket approach to calculate a price index known as the GNP deflator. (We discuss the GNP deflator in detail in Chapter 21.) Actually, the GNP deflator is the ratio of nominal GNP to real GNP. That is, the numerator in the current market-basket approach represents the market value of the current quantities at current prices (nominal GNP). The denominator represents the market value of the current quantities after removing the effects of the change in prices (real GNP).

Some economists favor using the GNP deflator instead of the CPI because the former covers a wider range of goods and services in the economy. (The CPI is based only on consumer goods and services.) Even more important, the constant market basket used in the CPI does not reflect changes in tastes and preferences or substitutions of relatively less for relatively more expensive items over time.

CONCLUSION

The two methods shown are alternative ways to calculate an index of the general price level. Both types of indexes hold quantity consumed constant, so that only price change is measured. In the constant market-basket approach, current- and base-year costs of the quantities from the base year are compared. In the current market-basket approach, current- and base-year costs of the quantities of the current year are compared. Each method yields an index, changes in which measure annual inflation rates. The Consumer Price Index follows the constant market-basket approach. The GNP deflator uses the current market-basket approach.

Gross National Product:
Measuring Aggregate Output

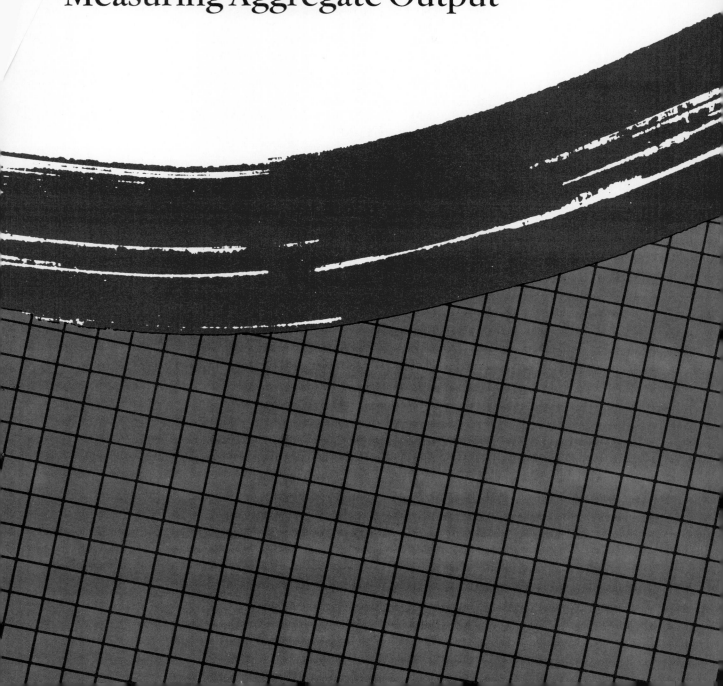

QUESTIONS TO CONSIDER

☐ What does GNP measure?

☐ How do economists measure GNP?

☐ What do the accounting identities tell us about the circular flow in a private-sector economy?

☐ In what ways do the government and foreign sectors affect the circular flow?

☐ How do national income accounting definitions differ from accounting identities?

I n Chapter 20 we introduced gross national product (GNP) as the statistical measure of aggregate output. In 1970, real GNP in the United States was $2.4 trillion, or an average of $11,800 per person. By 1986, real GNP had grown to $3.7 trillion, or $15,300 per person. In this chapter we consider how GNP is calculated and how useful it is as an indicator of economic activity.

Why do economists spend so much time defining and measuring gross national product? Because GNP is a key indicator of whether the economy as a whole is progressing toward society's economic goals. Government policy makers use past values of GNP to determine how well their policies worked. They use forecasts of future GNP to determine the potential effects of policies they are considering. Businesses use forecasts of GNP to predict future demand for their products. Economists use GNP to test the correctness of macroeconomic theories.

In addition, the measurement of GNP reveals a great deal about the relationships between resource markets and product markets. In Chapter 6 we showed how households, businesses, governments, and the foreign sector interact. As we discuss how GNP is calculated, you will learn how the interactions of these sectors, especially in financial markets, explain the operation of the macroeconomy.

DEFINING AND MEASURING AGGREGATE OUTPUT

In Chapter 20 we defined gross national product as the total *market value* of the *final* goods and services that an economy *produces during a particular period of time*. Each of the italicized phrases is important to your understanding the meaning of GNP.

GNP Measures Market Values

Measuring aggregate output—the quantity of all goods and services produced in the economy—presents a problem unlike that of measuring the output of individual markets. In Chapter 3 we used a physical measure of output (dozens of doughnuts) in studying the market for doughnuts. But to measure aggregate output (GNP) we must count not only the quantity of doughnuts but also the

		Apples	Wooden spoons		Gross national product (GNP)
Gross National **r a Two-Good**	Price (P)	$2.00/apple	$1.00/spoon		
	Quantity produced (Q)	200 apples	600 spoons		
	Market value (P × Q)	$ 400	+ $ 600	=	$1000

quantities of shoes, apples, and all other products. We cannot simply add physical quantities of different products and obtain a meaningful number. But we can calculate the market values (market price multiplied by physical quantity) of doughnuts, shoes, apples, and other products and then add these values to obtain total market value. Total market value is aggregate output, or GNP.

Exhibit 21.1 provides a simple example of how GNP is calculated. This hypothetical economy produces only two goods—apples and wooden spoons. Using the market-value approach, we first determine the total market value of each good by multiplying the market price and quantity produced (P × Q). To calculate GNP we add the market values of each product. In this example, $400 worth of apples and $600 worth of wooden spoons were produced during the period, giving a GNP of $1000.

Economists generally believe that market prices reflect the relative benefits consumers receive from different products. Thus a change in market values can help us determine whether the economy has satisfied more or less of society's wants. Of course, no measure—including GNP—is perfect. But economists generally believe that it is a good measure of aggregate output.

GNP Measures Output of Final Goods and Services

When calculating GNP, economists distinguish between final goods and intermediate goods. **Final goods** are (or will be) sold to their ultimate user. **Intermediate goods** are either used up completely in producing other goods or are purchased for resale. The value of intermediate goods is excluded from GNP. Including intermediate goods would double-count the value of resources used, since intermediate goods ultimately become part of the value of final goods.

Final goods. Products and services that are (or will be) sold to their ultimate user. GNP is a measure of the value of final goods produced.

Intermediate goods. Products and services that are used to produce other goods and services or are purchased for resale. The value of intermediate goods is excluded from GNP.

For example, if you buy a new car produced in the United States this year for $8000, we can say that a final good worth $8000 was produced. But several market transactions occurred before you purchased the car. The local car dealer purchased it from the manufacturer for $6000. At that stage, your car was an intermediate good because it was purchased for resale. If we added the $6000 and $8000 together we would overstate the value of goods produced. Only the $8000 value of the final good—the car purchased by its ultimate consumer—is counted in GNP. By the same logic, we exclude the value of steel and tires purchased by the car manufacturer. These, too, are intermediate goods because they are used to produce the car. They are already a part of the final $8000 value, and to count their purchases also would overstate GNP.

GNP Measures Goods and Services Produced in the Current Period

The definition of GNP also indicates that we want to calculate the economic value that an economy *produces in a particular period of time*, such as the current year. Thus GNP for this year does not count the $200 you paid for a new bicycle yesterday if the bicycle was produced last year. If your bicycle was produced in 1988, it is counted as part of GNP for 1988 even if it was not finally sold until 1989.

In addition, GNP is a measure of economic value *produced*, not *sold*, so we do not count the sale of secondhand items. The original sale of an item represents the value of the good produced. The $400 you paid for a new video cassette recorder in February is a part of GNP. But if you sell it to your roommate in June for $175, the value of VCRs produced does not increase. There are no additional VCRs, just a different owner.

Finally, GNP excludes financial transactions because they do not represent goods and services produced. Your purchase of 100 shares of common stock of a new corporation for $1000 or a bank loan of $50,000 to a business are purely financial exchanges. Neither transaction represents the production of additional goods or services. GNP focuses only on exchanges that occur in product markets, not financial markets.

Measuring GNP: Real versus Nominal GNP

Although market prices help us estimate the value of goods and services produced, market prices are a somewhat unstable measuring scale, as you saw in Chapter 20. When the general price level rises, average market price increases, but the higher price level does not necessarily reflect the production of more real economic value. (If the price of a pizza increases from $5 to $8, do you get more satisfaction from eating it?)

Thus if we use current market prices, measured GNP may increase, even if the economy's performance has not improved. Thus we must clearly distinguish changes in *nominal GNP* from changes in *real GNP*. (Recall that nominal values are expressed in current dollars. Real values are expressed in terms of dollars of constant purchasing power.) An increase in nominal GNP can occur even when fewer economic goods and services are produced. For example, nominal GNP increased by 3.7 percent in 1982. However, 1982 was a year of recession and real GNP actually decreased by 2.5 percent.

Exhibit 21.2 again illustrates a simple economy that produces only apples and wooden spoons. In the top half of the exhibit, current prices and current quantities are used to calculate *nominal GNP*. In this example, nominal GNP increased from $1000 in 1988 to $1320 in 1989, a 32 percent increase. But did the economy actually produce 32 percent more goods and services? We cannot use nominal GNP to answer that question because both output and price may increase (as they did in this example). You can see in the table that the quantity of apples produced increased by only 20 percent. The rest of the increase in the market value of apples occurred because the price of apples rose.

Year	Apples			Wooden spoons			Gross national product
	Price (P_a)	Quantity (Q_a)	Market value $(P_a \times Q_a)$	Price (P_s)	Quantity (Q_s)	Market value $(P_s \times Q_s)$	
Nominal GNP: Current quantities and current prices							
1988	$2.00	200	$400	$1.00	600	$600	$1000
1989	2.20	240	528	1.10	720	792	1320
Real GNP: Current quantities and 1988 prices							
1988	$2.00	200	$400	$1.00	600	$600	$1000
1989	2.00	240	480	1.00	720	720	1200

**Exhibit 21.2
Nominal and Real GNP for
a Two-Good Economy**

GNP deflator. The ratio of nominal GNP to real GNP expressed as a percentage; a measure of the general price level.

Since higher prices do not mean that more of society's wants have been satisfied, economists distinguish between changes in nominal GNP and changes in real GNP. To measure *real GNP,* economists use a constant set of prices. Because prices are held constant, real GNP changes only when the quantities produced rise or fall. We calculated real GNP in Exhibit 21.2 by determining how much GNP would have been in 1989 if prices had remained the same as they were in 1988. Using the 1988 price of apples and wooden spoons we calculated the real GNP for 1989 to be $1200, compared with $1320 for nominal GNP. Nominal GNP increased by $320 (32 percent). Of that increase, $200 represents a 20 percent increase in higher real value; $120 reflects the 10 percent increase in the average price of goods and services.

As we noted in Chapter 20, macroeconomic analysis often requires us to translate from nominal to real terms. As you saw, the CPI is sometimes used to deflate economic variables. When dealing with GNP, however, economists use the **GNP deflator**, that is, the ratio of nominal GNP to real GNP in a given year. In our example,

$$\text{GNP deflator, 1989} = \frac{\text{Nominal GNP, 1989}}{\text{Real GNP, 1989}} \times 100$$

$$= \frac{\$1320}{\$1200}(100) \quad \text{or} \quad 110$$

The value of the GNP deflator, like the value of the CPI, expresses the price level in any year as a percentage of the price level in a base year. In our example, we used 1988 prices to calculate real GNP; thus 1988 is the base year. The value of 110 for the GNP deflator indicates that the general price level increased by 10 percent between 1988 and 1989. (We can verify this rise, since Exhibit 20.2 shows that the price of each of the two products increased by 10 percent. However, it would be unusual for all prices to increase at the average rate.)

Currently, 1982 is used as the base year for the GNP deflator for the United States. We can calculate the value of the GNP deflator for 1985 by using the preceding formula and the value for nominal GNP ($3992.5 billion) and real GNP ($3573.5 billion). The GNP deflator for 1985 was 111.7, indicating that the general price level increased by 11.7 percent from 1982 to 1985. To check your understanding, verify this calculation using the same formula and the values given for nominal and real GNP in 1985.

First and Second Accounting Identities

The United States did not always have a measure of aggregate output. Many of the concepts and techniques used to measure GNP were developed in the 1930s, largely as a result of the efforts of Simon Kuznets. For his work, Kuznets was later awarded a Nobel Prize in Economics. Fundamental to Kuznets's measurements are two **accounting identities**, which are expressions that are *always true* by definition.

First accounting identity. The first identity states that aggregate output is always equal to actual aggregate expenditures. **Aggregate expenditures (AE)** are the total expenditures by all sectors of the economy on final goods in a specific period of time. Expressed in equation form,

First accounting identity

Aggregate output = Actual aggregate expenditures

Clearly, the amount spent on final goods sold is equal to the value of goods sold. (If you spend $300 to buy a color-TV set, the $300 represents both the amount you spent and the market value of what you bought.) But GNP is the value of final goods *produced*, not *sold*. What happens if businesses are unable to sell all that they have produced? Economists consider all final goods produced but not sold as though they had been bought by the business sector. This convention preserves the accounting identity and the objective of measuring the value of final goods produced in a particular period of time.

You may suspect (correctly) that aggregate expenditures are related to aggregate demand. But two differences are important. First, aggregate demand is a *relationship* between quantity of GNP demanded and general price level. Actual aggregate expenditures are a *single quantity* produced at the current price level. Second, actual aggregate expenditures may include "unplanned spending," or spending by businesses for goods produced but not sold. *Planned* aggregate expenditures at a certain price level and quantity of aggregate output demanded at that price level are, in fact, identical. (We discuss planned aggregate expenditures in detail in Chapter 22.)

Accounting identities. Relationships between macroeconomic variables that are always true by definition.

Aggregate expenditures (AE). Total expenditures on final goods by all sectors of the economy during a particular period of time.

National income (NI). Total income earned by the household sector; the sum of wages, rent, interest, and profits. It represents payment for resources used to produce final goods during a particular period of time.

Second accounting identity. The second identity recognizes that any market transaction involves two parties and can be examined from two perspectives. All dollars spent on aggregate output become dollars of income received by households in the economy. Thus aggregate output equals national income. **National income (NI)**—the total income earned by the household sector—is the sum of wages, rent, interest, and profits. Thus it represents payment for the resources used to produce final goods during a particular period of time. Expressed in equation form,

Second accounting identity

Aggregate output = National income

Together, the two accounting identities express fundamental macroeconomic relationships that help us understand how GNP is determined. Expressed in equation form, these relationships are

Accounting identities

Aggregate expenditures = Aggregate output = National income

$$AE \quad = \quad GNP \quad = \quad NI$$

Because of some real-world measurement problems, GNP as actually measured is not identical to national income. We identify these complications as we come to them in the following sections. Nevertheless, these problems do not disturb the fundamental equality between the concepts of aggregate output and national income.

Two Ways to Measure GNP

The equation combining the two accounting identities indicates that there are two ways to calculate GNP: (1) actual *expenditures* on final goods produced; and (2) total *income* received by owners of resources.

Exhibit 21.3 shows the values connected with the manufacture and final sale of a chair. The chair began life as a tree, which was harvested by the landowner and sold to a lumber mill. The tree became lumber, which was sold to the furniture manufacturer. The lumber was made into a chair, which was sold to a furniture store. Finally, the chair was sold for $55 to a family that put it in their living room.

Exhibit 21.3
Gross National Product:
Expenditure or Income

Revenues and costs of businesses			Income earned	
Landowner:				
Selling price		$ 5		
Less: Wages of lumberjack		2	Lumberjack	$ 2
Profit to landowner		$ 3	Landowner	3
Lumber mill:				
Selling price		$13		
Less: Cost of timber	$ 5			
Wages of mill workers	4	9	Mill workers	4
Profit to mill owner		$ 4	Mill owner	4
Furniture mfg.:				
Selling price		$35		
Less: Cost of lumber	$13			
Wages of factory workers	15	28	Factory workers	15
Profit to factory owner		$ 7	Factory owner	7
Furniture store:				
Selling price		$55		
Less: Cost of chair	$35			
Rent on building	4		Building owner	4
Wages of store employees	11	50	Store employees	11
Profit to store owner		$ 5	Store owner	5
			Total income earned	$55
Summary of incomes earned, all stages:			Wages	$32
			Rent	4
			Profit	19
			Total	$55

GNP equals actual aggregate expenditures. The first—and most obvious—way to arrive at the value of GNP associated with the chair is to equate the value to the amount spent by the family who bought it. After all, this amount is clearly the market value of a final good produced this year. What is true in this simple example is also true for the economy as a whole. We can determine the market value of final goods produced (GNP) by adding up the total amount that the household, business, government, and foreign sectors spent on the final goods produced in a particular year. We can use total spending as a measure of GNP because the first accounting identity, GNP equals actual aggregate expenditures, is always true.

GNP equals income received. We can also calculate GNP using the second accounting identity. That is, we add the income earned by owners of all the resources used to make the chair. In stage 1, the lumberjack earned $2 in wages and the landowner earned $3 in payment for her land and timber. In stage 2, the mill workers earned $4 in wages and the mill owner earned $4 in profits. In stage 3, the factory workers earned $15 in wages and the factory owner earned $7 in profits. In stage 4, the store employees earned $11 in wages, the building owner received $4 in rent, and the store owner earned $5 in profits. If we total the income earned by each person associated with producing and selling the chair—from landowner to furniture store worker—we arrive at the $55 value of the chair. This second accounting identity is true not only in this simple example, but also for the economy as a whole. (Actually, there are some measurement complications, as we discuss later in the chapter, but the basic relationship remains true.)

GNP: Does It Measure Social Value?

Before leaving the discussion of how GNP is measured, we should consider what it actually does and does not measure. Like any other economic measure, GNP is only one indicator of the economy's performance. Although economists generally believe that it is a good measure of aggregate output, GNP excludes certain factors that may cause it to inaccurately reflect how many of society's wants are satisfied.

GNP excludes nonmarket exchanges. First, GNP excludes values produced outside the marketplace, even if they add to social welfare. When individuals pay someone else to take care of their children or clean their houses, the expenditures are reflected in GNP. However, if individuals take care of their own children or clean their own houses, they satisfy wants but do not add to GNP. Likewise, almost all direct exchanges of services—you help me paint my house, I help you construct a garage for your house—satisfy wants but are not a part of GNP.

GNP also excludes some of the value of leisure time. If you go to the movies or play racketball in a local club, the payments you make are included in GNP. But if you watch TV or go for a walk in the woods, no market exchange occurs and no value is added to GNP. In fact, if each worker in the economy received one afternoon off (without pay) each week and spent it walking in the woods, measured GNP would fall. Fewer goods and services would be produced and less money would be exchanged in markets. Whatever value an afternoon in the woods might have, it is not reflected in GNP.

Such activities are not excluded from GNP because economists view them as unimportant or less valuable than goods and services exchanged in the market. Their exclusion is based on practical considerations: How can they be identified and what is their value? Even though their exclusion may underestimate the true wealth of a nation, it does not make GNP a less valuable measure. As long as such activities do not fluctuate much, GNP is still a good measure of how well the economy is performing.

GNP ignores external costs.   In addition, GNP fails to subtract external costs (see Chapter 6) from market value. Pollution and other external costs reduce social well-being but are not costs that producers or consumers pay for directly. Thus they are not reflected in the marketplace. As a result, measured GNP may somewhat overstate economic welfare.

GNP ignores the underground economy.   Some economists feel that the values exchanged in the underground economy are among the most important omissions from GNP. Statisticians measuring GNP must use recorded information to estimate actual expenditures and actual output. However, many economic exchanges are not a matter of public record.

Some underground exchanges are payments for illegal products or services such as drugs and prostitution. In addition, a significant amount of income received is never reported. For example, individuals working in restaurants or bars may not report all the tips they receive. Similarly, owners of retail stores may not record all their cash receipts. And individuals may perform various services for which they receive but do not report cash income. The size of this underground economy is difficult to estimate, but estimates run as high as $100 billion per year, or almost 3 percent of measured GNP. Its significance in distorting measures of economic activity is difficult to estimate.

GNP uses cost to value government goods and services.   Although most products are valued by their market prices when included in GNP, goods and services produced and consumed by government, such as highways and public education, are valued at their cost. But do government expenditures always reflect increases in social well-being? Some individuals question whether all the dollars spent on the latest weapon systems really add to social value. Others question the value of government expenditures to protect the environment or consumers. Since there is no direct market for these goods and services, economists must rely on costs to measure their contribution to GNP. Note, however, that this reliance deviates from the use of consumer demand to determine the economic values totaled to obtain GNP.

GNP does not indicate distribution or equity.   Finally, like most aggregate measures, GNP does not tell us whether various groups are better or worse off. That is, as a measure of aggregate output, it tells us nothing about the distribution of output and therefore nothing about equity. This difference is especially important in some of the poorer countries of the world. In considering whether these countries have improved or developed economically, economists watch not only the size but also the distribution of national income.

Despite the drawbacks, GNP remains an important indicator of an economy's growth or decline. Moreover, most economists agree that significant increases in real GNP in the United States over the past 50 years represent significant increases in the average standard of living. To this extent, the economy today appears to satisfy more of society's wants than before. But most economists agree that other indicators, such as the distribution of income, should also be used in any attempt to assess whether individuals are, in fact, better off.

CIRCULAR FLOW OF INCOME AND OUTPUT: A PRIVATE-SECTOR ECONOMY

Now that you have a better understanding of GNP, let's consider some of the fundamental macroeconomic relationships it reflects. We can use the circular-flow model introduced in Chapter 5 to illustrate how the household, business, government, and foreign sectors are related. This model will help you to see how the economy's gross national product is defined and measured. We can also use the model to indicate the fundamental truth of the two accounting identities.

A Simple Private-Sector Economy

Exhibit 21.4 shows a model of a simple economy that has no government or foreign sector. The household sector owns all the resources and spends all the income it receives. The business sector sells all the goods it produces to households. The bottom half of the model shows **consumption expenditures (C)**, which is the total amount spent by the household sector to purchase the final goods in product markets. With our simplifications, these dollars represent the only source of aggregate expenditures; that is, $AE = C$. According to the first accounting identity, these actual expenditures represent the value of the final goods produced during the period; that is, $AE = GNP$.

The top half of Exhibit 21.4 shows dollars flowing from the business sector to the household sector. In other words, dollars received by the business sector become dollars of income for people in the household sector. Revenues received by businesses either pay for labor (wages) and other resources (rent, for example) or pay the owners of businesses for the resources they supply (profits). With our simplifications, this dollar flow is also equal to national income; that is, $NI = $ Wages + Rent + Interest + Profits.

The second accounting identity tells us that the flow in the bottom half of Exhibit 21.4 (GNP) and the flow in the top half (NI) are identical amounts ($GNP = NI$). Thus we can view the flow in this economy as either the dollar amount of expenditures (the value of final goods exchanged) or as the dollar amount of income received (the value of resources exchanged).

Numerical example. We can illustrate these points using the example shown in Exhibit 21.5. The household sector has an income of $1000 ($NI = 1000), and according to our assumptions, the household sector spends all its income ($AE = C = 1000). These expenditures are received by the business sector as revenues, or receipts from sales. Because they measure the value of goods produced, these expenditures equal GNP ($AE = C = GNP$).

Consumption expenditures (C). Expenditures of households on final goods during a particular period of time.

Exhibit 21.4
The Circular Flow of Economic Activity: GNP and National Income
In the top half of this simplified circular-flow diagram, payments to resource owners by the business sector become income to the household sector. The total dollar amount is therefore national income. In the bottom half of the diagram, consumption expenditures by the household sector represent the total market value of goods and services produced by the business sector, or GNP. In this simplified model, all dollars received by households are spent and all dollars received by businesses become payments for resources used. Thus the total value of goods produced can be calculated either by adding expenditures in the product markets (GNP) or by adding incomes received (national income).

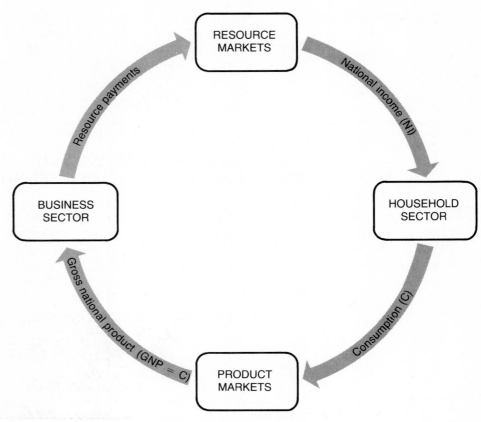

Exhibit 21.5 also shows that the business sector pays $1000 for resources such as labor, materials, buildings, and machinery used to produce final goods. The payments also include the profits paid to owners of businesses for the resources they contribute. In total, these resource payments are the $1000 of national income received by the household sector. Thus the example shows the fundamental accounting identity between aggregate expenditures, GNP, and national income: $AE = GNP = NI = \$1000$. Although the relationships among the various sectors get more complicated in our later discussions, these fundamental equalities are always true.

A More Realistic Private-Sector Economy

Although the basic accounting identities hold in all situations, a more realistic circular-flow model of economic activity requires that we complicate our example. We now add the factors of saving and investment to the model.

Income, consumption, and saving. Households do not typically spend their entire incomes. Most spend only a portion of what they earn and save the rest. When we relax our simplifying assumption to recognize saving, we must

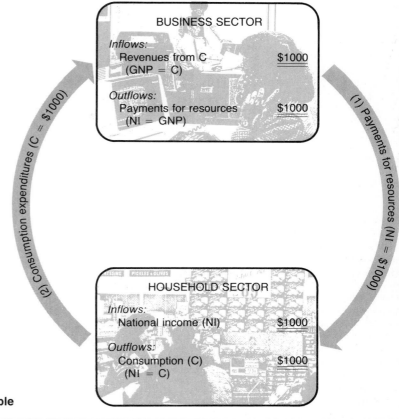

Exhibit 21.5
Simple Circular Flow: A Numerical Example

modify the circular-flow model. Exhibit 21.6 differs from our simple circular-flow model, reflecting the two possible uses for income. As you can see, the dollars that households receive as income are split into two flows: consumption expenditures (C) and **saving (S)**. Saving represents dollars received as income but not spent on consumer products. In other words, the income of the household sector flows out as consumption expenditures or saving. Expressed in equation form,

$$\text{National income} = \text{Consumption} + \text{Saving}$$
$$\text{NI} = \text{C} + \text{S}$$

Saving (S). The portion of income received by households during a particular period of time that is not spent on final goods.

Fixed investment. Expenditures by businesses for capital resources, such as new plants, equipment, or commercial buildings, and by households for residential construction during a particular period of time.

Business investment. Another simplification that we have used so far is the assumption that businesses produce only consumer goods for the household sector and that all goods produced are sold. However, some businesses produce capital resources (such as machinery and equipment) that are purchased by others in the business sector. Business expenditures for capital resources are called **fixed investment**. Like the purchase of consumer goods by the household sector, purchases of capital resources by the business sector are considered expenditures for final goods. (Household spending on residential construction is also included in fixed investment in government statistics. This fact does not affect the analysis or conclusions we reach, however.)

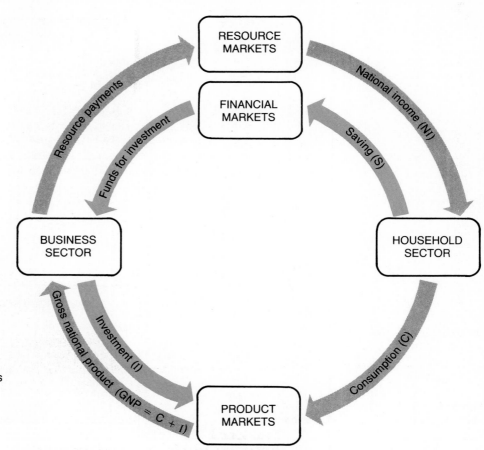

Exhibit 21.6
The Circular Flow of Economic Activity: Saving and Investment
Households receive disposable income, which they either spend on consumption or save. Dollars saved become dollars supplied to financial markets. In addition to dollars spent by consumers, businesses spend dollars (investment) for capital resources. Aggregate expenditures thus consist of both consumption (C) and investment (I).

Depreciation (capital consumption allowance). A business cost representing the value of capital resources used to produce goods; the fractional cost charged each year over the life of the resource to reflect both physical wear and tear and obsolescence. Unlike other costs, no payment is made for depreciation.

Why are capital resources not considered to be intermediate goods? After all, machinery, like materials, is used to produce final goods. Capital resources differ from intermediate goods in an important respect: They last for many years and are not completely used up in producing a batch of goods. Because capital resources last for years, expenditures on them—fixed investment—are considered to be expenditures on final goods and hence a part of GNP.

For example, a baker buys flour, yeast, and an oven. When the baker makes bread, the flour and yeast are completely used up. The total value of these products becomes part of the value of bread, as is true with any intermediate good. Although the oven is used, it is not used up and remains useful to the baker. By convention, we count only a fraction of the oven's value as a cost of producing the bread during a specific period of time. This amount, called **depreciation (capital consumption allowance)**, represents not only physical wear and tear but also the decrease in value when resources become outdated.

Depreciation is the second reason that national income and GNP are different numbers *as measured*. National income is calculated by adding up wages and salaries, rent, interest income, and profits. But profits equal revenues received *minus* all business costs. When capital resources wear out and become obsolete,

Net national product (NNP).
Gross national product minus depreciation (capital consumption allowance).

Inventory investment. The value of final goods produced in a particular period of time but not sold. The unsold goods are considered to have been "bought" by the businesses that produced them, and thus are counted as part of business investment expenditures.

Investment (I). Expenditures for fixed investment and inventory investment.

Financial markets. Markets in which lenders supply and borrowers demand loanable funds. In these markets, dollars saved become dollars invested.

the business assets are reduced. Thus depreciation is definitely a cost to the business sector.

Unlike other costs, however, depreciation does not also represent a payment to any resource owner and is not, therefore, a part of national income. Thus in order for GNP to equal national income, we must first subtract depreciation (the capital consumption allowance) from GNP. The resulting figure, called the **net national product (NNP)**, is in some ways a better measure than GNP of how much the economy has grown. To the extent that investment goes into replacing worn-out capital resources, the economy has not really increased its capacity to produce. We consider depreciation further, later in this chapter. But, in general, we continue to use GNP as our measure because it is difficult to measure depreciation and because GNP and NNP change together.

Another simplifying assumption that we have to reexamine is that of when final goods are sold. The fact is that businesses do not always immediately sell the final goods they produce; some goods are warehoused for future sale. As we mentioned earlier, economists by convention consider that businesses "buy" this inventory in the period in which it is produced. Any final goods produced but not sold are considered to be **inventory investment**.

In our more realistic economy, then, aggregate expenditures consist of two components: consumption (C) and **investment (I)**. Exhibit 21.6 shows investment—total fixed and inventory investment—as a second expenditure in the product-market portion of the model. Thus the first accounting identity can be expressed in this model as

$$\text{Aggregate output} = \text{Aggregate expenditures} = \text{Consumption} + \text{Investment}$$
$$\text{GNP} \quad = \quad \text{AE} \quad = \quad \text{C} \quad + \quad \text{I}$$

Financial Markets: The Link between Saving and Investment

One final and important complexity involves the link between saving and investment. Real-world economies contain financial markets, as well as product and resource markets. In **financial markets** borrowers and lenders exchange dollars for financial claims. Thus financial markets link dollars saved and dollars invested.

For example, if you save $1000 next year and decide to buy newly issued shares of stock in a corporation, you have exchanged savings for ownership claims in the business. If you put your money in a bank, you have exchanged savings for a claim on the assets of the bank. If the bank lends the money to a business, the bank exchanges funds for a claim on the business's assets.

Financial markets exist for two primary reasons. Individuals who save generally do not want to hide their savings in a mattress. Instead, they want their savings to grow. By trading their savings for claims in financial markets, households can earn additional income, either in the form of interest payments or growth in the value of their claims. Also, as the second accounting identity indicates, the revenues that businesses receive from selling their products represent income earned by households. If businesses want to make investments—buy additional equipment or build a new plant—they must acquire the necessary funds. Financial markets link households that want to save with businesses that require funds to make investments.

Note that we show all saving as originating from the household sector in Exhibit 21.6. However, businesses also save. Business saving is the sum of retained

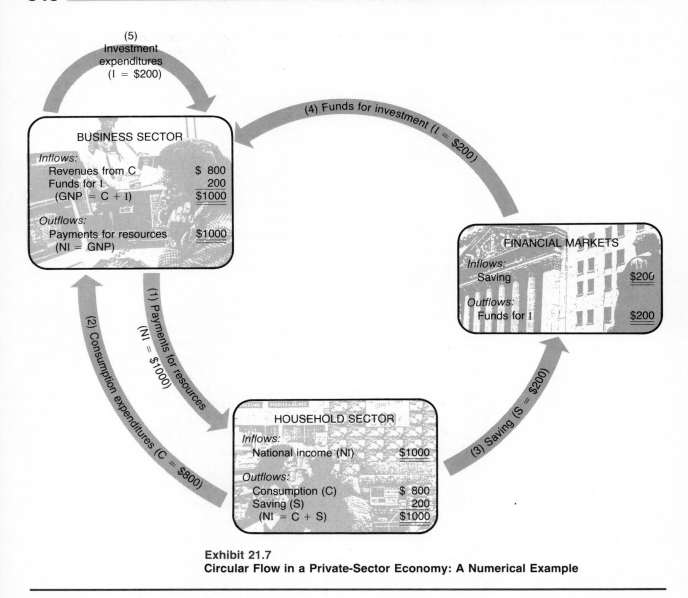

Exhibit 21.7
Circular Flow in a Private-Sector Economy: A Numerical Example

earnings—income earned but not paid out as dividends to stockholders—and depreciation—which is considered a cost but is not a cash payment. In fact, business saving is the largest source of funds used by the business sector to finance its investments.

We discuss financial markets in greater detail in the microeconomic portion of this textbook. For now, you should know that in financial markets, as in other markets, demand and supply of funds achieve equilibrium. In our simple economy, financial-market equilibrium equates the amount saved with the amount invested.

Numerical example. Exhibit 21.7 illustrates flows in a private-sector economy that includes both saving and investment. In this example you can see the equalities represented by the two accounting identities. Businesses producing

Stock. A quantity existing at some moment in time, such as the stock of capital resources or the stock of inventory possessed by the business sector on December 31 of any year.

Flow. A quantity or activity measured over a period of time, such as the gross national product produced in a particular year or the amount of income earned in a specific month.

consumer goods receive revenues of $800, which equal consumption expenditures (C). Businesses producing capital goods receive revenues equal to the $200 of investment (I).

As the first accounting identity indicates, GNP equals aggregate expenditures, which equals the sum of consumption and investment (GNP = AE = C + I). Exhibit 21.7 also shows that the entire $1000 of revenues received by the business sector for goods produced are matched by $1000 of payments to resource owners and therefore national income (GNP = NI = $1000). (This equality holds only if there is no depreciation, a simplification that we make here and in the following numerical examples.) Finally, the flows into and out of financial markets are equal. The household sector has income of $1000 and decides to spend $800 and save $200. The $800 spent flows into product markets and becomes $800 in revenues for businesses. The $200 saved flows into the financial market, where it becomes $200 of funds available for investment.

Stocks and Flows: Totals and Changes

The term *investment* has a special meaning in economics. Noneconomists often use the word to mean the total value of a firm's assets, or the stock of capital possessed by the firm. A **stock** is a quantity that exists at some moment in time— the stock of capital resources that businesses possessed on December 31, 1987, for example. In economics, however, investment refers to a **flow**, such as the total expenditure for new capital resources during the year 1987.

As you will see, macroeconomists focus on flows of economic activity, such as national income and gross national product. But flows are often related to stocks. For example, the quantity of products that businesses can produce in a year is a function of the stock of capital resources they possess during that year. The amount of interest income a household receives in a month depends, in part, on how much of its stock of wealth is in bank accounts, bonds, or other interest-paying forms of savings.

CIRCULAR FLOW: GOVERNMENT AND FOREIGN SECTORS

Thus far we have ignored the influence of the government and foreign sectors. Although we present a full discussion of how the government and the foreign sectors influence the economy in later chapters, we can illustrate their general effects in terms of our circular-flow model. We can also restate the accounting identities in view of the expanded circular-flow model.

Government and the Circular Flow

You can see the impact of government on the economy by relating the circular-flow model in Exhibit 21.8 to the basic elements of the government budget that we discussed in Chapter 6. On the receipts side, government obtains most of its ability to spend from tax payments made by individuals. (For simplicity, we ignore here all taxes not collected directly from households. We consider the effects of sales and other indirect taxes later in this chapter, however.) There are two kinds of government spending: transfer payments and purchases of goods and services.

Exhibit 21.8
The Circular Flow of Economic Activity: The Role of Government
Government constitutes a third sector in the circular flow. Government reduces the flow of national income at the top of the circular flow through taxes but injects additional income in the form of transfer payments. Dollars received by households (disposable income) therefore are national income less net taxes (taxes less transfer payments). Government is also a third source of expenditures in product markets at the bottom of the circular-flow diagram. With government considered, then, GNP is the sum of consumption, investment, and government expenditures. Finally, government participates in the financial markets.

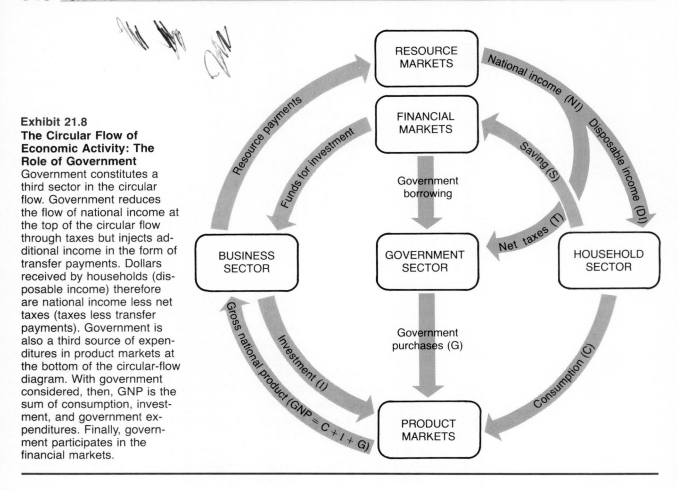

Disposable income (DI). Income received by households in a particular period of time and available to be spent or saved; household income after taxes have been deducted and transfer payments have been added.

Government purchases (G). Expenditures by the government sector to purchase final goods; a part of aggregate expenditures.

As we noted in Chapter 6, transfer payments represent payments to individuals for the purpose of redistributing income. They are not payments for resources provided.

In the top part of Exhibit 21.8, you can see that the flow to the household sector is decreased by the amount of taxes paid to government. The flow is increased by the transfer payments that government gives to households. Because taxes generally exceed transfer payments, national income is usually greater than disposable income. **Disposable income (DI)** is the income received by the household sector after taxes and transfer payments are accounted for. When considering how much households spend or save, we start with disposable income, not national income. We explore this difference in greater detail later in this chapter, but it does not affect the two accounting identities.

Government also buys goods and services, such as airplanes and missiles for national defense and asphalt and concrete for roads and sidewalks. **Government purchases (G)** are a third type of expenditure to be considered along with consumption and investment. Thus the first accounting identity between aggregate output and actual aggregate expenditures becomes

$$\text{Aggregate output} = \text{Actual aggregate expenditures}$$
$$\text{Gross national product} = \text{Consumption} + \text{Investment} + \text{Government purchases}$$
$$\text{GNP} = \text{C} + \text{I} + \text{G}$$

Note that this equation excludes transfer payments, although in Chapter 6 we included both transfer payments and government purchases as government expenditures. Transfer payments are excluded from GNP because they are not expenditures that are made to purchase final products. Their effect is to change the *distribution* of household income.

Finally, Exhibit 21.8 shows how government participates in financial markets. As in other sectors, funds entering and leaving the government sector are balanced. If outflows (for purchases and transfers) are less than inflows (taxes), government has a budget surplus. Government will then supply funds to financial markets to balance inflows and outflows. If outflows are greater than inflows, government has a budget deficit (as it has in recent years). The government budget deficit averaged $125 billion from 1982 to 1986. Government will then demand funds from the financial markets to balance inflows and outflows. We explain this impact of government on financial markets more fully in later chapters. For now you should recognize only that its role in financial markets greatly influences the macroeconomy's performance.

Numerical example. Exhibit 21.9 provides a numerical example of government's effect on the economy. Government directly affects the household sector in two ways: taxes and transfer payments. Net taxes (T), that is, taxes minus transfer payments (in this example, $125), are a flow from the household sector to the government. The government sector also affects the business sector in this example by purchasing goods and services. This expenditure on final products is a part of GNP. It adds $175 to the revenues of the business sector, just as consumption expenditures by the household sector do.

Finally, you can see the effect of government on financial markets. In this example, government has a budget deficit. Net taxes are $125; government purchases are $175, leaving a deficit of $50. The government will enter financial markets to borrow funds to make up this difference. Note that this action causes government to compete with the business sector for available funds. Of the $200 of saving available, the government takes $50 to finance its deficit, leaving $150 available for investment.

Foreign Trade and the Circular Flow

Imports (M). Expenditures by U.S. households, businesses, and governments for goods and services produced in other countries. These expenditures must be deducted from aggregate expenditures in order to measure GNP; they represent aggregate spending that is not used to purchase domestically produced goods.

To complete our overview of the economy, we add the foreign sector to the circular-flow model. Individuals, governments, and businesses of foreign countries comprise this sector. Flows to and from foreign economies are shown in a separate sector, but as Exhibit 21.10 indicates, foreign and domestic economies are closely related.

You can see the three effects of the foreign sector in Exhibit 21.10. First, some household expenditures flow to the foreign sector when households purchase **imports (M)**. (Domestic businesses and governments also buy foreign goods and

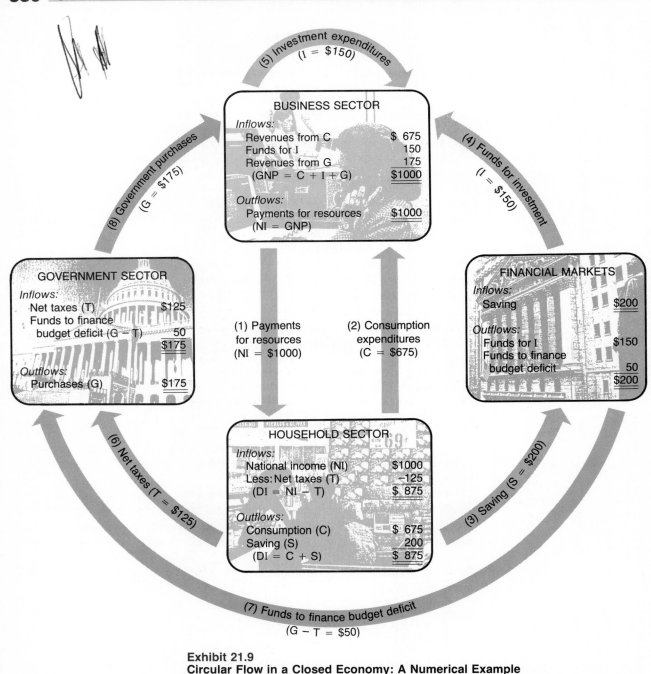

Exhibit 21.9
Circular Flow in a Closed Economy: A Numerical Example

Exports (X). Expenditures made by foreign households, businesses, and governments for goods produced domestically. Exports must be added to aggregate domestic expenditures when measuring GNP; they represent spending to purchase domestically produced goods.

services. We show all imports as consumer items only to keep the example simple.) Second, some goods and services produced by domestic businesses are sold to foreign households, businesses, and governments in the form of **exports (X)**. Finally, you can see the foreign sector also participates in domestic financial markets.

We want GNP to measure *domestic* aggregate output and must therefore measure spending on domestic goods and services. Thus we subtract the amount that U.S. households, businesses, and governments spend on foreign goods and services. We also add the amount spent by foreign households, businesses, and governments on goods and services produced in the United States. The difference between exports and imports (X − M) is called *net exports*. By subtracting imports and adding exports, we count expenditures on domestic products. The accounting identity of output and expenditures becomes

Aggregate output = Actual aggregate expenditures

$$\text{Gross national product} = \text{Consumption} + \text{Investment} + \text{Government purchases} + \text{Net exports}$$

$$\text{GNP} = \text{C} + \text{I} + \text{G} + (\text{X} - \text{M})$$

Exhibit 21.10
The Circular Flow of Economic Activity: The Foreign Sector
Dollars flow into the foreign sector in payment for imported goods. Dollars flow into the U.S. economy in payment for exported goods. The addition of these two dollar flows makes total spending (GNP) equal to the sum of consumption, investment, government purchases, and net exports (exports less imports). In addition, the foreign sector participates in U.S. financial markets.

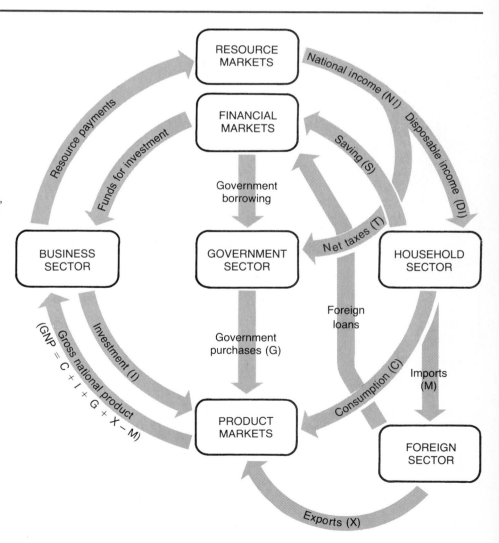

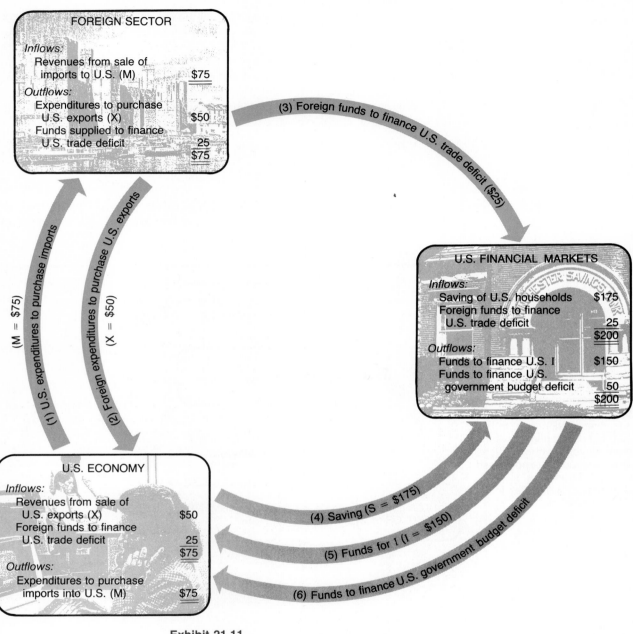

Exhibit 21.11
Circular Flow in an Open Economy: A Numerical Example

The foreign sector also affects financial markets. Foreign individuals, businesses, and governments may demand loanable funds (as Mexico, Brazil, Argentina, and other countries have done in recent years). They may also supply additional funds to U.S. borrowers. The net effect of the foreign sector in U.S. financial markets depends on the value of net exports. As in the other sectors, inflows and outflows must balance. (No sector can spend more than it receives without borrowing.) If net exports are positive, that is, exports exceed imports, the foreign sector will, on balance, borrow from U.S. financial markets to finance these additional purchases. If net exports are negative, that is, imports exceed exports, the foreign sector will, on balance, supply funds to U.S. financial markets. See A Case in Point: Additional Accounting Identities for other ways of looking at these relationships.

Numerical example.   Exhibit 21.11 illustrates the impact of the foreign sector on the domestic economy. At the left of the exhibit we see the trade flows. The $75 spent by U.S. individuals, businesses, and governments on imports represents a flow of dollars from the U.S. economy to the rest of the world. The $50 spent by foreign residents on U.S. exports is a flow of dollars into the domestic economy. Net exports are a negative $25, representing a trade deficit. As shown in the bottom of the exhibit, the trade deficit is matched by a $25 flow of funds supplied to U.S. financial markets from the foreign sector. Foreign-supplied funds, along with saving by U.S. households, are then available to finance investment and a government budget deficit.

The foreign sector has become increasingly important to the U.S. economy because the volume of imports and exports has grown. In 1986, over 11 percent

A Case in Point
Additional Accounting Identities

The two accounting identities that we have already introduced can be supplemented by a third one. It recognizes that the circular flow must be balanced overall. In the aggregate, if national income is $1000, then aggregate spending must be $1000.

Several of the flows that we have identified can be considered "leakages." For example, households do not spend all they receive as income. Saving constitutes a leakage from the circular flow. All of national income does not reach the household sector; government taxes represent a leakage. Imports represent a portion of consumption spending that leaks from the circular flow.

At the same time, inflows or "injections" add to the circular flow. Exports to the foreign sector and business investment inject spending, as do government purchases and transfer payments. These inflows or "injections" balance the outflows or "leakages." This idea is stated in the third accounting identity: actual leakages must equal actual injections. Expressed in equation form,

Third accounting identity

Actual leakages = Actual injections

As we noted, the leakages from the system are saving (S) and net taxes (T). The injections are invest-

ment (I), government purchases (G), and net exports $(X - M)$. Thus for the full circular-flow model, the third accounting identity is

Actual leakages = Actual injections

$$\text{Saving} + \text{Net taxes} = \text{Investment} + \text{Government purchases} + \text{Net exports}$$

$$S + T = I + G + (X - M)$$

Leakages and injections are also related to inflows and outflows in financial markets. Saving, for example, is an inflow; funds for investments is an outflow. Negative net exports (a trade deficit) means an inflow; positive net exports (a trade surplus) means an outflow. A government budget deficit (purchases exceed net taxes) means an outflow; a budget surplus means an inflow. These relationships can be expressed in a fourth identity as

Fourth accounting identity

$$\text{Financial market inflows} = \text{Financial market outflows}$$

$$\text{Saving} + \text{Trade deficit} = \text{Investment} + \text{Budget deficit}$$

$$S + (X - M) = I + (G - T)$$

of all U.S. final goods were exported, compared to less than 5 percent in 1960. In the mid-1980s, imports exceeded exports by a sizable amount; in 1986, for example, net exports were $106 billion. Thus the foreign sector helped to finance the large budget deficits of the federal government. We do not formally study the foreign sector until much later in this textbook. Learning some of the basic macroeconomic principles is easier when you study an economy without a foreign sector. Meanwhile, we point out, when appropriate, how the foreign sector influences the macroeconomy.

NATIONAL INCOME ACCOUNTING

As we noted earlier in this chapter, we can calculate GNP in two ways: (1) as a sum of expenditures on final goods; and (2) as a sum of income received by owners of resources. Combining the two accounting identities, we can express the GNP relationships as

Actual aggregate expenditures = Gross national product = National income

Using the first identity and referring to Exhibit 21.12, you can see that GNP in 1986 is equal to the sum of consumption, investment, government purchases, and net exports. According to the second identity, we should be able to calculate GNP by adding up various forms of income. That is, GNP should equal the sum of employee compensation (wages and salaries), rent, interest, and business prof-

Exhibit 21.12
Gross National Product and National Income in 1986 (billions of nominal dollars)

Expenditures approach			Income approach	
Consumption:			Employee compensation	$2498.3
Durable goods	$ 388.3		Rental income	15.6
Nondurable goods	932.7		Net interest	294.9
Services	1441.3		Business profits*	578.6
Total		$2762.4	National Income	$3387.4
Investment:			Plus: Indirect business taxes	366.0
Fixed investment	$ 675.1		Net National Product	$3753.4
Inventory investment	11.4		Plus: Capital consumption allowance	455.1
Total		686.4	Gross National Product	$4208.5
Government purchases:				
Federal	$ 367.2			
State and local	498.1			
Total		865.3		
Exports and imports:				
Exports	$ 373.0			
Less: Imports	−478.7			
Net exports		−105.7		
Gross National Product		$4208.5		

* Business profits include both corporate profits and proprietor income.
Source: Economic Report of the President, 1987 (Tables B-1, B-21, and B-23).

its. But this sum, national income, is less than GNP in Exhibit 21.12. If they are supposed to be identical, the logical question is: Why don't they add up? In Exhibit 21.12 you can see that the two differences between national income and gross national product are depreciation (the capital consumption allowance) and indirect business taxes.

We noted earlier that indirect business taxes, such as sales taxes, also cause GNP not to equal national income. They do not represent payments to resource owners and thus are not part of national income. But they are a part of actual aggregate expenditures and thus part of GNP. Exhibit 21.12 shows that in 1986, indirect business taxes amounted to $366.0 billion. (This figure also includes small adjustments for business transfers and net surpluses earned by government enterprises.) Adding these to national income gives net national product, that is, net of depreciation.

We also noted earlier that GNP includes all production of goods and services in a specific period of time—even production of capital resources that merely replaces those that are worn-out or obsolete. But because depreciation cost does not involve any payments, it is not income to anyone and so is excluded from national income. Thus we add the capital consumption allowance (total depreciation) to national income to get gross national product. The amount is not insignificant, as Exhibit 21.12 indicates: The capital consumption allowance in the U.S. economy amounted to $455.1 billion in 1986, or about 11 percent of total output.

National, Personal, and Disposable Income

We also gave little attention in our initial discussions to the distinction between national income and disposable income. *Income earned* by resource owners—the concept behind national income—differs from *income received*—the concept behind personal income (see Chapter 6)—in several ways. These differences are shown in Exhibit 21.13.

First, all business profits represent income earned and are therefore part of national income. But corporations usually do not distribute all their profits as dividends. Only the portion of corporate profits paid out as dividends counts as income received by the household sector. Thus to calculate personal income, we subtract corporate profits from national income and add dividends. Second, payments by businesses to help fund workers' social insurance (Social Security, for example) are counted in national income because they are payments for resources. Because the payments go to the government and not to households, however, they are excluded from personal income. Finally, personal income includes transfer payments, since such income can be spent or saved. But transfer payments are not income earned and thus are not included in national income.

Having accounted for the differences between national income and personal income, we next consider how personal income and disposable income differ. If you examine the definitions of these two terms side by side, the difference is obvious:

Personal income	**Disposable income**
Household income after transfer payments have been added but before personal income taxes have been subtracted.	Household income after transfer payments have been added and personal income taxes have been subtracted.

Gross National Product			$4208.5
Less: Capital consumption allowance			455.1
Net National Product			$3753.4
Less: Indirect business taxes			366.0
National Income			$3387.4
Less: Corporate profits	$299.7		
Contributions to social insurance	376.1		
		$675.8	
Plus: Dividend income	$ 81.2		
Transfer payments	513.7		
Other adjustments*	180.5		
		775.4	
			99.6
Personal Income			$3487.0
Less: Personal taxes			513.4
Disposable Income			$2973.6

* Other adjustments correct for the difference between net interest paid and interest income received by households.
Source: Economic Report of the President, 1987 (Tables B-21 and B-22).

Exhibit 21.13
Relationship of GNP to Disposable Income, 1986 (billions of nominal dollars)

In 1986, personal income taxes and other nontax payments to government (such as payments for automobile license plates) in the United States amounted to $513.4 billion, or 15 percent of personal income.

CONCLUSION

In this chapter, we previewed in general terms many of the basic economic relationships necessary to understand macroeconomics. We identified the major sectors of the economy—household, business, government, and foreign—and their most important interactions in product, resource, and financial markets. In Chapter 22 we begin to explore how decisions are made in each sector and how those decisions determine the macroeconomic performance of the economy. We also begin to show how different groups of economists have explained the workings of the macroeconomy.

SUMMARY

1. In this chapter we discussed the general concepts, definition, and measurement of aggregate output and some of the relationships among key macroeconomic variables.

2. Gross national product (GNP) is the market value of final goods produced in the economy in a particular period of time. Although market values are used to measure the value of the various products produced,

GNP is a measure of production—not sales. Goods and services produced in previous periods, goods that are resold, and intermediate goods are not included.

3. Nominal GNP is measured using current quantities and current prices. Changes in nominal GNP reflect changes in both prices and quantities. Real GNP is measured using a constant set of prices; it therefore reflects changes in quantities only. The GNP deflator, calculated as the ratio of nominal to real GNP, is a measure of the general price level.

4. Fundamental relationships between macroeconomic variables can be expressed in accounting identities that are always true. The first accounting identity states that aggregate output equals actual aggregate expenditures. It expresses the definition of GNP as the market value of final goods produced. To preserve the identity, any inventory produced but not sold is assumed to have been bought by the business sector.

5. The second accounting identity—aggregate output equals national income—expresses the concept that each dollar spent can be traced to a dollar of income. Although we use this identity for simplicity, technically we must subtract both depreciation and indirect business taxes from measured GNP in order to equate aggregate output and national income.

6. Gross national product can be calculated in two ways: (a) the sum of aggregate expenditures, or GNP = C + I + G + (X − M); or (b) the sum of incomes earned by resource owners, that is, GNP = Wages + Interest + Rent + Profits. The accounting identities show that the two ways are equivalent.

7. Although generally accepted as an important indicator of economic activity, GNP is not an accurate measure of social welfare for several reasons: (a) GNP does not measure all activity; (b) GNP does not subtract external costs such as pollution; (c) GNP does not account for the underground economy; (d) GNP does not count the costs of government services; and (e) GNP tells us nothing about the distribution of output or whether particular groups are better or worse off. Despite its limitations, GNP can be used to provide some direction for economic policy and to help determine whether economic activity is increasing or decreasing.

8. A purely private economy—one with no government and foreign sectors—has two types of aggregate expenditures: consumption (C) and investment (I). Thus GNP = C + I. The household and business sectors are related in that (a) household consumption expenditures become business revenues; (b) business costs and profits become household income; and (c) saving by households yields funds for business investment.

9. Financial institutions such as banks, savings and loan associations, and insurance companies help to channel saving into investment. They provide the link between those who save (and thus supply loanable funds) and those who demand loanable funds for investment, to finance government budget deficits, or to finance negative net exports.

10. A stock is an amount measured at some specific time; flows are amounts measured over a period of time. National income and GNP are flows.

11. A closed economy—one without a foreign sector—has three types of aggregate expenditures: consumption (C), investment (I), and government purchases (G). Thus AE = GNP = C + I + G. Disposable income received by households is less than national income because of net taxes (taxes minus transfer payments) paid to the government. Government demands funds from financial markets to finance budget deficits. Government supplies funds to financial markets when it has budget surpluses.

12. An open economy—one with a foreign sector—has four types of aggregate expenditures: consumption (C), investment (I), government purchases (G), and net exports (X − M). Thus GNP = C + I + G + (X − M). Imports are subtracted because part of domestic expenditures go to purchase foreign products and thus do not indicate domestic goods and services produced. Exports are added because some domestic goods and services produced are purchased by residents, businesses, and governments of other countries. If exports exceed imports (a trade surplus), the foreign sector will demand funds from financial markets. If imports exceed exports (a trade deficit), the foreign sector will supply funds to financial markets.

13. National income accounting requires us to account for depreciation and business taxes in order to make gross national product equal to national income.

KEY TERMS

QUESTIONS FOR REVIEW AND DISCUSSION

1. How much, if anything, do the following activities contribute to gross national product?
   a) A worker earned $300 working in a factory.
   b) A teenager mowed the family lawn; otherwise, the family would have had to hire someone for $10.
   c) An appliance store finally sold, for $200, a refrigerator that had been sitting in its warehouse for two years.
   d) A business produced $600 worth of consumer goods, but sold only $500 worth.
   e) An individual bought a new car produced this year in February for $8000. Not wishing to keep the car, she sold it for $6000 during the summer of the same year.
   f) An individual bought 100 shares of Zenon Corporation for $1500.
   g) A manufacturer of TV sets sold $3000 worth to Ned's Appliance Store.

2. How do you think GNP would be affected if the economy became more technically efficient? Can you think of any ways in which GNP can increase as a result of either allocative or technical inefficiency?

3. In each of the following cases, solve for the unknowns.

Case	Nominal GNP	Real GNP	GNP deflator
1	$3000	$2500	———
2	4000	———	125
3	———	3000	150

4. The owner and operator of Ned's Appliance Store decides to take off for a week and hires Kay Maree (who would have otherwise been unemployed) to operate the business. Is GNP affected?

5. Use the accounting relationships from the chapter to solve for the unknowns in each of the following cases and to answer questions (a) and (b). Note that these cases refer to a *closed economy*, that is, there is no foreign sector.

	Case 1	Case 2
Gross national product	$2000	$———
Consumption	1500	———
Net taxes	———	550
Saving	———	400
Investment	———	500
Disposable income	1700	———
Government purchases	350	———
National income	———	3700

   a) What is the size of the government budget deficit or surplus in each case?
   b) What are the inflows and outflows in the financial markets in each case?

6. Explain how whole-wheat flour can be either an intermediate good or a final good, depending on who purchases it and for what purpose.

7. The items in (a) and (b) are examples of costs that are not currently included in measuring GNP. For each example, answer the following questions: Should it be? If it were included, how would you measure it? Does its omission make any difference in our ability to determine whether economic activity has increased from one period to another? Why or why not?
   a) The value of services provided by homemakers.
   b) The external costs of pollution.

8. Use the accounting relationships from the chapter to solve for the unknowns in each of the following cases and to answer questions (a)–(c). Note that these cases refer to an *open economy*, that is, there is a foreign sector.

	Case 1	Case 2
Gross national product	$———	$4200
Exports	300	———
Government purchases	400	700
Saving	———	500
Net taxes	———	900
National income	———	———
Consumption	1500	———
Imports	200	450
Disposable income	2150	———
Investment	500	800

   a) What is the size of the government budget deficit or surplus in each case?
   b) What is the size of the trade deficit or surplus in each case?
   c) What are the inflows and outflows in the financial markets in each case?

Aggregate Expenditures and Equilibrium Output

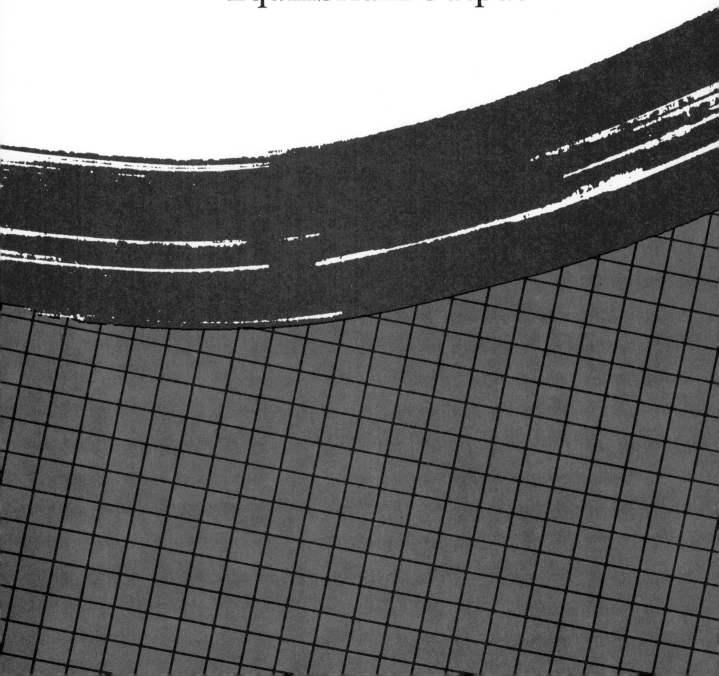

QUESTIONS TO CONSIDER

☐ How do the classical and Keynesian views of macroeconomic equilibrium differ?

☐ Why are economists interested in the marginal propensities to consume and save?

☐ What factors affect household consumption?

☐ What factors affect business investment?

☐ How does equilibrium output differ in the classical and Keynesian theories?

T hus far you have been exposed to several basic concepts of macroeconomics: aggregate demand and supply, gross national product, unemployment, and inflation. In Chapter 20 you learned that aggregate demand and supply determine macroeconomic equilibrium. In Chapter 21 you learned that actual aggregate expenditures always equal gross national product. But what is the connection between aggregate demand and actual aggregate expenditures? What determines aggregate supply? When an economy reaches equilibrium does it have stable prices and full employment? In order to answer these questions you must learn what affects aggregate demand and supply and how they determine macroeconomic equilibrium.

TWO VIEWS ON MACROECONOMIC EQUILIBRIUM

Over the years, economists have given different answers to those same questions. In this section, we consider two of the dominant theories: that of the classical economists and that of John Maynard Keynes and his followers. As you will see later in this textbook, modern economic theory incorporates elements of both the classical and Keynesian theories.

Classical View: Full-Employment Equilibrium

Prior to the 1930s, mainstream economic theory concluded that an economy would automatically reach macroeconomic equilibrium at the full-employment level of output. Keynes referred to economists who held this view as classical economists. (Actually, he applied that term to any economist who held views counter to his own. Not all economists at the time held precisely the same views that we generally attribute to this group.)

To simplify our explanation of **classical economic theory**, let's consider an economy having only a business sector and a household sector. We consider the roles of the government and foreign sectors in later chapters, but the explanation is easier to follow when there are only two sectors.

Classical economic theory. Macroeconomic theories of economists in the late 1800s and early 1900s who assumed that interest rates, wages, and prices were flexible; this theory predicts that the economy will tend to operate at full employment.

Say's law. The proposition, popularized by nineteenth-century French economist Jean Baptiste Say, that supply creates its own demand.

Say's law. Why did the classical economists believe that an economy would reach a full-employment equilibrium? Why would businesses produce that particular amount and why would households demand the same amount? We can summarize the classical school's conclusion by stating **Say's law**, named for Jean Baptiste Say (1767–1832), to whom it is attributed. Simply put, Say's law says that *supply creates its own demand*.

That is, as the accounting identities indicate, when businesses produce $1000 billion of goods, they simultaneously create an equivalent amount of income (GNP = NI). In other words, households receive enough income to buy all that is produced. For example, when businesses produce $1000 billion of output, households receive $1000 billion of income in wages, rent, interest, or profits. If there is no saving, households will spend all $1000 billion of their income, exactly the amount necessary to buy all that is produced. If businesses increase production to $1500 billion, income and expenditures will rise to match. Say's law, in effect, says that total spending (demand) is determined by total output (supply).

But the classical economists were aware that households tend to save a portion of their incomes. When there is saving, the economy cannot reach macroeconomic equilibrium unless saving equals investment (S = I). For example, if households save $200 billion of their $1000 billion of income, consumption will be only $800 billion, or $200 billion less than output. For equilibrium to occur, businesses must be willing to invest the same amount that households save—in this case, $200 billion. But if businesses invest only $150 billion, total spending will be only $850 billion, which is not enough to buy all that is produced. Classical economists believed that saving would equal investment because financial markets make household saving available to businesses for investment, as you learned in Chapter 21.

Flexible interest rates mean that saving equals investment. Exhibit 22.1 shows household saving flowing through financial markets to supply funds for business investment. Classical economists viewed saving as positively related to interest rates and investment as negatively related to interest rates. An increase in interest rates means a greater reward for saving, that is, greater interest income in the future. Thus saving increases as interest rates rise and decreases as interest rates fall. A decline in interest rates lowers the cost of borrowing and increases the profits that businesses expect from investing. Thus investment increases as interest rates fall and decreases when interest rates rise.

If interest rates are flexible, as classical economists believed, the rate will adjust to make the quantity of funds supplied (saving) equal to the quantity demanded (investment). Any change in supply (or demand) will cause adjustments that return financial markets—and therefore the economy—to equilibrium. Thus flexible interest rates help make Say's law true.

Flexible wages and prices guarantee full employment. Classical economic theory is also based on the assumption that wages and prices are flexible. Classical economists concluded that an economy tends to produce at its potential, or full-employment, output level. To see why, let's consider what flexible wages and prices mean in the labor market and in the macroeconomic model of aggregate demand and supply.

Businesses demand labor to produce goods and services; households supply labor to obtain income. Both labor demand and supply decisions are influenced

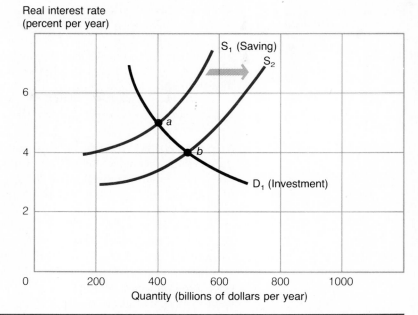

Exhibit 22.1
Financial Market Equilibrium and Classical Theory
In classical economic theory flexible interest rates automatically equate saving and investment in the market for loanable funds. Initially this market is in equilibrium at point *a*, where S_1 intersects D_1. An increase in saving shifts the supply of loanable funds to S_2. The initial surplus of funds is eliminated as the interest rate falls, restoring the market to equilibrium at point *b*.

by the level of *real wages*. If real wages increase, higher wage costs will cause businesses to demand less labor. But higher wages also mean greater rewards for working, so households will supply more labor. If wages are flexible, the labor market will reach equilibrium where quantity of labor supplied equals quantity demanded. The classical economists associated this result with "full employment" because everyone who wants to work for the existing wage is employed. Anyone still without a job is, according to the classical economists, voluntarily unemployed.

If the labor market is operating at full employment, the business sector is also producing at the full-employment level of output, or at what we called potential GNP in Chapter 20. No more could be produced without additional labor, but labor is fully employed. Will this quantity of output be bought? The answer, according to the classical school is *yes*. The flexibility of interest rates and prices ensures the necessary adjustment to "full-employment" equilibrium.

Full-employment equilibrium in classical theory. Exhibit 22.2 illustrates the classical theory of aggregate demand and supply. Note that aggregate supply in this model is a vertical line at the economy's potential GNP of $3000 billion per year. If wages are flexible, the labor market will adjust to full employment and the business sector will tend to produce at the "full-employment" level of output, or potential GNP. This result will occur regardless of price. Real, not nominal, wages determine the level of employment and therefore the level of output.

With flexible interest rates, wages, and prices, equilibrium will occur at an economy's potential GNP. Classical economists did not suggest that the economy would operate constantly at full-employment equilibrium. They recognized that various "shocks" to the system might occur. Consumers, for example, might decide to save more or save less; businesses might change the level of their desired investments. But classical economists did believe that full employment was the "normal," or equilibrium, condition of an economy. They believed that a departure from equilibrium would result in *automatic adjustments* that would return the economy to full-employment equilibrium. And they believed that these adjustments would occur rapidly enough for the economy to be considered self-correcting. As a result, they considered government intervention both unnecessary and undesirable.

Suppose, for example, that households decide to spend less and, as a result, aggregate demand decreases (from AD_1 to AD_2 in Exhibit 22.2). The economy is no longer in equilibrium. At the old price level (115), quantity of output demanded ($2900 billion) is less than quantity supplied ($3000 billion). However, this disequilibrium is only temporary. The economy would automatically and rapidly begin to adjust and restore equilibrium. The decline in spending causes saving to increase, driving down interest rates and causing investment spending to rise. As output falls, so does demand for labor. Surpluses in labor and product markets force wages and prices to fall. As these changes occur, the general price level falls (to 110), and output returns to the full-employment level.

Most economists today believe that automatic adjustment mechanisms will eventually restore an economy to full-employment equilibrium. But unlike classical economists, not all modern theorists assume that interest rates, wages, and prices are perfectly flexible, nor do they all believe that the adjustment will be rapid.

Exhibit 22.2
Macroeconomic Equilibrium and Classical Theory
In classical economic theory aggregate supply equals potential GNP. Changes in aggregate demand affect the general price level but not real output. If aggregate demand falls to AD_2, a temporary surplus is created in both labor and product markets. But as real wages fall, the labor market returns to full employment. As prices fall, the economy adjusts to produce at potential GNP. With flexible wages and prices, the economy returns to full employment quickly and automatically.

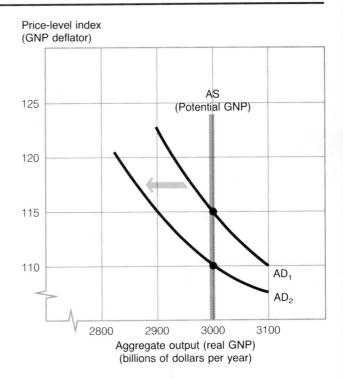

Keynesian View: Equilibrium below Full Employment

Doubts about the speed of automatic adjustment mechanisms were generated by events of the Great Depression. Between 1929 and 1933, real output in the United States fell by 30 percent, and unemployment rose to 25 percent. Prices and interest rates fell, as classical economic theory predicted. But still the economy lingered in a deep and prolonged depression.* To the classical assertion that the economy would automatically adjust to full employment in the long run, economist John Maynard Keynes replied: "In the long run we are all dead."

Faced with circumstances that seemed to contradict the classical view, Keynes challenged the very premises of classical theory. First, he turned Say's law upside down. In Keynesian theory, aggregate demand determines the quantity of output businesses produce. If aggregate demand is insufficient, the economy will not achieve full employment. Keynes argued that demand creates supply, not the other way around as Say's law suggests.

But what of the automatic adjustments that supposedly lead to full employment, according to the classical view? Keynes attacked the notions that wages, prices, and interest rates were flexible enough to guarantee full employment. Unions, for example, may strongly resist nominal wage cuts, even if theory suggests that falling prices will keep real wages the same. If wages are not flexible enough, the labor market may not adjust to full employment. Keynes disagreed that saving and investment respond to interest rates. In the **Keynesian theory**, saving depends most heavily on current income. Investment is largely determined by expected future demand. Under these conditions, financial markets may fail to adjust to a full-employment equilibrium.

Keynes's theory can be expressed in terms of the aggregate demand and supply diagram in Exhibit 22.3. Note that the Keynesian aggregate supply (AS) curve is horizontal across a considerable range of output. It is vertical at the full-employment, or potential GNP, output level.

The horizontal portion of the aggregate supply curve reflects Keynes's view of an economy in the midst of a deep depression. With many people out of work, businesses could hire more workers at the current wage. With many plants and factories operating well below their capacity, producing more at the same cost would be possible. Thus output is determined by aggregate demand. If wages and prices do not fall, the economy will reach equilibrium (where AD_1 intersects AS) below the full-employment level. Without flexible wages and prices, the economy has no automatic mechanism to return it to full employment.

Keynes placed great stress on aggregate demand. In the Great Depression he saw proof that aggregate demand could be inadequate and that the economy could reach equilibrium despite considerable unemployment. Classical economists classified this unemployment as voluntary because they believed that the unemployed could get jobs if they were willing to accept a lower wage. Keynes classified this unemployment as involuntary, expressing his belief that low aggregate demand was not the fault of the unemployed. Keynes suggested that increases in aggregate demand, not lower wages, was the best way to return the economy to full em-

Keynesian theory. The economic propositions of John Maynard Keynes, including the belief that fluctuations in aggregate output are generally caused by changes in private-sector demand. Keynesian economists generally recommend government policies to boost aggregate demand during recessions.

---

* The difference between a depression and a recession (a fall in GNP as defined in Chapter 20) is a matter of semantics. A depression is just a severe and prolonged recession. A classic economics joke is that the economy is in a recession when your neighbor is out of work. It is in a depression when you lose your job.

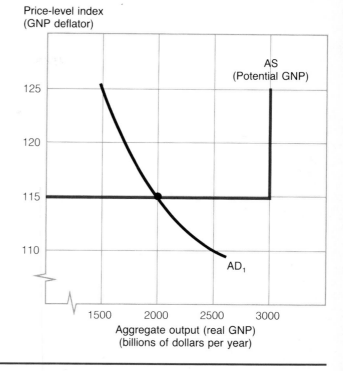

Price-level index
(GNP deflator)

Exhibit 22.3
Macroeconomic Equilibrium and the
Keynesian Model
In the simple Keynesian model a fall in aggregate demand causes a drop in real output. Because wages and prices are inflexible, the general price level is unaffected. The downward inflexibility of prices makes the Keynesian aggregate supply curve horizontal below full-employment output. However, as with classical theory, aggregate supply becomes vertical when the economy reaches full employment.

ployment. To raise aggregate demand, he suggested that government increase its spending, an idea that remains controversial.

In the rest of this chapter, we follow the Keynesian approach to macroeconomic equilibrium. For simplicity, we continue to describe the operation of a private-sector economy (no government or foreign sectors). Since Keynesian theory focuses on aggregate demand, let's begin by considering factors that influence the spending decisions of households and businesses.

CONSUMPTION AND SAVING: THE HOUSEHOLD SECTOR

We begin our survey of aggregate demand by looking at the household sector. To keep our analysis simple, we temporarily make several simplifying assumptions:

1. The economy consists of business and household sectors only. (That is, we ignore the influence of the government and foreign sectors.)

2. The general price level is constant.

3. There is no capital consumption allowance, nor are there any business taxes. (This allows us to equate real GNP, aggregate output, and national income, in keeping with the accounting identity introduced in Chapter 21.)

Although we relax some of these assumptions later, they make understanding macroeconomic principles a bit easier. After you have grasped some of the essentials of macroeconomic analysis, using this simplified economy, we can consider a more realistic and complete model of the economy. In particular, we can consider what happens when the price level varies.

When looking at the effect of households on aggregate demand, we have to consider the determinants of household consumption expenditures. As we noted in Chapter 21, household expenditures for final consumer goods and services are a component of aggregate demand. In fact, consumption accounts for over 60 percent of the total purchases of final goods. An understanding of what determines consumption is crucial to understanding what determines aggregate demand.

Consumption, Saving, and Disposable Income

Among the factors that influence household consumption and saving decisions, the most important by far is the level of disposable income (DI). Since we are ignoring government at this point, disposable income (income less taxes plus transfer payments) is equal to national income. As you might suspect, *the greater the level of disposable income, the greater is the level of consumption*. Keynes argued that this relationship between consumption and disposable income was a "fundamental psychological law." Households, he said, "are disposed, as a rule and on the average, to increase their consumption as their income increases, but not by as much as their income increases."[*]

Exhibit 22.4 illustrates the basic relationship between disposable income and consumption as a **consumption schedule**. You can see that the household sector spends more as disposable income increases, as Keynes observed. When income increases from $1200 billion to $1600 billion, for example, consumption rises from $1100 billion to $1400 billion per year. Note that we singled out disposable income and made the "all-other-factors-unchanged" assumption. We consider other factors that affect the level of consumption—such as wealth and the availability of credit—later in this chapter.

Marginal propensity to consume. Exhibit 22.4 also supports Keynes's second proposition: Households spend only part of any increase in disposable income. While disposable income increases from $1200 billion to $1600 billion— a $400 billion increase—consumption increases by $300 billion—from $1100 billion to $1400 billion per year. Because of its importance, Keynes gave the relationship between a change in disposable income and a change in consumption a specific name: the **marginal propensity to consume (MPC)**. In Exhibit 22.4, when disposable income rises from $1200 billion to $1600 billion, the marginal propensity to consume is 0.75, calculated as

Consumption schedule. A table showing the level of consumption expenditures at various levels of disposable income.

Marginal propensity to consume (MPC). The ratio of changes in consumption to changes in income; indicates the proportion of any additional income that will be spent on consumption.

$$\text{Marginal propensity to consume} = \frac{\text{Change in consumption}}{\text{Change in disposable income}} \quad \text{or} \quad \frac{\text{Change in C}}{\text{Change in DI}}$$

$$\text{MPC} = \frac{(\$1400 - \$1100)\text{ billion}}{(\$1600 - \$1200)\text{ billion}}$$

$$= \frac{\$300\text{ billion}}{\$400\text{ billion}} \quad \text{or} \quad 0.75$$

---

[*] John Maynard Keynes, *The General Theory of Employment, Interest, and Money*. New York: Harcourt, Brace & World, 1936, p. 96.

Disposable income (DI)	Consumption (C)	Saving (S = DI − C)
0	200	−200
400	500	−100
800	800	0
1200	1100	100
1600	1400	200
2000	1700	300

Exhibit 22.4
Consumption, Saving, and Disposable Income (billions of dollars per year)

The marginal propensity to consume shows what proportion of a change in disposable income will be spent. The MPC of 0.75 in this example means that every $100 billion of extra disposable income will cause consumption to increase by $75 billion. To check your understanding of this concept, apply the formula to other data in Exhibit 22.4 and calculate the marginal propensity to consume for several changes in disposable income. (We assumed a constant MPC, so you should obtain 0.75 in each case.)

Average propensity to consume. It is important to distinguish the marginal propensity to consume from the average propensity to consume. The marginal propensity to consume indicates how much a *change* in disposable income will *change* consumption. The **average propensity to consume (APC)** is the ratio of consumption to disposable income at some specified level of income. Or if you divide the *level* of consumption in any year by disposable income in that same year, you get the average propensity to consume. In Exhibit 22.4, the average propensity to consume is 0.85 when disposable income is $2000 billion per year, calculated as

$$\text{Average propensity to consume} = \frac{\text{Level of consumption}}{\text{Level of disposable income}} \quad \text{or} \quad \frac{C}{DI}$$

$$APC = \frac{\$1700\,\text{billion}}{\$2000\,\text{billion}} \quad \text{or} \quad 0.85$$

The average propensity to consume shows how much of a specified level of disposable income will be spent. In this case, the household sector will spend 85 percent of disposable income if it is $2000 billion per year. Although the marginal propensity to consume is the same at each level of income, the average propensity to consume is not. If disposable income is $800 billion, consumption will also be $800 billion, and the average propensity to consume will be 1.0.

In this example, when disposable income falls below $800 billion, the average propensity to consume exceeds 1.0. For example, average propensity to consume is 1.25 when disposable income is $400 billion. This figure indicates that the household sector is *dissaving,* that is, spending more than its current income. To

Average propensity to consume (APC). The ratio of consumption to income at some specified level of income; indicates the proportion of a specified level of income that will be spent on consumption.

Saving schedule. A table showing the level of saving for various levels of disposable income.

Marginal propensity to save (MPS). The ratio of changes in saving to changes in disposable income; shows the proportion of any additional disposable income that will be saved.

check your understanding, calculate the average propensity to consume when disposable income is $1600 billion. (You should find APC to be 0.875.)

Saving Schedules and the Marginal Propensity to Save

Exhibit 22.4 also shows a **saving schedule**, that is, the amounts that will be saved at various levels of disposable income. By definition, households have only two options for their disposable income: consumption or saving. That is, disposable income always equals consumption plus saving, or DI = C + S.

Note that by rearranging terms in the equation, we can calculate saving as the difference between disposable income and consumption, or S = DI − C. For example, when disposable income is $1600 billion per year, the household sector will consume $1400 billion. Saving, therefore, is $200 billion. Because of this relationship, the factors that determine saving are really the same as those that determine consumption.

The data in Exhibit 22.4 show that households not only spend more when their disposable income rises, but they also save more. The change in saving, like the change in consumption, is less than the change in disposable income. As for the marginal propensity to consume, we can define the **marginal propensity to save (MPS)** as the relationship between changes in disposable income and changes in saving.

In Exhibit 22.4, the marginal propensity to save for an increase in disposal income from $1200 billion to $1600 billion per year is 0.25, calculated as

$$\text{Marginal propensity to save} = \frac{\text{Change in saving}}{\text{Change in disposable income}} \quad \text{or} \quad \frac{\text{Change in S}}{\text{Change in DI}}$$

$$\text{MPS} = \frac{(\$200 - \$100)\,\text{billion}}{(\$1600 - \$1200)\,\text{billion}}$$

$$= \frac{\$100\,\text{billion}}{\$400\,\text{billion}} \quad \text{or} \quad 0.25$$

The marginal propensity to save shows the proportion of a change in income that will be saved. In this example, the MPS of 0.25 indicates that a $100 billion change in disposable income will cause a $25 billion change in saving. You should verify that the marginal propensity to save is 0.25 at each level of disposable income shown in Exhibit 22.4.

Because any change in disposable income will be either spent or saved, the sum of the proportion consumed (MPC) and the proportion saved (MPS) always equals 1 (MPC + MPS = 1). For example, if your marginal propensity to consume is 0.75, you will spend $0.75 of every $1 of additional disposable income you receive and save the balance of $0.25.

Consumption and Saving: A Graphic View

The relationship between disposable income and consumption in Exhibit 22.4 is shown graphically in Exhibit 22.5(a). The horizontal axis shows disposable income in billions of dollars. The vertical axis shows consumption expenditures

(a) Consumption

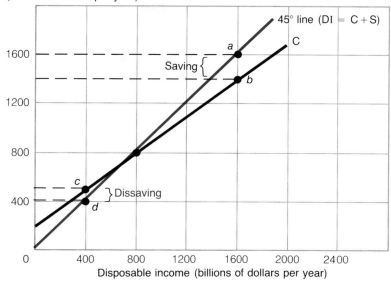

(b) Saving

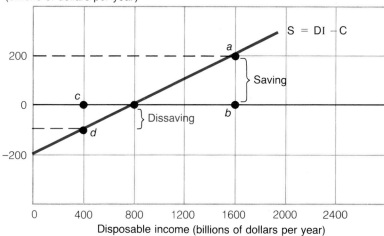

Exhibit 22.5
Consumption and Saving: A Graphic View
Part (a) shows consumption and saving at various levels of disposable income. The red 45° line indicates points at which expenditures and income are identical. For example, at $800 billion of income where C intersects the 45° line, consumption will also be $800 billion, indicating zero saving. At $1600 billion of income, consumption is $1400 billion—the difference between points *a* and *b*—indicating saving of $200 billion. At $400 billion of income, consumption is $600 billion—the difference between points *c* and *d*—indicating dissaving of $200 billion. The amount of saving is shown in part (b).

RECAP

Disposable income is the most important component of consumption. Consumption tends to rise as disposable income rises, but not as quickly.

The marginal propensity to consume (MPC) indicates the proportion of any additional disposable income that will be spent. The average propensity to consume (APC) indicates the proportion of some specified level of income that will be spent. The aggregate consumption line indicates how the level of consumption varies with disposable income for the entire household sector.

The marginal propensity to save (MPS) indicates the proportion of any additional income that will be saved. The 45° line indicates how the level of saving varies with disposable income for the entire household sector.

in billions of dollars. You can read the level of consumption spending at any level of disposable income from the blue line (labeled C) on the graph.* For example, locate disposable income of $1600 billion per year on the horizontal axis. Then move vertically from that point to the consumption line, and from there horizontally to the vertical axis. Consumption expenditures are $1400 billion per year. To check your understanding, try reading other points on the graph.

Another line on the graph is also important to our analysis. Because of its angle, this line is labeled "45° line." Its significance for graphic analysis is that each point on the line is the same distance, measured in dollars, from both the vertical and horizontal axes. Thus the height of the 45° line (above the horizontal axis) measures disposable income. Using the 45° line and the consumption line, we can identify the level of saving for any level of disposable income. For example, suppose that disposable income is $1600 billion. The height of the 45° line at that level of income is also $1600 billion. We can divide that height into two parts: consumption and saving. Consumption, indicated by the height of the consumption line, is $1400 billion. The vertical distance between consumption and the 45° line, $200 billion in this case, indicates the amount of disposable income saved.

Where the consumption line intersects the 45° line (at $800 billion), consumption and disposable income are equal and saving is zero. When disposable income is above the point of intersection, the consumption line lies below the 45° line, indicating that the household sector is saving some portion of its current disposable income. When disposable income is below the point of intersection, however, the consumption line lies above the 45° line, indicating that consumption exceeds disposable income.

In this example, when disposable income is $400 billion, consumption is $500 billion. Thus saving is −$100 billion. Negative saving (called *dissaving*) means that households are spending more than their current disposable income. If you are like many college students, you work during the summer, putting at least part of your earnings in the bank. By saving during the summer, you are able to spend more than your income during the school year. During the summer you save; during the school year, you dissave.

Although they can read the level of saving from a consumption graph, economists sometimes find it convenient to display saving as shown in Exhibit 22.5(b). Again the horizontal axis represents the level of disposable income. The vertical axis shows the level of saving. The graph indicates, for example, that saving will be $200 billion if disposable income is $1600 billion and that dissaving of $100 billion will occur if disposable income is $400 billion.

Other Determinants of Consumption Expenditures

Although disposable income is the most important determinant of consumption, several other factors influence consumption. These factors include wealth, the general price level, and expectations about future income and price levels. They are the "all-other-things-unchanged" factors that we have held constant while

---

* The ratio of the change in consumption to the change in disposable income is the marginal propensity to consume. Hence the slope (see the Appendix to Chapter 1) of the consumption line measures MPC. The intercept (see also the Appendix to Chapter 1) shows the portion of consumption spending that depends on factors other than current disposable income, that is, the factors held constant along the consumption line. A change in any of these factors will change the intercept and shift the consumption line.

discussing the relationship between consumption and income. Let's now consider their effects.

Wealth.   If you or your family have put aside some income in past years, you have accumulated wealth. Your wealth may include a savings account in a local bank, stocks and bonds of corporations, and equity in a house (the part of the house that belongs to you, not the bank). If you have wealth, you can spend more than your current income. Individuals who lose their jobs and thus their current income, for example, often spend more than their income by withdrawing funds from their savings.

The determinants of consumption are also determinants of saving. Households save for many reasons, but two of these are to build up security against job losses and to provide for retirement. The more wealth a household has, the greater its financial security. Thus we can expect that *greater wealth will decrease saving, and therefore increase consumption at each level of income.*

Two historical examples show the relationship between wealth and consumption. Between 1973 and 1975, the value of stocks traded on the New York Stock Exchange declined significantly, lowering the real wealth of the household sector. For that reason (and perhaps others), consumption expenditures were $17–$20 billion per year lower than might have been expected for the level of income.

During World War II, production of war materials had high priority. The economy produced few consumer durable goods, especially cars and household appliances. With few goods to buy, households saved nearly 25 percent of their disposable income (compared to an average of about 6 percent in the past 10 years). A backlog of demand for durable goods grew, and when the war ended and production of consumer goods resumed, consumption expenditures increased dramatically. Saving fell to a historic low of only 3.1 percent of disposable income in 1947 as households spent accumulated wealth. Some economists and politicians had been concerned that the economy might slip into a depression after the war. Instead, increased consumption made inflation and excess demand a more serious concern.

Price level.   Consumption expenditures are also affected by price level because a change in the general price level causes a change in real wealth. Households hold a great deal of their wealth in the form of **monetary assets**, such as bonds or other debt obligations of businesses and governments. Such assets are essentially promises to make payments that are fixed in nominal terms.

For example, suppose that you hold a $1000, 10-year government bond with an 8 percent interest rate. The government has promised to pay you, the holder of the bond, $80 each year for the next 10 years and to return your $1000 at the end of the 10-year period. The *nominal* value of the interest and principal payments is fixed, but the *real* value of these promised payments depends on the general price level. If it increases, the purchasing power of money falls. As we noted in Chapter 20, you then would not be able to buy as much with the $80 interest payment as you could before. An increase in the general price level reduces the purchasing power of a dollar and therefore the real value of the promised payments. As a result, *an increase in the general price level reduces the real wealth of bondholders and consequently reduces consumption expenditures.*

Monetary assets. Bonds or other debt obligations that promise the holders future payments that are fixed in nominal terms.

Expectations. Household spending is also affected by expectations about income and prices. Expected changes in income cause households to change their consumption patterns in the same direction as do changes in current income. Thus if households are pessimistic about the future—for example, if they believe that a recession is coming and income will fall—they tend to save more and spend less current income. On the other hand, if households have confidence in the future, consumption will rise. *If future income is expected to rise, current consumption will also rise.*

The aggregate response to expectations of future price levels is not easy to predict. Usually, consumption is lower than normal during bursts of inflation, perhaps in part because people expect government to invoke policies to reduce prices. But during the burst of inflation in 1979–1980, consumption was higher than usual. Some economists viewed this reaction as household fears that even higher prices were coming. Although economists have some difficulty understanding exactly how expectations are determined, they agree that consumer and business expectations have important effects on the economy.

Cost and availability of credit. A change in *real* interest rates can have two conflicting effects on consumption. On the one hand, a higher interest rate means an increased reward for saving. At the same time, the higher rate increases the cost to consumers who borrow to finance cars, appliances, and other purchases. As a result of the higher rate, saving will increase and consumption will decrease.

On the other hand, consider the effect on a family that is saving with a particular objective in mind: to buy a car or put a son or daughter through college. For that family, a higher interest rate would raise future interest income and reduce the amount of saving required to achieve their objective. Although Keynes did not believe that consumption or saving was strongly influenced by interest rates, classical economists did. More recent studies of interest effects and the availability of credit have reached conflicting conclusions.

Movement along Consumption Curve versus Shifts in Consumption

The factors affecting the level of consumption can be grouped into two categories: disposable income and all others. Recall that Exhibit 22.5(a) focuses on the relationship between consumption and disposable income and that all other factors—wealth, price level, and expectations—remain constant. In Chapter 3 we made a similar distinction with regard to demand. We concentrated on the relationship between price and quantity consumed while holding prices of substitutes and complements, income, and other factors constant. Recall that we distinguished movement along a curve from a shift in the curve. Movement along a product demand curve occurs when product price changes. A shift in a product demand curve results from a change in one of the other factors that we assume are unchanged along any demand curve.

Similarly, we distinguish movement along a consumption line from a shift in the line. When drawing a consumption line, we hold factors other than income constant. A change in consumption caused by a change in the level of disposable income results in *movement along* the consumption line. This change is called

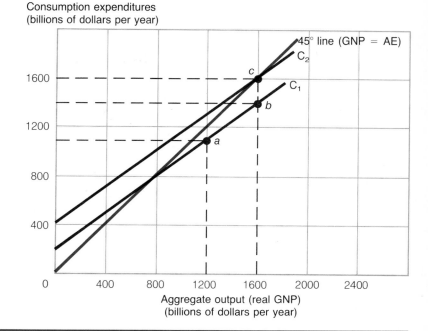

Exhibit 22.6
Movement along versus a Shift in the Consumption Line
The consumption line shows the response of households to a change in GNP, all other factors affecting consumption remaining constant. When GNP increases from $1200 to $1600 billion, consumption rises from $1100 to $1400 billion as the economy moves along C_1 from point a to point b. If autonomous consumption increases (greater wealth, more optimistic expectations, lower interest rates), the consumption line shifts upward (to C_2) indicating more consumption at each level of income. Compare point b on C_1 to point c on C_2, for example.

induced consumption because additional consumption is *induced* by the change in disposable income. On the other hand, changes in wealth, price levels, or expectations cause a shift in the consumption line, also known as a change in **autonomous consumption**. When the consumption line shifts, more or less is consumed at every level of disposable income.

In Exhibit 22.6, C_1 is the initial consumption line. If all other factors remain constant as disposable income rises from $1200 billion to $1600 billion, consumption will rise from $1100 billion to $1400 billion. That is, we *move along* C_1 from a to b. We can also predict the size of the change in consumption by knowing that the marginal propensity to consume is 0.75. Since each $100 increase in disposable income results in a $75 increase in consumption, a $400 billion rise in disposable income (from $1200 billion to $1600 billion) will increase consumption by $300 billion. Using the formula for MPC,

Induced consumption. A change in consumption in response to a change in income (holding other factors constant); results in a movement along a consumption line.

$$\text{Marginal propensity to consume} = \frac{\text{Change in consumption}}{\text{Change in disposable income}}$$

$$\text{MPC} = \frac{\text{Change in C}}{\text{Change in DI}}$$

Thus

Autonomous consumption. The portion of consumption that is independent of the level of income. A change in a factor other than income causes a change in autonomous consumption and results in a shift in a consumption line.

$$\text{Change in C} = \text{MPC} \times \text{Change in DI}$$

$$= 0.75(\$400 \text{ billion}) \quad \text{or} \quad \$300 \text{ billion}$$

By contrast, suppose that households simply become more optimistic about the future, based perhaps on Wall Street analyst Rosie Scenario's forecast of strong economic growth. With the expectation that *future* income will be greater, households are likely to spend more *now* at each level of income. Exhibit 22.6 shows that households will spend $1600 billion per year if disposable income is $1600 billion (point *c* on C_2), compared to $1400 billion (point *b* on C_1) under the old expectations. This change causes the consumption line to *shift* from C_1 to C_2, indicating that consumption will be $200 billion higher *at each level of disposable income*. This change in one of the other factors results in a $200 billion change in the intercept of the consumption line. The intercept represents the portion of consumption that does not depend on current income. As we noted earlier, economists refer to spending that is independent of the level of income as *autonomous*. Therefore the intercept represents autonomous consumption.

Long-Run and Short-Run Views of Consumption

Exhibit 22.7 shows the historical relationship between consumption and disposable income for the years 1929–1986. It supports the idea that consumption rises with income but by less than the increase in disposable income. For example, between 1972 and 1982, disposable income increased by $1421.8 billion and consumption expenditures by $1293.1 billion. Using the formula for marginal propensity to consume, we obtain an MPC of about 0.91. This figure has remained fairly steady over time. Although the consumption line is not exactly straight, the relationship between consumption and disposable income appears to be reasonably stable and predictable.

However, there is a major difference between this plot of historical data and the consumption lines shown in Exhibit 22.6. That graph shows that households will maintain some minimum level of spending even if they must dissave to do so, and observations of individual households confirm such a relationship. In contrast, the historical graph in Exhibit 22.7 shows no significant dissaving at any income level. (In fact, for the entire period shown, dissaving occurred only in 1932–1933, and even then it was less than 2 percent of income.)

Economists have explained this puzzle by distinguishing between long-run and short-run consumption. The historical relationship measures long-run reactions; the hypothetical consumption line indicates short-run reactions. This difference explains the extent of dissaving shown in both graphs. When disposable income declines temporarily, households can maintain some level of spending by dissaving. However, if disposable income remains quite low for a long period of time, households will deplete much or all of their savings. Thus they will be unable to consume more than their current disposable income (without borrowing).

You can see the distinction by considering how you might react to a long-run increase in your income—a $1000 per year raise—and a short-run change—a legacy of $1000 from your rich Uncle Sam. In either case, your income this year is $1000 greater than last year's. However, the check from Uncle Sam is a temporary change that affects only your current income. In contrast, the raise affects your permanent (long-run) income, so you can expect higher disposable income not only this year but also in the future. A change in your permanent income is obviously worth more to you and thus tends to result in a greater increase in spending. Economists generally agree that *a change in permanent income will stimulate a greater change in consumption than will a change affecting current income only*.

Exhibit 22.7
Historical Consumption Function, 1929–1986

Historically, the marginal propensity to consume has been a relatively consistent 0.91, indicating that increases in disposable income cause smaller increases in consumption. For example, between 1972 and 1982, consumption increased by $1293.1 billion, while disposable income increased by $1421.8 billion. Unlike the hypothetical relationship, the historical relationship does not indicate dissaving at low levels of income (although dissaving did occur in 1932–1933). Economists believe that the historical relationship indicates how consumption responds to long-run or permanent changes in disposable income.

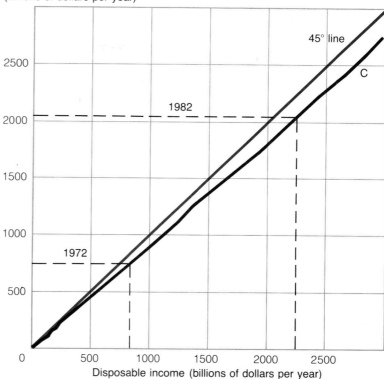

Sources: U.S. Department of Commerce, *The National Income and Product Accounts of the United States, 1929–82* (Table 2.1); *Economic Report of the President, 1987* (Table B-26).

RECAP

Long-run or permanent changes in income cause greater changes in consumption than do short-run or temporary changes.

In addition to the level of income, consumption spending is affected by wealth, the general price level, expectations, interest rates, and availability of credit.

Induced changes in consumption result from an increase or a decrease in income. They cause movement along a given consumption line, with all other factors held constant. Autonomous changes in consumption result from a change in a factor other than income. They cause the aggregate consumption line to shift.

Two historical examples illustrate the importance of distinguishing between temporary and permanent changes in income. In 1964, Congress approved a permanent tax cut. In estimating its effect—how much consumption spending would increase initially—economists used a marginal propensity to consume of roughly 90 percent, based on the historical, or long-run relationship. The actual results were not very different from that prediction.

In 1968, Congress enacted a temporary tax increase. The initial decrease in consumption spending was far less than would have been projected by the long-run relationship. Because the 1964 cut was a permanent change (or as permanent as any tax changes ever are), it increased the household sector's estimate of its permanent income. The 1968 tax increase, clearly labeled as a temporary increase, affected only current income and thus caused a smaller change in consumption. Despite the economic lessons of the 1968 temporary tax increase, a temporary tax cut was approved in 1975. The results were disappointing to the politicians who expected a greater increase in consumption but were perfectly understandable to those familiar with economic analysis.

INVESTMENT AND THE BUSINESS SECTOR

As consumers of most final goods, households are clearly a major force in determining aggregate demand. However, investment spending by the business sector is another significant part of aggregate demand. Businesses make *fixed investments* in capital resources, such as buildings and equipment, and *inventory investments* in quantities of goods held for future sale. To understand aggregate demand, we must examine the factors that influence business investment decisions.

Autonomous Nature of Investment Decisions

Unlike household consumption decisions, business investment decisions are not greatly affected by current levels of output. Once resources such as labor hours and materials are purchased and used, they are gone. Thus demand for such resources is based largely on *current* levels of aggregate output and expected levels of *current* sales. But capital resources are by definition long-lasting; they provide services both now and in the future. Thus demand for them is based largely on expected *future* sales.

Similarly, decisions to change inventory levels are influenced mostly by expected future sales, not just by current levels of income and sales. Businesses typically add to inventories at the beginning of the recovery phase of a business cycle, for example. Even though current sales and income are low, businesses build up inventories because they anticipate an increase in future sales (or perhaps higher future costs).

Neither demand for fixed investment nor demand for inventory investment is closely related to current sales. For simplicity, then, we assume that investment in both capital resources and inventory is completely autonomous. In other words, we assume that the business sector will invest the same amount at all levels of GNP. Although current sales may have some influence on investment, historical data support the assumption that the influence is small.

Historical relationship between investment and real GNP. When we looked at the historical data on consumption, we found a fairly stable relationship between consumption and disposable income. In contrast, the relationship between investment and real GNP is anything but stable. Exhibit 22.8 shows percentage changes in real GNP and in investment from 1955 to 1986. We can draw two conclusions from these data: (1) there is no consistent relationship between investment and real GNP; and (2) investment is much more volatile than real GNP. Over the 1955–1986 period, annual changes in real GNP ranged from a low of −2.6 percent to a high of 6.4 percent. Changes in investment ranged from a low of −20.4 percent to a high of 29.4 percent.[*]

Economists differ sharply over the cause of this instability. Keynesians believe that these fluctuations reflect unstable spending by the private sector and support

---

[*] As we noted in Chapter 21, investment in national income and product accounts includes not only business spending for capital resources and inventory but also housing investment by households. Although the level of investment in housing is very unstable, eliminating this category would not greatly change the central point of the graph.

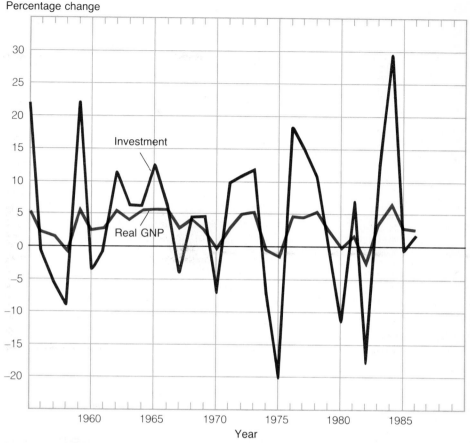

Percentage change

Exhibit 22.8
Volatility of Investment Spending, 1955–1986
This graph shows annual percentage changes in real GNP and investment. Note that there is no consistent relationship between investment and real GNP and that investment is much more volatile than real GNP. Between 1955 and 1986, annual changes in real GNP ranged from a low of −2.6 percent to a high of 6.4 percent. During the same period, changes in investment ranged from a low of −20.4 percent to a high of 29.4 percent.

Sources: U.S. Department of Commerce, *The National Income and Product Accounts of the United States, 1929–82* (Table 1.2); *Economic Report of the President, 1987* (Table B-1).

government policies to correct for the instability. Other economists, however, believe that government policies are themselves an important source of the instability. We return to this controversy when we have given you the necessary tools to analyze the arguments.

Determinants of Investment Expenditures

Although investment is not closely related to current levels of aggregate output, it is sensitive to several factors. These factors are expectations, real interest rates, current capacity and future demand, technological change, and tax policies.

Expectations (business confidence). As we noted previously, both fixed investment and inventory investment decisions are heavily influenced by expected

Nominal interest rate. The actual or market interest rate charged for borrowed funds; determines how many dollars must be paid in interest.

Real interest rate. The cost of borrowed funds stated in real terms; the nominal rate of interest minus the expected rate of inflation; reflects the amount of real purchasing power a borrower can expect to pay in interest.

sales. Investment tends to rise when businesses expect sales to increase in the future.

Real interest rates. Another important determinant of investment spending is the real interest rate. The **nominal interest rate** is the market rate and indicates the actual or nominal cost of financing. The **real interest rate** has been adjusted for expected inflation and shows the real cost of financing.

Why is the real interest rate important? Businesses often borrow to purchase capital resources or more inventory. When they obtain funds from their shareholders, the interest rate represents the opportunity cost of using those funds. In either case, an increase in real interest rates means greater real costs for funds. As a result, investment will decrease.

Although nominal interest rates determine how many dollars of interest must be paid, an increase in the general price level reduces the real value of a dollar. Both borrowers and lenders are aware of this fact, so nominal interest rates are not accurate estimates of real costs. Remember that it is real—not nominal—interest rates that influence business investment.

Current capacity and future demand. An expected increase in aggregate demand also increases investment spending for new plant and equipment. When considering how much to invest, businesses compare current capacity to expected sales. If they have significant unused capacity, they can meet increased sales without further investment. But if they have no excess capacity, businesses must make additional investments if they are to meet future demand.

Rate of technological change. As you might expect, a firm having machines or other equipment that is in danger of becoming obsolete in the near future is likely to invest in new capital resources. When new technology allows for either lower costs or better quality products, firms that want to remain in business have little choice but to invest. But when technological change is very rapid, firms may hesitate to invest large sums in equipment that may soon become obsolete.

Government tax policy. Although we are not ready to bring the government sector into our analysis, we should note that government tax policy can affect investment decisions. In the past, businesses have been granted special tax incentives to encourage new investment. The tax changes in 1986 removed some of these incentives and caused some economists to predict a decline in investment.

RECAP ▰▰▰▰▰

Unlike consumption, investment is not very responsive to changes in the current level of aggregate output or income.

Investment spending by the business sector is influenced by expectations (business confidence), interest rates, current capacity and future demand, the rate of technological change, and government tax policies.

Historically, investment has been much less stable than real GNP, but economists disagree over why.

EQUILIBRIUM OUTPUT IN THE SIMPLE KEYNESIAN MODEL

Now that you have a better understanding of two of the determinants of aggregate demand—consumption and investment—we can consider the determination of macroeconomic equilibrium. As the title of this section indicates, we explore equilibrium in terms of the simple Keynesian model of the economy. Thus we assume that the general price level is fixed. For the moment we also ignore the effects of the government and foreign sectors.

Although we relax these unrealistic assumptions later, you can learn a great deal about macroeconomic equilibrium from this over-simplified model. In particular, we consider why Keynes believed that the economy could reach equilibrium below the full-employment, or potential output, level.

Macroeconomic Equilibrium

Before seeing how equilibrium is achieved in this Keynesian model, you must understand what macroeconomic equilibrium means. This requires that you clearly distinguish between the *accounting identity* we used in Chapter 21 to measure GNP and the *equilibrium condition* we use in this chapter to determine equilibrium GNP.

In Chapter 21 you saw that GNP, the level of output produced, is by definition identical to the level of *actual* aggregate expenditures. In the purely private-sector economy that we are considering, there are three components of actual aggregate expenditures: consumption expenditures (C), *planned* (or desired) investment (I), and *unplanned* (or undesired) inventory investment (I_u). To make the relationship between GNP and actual expenditures an identity, economists count unplanned inventory investment as an expenditure by the business sector. In equation form,

Accounting identity

Aggregate output = Actual aggregate expenditures

$$= \text{Consumption} + \frac{\text{Planned}}{\text{investment}} + \frac{\text{Unplanned}}{\text{inventory investment}}$$

$$\text{GNP} = C + I + I_u$$

However, macroeconomic equilibrium occurs only when quantity produced equals quantity *demanded*. Businesses are forced to make unplanned inventory investments when the quantities they supply are different from quantity demanded. We would not expect businesses to be satisfied, however, if they produced more (or less) than could be sold at current prices. The economy will not be in macroeconomic equilibrium unless unplanned inventory investment (I_u) is zero. Thus

Equilibrium condition

Aggregate output = Planned aggregate expenditures

$$= \text{Consumption} + \text{Planned investment}$$

$$\text{GNP} = C + I$$

Keynesian Equilibrium

We can use the data in Exhibit 22.9 to see how equilibrium is reached in the simple Keynesian model. Exhibit 22.9(a) shows planned aggregate expenditures at several levels of output. In this private-sector economy, planned aggregate expenditures are the sum of planned spending by the household and business sectors (AE = C + I). Note the assumption that planned investment (I) is $400 billion at each level of GNP. That is, following the assumptions of Keynesian theory, we assume that investment is unrelated to current output. Planned aggregate expenditures increase as output increases because consumption spending increases.

Exhibit 22.9
Equilibrium in the Simple Keynesian Model (billions of dollars per year)
For the economy to attain macroeconomic equilibrium in the simple Keynesian model, quantity of output demanded must equal quantity of output supplied. The aggregate expenditures curve (AE = C + I) shows planned spending, or quantity of output demanded. If actual GNP is $3200 billion, planned spending is only $3000 billion; that is, $200 billion of planned inventory investment exists (the difference between points *a* and *b*). Businesses will reduce output to $2400 billion to achieve equilibrium. If actual GNP is $1600 billion, planned spending is $1800 billion; that is, $200 billion of unplanned inventory disinvestment exists (the difference between points *c* and *d*). Businesses will increase output to $2400 billion to restore equilibrium.

(a)

| Aggregate output (GNP) | Planned expenditures | | | Unplanned inventory investment (I_u = GNP − AE) |
	Consumption (C)	Planned investment (I)	Aggregate expenditure (AE = C + I)	
0	200	400	600	−600
800	800	400	1200	−400
1600	1400	400	1800	−200
2400	2000	400	2400	0
3200	2600	400	3000	200
4000	3200	400	3600	400

(b)

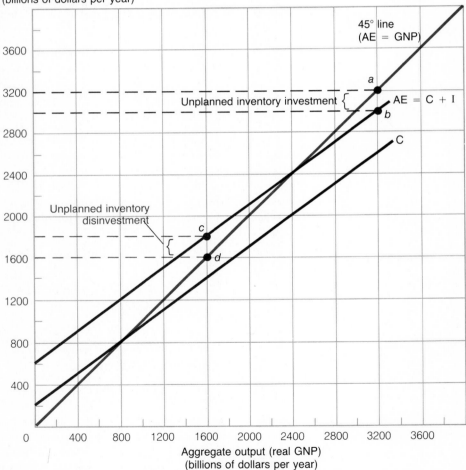

Expenditures
(billions of dollars per year)

Both consumption (C) and planned aggregate expenditures (AE) are plotted in Exhibit 22.9(b). Planned investment (I) is not plotted, but if it were, it would appear as a horizontal line at $400 billion. The vertical distance between the consumption and planned aggregate expenditures lines represents that $400 billion of investment. As we discuss the determination of equilibrium, you should be sure you understand the reasoning in terms of both the graph and the table.

The last column in Exhibit 22.9(a) shows *unplanned inventory investment* at each level of output. Unplanned inventory investment represents output produced but not sold. We can calculate it as the difference between aggregate output and planned aggregate expenditures ($I_u = GNP - AE$). For example, when GNP is $3200 billion, planned expenditures are only $3000 billion. That is, $200 billion of output produced would not be sold, and warehouses would be filled with products that could not be sold at existing prices. (In Exhibit 22.9(b), unplanned inventory investment is the vertical distance between aggregate expenditures and the 45° line. Recall that expenditures are equal to output on the 45° line.)

At this point, the economy clearly is not in equilibrium because businesses do not want this extra inventory. What can they do to get rid of the surplus? One possible action is to reduce quantity produced. If businesses reduce output from $3200 billion to $2400 billion, unplanned inventory investment would disappear. (Recall that in this simple Keynesian model, the general price level is fixed. While you might expect to see businesses lowering price to achieve equilibrium, we have assumed that this option is unavailable. Keynes assumed that workers would not accept a cut in nominal wages. Thus businesses would be reluctant to lower prices, because their profits would fall.)

Similarly, the economy would not be in equilibrium if GNP were only $1600 billion per year because planned spending ($1800 billion) exceeds aggregate output. As a result, unplanned inventory investment is a −$200 billion, or what economists call unplanned inventory *disinvestment*. (Note in Exhibit 22.9(b) that planned aggregate expenditures are $200 billion above the 45° line at a GNP of $1600 billion.)

The resulting good news for businesses is that sales are high. But the bad news is that warehouses are not holding the quantity of goods that businesses want. Businesses can expand production by hiring unemployed workers and putting idle capacity to use. Because we are assuming costs do not increase, the increase in output will not require higher prices. When output is increased to $2400 billion, unplanned inventory investment is zero. The stock of goods held in warehouses is exactly what businesses want. Aggregate output is equal to planned aggregate expenditures ($GNP = AE = C + I$) and macroeconomic equilibrium has been reached. An alternative way of finding equilibrium is given in A Case in Point: Equilibrium—Planned Leakages and Injections.

RECAP

The accounting identity between aggregate output and actual aggregate expenditures is always true because unplanned inventory investment is, by definition, part of actual expenditures.

Macroeconomic equilibrium exists only if there is no aggregate unplanned inventory investment, so aggregate output must equal planned aggregate expenditures.

The equilibrium level of aggregate output lies at the intersection of the 45° line and the planned aggregate expenditures line in the Keynesian output–expenditure graph.

EQUILIBRIUM OUTPUT AND FULL EMPLOYMENT

We have just shown that businesses adjust quantity of output to match quantity demanded. This adjustment produces macroeconomic equilibrium in the simple Keynesian model. But what about the macroeconomic goal of full employment? In this section we indicate why, in this model, the equilibrium level of output may not be the same as the full-employment level of output.

A Case in Point
Equilibrium—Planned Leakages and Injections

We can determine the conditions for equilibrium using the concept of leakages and injections presented in A Case in Point in Chapter 21. There we noted that according to the third accounting identity, *actual leakages* always equal *actual injections*. If we consider a simple private-sector economy, saving is the only leakage and investment the only injection. Thus

Accounting Identity

Actual leakages	=	Actual injections
Saving	=	Planned investment + Unplanned inventory investment
S	=	I + I_u

This identity is always true, but the economy cannot achieve equilibrium unless unplanned inventory investment is zero. That is, equilibrium requires that *planned leakages* equal *planned injections*. Thus

Equilibrium condition

Planned leakages = Planned injections
Saving = Planned investment
S = I

In the table below, we show planned saving as the difference between GNP and consumption (C) because we are using a private-sector economy only. (To consider an economy that also has a government sector, we would have to distinguish between GNP and disposable income.) We also use the accounting identity to find unplanned inventory investment.

In the graph, unplanned inventory investment is the difference between the saving (S) curve and the investment (I) curve. When saving is above investment (when

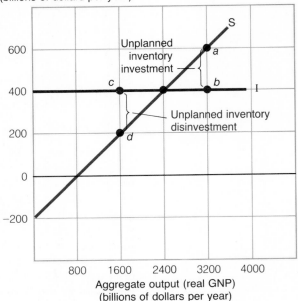

Leakages and injections
(billions of dollars per year)

Aggregate output (real GNP)
(billions of dollars per year)

GNP is $3200 billion, for example), unplanned inventory investment results. When saving is below investment, unplanned inventory disinvestment results. When the saving and investment curves intersect (where GNP equals $2400 billion), unplanned inventory investment is zero. Planned investment, the only planned injection, equals planned saving, the only planned leakage. Thus the economy is in equilibrium.

Equilibrium: Leakages and Injections (billions of dollars per year)

Actual output (GNP)	Consumption (C)	Planned leakages: Saving (S = GNP − C)	Planned injections: Investment (I)	Unplanned inventory investment ($I_u = S − I$)
0	200	−200	400	−600
800	800	0	400	−400
1600	1400	200	400	−200
2400	2000	400	400	0
3200	2600	600	400	200
4000	3200	800	400	400

GNP Gaps and Cyclical Unemployment

Exhibit 22.10 shows the same planned aggregate expenditures (AE = C + I) that we used in Exhibit 22.9. As noted, we can express equilibrium as planned expenditures equal actual output. Thus the equilibrium level of aggregate output is the intersection of the planned aggregate expenditures curve (AE = C + I) and the 45° line. In this case, equilibrium output is $2400 billion per year.

But what if the full-employment level of output (the level of potential output) is $3200 billion per year? The difference between the equilibrium level of output ($2400 billion) and potential output ($3200 billion) is what we called the GNP gap in Chapter 20. In this case the GNP gap is $800 billion. A positive GNP gap is called a **contractionary gap**.

Why will the economy not reach full employment? Note that at full employment, actual aggregate output ($3200 billion) is greater than planned aggregate expenditures ($3000 billion). As a result, unplanned inventory investment equals $200 billion. Businesses would try to eliminate unplanned inventory investment by reducing aggregate output. The economy will not be in equilibrium unless output falls to $2400 billion per year. A decline in output is what happens when the economy contracts, hence the term *contractionary gap*. In the Keynesian view, this decline in output also results in cyclical unemployment, as output and employment fall below their full-employment levels.

Contractionary gap. The amount by which potential GNP exceeds the equilibrium level of aggregate output.

Exhibit 22.10
A Contractionary Gap: Equilibrium at Less than Full Employment
In this graph, full employment, or potential GNP, is shown as $3200 billion. However, for current planned spending (AE = C + I), the economy reaches equilibrium at a GNP of $2400 billion, which falls below full employment. The result is a positive GNP gap of $800 billion (the difference between potential GNP and equilibrium GNP). In this simple Keynesian model, which assumes a constant general price level, the economy has no automatic way of adjusting to full employment. Therefore Keynes predicted that the economy could be stuck for an indefinite period operating below full employment.

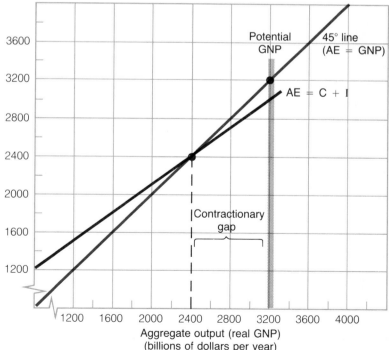

Equilibrium Adjustments: Keynes and the Classical Economists

The classical economists agreed with Keynes that the economy might contract as a result of a decline in aggregate demand. But they disagreed with Keynes's analysis of how the economy would react. And they strongly disagreed with Keynes about whether government action was necessary or desirable.

What causes a contractionary gap at a particular price level? Keynes viewed inadequate aggregate demand as the cause of such gaps. He argued that equilibrium falls below the full-employment level because planned spending by households and businesses is too low. If planned aggregate expenditures were greater, the economy would achieve full employment. To close the gap and achieve full employment, aggregate demand must be increased.

Note that this conclusion rests on two assumptions of the simple Keynesian model: (1) wages and prices will not fall; and (2) saving depends on the level of income and not on interest rates. With these assumptions, there is only one way for the economy to achieve equilibrium: Businesses must adjust output to match the level of planned spending. But there is no guarantee that the economy will achieve full employment. The mechanisms that produce full employment in the classical view—flexible interest rates, wages, and prices—are assumed not to operate.

Actually, Keynes (and current Keynesians) recognized that wages and prices are likely to adjust. But he also believed that these adjustments may be slow and uncertain. In Keynes's view, there was no reason for the economy to endure a lengthy recession. His solution? Add government spending to private-sector spending to increase aggregate demand.

The classical economists (and their modern counterparts) did not accept Keynes's conclusion or his solution. Instead of inadequate demand, they suggested that a contractionary gap is a temporary situation in which the existing price level is too high. If wages and prices are flexible, as classical theory assumes, the contractionary gap will close automatically as the general price level falls. Government action is unnecessary because the economy is self-correcting.

The models of Keynes and the classical economists begin with different assumptions and lead to different conclusions. Because Keynes assumed wages and prices were inflexible, he concluded that the economy may require an occasional prod from the government to attain full-employment equilibrium. The classical economists assumed flexible wages and prices and concluded that the economy is self-correcting.

Which of these analyses best represents the economy? That question is still being debated by economists. In fact, modern variations of both the Keynesian and classical arguments are not quite as simple as we have indicated here. We can, however, trace the assumptions and analysis of modern economists to those roots. We continue the comparison of the classical and the Keynesian views as we build our economic model in the following chapters.

CONCLUSION

In this chapter, you saw how the economy achieves equilibrium in the models of both Keynes and the classical economists. In the Keynesian analysis, a change in one of the factors that determine planned consumption and planned investment will cause a change in planned aggregate expenditures. But *how much* will a change in planned aggregate expenditures change the equilibrium level of aggregate output? As you will see in Chapter 23, an initial change in autonomous spending causes aggregate output to expand by more than just the initial change in spending.

We also introduced you to an important, but highly controversial macroeconomic question: Does the economy have quick and automatic adjustment mechanisms that will help to achieve full employment? The answer to this question is very important for determining the desirability of various macroeconomic policies. Although neither Keynes or his contemporaries are alive today, the debate they engaged in is very much alive. Modern economists who believe, as Keynes did, that the adjustment mechanism is slow and uncertain, continue to argue for government action to stabilize the economy. Economists who believe that automatic adjustment mechanisms are strong and quick side with the classical economists and argue that government should play a passive role in the macroeconomy.

SUMMARY

1. In this chapter we discussed some of the differences between the models of Keynes and the classical economists. We discussed the factors that determine consumption and investment and showed how a private-sector economy reaches macroeconomic equilibrium in the simple Keynesian model.

2. Classical economists viewed interest rates, wages, and prices as flexible. They expected interest rates to adjust automatically to equate saving and investment at any level of output and real wages to adjust automatically to create full employment. In the classical model, output is determined strictly by the factors that determine the economy's potential output. The classical aggregate supply curve is a vertical line at potential GNP.

3. Keynes disputed the classical assumptions. He believed that saving was largely determined by current income and investment by expected future demand. He saw no reason to believe that the two would necessarily coincide at potential GNP. He also believed that during a depression, wages and prices might not fall, which could lead to equilibrium at less than full employment. In the simple Keynesian model, aggregate supply is a horizontal line below full employment, but a vertical line at potential GNP.

4. The most important determinant of consumption spending is disposable income. Consumption tends to increase as income rises but at a slower rate. Saving is the difference between income and consumption. The marginal propensity to consume (MPC) indicates what proportion of any change in disposable income will be spent. The marginal propensity to save (MPS) indicates what proportion will be saved.

5. When the consumption–income relationship is shown on a graph, an additional line—the 45° line—is added to show points at which expenditures equal income. The difference between the 45° line and the consumption line measures the amount of saving (or dissaving if income is less than consumption) at any level of income.

6. Based on historical data, the marginal propensity to consume for the U.S. economy appears to be 0.91 on the average. However, historically there has been no tendency for dissaving to occur at low levels of income. Households will change consumption more if a change in disposable income is considered to be permanent or long run. Consumption will change less if the change in disposable income is considered to be short run or temporary.

7. Consumption also responds to wealth, the general price level, expectations, interest rates, and the availability of credit.

8. Economists distinguish between induced and autonomous changes in consumption. Induced changes result from a change in the level of disposable income and cause a movement along a consumption line. Autonomous changes result from a change in a factor other than disposable income and cause a shift in the consumption line. An increase in autonomous consumption means higher consumption at every level of income.

9. Investment spending by the business sector is influenced by expectations, interest rates, current capacity and future demand, the rate of technological change, and government tax policies. Historically, changes in

investment spending have been more volatile than changes in real GNP.

10. Accounting identities are always true. Equilibrium conditions are true only when equilibrium exists. By the first accounting identity, aggregate output is always identical to actual aggregate expenditures because unplanned inventory investment is considered to be an actual expenditure. Aggregate output is equal to planned aggregate expenditures (equilibrium condition), only if unplanned inventory investment is zero. If unplanned inventory investment is not zero, an adjustment can be expected in output to return the economy to equilibrium.

11. In the simple Keynesian model, the equilibrium output may not be the full-employment, or potential, output. A contractionary gap exists if potential GNP is greater than the equilibrium output. In the classical model, a contractionary gap will cause wages and prices to fall. This automatic adjustment returns the economy to full-employment equilibrium. In the simple Keynesian model, wages and prices will not fall (or at least not quickly). Government spending may be desirable to return the economy quickly to full employment.

KEY TERMS

Classical economic theory, 560
Say's law, 561
Keynesian theory, 564
Consumption schedule, 566
Marginal propensity to consume (MPC), 566
Average propensity to consume (APC), 567
Saving schedule, 568
Marginal propensity to save (MPS), 568
Monetary assets, 571
Induced consumption, 573
Autonomous consumption, 573
Nominal interest rate, 578
Real interest rate, 578
Contractionary gap, 583

QUESTIONS FOR REVIEW AND DISCUSSION

1. Why was consumption in 1932–1934 (during the Great Depression) higher than the long-run relationship would predict? Why was consumption much lower between 1942 and 1945 (during World War II) and somewhat higher between 1946 and 1947 than the long-run relationship would predict?

2. The average propensity to consume (APC) tends to change along the short-run consumption line. Would you expect it to rise or fall during a recession? Why?

3. Answer the following questions for an economy for which the marginal propensity to consume has a value of 0.80.
   a) What does a marginal propensity to consume of 0.80 mean?
   b) What change would you expect in consumption if disposable personal income increased by $400 billion? What change in saving?
   c) What change in saving would you expect if disposable personal income decreases by $300 billion? What change in consumption?

4. Consider the data for the hypothetical economy shown in the following table. (In answering the questions that follow, use the assumptions of the simple Keynesian model as in the chapter.)

Aggregate output (GNP)	Consumption (C) (billions per year)
400	$ 520
800	840
1200	1160
1600	1480
2000	1800
2400	2120

   a) If planned investment is $120 billion, what will the equilibrium level of output be? What will the level of saving be when aggregate output is $800 billion? When aggregate output is $1600 billion?
   b) What will unplanned inventory investment be when aggregate output is $1200 billion? When aggregate output is $1600 billion?
   c) What will the average propensity to consume be when aggregate output is $2000 billion? When aggregate output is $800 billion? What does it mean if the average propensity to consume exceeds 1.0?
   d) What is the marginal propensity to consume in this economy? (*Hint:* Use the formula for the marginal propensity to consume, choose any two levels of output, and remember that aggregate output equals income in this simplified economy.) What is the marginal propensity to save? Below what level of income does dissaving occur?
   e) If potential GNP is $2000 billion, what is the size of the contractionary gap?
   f) For equilibrium level of output to be $2000 billion, what change in autonomous consumption or planned investment is necessary?

5. Use the graph below to answer the questions in (a)–(c).

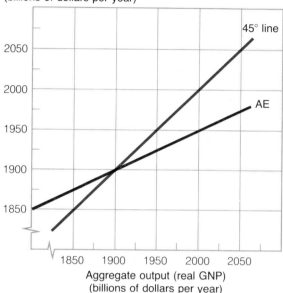

Expenditures
(billions of dollars per year)

Aggregate output (real GNP)
(billions of dollars per year)

a) What is the equilibrium level of output?
b) What is the level of unplanned inventory investment (or disinvestment) when aggregate output (real GNP) is $1850 billion? What automatic adjustment would you expect to happen in this simple Keynesian model to bring the economy to equilibrium?
c) If potential GNP (full-employment output) is $2000 billion, what is the size of the contractionary gap? What is the level of unplanned inventory investment (or disinvestment) at full-employment output? What

automatic adjustment would you expect in this Keynesian model if the economy were currently producing this full-employment output?

6. Investment spending tends to increase as interest rates fall. In the 1930s—during the Great Depression—however, investment spending and interest rates fell at the same time. What factors explain the fall in investment? Does this situation mean that investment does not respond to interest rates?

7. Explain why each of the following statements is false.
a) An increase in the general price level tends to raise the real wealth of households and thus increases consumption.
b) If planned aggregate expenditures exceed actual aggregate output, the current level of aggregate output is above the equilibrium level.
c) If actual aggregate expenditures are greater than planned aggregate expenditures, there is currently unplanned inventory disinvestment.
d) If planned investment is greater than planned saving, the current level of aggregate output is below the equilibrium level.

8. Use the information presented in the appendix to this chapter and the consumption relationship for a hypothetical economy expressed below to answer questions (a)–(d).

$$C = \$320 \text{ billion} + 0.60GNP$$

a) If planned investment is $400 billion, what is the equilibrium level of GNP?
b) If equilibrium GNP is $1200 billion, what is the level of investment?
c) What is the equation for saving?
d) Using the equilibrium condition that planned leakages must equal planned injections, calculate the equilibrium value if planned investment is $240 billion.

Appendix to Chapter 22

Algebra of Keynesian Equilibrium

In this chapter, you learned to determine macroeconomic equilibrium in the simple Keynesian model and to locate the equilibrium level of aggregate output both in a table and on a graph. In this appendix we examine the same concepts using algebraic representations of consumption, investment, and saving. As in the chapter, we assume a private-sector economy with a constant price level.

EXPRESSION FOR CONSUMPTION

Holding all other factors constant, we express consumption in terms of GNP. We can express algebraically the same consumption relationship we used in Exhibit 22.9(a) and (b) as

$$C = 200 + 0.75 \text{ GNP}$$

where C is consumption expenditures and GNP is aggregate output (in billions of dollars per year). The 0.75 in the expression is the value of the marginal propensity to consume. To check your understanding, verify that this expression is the same as the one used in the chapter. Plug in several values for aggregate output (GNP) and compare the values you obtain for consumption expenditures (C) with the data in Exhibit 22.9.

EXPRESSION FOR PLANNED AGGREGATE EXPENDITURES

As we did in the chapter, we assume that planned investment is completely autonomous (that is, unrelated to aggregate output) and has a given value of 400. Since consumption and investment are the only expenditures in this simple economy, we can write the expression for planned expenditures as

$$\text{Aggregate expenditures} = \text{Consumption} + \text{Planned investment}$$
$$\text{AE} = \text{C} + \text{I}$$
$$= 200 + 0.75\text{GNP} + 400$$
$$= 600 + 0.75\text{GNP}$$

EQUILIBRIUM: PLANNED EXPENDITURES EQUAL AGGREGATE OUTPUT

As noted in the chapter, we can express equilibrium in one of several ways. First, recognizing that there can be no unplanned expenditures when equilibrium is reached, we equate planned aggregate expenditures (AE) with aggregate output (GNP). Thus we can determine equilibrium as follows:

$$\text{Aggregate output} = \text{Planned aggregate expenditures} \quad \text{or} \quad \text{GNP} = C + I$$
$$\text{GNP} = 600 + 0.75\,\text{GNP}$$
$$(1 - 0.75)\,\text{GNP} = 600$$
$$0.25\,\text{GNP} = 600$$
$$\text{GNP} = 2400$$

In this case, the equilibrium level of aggregate output—the level at which planned expenditures equal aggregate output—is 2400.

EQUILIBRIUM: PLANNED LEAKAGES EQUAL PLANNED INJECTIONS*

We can also express the equilibrium condition in terms of leakages and injections. In this simple model, saving is the only leakage and investment the only injection. We already have the value of 400 for investment. We must now derive an expression for saving.

First, we recognize that our simplifying assumptions make GNP identical to national income and national income identical to disposable income (GNP = NI = DI). (We continue to ignore depreciation, and with no government there are no taxes and transfers.) Second, we know that households will either spend (C) or save (S). Thus we can conclude that GNP is equal to the sum of consumption expenditures (C) and saving (S). That is,

$$\text{GNP} = C + S$$
$$= (200 + 0.75\,\text{GNP}) + S$$

Solving for S, we have

$$S = 0.25\,\text{GNP} - 200$$

Note that the value 0.25 in the expression for saving represents the marginal propensity to save, or the same value we obtained in the chapter. To check your understanding, plug a few values for aggregate output into the expression and compare the values you calculate with those in Exhibit 22.9.

We now have expressions for planned leakages since saving is the only actual or planned leakage in this case. There are two possible actual injections: planned investment (I) and unplanned inventory investment (I_u). We noted in Chapter 21 that there is a third accounting identity: Actual leakages equal actual injections.

---

*Before reading this section, be sure to read A Case in Point: Equilibrium—Planned Leakages and Injections, which appears on p. 585.

Thus it is always true that

Accounting identity

$$\text{Actual leakages} = \text{Actual injections}$$
$$\text{Saving} = \text{Planned investment} + \text{Unplanned inventory investment}$$
$$S = I + I_u$$

But in equilibrium, unplanned inventory investment is zero, and planned leakages equal planned injections. Using this condition and the expressions for saving and investment,

$$\text{Planned leakages} = \text{Planned injections}$$
$$S = I$$
$$0.25\,\text{GNP} - 200 = 400$$
$$0.25\,\text{GNP} = 600$$
$$\text{GNP} = 2400$$

This is the same equilibrium level of aggregate output we obtained previously, supporting the notion that equilibrium can be expressed in two ways.

CONCLUSION

In this appendix we demonstrated algebraically equilibrium in a simple Keynesian model for a private-sector economy. We obtained equilibrium values by using two different forms of the equilibrium condition: Planned expenditures equal aggregate output, and planned leakages equal planned injections.

We can demonstrate algebraically that the two equilibrium conditions are really the same by recognizing the following identity:

$$\text{GNP} = C + S \quad \text{or} \quad C = \text{GNP} - S$$

If we substitute the expression for C into the first equilibrium condition, we get the second equilibrium condition:

$$\text{Aggregate output} = \text{Planned expenditures}$$
$$\text{GNP} = C + I$$
$$\text{GNP} = \text{GNP} - S + I$$

or

$$S = I$$
$$\text{Planned leakages} = \text{Planned injections}$$

CHAPTER 23

Changes in Spending and the Multiplier Effect

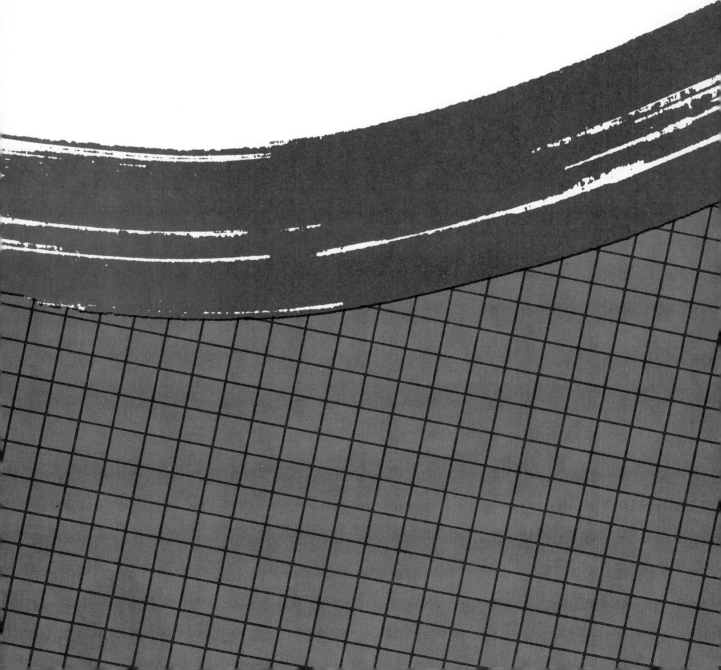

QUESTIONS TO CONSIDER

☐ What is the multiplier and what does it predict about an initial change in spending?

☐ Why did Keynes conclude that the absolute level of saving cannot be increased?

☐ How do government fiscal policies affect the equilibrium level of output in an economy?

☐ What does the multiplier predict about government attempts to close a contractionary gap with discretionary fiscal policies?

☐ How do imports and exports affect the equilibrium level of output in an economy?

Recall that in Chapter 22 we discussed how the economy adjusts to equilibrium in the simple Keynesian model. We observed that a change in a factor such as wealth, expectations, or interest rates would change planned aggregate expenditures and thus equilibrium output (GNP). In this chapter you will see *how much* equilibrium output will change. We can expect equilibrium output to increase by more than the initial change in spending. Using this principle, we can answer the following questions: Why did a $116 billion decrease in investment between 1929 and 1933 result in a $211 billion decrease in GNP? Why did President Kennedy's advisors recommend a $15 billion tax cut to increase GNP by $30 billion?

MULTIPLIER EFFECT

For the time being, we continue to examine an economy having only household and business sectors. In addition, we continue to follow the simple Keynesian model and assume that the general price level is constant.

Multiplier Effect of a Change in Investment

Before examining the effect of a change in aggregate expenditures on the total economy, let's consider the effect that a single firm has on the economy when it changes its spending plans. Suppose Dynamic Enterprises expects the economy to grow rapidly. As a result, the firm decides to invest in a new plant—at a cost of $1 million. The $1 million that Dynamic pays to have the plant built will, from the macroeconomic perspective, raise GNP *initially* by $1 million. In addition the accounting identity between GNP and national income indicates that the $1 million expenditure causes income to increase by $1 million *to begin with*. That is, the expenditure becomes income for the owners and workers of the construction company and the owners and workers of firms supplying building materials.

Multiplier. The amount that equilibrium GNP will change as a result of a change in autonomous expenditures. Measured as the ratio of the change in equilibrium GNP to the change in autonomous expenditures. The simple multiplier effect, assuming a constant price level, can also be calculated as $1 \div (1 - MPC)$.

Thus far we have gone around the circular flow once—from an increase in spending to an increase in national income. But the flow continues because we can expect the individuals who received the $1 million to spend part of their new income. If the marginal propensity to consume is 0.75, each dollar of extra income results in an additional $0.75 worth of consumption. The $1 million initial increase in income causes consumption to rise by $750,000 (0.75 × $1 million). At this point the initial $1 million increase in investment has induced additional consumption of $750,000, making a total increase in aggregate expenditures and GNP of $1.75 million.

As Exhibit 23.1 illustrates, the process does not stop there. The $750,000 increase in consumption raises GNP and national income by $750,000. This increase in income, in turn, induces additional consumption of $562,500 (0.75 × $750,000) in the third round, which induces an additional $421,875 (0.75 × $562,500) of consumption in the fourth round, and so on. Although the process has no end, the effects eventually become quite small. In Exhibit 23.1, for example, you can see that the increase in consumption in the twenty-fifth round is only $1003.

Exhibit 23.1 shows that the process ultimately means a $4 million increase in aggregate expenditures, GNP, and national income. In other words, the increase in GNP was four times as large as the initial increase in investment expenditures by Dynamic. The total change in aggregate expenditures represents the sum of the initial (autonomous) increase in investment ($1,000,000) and the subsequent (induced) increase in consumption ($3,000,000).

The principle that an initial increase in autonomous spending results in an even greater change in equilibrium output, is called the *multiplier effect*. The **multiplier** is the ratio of the change in equilibrium GNP to the change in autonomous spending. Thus it indicates how much equilibrium GNP changes because of a change in autonomous spending. Any change in autonomous spending—whether consumption, investment, government purchases, or net exports—can have a multiplier effect.

Now that you have some understanding of why a multiplier effect occurs, let's consider *how strong* the effect is by measuring a multiplier for a change in

Exhibit 23.1
The Multiplier Effect of a Change in Autonomous Spending

Round	Initial increase in investment	Additional induced consumption	Increase in income this round	Cumulative increase in aggregate expenditures and GNP
1	$1,000,000	$ 0	$1,000,000	$1,000,000
2	0	750,000	750,000	1,750,000
3	0	562,500	562,500	2,312,500
4	0	421,875	421,875	2,734,375
.	.	.	.	.
.	.	.	.	.
.	.	.	.	.
25	0	1,003	1,003	3,997,742
.	.	.	.	.
.	.	.	.	.
.	.	.	.	.
Total	$1,000,000	$3,000,000	$4,000,000	$4,000,000

Exhibit 23.2
Multiplier Effect of a Change in Planned Investment
Initially, the economy's equilibrium GNP is $1600 billion. Part (a) shows that a $200 billion increase in investment raises aggregate expenditures by $200 billion at each level of output. In part (b) the aggregate expenditures curve shifts upward by $200 billion from AE_1 to AE_2. As a result, equilibrium GNP increases to $2400 billion. Thus the $200 billion increase in planned investment causes an $800 billion increase in equilibrium GNP, indicating a multiplier of 4.0. That is, equilibrium GNP increases by $4 for each $1 increase in autonomous spending.

(a) Output and expenditures data
(billions of dollars per year)

Aggregate output (GNP)	Planned expenditures			Unplanned inventory investment (I_u)
	Consumption (C)	Planned investment (I)	Aggregate expenditures (AE = C + I)	
Original investment (I = $200); Equilibrium GNP = $1600				
0	200	200	400	−400
800	800	200	1000	−200
1600	1400	200	1600	0
2400	2000	200	2200	200
3200	2600	200	2800	400
New investment (I = $400); Equilibrium GNP = $2400				
0	200	400	600	−600
800	800	400	1200	−400
1600	1400	400	1800	−200
2400	2000	400	2400	0
3200	2600	400	3000	200

(b) Output–expenditures graph

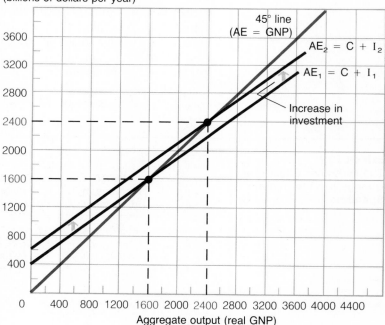

Expenditures
(billions of dollars per year)

Aggregate output (real GNP)
(billions of dollars per year)

autonomous spending. We begin with an economy in equilibrium. Exhibit 23.2 shows that, initially, equilibrium GNP is $1600 billion—where the aggregate expenditures line intersects the 45° line on the graph, and where unplanned inventory investment is 0 in the table.

Suppose that businesses expect demand to increase, and as a result, they want to invest in new machinery. Exhibit 23.2(a) shows that if investment spending increases by $200 billion, aggregate expenditures will also increase by $200 billion at each level of output. In Exhibit 23.2(b), the planned expenditures line shifts upward by $200 billion (from AE_1 to AE_2). The increase in autonomous expenditures raises equilibrium GNP to $2400 (where the AE and 45° lines intersect). In other words, businesses decided to spend an additional $200 billion, but this increase ultimately resulted in an increase of $800 billion in output and spending. Thus the multiplier has a value of 4.0, calculated as

$$\text{Multiplier} = \frac{\text{Change in equilibrium GNP}}{\text{Change in autonomous expenditures}}$$

$$= \frac{\$800 \text{ billion}}{\$200 \text{ billion}} \quad \text{or} \quad 4.0$$

The value of the multiplier measures the additional aggregate output resulting from each dollar of initial spending. In this case, the value of 4.0 indicates that for each $1 increase in planned investment, aggregate output will increase by $4. Check your understanding by returning to Exhibit 23.2 and raising investment spending by $400 billion instead of $200 billion per year. (You should find that equilibrium GNP will increase to $3200 billion, an increase of $1600 billion, or four times the increase in autonomous expenditures.)

This example shows that when businesses spent only an additional $200 billion, total output and spending increased by $800 billion. The important question is: Where did the other $600 billion come from and what determines the size of the multiplier effect?

Marginal propensity to consume and the multiplier. The multiplier effect depends on how much new spending is generated in each round. As the example of Dynamic Enterprises indicated, this depends on the marginal propensity to consume. If the marginal propensity to consume in that example had been 0.80 instead of 0.75, $800,000 of consumption would have been induced in the second round instead of $750,000. Each round would have increased consumption even more than it did. Ultimately, aggregate expenditures and GNP would have increased by five times.

We can express the relationship between the autonomous expenditures multiplier and the marginal propensity to consume (MPC) mathematically. For example, when the marginal propensity to consume is 0.75, the multiplier is 4, which we calculate as follows:

$$\text{Multiplier} = \frac{1}{1 - \text{Marginal propensity to consume}} \quad \text{or} \quad \frac{1}{1 - \text{MPC}}$$

$$= \frac{1}{(1 - 0.75)}$$

$$= \frac{1}{0.25} \quad \text{or} \quad 4.0$$

The appendix to this chapter explains how we arrived at this formula. From the formula we can see an important economic principle: *The larger the value of the marginal propensity to consume, the larger is the value of the multiplier*. This relationship is logical because a greater proportion of each dollar of income is spent in each round and thus in total. To check your understanding of this point, calculate the value of the multiplier when the marginal propensity to consume is 0.80. (Your answer should be 5.0.)

The multiplier is important because we can use it to predict the change in output caused by a change in autonomous expenditures. If the multiplier has a value of 4.0, we can predict that a $100 increase in autonomous expenditures will result in a $400 billion increase in equilibrium GNP. We can express this relationship as

$$\text{Change in equilibrium GNP} = \text{Change in autonomous expenditures} \times \text{Multiplier}$$

$$= \$100 \text{ billion} \times 4.0 \quad \text{or} \quad \$400 \text{ billion}$$

The multiplier effect also works in reverse. That is, a $100 *decrease* in autonomous expenditures will cause a $400 *decrease* in equilibrium GNP when the multiplier has a value of 4.0. See A Case in Point: Keynesian Analysis of the Great Depression for an example of the multiplier effect in reverse.

Saving and the Paradox of Thrift

We have seen how a change in autonomous investment has a multiplier effect. The same is true for a change in autonomous consumption or saving, a fact that is helpful in answering the following question: Individuals may increase their personal wealth by saving more, but can an economy also increase its wealth through saving? If the household sector overall attempts to save more, will the level of saving actually rise?

The obvious answer, *yes*, is the answer that economists typically gave prior to the 1930s. The classical economists emphasized that an economy grows when it produces more capital resources. If the economy is operating at full employment, more capital resources can be produced only by sacrificing current consumption. In other words, the economy must save in order to grow. In fact, classical economists believed that if most households saved more (that is, more at each level of income) the economy would grow faster.

Recall, however, that the classical economists assumed that saving and investment are directly linked through financial markets: More saving reduces interest rates and causes investment to rise. In the classical model total output does not change; only the mix changes—more capital resources and fewer consumer goods and services. By producing fewer video cassette recorders and clothes and more machines and factories, the economy's future production possibilities increase.

In contrast, Keynes suggested that the classical model reflected the *fallacy of composition*: What is true for an individual is not necessarily true for the whole economy (see Chapter 1). Let's consider Exhibit 23.3, for example. Under the original conditions (AE_1), equilibrium GNP is $2400 billion. At that level of output, the actual level of saving is $200 billion per year.

Now suppose that households decide to save $200 billion more at the current level of output. This change shifts the planned expenditures line down by $200 billion (to AE_2). At each level of output, saving is $200 billion more and con-

RECAP

Changes in autonomous expenditures cause equilibrium GNP to change by a multiple of the change in expenditures.

The multiplier is the ratio of the change in equilibrium GNP to the change in autonomous expenditures. That is,

$$\text{Multiplier} = \frac{\text{Change in equilibrium GNP}}{\text{Change in autonomous expenditures}}$$

The multiplier can be used to predict the change in output from an initial change in spending. That is,

$$\text{Change in equilibrium GNP} = \text{Change in autonomous expenditures} \times \text{Multiplier}$$

In a simple, private-sector economy, the multiplier is

$$\text{Multiplier} = \frac{1}{1 - \text{MPC}}$$

A Case in Point
Keynesian Analysis of the Great Depression

Together, the simple Keynesian model and the multiplier provide an easily understood (but incomplete) description of what actually happened to the U.S. economy during the early years of the Great Depression. In order to use the multiplier we have to know its value. As we have stated, the multiplier depends on the marginal propensity to consume. Between 1929 and 1933, real GNP decreased by $211.1 billion—from $709.6 billion to $498.5 billion. During the same period, consumption declined by $92.7 billion—from $471.4 to $378.7 billion. Using the formulas for MPC and the relationship between MPC and the multiplier, we can estimate the multiplier for the years 1929–1933 at 1.8, calculated as

$$\frac{\text{Marginal propensity}}{\text{to consume}} = \frac{\text{Change in consumption}}{\text{Change in GNP}}$$

$$= \frac{471.4 - 378.7}{709.6 - 498.5}$$

$$= \frac{92.7}{211.1} \quad \text{or} \quad 0.44$$

and

$$\text{Multiplier} = \frac{1}{1 - \text{MPC}}$$

$$= \frac{1}{1 - 0.44}$$

$$= \frac{1}{0.56} \quad \text{or} \quad 1.78$$

The multiplier helps us connect two important facts about the Great Depression: (1) real GNP fell by $211 billion; and (2) real investment fell by $116 billion. (Other components of aggregate expenditures were fairly stable, falling less than $2 billion.) The multiplier effect suggests that a $118 billion change in autonomous expenditures would result in a $212 billion ($118 × 1.8) change in real GNP, which is almost identical to the change that actually occurred.

While this example shows the usefulness of the multiplier, it does not fully explain the Great Depression. Why did investment decrease by $116 billion? Did other important changes occur? Why did the economy not adjust as classical theory predicts? We consider the answers to these questions as we develop a more complete model of the macroeconomy. Economists have had much to say about the causes of the Great Depression and disagree sharply on the best explanation for it. While the simple Keynesian approach is incomplete, it did seem to explain the Great Depression better than the classical approach. As a result, Keynesian economics became, for a time, the mainstream of U.S. economic thought.

sumption is $200 billion less. The new equilibrium GNP is $1600 billion. But what happened to the absolute level of saving? In this example, the level of saving remained the same. But why? If income had been unchanged, there would have been $200 billion more in saving. Because higher saving means lower consumption, however, equilibrium output and income decreased. As a consequence, the absolute amount saved by the household sector was unchanged.

This conclusion depends on the assumption that investment remains constant as saving increases. In fact, Keynes argued that the drop in consumption might make businesses pessimistic about future demand for their products. If this occurs, investment may actually fall, leading to even lower output and a decrease in the level of saving. In the simple Keynesian model, the household sector cannot increase the absolute amount of saving because any attempt to do so reduces equilibrium output. This result is known as the *paradox of thrift*.

Who is right? Modern economists agree and disagree with both theories. Most economists now agree with the classical economists that higher saving leads to

Exhibit 23.3
Paradox of Thrift
Initially, equilibrium GNP is $2400 billion and saving is $200 billion. If households increase saving by $200 billion at each level of GNP, the Keynesian model predicts that equilibrium GNP will fall (to $1600 billion in this case). Thus the actual level of saving is unchanged, a result known as the paradox of thrift. This result depends on the assumption that investment will be unchanged.

(a) *Output and expenditures data*
(billions of dollars per year)

Aggregate output (GNP)	Planned expenditures				Unplanned inventory investment (I_u)
	Consumption (C)	Saving (S = GNP − C)	Planned investment (I)	Aggregate expenditures (AE = C + I)	
Original consumption and saving; Equilibrium GNP = $2400					
0	400	−400	200	600	−600
800	1000	−200	200	1200	−400
1600	1600	0	200	1800	−200
2400	2200	200	200	2400	0
3200	2800	400	200	3000	200
New consumption and saving; Equilibrium GNP = $1600					
0	200	−200	200	400	−400
800	800	0	200	1000	−200
1600	1400	200	200	1600	0
2400	2000	400	200	2200	200
3200	2600	600	200	2800	400

(b) *Output–expenditures graph*

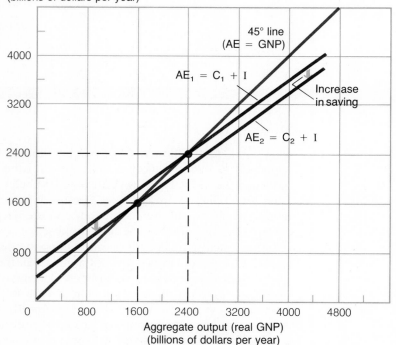

greater investment and economic growth in the long run. But some economists believe that the link between saving and investment is imperfect. They argue that these imperfections may cause the short-run response of investment to be slow or limited. As a consequence, the immediate effect of higher saving may be a decrease in planned spending and a drop in output.

The key point is that to be effective, any increase in saving must be channelled into investment. This channelling is easily done in a planned economy like the Soviet Union, where government officials control both the level of investment and the level of saving. It is more uncertain in a market economy, where the individuals who save and those who invest are not the same.

GOVERNMENT FISCAL POLICIES AND EQUILIBRIUM

Until now we have explored macroeconomic theory by focusing only on the private sector. Although we are not yet ready to tackle all the important questions about government's impact on the economy, we can take a first look. In this section we again utilize the simple Keynesian model. And again we assume that the general price level is constant and that investment is determined independently from saving.

Government and the Circular Flow

To begin, let's reexamine the circular-flow diagram from Chapter 20, as shown in Exhibit 23.4. Adding government to the circular flow changes three elements in the analysis. First, disposable income (DI)—the income received by the household sector—no longer equals aggregate output and national income. Recall that the government takes part of national income in the form of net taxes (T), or the difference between taxes and transfer payments. Second, government purchases of final goods and services are a part of planned aggregate expenditures (AE = C + I + G). Finally, government demands funds in the financial market when it has a budget deficit and supplies funds when it has a budget surplus.

Government Purchases and Equilibrium Output

Most economists agree that government can affect the overall economy by changing the size of elements in its budget. To illustrate how, let's look at the elements one at a time, beginning with government purchases (G). As the circular-flow diagram indicates, government purchases represent demand by the public sector for final goods and services. Exhibit 23.5(a) shows that the addition of government purchases to private sector expenditures means that AE = C + I + G. Equilibrium GNP initially is $1600 billion, where the aggregate expenditures line intersects the 45° line.

Multiplier effect of a change in government purchases. An increase in government purchases (with all other factors unchanged) will increase planned aggregate expenditures—and thus equilibrium GNP. Like a change in investment,

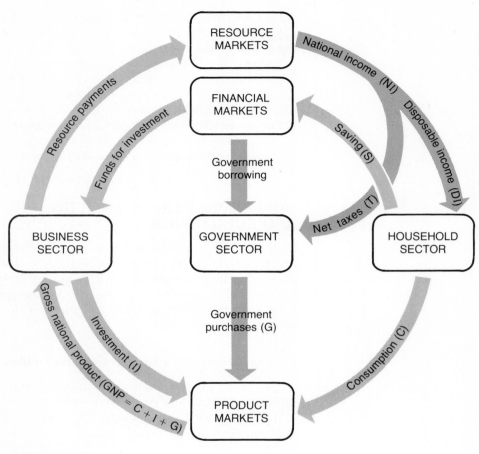

Exhibit 23.4
Circular Flow with a Government Sector

a change in government purchases will have a multiplier effect. Exhibit 23.5(b) shows that increasing government purchases by $400 billion—from $200 billion to $600 billion—shifts aggregate expenditures from AE_1 to AE_2. That is, aggregate expenditures increase by $400 billion at each level of aggregate output. The new equilibrium GNP is $3200 billion, or $1600 billion more than it was initially.

We can use the multiplier to predict this change in GNP. As shown earlier, when MPC is 0.75 the multiplier is 4.0. In this case the only change we made was to add government purchases, so the change in aggregate output will be $1600 billion, which we calculate as

Change in equilibrium GNP = Change in autonomous expenditures × Multiplier

= Change in G × Multiplier

= ($600 billion − $200 billion) × 4.0

= $400 billion × 4.0   or $1600 billion

Exhibit 23.5
Multiplier Effect of a Change in Government Purchases
A $400 billion increase in government purchases will increase planned aggregate expenditures by $400 billion at each level of output. In part (b) this change shifts the aggregate expenditures line upward (from AE_1 to AE_2). The $400 billion increase in government purchases causes a $1600 billion increase in equilibrium GNP, indicating a multiplier of 4.0.

(a) Output and expenditures data
(billions of dollars per year)

| Aggregate output (GNP) | Planned expenditures | | | Aggregate expenditures (AE = C + I + G) |
	Consumption (C)	Planned investment (I)	Government purchases (G)	
Original government purchases (G = $200); Equilibrium GNP = $1600				
0	50	150	200	400
800	650	150	200	1000
1600	1250	150	200	1600
2400	1850	150	200	2200
3200	2450	150	200	2800
New government purchases (G = $600); Equilibrium GNP = $3200				
0	50	150	600	800
800	650	150	600	1400
1600	1250	150	600	2000
2400	1850	150	600	2600
3200	2450	150	600	3200

(b) Output–expenditures graph

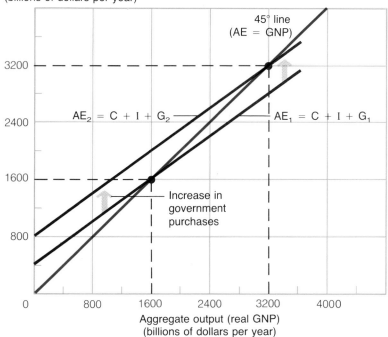

Taxes, Consumption, and Aggregate Expenditures

Let's also consider the effects of a change in net taxes.* The basic effect of higher taxes is straightforward: They lower disposable income received by the household sector and thus consumption at each level of output. When taxes are zero, as shown in the top part of Exhibit 23.6(a), aggregate output, national income, and disposable income are identical. When taxes are imposed, as in the bottom part of Exhibit 23.6(a), we must recognize that a part of national income flows to the government sector as taxes. Thus we subtract taxes from output to get disposable income. If taxes are $400 billion, disposable income is $400 billion less than GNP at each level. In Exhibit 23.6(b) the taxes cause a downward shift in the aggregate expenditures line from AE_2 to AE_1.

Note that consumption is lower at each level of aggregate output because taxes reduce disposable income. The relationship between consumption and disposable income is the same in both the top and bottom parts of Exhibit 23.6(a). In both cases consumption is $1550 billion when disposable income is $1600 billion and $1850 billion when disposable income is $2000 billion. But consumption at each level of aggregate output falls when taxes are imposed because disposable income is lower. For example, at $2000 billion of output, disposable income is $1550 billion with taxes but is $1850 billion without taxes.

This example shows the effect of a **lump-sum tax**. Unlike a sales or income tax, the amount of lump-sum taxes paid is not affected by the level of aggregate output or income. The property tax, a major source of state and local government revenues, is an example of a lump-sum tax.

Multiplier effect of a change in taxes.   Exhibit 23.6 also shows that a change in lump-sum taxes, like changes in spending, has a multiplier effect. To calculate the effect, we first determine the change in autonomous expenditures, that is, the change in planned spending at each level of output when taxes change. Second, we multiply this change by the multiplier to obtain the change in equilibrium GNP.

In the example shown in Exhibit 23.6, a $400 billion increase in lump-sum taxes produces a $300 billion change in consumption at each level of GNP. Why does a $400 billion increase in taxes cause only a $300 billion decrease in consumption? Because a change in taxes does not affect aggregate expenditures directly (as a change in investment or government purchases does). Rather, by changing disposable income at each level of output, it reduces consumption. But with a marginal propensity to consume of 0.75, each $100 of lump-sum taxes causes only a $75 decline in consumption. Thus the multiplier effect of a change in taxes is less than that of a change in investment or government purchases.

With a multiplier of 4.0, we can predict that a $300 billion drop in autonomous expenditures will result in a $1200 billion drop in equilibrium GNP. That is,

$$
\begin{aligned}
\text{Change in equilibrium GNP} &= \text{Change in autonomous expenditures} \times \text{Multiplier} \\
&= (\text{Change in taxes} \times \text{MPC}) \times \text{Multiplier} \\
&= (\text{Change in disposable income} \times \text{MPC}) \times \text{Multiplier} \\
&= -\$400 \text{ billion} \times 0.75 \times 4.0 \\
&= -\$300 \text{ billion} \times 4.0 \quad \text{or} \quad -\$1200 \text{ billion}
\end{aligned}
$$

Lump-sum tax. A tax, such as the property tax, that is unaffected by the level of aggregate output.

*Note that an increase in net taxes can represent either higher taxes or lower transfer payments. We make no distinction between them in this analysis because the effects are the same.

*(a) Output and expenditures data
    (billions of dollars per year)*

Aggregate output (GNP)	Net taxes (T)	Disposable income (DI = GNP − T)	Consumption (C)	Investment (I)	Government purchases (G)	Aggregate expenditures (AE = C + I + G)
Original equilibrium (No lump-sum taxes); Equilibrium GNP = $3200						
1600	0	1600	1550	50	400	2000
2000	0	2000	1850	50	400	2300
2400	0	2400	2150	50	400	2600
2800	0	2800	2450	50	400	2900
3200	0	3200	2750	50	400	3200
3600	0	3600	3050	50	400	3500
New equilibrium (Lump-sum taxes = $400); Equilibrium GNP = $2000						
1600	400	1200	1250	50	400	1700
2000	400	1600	1550	50	400	2000
2400	400	2000	1850	50	400	2300
2800	400	2400	2150	50	400	2600
3200	400	2800	2450	50	400	2900
3600	400	3200	2750	50	400	3200

**Exhibit 23.6
Multiplier Effect of a Change in Lump-Sum Taxes**
Lump-sum taxes are the same at each level of GNP. Disposable income is less than GNP by the level of net taxes. As lump-sum taxes increase from zero to $400 billion, equilibrium GNP falls from $3200 billion to $2000 billion. The $400 billion increase in taxes causes a $400 billion decrease in disposable income and an initial decrease in consumption of $300 billion because the marginal propensity to consume is 0.75. The $300 billion reduction in autonomous expenditures causes a $1200 billion decrease in equilibrium GNP.

(b) Output–expenditures graph

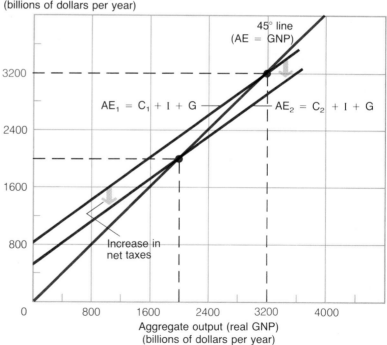

Expenditures
(billions of dollars per year)

Government purchases are another part of aggregate expenditures. When they are included, aggregate expenditures become AE = C + I + G. Changes in government purchases have a multiplier effect as do changes in autonomous consumption and investment.

Changes in net taxes have a smaller multiplier effect than do government purchases. A change in net taxes changes disposable income, but only part of any increase in disposable income is spent.

The change in autonomous expenditures caused by a change in lump-sum taxes equals the change in taxes multiplied by the marginal propensity to consume.

Because income taxes increase with GNP, a smaller increase in aggregate expenditures is associated with a change in GNP as is a smaller multiplier effect than with lump-sum taxes.

Multiplier effect of income taxes. Thus far we have focused on lump-sum taxes—taxes that are independent of the level of aggregate income. But both income taxes and sales taxes increase with the level of GNP. And these taxes account for most of the federal government's revenues and a large part of state and local government revenues. Both income taxes and lump-sum taxes reduce disposable income to less than aggregate output. However, lump-sum taxes are a constant amount at all levels of income; income taxes increase with income. Because income taxes change the relationship between consumption and GNP, income taxes change the multiplier effect.

In Exhibit 23.7, the marginal propensity to consume—the relationship between disposable income and consumption—is 0.75. Every $400 billion increase in disposable income results in $300 billion of additional consumption ($400 billion × 0.75). However, with an income tax of 20 percent, each $500 billion increase in GNP results in $100 billion more in taxes and only $300 billion more in consumption. In other words, an income tax means that a smaller change in consumption is associated with each change in GNP. Because the consumption change is smaller, the multiplier effect is also smaller.

We can observe the multiplier effect by noting the increase in equilibrium GNP associated with an increase in investment. In Exhibit 23.7 you can see that equilibrium GNP increases from $2000 billion to $3000 billion when investment increases by $400 billion. In other words, the $400 billion increase in autonomous expenditures resulted in a $1000 billion increase in real GNP. The effect is a multiplier of 2.5, which we calculate as follows:

$$\text{Multiplier} = \frac{\text{Change in equilibrium GNP}}{\text{Change in autonomous expenditures}}$$

$$= \frac{\$1000 \text{ billion}}{\$400 \text{ billion}} \quad \text{or} \quad 2.5$$

Note that the marginal propensity to consume has not changed, but the multiplier is smaller than in the earlier example because tax revenues increase as GNP increases.

Fiscal Policy and a Contractionary Gap

So far we have shown that a change in government purchases or a change in taxes can have a multiplier effect on aggregate output. In other words, government can increase aggregate expenditures by deliberately changing taxes and/or government purchases. Economists call such actions **discretionary fiscal policy**.

Keynes and his followers argued that changes in fiscal policy can and should be used to stabilize the economy. Most (but not all) economists today believe that changes in the government's budget *can* affect the level of planned spending. But not all of them believe that government *should* use discretionary fiscal policies. We return to this important debate in Chapter 26. But for the moment we ask why, according to Keynes, would an increase in government spending (or a decrease in taxes) close a large contractionary gap, such as the one that occurred in the Great Depression?

Discretionary fiscal policy. Deliberate changes made in elements of the federal government's budget—taxes, transfer payments, and/or government purchases of goods and services—to affect the level of aggregate demand. The aim of such policies is to achieve macroeconomic stabilization—full employment and stable prices.

(a) Output and expenditures data
  (billions of dollars per year)

Aggregate output (GNP)	Income taxes (T = 0.20 × GNP)	Disposable income (DI = GNP − T)	Consumption (C)	Investment (I)	Government purchases (G)	Aggregate expenditures (AE = C + I + G)
Original equilibrium (Investment = $100); Equilibrium GNP = $2000						
1000	200	800	900	100	400	1400
1500	300	1200	1200	100	400	1700
2000	400	1600	1500	100	400	2000
2500	500	2000	1800	100	400	2300
3000	600	2400	2100	100	400	2600
3500	700	2800	2400	100	400	2900
New equilibrium (Investment = $500); Equilibrium GNP = $3000						
1000	200	800	900	500	400	1800
1500	300	1200	1200	500	400	2100
2000	400	1600	1500	500	400	2400
2500	500	2000	1800	500	400	2700
3000	600	2400	2100	500	400	3000
3500	700	2800	2400	500	400	3300

(b) Output–expenditures graph

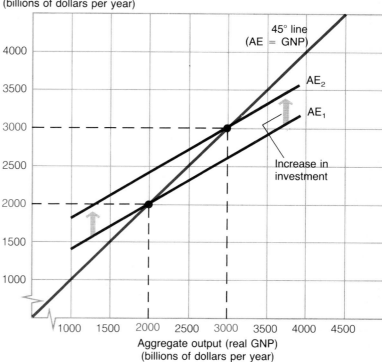

Exhibit 23.7
Multiplier Effect of Income Taxes
Income tax receipts, unlike lump-sum tax receipts, rise as GNP increases. As a result, the change in consumption associated with a change in GNP is smaller. That is, the multiplier effect is reduced. In this case, a $400 billion increase in investment causes equilibrium GNP to increase by $1000 billion (from $2000 billion to $3000 billion), a multiplier effect of 2.5.

Expenditures
(billions of dollars per year)

Exhibit 23.8
Closing a
Contractionary Gap
Initially, equilibrium GNP is
$2400 billion (where AE$_1$ in-
tersects the 45° line). With
potential GNP at $3600 bil-
lion, however, there is a contractionary gap of $1200 bil-
lion. Keynes suggested that
discretionary fiscal policy—
deliberate changes in government purchases or
taxes—be used to close the
gap. A $300 billion increase
in government purchases or
a $400 billion decrease in
lump-sum taxes would shift
the aggregate expenditures
line to AE$_2$. With a multiplier
of 4.0, government policies
that increase autonomous
expenditures by $300 billion
will close the contractionary
gap of $1200 billion.

Consider the situation in Exhibit 23.8. Initially, real (equilibrium) GNP is $2400
billion. Full employment, or potential GNP, however, is $3600 billion. As we noted
in Chapter 22, when potential GNP is greater than real GNP, a contractionary gap
exists (in this case, a gap of $1200 billion). Keynes believed that in the Great
Depression the economy had reached such a position.

Recall that Keynes assumed that wages and prices would not fall in a recession.
Thus he believed that the economy has no automatic mechanism to quickly restore
the economy to full-employment equilibrium. However, he believed that either a
decrease in taxes or an increase in government purchases (or a combination of
both) could be used to close a contractionary gap. In this example, we know the
multiplier—4.0, as in our earlier examples—and the desired change in equilibrium
GNP—$1200 billion, or the size of the contractionary gap. Using the multiplier
formula, we can show that a $300 billion change in autonomous expenditures
would increase equilibrium GNP by the required amount. That is,

Change in equilibrium GNP = Change in autonomous expenditures × Multiplier

$1200 billion = Change in AE × 4.0

Change in AE = $300 billion

The government could generate the required increase in autonomous expenditures by either a $300 billion increase in government purchases (G) or a $400

billion decrease in lump-sum taxes. (A $400 billion decrease in lump-sum taxes leads to an initial $300 billion change in consumption, if the marginal propensity to consume is 0.75.) As discussed in A Case in Point: The 1964 Tax Cut, a similar analysis of the position of the U.S. economy in the early 1960s, led Keynesian economists to suggest a tax cut in 1964.

A Case in Point
The 1964 Tax Cut

One of the factors that helped elect John F. Kennedy president in 1960 was general dissatisfaction over economic conditions. During the preceding four years (1956–1960), there had been two recessions and relatively slow economic growth. Kennedy's advisors were Keynesians; they argued that aggregate demand was inadequate to maintain full employment. They believed that the economy was facing a contractionary gap, that is, that actual output was below potential output.[*]

To develop what they saw as a desirable change in fiscal policy, the president's advisors had to have two basic measures: (1) an estimate of the size of the contractionary gap; and (2) an estimate of the multiplier effect. They attacked the first problem by attempting to estimate full-employment output. Their studies suggested that the full-employment unemployment rate (what economists later came to call the natural rate of unemployment) was 4 percent. They then estimated potential GNP at that rate of unemployment and, comparing actual and potential GNP, estimated the contractionary gap at $30 billion.

In addition, the president's advisors estimated the multiplier to be 2.5.[†] Putting these two estimates together—and assuming a marginal propensity to consume of 0.80—they suggested that a tax cut of $15 billion would completely close the contractionary gap. That is,

$$\text{Change in equilibrium GNP} = \text{Change in autonomous expenditures} \times \text{Multiplier}$$

[*] For more details about the 1964 tax cut, see Charles McClure, Jr., "Fiscal Failure: Lessons of the Sixties," in *Economic Policy and Inflation in the Sixties*. Washington, D.C.: American Enterprise Institute, 1972. Although basically a critical analysis of the 1964 tax cut, the article explains the Keynesian rationale for it.

[†] The Council of Economic Advisors did not actually provide an estimate of the multiplier but did indicate that every dollar of tax cut would generate two dollars of extra output. Assuming that the marginal propensity to consume is 0.80, the multiplier is 2.5.

$$\text{Change in equilibrium GNP} = \left(\text{Change in taxes} \times \text{MPC} \right) \times \text{Multiplier}$$

$$\$30 \text{ billion} = \left(\text{Change in taxes} \times 0.80 \right) \times 2.5$$

$$\text{Change in taxes} = \$30 \text{ billion} \div 2.0$$

$$= \$15 \text{ billion}$$

Of course, the president's advisors could also have proposed a $12 billion increase in government expenditures to obtain a $30 billion increase in GNP. However, they believed that they could more easily get Congress to agree to a tax cut than to an increase in spending. Many of those who supported the tax cut did so for other reasons. Some—using arguments similar to those used by President Reagan in the 1980s—wanted a tax cut to boost incentives to work, save, and invest. Others hoped that the tax cut would reduce the overall size of the government.

Although the motives of its supporters in Congress differed, the bill gathered enough support to be enacted into law. The tax cut reduced personal taxes by 20 percent and corporate taxes by 10 percent. The contractionary gap was effectively closed by 1965. Unemployment, which had been at over 5 percent in the early 1960s, stood below the full employment target, prompting *Time* magazine to put John Maynard Keynes on its cover.

Although the tax cut clearly increased aggregate demand, it now appears to have been too much for the economy to handle. Coupled with rising government expenditures to pay for the Vietnam War, the tax cut helped create excess demand, which fueled the fires of inflation. There are at least two lessons to be learned from this experience: (1) tax cuts can increase aggregate demand; and (2) predicting the effects of discretionary fiscal policies is more difficult than the architects of the 1964 tax cuts believed at the time.

Fiscal Policy and Timing of the Multiplier Effect

Any attempt to use discretionary fiscal policy must be based on an estimate of the multiplier, the size of the gap to be closed, and the speed with which the multiplier works. The quicker and more certain the response of the economy to policy action, the better is the case for discretionary fiscal policy. The slower and less certain the response, the weaker is the case.

When we introduced the multiplier earlier in this chapter, we discussed its effects in terms of *rounds* of the circular flow. But how long does a round of spending take to work its way around the circular flow. Some economists suggest that, roughly, a round might take three or four months. Thus the full impact of a change in fiscal policy is not immediately felt, but is spread over a considerable period of time. As we discuss in Chapter 26, the delayed effect weakens the case for fiscal policy action to close contractionary gaps.

EQUILIBRIUM IN AN OPEN ECONOMY

To complete our model of the economy we must also include the foreign sector. As we noted in Chapter 20, the impact of this sector on spending is measured as *net exports* (X − M), the difference between imports (M) and exports (X).

Exhibit 23.9 shows the effects of adding net exports to our model (maintaining the Keynesian assumptions). Planned aggregate expenditures is greater by the

Exhibit 23.9
Keynesian Equilibrium in an Open Economy
Adding net exports (X − M) to total planned aggregate expenditures (AE = C + I + G + X − M) shifts the aggregate expenditures line. Equilibrium GNP will rise to $2400 billion in this case because exports exceed imports.

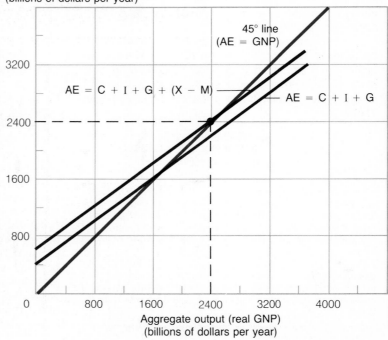

amount of net exports ($AE = C + I + G + X - M$). We add spending by foreign individuals, businesses, and governments on domestic goods and services (exports) because the goods are produced in the United States. We subtract spending by domestic households, businesses, and government (imports) because those goods and services are produced in other countries. The net result shows spending for domestically produced goods and services, that is, domestic GNP.

Equilibrium is still the point at which planned aggregate expenditures equal aggregate output. Note, however, that in this example we show net exports as a constant amount, unaffected by the level of output. In the real world, imports tend to rise as output (GNP) and income increase. Why? When GNP increases, businesses buy and use more foreign resources (such as tin from Bolivia). Households buy and consume more foreign goods (such as coffee from Brazil and automobiles from Japan and South Korea).

CONCLUSION

In this chapter, you learned that changes in spending have a multiplier effect on equilibrium GNP. An initial boost in spending creates more income and therefore even more spending. Our analysis of the multiplier was based on the simple Keynesian model. The simplifications—especially the fact that the general price level is held constant—made the introduction of macroeconomics easier. To study the actual behavior of the U.S. or any other modern economy, however, we must use a more complete and realistic model.

One important factor that we have ignored so far is money. To complete our macroeconomic model we have to consider the role of money and how a change in the amount of money supplied affects economic activity. Moreover, if we are to study inflation, we must allow the price level to vary. Thus we must discuss the factors behind the full-scale aggregate demand and supply model introduced in Chapter 20 and how we can use that model.

As we proceed, you will encounter the multiplier effect again and again. As we modify our model, you will find that many elements reduce the overall multiplier effect in the real world. Only after making the model more realistic and complete can we return to the idea of government policies and whether they can improve economic performance—a controversial but exciting issue.

SUMMARY

1. In this chapter we discussed how a change in autonomous expenditures has a multiplier effect on equilibrium GNP, based on the Keynesian assumptions of inflexible wages and investment which is independent of current income and saving.

2. The multiplier is the ratio of the change in equilibrium GNP to the change in autonomous expenditures. The multiplier effect results from an initial increase in spending that causes an increase in income and therefore generates further increases in spending. But because the household sector spends only a portion of the increase in income, subsequent rounds of spending are smaller and smaller. The greater the marginal propensity to consume, the greater is each round of spend-

ing and the larger the eventual multiplier effect. The product of the multiplier and the change in autonomous expenditures predicts the change in equilibrium GNP.

3. Classical economists believed that more saving increases investment and therefore the economy's potential GNP. In the simple Keynesian model, investment is constant; an initial increase in saving reduces consumption, causing equilibrium GNP to decline and thus the total level of saving to be unchanged. This effect is called the paradox of thrift. But if investment falls as firms become pessimistic about the future, the level of both saving and GNP may fall.

4. When the government sector is added to the model, disposable income is less than national income (and GNP) by the amount of net taxes (taxes less transfer payments). And government purchases are added to consumption and investment to determine planned aggregate expenditures (AE = C + I + G).

5. Changes in government purchases and in net taxes, like changes in other autonomous expenditures, have a multiplier effect. A change in lump-sum taxes (taxes unrelated to aggregate output) first affects disposable income. Because households spend only a portion of any change in income, the initial change in spending is the product of the change in taxes and the marginal propensity to consume.

6. The amount of income taxes paid increases with aggregate output, as does the difference between GNP and disposable income. A smaller increase in aggregate expenditures is associated with a change in GNP and the multiplier effect is less.

7. Because wages and prices are inflexible in the simple Keynesian model, the economy could reach equilibrium at less than full employment. Using discretionary fiscal policy—deliberate changes in government purchases and/or taxes—the government can increase expenditures and push the economy to the full-employment, or potential GNP, level.

8. Adding the foreign sector to the simple Keynesian model requires adding net exports (X − M) to aggregate expenditures. Exports represent foreign spending on domestic goods and services; imports represent domestic spending on foreign goods and services. In this expansion of the model, AE = C + I + G +(X − M).

KEY TERMS

Multiplier, 593
Lump-sum tax, 602
Discretionary fiscal policy, 604

QUESTIONS FOR REVIEW AND DISCUSSION

1. A small city is considering trying to attract additional industry. A city council member argues: "If we attract a firm with an annual payroll of $2 million, local merchants will find their sales rising by $2 million as well." Based on the concepts presented in this chapter, how would you respond to the city council member and help the council analyze the effect of a new firm on the local economy? How would the closing of a similar plant affect the local economy?

2. Suppose that the marginal propensity to consume is 0.80. Complete each of the following statements.

a) If disposable income increases by $400 billion, consumption will (increase/decrease) by $_____ billion.

b) If disposable income decreases by $300 billion, saving will (increase/decrease) by $_____ billion.

c) If there is no government or foreign sector and if investment is unaffected by current output, the multiplier will have a value of _____.

d) Based on the answer to (c), a $150 billion increase in planned investment would increase equilibrium GNP by $_____.

e) If equilibrium GNP increases by $300 billion because of a change in planned saving, then saving must have (increased/decreased) by $_____ billion.

3. Use the following graph to complete the statements in (a)–(f).

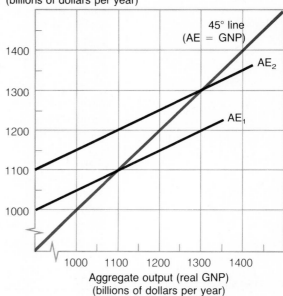

Expenditures
(billions of dollars per year)

Aggregate output (real GNP)
(billions of dollars per year)

a) The change in planned expenditures caused equilibrium GNP to increase from $_____ billion to $_____ billion.

b) Autonomous expenditures increased by $_____ billion.

c) The multiplier is _____.

d) If government purchases were to decline by $50 billion, equilibrium GNP would (increase/decrease) by $_____ billion.

e) Suppose that potential GNP is $1400 billion. The contractionary gap that initially existed (AE₁) was $_____ billion. Indicate the size of the gap on the graph.

f) Draw a new AE line that shows the level of planned aggregate expenditures required to close the gap. Planned aggregate expenditures would have to increase by $_____ (from AE₂) to close the gap and bring the economy to full employment.

4. The following table shows planned aggregate expenditures by the household and business sectors in the economy of Orcam, both before (case 1) and after (case 2) an increase in investment.

Aggregate output (GNP) (millions)	Planned aggregate expenditures (millions)	
	Case 1	Case 2
$ 500	$ 600	$ 650
750	800	850
1000	1000	1050
1250	1200	1250
1500	1400	1450

Answer the following questions, assuming that there is no government or foreign sector.
a) What is the equilibrium GNP in each case?
b) By how much did autonomous expenditures increase between case 1 and case 2?
c) What is the marginal propensity to consume?
d) What is the value of the multiplier?
e) If potential GNP is $1500 million, what is the size of the contractionary gap in each case? By how much must autonomous expenditures be increased to close the gap?

5. The macroeconomy of Lower Bakpayne is described as follows:

Aggregate output (GNP) (millions)	Planned aggregate expenditures (millions)
	Current
$ 600	$640
700	720
800	800
900	880
1000	960

a) What is the current equilibrium level of GNP?
b) If investment, government purchases, taxes, and net exports are fixed, what is the value of the marginal propensity to consume? What is the value of the multiplier?

c) If net taxes are $125 billion, what is disposable income when GNP is $1000 billion? What is consumption?
d) If potential GNP is $1000 billion, how big is the current contractionary gap? By how much would government purchases have to increase to close the gap? What change in lump-sum taxes would close the gap?
e) What would the new equilibrium GNP be if government purchases decreased by $20 billion? (Answer this part both by adding another column to the table and using the formula for the multiplier.)
f) Starting from the initial conditions given, what will be the new equilibrium GNP if net taxes decreased by $50 billion? (Answer this part both by adding another column to the table and by using the formula for the multiplier.)

6. Explain whether each of the following statements is true, false, or debatable in the context of the simple Keynesian model.
a) The greater the marginal propensity to consume, the smaller is the multiplier.
b) An increase in lump-sum taxes has the same effect on equilibrium GNP as a change in government purchases.
c) The multiplier effect tends to be smaller when the government relies on income taxes instead of lump-sum taxes.

The following questions are based on the appendix to this chapter.

7. Suppose that planned investment and planned consumption are expressed as follows:

$$C = 650 + 0.60\text{GNP} \quad \text{and} \quad I = 150$$

a) If this is a purely private-sector economy, what is the equilibrium level of GNP?
b) What is the marginal propensity to consume? What is the multiplier?
c) If planned investment rises by $50, how much will equilibrium GNP increase? (Answer this part both by using the multiplier and by solving for the new equilibrium level of aggregate output.)

8. Suppose that planned expenditures are expressed as

$$C = 250 + 0.75\text{DI} \quad G = 150 \quad X = 100$$
$$I = 125 \quad T = 100 \quad M = 75$$

a) What is the equilibrium level of GNP?
b) If potential GNP is $2320, what is the size of the contractionary gap?
c) By how much would government purchases (G) have to increase to close the contractionary gap? How much would net taxes (T) have to fall?

Appendix to Chapter 23

Algebra of the Multiplier Effect

In this chapter, you saw that a change in autonomous expenditures has a multiplier effect, increasing the equilibrium level of aggregate output by more than the initial change in spending. In this appendix, we demonstrate the multiplier effect and derive the multiplier using an algebraic representation of aggregate expenditures.

AGGREGATE EXPENDITURES: A NUMERICAL EXAMPLE

In the Appendix to Chapter 22, we used the following consumption (C) function:

$$C = 200 + 0.75GNP$$

where C is consumption and GNP is aggregate output. As we noted in that appendix, the figure 200 represents autonomous consumption (the portion that does not vary with aggregate output). As before, the coefficient of GNP (0.75) is the value of the marginal propensity to consume (MPC).

If we assume an initial value of investment (I_1) of 400, we derive the formula for aggregate expenditures (AE_1) as follows:

$$\text{Aggregate expenditures} = \text{Consumption} + \text{Investment}$$
$$AE_1 = C + I_1$$
$$= 200 + 0.75GNP_1 + 400$$
$$= 600 + 0.75GNP_1$$

Note that the figure 600 in the equation represents total autonomous expenditures, that is, the sum of autonomous consumption and autonomous investment. If businesses become more optimistic about the future and investment rises to 600 as a result, we can express the new aggregate expenditures (AE_2) as

$$AE_2 = 800 + 0.75GNP_2$$

Note that the $200 billion increase in planned investment raised the autonomous portion of aggregate expenditures (the part not related to GNP) from $600 to $800 billion.

CHANGE IN EQUILIBRIUM: THE MULTIPLIER EFFECT

As in the chapter, we want to know how the change in investment affects equilibrium. Equilibrium requires that

$$\text{Aggregate output} = \text{Planned aggregate expenditures}$$
$$GNP = AE$$

Thus

$$\text{When I} = 400: \quad \text{GNP}_1 = 600 + 0.75\text{GNP}_1$$
$$\text{When I} = 600: \quad \text{GNP}_2 = 800 + 0.75\text{GNP}_2$$

Solving each equation, we find that equilibrium GNP will increase from $2400 to $3200. That is

When I = 400	**When I = 600**
$\text{GNP}_1 = 600 + 0.75\text{GNP}_1$	$\text{GNP}_2 = 800 + 0.75\text{GNP}_2$
$(1 - 0.75)\text{GNP}_1 = 600$	$(1 - 0.75)\text{GNP}_2 = 800$
$\text{GNP}_1 = 600/(0.25)$	$\text{GNP}_2 = 800/(0.25)$
$= \$2400$	$= \$3200$

This analysis indicates that the multiplier is 4.0 because a $200 increase in investment increased equilibrium GNP by $800.

We can also find the change in equilibrium GNP directly by subtracting the expression for GNP_1 from that for GNP_2, or

$$(\text{GNP}_2 - \text{GNP}_1) = (800 + 0.75\text{GNP}_1) - (600 + 0.75\text{GNP}_2)$$
$$= 200 + 0.75(\text{GNP}_2 - \text{GNP}_1)$$
$$(1 - 0.75)(\text{GNP}_2 - \text{GNP}_1) = 200$$
$$(\text{GNP}_2 - \text{GNP}_1) = 200/0.25 \quad \text{or} \quad 800$$

ALGEBRAIC DERIVATION OF THE MULTIPLIER

We can derive a more general expression for the multiplier by first rewriting the expression for aggregate expenditures, substituting general terms for the numbers we used previously.

Original expression	**General expression**
$\text{AE}_1 = 200 + 0.75\text{GNP}_1 + \text{I}_1$	$\text{AE}_1 = \text{AC} + (\text{MPC} \times \text{GNP}_1) + \text{I}_1$
	$= (\text{AC} + \text{I}_1) + (\text{MPC} \times \text{GNP}_1)$

where AC represents autonomous consumption, MPC represents marginal propensity to consume, and AE represents aggregate expenditures. Then using the general expression and the equilibrium condition, we obtain a general expression of the multiplier, assuming an increase in investment from level I_1 to level I_2.

Original expression

$$\text{GNP}_2 - \text{GNP}_1 = 200 + (0.75)(\text{GNP}_2 - \text{GNP}_1)$$

General expression

$$\text{GNP}_2 - \text{GNP}_1 = (\text{I}_2 - \text{I}_1) + \text{MPC}(\text{GNP}_2 - \text{GNP}_1)$$
$$(1 - \text{MPC})(\text{GNP}_2 - \text{GNP}_1) = \text{I}_2 - \text{I}_1$$

and

$$\text{Multiplier} = \frac{\text{GNP}_2 - \text{GNP}_1}{\text{I}_2 - \text{I}_1} = \frac{1}{1 - \text{MPC}} \quad \text{or} \quad \frac{1}{\text{MPS}}$$

Note that any change in income will either be spent or saved. As a result, the proportion spent (MPC) plus the proportion saved (MPS) equals 1. Thus

$$1 - \text{MPC} = \text{MPS} \quad \text{and} \quad \frac{1}{1 - \text{MPC}} = \frac{1}{\text{MPS}}$$

EQUILIBRIUM IN A PUBLIC-SECTOR ECONOMY

When we add the public sector to our model we must make two important changes. First, we subtract net taxes (T) from aggregate output (GNP) to obtain disposable income (DI). That is,

$$C = 200 + 0.75(\text{GNP} - T)$$
$$= 200 + 0.75\text{DI}$$

Note that this expression assumes lump-sum, not income, taxes. That is, the amount of net taxes is unaffected by changes in income.

Second, we add government purchases to consumption and investment to obtain aggregate expenditures. Thus if investment (I) is 350 and both government purchases (G) and net taxes (T) are 200, planned aggregate expenditures (AE) are

$$\text{AE} = C + I + G$$
$$= 200 + 0.75(\text{GNP} - 200) + 350 + 200$$
$$= 600 + 0.75\text{GNP}$$

For these conditions equilibrium GNP will be $2400, calculated as

$$\text{Aggregate output} = \text{Planned aggregate expenditures}$$
$$\text{GNP} = \text{AE}$$
$$(1 - 0.75)\,\text{GNP} = 600$$
$$\text{GNP} = \frac{600}{0.25} \quad \text{or} \quad \$2400$$

CONCLUSION

In this appendix we showed how to use the equilibrium condition and expressions for planned aggregate expenditures to derive the multiplier. You saw that in a simple, private-sector economy the value of the multiplier is determined by the value of the marginal propensity to consume (MPC).

SEVEN

Money, Banking, and Economic Activity

Money and the
Banking System

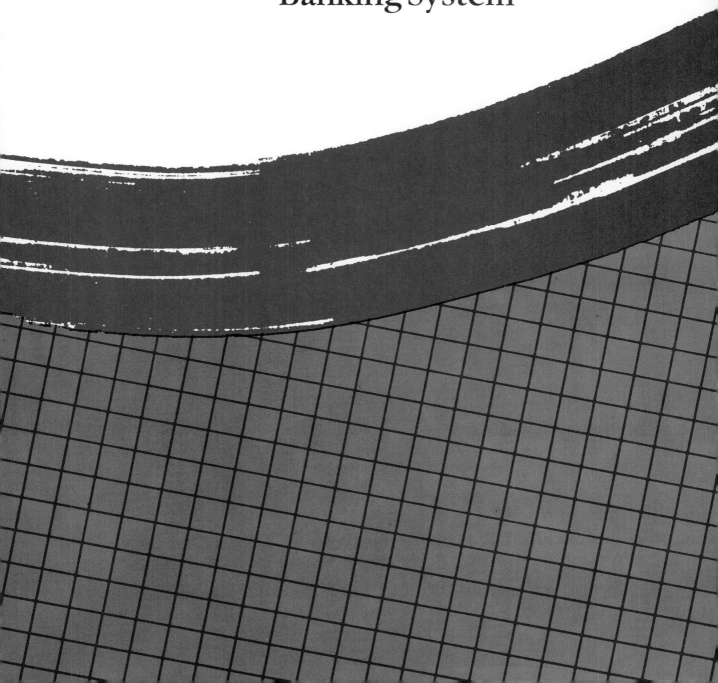

QUESTIONS TO CONSIDER

☐ In what ways have definitions of money changed from time to time and place to place?

☐ How do banks create money?

☐ What are the functions of the Federal Reserve System?

☐ How and to what degree does the Fed control the money supply?

☐ What does the deposit multiplier predict about a change in the money supply?

We take a look at money and its effects on a macroeconomy in this chapter and Chapter 25. In previous chapters we stated values of certain economic variables in terms of dollars (prices and GNP, for example). But we did not define money or discuss its role in the economy. You might think that everyone knows what money is. But in this chapter you will discover that economists use the term *money* in a special, technical way. So, what is money and what functions does it serve? Where does money come from? How do banks create money?

As we answer these questions you will learn that economists generally agree that money can play an important role in our quest for macroeconomic stability. When we lose control of money, we face serious economic consequences. For example, economists generally agree that too fast a growth in the supply of money causes high rates of inflation. And most severe economic recessions (depressions) have been accompanied by a collapse of the banking system and a sharp reduction in the supply of money. But to understand why, you must first learn what money is and how its supply is determined.

WHAT IS MONEY?

We begin our discussion with a simple question: What is money? As you will see, the answer to this question depends on the time and place, as well as the person you ask.

Commodity Money

The earliest forms of money were items such as cattle, animal hides, large stone wheels, and salt. The Case in Point in Chapter 5 showed how prisoners in World War II POW camps used cigarettes as money. Economists call such items **commodity money**. Various types of commodity money may have very different physical characteristics, but they all meet the broad economic definition of **money**: They serve as a medium of exchange. That is, buyers may use these items to purchase goods and services and sellers will accept them in payment.

Commodity money. An item used as a medium of exchange that also has significant value for other uses.

Money. Any item used as a medium of exchange.

618

Consider for a moment how an economy without a system of money might function. If you wanted to buy a shirt, for example, you would still go to a store and pick one out. But when you asked the clerk how much it cost, he might reply, "I'll trade you the shirt for 2 history textbooks. You're actually getting a bargain. Last week the price was 3 bushels of apples." In this moneyless economy, there is no standard unit of account; last week it was apples, this week textbooks. Regardless of what you receive in payment for your work, you are going to have trouble buying what you want. If you are paid in apples and want to buy a shirt this week, you must first find someone who will trade you history textbooks for apples and then go back to the store and buy the shirt. If this process takes a while, by the time you get back, the clerk may now want razors instead of textbooks.

Arranging trades can be difficult and time-consuming. But if any one item is generally accepted in exchange, these costs can be greatly reduced. That is, instead of trading apples for textbooks and textbooks for a shirt, you can, like the Roman legionnaires, be paid in salt and use salt to buy the things you want. *By serving as a standard unit of account and a medium of exchange, money makes trading much easier.* As a result, money improves the efficiency of the economic system.

To be a useful medium of exchange, an item must be relatively standardized and easily transported. It must be easily divisible, so that it can be used for both small and large purchases. However, many commodities have drawbacks as media of exchange. No two cows or pelts are identical; stone wheels are heavy and bulky; and a tenth of a cigarette is of little use. Money also offers a way to store wealth. By saving some of what you earn today, you can buy more-expensive items—houses, cars, education—tomorrow. But salt is subject to moisture, apples rot, cigarettes go stale, and cows grow old and die.

Because of these difficulties, gold and silver historically have been the most common forms of commodity money. Gold and silver coins have been minted for at least 2500 years. However, like all commodities used as money, gold and silver have other valuable uses. Thus if the value of the gold in $10 gold coins increases to $15, the coins will be melted down and the gold used to make candlesticks, jewelry, or other products. Moreover, significant amounts of real resources are required to discover, mine, and smelt gold and silver. Those resources cannot then be used in other ways.

These two problems point out another drawback to commodity money. In order to serve as a medium of exchange, money must maintain a relatively stable or predictable value. If the value of money falls dramatically—as occurs during very rapid inflation—it may not be accepted in exchanges. But in order to maintain a stable value, the **money supply**—the quantity of money in circulation at any time—cannot fluctuate wildly. And it is very difficult to control the supply of most commodities. For example, Spanish looting of the New World in the sixteenth century dramatically increased the supply—and decreased the value—of gold.

Goldsmiths and the First Bank Money

Some of the disadvantages of commodity money led to the creation of the first paper currency and early banking. In the fifteenth and sixteenth centuries, gold and silver coins were common forms of money. But traders soon discovered that transporting gold over large distances was expensive and the risks of theft high.

Money supply. The total quantity of money in circulation at any time.

(a) 100 percent reserve system

Balance sheet at 12/31/1578

Assets		Liabilities	
Gold in vault (reserves)	$1000	$1000	Bank money (receipts)

(b) Fractional reserve system

Balance sheet at 12/31/1588

Assets		Liabilities	
Reserves	$1000	$5000	Bank money (paper currency)
Loans	4000		

Exhibit 24.1
Financial Position of A. U. Smith

Assets. Items of value.

Liabilities. Claims on assets.

Reserves. Funds held by banks in order to meet the demands of their depositors and the legal requirements of the Federal Reserve System.

European goldsmiths, however, had relatively secure locations in which to store the gold they used in their work. Individuals began depositing their gold at goldsmiths' shops for safe keeping. In return, they were given a receipt that was, in effect, an IOU or a claim from the goldsmith for so many ounces of gold. Soon traders found it more convenient to trade the receipts than to exchange quantities of gold. Thus goldsmiths' receipts became an early form of paper money.

Paper money has several advantages as a medium of exchange. First, it is easy to transport and store. Second, it has a constant nominal value. (However, as you will see later, its real value can change.) And third, it need not depend on the supply of any commodity, even though the earliest paper money was based on gold.

Exhibit 24.1(a) shows a balance sheet for A. U. Smith, which illustrates these early banking activities. The balance sheet, as we discussed it in Chapter 6, is simply a listing of a business's **assets**—items of value—and **liabilities**—claims against the assets. It is a useful way both to view the current financial position of any business and to follow the evolution of money and banking.

Smith's assets are the $1000 of gold stored in his vault. The gold is identified as **reserves**, indicating that he is holding this amount of gold to pay anyone who presents a claim against the gold. The other side of the balance sheet shows Smith's liabilities. In this case, his only liabilities are the receipts representing claims to the gold in his vaults. Anyone holding $100 of Smith's currency could present it to Smith and receive $100 worth of gold in exchange. The paper money has been identified as *bank money.* Later in this chapter when we discuss modern banking, you will see that Smith and banks operate in much the same way.

The balance sheet shows the effect of having a banking system with a 100 percent reserve. As long as Smith holds $100 of gold in reserve for every $100 of claims on his gold, his activities do not affect the money supply. At first, goldsmiths and traders simply used one form of money (goldsmiths' notes or bank money) for another (gold or commodity money). However, there is an important difference. Although both gold and paper money are assets (items of value) to those who hold them, paper money is a liability to the bank (goldsmith) that issued it. Whether these pieces of paper are acceptable in exchanges depend on the reliability of the issuer. As long as traders believed that Smith would make good his promises, his paper money was acceptable.

RECAP

Money is a medium of exchange that serves the economy by facilitating trades.

To be useful as money, an item must be standardized, easily stored and transported, and easily divisible for small as well as large purchases and have a reasonably stable, predictable value.

Commodities such as tobacco, cattle, gold, and silver have been used as money.

Goldsmiths were the early bankers, accepting deposits of gold and issuing bank money in the form of deposit receipts. These receipts became acceptable in trades as an early form of paper money.

Creating Money in a Fractional Reserve System

Eventually, some enterprising goldsmith noticed that depositors typically demanded only a fraction of the amount of gold held on deposit. Thus it was possible—and profitable—for "bankers" like A. U. Smith to loan out some of the "extra" gold. The interest they earned on loans increased their income. Moreover, those seeking loans did not always demand gold. Many were willing to trade a financial claim on their own assets (their promise to pay the goldsmith back with interest) for a financial claim on the goldsmith's assets (the goldsmith's paper money).

The balance sheet in Exhibit 24.1(b) shows Smith's position 10 years after he learned how profitable it was to make loans. He now has two types of assets: $1000 of gold in his vaults and $4000 in loans. Loans are promised future payments of interest on and the return of principal to Smith.

Although Smith has only $1000 of gold on reserve in his vaults, he has issued $5000 of paper money. This arrangement is what economists refer to as a **fractional reserve banking system**. In this case, Smith's reserves are only 20 percent of the deposits, or the claims against reserves. The fraction of bank money backed by reserves (0.20, or 20 percent, in this case) is called the *reserve ratio*. (We return to the idea of a reserve ratio later in this chapter when we consider current legal requirements for reserves.)

Moving from a 100 percent reserve to a fractional reserve system has two important implications. First, in a fractional reserve banking system, *banks create money and increase the money supply*. Smith accepted $1000 in gold but issued $5000 in paper money. As a result, he increased the money supply by $4000. (The money in Smith's vault is not in the hands of the public, that is, not in circulation, and thus is not part of the money supply.)

Second, because banks hold insufficient reserves to pay all claims at one time, *banks and their depositors are exposed to risks*. Smith holds only $1000 in reserves. If all $5000 of claims (paper money) were presented at the same time, Smith could not pay the full amount of those claims. A large part of his assets are loans, which represent *future* cash payments. The value of the money issued by Smith now depends on trust—trust that Smith is a competent manager, that he has not made too many loans, and that the loans will be repaid.

This example of a fractional reserve banking system, also illustrates two difficulties in controlling the quantity of money in circulation. First, to a large degree, the quantity of bank money depends on the risks Smith and other bankers are willing to accept. Note that Smith's income depends on accepting risks—both the risk that depositors may want all their gold at once and the risk the loans may not be repaid. The more risks that Smith is willing to accept, the smaller is the fraction of reserves he will hold and the greater the amount of bank money he will issue.

Second, the money supply depends on public trust in banks. For example, if depositors learned that Smith had loaned $2000 to finance a ship lost at sea, they might rush down to Smith and demand their gold. But there would be only $1000 with which to satisfy their claims. Smith might be able to get some borrowers to pay early, or he might borrow from another goldsmith and thus pay off some of his depositors.

Fractional reserve banking system. A system in which banks hold reserves that are only a fraction of their deposits.

If Smith cannot raise enough gold to satisfy his depositors, he will be forced to close his doors. His paper money would then be worthless, and no one would accept it as a medium of exchange. As a result, the money supply would fall by $4000 ($1000 in gold would return to circulation but $5000 of paper currency would disappear). If distrust of banks spread, the entire banking system could fail. Only confidence in Smith and in the system as a whole can prevent such problems.

Checking Deposits: Modern Bank Money

The example of the goldsmiths is true and is one way banks in the United States created money in the first half of the 1800s. At that time, U.S. banks accepted deposits of gold, made loans, and issued paper money just like their earlier European counterparts, the goldsmiths. Just prior to the Civil War there were over 9000 different types of banknotes, as well as 3000 known types of counterfeit notes. Some of them were not worth much more than the paper on which they were printed.* Then in 1864, Congress passed the National Banking Act, effectively eliminating private banknotes. At the same time it restricted the power to issue paper money to the Federal government. (Currently all paper money is issued by the Fed and all currency is minted by the U.S. Treasury Department.)

In place of paper notes, banks in the nineteenth century expanded the use of another form of bank money: **checking deposits**. A check is essentially an order to your bank to pay funds that you have previously placed in a checking deposit at the bank. Most of the time when you pay by check, no coins or paper bills are involved at all. If you write a check to pay the bookstore for your textbooks, the bookstore will probably deposit the check in their account at the same or another bank. The bank (or banks) will make bookkeeping entries that decrease the funds in your checking account and increase the funds in the bookstore's account.

A check is a very good substitute for cash, and, for many purposes, is actually superior. Checks are a relatively safe form of payment because it is difficult for someone who finds a lost or stolen check to get funds from your account. Checks also provide a record of payments. Because checks are widely used to make payments and are easily converted into cash, checking deposits, like the paper money that banks used to issue, are recognized as money. In fact, almost 90 percent of the dollar amount of payments in the United States are now made by check. Checking deposits (bank money) account for most of the money in circulation.

Official measures of the money supply. The growth in use of checking accounts changed the way economists measure the money supply, that is, the quantity of money in circulation at any time. Measuring the money supply is important because changes in it affect the number and type of economic exchanges. However, economists do not agree on the best measure of the money supply for purposes of predicting economic activity.

Most economists accept currency (coins and paper money) in circulation and checking deposits as money. Indeed, this definition is the **M-1** measure of money, one of several official measures of the money supply. The term *in circulation* is important; cash held in bank vaults is not considered part of the money supply. Although checking deposits are a medium of exchange, the distinction between a

Checking deposits. Funds held in checking accounts by banks; may be transferred by writing a check; included in the M-1 definition of money.

M-1. The narrow official definition of money, which includes only currency held by the public and checking deposits.

*Robert Puth, *American Economic History*. New York: Dryden Press, 1982, p. 175.

A Case in Point
Financial Innovation and the Supply of Bank Money

In this and subsequent chapters, we focus on how money is created and why it is important that a nation control its money supply. In order to control its money supply, a nation must be able to define and measure that supply. As we noted in the text, one official measure is based on the M-1 definition of money. But changes in financial institutions and the characteristics of deposit accounts they offer have caused substantial changes in the M-1 money supply in recent years.

Prior to the 1930s, government regulation of the banking industry made it relatively easy to define money. Commercial banks were permitted to provide checking deposits, but could not pay interest on those deposits. Thrift institutions—savings-and-loan associations, credit unions, and mutual-savings banks—could not offer checking accounts. As a result, the money supply was simply the currency held by the public plus checking deposits in commercial banks, which paid zero interest.

Financial institutions are in business to earn profits, which they do by attracting funds that they can in turn lend or invest. Thus an institution that can attract more funds can earn more profits. During the 1970s and 1980s, high inflation rates led the public to demand high interest payments as an incentive to deposit their funds. But government regulations limited the rate of interest that thrift institutions could pay. In order to remain competitive, these institutions sought ways around the restrictions. In particular, they wanted to offer the services of a commercial bank, while paying interest on deposits.

In 1972, courts in Massachusetts and New Hampshire ruled that savings banks could set up *NOW accounts*. Like savings deposits, NOW accounts pay interest. But as with checking accounts, NOW depositors can write "negotiable orders of withdrawal" that are, for all practical purposes, checks. In 1974, credit unions started providing comparable services in the form of *share draft accounts*. Finally, in 1978 some savings banks began to offer *automatic transfer services (ATS)*, which automatically transfer funds from savings accounts to cover checks written.

These new substitutes for commercial bank checking deposits caused many people to withdraw their funds from commercial banks. In response, in 1980 Congress empowered all types of depository institutions to offer NOW and ATS accounts. As a result, the government definition of M-1 now includes all such accounts. Commercial banks and thrift institutions are not the only financial institutions, however. Investment firms also compete for the public's funds. To counteract the surge of interest in new bank accounts, in the 1970s investment firms established *money market mutual funds*. Buying shares in a money market mutual fund enabled small investors to earn higher rates of interest than they could on savings accounts. From 1977 to 1982 these funds grew from $4 billion to $232 billion, largely because individuals withdrew funds they had formerly deposited in commercial banks and savings-and-loan associations. In 1982, banks were allowed to compete with these new funds by offering *money market deposit accounts*.

The addition of money market accounts complicated the measuring of the money supply. Both money market mutual funds and money market deposit accounts offer only limited checking privileges. Although these are certainly close substitutes for checking deposits, they are included in the M-2 but not the M-1 definition of money. These and other innovations have so blurred the dividing line between M-1 and other definitions of money that the Fed has decided to stop using M-1 as its principal measure of the money supply.

checking deposit and other kinds of deposits is not as clear-cut as it might seem. In A Case in Point: Financial Innovation and the Supply of Bank Money, we discuss how innovations in financial services have created many new forms of deposit accounts. Exhibit 24.2 shows the money supply as defined by M-1 in 1986. As you can see, checking deposits account for approximately 75 percent of the M-1 money supply.

The currency and checking deposits that make up M-1 are not only interchangeable, they also share a common characteristic: high **liquidity**, or spendability. We noted earlier in this chapter that in an economy without money, you might find it difficult to use the assets you own to buy the goods and services you

Liquidity. How quickly and inexpensively an asset may be turned into money without risk of loss of value. Money has perfect liquidity; other assets, less liquidity.

	1970		1986	
	Billions of dollars	Percentage	Billions of dollars	Percentage
Components of M-1				
Currency	49.2	22.7	183.5	25.1
Checking deposits	167.4	77.3	546.9	74.9
Total M-1	216.6	100.0	730.4	100.0
Components of M-2				
Total M-1	216.6	34.5	730.4	26.1
Savings deposits	261.0	41.5	371.5	13.2
Small time deposits	151.1	24.0	852.4	30.4
Money market mutual funds	0.0	0.0	207.2	7.4
Money market deposit accounts	0.0	0.0	570.7	20.3
Other	−0.5	0.0	72.5	2.6
Total M-2	628.2	100.0	2804.7	100.0

Source: *Economic Report of the President, 1987* (Tables B-64 and B-65).

Exhibit 24.2
The Money Supply, 1970 and 1986 (at December 31)

want. The easier it is to convert an asset to immediately spendable form *without risk of loss of value*, the more liquid the asset is. Currency is perfectly liquid, checking deposits only slightly less so, stocks still less so, and land and jewelry even less so.

Exhibit 24.2 also shows a broader official measure of the money supply, **M-2**. This measure includes all items that are in M-1 plus savings deposits, small time deposits, money market mutual fund shares, and money market deposit accounts. Some economists believe that M-2 is a better measure of the money supply because there is very little difference between funds held in these accounts and the items included in M-1.

For example, savings deposits are part of M-2 but not M-1. You cannot directly spend funds held in your savings account, but they are very close substitutes for M-1 money. Technically, a bank may require 30 days notice before allowing a withdrawal from a savings account. In practice, such rules are rarely enforced. Most banks allow depositors to withdraw cash immediately at the bank, at automatic teller machines, or even over the telephone.

Similarly, money market mutual fund shares and money market deposit accounts are almost as spendable as checking deposits because most mutual funds and banks allow some check-writing privileges. (They often place limits on the minimum size of the check or the number of checks than can be drawn per month, however.) Because these accounts allow ready access to funds and pay higher interest rates than conventional checking deposits, they are attractive substitutes for M-1 money. These and other financial innovations have blurred the distinction between M-1 and M-2.

Even broader measures of the money supply, known as M-3 and L, include additional, progressively less liquid, items. Economists continue to debate which

M-2. A broader official definition of money, including not only currency held by the public and checking deposits (M-1 money) but also savings deposits, small time deposits, money market mutual fund shares, and money market deposit accounts.

measure is the best predictor of changes in economic activity. For our purposes the simplest definition and measure of money is the best. Thus in this textbook *money is defined as items used as media of exchange and is measured as M-1, or currency in the hands of the public and checking deposits.*

Whether banks issue paper currency or accept checking deposits, they still create bank money—M-1—just as the goldsmiths did. Moreover, because the modern banking system is a fractional reserve system, it is subject to the same potential problems that the goldsmiths faced. Because the quantity of bank money (checking deposits) depends on the willingness of banks to accept risks, controlling the money supply can be difficult. In addition, widespread concern over the integrity of several banks can cause individuals to lose confidence in bank money. As a result, the money supply may fall rapidly. Several such "panics" and runs on banks in the latter part of the 1800s caused serious economic recessions.

THE FEDERAL RESERVE SYSTEM

The panic of 1907 finally prompted Congress to seek a way to avoid such problems. In 1913, a new financial institution was created: the Federal Reserve System, commonly referred to as the Fed.

Structure of the Fed

The Federal Reserve System has several components. The 12 regional Federal Reserve Banks are located in Atlanta, Boston, Cleveland, Chicago, Dallas, Kansas City, Minneapolis, New York, Philadelphia, Richmond, St. Louis, and San Francisco. These regional banks have only limited authority to act independently. Actually, they are more like branches of a single central bank.

The Board of Governors sets policy for the Fed and is headed by a chairman, who is the most powerful member of the board. The chairman and the other six board members are appointed by the president for 14-year terms of office. The original intent behind the long terms was to give the Fed's officers experience and independence. But while it is theoretically independent and is generally considered to act professionally, the Fed is not immune to political pressure. Moreover, because most board members have resigned before completing a full 14 years of service, the Fed has not had the depth of experience originally envisioned.

The Federal Open Market Committee (FOMC) consists of the Board of Governors and five of the 12 presidents of the regional banks. The president of the New York regional bank is always on the FOMC; the other presidents serve on a rotating basis. All 12 regional presidents usually meet with the Open Market Committee, although only five may vote on committee business. The FOMC is perhaps the most powerful committee of the Fed. The committee meets regularly to decide whether to change the money supply and, if so, by how much.

Functions of the Fed

The Federal Reserve System is the nation's central bank. Like central banks in other countries, the Fed has two principal responsibilities: (1) to help the banking system operate smoothly and safely; and (2) to control the supply of money.

Helping the financial system work. When it established the Fed in 1913, Congress's objective was to help ensure the smooth and safe functioning of the nation's financial system. In doing so the Fed provides banking services for the federal government. The Treasury Department and other federal agencies have checking deposits at the Fed. The Fed is also your banker's bank. Banks maintain deposit accounts at the Fed. A bank that is temporarily short of reserves can get a temporary loan from the Fed. (However, nonbank businesses and private citizens cannot have accounts at the Fed.)

The Fed also provides check-clearing services. For example, suppose that you write a $100 check on your account at the Northeast Bank to pay for some clothes you bought at the Farout Place. The owner of the Farout Place deposits your check in her account at the Southwest Bank. The Southwest Bank will send your check to the Fed. The Fed will then add $100 to the deposit account of the Southwest Bank, subtract $100 from the deposit account of the Northeast Bank, and send your check to the Northeast Bank. In this way the Fed helps to transfer $100 from your account to that of the Farout Place.

To help the financial system function safely, the Fed also oversees the activities of member banks (in conjunction with various other government agencies). When discussing the goldsmiths, we noted that risks and bank profits are linked; so too are risks and bank failures. To keep these risks within acceptable limits, agents of the government periodically (usually once a year) conduct financial audits of banks. They check on the quantity of cash on hand, the riskiness of loans, and generally assess the performance of the bank's management. These activities are designed to spot banks that may be headed for trouble before they actually fail.

However, even the closest monitoring cannot prevent all failures. Recognizing that, Congress established two independent federal agencies, the Federal Deposit Insurance Corporation (FDIC) and the Federal Savings and Loan Insurance Corporation (FSLIC), to insure most deposit accounts at banks. Currently, this insurance covers accounts up to $100,000. Thus most depositors will suffer no loss even if their banks fail, and so are less likely to try to withdraw all their funds, which could cause a bank failure. This protection does not extend by law to accounts larger than $100,000. Recently, large depositors in some large banks were given full protection. But similar protection has not been extended to large depositors in smaller banks. As a result, smaller banks have complained they have lost large accounts.

Controlling the money supply. When it established the Fed, Congress appeared to be most concerned about preventing panics in the banking system that would result in large-scale contractions in the money supply. Now, however, economists believe that the Fed's most important macroeconomic role is implementing **monetary policy**, that is, controlling the size and growth rate of the money supply.

Why are economists concerned about the size of the money supply? The size of the money supply determines the value of money. The value of money determines how much you can buy with a dollar (or franc, or pound, or lira, or yen, depending on the nation involved). A $20 bill will always buy $20 worth of goods and services, but the quantity of such products may vary. For example, a $20 bill that bought two sacks full of groceries 10 years ago can buy only one sack full today.

Monetary policy. Federal Reserve System actions taken to influence the size or growth rate of the money supply.

When the money supply grows rapidly, the purchasing power of money declines. If the money supply grows extremely rapidly, people may lose confidence in the value of paper money and refuse to accept it in exchange. If so, it will cease to be money and exchanges will be less efficient. (This, in fact, occurred in Bolivia in the mid-1980s when prices rose by several hundred percent *per month.*) To maintain the dollar's value, the Fed uses a variety of economic tools to control the money supply, which we discuss in the next section.

MONETARY POLICY AND THE MONEY SUPPLY

How does the Fed control the M-1 money supply in the United States? How complete is that control? As is so often the case in economic discussions, the answer to the first question is easy, the answer to the second is debatable.

Factors Determining the Quantity of Checking Deposits

In considering the Fed's control of the money supply, we focus on its control of checking deposits. Although the Fed is responsible for issuing currency—one other part of M-1—it readily supplies currency on demand. For example, in peak trading months (such as December) the quantity of currency in circulation expands. Thus to control the size of the money supply, the Fed seeks to influence the quantity of checking deposits, or bank money. But if bank money is created by banks, how does the Fed influence the quantity of checking deposits?

To understand how, recall the two factors that determined how much bank money A. U. Smith created in our earlier example: the size of his reserves and the reserve ratio. Smith had $1000 in reserves, which represented 20 percent of his bank money. Reserves, the reserve ratio, and the quantity of bank money are related as follows:

$$\text{Reserves} = \text{Bank money} \times \text{Reserve ratio}$$
$$\$1000 = \$5000 \times 0.20$$

Although the Fed cannot directly increase or decrease the quantity of bank money, it can change the reserve ratio and the quantity of reserves in the banking system. In response, banks will change the quantity of bank money. By influencing the quantity of bank money, the Fed's monetary policy changes the money supply.

Required reserve ratio. The minimum portion of deposits that must be legally held as reserves, as set by the Fed.

Legal reserves. Reserves held by banks to satisfy legal minimums imposed by the Fed. They include currency held in bank vaults and banks' deposits held at the Fed.

Open-market operations. The buying and selling of government securities by the Fed; used to change the quantity of bank reserves and hence the supply of money.

Monetary-Policy Tools of the Fed

The Fed has three basic monetary-policy tools. First, it has the legal power to establish and enforce a **required reserve ratio**, which is the minimum percentage of deposits that banks must maintain in **legal reserves**. (Both currency held in a bank's vault and the bank's deposits at the Fed are counted as part of its legal reserves.) Second, the Fed can increase banks' reserves by granting them loans. But the most common monetary policy tool is **open-market operations**, which involves changing the quantity of bank reserves by buying or selling government securities from the public.

(a) Initial balance sheet

Assets		Liabilities	
Reserves	$1000	$5000	Deposits
Loans	4000		

Reserves: Actual $1000
         Required   1000   (= 5000 × 0.20)
         Excess $ 0

(b) Deposit of Fed's $200 check

Assets		Liabilities	
Reserves	$1200	$5200	Deposits
Loans	4000		

Reserves: Actual $1200
         Required   1040   (= 5200 × 0.20)
         Excess $ 160

(c) After $160 loan to Ms. MacBeth

Assets		Liabilities	
Reserves	$1040	$5200	Deposits
Loans	4160		

Reserves: Actual $1040
         Required   1040   (= 5200 × 0.20)
         Excess $ 0

Exhibit 24.3
Effect of Open-Market Operations on the Goldsmith National Bank

Creating Money in the Banking System by Open-Market Operations

To see how the money supply increases, let's consider how the Goldsmith National Bank reacts to an initial increase in its deposits. In tracing these effects we will consider reserves and loans as the only two assets of the bank and checking deposits as the only liability. This simplification allows us to focus on the important elements of the process. In addition, we make three assumptions:

1. The public—individuals and nonbanking businesses—does not want to hold any additional currency.

2. Banks do not want to hold any excess reserves.

3. The required reserve ratio is 20 percent.

Open-market operations—First round. Initially, Goldsmith National Bank has $1000 of reserves, $4000 in loans, and $5000 of checking deposits, as shown in Exhibit 24.3(a). With a required reserve ratio of 20 percent, the bank's actual and required reserves are equal, and it has no excess reserves.

Suppose that the Fed wants to increase the money supply through open-market operations. To initiate the increase, the Fed purchases $200 of government securities held by Mr. H. I. Roller, paying him with a check. Mr. Roller deposits the Fed's check in the Goldsmith National Bank. The bank sends the check back to the Fed, which increases Goldsmith National Bank's deposits at the Fed by $200. The effect of this initial (first-round) action is shown in Exhibit 24.3(b). The Goldsmith National Bank now has $200 more of actual reserves (since deposits at the Fed are reserves) and $160 of excess reserves. The amount of currency in circulation did not change, but the $200 increase in checking deposits increased the money supply by $200.

Second-round increase in money and reserves. The money creation process is not over, however, because Goldsmith National Bank does not want to hold any excess reserves. To increase its profits, the bank loans the $160 of excess reserves to Ms. MacBeth, who runs the local dry cleaners. To keep the example simple, we assume that she receives $160 in cash. With this exchange of cash (reserves) for a financial claim (the loan), Goldsmith has eliminated its excess reserves as shown in Exhibit 24.3(c).

Ms. MacBeth did not take out the loan so she could carry $160 around in her purse. She took out the loan to spend it, as borrowers typically do. Suppose that she spends the money on an elaborate macrame wall-hanging made by Shirley Knott, a local artist. Because Ms. Knott does not want to hold cash, she deposits the money in her bank account at the Silversmith National Bank. With her deposit, the second round ends.

What is the effect on the money supply so far? The Fed's initial action increased checking deposits and the money supply by $200. But the Goldsmith National Bank ended up with excess reserves, which it loaned out, causing the money supply to grow by another $160. Thus far the money supply has grown by a total of $360: the $200 in Mr. Roller's checking account plus the $160 in Ms. Knott's checking account. Note that the Fed is directly responsible for the first $200 of new money created. But the profit-seeking activities of the Goldsmith National Bank led it to make a new loan, which led to the creation of $160 of new deposits.

Before moving on, we might ask: What would happen if Goldsmith National Bank had created new money by giving Ms. MacBeth a loan in the form of a checking deposit? Wouldn't this maintain the bank's reserves and allow it to create more money? Giving Ms. MacBeth checking deposits instead of cash would *temporarily* keep the bank's reserves from decreasing. But Ms. MacBeth wants to spend the money she has borrowed. If the person receiving Ms. MacBeth's money has an account in another bank (as in our example), the Goldsmith National Bank will eventually lose reserves, just as if the loan had been made in cash. Thus *in a banking system that has many banks, a single bank can increase loans only to the extent that it has excess reserves.*

Third-round increase in money and reserves. The money creation process continues beyond the second round. Exhibit 24.4 shows changes in Silversmith National Bank's balance sheet. The bank had no excess reserves initially. However, the $160 deposit by Ms. Knott increases the bank's deposits and reserves by $160, as shown in Exhibit 24.4(b). The increase in deposits raises the bank's required reserves by $32 ($0.20 \times \$160$), but leaves it with $128 in excess reserves. To eliminate this excess and increase its profits, the bank makes a $128 loan to Ed Satera. Mr. Satera takes the loan in cash, thus eliminating Silversmith National Bank's excess reserves. He then uses the cash to buy a curio cabinet from Hu's Whatnots. When Mr. Hu deposits the $128 in the store's account at the Coppersmith National Bank, the third round ends.

What is the effect on the money supply so far? At the end of the second round it had grown by $360. During the third round, it grows another $128 for a total of $488 in additional deposits at the end of the third round.

(a) Initial balance sheet

Assets		Liabilities	
Reserves	$ 800	$4000	Deposits
Loans	3200		

Reserves:	Actual	$800	
	Required	800	(= 4000 × 0.20)
	Excess	$ 0	

(b) Deposit of $160 by Shirley Knott

Assets		Liabilities	
Reserves	$ 960	$4160	Deposits
Loans	3200		

Reserves:	Actual	$960	
	Required	832	(= 4160 × 0.20)
	Excess	$128	

(c) After loan of $128

Assets		Liabilities	
Reserves	$ 832	$4160	Deposits
Loans	3328		

Reserves:	Actual	$832	
	Required	832	(= 4160 × 0.20)
	Excess	$ 0	

Exhibit 24.4
Effect of Open-Market Operations on the Silversmith National Bank

Multiplier Effect on Deposit Expansion

After accepting Hu's deposit, Coppersmith National Bank holds $26 in excess reserves. We can expect the bank to loan out this excess, which will again increase deposits and excess reserves. The deposit-expansion process, like that of the expenditures multiplier in Chapter 23, goes on endlessly.

As Exhibit 24.5 indicates, however, changes in excess reserves and deposits get smaller with each round. Why? Because the 20 percent required reserve ratio means that in each round excess reserves and subsequent expansion in loans and the money supply are only 80 percent as large as in the previous round. By the end of the twenty-fifth round, there will be virtually no increase in deposits and in the money supply.

What is to be learned from this example? First, an initial increase in deposits and reserves leads to a multiple expansion in deposits and therefore in the money supply. In this case, the ultimate increase in deposits (roughly $1000) is five times larger than the initial increase in bank reserves ($200). We can express this relationship using the **deposit multiplier**, calculated as

Deposit multiplier. The ultimate change in checking deposits (bank money) caused by a $1 initial change in bank reserves; in a simple banking system, equal to 1 ÷ required reserve ratio.

$$\text{Deposit multiplier} = \frac{\text{Total increase in deposits}}{\text{Initial increase in reserves}}$$

$$= \frac{\$1000}{\$200} \quad \text{or} \quad 5.0$$

Economists—especially those at the Fed—use the deposit multiplier to predict the increase in deposits in response to an initial change in reserves. For example, if the deposit multiplier is 5.0, an increase of $300 million in reserves will result in a $1500 million increase in deposits, calculated as

$$\text{Deposit multiplier} = \frac{\text{Total increase in deposits}}{\text{Initial increase in reserves}}$$

$$5.0 = \frac{\text{Total increase in deposits}}{\$300 \text{ million}}$$

$$\$1500 \text{ million} = \text{Total increase in deposits}$$

In order to use this formula to predict changes in deposits, economists first have to determine the deposit multiplier. In the example above, a deposit multiplier of 5.0 resulted from a required reserve ratio (rrr) of 20 percent. We can state this relationship mathematically as

$$\text{Deposit multiplier} = \frac{1}{\text{Required reserve ratio}} \quad \text{or} \quad \frac{1}{\text{rrr}}$$

Thus the deposit multiplier is inversely related to the required reserve ratio. The larger the required reserve ratio, the smaller is the multiplier. To check your understanding, calculate the deposit multiplier if the required reserve ratio is 25 percent. (Your answer should be 4.) And the smaller the deposit multiplier, the smaller is its effect on growth of the money supply, since in each round a bank would have to hold back more and lend out less of new deposits. For example, at a 20 percent required reserve ratio, a bank can lend $80 of each $100 of deposits. At a 25 percent required reserve ratio, it can lend only $75 of each $100 of deposits.

Exhibit 24.5
Summary of Deposit Expansion Process

	Changes in				Money supply	
Round	Actual reserves	Checking deposits	Required reserves	Loans	(This round)	(Cumulative)
1	$200.00	$ 200.00	$ 40.00	—	$ 200.00	$ 200.00
2	—	160.00	32.00	$ 160.00	160.00	360.00
3	—	128.00	25.60	128.00	128.00	488.00
.	.	.	.	.	.	.
.	.	.	.	.	.	.
.	.	.	.	.	.	.
25	—	0.76	0.15	0.76	0.76	996.98
.	.	.	.	.	.	.
.	.	.	.	.	.	.
.	.	.	.	.	.	.
Total	$200.00	$1000.00	$200.00	$1000.00	—	$1000.00

(a) Initial balance sheet

Assets		Liabilities	
Reserves	$1000	$5000	Deposits
Loans	4000		

Reserves:	Actual	$1000	
	Required	1000	(= 5000 × 0.20)
	Excess	$ 0	

(b) After the Fed cashes Mr. Roller's $100 check

Assets		Liabilities	
Reserves	$ 900	$4900	Deposits
Loans	4000		

Reserves:	Actual	$ 900	
	Required	980	(= 4900 × 0.20)
	Excess	$−80	

(c) After Goldsmith reduces its loans by $80

Assets		Liabilities	
Reserves	$ 980	$4900	Deposits
Loans	3920		

Reserves:	Actual	$980	
	Required	980	(= 4900 × 0.20)
	Excess	$ 0	

Exhibit 24.6
Deposit Contraction Process

Multiplier Effect on Deposit Contraction

The deposit-multiplier process also works in reverse. Suppose, for example, that the Fed sells Mr. Roller $100 of government securities, accepting his check drawn on the Goldsmith National Bank. The Fed will decrease the bank's deposits at the Fed by $100 and send the check to the bank. The bank will deduct $100 from Mr. Roller's checking deposit.

But this transaction decreases reserves and deposits at Goldsmith National Bank by $100, leaving the bank with *negative* excess reserves (− $80), as shown in Exhibit 24.6. That is, the bank does not have enough reserves to meet the legal requirement. To remedy this situation, the bank will reduce its outstanding loans enough to meet the reserve requirement. For example, suppose that the next customer to enter the Goldsmith National Bank, Ernie Frankly, gives the bank a check drawn on the Silversmith National Bank for $80, representing the last payment on his car loan. The Goldsmith National Bank sends his check to the Fed, which transfers $80 from the Silversmith National Bank's deposit account to Goldsmith's account. This action brings Goldsmith's reserves back to the required level, but leaves Silversmith $64 short of the required reserve ratio.

So far deposits (and the money supply) have decreased by $180 ($100 from Mr. Roller's account and $80 from Mr. Frankly's account). As with the expansion process, the contraction process continues until the banking system has eliminated all negative excess reserves. Since the required reserve ratio is 0.20, the deposit multiplier is 5.0, so the $100 initial decrease in reserves will lead to a $500 decrease in deposits, calculated as

$$\text{Deposit multiplier} = \frac{\text{Total decrease in deposits}}{\text{Initial decrease in reserves}}$$

$$5.0 = \frac{\text{Total decrease in deposits}}{\$100}$$

$$\$500 = \text{Total decrease in deposits}$$

Other Monetary-Policy Tools

The Fed has two other monetary policy tools that it can use: loans to banks and changes in reserve requirements. Typically, the Fed makes loans only to banks requiring temporary help, acting as a lender of last resort. But additional loans would, like the purchase of securities in the open market, inject additional reserves into the banking system.

Exhibit 24.7(a) shows the effect on Goldsmith National Bank of a $200 loan from the Fed. The loan adds $200 to the bank's actual and excess reserves and $200 to its liabilities. We can expect the bank to loan out its excess reserves, an action that will trigger the deposit-multiplier process. Exhibit 24.7(a) does not trace all the steps in the process but for a deposit multiplier of 5.0, the final increase in the money supply will be $1000—the $200 initial increase in reserve times 5.0, the deposit multiplier.

The Fed may also affect the money supply by changing the required reserve ratio. Exhibit 24.7(b) shows that if the Fed raises the required reserve ratio from 20 to 25 percent, Goldsmith National Bank will have negative excess reserves (-250). Thus the increase in the required reserve ratio means that it must decrease its loans by $250. The cash it receives when the loan is repaid will add $250 to its reserves. Once again this initial action is only the first step in the deposit-expansion process. Note that the change in the required reserve ratio to 25 percent decreases the deposit multiplier to 4.0. Thus the initial drop of $250 will eventually cause the money supply to contract by $1000 ($250 × 4.0).

Some Real-World Complications

What we have illustrated is the simplest form of the deposit multiplier. In deriving the formula, we made two important assumptions. First, we assumed that *the public does not want to hold additional currency*. This assumption means that every additional dollar the public receives will be deposited in the banking system. However, if individuals and businesses hold some or all of the increase in currency, the change in reserves will be smaller and deposits will expand less.

Second, we assumed that *banks do not want to hold excess reserves*. This assumption is reasonable, in terms of normal banking practices. But banks sometimes do maintain excess reserves. To the extent that they do so, the value of the deposit multiplier is lowered. For example, what if Goldsmith National Bank holds reserves equal to 22 percent of deposits (despite a required reserve ratio of only 20 percent)? In the first round, the bank would have increased loans by only $156

RECAP

The Fed has three tools with which to control the money supply: setting the required reserve ratio, making loans, and buying and selling government securities on the open market. The Fed's principal tool for managing the money supply is open-market operations.

The quantity of bank money created can be expressed by the following relationship: Reserves = Bank money × Reserve ratio. The smaller the quantity of reserves and the larger the ratio of bank money to reserves, the smaller is the quantity of bank money.

The Fed's control is indirect. Changes in monetary policy change either the level of actual or required reserves. Banks then respond by making new loans and creating new deposits (bank money).

Because reserves are a fraction of deposits, changes in reserves have a multiplier effect on total deposits. The deposit multiplier is 1 ÷ required reserve ratio.

(a) Effect of a Fed loan of $200 to the Goldsmith National Bank

Initial balance sheet			
Assets		**Liabilities**	
Reserves	$1000	$5000	Deposits
Loans	4000		

Reserves: Actual $1000
Required   1000   (= 5000 × 0.20)
Excess $ 0

After the Fed's $200 loan			
Assets		**Liabilities**	
Reserves	$1200	$5000	Deposits
Loans	4000	200	Fed's loan

Reserves: Actual $1200
Required   1000   (= 5000 × 0.20)
Excess $ 200

(b) Fed raises required reserve ratio from 20 to 25 percent

Initial balance sheet			
Assets		**Liabilities**	
Reserves	$1000	$5000	Deposits
Loans	4000		

Reserves: Actual $1000
Required   1000   (= 5000 × 0.20)
Excess $ 0

After the Fed raises the reserve ratio			
Assets		**Liabilities**	
Reserves	$1000	$5000	Deposits
Loans	4000		

Reserves: Actual $ 1000
Required   1250   (= 5000 × 0.25)
Excess $ −250

Exhibit 24.7
Effects of Other Monetary Policies

instead of $160 (see Exhibit 24.3). If other banks also hold higher reserves, expansions in later rounds will also be smaller.

In fact, the simple deposit-multiplier formula that we used indicates only the *potential* change in the money supply. The *actual* multiplier effect depends on real-world actions. However, the ultimate effect of Fed policies on the money supply cannot be predicted as precisely as our examples might suggest. This uncertainty is an important limitation on the Fed's policy making, which we discuss in Chapter 27. Nevertheless, the basic principle remains true: Any excess reserves (whether positive or negative) in the banking system will cause a multiple change in deposits and thus in the money supply.

CONCLUSION

In this chapter we began to explore the role of money in macroeconomic analysis. We showed how the quantity of money in circulation at any time depends on the current size of bank reserves, the required reserve ratio, and banks' desire to create excess reserves. As we have seen, the Fed has a major influence on each of these factors through its various monetary-policy tools.

In Chapter 25 we consider a fourth factor affecting the quantity of money in circulation at any time: the public's desire to hold currency. Here, too, the Fed plays a role by instilling public confidence in the banking system and the economy in general. By considering demand for money we can demonstrate how the money market reaches equilibrium and how changes in the money supply affect aggregate expenditures.

Once we make that connection, we can fully explore the operation of aggregate demand and aggregate supply (Chapter 26). We return to the topic of monetary policy in Chapter 27. There we discuss how the Fed decides how much money to supply and consider how and why economists disagree about monetary policy. As you will see, the Fed's inability to directly change the supply of money has important implications for monetary policy.

SUMMARY

1. In this chapter we explored the history, functions, and definition of money and how the actions of banks and the Federal Reserve System determine the quantity of money in circulation.

2. Some early forms of money actually were commodities: tobacco, cattle, or stone wheels. For many centuries gold and silver were used as money. The basic function of money is to facilitate exchanges, reducing the difficulty and time required in bartering. Any item used as a medium of exchange is considered money. To be most useful as a medium of exchange, however, an item must be relatively standardized, easily stored and transported, and easily divisible so that it can be used for both small and large purchases. For money to be an acceptable medium of exchange, its supply and value must remain relatively stable.

3. Goldsmiths in the fifteenth and sixteenth centuries stored gold in their vaults and issued receipts that could be exchanged for a given quantity of gold. Traders found it convenient to trade these receipts rather than the actual gold, and the receipts became the first form of bank money. The value of this bank money depended on the honesty and reputation of the goldsmiths who issued it.

4. Because only a fraction of the gold was ever demanded at one time by depositors, goldsmiths began to loan out their "extra" gold. The quantity of reserves maintained became only a fraction of the bank money issued. This fractional reserve banking system allowed goldsmiths to expand the money supply. Fractional reserve systems involve risks, since a bank has insufficient reserves to meet the claims of all depositors at any one time. The total quantity of bank money depends on the reserve ratio (proportion of bank money represented by reserves) and the level of reserves.

5. Banks today act in much the same way that the early goldsmiths did. Instead of paper money, banks today create checking deposits, which is simply another form of bank money. The value of this bank money depends on the integrity and skills of bank management. Official definitions of money reflect liquidity. Liquidity expresses the ease and expense of converting an asset into money with little risk of loss of value. The most narrow official definition of money (M-1) indicates high liquidity: only currency in circulation and checking deposits. A broader, somewhat less liquid official measure of the money supply (M-2) includes all items in M-1 plus savings deposits, deposits in money market mutual fund shares and money market deposit accounts, and small time deposits.

6. The Federal Reserve System (the Fed) was created by Congress in 1913 to help the banking system function smoothly and safely and to control the money supply. There are 12 regional Federal Reserve Banks, but power in the Fed is centralized. The Board of Governors is the chief policy-making committee; the Federal Open Market Committee is the group most responsible for setting monetary policy.

7. The Fed issues all paper money, supplies currency as demanded, provides banking services for the federal government, clears checks, holds bank reserves, makes loans to banks, and oversees banking activity. The FDIC and FSLIC insure most types of deposits in member banks and savings and loan associations.

8. The Fed's major economic role is to control the money supply, which it does by regulating the quantity of bank money represented by checking deposits. The quantity of bank money created can be expressed by the following relationship: Reserves = Bank money × Reserve ratio. The smaller the reserves and the larger the ratio

of bank money to reserves, the smaller is the quantity of bank money.

9. The Fed's three monetary-policy tools are (a) changes in the required reserve ratio; (b) increasing reserves through loans; and (c) open-market operations, that is, buying and selling government securities. The principal tool is open-market operations.

10. Excess reserves in the banking system lead to a multiple expansion of loans and deposits. If the public does not want to hold additional currency and banks do not want excess reserves, the deposit multiplier is equal to 1 ÷ required reserve ratio. The deposit multiplier will overstate the actual expansion in the money supply if the public increases its desire for currency and/or if banks wish to hold some excess reserves. The deposit-multiplier process also works in reverse to contract the money supply when there are negative excess reserves.

KEY TERMS

Commodity money, 618
Money, 618
Money supply, 619
Assets, 620
Liabilities, 620
Reserves, 620
Fractional reserve banking system, 621
Checking deposits, 622
M-1, 622
Liquidity, 623
M-2, 624
Monetary policy, 626
Required reserve ratio, 627
Legal reserves, 627
Open-market operations, 627
Deposit multiplier, 630

QUESTIONS FOR REVIEW AND DISCUSSION

1. If you were to ask people how much money they have in the bank, do you think they would differentiate between money held in savings and checking accounts? In what way are savings accounts like currency and checking deposits? In what way are they different? Substituting shares of common stock for savings deposits, answer the same questions.

2. Comment on the statement: "The concept of scarcity certainly applies to money. I could never have enough." If you had more money (as economists define it) today than you did 10 years ago, would you necessarily be better off? Explain. (Be sure to distinguish money from income and real from nominal income.)

3. Almost anything can serve as money. If you were choosing a commodity to use as money, what physical attributes would be important? What limitations do the following commodities have as money: rice, carved stones, whiskey, personal IOUs, and furs?

4. Comment on the statement: "Banks can create money from nothing." Explain how banks create money. What limits the amount of money that a bank can create? What is the connection between the amount of money banks create and their income?

5. Explain why each of the following statements is true.
   a) An individual bank reduces its reserves when it makes a new loan.
   b) The banking system as a whole can't change the quantity of actual reserves.
   c) Banks can eliminate excess reserves.

6. Explain whether the money supply will increase, decrease, or be unaffected by each of the following actions.
   a) The Fed sells $100 million of government securities.
   b) The public decides to hold less currency (and the Fed takes no offsetting action).
   c) A business in California sends a large check to a business in New York, which deposits the check in its local bank.
   d) Banks decide to hold more excess reserves.
   e) The Fed lowers the required reserve ratio.
   f) The Fed prints new paper money and stores it in its vaults.
   g) New supplies of gold are discovered in Vermont.

7. Suppose that the public does not want to hold additional currency and that the banking system does not want to hold excess reserves.
   a) If the required reserve ratio is 0.25 and the Fed buys $50 billion worth of securities from the public, what happens to the money supply?
   b) If the required reserve ratio is 0.15 and the Fed sells $75 billion worth of securities to the public, what happens to the money supply?
   c) If the required reserve ratio is 0.15 but banks decide to hold 0.20 in reserves, what happens to the money supply if the Fed sells $150 billion in securities?

8. Explain how the following statement can be true: "Financial claims are both liabilities and assets at the same time." For which groups are the following claims either liabilities or assets: checking deposits, U.S. government

securities, bank loans, a $5 bill held by the public, deposits held at the Fed?

9. How would you explain the fact that during the 1930s (the period of the Great Depression) banks held significant excess reserves? Why do banks typically hold almost no excess reserves today? Are banks with no excess reserves safe places to keep your money?

10. Explain the statement: "The quantity of checking deposits in the banking system depends on the quantity of loans made by banks and the confidence the public has in the security of bank deposits." Between 1929 and 1933 (the period of the Great Depression) the U.S. money supply dropped by 25 percent (although currency in the hands of the public increased). How does the statement explain why the quantity of bank money (checking deposits) may have fallen?

11. Use the following information to answer the questions in (a)–(e).

Loans issued by banks	$2600 billion
Currency held in bank vaults	90 billion

Checking deposits	1600 billion
Currency held by the public	450 billion
Savings deposits	500 billion
Bank deposits held by the Fed	150 billion
Currency in the Fed's vaults	50 billion
Government securities held by banks	600 billion
Small time deposits	800 billion

a) Using the M-1 definition, what is the stock of money?
b) What is the amount of actual reserves held by banks? If the required reserve ratio is 0.125, what are the amounts of the required reserves and excess reserves? (Assume there are no required reserves for savings deposits.)
c) Based on your answer to (b), by how much would you expect the money supply to change if banks do not want to hold excess reserves (assuming no change in the public's desire to hold currency)?
d) How would your answers to (b) and (c) change if the required reserve ratio were 0.20?
e) What steps can an individual bank take to eliminate negative excess reserves?

Economic Encounters
Inside the
Underground Economy

The underground economy isn't just organized crime, like gambling or prostitution. It's the street vendor peddling sunglasses and watches outside your office building. It's farmers selling home-grown vegetables from roadside stands. It's musicians playing in subways and city squares for spare change, and it's fairly ordinary people who work "under the table" as waitresses, carpenters, or babysitters.

Estimates place the worth of the underground economy at around $500 *billion* annually, a figure that, because it cannot be verified, is not included in the GNP. This segment of the economy has two basic components: money earned from illegal activity (such as drug trafficking or prostitution) and nonreporting of money earned legally (for example, by cab drivers who don't run their meter, or by waiters who don't report tips). The Internal Revenue Service estimates that unreported income from *legal* sources grew by 13 percent per year from 1973 to 1981—or from $94 billion to $250 billion. Unreported income from three *illegal* activities—prostitution, drug trafficking, and gambling—grew even more rapidly: by 18 percent per year, or from $9 billion to $34 billion.

The only good news about this situation is that we therefore may be overestimating national unemployment (of the 20 million estimated underground workers in the U.S., 1 million may be listed on official records as unemployed) and underestimating our actual GNP. But the good news ends there.

Sources: "A Monetary Perspective on Underground Economic Activity in the United States," *Federal Reserve Bulletin,* March 1984, pp. 174–190; "Inching Down the Capitalist Road," by James O. Jackson. *Time,* May 4, 1987, p. 42; and "In Defense of the Black Market," by Mario Vargas Llosa. *The New York Times Magazine,* February 22, 1987.

Playing by Their Own Rules In many of the nation's cities, hundreds of thousands of people have dropped out of the legitimate economy to earn a living in any number of illegal ways: prostitution, street vending, drug dealing, or petty theft. One expert estimates that 30 percent of youths in Boston, Philadelphia, and Chicago claim that crime (like running numbers and other gambling activities) is more lucrative than legitimate work. Shoplifting and mugging are also high on the list of "careers" in the underground economy.

A Worldwide Underground The underground economy is a problem everywhere, not just the U.S. In Bolivia, a country wracked by economic troubles, experts estimate that a whopping 60 percent of the labor force works in the underground economy, many in illegal drugs, like cocaine.

Sometimes the underground economy results from frustration with the myriad rules and regulations set down by a nation's government. For instance, Peru's 500,000 laws and executive orders seem to favor the already privileged. With no education, no training, and no chance of obtaining credit, the poor find occupations outside the mainstream of Peru's society. By one estimate, 95 percent of Lima's

> **The underground economy isn't just organized crime, like gambling and prostitution.**

public transportation is provided by underground businessmen.

The U.S.S.R.'s underground economy is estimated to include 40 percent of all household services; the average citizen, it is estimated, obtains about 12 percent of his income from underground activities. To discourage moonlighters and other underground workers by giving them a share of the legitimate economic pie, the Soviets

Street vendors are an integral part of the New York City scene. They, too, are a part of the underground economy. (Naoki Okamoto/Black Star)

began to lean more toward capitalism than ever before, approving plans to allow for some small private enterprises—"mom and pop" operations like shoe repair shops, jewelry studios, or vegetable markets.

The actual success of the Soviet measures to coax the underground economy above ground is in question, especially since the government plans to tax legitimized businesses that register with authorities. One moonlighter, an interior decorator, explained, "This law is for old ladies who knit socks, not for people doing real jobs. We don't plan to register."

Avoiding Uncle Sam   Of Ben Franklin's two "certainties" of life—death and taxes—at least one seems avoidable by some people. Tax evasion occurs most frequently when taxes are deemed too high by potential taxpayers. In Sweden—where tax rates skyrocket to about 80 percent of income—citizens often resort to nonmonetary types of income, or payments "under the table." For example, a plumber might repair a carpenter's plumbing in return for repairs on his home. When asked to bid on a job, a worker might submit two figures: a high one if the transaction is to be reported to the government, a much lower one if the job is to be paid for in cash.

Even if a person's entire income isn't obtained "underground," he or she might easily be tempted to temporarily join the ranks when receiving an unexpected cash windfall from gambling at cards or horses. A day at the races or a night in Las Vegas may never be reported to the IRS—cold cash without taxation.

In 1981, the IRS estimated that unreported legal income totalled 250 billion dollars. Government agencies have almost no recourse because people who work off the books are almost impossible to trace. One New York auto mechanic claims to earn $30,000 yearly in unreported income; the owner of the body shop where he

Police destroy the plunder of a recent cocaine bust in Columbia by dumping the drug into the Caribbean Sea. Drug traffickers comprise a sizeable portion of the underground economy. (Matthew Naythons/Gamma-Liaison)

works pays him, in cash, 60 percent of the bill for each car he repairs. With his earnings (and remember, none of it goes to Uncle Sam), he's bought a three-bedroom home with hot tub and Jacuzzi, rents a two-bedroom apartment in Greenwich Village, and drives a snazzy foreign car. No disadvantages to the mechanic's situation, you say? He says there *are* a few—he gets no health benefits or pension program.

A day at the races or a night in Las Vegas may never be reported to the IRS.

Because they cannot list legitimate jobs and don't want to leave a trail of records behind, participants in the underground economy can't apply for credit cards or use checks. Cash is the lifeblood of the underground economy. Transactions paid in cash are easy to hide from authorities and difficult to trace. Some economists believe the increased demand for currency in recent years—especially large-denomination bills—is evidence of a growing underground economy. Currency as a percentage of the total money supply increased from 20 percent in 1960 to 28

percent in 1984, despite the growing popularity of interest-paying checking accounts during this period.

The IRS and other concerned agencies say that income tax evaders not only damage the government, but they cheat honest taxpayers and erode national morals. As one solution, authorities have proposed a shift from income tax to a tax on spending. That means every time anyone made a purchase, they would pay a tax. This way, whether our money came from "honest" labor or underground activities, we'd all contribute to the government's coffers—at an estimated rate of $20 billion a year. In addition, proponents argue that a consumption tax would encourage saving, and could allow lower-income Americans to be eliminated from the income tax rolls.

Remember, the next time you buy a pair of earrings or necklace from a street vendor, or pay your gardener under the table, you are contributing to an underground network that has large repercussions for the entire economy. One last statistic: The underground economy in the U.S. causes tax revenues to be underpaid by as much as $100 billion yearly—an amount that, if channeled properly, could make a substantial dent in the national deficit.

Money and
Economic Activity

QUESTIONS TO CONSIDER

☐ Why do individuals and businesses hold money?

☐ What factors influence the demand for money?

☐ How does the market for money adjust to achieve equilibrium?

☐ What did the classical economists conclude from the equation of exchange?

☐ How do modern economists believe the economy responds to a change in the money supply?

Our discussion of money is continued as we answer the following questions: Can you ever have too much money? Can the economy ever have too much money? What happens if there is more money in circulation than households and businesses demand? How does a change in the supply of money affect economic activities such as spending, lending, and output decisions?

In Chapter 24 you learned what money is and how the Fed and the banking system can expand or contract the money supply. To study the market for money, however, we must consider why money is demanded and what factors affect that demand. Only then can we consider how demand for and supply of money interact and answer the preceding questions.

RATIONAL CHOICE AND DEMAND FOR MONEY

Beginning students in economics sometimes believe that money is one item with unlimited demand. Part of that confusion comes from a failure to distinguish money—currency and checking deposits—from income. We do, of course, receive much of our income in the form of money. And all of us want more income so we can buy more goods and services and increase our stock of savings. But a desire for more income is not the same as a desire to hold more money. In fact, the fraction of our income we hold as money—currency and checking deposits—is quite small.

As you study this chapter, do not confuse wanting more income with wanting to hold additional quantities of money. When economists talk about demand for money, they mean the *willingness to hold currency and checking deposits*—the two items in the M-1 definition of money. But why do individuals and businesses demand money? What causes demand for money to change? Economists believe that demand for money can best be predicted by assuming that households and businesses apply the principles of rational choice. That is, households and businesses weigh the extra benefits against the extra costs of holding money.

Benefits of Holding Money

Two of the principal uses of money suggest benefits of holding it. Because money is a medium of exchange, there is a **transactions motive** for holding

Transactions motive. The desire to hold money in order to make economic transactions, that is, to buy resources and products in economic markets. This motive is related to money's function as a medium of exchange.

641

Precautionary motive. Holding money to meet unexpected expenditures; related to money's function as a liquid store of value.

money. That is, individuals and businesses want to hold money so they can exchange it for goods and services. The more you expect to spend in the coming week, the more money you are likely to hold. For example, if you expect to spend $100 on groceries during the next week, you are likely to hold $100 of money, either in cash or in your checking account.

Not all expenditures can be fully anticipated, of course. Because money is a liquid store of value, there is a **precautionary motive** for holding it. For example, you may choose to hold more money in your checking account than you expect to spend next week in case your car suddenly breaks down and must be repaired. Businesses also maintain precautionary balances because they cannot predict exactly when they will receive money from their customers, yet they must have money to pay their own bills.

GNP or national income. The transactions motive helps explain why demand for money depends in part on nominal GNP (nominal national income). Think about how you might change your transactions demand for money as your income rises. Suppose that each Friday you deposit your weekly earnings of $350 in the bank. If you spend your income at a rate of $50 each day, you hold an average of $175 (three and one-half days of expenditures) in the bank as money.

What will happen to your demand for money if your nominal income doubles to $700 per week? You will probably spend more each week. If you deposit $700 each Friday and spend $100 each day, you will hold an average of $350 (still three and one-half days of expenditures) in the bank as money. In this case, your demand for money has doubled because your income (and your spending) has doubled. Even if your spending does not exactly double, we would expect your demand for money to vary directly with changes in your nominal income.

Note that spending should increase regardless of how your real income is affected. If your real income is rising—say, prices increase by 5 percent while your paycheck increases by 10 percent—you may spend more because you buy more steak and less hamburger or more-expensive clothes. If your real income declines—say, prices increase by 10 percent and you receive a 5 percent raise— you will have to spend more money (write a larger check) to buy hamburger and a less expensive brand of clothes.

What is true for an individual is, in this case, true in the aggregate. As nominal national income increases, the dollar volume of aggregate expenditures will increase. In response, more money will be demanded to support the greater volume of transactions. Thus we can conclude that *an increase in nominal GNP will increase the quantity of money demanded.*

Frequency of payment. The average balance in your checking account will also depend on how often you are paid. In the preceding example, we said that if you deposited your salary of $700 every week and spent it at $100 per day, your average checking deposit balance would be $350. If you receive the same annual salary but are paid $1400 every two weeks, your average checking account balance (the money you hold) will be $700. In general, *the more frequently that individuals are paid, the less money they will hold.* Similarly, businesses that expect to receive frequent cash payments will hold less money.

Costs of Holding Money

As much as we all like money, economists recognize that people may sometimes have more money than they want to hold. To understand why, we must recognize that there are costs to holding money. The costs depend on current interest rates, expected inflation rates, and availability of close substitutes for money.

Nominal interest rates. A major cost of holding money is the opportunity cost of not earning interest, or some other return, on that portion of your wealth. Even interest-bearing checking accounts (such as NOW accounts) involve some costs because they pay lower interest rates than time deposits and money market accounts. We can expect that *higher interest rates will cause a decrease in the quantity of money demanded* because higher rates increase the opportunity cost. In other words, higher interest rates offset the inconvenience and risk of not holding assets in a more liquid form.

Expected price levels. In Chapter 24 we observed that the real value of money (its purchasing power) decreases when the general price level rises. In contrast, the nominal value of some assets, such as stocks and real estate, typically increases along with the price level, often by enough to maintain their real value. *Thus an expected increase in the general price level will raise the cost of holding money and thus lower demand for money.*

But we said in Chapter 22 that nominal interest rates typically reflect expected changes in the general price level. However, economic studies show that nominal interest rates on checking deposits tend to adjust more slowly than other interest rates. As a result, the opportunity cost of holding money increases when the general price level increases.

In the United States, the annual increase in the general price level in the mid-1980s has been less than 5 percent, making the cost of holding money relatively low. But in Bolivia, where consumer prices rose by 12,000 percent in 1985, people began leaving work early on payday and spending their income before prices rose further. Under such unusual circumstances, there is virtually no demand for money.

Availability of close substitutes. Rapid price-level increases also increase demand for highly liquid, interest-earning alternatives to money. In the late 1970s, the relatively high rates of inflation (by U.S. standards) led banks and other financial institutions to create many new substitutes for money. For example, money market mutual funds and money market deposit accounts both emerged during this period of time. These accounts allow limited check writing but pay higher interest rates than standard checking deposits. Although somewhat less liquid than cash or checking deposits, they offered higher interest as a protection against inflation.

Credit cards are another substitute for money. Credit cards allow you to spend your income before you receive it. And if you pay your bill in full each month, the cost of using the card is just a small annual fee. Credit cards have reduced both transactions demand and precautionary demand for money. By paying with "plastic" you can hold very little cash and maintain small amounts in your checking account. In many cases unused credit is also a very good substitute for holding precautionary money. Similarly, a business that has arranged to borrow money (a line of credit) as necessary to meet its bills can satisfy its demand for liquidity without holding money. As these examples indicate, *increased availability of close substitutes decreases demand for money.*

EQUILIBRIUM IN THE MARKET FOR MONEY

You should not be too surprised to learn that economists study the interaction between demand for and supply of money in the money market. As in product markets, equilibrium in the money market occurs when quantity demanded equals quantity supplied. Moreover, the market automatically adjusts to equilibrium as individuals and businesses respond to shortages and surpluses. In this section we describe how the money market reaches equilibrium and what this process means for aggregate spending.

Supply of Money

Before we can consider equilibrium, however, we must expand on our discussion of the money supply. In Chapter 24 we said that the money supply depends on the current size of bank reserves, the required reserve ratio, and the banking system's desire to create excess reserves. We also noted that the Fed seeks to control the money supply, using its monetary-policy tools. The Fed sets required reserve ratios and manipulates bank reserves primarily through open-market operations.

But the supply of money also depends on the public's desire to hold currency. The Fed can influence this demand (by assuring confidence in the security of the banking system, for example). Because factors other than Fed policies affect the money supply, the Fed's control is incomplete. In the following discussion, however, we will assume that the money in circulation is the quantity decided on by the Fed. (You can believe that the Fed wishes this assumption were true.) Although a simplification, this assumption lets us focus on the relationship between changes in the money supply and changes in aggregate spending and output. In Chapter 27 we will consider the implications of the Fed's inability to control the money supply exactly.

What Is the Money Market?

Exhibit 25.1 shows a hypothetical money market, illustrating the relationship between quantity of money demanded and supplied and nominal interest rates. (There are many interest rates in an economy, and they all tend to move up and down together, though not always at the same speed.) Because we assume that the Fed fixes the supply of money, the money supply curve (Ms) is a vertical line at $600 billion. And since we expect quantity of money demanded to fall as the interest rate rises, the money demand curve (Md) slopes downward and to the right, like a typical demand curve. The money market is in equilibrium when quantity demanded equals quantity supplied (where Md intersects Ms). As shown in Exhibit 25.1, equilibrium occurs when the interest rate is 8 percent.

For any money demand curve we again make the all-other-things-unchanged assumption. That is, we hold constant the level of nominal GNP, expectations, and

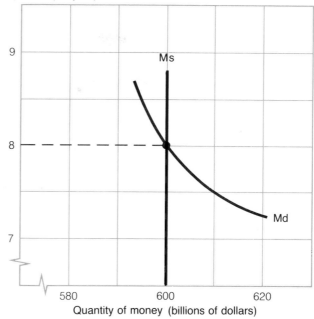

Nominal interest rate
(percent per year)

Exhibit 25.1
Market for Money
The market for money indicates how the demand and supply of money determines
the nominal rate of interest. Although the Fed's control over the money supply is
imperfect, we assume here that the quantity of money supplied will be established by
the Fed's monetary policies. Thus the money supply (Ms) is a vertical line. An increase in the nominal interest rate means an increase in the opportunity cost of holding money and causes quantity of money demanded to fall. When drawing the demand for money curve (Md), we hold all other factors constant—especially nominal
GNP and price level expectations. The money market will reach equilibrium when
quantity of money demanded equals quantity supplied, or at an interest rate of 8
percent in this case.

the other factors that affect demand. A change in any of these factors will cause a
shift in the money demand curve. For example, an increase in nominal GNP will
increase demand of money, shifting the curve to the right.

To understand the market for money you must be able to answer the following
question: If the Fed's policies determine how much money is supplied, what
forces will automatically adjust quantity demanded to match quantity supplied? As
you will discover, there are actually two adjustments that can bring the money
market to equilibrium. One involves changes in the interest rate; the other involves
changes in nominal GNP.

Before we go into detail about the adjustments, ask yourself what you would
do if you had too much money? (Recall, we are *not* talking about having too much
income or wealth.) Suppose that your rich Uncle Sam just handed you a nice
surprise—a $1000 bill. But this is more money than you want to hold as cash or
in your checking account. What can you do with it? To oversimplify, you can either

spend the money—perhaps buy a new stereo system—or *lend* it—perhaps put it in a money market account or buy some shares of common stock. (Note that we use the term *lend* broadly here. Lending includes a loan you make to your roommate whose allowance check has not arrived. But it also includes your purchase of savings bonds or shares of common stock.)

By either spending or lending the money, you can eliminate the excess money you are holding. But the money you spend or lend does not disappear; it winds up in the hands of others. If they do not want more money, they will also spend or lend the excess. The important principle is that the spending and lending actions of the household and business sectors do not affect the quantity of money in circulation. These actions just move the existing quantity of money around. The public as a whole cannot get rid of money (except by using paper currency to start fires or as wallpaper).

How, then, does the money market ever reach equilibrium? As you will see shortly, spending and lending activities change nominal GNP and interest rates and thus the demand for money. (In the following discussion we continue to hold constant expected price levels, frequency of payment, and substitutes for money.)

Adjusting to a Surplus of Money by Increasing Spending

Exhibit 25.2(a) shows a market initially in equilibrium at 8 percent interest and $600 billion supplied (where Md_1 intersects Ms_1). But what if the Fed lowers the reserve ratio or buys government securities in the open market? Either of these actions would give banks excess reserves and set in motion an expansion of loans and checking deposits. In this case the money supply would increase to $620 billion (step 1, a shift from Ms_1 to Ms_2).

As a result of the Fed's policy change (and the banks' response), the money market is not in equilibrium. A surplus of $20 billion exists at the current nominal GNP and interest rate. Anyone holding too much money will either spend it or lend it. By tracing both paths, you can see how each action increases quantity of money demanded and brings the money market into equilibrium. At the same time, you can see how money affects aggregate expenditures.

What happens if households and businesses spend the $20 billion surplus? More spending means an increase in planned aggregate expenditures—more consumption and/or investment—shown as step 2, the shift from AE_1 to AE_2 in Exhibit 25.2(b). An increase in aggregate expenditures raises nominal GNP. As nominal GNP increases, so will the number of transactions and transactions demand for money. (Although we will continue to refer to nominal GNP, the graphs in Exhibits 25.2 and 25.3, like all our Keynesian output–expenditures graphs, show output as real GNP. Higher real GNP is also higher nominal GNP because we are holding the general price level constant.)

As long as there is a surplus of money, aggregate expenditures and nominal GNP will rise. The result will be a new money demand curve—step 3, the shift from Md_1 to Md_2 in Exhibit 25.2(a)—and a new equilibrium in the money market. The adjustment process can be summarized as:

Spending response to an increased supply of money

Increased money supply	*causes*	Increased aggregate expenditures	*causes*	Increased nominal GNP	*causes*	Increased demand for money

(a) *Money market*

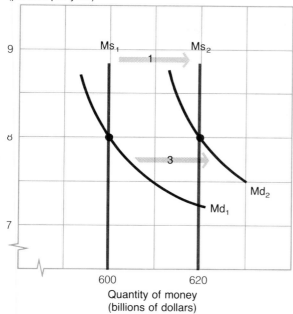

Nominal interest rate
(percent per year)

(b) *Market for final goods*

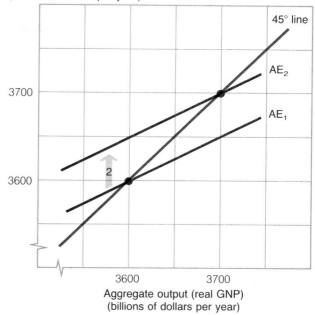

Aggregate expenditures
(billions of dollars per year)

Exhibit 25.2
Spending Response to Increased Supply of Money
If Fed policies increase the money supply (step 1, shift from Ms_1 to Ms_2), a surplus of
money will exist at the initial interest rate (8 percent). If the public attempts to get rid
of the surplus by increased spending, planned aggregate expenditures increase [step
2, shift from AE_1 to AE_2 in part (b)] raising the equilibrium level of GNP. The increase
in GNP, in turn, increases money demand (step 3, shift from Md_1 to Md_2) and restores
equilibrium.

The adjustment process works in a similar fashion when the money supply
decreases. That is, a smaller money supply reduces aggregate expenditures and
decreases nominal GNP. As a result, demand for money decreases, returning the
money market to equilibrium. (You might test your understanding of this process
by drawing the shifts in money supply, aggregate expenditures, and money demand
that illustrate this adjustment.)

Adjusting to a Surplus of Money by Increasing Lending

Instead, what if households and businesses *lend* the excess $20 billion? As we
noted earlier, we are using the term lend broadly to reflect not only a direct loan
to a friend but also the purchase of a government bond or new shares of common
stock. In an important way all such purchases are alike: Any increase in lending
can be considered an increase in demand for financial claims, such as government
bonds. And as in any market, we can expect an increase in demand for bonds to

Yield. The interest rate (return) received from the purchase of a financial claim; varies inversely with the price of the financial claim. Market interest rates are yields.

raise their price. But what is the relationship between the price of a bond and interest rates?

Suppose that you decide to buy a bond representing the government's promise to pay you a fixed sum of $100 in interest each year. If you can buy the bond for $1000, you will earn a 10 percent return on your purchase ($100 ÷ $1000 = 0.10, or 10 percent). Economists call the return actually earned on a bond the **yield**. The yield on a bond is *inversely* related to the price of the bond. Suppose, for example, that the price of the bond for sale increases to $1250. In that case, the fixed annual interest payment of $100 represents a yield of only 8 percent per year ($100 ÷ $1250 = 0.08, or 8 percent).

The yield on any particular bond partially reflects the risk the bondholder accepts in holding that bond (which can be substantial for some corporate or foreign securities). It also reflects the real return that bondholders require to justify parting with their money. The yield is the same as the money market interest rate.

We can now state how lending helps the money market reach equilibrium. *A surplus of money increases lending and therefore the demand for financial claims. As a result, the prices of financial claims rise and the yield or interest rate falls. A drop in the interest rate reduces the opportunity cost of holding money, making people willing to hold more money.* Exhibit 25.3(a) shows this effect as step 2, a movement along the money demand curve (Md).

Although we show the money market in equilibrium, the economy has not finished its adjustments. Because we have assumed that the general price level will remain constant, a drop in the nominal interest rate represents a drop in the *real interest rate*. Lower real interest rates decrease the cost of borrowing. Thus businesses will find more investment projects profitable, and households can afford to borrow money to buy durable goods, such as cars and appliances. (Demand for housing is particularly sensitive to changes in interest rates, but housing purchases are part of investment spending in GNP accounting.) In other words, as interest rates fall we can expect an increase in aggregate expenditures and an increase in nominal GNP, shown as step 3 in Exhibit 25.3(b).

Lending response to an increased supply of money

Increased money supply	*causes*	Decreased interest rates	*causes*	Increased aggregate expenditures	*causes*	Increased nominal GNP

Comparison of Spending and Lending Responses

The reactions of households and businesses to an increase in the money supply—either spending or lending—cause the money market to adjust to equilibrium. In addition, both spending and lending increase aggregate expenditures and nominal GNP. Higher spending directly increases aggregate expenditures and nominal GNP. The money market adjusts as higher nominal GNP increases money demand. Higher lending reduces interest rates (yields), indirectly stimulating an increase in aggregate expenditures. Lower interest rates result in a movement along the money demand curve, helping to restore money market equilibrium.

(a) Money market

Nominal interest rate
(percent per year)

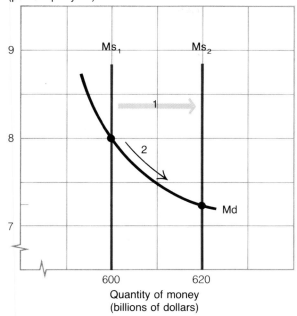

Quantity of money
(billions of dollars)

(b) Market for final goods

Aggregate expenditures
(billions of dollars per year)

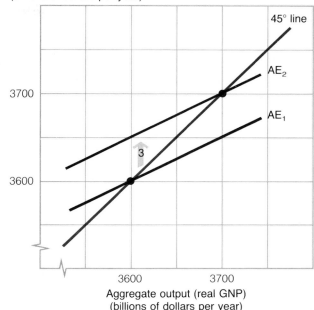

Aggregate output (real GNP)
(billions of dollars per year)

Exhibit 25.3
Lending Response to Increased Supply of Money
An increase in the money supply (step 1, shift from Ms_1 to Ms_2) leaves a surplus in the money market at the initial interest rate (8 percent). If the public uses the surplus to buy financial claims—savings bonds or shares of stock, for example—the increased demand for financial claims raises their price and lowers their yield (the interest rate). That persuades the public to hold more money (step 2, shown as movement along the money demand curve) and restores equilibrium in the money market. But the lower interest rate also stimulates additional investment and interest-sensitive consumption spending. The consequent rise in aggregate expenditures [step 3, shift from AE_1 to AE_2 in part (b)] causes GNP to increase.

Although we have discussed the responses separately, most economists believe that an increase in the supply of money will cause both more spending and more lending. That is, actual adjustment to equilibrium appears to result from a combination of a shift in the demand curve *and* movement along the money demand curve. But as we discuss in the next section, economists differ in the emphasis they place on the two adjustment processes.

Finally, it is important to note that the economy will continue adjusting until *both* the money market and the market for final goods are in equilibrium. That is, quantity of money demanded must equal quantity supplied *and* aggregate expenditures must equal quantity of output supplied. Moreover, these two markets are interrelated. An increase in nominal GNP will increase demand for money. Increased demand for money increases interest rates, which in turn decreases

An increase in the money supply will create a surplus. If individuals do not want to hold more money, they will spend it or lend it. Lending activities include the purchase of any financial claim—savings bonds or shares of stock, for example.

Additional spending—more planned aggregate expenditures—raises nominal GNP, which in turn increases demand for money (shifts the money demand curve), helping to restore equilibrium in the money market.

Additional lending raises the price of financial claims and lowers their yields, or interest rates. As interest rates fall, the quantity of money demanded increases (movement along the curve), helping to restore equilibrium in the money market. Lower interest rates also stimulate additional spending and raise nominal GNP.

Full macroeconomic equilibrium requires that both the money market and the market for final goods be in equilibrium simultaneously.

Velocity (V). The average number of times each dollar in the money supply is spent during a specific period of time; calculated as the ratio of nominal GNP to the money supply, that is, $V = (P \times Q) \div Ms$.

Equation of exchange. The identity of total spending and nominal GNP, or

$$Ms \times V = P \times Q$$

planned aggregate expenditures. In other words, changes in the money market cause changes in nominal GNP, and changes in nominal GNP cause changes in the money market. Economists are well aware of these interconnections. (In the appendix to this chapter we describe how interest rates and nominal GNP are determined simultaneously.)

MONEY AND ECONOMIC ACTIVITY: CLASSICAL AND MODERN VIEWS

You now know something about demand, supply, and equilibrium in the money market. But two important questions remain unanswered. First, how much will aggregate expenditures increase when the money supply is increased? Second, how much of any increase in nominal GNP represents higher real GNP and how much represents higher prices?

The modern answer to the second question is presented in Chapter 26. However, the classical economists believed that these questions had fairly simple answers. Their analyses suggested that an increase in the money supply would not affect real GNP but would cause a proportional increase in the general price level. To understand this conclusion, we must consider yet another accounting identity.

Equation of Exchange

We can view any market exchange from two perspectives: what is bought and what is spent. For example, suppose that you go to the local music shop and buy 3 tapes for $20, giving the sales clerk a $20 bill. We can look at this exchange as your *buying* $20 worth of tapes. (Since tapes are a final good, you have also added $20 to nominal GNP.) We can also look at this exchange as your *spending* one $20 bill.

Of course, the $20 bill that you gave the clerk will be spent over and over again during a year. For example, the store owner may put the same $20 bill (along with a few more) into the clerk's pay envelope on Friday. On Saturday, the clerk may go to a clothing store and exchange the same $20 bill for a new sweater. Again, the same $20 bill is exchanged for $20 of final goods. The two purchases—yours and the clerk's—represent a total of $40 of consumption, or $40 of nominal GNP. But it was the same $20 bill that was spent twice. The number of times the average dollar of money in the economy is spent to buy a final good in a year is what economists call **velocity (V)**.

The two ways of looking at exchanges give us two identical dollar values. On the one hand, we have $40 of final goods bought—3 tapes for $20 and 1 sweater for $20. On the other hand, we have $20 of money spent twice, which also equals $40. If we followed the circulation of every dollar in the economy, we would find that the value of what is spent *always* equals the value of what is bought. We can express this relationship as an accounting identity (which is always true by definition) called the **equation of exchange**:

Value of money spent = Value of goods bought   or   nominal GNP
Money supply × Velocity = General price level × Real GNP
Ms   ×   V   =   P   ×   Q

Classical quantity theory. The proposition of the classical economists that changes in the money supply cause proportional changes in the price level; based on the equation of exchange (M × V = P × Q) assuming velocity (V) is constant and real GNP (Q) equals potential GNP.

It is possible to estimate the size of the money supply, real GNP, and the general price level. But velocity cannot be directly measured. (How much time and effort would it take to trace the flow of even a few dollar bills for one year?) Instead economists calculate velocity by rearranging the equation of exchange. Thus in 1986 the M-1 money supply averaged $672.5 billion and real GNP was $3674.9 billion. The general price level (the GNP deflator in proportionate, *not* percentage terms) was 1.145. So the velocity of money (the number of times an average dollar was spent on final goods and services) was 6.26, calculated as

$$\text{Velocity (V)} = \frac{\text{Nominal GNP}}{\text{Money supply}} \quad \text{or} \quad \frac{P \times Q}{M\text{-}1}$$

$$= \frac{1.145(\$3674.9)}{\$672.5} \quad \text{or} \quad 6.26$$

Classical Quantity Theory

The equation of exchange is an identity, not a theory. To construct a theory from the equation of exchange, we have to specify which variables affect which other variables. The classical economists turned the equation of exchange into **classical quantity theory** by assuming that both velocity and real GNP are constant in the short run.

You may be wondering why the classical economists believed velocity and real GNP to be constant. They thought that velocity was determined largely by how often people were paid, how long banks took to process checks, and personal preferences for holding and spending money. These factors generally change quite slowly, so classical economists assumed that velocity was constant. Recall that classical economists also believed that flexible wages, prices and interest rates would cause the economy to produce at its potential GNP level. Potential GNP can be considered constant in the short run, and the classical economists assumed that real GNP was also fixed.

Accepting these assumptions for the moment, we can see why changes in the money supply are directly related to changes in the general price level. For example, suppose that potential GNP is $2000 billion. Because the classical assumption is that the economy will adjust to full employment, real GNP is also $2000 billion. If the supply of money is $500 billion and velocity is 5, the equation of exchange indicates a general price level index of 1.25, calculated as

Money supply	×	Velocity	=	General price level	×	Real GNP
Ms	×	V	=	P	×	Q
$500 billion	×	5	=	P	×	$2000 billion
1.25			=	P		

Classical economists were very much impressed by indications that the money supply and the general price level fluctuated together. This relationship is approximately true, but unfortunately for classical quantity theory, changes in the money supply are not *always* exactly proportional to changes in prices. The classical version of the quantity theory is, in fact, too simple to explain the relationship between the money supply and the general price level.

RECAP

The equation of exchange (Ms × V = P × Q) is an identity. It recognizes the fact that the total value spent and received on final goods are equal. Total value spent (Ms × V) is the product of the money supply (Ms) and velocity (V). Total value received—nominal GNP—is the product of the general price level (P) and real output (Q).

Classical quantity theory is based on the assumptions that velocity is constant and that real GNP equals potential GNP. It predicts that increases in the money supply will result in proportional increases in prices.

The modern view of money recognizes that velocity can change as nominal interest rates change. It also recognizes that increases in the money supply can cause real GNP to increase in the short run, although increases in the money supply cause a higher general price level in the long run.

Modern Monetary Theories

The simple theory of the classical economists has been replaced by modern monetary theories. These theories recognize that velocity is not constant. Changes in nominal interest rates may change money demand, thereby offsetting part or all of any change in money supply and reducing the impact on nominal GNP. In addition, modern theories recognize that the economy does not always operate at full employment and that a change in money supply may increase real GNP in the short run. Although most modern monetary theories are based on these principles, economists do not agree on some important details, as you will see.

Changes in velocity. Economists now maintain that velocity is not constant because demand for money is not constant and money and velocity are linked. At the beginning of this chapter, we noted that demand for money depends on how frequently people are paid—a factor that also affects velocity. Consider that if you spend $36,000 per year and are paid once a month, your average demand for (holding of) money is $1500. If you are paid twice a month, your demand for money falls to $750. But your personal velocity of money—the number of times you spend essentially the same dollar—rises from 24 ($36,000 ÷ $1500) to 48 ($36,000 ÷ $750). Thus we can conclude that *velocity is inversely related to quantity of money demanded*.

Historically, the evidence supports the modern economic contention that velocity is not constant. Exhibit 25.4 shows two measures of velocity: one based on the M-1 definition of money and one based on the M-2 definition. (In each case, velocity is calculated by dividing yearly averages of nominal GNP by the average supply of money, either M-1 or M-2.) The graphs reveal several interesting facts.

First, the velocity of M-1 money increased during most of the period shown, rising from 3.5 in 1959 to peak at 7.1 in 1981. This increase reflects declining demand for M-1 money, which many economists attribute to the increased availability of interest-paying substitutes. In addition, households have held less and less money for transactions and precautionary purposes by relying increasingly on credit cards. Finally, because nominal interest rates generally increased, businesses reduced the quantity of money they held.

The velocity of M-2 money fluctuated within a fairly narrow range during the same period. The stability of the M-2 velocity reflects the fact that many substitutes for M-1, especially money market mutual funds and money market deposit accounts, are included in the M-2 measure of the money supply. Thus a switch of funds from checking deposits to these new funds decreased M-1 but had no effect on M-2.

However, since 1981, M-1 velocity has fallen significantly, representing an increase in demand for money. Economists do not agree on whether this change represents a temporary or more permanent change in money demand. Whatever the cause, M-2 velocity has been more stable than M-1 velocity during this period. How important is the change in velocity of money? For economists who want to predict changes in the money supply, the more important question is whether changes in velocity are predictable. To the extent that changes in velocity are predictable, the effects of a change in the money supply on nominal GNP are also predictable. But if velocity changes are erratic, the Fed has difficulty knowing how much to change the money supply to achieve the results it seeks.

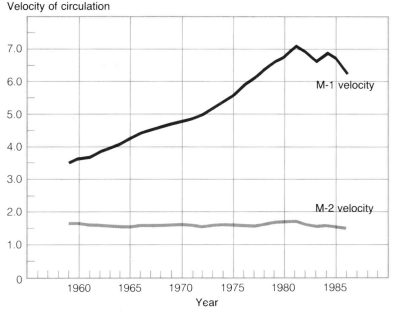

Exhibit 25.4
Velocity of Circulation: 1959–1986
The graph indicates that velocity, as measured by the ratio of nominal GNP to the M-1 stock of money, has a clear upward trend until 1981, reflecting in part the development of substitutes, especially money market mutual funds and money market deposit accounts. Velocity based on the M-2 stock of money is more stable, although certainly not constant.

Sources: Economic Report of the President, 1987; U.S. Department of Commerce, *The National Income and Product Accounts of the United States, 1929– 1982;* Federal Reserve Bank of Boston.

Some economists prefer to focus on M-2, which has been relatively stable. They argue that updating classical quantity theory to use M-2 as a measure of money makes the effect of velocity change predictable. But economists are very much divided on the question of how accurately velocity can be predicted.

Short-run changes in real output. A second difference between the classical and modern views of money is the classical assumption that the economy operates at full employment. Based on that assumption, the classical economists concluded that changes in the money supply primarily affect the general price level. However, most modern theories consider a change in the general price level to be the most significant *long-run* effect of a change in the money supply. But modern theories also recognize that changes in the money supply can have important short-run effects on real GNP, especially if the economy is operating below potential GNP.

As we noted in Chapter 23, if an economy is operating below its potential GNP level, a contractionary gap exists. Increasing the money supply can help close the gap by increasing aggregate expenditures. Although an increased money supply means a higher general price level, it also means lower interest rates and greater real output, at least in the short run. Those who advocate monetary policy to offset falling demand during recessions want to take advantage of this short-run effect.

Monetarists and Keynesians: A contrast. Economists now generally agree with the modern theories that we have stated, although complete agreement

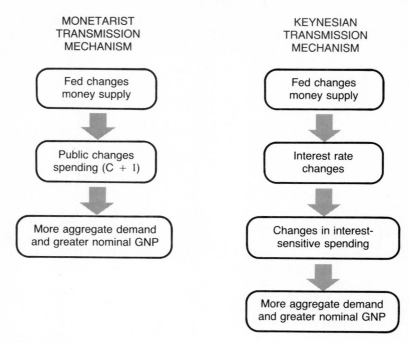

Exhibit 25.5
Monetarist and Keynesian Monetary Transmission Mechanisms

does not exist. During the 1950s and 1960s, however, economists disagreed strongly about the importance of money. Economists who followed the Keynesian tradition argued that monetary policy was largely ineffective. A rival school of economists, the **monetarists**, countered with the argument that changes in the money supply were the most significant cause of short-run changes in nominal GNP.

Both monetarists and Keynesians now believe that money matters. However, as Exhibit 25.5 shows, the two groups tend to differ over how a change in the money supply affects aggregate expenditures. Monetarists generally emphasize the direct connection between changes in the money supply and changes in aggregate expenditures. In their view—based on a modern version of classical quantity theory—interest rates do not have to fall to stimulate additional spending. In contrast, Keynesians emphasize lending, stressing the connection between changes in spending and changes in interest rates caused by changes in the money supply. Both groups contend that more money leads to more aggregate expenditures. But the link between money and spending is somewhat weaker and looser in the Keynesian view. As a result, Keynesians are more likely to look for changes in factors other than the money supply when seeking to explain short-run changes in output.

While consensus was being reached on some issues, new controversies emerged. Most economists agree that Keynesian theory focused attention on the short-run behavior of the economy in contrast to the long-run behavior analyzed by the classical theories. Indeed, much of modern macroeconomics, as you will

Monetarists. Economists who believe that fluctuations in aggregate output are generally caused by changes in the money supply.

see in the remaining chapters, is devoted to analyzing the short-run behavior of the economy. Although monetarists recognize the importance of short-run analysis, they often accuse Keynesians of not emphasizing the long run enough. As part of this difference in focus, Keynesians are generally more supportive of the use of monetary and fiscal policies to correct short-run problems. Monetarists and their allies tend to stress that most problems will be taken care of automatically in the long run. They show less enthusiasm for policies to smooth out economic fluctuations. We return to this argument when we consider monetary and fiscal policies in Chapter 27.

CONCLUSION

In this chapter we showed that economists generally agree that changes in the supply of money will increase aggregate expenditures, hence nominal GNP. Thus we know that the money supply is important. But our model so far is inadequate to address an important question: How much of any change in nominal GNP will be a general price-level change and how much will reflect a change in real GNP?

Throughout this chapter, we have assumed that the Fed can increase the money supply without affecting general price-level expectations. But in fact, an increase in the money supply tends to raise the general price level. If households and businesses react to an increase in the money supply with expectations of higher prices, interest rates may not fall and the Fed's policy may have less impact than we have suggested. To consider this most important issue, we explore in some detail in Chapter 26 the modern macroeconomic model of aggregate demand and supply.

Moreover, we have to consider how the Fed can best use its monetary-policy tools to help the economy achieve full employment, price stability, and growth. Economists generally agree that both monetary and fiscal policies affect aggregate spending. However, they do not agree on how, or if at all, these policies should be used. We explore these issues in Chapter 27.

SUMMARY

1. In this chapter we explored the factors affecting demand for money; how equilibrium is achieved in the money market; and how economic views of the effects of money have changed over the years.

2. Demand for money reflects the willingness of households and businesses to hold money. They hold money for transactions and precautionary reasons. That is, they hold money to make purchases and to guard against unforeseen expenses. When nominal GNP increases, so does demand for money. When individuals or businesses receive more frequent payments, demand for money decreases.

3. When nominal interest rates rise and when the general price level is expected to increase, the opportunity cost of holding money rises and demand for money falls.

When good substitutes for money—such as money market funds and credit—are developed, demand for money decreases.

4. The money supply depends on the current size of bank reserves; the banking system's desire to hold reserves in excess of the required reserve ratio; and the public's desire to hold currency. The Fed's control of the money supply, while not absolute, is extensive.

5. The economic model of the money market shows the relationship between the nominal rate of interest and quantity of money demanded and supplied. If there is too much money in the economy, individuals and businesses will either spend it on final goods or lend it by purchasing a financial claim. Either activity results in money market equilibrium.

6. Additional spending on final goods (more planned aggregate expenditures) causes nominal GNP to increase, which in turn increases demand for money (shifts the demand curve), restoring equilibrium in the money market.

7. Additional lending increases prices and lowers interest rates (yields) on financial claims, lowers the cost of holding money, and increases the quantity of money demanded (a movement along the money demand curve), restoring equilibrium. In addition, lower interest rates stimulate more investment and interest-sensitive consumption, increasing aggregate expenditures and thus nominal GNP.

8. The money market and the market for final goods are related. A change in the money market affects planned spending (by affecting spending and/or lending) and thus affects the market for final goods. Changes in the market for final goods cause changes in nominal GNP and therefore in money demand. For an economy to reach equilibrium, both markets must achieve equilibrium simultaneously.

9. The equation of exchange (Ms × V = P × Q) is an identity, expressing the fact that identical values are spent and received in market exchanges. The total value spent (Ms × V) depends on the quantity of money (Ms, the money supply) and the average number of times it is spent (V, the velocity). The total value received (P × Q) is the product of the general price level (P) and real output (Q), that is, nominal GNP.

10. The classical economists assumed that velocity and real GNP were constant in the short run. Thus classical quantity theory concludes that increases in the money supply result in proportional increases in prices.

11. The modern view of money recognizes that velocity (and demand for money) can change in response to changes in nominal interest rates. It also recognizes that an economy may operate below potential GNP in the short run. And finally, it recognizes that increases in the money supply may cause higher real output in the short run, although most of the long-run influence is on prices.

12. Both Keynesians and monetarists agree that changes in the money supply can change nominal GNP. Keynesians tend to stress lending, emphasizing that an increase in the money supply lowers interest rates and stimulates interest-sensitive spending. Monetarists tend to stress spending, emphasizing that an increase in the money supply leads to more aggregate expenditures.

KEY TERMS

Transactions motive, 641
Precautionary motive, 642
Yield, 648
Velocity (V), 650
Equation of exchange, 650
Classical quantity theory, 651
Monetarists, 654

QUESTIONS FOR REVIEW AND DISCUSSION

1. Consider each of the following statements. Using the concepts of this chapter, explain why the person making each statement is confused.
   a) How can economists believe that there can ever be too much money? This notion could only apply to the richest people in our society.
   b) Economists speak of a demand for money, but the only reason I want money is to spend it as fast as I get it. After all, I can't eat, wear, or enjoy money. But I can eat, wear, and enjoy the things I can buy with money.
   c) Economic theory shows that increases in the supply of money result in greater aggregate output. Thus the solution to the problem of scarcity is for Congress to require the Fed to increase the supply of money.

2. What effect will each of the following changes have on quantity of money demanded? On velocity?
   a) An increase in interest rates.
   b) An increase in credit card use.
   c) Growth in real output.
   d) Expectations of a higher general price level.
   e) An increase in the general price level (assuming that expectations do not change).

3. Is each of the following statements true, false, or uncertain? Explain why.
   a) An increase in the money supply will result in a smaller increase in nominal GNP if velocity increases as well.
   b) An increase in bond prices will increase the yield on bonds and thus result in higher market interest rates.
   c) An increase in velocity means the demand for money has decreased.

4. Suppose that the U.S. government sends each of its citizens five newly printed $100 bills. (That would total some $125 billion, or represent about a 20 percent increase in the money supply.)
   a) Predict the effect of this action on demand for goods and services. The general price level. Nominal interest rates.
   b) Would you be any better off than you were the day before? (Explain why your answer might depend on whether the economy were producing at its level of potential GNP.)

5. Suppose a business is considering selling some bonds to finance a new plant. Explain how each of the following would affect the price of its bonds. The yield received by someone buying the bonds.
   a) The Fed increases the money supply (but does not cause individuals to expect an increase in the price level).
   b) The Fed increases the money supply setting off expectations that future price levels will increase.
   c) The firm announces its new plant will be built in a foreign country with a highly unstable economy.
6. Ambrose Bierce, an American short-story author (but not an economist), defined money as "a blessing that is of no advantage to us excepting when we part with it." Would you expect economists to accept or reject Bierce's definition? Why?
7. Use the information presented in the appendix to this chapter, as well as the following equations, to answer questions (a)–(c). Suppose that the money market and

market for final goods of the economy can be described as follows:

Final goods market

$C = 150 + 0.7GNP$
$I = 75 - 4r$
$G = 100$

Money market

$Ms = 500$
$Md = 160 - 8r + 0.4GNP$

where C, I, G, Md, and Ms are expressed in millions of dollars.
a) What is the equilibrium level of GNP and the interest rate?
b) What will the equilibrium level of output and the interest rate be if the money supply rises by $20 million?
c) What will the equilibrium level of output and the interest rate be if government expenditures rise by $10 million? Explain why the expenditures multiplier cannot be expressed as $1 \div (1 - MPC)$. [*Hint:* What is investment (I) at the new equilibrium?]

Appendix to Chapter 25

Algebra of Joint Equilibrium in the Final Goods and Money Markets

In this chapter we observed that macroeconomic equilibrium requires that both the final goods and money markets be in equilibrium. In this appendix, we demonstrate how these two markets achieve equilibrium simultaneously. In doing so, we will show how interest rates and aggregate output connect the final goods and money markets.

EQUILIBRIUM IN THE FINAL GOODS MARKET

As we noted in Chapters 22 and 23, equilibrium in the final goods market is reached when GNP = C + I + G, where C is consumption, I is investment, and G is government expenditures. (For simplicity we ignore the foreign sector.)

Consumption is directly related to GNP, if we ignore consumption sensitive to interest rates.

In previous appendixes we considered investment to be constant. But now that we have included the money market in our model, we must recognize the relationship between investment and the interest rate, r. Since money markets have a major influence on interest rates, interest rates link final goods and money markets. We continue to assume that government expenditures (G) are not related to other variables in the model.

In the final goods market, equilibrium requires that the quantity of output produced be equal to the quantity of planned expenditures (GNP = AE). Thus, if

$$C = 100 + 0.75GNP$$
$$I = 100 - 5r$$

we can express *equilibrium in the final goods market* as

$$\text{Aggregate output} = \text{Planned aggregate expenditures}$$
$$GNP = AE$$
$$= C + I + G$$
$$= (100 + 0.75GNP) + (100 - 5r) + G$$
$$= 200 + 0.75GNP - 5r + G$$
$$0.25GNP = 200 - 5r + G$$

EQUILIBRIUM IN THE MONEY MARKET

As noted in the chapter, equilibrium in the money market requires that quantity of money supplied equals quantity of money demanded (Ms = Md). To keep the analysis simple, we continue to assume that the Fed determines the supply of money. But we must recognize that demand for money varies directly with aggregate output (GNP) and indirectly with the rate of interest r. Thus if

$$Md = 200 - 10r + 0.30GNP$$

we can describe *equilibrium in the money market* as

$$\text{Supply of money} = \text{Demand for money}$$
$$Ms = Md$$
$$Ms = 200 - 10r + 0.30GNP$$
$$0.30GNP = -200 + 10r + Ms$$

MACROECONOMIC EQUILIBRIUM

To reach macroeconomic equilibrium, the final goods and money markets must reach equilibrium simultaneously. Since both equilibrium equations contain the same variable, r, we first solve each for r, as follows:

Final goods market	Money market
$0.25GNP = 200 - 5r + G$	$0.30GNP = -200 + 10r + Ms$
$5r = 200 + G - 0.25GNP$	$10r = 200 - Ms + 0.30GNP$
$r = 40 + 0.2G - 0.05GNP$	$r = 20 - 0.1Ms + 0.03GNP$

If the economy is to reach equilibrium, r must have the same value in each equation. And assuming that government purchases (G) are 75 and the money supply (Ms) is 450, the equilibrium level of GNP is 1000, calculated as

$$\text{Interest rate in money market} = \text{Interest rate in final goods market}$$
$$20 - 0.1\text{Ms} + 0.03\text{GNP} = 40 + 0.2\text{G} - 0.05\text{GNP}$$
$$20 - (0.1)(450) + 0.03\text{GNP} = 40 + (0.2)(75) - 0.05\text{GNP}$$
$$0.08\text{GNP} = 80$$
$$\text{GNP} = 1000$$

We can then determine the interest rate at this equilibrium level of output by using either the equation for money market equilibrium (shown below) or the equation for final goods market equilibrium. Thus

$$r = 20 - 0.1\text{Ms} + 0.03\text{GNP}$$
$$= 20 - (0.1)(450) + (0.03)(1000)$$
$$= 5\%$$

To check your understanding, verify this equilibrium level by substituting the equilibrium values for GNP and r into the final goods and money markets equilibrium equations.

CONCLUSION

In this appendix we considered a more complete model of the economy than those in previous appendixes. We demonstrated how macroeconomic equilibrium requires that both final goods and money markets be in equilibrium and showed how interest rates and aggregate output link these two markets. Thus a policy change—an increase in the money supply by the Fed, for example—will affect both markets and macroeconomic equilibrium. We explore the issues involved with such policies in Chapter 27.

Aggregate Demand and
Aggregate Supply

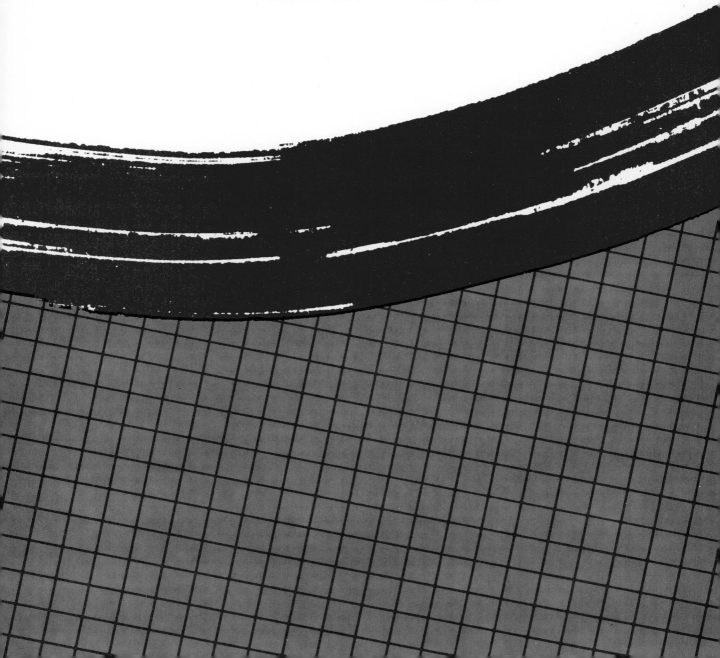

QUESTIONS TO CONSIDER

☐ How are aggregate expenditures and aggregate demand related?

☐ What factors affect aggregate demand?

☐ In what ways do long-run and short-run aggregate supply and equilibrium differ?

☐ How does an economy respond to an expansionary or contractionary gap?

☐ Why do economists disagree about the speed of the economy's automatic response to a contractionary gap?

R ecall that in Chapters 22–25 we explored aggregate expenditures, including the role of money in the economy. At this point you know that changes in spending—caused by changes in the money supply or other factors—will change aggregate expenditures and lead to changes in nominal GNP. But *how much* does real output change when aggregate expenditures change? And *how much* of any change in aggregate expenditures is simply a change in the general price level? Why did the U.S. economy experience both higher prices and lower output in 1974–1975? Why did the high growth in real output in the mid-1960s have little effect on inflation? Why did both real output and inflation fall in the early 1980s?

To be able to answer these and similar questions we must have a model of the economy that incorporates both real output and the general price level. In this chapter, we return to the aggregate demand/aggregate supply diagram introduced in Chapter 20. By looking more closely at aggregate demand and supply and how they interact, we can develop a model to use in looking at the economic history of the United States. More importantly, the model can help us predict the types of changes that will accompany future economic events.

AGGREGATE DEMAND

In Chapter 20 we introduced the aggregate demand curve and some of the reasons for its shape. Now that we have considered the role of money in the economy, we can return to these reasons and consider them in greater detail. Moreover, we can now consider the factors that cause aggregate demand to increase or decrease. First, however, you must understand how aggregate expenditures and aggregate demand are linked.

Connecting Aggregate Expenditures and Aggregate Demand

Before exploring their details, take a quick look at Exhibit 26.1. Exhibit 26.1(a) shows the familiar output–expenditures model that relates planned aggregate expenditures to the level of aggregate output (real GNP). The aggregate expen-

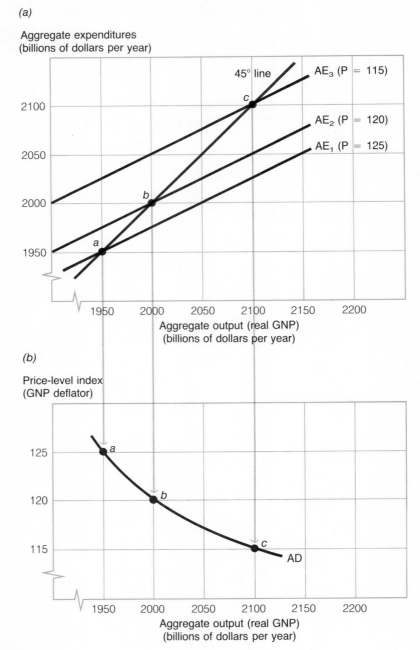

Exhibit 26.1
Relating Aggregate Expenditures to Aggregate Demand
Along each aggregate expenditures curve shown in part (a) the price level is held constant. (Note that AE₁ corresponds to the price level of 125.) Only one point on each aggregate expenditures curve–where AE intersects the 45° line—represents a potential point of equilibrium. These intersections represent points on the aggregate demand curve shown in part (b).

ditures curve (AE₁) indicates how much the economy—household, business, government, and foreign sectors combined—will be willing and able to spend on real output.

Exhibit 26.1(b) shows aggregate demand. As defined in Chapter 20, aggregate demand shows *the relationship between the total quantity of goods and services demanded and the general price level*. The definitions of the two relationships indicate their close connection. The total quantity of aggregate output demanded at any price level is the same as the total amount of planned expenditures at that price level. In other words, both curves represent the output demanded by all sectors of the economy combined. But what is the precise connection between the two curves?

First, you should recognize that any point along an aggregate demand curve could be a point of equilibrium, where quantity of output demanded and supplied are equal. However, only one point along an aggregate expenditures curve satisfies this condition for equilibrium. For example, at the intersection of AE₁ and the 45° line (point *a*), the economy is willing to buy $1950 billion of real output if $1950 billion is supplied. But at any other level of output, quantity produced would not match quantity demanded. There would be unplanned inventory investment or disinvestment—too much or too little supplied.

Second, recall that along an aggregate expenditures curve, *the price level is constant*. In deriving AE₁, for example, we asked how much planned spending would be associated with a price level of 125 (which is why you see P = 125 in parentheses after AE₁). Exhibit 26.1(a), then, indicates that if the price level were 125, planned spending would equal aggregate output at $1950 billion. Since we know that the economy demands $1950 of output at a price level of 125, we know one point on the aggregate demand curve. Note that point *a* in Exhibit 26.1(a) is directly related to point *a* in Exhibit 26.1(b).

Changing the price level will shift the planned expenditures curve in Exhibit 26.1(a) and cause movement along the aggregate demand curve in Exhibit 26.1(b). For example, if the price level falls to 120, the aggregate expenditures curve shifts upward to AE₂ (P = 120). At the higher level of planned spending, the new quantity demanded is $2000 billion, or point *b* on both graphs. If the price level falls to 115, the aggregate expenditures curve shifts again, this time to AE₃ (P = 115). The new quantity of output demanded ($2100 billion) is represented by point *c* on both graphs.

This analysis shows that higher price levels are associated with lower spending levels and vice versa. But why? What is it about a higher price level that makes planned spending (and quantity of output demanded) fall?

Negative Slope of the Aggregate Demand Curve

The aggregate demand curve shown in Exhibit 26.1(b) has the same downward slope as the aggregate demand curves we drew in Chapter 20. This negative slope—an inverse relationship between the price level and quantity of aggregate output demanded—results from three effects of a change in the price level. First, an increase in the price level decreases the purchasing power of money and wealth held by the household sector. Second, an increase in the price level increases the nominal interest rate in the money market. And third, an increase in the price level decreases the relative prices of foreign goods.

To understand aggregate demand, you must understand how and why an increase in the price level leads to lower planned spending—less output demanded—by all sectors of the economy combined.

Real wealth or real balances effect. The wealth of the household sector is held in many forms: houses, land, stocks, bonds, and money, to name a few. What happens to this wealth when the price level increases? Typically, an increase in the price level brings an increase in the price of many assets. For example, housing and land are often viewed as inflation-proof assets because their market value tends to rise with the general price level. However, households also hold part of their wealth as money, checking deposits, and bonds. These monetary assets represent a claim that is fixed in *nominal* terms. Thus a rise in the price level means a drop in the *real* value of monetary assets and real wealth.

For example, suppose that your wealth consists of $500 in a checking account and a government bond that promises you $100 in interest payments over the next five years plus a final payment of $1000. What happens to the real value—the purchasing power—of your wealth if the price level doubles? You will still have a $500 nominal balance in your checking account and can still buy $500 worth of goods and services. But with most items costing twice as much, you can buy only one-half as much with $500 as you could before. The *real balance* in your account has decreased. Similarly, you will still receive the promised interest and return of principal on the bond. But these sums are also worth only half as much as before. Your *real wealth*—what you can buy with the assets you own—is only one-half as large as before.

As we noted in Chapter 22, consumption is directly related to wealth: More wealth means more spending. Because households hold much of their wealth as monetary assets, household wealth falls when the price level rises. Thus *if the price level rises, real wealth and hence consumption will fall, and less aggregate output will be demanded*. In Exhibit 26.1, the effect on real wealth is one reason that an increase in the price level from 120 to 125 would shift the aggregate expenditures curve from AE_2 to AE_1. This shift would also cause a movement along the AD curve from point *b* to point *a*. Conversely, *a decline in the price level will increase real wealth and hence consumption, causing quantity of aggregate output demanded to rise*. In Exhibit 26.1, a decline in the price level from 120 to 115 shifts the aggregate expenditures curve from AE_2 to AE_3 and results in movement along the AD curve from point *b* to point *c*.

Interest-rate effect. An increase in the price level also means a greater nominal GNP at every level of real output. (Recall that nominal GNP represents the price level times real GNP.) But, as you learned in Chapter 25, higher nominal GNP means a greater volume of transactions and therefore an increase in demand for money. If the money supply remains fixed, greater money demand will cause real interest rates to rise. Higher interest rates, in turn, reduce both business investment and interest-sensitive household consumption. Thus *an increase in the price level raises nominal GNP and hence demand for money. The consequent increase in interest rates reduces quantity of aggregate output demanded*. The interest-rate effect is thus another reason for the downward slope of the aggregate demand curve.

Foreign-prices effect. Finally, a change in the U.S. price level changes the *relative* prices of foreign goods and services. Higher prices for U.S. products means that foreign products are relatively less expensive. For example, as foreign cars become relatively less expensive, you may buy a Toyota instead of a Ford. And U.S. businesses may buy more German steel and less U.S. steel. But foreigners will also buy fewer U.S. products. That is, *an increase in the U.S. price level will raise imports (M) and lower exports (X). This reduction in net exports (X − M) represents a drop in planned spending—less U.S. output demanded.*

Factors that Shift the Aggregate Demand Curve

When drawing an aggregate demand curve, we want to focus only on the changes in spending caused by a change in the price level. Thus we make an all-other-things-unchanged assumption, holding monetary and fiscal policies, expectations, foreign income, and price levels in other countries constant. Changes in any of these factors will cause a change in planned spending *at each and every price level.* That is, changes cause a shift in the aggregate demand curve.

Monetary and fiscal policies. In Chapter 25 we noted that changes in the money supply cause changes in the level of aggregate expenditures. If Fed policies increase the money supply, households and businesses will increase their spending at each and every price level. Thus an increase in the money supply means an increase in aggregate demand (a shift to the right of the AD curve).

Conversely, if Fed policies decrease the money supply, households and businesses will decrease their spending at each and every price level, causing a decrease in the aggregate demand curve (a shift to the left). Thus to draw an aggregate demand curve, we hold monetary policy constant because a change in monetary policy causes a shift in the aggregate demand curve.

We also hold fiscal policies—both taxes and government purchases—constant. Any change in fiscal policies changes the level of spending at any given price level, that is, shifts the aggregate demand curve. For example, a decrease in tax rates raises household income and the profits businesses can expect to earn on any new investment. As a result, decreased tax rates will increase consumption and investment at all price levels. A change in government purchases directly changes planned spending and aggregate demand; thus if government purchases increase, so will aggregate demand.

Expectations. Spending decisions are strongly influenced by expectations. Suppose that the Fed announces plans to reduce the money supply. As we showed in Chapter 25, the reduction in money supply will reduce planned spending. Thus businesses may expect the demand for their products will fall. As a result, businesses may reduce their inventories and halt plans to build new plants and buy new machinery, that is, investment will fall. Households may expect the reduction in the money supply to raise unemployment and lower future prices. If so, current consumption will decrease.

To draw any particular aggregate demand curve, therefore, we hold expectations constant—expectations both about future price levels and future real income. Note that a change in expectations causes a reduction in investment and consumption even before the Fed actually takes any action to reduce the money supply.

Income and price levels in foreign economies.   You have already seen how changes in net exports affect aggregate expenditures and thus aggregate demand. Net exports might increase, for example, if price levels in Western Europe increase rapidly, making U.S. goods relatively less expensive. Net exports might fall if income in Latin America falls, decreasing the quantity of U.S. exports purchased. Any change in foreign income and foreign price levels will shift the aggregate demand curve.

All these factors—monetary and fiscal policies, expectations, and foreign income and price levels—are held constant for an aggregate demand curve. Be alert for these factors. When they change, they shift the aggregate demand curve and cause adjustments in the macroeconomy.

Changes in Aggregate Demand: The Multiplier Effect

In Chapter 23, we noted that a change in planned expenditures (a shift in the AE curve) has a multiplier effect. That is, an initial change in spending causes a much larger final change. For example, if businesses expect the economy to boom in the next several years, they may increase their investments in new machinery now. As a result, they will earn more profits, create more jobs, and generate more household income and more consumption spending. In Exhibit 26.2(a) the $50 billion increase in investment causes a $100 billion increase in total spending. (Note that AE_2 is $50 billion above AE_1 at each level of output and that AE_2 intersects the 45° line at $100 billion more output.) This movement from point *a* on AE_1 to point *b* on AE_2 represents a multiplier effect of 2.

Importantly, both the initial increase in investment and the resulting increase in consumption represent greater output demanded *at the current price level*. (Note that both AE_1 and AE_2 refer to planned spending at a price level of 125.) As you can see in the bottom graph, this increase in aggregate expenditures causes aggregate demand to increase (a shift from AD_1 to AD_2).

The amount by which the aggregate demand curve shifts is determined by the multiplier effect. That is, the curve will shift by the full amount of the final change in spending. In other words, *the multiplier indicates how much the aggregate demand curve shifts as a result of a change in planned aggregate expenditures*. Note that in both graphs movement is from point *a* to point *b*, and output demanded increases by $100 billion. However, as you will discover when we add aggregate supply to the diagram, the actual change in real output will be less than this change in planned expenditures.

Note that any change in planned expenditures affects the quantity of output demanded. When aggregate expenditures change because the price level changes, there is a movement along an aggregate demand curve. A change in aggregate expenditures caused by changes in monetary policies, expectations, or factors other than the price level results in a shift in the aggregate demand curve.

RECAP

The aggregate demand curve (AD) is directly related to the aggregate expenditures curve (AE). Each AE curve is drawn for one particular price level. The intersection of an AE curve and the 45° line represents a single point on an AD curve. A change in the price level shifts the AE curve but causes movement along the AD curve.

An increase in the price level lowers the real value of money and monetary assets held by households, raises demand for money and real interest rates, and raises the relative prices of U.S. versus foreign goods and services. These changes reduce spending and cause movement along the AD curve.

An increase in the money supply, lower taxes, higher government purchases, expectations of price level increases or real income increases, and higher income and price levels in foreign countries all increase aggregate demand (shift the curve to the right).

An initial change in spending has a multiplier effect. The multiplier effect determines how much the aggregate demand curve shifts.

(a) Shift in aggregate expenditures

(b) Shift in aggregate demand

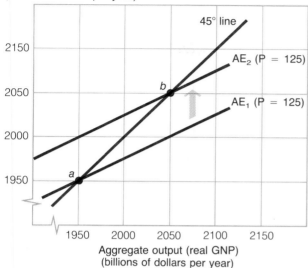

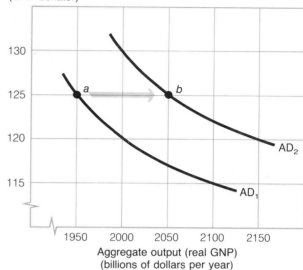

Exhibit 26.2
The Multiplier Effect: Changing Aggregate Demand
In part (a) a $50 billion increase in planned investment shifts the aggregate expenditures line upward by $50 billion. The quantity of aggregate output demanded increases by $100 billion—a multiplier effect of 2. In part (b) we see that this shift represents a $100 billion increase in the quantity of aggregate output demanded at the (constant) price level of 125. Aggregate demand shifts by the full extent of the multiplier effect.

LONG-RUN AGGREGATE SUPPLY AND EQUILIBRIUM

So far in our study of macroeconomics we have concentrated on the demand side of the economy. But as we noted in Chapter 20, the equilibrium level of real GNP and the price level lies at the intersection of the aggregate demand and aggregate supply curves. To complete our model, then, we must consider aggregate supply: how the quantity of aggregate output produced and the price level are related.

Macroeconomists distinguish *two* aggregate supply curves. One, following classical theory, describes the *long-run* relationship between the price level and aggregate output. The other, following the Keynesian tradition, describes the *short-run* relationship. In this section we consider the long-run aggregate supply curve and in the following section, the short-run aggregate supply curve. Both supply curves are useful in describing and predicting macroeconomic events.

According to classical economics, the level of aggregate output is completely determined by factors on the supply side. Regardless of the level of aggregate demand, classical economists believed that automatic adjustment mechanisms—changes in wages, prices, and interest rates—would restore the economy to full employment (potential GNP). Many present-day economists argue that classical theory does not describe the short-run behavior of the economy. But most accept the classical conclusion that the economy tends to produce at its potential GNP level in the long run, that is, after making a full and complete adjustment to current economic conditions. To understand the long-run aggregate supply curve, then, we must answer two questions: What determines the level of the economy's potential GNP? Why is the level of output produced unrelated to the price level in the long run?

Factors that Change Potential GNP

In Chapter 20 we associated potential GNP with the economy's production possibilities curve. Economists also identify four factors that determine the economy's potential GNP: supplies of natural resources, supplies of labor, supplies of capital resources, and technology.

Supplies of natural resources. The amount and types of final goods an economy can produce are affected by the available supplies of natural resources. This factor includes the amount and quality of land and water, as well as supplies of oil, iron ore, and other important minerals. Although an economy can import natural resources, it must pay for them, reducing its ability to produce goods and services to satisfy domestic demands.

Supplies of labor. The size and skills of the labor force affect potential output. Thus education and job training can increase the potential GNP of an economy. Indeed, much of the growth in potential output in the U.S. economy has been credited to the increased skills of its work force. Attitudes about who should work and how much they should work also affect the amount of labor supplied. For example, the United States has laws requiring children under 16 to attend school and forbidding them to hold most jobs. And how many hours per week do you associate with a full-time job? Many individuals view full-time work as 40 hours per week. But 100 years ago the normal workweek was closer to 60 hours. The more hours that individuals are willing to work the larger the supply of labor. Similarly, the increasing proportion of women seeking work in the labor market in the 1960s and 1970s added to the economy's potential GNP.

Supplies of capital. The economy's potential output is also limited by the quantity and quality of existing capital resources—machinery, buildings, and transportation and communications systems. However, these resources can certainly be changed over time. Increases in capital resources allow more output to be produced with the same amounts of labor and natural resources. In fact, private and public investments in capital resources are a major source of economic growth.

Technology. The final factor affecting potential output is technology. Technology determines how much output can be obtained from the supplies of other resources that are available. Technological progress can increase potential output even if supplies of resources remain constant.

We will explore the determination of potential output further in Chapter 30. Economic growth—the subject of that chapter—depends on the steps an economy takes to increase its potential output. In this chapter, our interest is in aggregate supply—how the quantity of aggregate output supplied changes with the price level.

Long-Run Aggregate Supply and Potential GNP

Now that you understand the factors that affect potential GNP (output), we can consider how potential GNP affects the economy's long-run aggregate supply curve. We can also show why quantity of aggregate output supplied is unrelated to the price level in the long run.

When discussing the shape of the economy's long-run aggregate supply curve, we hold the factors that determine potential GNP constant. Then we ask how, if at all, the quantity of aggregate output produced is related to the price level when the economy has adjusted completely to current economic conditions. To understand the shape of the long-run aggregate supply curve we must ask, as the classical economists did: Does a change in aggregate demand affect quantity of output produced? Suppose, for example, the economy shown in Exhibit 26.3 is initially operating where aggregate demand (AD_1) intersects the potential GNP line (point *a*). Because the quantity produced (2000 billion) is equal to the quantity demanded at the initial price level of 120, the economy is in equilibrium.

What happens, however, if aggregate demand increases to AD_2? At the original price level, quantity of aggregate output demanded exceeds the economy's potential GNP. Thus many, if not most, markets will experience shortages which put upward pressures on wages and prices. Employers will bid against each other for available workers; consumers will bid against each other for available products. As wages and prices increase the price level will rise. At the same time, higher prices reduce quantity of aggregate output demanded. When the price level reaches 130, the aggregate shortage disappears and the economy once again produces and sells its potential output of $2000 billion (point *b*). The increase in aggregate demand has increased the price level, but had no effect on GNP.

What if aggregate demand decreases to AD_3? At the original price level (120), quantity of aggregate output demanded will be less than the economy's potential GNP. Thus many, if not most, markets will experience surpluses which put downward pressure on wages and prices. Rather than face unemployment, workers will accept lower nominal wages. As labor costs fall, businesses will lower prices to keep sales from falling. As wages and prices decrease, the price level will fall. At the same time, lower prices increase quantity of aggregate output demanded. When the price level reaches 110, the surplus disappears and the economy once again produces and sells at its potential output of $2000 billion (point *c*). Again, the change in aggregate demand affects only the price level, not real GNP.

What does this analysis tell us? First, it suggests that changes in aggregate demand set in motion automatic adjustments, principally changes in wages and prices. When the economy has made a full and complete adjustment, it will produce and sell its potential GNP. In the view of most economists, this full and complete adjustment does not take place instantly, but it does occur eventually. Reflecting the period of time this adjustment may take, economists say that the economy has reached **long-run equilibrium** when quantity of output demanded equals potential GNP.

Long-run equilibrium. A position in which quantity of aggregate output demanded at the current price level equals the economy's potential output; graphically, when the aggregate demand and short-run aggregate supply curves intersect at the potential output level. The position the economy will achieve if wages and prices fully adjust to aggregate demand.

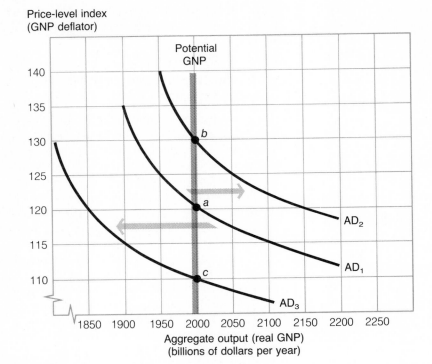

Exhibit 26.3
Long-Run Aggregate Supply and Potential GNP
An increase in aggregate demand (from AD_1 to AD_2) creates excess demand pressures. Shortages put upward pressure on input prices. The price level rises (to 130 in this case) but the economy produces and sells its potential GNP. Similarly, a decrease in aggregate demand (from AD_1 to AD_3) creates surpluses and puts downward pressure on wages and prices. As the price level falls, the economy returns to long-run equilibrium at the potential GNP level (although at a lower price level). Hence the economy's long-run aggregate supply curve is a vertical line at potential GNP.

RECAP

The long-run aggregate supply curve is a vertical line at the economy's potential GNP. Given time to make a full adjustment, the economy will produce this full-employment level of output.

Potential GNP will change when supplies of natural, capital, or labor resources change or when technology changes.

Potential GNP is not a technological maximum. More than this level of output can be produced in the short run. In the long run, potential GNP is the only level of output that can be sustained.

Second, in the long run an economy's equilibrium output is its potential GNP, regardless of the level of demand and the price level. There is no long-run relationship between the price level and real GNP. That is, *the economy's long-run aggregate supply curve is a vertical line at potential GNP.*

SHORT-RUN AGGREGATE SUPPLY AND EQUILIBRIUM

Our analysis in the previous section followed classical economic theory. Most economists now generally accept the notion that the economy will produce its potential GNP when the economy has fully adjusted to economic conditions. But there is clear evidence that the economy does not always produce at its potential GNP level. Thus economists—at least since Keynes—have explored factors that may explain why the general price level appears to be directly related to quantity of output supplied in the short run.

Factors that Shift the Short-Run Aggregate Supply Curve

To derive a short-run aggregate supply curve, we must first define the short-run relationship between aggregate output supplied and the general price level. We focus only on the response to changes in the price level by holding the other factors that influence quantity supplied constant. We expect the short-run aggregate supply curve to shift if there is a change in the prices of resources, price-level expectations, or the economy's potential GNP.

Resource prices. There is some evidence to indicate that resource prices, especially labor prices, in the short run are reasonably constant. That is, the economy can produce somewhat more or less aggregate output without having a serious impact on resource prices. In the case of materials and intermediate goods, the adjustment may be slow because many producers will have existing contracts with suppliers that specify resource price levels and must be honored. Automakers, for example, may have already contracted for next month's supplies of steel.

Many wages are also fixed in the short run. In unionized companies, wage rates are written into formal contracts. And many nonunion workers have their wages reviewed and adjusted only once a year, during an annual performance appraisal. Thus the assumption that resource prices are fixed is realistic for the short run, and we hold them constant when drawing a short-run aggregate supply curve. However, it is unrealistic to believe that resource prices will remain unchanged for very long. And when resource prices change, the short-run aggregate supply curve shifts: *Increases in resource prices decrease aggregate supply, and decreases in resource prices increase aggregate supply in the short run.*

Price-level expectations. Economists believe that quantity of labor supplied depends on the *real wages* that workers receive. In other words, people work to earn income in order to consume. Higher real wages increase the quantity of goods and services that can be purchased. Thus more labor will be supplied when real wages increase, and less labor will be supplied when real wages fall.

However, workers are typically promised a certain nominal, or dollar, wage over the next year. How much the real wage is, therefore, depends on how the price level changes over the next year. While the future price level is unknown to those of us without accurate crystal balls, individuals tend to translate nominal wage offers into real terms based on what they *expect* average prices to be. The higher the expected price level, the lower is the expected real value of any nominal wage offer.

In drawing an aggregate supply curve, we hold both price-level expectations and nominal wages constant. We assume that workers believe that they are facing a specific and constant real-wage offer. Workers are likely to change their expectations, however, if they observe that actual price changes are slower or faster than they expected. If they expect a greater increase in prices, they will recognize that their expected real wage is lower than anticipated. They may therefore refuse to work unless they receive a matching increase in nominal wages.

Higher wages raise costs to businesses, which respond by raising prices. Thus a change in expectations about future prices will cause the short-run aggregate supply curve to shift: *An increase in the expected price level will cause a decrease in aggregate supply; a decrease in the expected price level will cause an increase in aggregate supply.*

Potential GNP. When drawing a short-run aggregate supply curve we also assume that the economy's productive potential is constant. We noted earlier in the chapter that potential GNP depends on supplies of natural resources, supplies of labor, supplies of capital resources, and technology. A change in any of these factors also shifts an economy's short-run aggregate supply curve. That is, *increases in potential GNP increase the short-run aggregate supply curve. Decreases in potential GNP decrease the short-run aggregate supply curve.*

Slope of the Short-Run Aggregate Supply Curve

Although potential GNP is fixed in the short run, businesses can supply a wide range of aggregate output. In fact, quantity supplied in the short run depends on the price level. The higher the price level, the more output businesses will offer for sale. As a result, the short-run aggregate supply curve drawn by most economists slopes upward and to the right, as shown in Exhibit 26.4. (Note that the short-run curve is labeled AS. Long-run supply curves are labeled Potential GNP.)

Following the principles of rational choice, we can expect businesses that seek to maximize profits to supply more when real profits rise and to supply less when real profits fall. But, as we noted in Chapter 20, real profits are linked to both cost and price. Thus the shape of the short-run aggregate supply curve depends on how businesses respond in the short run to changes in aggregate demand.

Consider what happens to profits if aggregate demand increases (holding resource prices, price-level expectations, and potential GNP constant). Businesses first observe the increase in demand when inventories fall and orders for their products increase. More demand puts upward pressure on product prices. With resource prices fixed, however, a higher product price means a greater real profit for producers, who are then willing to supply more for sale. That is, higher demand results in an increase in both price and real output in the short run. This response is consistent with a short-run aggregate supply curve having a positive slope.

Similarly, a decrease in aggregate demand puts downward pressure on product prices. But with resource prices fixed, lower product prices mean lower real profits for producers. Their short-run response is to lower quantities offered for sale. Thus the positive slope of the short-run aggregate supply curve reflects the positive relationship between profits and product prices when resource prices are fixed.

Note that, like the Keynesian view of aggregate supply presented in Chapter 22, the curve in Exhibit 26.4 is relatively flat at very low levels of output. At higher levels of output, it has a relatively steep slope, like the classical supply curve in Chapter 22. The overall shape also reflects costs and profits. For any short-run aggregate supply curve, the economy's production possibilities are fixed. At very low levels of output, many machines and factories are unused and many workers are unemployed. In such circumstances, we can predict that businesses and work-

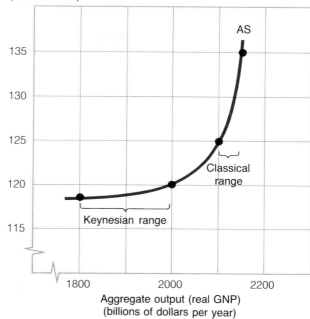

Price-level index
(GNP deflator)

Exhibit 26.4
Shape of the Short-Run Aggregate Supply Curve
The short-run aggregate supply curve (AS) shows the relationship between output supplied and price level in the short run. At low levels of output (from $1800 to $2000 billion in this case), the AS curve indicates that changes in aggregate demand largely affect real GNP. This portion of the curve is labeled the Keynesian region because Keynes' theory suggested that in a recession, when there are substantial unemployed resources, increases in output could be obtained with relatively little or no increase in cost. At relatively high levels of output (above $2100 billion on this curve), the AS curve is quite steep. This portion of the curve is labeled the classical region because the theories of the classical economists stressed that, when the economy is near full employment, an increase in aggregate demand would largely result in higher prices. Increases in output in this region can be obtained only by employing less-efficient machinery and labor, and thus at sharply rising costs. Therefore more will be supplied only with substantial increases in prices.

ers will be eager to respond to higher demand, even if prices increase only a small amount.

On the other hand, at high levels of output most resources are employed. Thus increases in output are likely to require the use of some less efficient—and hence more expensive—resources. Businesses will demand higher prices to cover this increase in costs.

Short-Run Equilibrium

The short-run aggregate supply curve does not tell us how much real output the economy will produce or what the price level will be. But it does tell us how the economy can be expected to react in the short run to changes in aggregate

Short-run equilibrium. A position in which quantity of aggregate output demanded at the current price level equals quantity supplied; graphically, where the aggregate demand and short-run aggregate supply curves intersect.

demand. The price level and quantity of real GNP produced are jointly determined by aggregate demand and the short-run aggregate supply curve.

For example, consider Exhibit 26.5. Under the initial conditions (AD_1 and AS_1), the economy is in **short-run equilibrium**; aggregate output is $2000 billion and the price level is 120 (point a). But what if planned investment increases by $25 billion per year (perhaps because lower interest rates make purchases of capital resources more profitable)? If the multiplier is 4.0, planned aggregate expenditures (quantity of aggregate output demanded at the current price level) will increase by $100 billion, shifting the aggregate demand curve to the right (to AD_2).

Because demand has increased, the economy is no longer in equilibrium at the old price level of 120. Quantity of aggregate output demanded *at the current price level* is greater than quantity supplied. In response, producers will expand

Exhibit 26.5
Short-Run Equilibrium
The intersection of aggregate demand and the short-run aggregate supply curve determines short-run equilibrium. A change in aggregate demand (a shift in the curve from AD_1 to AD_2) will cause the economy to move along its short-run aggregate supply curve (from point a to point b). The simple multiplier indicates how much aggregate demand shifts (in this case, by a factor of 4). The real-output multiplier is smaller (a factor of 2) because the price level absorbs part of the change in demand.

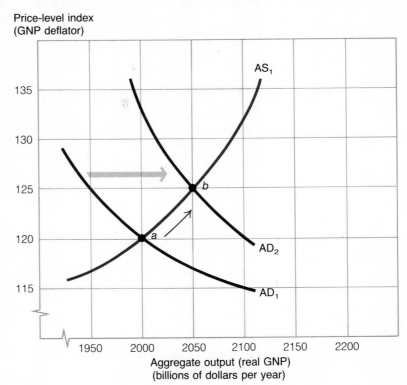

output. But the slope of the aggregate supply curve means that costs rise as output increases causing producers to raise prices. To restore short-run equilibrium, both aggregate output and the general price level will increase. The changes that occur represent movement along the short-run aggregate supply curve from point *a* to point *b*.

This example shows why the simple multiplier we used in Chapters 22 and 23 overstates the short-run effect of spending changes on real output. In Exhibit 26.5 the $25 billion increase in investment increased aggregate demand by $100 billion. Because the short-run aggregate supply curve is positively sloped, however, the change in aggregate demand affected both real output and the price level. After the economy adjusted to equilibrium, real GNP increased by only $50 billion, a real-world multiplier effect of only 2.

This real-world multiplier effect depends on the shape of the short-run aggregate supply curve. If the economy is operating at far below its full-employment level, the short-run aggregate supply curve is, as you have seen, relatively flat. In that case a change in demand primarily affects real output. But if the economy is operating somewhere on the sharply upward sloping portion of the aggregate supply curve, an increase in demand primarily affects the price level.

We showed that in the short run, changes in aggregate demand result in movement along the short-run aggregate supply curve. An increase in aggregate demand raises both real output and the price level. A decrease in aggregate demand lowers both aggregate output and the price level. These adjustments explain how the economy reaches short-run equilibrium. But, as you have also seen, most economists expect further adjustments to take place in the long run. In order to predict the long-run adjustments that may occur, we have to compare current output to potential GNP, as indicated in the next section.

ADJUSTMENTS TO GNP GAPS

The short-run response of the economy depends on the short-run aggregate supply curve, which in turn depends on holding resource prices and price-level expectations constant. We showed earlier that after the long-run adjustments are complete the economy will produce its potential GNP. But how quickly can the economy adjust? To see how and why economists give different answers to this question, let's consider how the economy makes first a short-run, then a long-run, response to a change in aggregate demand.

Adjustments to an Expansionary Gap

What changes can we expect if aggregate demand increases? Exhibit 26.6 shows an economy initially in a long-run equilibrium position (point *a*). If aggregate demand increases (from AD_1 to AD_2), the short-run response of the economy is to move along the initial short-run aggregate supply curve (AS_1) to a new *short-run* equilibrium (point *b*). This short-run equilibrium is not likely to last, however, since actual output is greater than potential output. In Chapter 20 we introduced the concept of a GNP gap, which we defined as the difference between potential

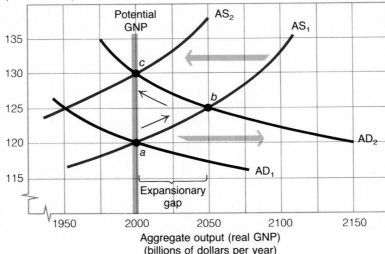

Exhibit 26.6
Long-Run Response to an Expansionary Gap
If the economy begins from a long-run equilibrium position (point *a*), an increase in aggregate demand will cause the economy to move along its short-run aggregate supply curve (to point *b*). Real GNP increases along with the price level, opening an expansionary gap (actual GNP exceeds potential GNP). This gap is possible in the short run, but excess demand pressures will cause input prices to rise, decreasing aggregate supply (shifting the curve to AS$_2$). As the economy makes a full adjustment, it will return to long-run equilibrium and produce and sell its potential GNP (point *c*).

output and the current level of GNP. In its current position (point *b*) the GNP gap is − $50 billion, calculated as

$$\text{GNP gap} = \text{Potential GNP} - \text{Actual GNP}$$
$$= \$2000\,\text{billion} - \$2050\,\text{billion}$$
$$= -\$50\,\text{billion}$$

We refer to a negative GNP gap—when actual GNP exceeds potential GNP—as an **expansionary gap** because it occurs as the economy attempts to expand beyond potential GNP. We can also describe this situation as one of *excess aggregate demand*. That is, the level of output demanded at the existing price level (125 in our example) exceeds the full-employment, or potential GNP, level.

Although the economy has reached short-run equilibrium, we still have to answer two important questions: Just how can the economy produce more than its potential output? What adjustments can we expect the economy to make in the long run?

Expansionary gap. When actual GNP exceeds potential GNP; a negative GNP gap. When actual unemployment is below the natural rate of unemployment.

Recall that potential GNP is not a physical maximum. An economy can produce more than this level if workers temporarily agree to work longer than normal hours or if higher nominal wages attract additional people to jobs that they would normally reject. This higher level of output may also be reached if employers are temporarily willing to take on workers they might normally refuse to hire and thus accept temporarily lower profits. Although these measures allow the economy to reach short-run equilibrium above its potential output, excess demand pressures will put upward pressure on prices.

Note that as output expands beyond potential GNP, unemployment falls below the natural rate of unemployment we associated with the frictional and structural unemployment in Chapter 20. Jobs are plentiful, but workers are relatively scarce. As businesses compete against each other for available resources, resource prices will rise. Moreover, workers will realize that the increase in the price level has reduced their real wages. Accordingly, they will revise their expectations and ask for higher nominal wages in order to restore real wages to their former level. In other words, we can expect increases in both resource prices and price-level expectations, two factors that we had assumed to be constant for any particular short-run supply curve.

As resource prices increase, short-run aggregate supply will decrease; that is, the curve will shift to the left. This pattern of upward pressure on prices—raising costs and lowering supply—will continue until there is no longer any excess demand. In Exhibit 26.6 excess demand—the expansionary gap—is gone when aggregate supply reaches the level of AS_2. The economy will thus reach long-run equilibrium at a price level of 130 (where AD_2 intersects AS_2).

This analysis indicates that the economy cannot reach a stable equilibrium position beyond potential GNP. Left to its own devices, the economy will automatically adjust to relieve excess demand pressures. Although both real GNP and the price level increase in the short run, the increase in aggregate demand affects only the price level in the long run. This result usually occurs when the economy starts from a long-run equilibrium position.

Note also that this one-time increase in aggregate demand causes only a one-time increase in the price level. There is no reason to expect such a change to cause inflation, that is, a sustained increase in the price level. However, if demand increases continually, the economy may experience a series of expansionary gaps and a series of price level increases, as A Case in Point: Expansionary Gaps indicates.

Adjustments to a Contractionary Gap

Economists basically agree that adjustments to expansionary gaps are relatively quick. In contrast, economists are sharply divided over how quickly and easily an economy adjusts to a contractionary gap. Let's first consider the adjustment process and then why some economists believe that the economy adjusts quickly, while others believe that adjustment is long and costly.

Consider, for example, the economy shown in Exhibit 26.7. Under initial conditions (AD_1 and AS_1), the economy is operating at its potential output level of $2000 billion (point *a*). If aggregate demand decreases to AD_2, the economy

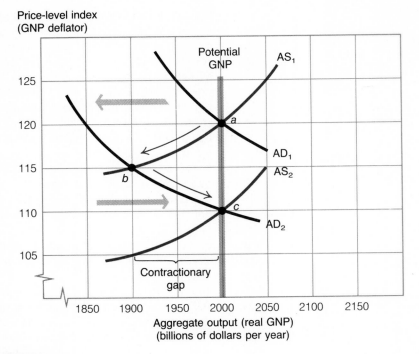

Exhibit 26.7
Long-Run Response to a Contractionary Gap
As aggregate demand decreases (as the curve shifts from AD₁ to AD₂), the economy
moves along its short-run aggregate supply curve. Real GNP falls, along with the
price level, opening a contractionary gap (actual GNP is less than potential GNP).
This gap puts downward pressure on wages and prices. A fall in wages and other
input prices will increase aggregate supply (to AS₂) and restore long-run equilibrium.

will move along the AS₁ curve to reach short-run equilibrium at point *b*. But at
this point, potential output exceeds actual output by $100 billion. This positive
gap between potential and actual GNP is a **contractionary gap**. (Use the formula
for the GNP gap and the data in Exhibit 26.7 to demonstrate that there is a positive
gap of $100 billion.)

As output demanded falls, producers will cut back on production, laying off
or firing some of their workers. As unemployment rises, workers may be willing
to accept lower nominal wages. The surpluses in product markets and other
resource markets put downward pressure on prices. Eventually, resource costs
(including wages) and prices—which we held constant in the short run—will
begin to fall. Moreover, the downward movement in prices should cause workers
to lower their price-level expectations. Together, these changes cause aggregate
supply to increase; that is, the curve will shift to the right. The pressures of the
contractionary gap continue until the short-run aggregate supply curve reaches
AS₂ and the economy returns to long-run equilibrium at point *c*.

Contractionary gap. When potential GNP exceeds actual GNP; a
positive GNP gap. When the actual
unemployment rate is greater than
the natural rate of unemployment.

Automatic Adjustments— Fast or Slow?

The preceding description of the economy's response to a contractionary gap basically reflects the classical viewpoint. Indeed, if wages and prices are flexible, the economy should make the adjustment to long-run equilibrium rather quickly. For classical economists, the contractionary gap was merely a short-run surplus of labor (and other resources). They believed that workers would recognize that if both nominal wages and prices fall at the same rate, they could return to work at the same real wages.

But the experience of the U.S. and British economies during the Great Depression in the 1930s suggested that the classical view was incorrect. That prolonged and deep recession suggested that the automatic adjustment mechanism operated slowly in the face of a contractionary gap—if it worked at all. Keynes concluded that wages and prices were not flexible enough to permit rapid adjustment,

A Case in Point
Expansionary Gaps: A Historic Example

Economic events during 1966–1969 provided a real-world example of adjustments to an expansionary gap. In this period, U.S. government spending increased. More was spent on social programs—President Johnson's War on Poverty—and on national defense—the Vietnam War. The increase in government expenditures was supported by an increase in the money supply. The increase in both government expenditures and the money supply caused aggregate demand to increase. As a result, the economy was pushed beyond its potential output level. The expansionary gap in 1968 is shown in the graph. From 1966 to 1969 the GNP gap averaged −$103.9 billion per year or 4.7 percent of potential GNP. As a result, the rate of inflation (as measured by the GNP deflator) more than doubled, rising from 2.7 percent in 1965 to 5.6 percent in 1969.

We noted in this chapter that a one-time increase in aggregate demand should cause only a one-time increase in the price level. As the economy returns to its potential output level, the expansionary gap is eliminated. To get inflation—a sustained upward movement in prices—requires continued excess demand pressure. But such sustained excess demand is exactly what happened in 1966–1969. Continued increases in government spending and in the money supply kept increasing aggregate demand beyond the potential output level. The result was a high rate of inflation.

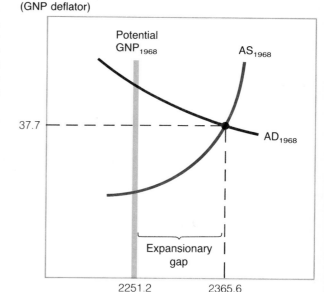

Price-level index (GNP deflator)

Potential GNP$_{1968}$ · AS$_{1968}$

37.7

AD$_{1968}$

Expansionary gap

2251.2   2365.6

Aggregate output (real GNP) (billions of dollars per year)

perhaps because workers may believe that lower nominal wages would mean a decline in real income. This reluctance to accept lower nominal wages—a necessary condition for shifting the short-run aggregate supply curve—may cause the economy to remain in a recession for an indefinite (or prolonged) period of time.

Since Keynes, most economists have recognized that wages and prices do not respond quickly enough to prevent significant short-term reductions in output. However, many economists now reject Keynes's conclusion that the inflexibility reflects irrational behavior by workers. Some economists put the blame on inaccurate price-level expectations. Others point to contracts and other arrangements that limit short-run adjustments in wages and prices. These arguments deserve further explanation because each results in different policy recommendations.

Sluggish adjustment: Expectations theory. Workers are presumed to respond to changes in real wages. Because wage and salary offers are stated in nominal (not real) terms, however, workers must translate a nominal wage offer into an expected real wage. Suppose that workers are promised a 5 percent increase in nominal wages. If they expect the price level to rise 3 percent, they will consider this offer to represent higher real wages. If they expect prices to rise 8 percent, they will consider the offer to represent lower real wages. The response of workers to a change in nominal wages, then, depends on their price-level expectations.

But what if workers' price-level expectations are wrong? For example, what if workers are offered a 10 percent increase in nominal wages and the general price level increases by 10 percent? In real terms, wages are unchanged. Workers will certainly notice the increase in nominal wages, but may not immediately or correctly notice the increase in prices. If they believe that prices are rising more slowly than 10 percent, they will believe real wages are rising and respond by increasing the quantity of labor they supply. As a result, the economy will be able to produce more.

However, this increase in labor supplied and output will only be temporary. Eventually, workers will realize that real wages are unchanged. They will then respond by offering the initial quantity of labor, and output will fall back to the original level.

Likewise, businesses seek real profits, but their forecasts of the price level may also be incorrect. Thus they may reject nominal wage or other resource prices that actually represent constant or lower real costs to the firm. As for workers, however, we can predict that such behavior will be corrected when better information is available.

The economy should operate at the potential GNP level whenever expectations match reality. If the price level is expected to rise faster than it actually does, workers may believe that real wages are falling, and businesses may believe that real profits are falling. As a result, real output may drop below the potential GNP level. If price-level expectations are lower than actual changes, workers may view real wages as rising, and businesses may view real profits as rising. As a result, real output may increase above the potential GNP level.

Expectations theory provides an explanation for why a decrease in demand lowers real output and increases unemployment in the short run. It attributes this relationship to inaccurate perceptions about actual changes in the price level. But it predicts that the fall in output will be only temporary. As expectations adjust to reality, the short-run aggregate supply will increase, bringing the economy back to potential GNP.

Expectations theory has been used to explain the economy's behavior in 1969 and 1970. Increased government spending in 1966–1969 fueled inflation. The Fed reacted by reducing the money supply, and the economy went into a recession. However, prices and unemployment continued to rise. Milton Friedman and others argued that this behavior reflected incorrect expectations. Friedman suggested that workers and businesses believed that the inflation of the late 1960s would continue, in part because they expected government to continue to increase aggregate demand. Expecting higher price levels, workers continued to demand higher nominal wages and producers kept raising prices despite the recession.

Sluggish adjustment: Contracts theory. Other economists, while not rejecting the importance of expectations, argue that wages are often set by contract. Union contracts may fix nominal wages for two or even three years. Some wage contracts call for indexing nominal wages to changes in the general price level, but these adjustments occur only once or twice a year. Even nonunion employees not covered by formal wage contracts often have their salaries set once a year at performance-review time. These arrangements may be viewed as informal wage contracts.

Whether wage contracts are formal or informal, changes in aggregate demand have a much greater effect on employment (and real output) than on wages and prices in the short run. Wages eventually adjust to reflect labor-market conditions, but the speed of the adjustment is slowed by the length of time that wages are fixed by contracts. Although expectations may be important, changes in expectations can affect only those contracts that are up for change.

Contracts and expectations theories compared. Both the contracts and expectations theories are consistent with a short-run aggregate supply curve that slopes upward. However, their implications for macroeconomic adjustments and policy are quite different.

According to expectations theory, the obstacle to a return to full-employment is inaccurate expectations. Because of the publicity given to inflation rates by the news media, it is unlikely that many people can hold incorrect expectations for long. Thus advocates of expectations theory believe that the short run is only a brief period of time. And since the economy's automatic adjustment mechanism works quickly, the economy will not remain below full employment for very long. Costs to the economy—both opportunity costs of lost production and associated costs to individuals of unemployment—should be reasonably small according to expectations theory.

According to contracts theory, however, adjustment to full employment depends on the length of wage contracts. Advocates of contracts theory thus believe that the short run may be a relatively long period of time. Because the adjustment is slow, the costs to the economy—lost output and unemployment—are high. As you will see in Chapter 27, some economists use the likelihood of slow adjustment to justify macroeconomic policies to shift the aggregate demand curve.

Does the economy adjust quickly or slowly to contractionary gaps? Can past experience help us choose between the two competing theories? Since the 1950s,

RECAP

If short-run equilibrium occurs beyond potential GNP, an expansionary gap results. This excess demand pressure causes increases in input prices and/or upward adjustments in price-level expectations. As the economy automatically adjusts, aggregate supply decreases, closing the gap.

If short-run equilibrium occurs below potential GNP, a contractionary gap results. This excess supply pressure causes decreases in wages and prices and/or downward adjustments in price-level expectations. As the economy automatically adjusts, aggregate supply increases, closing the gap.

Economists agree that the economy adjusts quickly to expansionary gaps. They disagree about whether contractionary gaps are quickly and easily closed. Some attribute contractionary gaps to temporarily incorrect expectations; others attribute such gaps to contracts that limit short-run changes in resource prices.

the largest initial effects of an actual decrease in demand have been a drop in output and a rise in unemployment. Moreover, the price level stubbornly resists an actual decline. (The GNP deflator last fell in 1949.) Thus history would seem to support those who believe that the adjustment process is slow.

But proponents of expectations theory believe that at least some of this price level behavior reflects private-sector expectations that government policies will increase demand and push prices up. This expectation prevents the downward adjustment in aggregate supply necessary to automatically restore full employment. These economists also point to the rapid fall in inflation rates in 1981–1982, when the Fed's monetary policies were clearly aimed at slowing price increases. Who, then, is right? The contradictory evidence and the difficulty of measuring expectations may make agreement impossible.

A Case in Point
Aggregate Demand and Supply in Action

We can use aggregate demand and supply to answer some of the real-world questions raised in the introduction to this chapter. Why did real output grow in the mid-1960s without causing much inflation? Why did both real output and the rate of inflation fall in the early 1980s?

The late 1950s and early 1960s were a period of slow and erratic growth, with low rates of inflation. With a few exceptions, the annual change in the Consumer Price Index was less than 2 percent. But the economy appeared to be operating below its potential output level.

(a) The economy in 1962

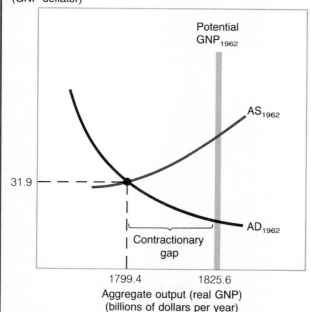

(b) The economy in 1968

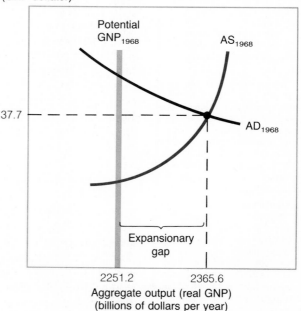

Exhibit 26C.1
The 1964 Tax Cut

Supply Shocks: Double Whammy

Thus far we have focused on how the economy adjusts to changes in aggregate demand. In some cases, however, it must also adjust to changes in aggregate supply. As A Case in Point: Aggregate Demand and Supply in Action indicates, economies have experienced **supply shocks**, or sudden and sharp increases in resource prices. Exhibit 26.8 shows how a supply shock decreases aggregate supply, causing real GNP to fall and the price level to rise. A supply shock also opens a contractionary gap, as real GNP falls below the potential GNP level.

Supply shocks. Sharp declines in aggregate supply caused by a decrease in the supply of key resources; may cause a decline in potential output.

The long-run effect of a supply shock depends in part on the policy response. As you will see in Chapter 27, monetary and fiscal policies can be used to increase demand, or the economy can be allowed to adjust on its own. If higher prices are

---

The economy's position in 1962 is shown in Exhibit 26C.1(a). Between 1958 and 1962 the economy experienced a contractionary GNP gap averaging $45.7 billion or 2.6 percent of potential GNP. The remedy suggested by President Kennedy's Keynesian advisors was a tax cut, which was finally passed in 1964.

A tax cut tends to raise aggregate demand, resulting in movement along the short-run aggregate supply curve. The 1964 tax cut closed the contractionary gap that had existed and caused real GNP to grow at an average rate of 4.5 percent between 1964 and 1967. As the economy moved along the short-run aggregate supply curve, the price level also rose, causing the rate of inflation to increase from 1.9 percent in 1965 to 3.4 percent in 1966. Unfortunately, as Exhibit 26C.1(b) shows, the economy was stimulated beyond the point of potential output. As the graph indicates, this can (and did) cause excess aggregate demand, resulting in the rapid inflation of the late 1960s.

The U.S. economy was rocked again in 1979 by a second oil-induced supply shock, this time caused by the revolution in Iran that disrupted oil supplies and doubled oil prices. Inflation accelerated into double digits, averaging 13.3 percent in 1979 and 12.4 percent in 1980. Opinion polls indicated that the general population believed inflation to be the country's major economic problem.

In an effort to bring down inflation, the Fed reduced the growth of the money supply. Exhibit 26C.2 shows the effects of this policy change on the economy's position in 1982. Decreased aggregate demand opened up a sizable contractionary gap. Unemployment rose significantly, exceeding 10 percent for several months.

But the policy change also put significant downward pressure on wages and prices. As a result, inflation, which had averaged nearly 9 percent in 1981, fell below 4 percent in 1982. The policy was clearly successful in eliminating inflationary pressures, although at a cost of high unemployment and lower output for a period of time.

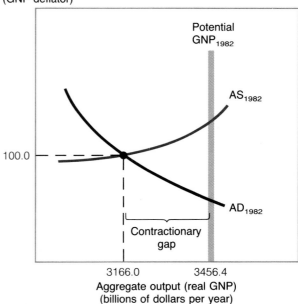

Price-level index (GNP deflator)

Exhibit 26C.2
Fed Policies and the Economy in 1982

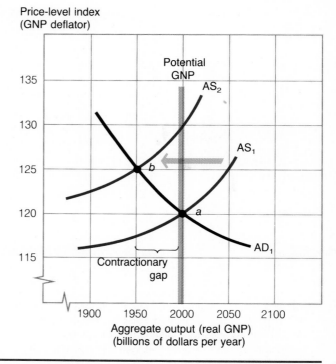

Exhibit 26.8
Supply Shock—A Decrease in Aggregate Supply
A sharp increase in input prices causes a supply
shock—a decrease in aggregate supply (a shift in the
curve from AS₁ to AS₂). As a result, real output falls and
the price level rises. The supply shock also opens a
contractionary gap. The economy will have to adjust by
increasing aggregate supply (back to AS₁) unless aggregate demand is increased.

paid to foreign owners for resources (as they were in the 1970s), real wages and
profits may have to fall before aggregate supply can increase. Whatever policy is
followed, the effects of a supply shock will be unpleasant.

The U.S. economy was subjected to supply shocks in 1973–1975. In 1973–
1974 the price of imported oil quadrupled as a result of OPEC action. The result
was a recession that lasted from November 1973 until March 1975. In many respects
it was the worst recession since the Great Depression of the 1930s. Real output
fell by almost 5 percent, and unemployment climbed to nearly 9 percent. In early
1975, real output was $140 billion below potential output. At the same time, the
price level increased by nearly 9 percent in 1973 and over 12 percent in 1974.
(As we noted in Chapter 20, this double dose of bad news is termed *stagflation*.)

CONCLUSION

In this chapter we considered how the macroeconomy reaches equilibrium in the
face of changing aggregate demand and supply. In doing so, we took special note
of the difficulty the economy may have in adjusting to a contractionary gap. We
know that monetary and fiscal policies can increase aggregate demand and bring
about faster adjustment to long-run equilibrium. But should government try to
speed the adjustment process? Or is the short run so short that intervention is
unnecessary? In the next part of this textbook, we consider the issues surrounding
macroeconomic policy. Only then can you understand why economists disagree
strongly over the desirability of government intervention.

SUMMARY

1. In this chapter we explored aggregate demand and supply and how the macroeconomy adjusts to equilibrium in both the short run and the long run.

2. For any aggregate expenditures (AE) curve we hold the price level constant. Each point of equilibrium between an AE curve and the 45° line is a single point on the aggregate demand (AD) curve, since such points represent quantity demanded at some particular price level. A change in the price level shifts the AE curve and results in movement along the AD curve.

3. Three factors explain why quantity of aggregate output demanded falls when the price level rises. Higher prices lower the real value of money and monetary assets held by the household sector, causing wealth and thus consumption to fall. Higher prices also increase nominal GNP and thus transactions demand for money and interest rates, lowering investment and interest-sensitive consumption. And higher prices in the United States make foreign goods more attractive, which decreases exports and increases imports.

4. For any aggregate demand curve we hold monetary and fiscal policies, expectations, and income and price levels in foreign countries constant. A change in any of these factors will increase or decrease aggregate demand and shift the AD curve.

5. An initial change in spending has a multiplier effect that determines how much more or less aggregate output will be demanded at the current price level, that is, how much the aggregate demand curve will shift.

6. The long-run aggregate supply curve is a vertical line at the economy's potential GNP level. Given sufficient time to adjust, the economy will reach a long-run equilibrium at potential GNP. Potential GNP changes when technology or resource supplies change.

7. The short-run aggregate supply curve shows how the economy will initially respond to a change in aggregate demand. The curve will shift if resource prices, price-level expectations, or potential GNP change.

8. Short-run equilibrium occurs at the intersection of the aggregate demand and short-run aggregate supply curves. An increase in aggregate demand causes movement along the short-run aggregate supply curve. Both real GNP and the price level will rise. The simple multiplier predicts how much aggregate demand increases as a result of an increase in planned spending. The real-world multiplier effect—the final change in real output—will be less because price increases absorb a part of the demand impact.

9. If short-run equilibrium occurs at the economy's potential GNP level, the economy is also in long-run equilibrium. If short-run equilibrium occurs beyond potential GNP, an expansionary gap results. This gap will be closed by excess demand pressures that raise resource prices and/or price-level expectations and decrease aggregate supply. If short-run equilibrium occurs below potential GNP, a contractionary gap results. This gap will be automatically closed by excess supply pressures that lower wages and prices and raise aggregate supply, returning the economy to long-run equilibrium.

10. Economists generally agree that the economy adjusts quickly and automatically to close an expansionary gap. But they disagree about how quickly the economy's automatic adjustments will close a contractionary gap. Proponents of a speedy reaction believe that the gap occurs because households and businesses incorrectly forecast price-level changes for a brief time. Proponents of a slow reaction argue that many resource prices are fixed by contracts for longer periods.

11. Sharp increases in resource prices—such as the oil-price increases in the 1970s—result in supply shocks. As aggregate supply decreases, real GNP falls and the price level rises. How the economy adjusts depends in part on government economic policies.

KEY TERMS

Long-run equilibrium, 669
Short-run equilibrium, 674
Expansionary gap, 676
Contractionary gap, 678
Supply shocks, 683

QUESTIONS FOR REVIEW AND DISCUSSION

1. Explain the effect that each of the following changes will have on aggregate demand, aggregate supply, the price level, and equilibrium GNP level in the short run. If the effect is uncertain, state why. Draw a graph showing the changes in aggregate demand and/or aggregate supply that illustrate your answer.
   a) The money supply increases.
   b) Workers demand higher real wages.
   c) Households and businesses expect the economy to expand in the near future.
   d) Real interest rates increase.
   e) The real cost of resources increases.
   f) An increase in the price level is expected for the future.
   g) Foreign incomes increase.

2. Explain how, if at all, potential GNP is affected by the following:
   a) An improvement in production technology.
   b) A significant decrease in resource supplies.

c) An increase in the number of skilled workers.

d) An increase in the general price level.

3. What change in aggregate demand and/or aggregate supply would explain each of the following:

a) Aggregate output increases.

b) The general price level falls.

c) Real GNP increases and the price level falls.

d) Both real GNP and the price level increase.

4. Use the following graph to help you answer the questions in (a)–(e).

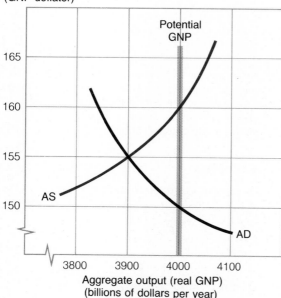

Price-level index
(GNP deflator)

a) What is the current equilibrium GNP and general price level?

b) Is this economy in long-run equilibrium? How do you know?

c) Indicate on the graph the existing GNP gap. Is this a contractionary or an expansionary gap? Is this a positive or a negative GNP gap?

d) On the graph, draw the changes that will occur as the economy's automatic adjustment mechanism operates. Describe the changes, that is, what is happening in the labor and product markets.

e) Suppose that instead of relying on the automatic adjustment mechanism, the Fed takes action to eliminate the gap. Would the Fed increase or decrease the money supply? What specific actions might the Fed take to accomplish this change?

5. Explain whether each of the following statements is true, false, or debatable.

a) An increase in the price level decreases planned spending. Therefore aggregate demand will fall.

b) If aggregate demand doesn't rise as fast as potential output, the economy can't maintain full employment unless the price level falls.

c) Starting from a position of long-run equilibrium, an increase in aggregate demand will be followed by a decrease in short-run aggregate supply as the economy adjusts to long-run equilibrium.

d) Changes in aggregate demand affect the price level less in the short run than in the long run.

6. The following table shows aggregate supply and demand both before and after a change in demand.

General price level	Aggregate supply	Aggregate demand	
		AD$_1$	AD$_2$
80	800	1200	1400
90	1000	1000	1200
100	1100	900	1100
110	1150	800	1000

a) Did aggregate demand increase or decrease? How do you know?

b) What is the equilibrium level of output under both the original and new conditions?

c) If potential GNP is $1000, will there be a contractionary or expansionary gap under the new aggregate demand conditions? Of what size? What do you predict about the economy's future adjustment to long-run equilibrium?

d) If potential GNP is $1200, will there be a contractionary or expansionary gap under the new aggregate demand conditions? Of what size? What do you predict about the economy's future adjustment? How, if at all, does your prediction depend on what you assume about the flexibility of wages and prices?

7. Explain how a contractionary gap can be created by a decrease in aggregate demand or an increase in potential output. (Draw two graphs: one depicting a decrease in aggregate demand, the other showing an increase in potential output.) Explain how a contractionary gap can be closed by either an increase in aggregate demand or an increase in aggregate supply. Why might economists who stress the contracts theory recommend an increase in aggregate demand in response to a contractionary gap?

8. For each of the following situations, start by drawing aggregate demand and aggregate supply curves for an economy in equilibrium. Then add curves as needed to reflect the following conditions:

a) The economy experiences an increase in real output, but the price level falls (short-run analysis only).

b) The economy experiences an increase in both the price level and real output (short-run analysis only).

c) The economy experiences a decline in output and the price level (short-run analysis only).

EIGHT

Macroeconomic Role of Government

Macroeconomic Policy:
Theory and Practice

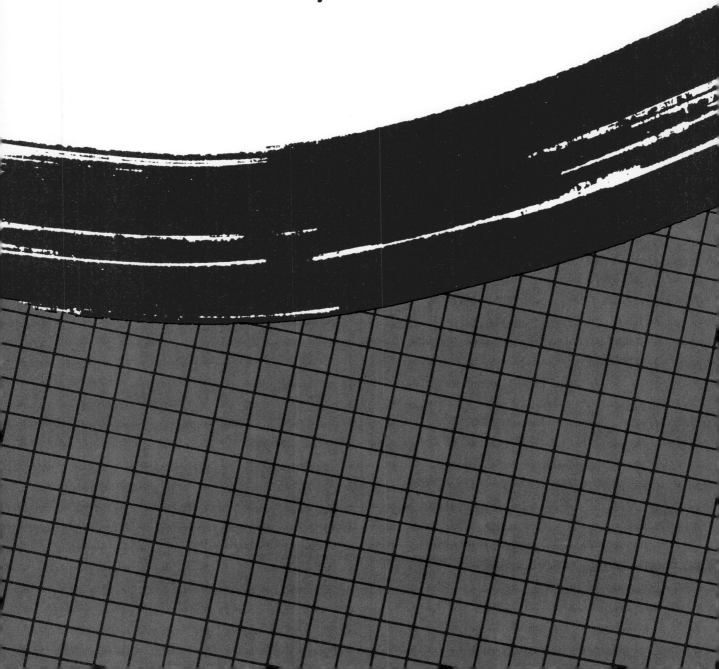

QUESTIONS TO CONSIDER

☐ How do macroeconomic government policies affect the federal budget and government's interaction with the private sector?

☐ What types of fiscal and monetary policies might be used to close GNP gaps and what are the alternatives?

☐ How do the effects of automatic stabilizers, crowding out, and rational expectations limit discretionary fiscal policy?

☐ Why do economists disagree about whether the government should take an active role in counteracting business-cycle fluctuations?

☐ Is the growing national debt a macroeconomic problem and, if so, what can be done about it?

In Chapter 26 we showed how the automatic adjustment mechanism eventually stabilizes prices and returns an economy to equilibrium at its potential or full-employment GNP. But we also noted that the U.S. economy has suffered through periods of recession and inflation. Could government actions have avoided some of these problems? Or were they a cause? What policies should government pursue in the future in order to obtain what the Employment Act of 1946 called "maximum employment, production, and purchasing power"?

In this chapter, we consider issues surrounding the use of macroeconomic policies to counteract the business cycle. We first consider the underlying economic principles, that is, the theory behind macroeconomic policies. How does a government budget deficit affect the economy? How does the economy's performance affect the federal government's budget? What can the Fed do to stabilize the economy?

After considering the theory of macroeconomic policy, we can turn to practical questions and problems facing policy makers and the subject of economic policy debates. *Can* government affect macroeconomic conditions? *Should* it try to? These are important and controversial questions. In fact, they are the very questions that led to the development of macroeconomics. Keynes got economists and politicians interested in the notion that government could and should play an active role in managing the macroeconomy. Macroeconomists since then have been busy either defending or attacking his assertion.

GOVERNMENT AND MACROECONOMIC POLICY

The public sector—government at the local, state, and federal levels—is very much involved in the macroeconomy. In 1986, total government expenditures in the United States were almost $1.5 trillion dollars. At the same time, government receipts—taxes and other fees—totaled $1.34 trillion. Some 20 percent of total output in the United States was purchased by government. One-fifth of all working individuals were employed by government. Governments establish laws and regulations with far-reaching effects on economic decisions of households, banks and other businesses, and the foreign sector. Recall that an agency of the federal government—the Federal Reserve System (the Fed)—has the power to increase or decrease the money supply, which has important effects on the economy.

Government and the Circular Flow

Exhibit 27.1 shows an overview of the macroeconomic roles of government. The flows at the bottom show the effects of government interactions in financial markets. These include the sale of government bonds to finance a budget deficit as well as monetary policies affecting the supply of money. The flows at the top and the summary in the box at the right show the effects of government's *fiscal policies,* that is, its taxing and spending activities. Government purchases are, of course, a component of and directly affect aggregate demand. Transfer payments and taxes directly affect income in the private sector and, consequently, consumption and investment. Interest payments on the national debt are another source of income for the private sector. Purchases, taxes, and transfer payments are elements of government's current fiscal policies. But interest payments reflect the effects of past policies, as you will see.

Government Budget Deficits and Surpluses

The federal government's budget summarizes the receipts and expenditures resulting from its fiscal policies. We are particularly interested in the **budget balance**, that is, the difference between receipts (taxes and fees) and expenditures (purchases, transfers, and interest paid), or

$$\text{Budget balance} = \text{Receipts} - \text{Expenditures}$$
$$= \text{Taxes} - (\text{Purchases} + \text{Transfers} + \text{Interest})$$

If the government's budget balance is positive (receipts exceed expenditures) government has a **budget surplus**. If the balance is negative (expenditures exceed receipts) government has a **budget deficit**. Large federal budget deficits have been common in recent years. As shown in Exhibit 27.1, the government sector—including state, local, and federal governments—had a combined budget deficit of $143.1 billion in 1986. The federal government ran a deficit of $204 billion, but state and local governments collectively had a $61 billion surplus. At the end of 1986, the public held approximately $1750 billion of federal government debt representing an average of $7250 per person in the United States.

Methods of financing government spending. The government—like individuals or households—cannot spend more money than it receives. But if you have a personal deficit (spend more than your current income), you may convince someone to lend you money. In contrast, the government can raise money by taxing or by printing more money, as well as by borrowing.

Local, state, and federal governments all have the power to impose and collect taxes. In fact, taxes and other fees provide over 90 percent of the money that government spends. However, in the United States, only the federal government

Budget balance. The difference between government receipts (taxes and fees) and expenditures (purchases, transfers, and interest payments on national debt).

Budget surplus. A positive budget balance, when receipts exceed expenditures.

Budget deficit. A negative budget balance, when expenditures exceed receipts.

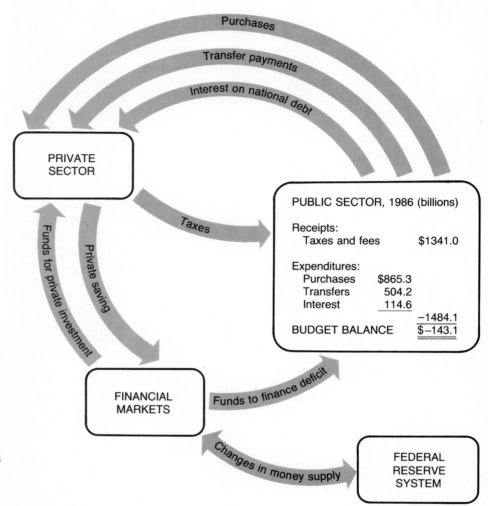

Exhibit 27.1
Government's Impact on the Macroeconomy
The government has a direct impact on the private sector through its purchases, transfer payments, taxes, and interest payments on the national debt. Purchases add directly to aggregate demand. Taxes, transfer payments, and interest payments directly affect income and indirectly affect aggregate demand. These flows represent the government's fiscal policies.

Source: Economic Report of the President, 1987, Table B-77.

has an option of "printing" its way out of a deficit. That is, it can mint coins and print paper money. As we discussed in Chapter 24, the Federal Reserve System has control over *monetary policy* in the United States. The Fed determines how much government money (coins and paper money) circulates. It also influences the quantity of bank money (checking deposits). By changing the money supply the Fed can affect aggregate demand.

Although the Fed is a government agency, it operates independently. Congress and the president determine fiscal policy, but the Fed determines monetary policy. This separation of powers is important: In the United States, that part of government responsible for spending cannot simply print money to spend. Congress and the president can (and have) put pressure on the Fed to "monetize" a deficit by purchasing some of the government's debt. As we explained in Chapter 24,

National debt. The total amount owed by the federal government; the cumulative effect of past budget deficits and surpluses.

when the Fed buys government securities it sets in motion a deposit expansion process that increases the money supply. Fiscal and monetary powers are not separate in all other countries, however. Where government directly controls the "printing press" it can easily create government money. The result is often a continual rapid increase in the money supply and, consequently, inflation.

But if the Fed is unwilling to lend enough to cover the deficit, the government must enter the financial market and borrow from U.S. households or businesses. (The federal government increasingly has also borrowed from the foreign sector.) Borrowing is the only alternative to taxing for state and local governments. And these governments are often strictly limited by state law in their ability to spend more than they receive in taxes and other receipts. Typically, borrowing is limited to funding capital expenditures—to finance a new school building, for example— by issuing bonds.

Additional borrowing to finance a federal government deficit adds to the **national debt**, that is, the total amount owed by the government. The federal debt ceiling is set—and, in recent years, raised—by Congress each year. Government borrowing often reduces the amount of saving available to finance private-sector spending. (A budget surplus has the opposite effect: reducing the national debt and increasing the funds available for private investment.)

Do not confuse the terms deficit and debt. They are connected, but different. A deficit refers to the excess of expenditures over receipts during one budget (fiscal) year. The national debt is the total amount owed by the federal government as of a particular date. A deficit financed by borrowing increases the national debt. The national debt reflects the cumulative effect of all past deficits and surpluses.

Historically, the national debt increased primarily during wartime and recessions. During World War II, the national debt increased from $43 billion in 1940 to $235 billion in 1945. During the Great Depression, the national debt increased from $17 billion in 1929 to $48 billion in 1939. However, the federal government has run huge budget deficits in the 1980s, only a small part of which can be attributed to the recession of 1982. As a result, the national debt increased by over 250 percent from fiscal year 1980 to fiscal year 1987. The size of the budget deficits has created special problems, as you will see later in this chapter.

Each method of financing government expenditures has, to some extent, a negative effect on the economy. Taxes reduce private spending directly. Increases in the money supply may lower the purchasing power of money and monetary assets held by households. Borrowing raises interest rates and indirectly reduces private spending. On the other hand, government spending also offers benefits to society. To identify the best level of spending and the best means of financing, these benefits and costs must be considered.

Government Stabilization Policies

With this background on the federal government's budget, we can now consider how government policies—both fiscal and monetary—affect the budget and the economy as a whole. Government macroeconomic policies can influence the economy in both the short run and the long run. The long-run macroeconomic goal of economic growth is the topic of Chapter 30. In this chapter we focus mostly on the short-run goals of price stability and full employment. To achieve these goals, the economy must avoid contractionary and expansionary GNP gaps.

RECAP

The federal government's budget summarizes its fiscal policies. Taxes and fees are receipts; expenditures include purchases of final goods, transfers, and interest paid on the national debt.

The budget balance is the difference between receipts and expenditures. A positive balance is a budget surplus; a negative balance is a budget deficit.

Governments have three ways to raise money to spend: taxes, borrowing, and printing new money. Because the Fed has independent responsibility for the money supply, Congress, the president, and state and local governments can spend only by taxing and borrowing.

Although government spending may be beneficial, each method of financing government spending has a negative effect on the economy. Taxes directly reduce private spending; borrowing raises interest rates and indirectly reduces private spending; increases in the money supply may lower the purchasing power of money and monetary assets held by households.

Recall that the macroeconomy is subject to sudden changes or shocks. A sudden, large increase in investment or in the money supply will increase aggregate demand, creating a demand shock. The increase in aggregate demand may open an expansionary gap (actual GNP rises above potential GNP). Although this results in a temporary increase in real GNP and a fall in unemployment, the expansionary gap puts upward pressure on prices. A sudden decrease in aggregate supply (a supply shock) or in aggregate demand will open a contractionary gap (actual GNP falls below potential GNP) and cause unemployment to increase.

When either a contractionary or an expansionary gap opens, policy makers have two basic options. First, they can *do nothing* and allow the economy's automatic adjustment mechanism to operate; eventually, the economy will return to full employment. Second, government can *enact fiscal or monetary policies* that shift aggregate demand and reduce or eliminate the gaps.

Exhibit 27.2
Policy Responses to a Contractionary Gap
The initial equilibrium (point *a*) shows the economy in a contractionary gap; actual GNP ($1900 billion) is $100 billion below potential GNP. If no action is taken, automatic adjustment mechanisms decrease wages and prices and ultimately increase aggregate supply (to AS_2). If government uses expansionary fiscal and/or monetary policies, aggregate demand will increase (to AD_2). Either response will eventually restore the economy to long-run equilibrium, producing and selling at its potential GNP. Automatic adjustments will result in lower prices (to point *b*) but may take considerable time and result in higher unemployment. Expansionary policies produce rapid adjustments but put upward pressure on prices (point *c*).

(a) Rely on automatic adjustment

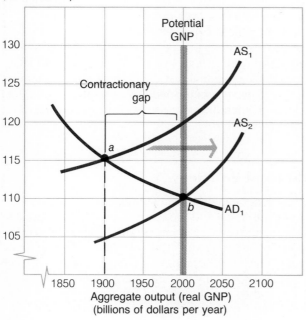

(b) Use expansionary policies

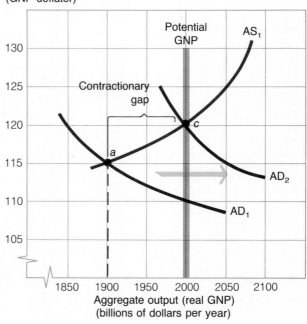

Expansionary policies. Changes in fiscal and/or monetary policies that increase aggregate demand. Lower taxes and higher spending are expansionary fiscal policies; reducing the required reserve ratio and buying government securities are expansionary monetary policies.

Eliminating contractionary gaps with expansionary policies. Exhibit 27.2 shows an economy initially facing a contractionary gap. Actual GNP ($1900 billion) is $100 billion less than potential GNP, and the actual unemployment rate is more than the natural rate. If the government did nothing, relying on the automatic adjustment mechanism, the contractionary gap would put downward pressure on wages and prices. This pressure would eventually cause an increase in aggregate supply (to AS_2), as shown in Exhibit 27.2(a).

Some economists argue that automatic adjustments take too long. They suggest that government use **expansionary policies** to increase aggregate demand (to AD_2 in Exhibit 27.2b). If Congress and the president agree to increase purchases or lower taxes to stimulate private-sector spending, they are using expansionary *fiscal* policies. If the Fed buys government securities in the open market or lowers the required reserve ratio to increase the money supply and stimulate private-sector spending, it is using expansionary *monetary* policies. As illustrated in A Case in Point: Closing a Contractionary Gap, an expansionary policy, such as a tax cut, can increase aggregate demand enough to close a contractionary gap and restore full employment. Although expansionary policy may enable the economy to return to full employment more quickly, the price level will rise as well.

A Case in Point
Closing a Contractionary Gap: The 1964 Tax Cut

One of the factors that helped elect John F. Kennedy to the presidency in 1960 was a general dissatisfaction with economic conditions. In particular, two recessions and relatively slow economic growth had occurred during the preceding four years (1956–1960). At the time, Keynesian economists dominated economic thought. Kennedy's advisors were no exception. They argued that aggregate demand was generally inadequate to maintain full employment. In other words, they believed that the economy was facing a contractionary gap. Because they assumed that wages and prices would fall too slowly to allow a return to full employment, they recommended that government enact expansionary fiscal policies to stimulate aggregate demand.[*]

As a first step in developing such a fiscal policy, the economists required two basic measures: (1) an estimate of the size of the contractionary gap; and (2) an estimate of the multiplier effect. They attacked the first problem by attempting to discover what full-employment

[*] For more details about the 1964 tax cut, see Charles McClure, Jr., "Fiscal Failure: Lessons of the Sixties" in *Economic Policy and Inflation in the Sixties*. Washington, D.C.: American Enterprise Institute, 1972. McClure is critical of the tax cut but explains the thinking of the Keynesian advisors who recommended this fiscal policy.

output would be. Based on their studies, they concluded that full employment could be roughly measured as the output associated with a 4 percent unemployment rate. Translating this figure into the level of output that could be produced with full employment, they arrived at a contractionary gap of $30 billion.

In addition, they estimated the multiplier effect to be 2 for the change in taxes. (Although the multiplier they used is not the simple multiplier we discussed in Chapter 23, it is based on the same principles.) Putting these two estimates together, they recommended a tax cut of $15 billion to close the contractionary gap. That is,

Change in GNP = Change in taxes × Multiplier
$30 billion = Change in taxes × 2.0
$15 billion = Change in taxes

President Johnson and Congress accepted the argument, enacting the 1964 tax cut. Initially, the tax cut met its goals: The contractionary gap closed and unemployment fell. However, over the next several years, the stimulus of the tax cut—coupled with increases in spending for the Vietnam War and for President Johnson's War on Poverty—opened an expansionary gap.

(a) Rely on automatic adjustment

Price-level index
(GNP deflator)

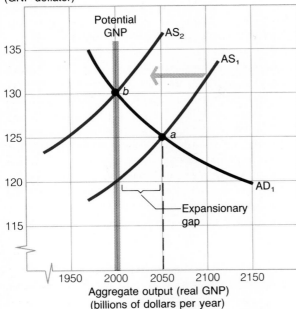

(b) Use contractionary policies

Price-level index
(GNP deflator)

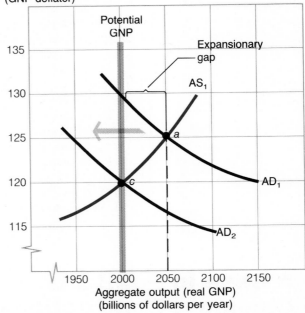

Exhibit 27.3
Policy Responses to an Expansionary Gap
The initial equilibrium (point *a*) shows the economy in an expansionary gap; actual GNP ($2050 billion) is $50 billion above potential GNP. If the government takes no action, automatic adjustment mechanisms increase wages and prices and ultimately decrease aggregate supply (to AS₂). If the government uses contractionary fiscal and/ or monetary policies, aggregate demand will decrease (to AD₂). Either response will eventually restore the economy to long-run equilibrium, producing and selling at its potential GNP. Automatic adjustments result in higher prices (point *b*). Contractionary policies reduce the upward pressure on prices (point *c*).

Contractionary policies.
Changes in fiscal and/or monetary policies that decrease aggregate demand. Higher taxes and lower spending are contractionary fiscal policies; raising the required reserve ratio and selling government securities are contractionary monetary policies.

Eliminating expansionary gaps with contractionary policies. Similarly, the government has two policy options when an increase in aggregate demand opens an expansionary gap, as shown in Exhibit 27.3. The initial short-run equilibrium (where AD₁ intersects AS₁) is $50 billion above potential GNP, indicating that actual unemployment is less than the natural rate. If government takes no action, as illustrated in Exhibit 27.3(a), automatic adjustments will eventually decrease aggregate supply (to AS₂) as wages and prices adjust upward.

On the other hand, government may use **contractionary policies**, as illustrated in Exhibit 27.3(b). If Congress and the president increase taxes or decrease government purchases to lower aggregate demand, they are using contractionary *fiscal* policies. If the Fed sells securities or raises the required reserve ratio (thereby lowering bank reserves, the money supply, and hence aggregate demand), it is using contractionary *monetary* policies. Contractionary policies will also

The government has two options when the economy is not in long-run equilibrium: do nothing and rely on the automatic adjustment mechanism, or take discretionary action using fiscal or monetary policies to change aggregate demand and close the GNP gap.

In response to a contractionary gap, automatic adjustments lower wages and prices and increase aggregate supply.

Expansionary fiscal policies (increased spending or lower tax rates) or expansionary monetary policies (lower reserve requirements or buying government securities) increase aggregate demand. Expansionary policies may cause change more quickly than automatic adjustment, but they raise the price level.

In response to an expansionary gap, automatic adjustments increase wages and prices and decrease aggregate supply.

Contractionary fiscal policies (higher taxes or lower spending) or contractionary monetary policies (higher reserve requirements or selling government securities) decrease aggregate demand. Contractionary policies lower the price level.

restore the economy to its potential output, but at a lower price level than the do-nothing policy.

MACROECONOMIC POLICY: SOME COMPLICATIONS

The belief that government can take effective action to reduce the swings in the business cycle dates from the Great Depression. Before then, most economists believed that the economy's automatic adjustment mechanism was sufficient to restore full employment. But the experience of the Great Depression shook the faith of many economists and politicians in the automatic adjustment process. Keynes and his followers argued that government could and should take action in a deep recession to boost aggregate demand and help the economy recover to full employment. In fact, during the 1960s many economists believed that government policies could be changed easily and quickly to counterbalance virtually any shift in aggregate demand.

Today few economists believe that it is desirable or even possible for government to react to every fluctuation in the economy. But economists continue to debate whether government should rely exclusively on the automatic adjustments or, under some circumstances, take discretionary policy actions. The following questions are important to this debate: To what extent will changes in actual GNP *automatically* result in stabilizing changes in the federal government's budget? To what extent will expansionary fiscal policy reduce private-sector spending? And to what extent will households and businesses take rational actions that offset the effects of anticipated policies? These complications, discussed in this section, affect the benefits and costs of discretionary policy actions.

Budget Deficits and the Business Cycle

An increase in the budget deficit results from greater expenditures (purchases, transfers, and interest payments) and/or lower receipts (taxes and fees). Either change is expansionary, but an increase in the deficit can occur for two different reasons.

Discretionary fiscal policies and budget deficits. First, the deficit will increase if Congress and the president decide to increase government spending or lower tax rates. Because these budget changes require deliberate decisions, economists refer to them as **discretionary policies**. Discretionary fiscal policies that are expansionary will increase aggregate demand and the size of the government's budget deficit (or lower its budget surplus) *at the existing level of GNP*.

Contractionary policies can also be discretionary, as, for example, a decision by government to cut spending or increase tax rates. Discretionary fiscal policies that are contractionary tend to reduce a budget deficit at the existing level of GNP. To check your understanding, refer to the budget equation at the beginning of this chapter. Demonstrate how expansionary fiscal policies would increase (and contractionary policies reduce) a budget deficit.

Discretionary policies. Deliberate changes in monetary and/or fiscal policies to counteract cyclical changes in economic activity, that is, to reduce or eliminate expansionary and contractionary gaps. Also called countercyclical policies.

Automatic stabilizers. Taxes and expenditures that automatically change when economic activity changes. Stabilizers cause a decrease in the actual budget balance when GNP falls and an increase when GNP rises. These changes reduce cyclical changes in aggregate demand. Important stabilizers are income taxes, unemployment compensation, and welfare.

Automatic stabilizers and budget deficits. But discretionary fiscal policies are only one cause of a change in the deficit. The deficit will also increase if the level of GNP falls, because lower GNP means lower income and higher unemployment. Thus a drop in GNP automatically lowers tax receipts and increases government transfer payments. Because income taxes, unemployment compensation, welfare, and other government revenue and transfer programs respond spontaneously *to a change in GNP*, economists refer to them as **automatic stabilizers**. That is, these programs automatically cause changes in aggregate demand that offset contractionary and/or expansionary gaps. Do not confuse automatic stabilizers with the automatic adjustment mechanism. The automatic adjustment mechanism works in a private-sector economy. Automatic stabilizers are aspects of government policy.

To see the effect of automatic stabilizers, let's suppose that aggregate demand falls and the economy slips into a recession. Unemployment will rise, and GNP and national income will fall. Because federal government revenues are largely dependent on income taxes (both individual and business), the decline in income will lower tax receipts even if tax rates remain constant. Since 1960, government tax receipts have been approximately 20 percent of GNP. If this relationship was constant, tax receipts would fall from $440 billion to $400 billion as GNP falls from $2200 billion to $2000 billion.

At the same time—because unemployment is increasing—government transfer payments for unemployment compensation and welfare will rise. This increase in transfer payments happens even if the policies that determine eligibility and the level of individual benefits remain constant. Both the decline in tax receipts and the increase in transfer payments will increase a budget deficit. But these automatic changes in the budget are also expansionary. Thus they offset to some extent the decline in private-sector income, helping to lessen the decrease in aggregate demand.

Automatic stabilizers also help close an expansionary gap caused by an increase in aggregate demand. Rising income and falling unemployment automatically increase tax receipts and lower transfer payments. These automatic changes in the budget will somewhat offset the rise in private-sector income, limiting the increase in aggregate demand and reducing excess demand pressures.

Discretionary policies and automatic stabilizers compared. The distinction between automatic and discretionary changes in the government's fiscal policies is important. An increase in the federal budget deficit may result from either a change in tax or spending policies or from a decrease in GNP unrelated to changes in fiscal policy. But the meaning of and appropriate response to the deficit are quite different.

Suppose, for example, that aggregate demand drops, reducing output and employment. Automatic stabilizers will increase the budget deficit. If Congress responds with contractionary policies—raising taxes or lowering spending—aggregate demand will decrease. As a result, the recession will worsen, increasing the deficit. A similar failure to recognize the distinction between discretionary policies and automatic stabilizers caused a serious policy mistake in 1932, as A Case in Point: Response to a Budget Deficit illustrates.

Full-employment budget. Government receipts and expenditures that would occur under existing fiscal policies if the economy were producing at its potential GNP level. Changes in the full-employment budget reflect discretionary changes in fiscal policies.

Full-employment budget and fiscal policies. To distinguish discretionary fiscal policy changes from the operation of automatic stabilizers, economists use the concept of a **full-employment budget**. This budget is an estimate of what government expenditures and receipts would be *under existing tax and spending laws if the economy were producing at its potential GNP level.* The full-employment budget gets its name from the relationship of potential GNP to full employment (the natural rate of unemployment). Because a full-employment budget eliminates the effects of cyclical changes in GNP—movement above and below potential GNP—it is sometimes called a *cyclically adjusted* budget. (Like potential GNP, the concept of a full-employment budget is widely accepted, although there is considerable debate over how to measure it.)

Expansionary fiscal policies will worsen the full-employment budget balance (a deficit will increase or a surplus will decrease). Contractionary fiscal policies will improve the full-employment budget balance (a deficit will decrease or a surplus will increase). On the other hand, because the full-employment budget

A Case in Point
Response to a Budget Deficit:
The 1932 Budget Changes

In 1930 the federal government's budget was nearly in balance. In 1931, however, government expenditures were twice the size of tax receipts, leaving a budget deficit of $2.1 billion. In today's world of $200 billion deficits, $2.1 billion may sound like a rather small amount. However, that deficit was 2.8 percent of nominal GNP in 1931 and therefore was equivalent to a $112 billion deficit in 1985.*

President Herbert Hoover and his economic advisors—like most classical economists—viewed the deficit as poor fiscal management and were determined to eliminate it. Hoover pushed for and Congress accepted an increase in taxes and a decrease in government expenditures in 1932. But Hoover and his advisors did not realize that the deficit was caused largely by the recession and consequent fall in income tax receipts.

Hoover's choice of a contractionary fiscal policy helped to turn the recession into the Great Depression. The deficit fell only to $1.4 billion because tax receipts decreased as GNP fell. Personal tax receipts in 1932 were only one-half those in 1931. In fact, if transfer payments had not fallen (unemployment compensation and other automatic stabilizing expenditure programs

did not exist at that time), the deficit would have been almost identical in 1931 and 1932.

By November 1932, U.S. citizens had begun to blame Hoover for their economic woes and voted him out of office in favor of Franklin Delano Roosevelt, who promised action. Interestingly, Roosevelt agreed with Hoover's fiscal policy. In fact, during the 1932 campaign Roosevelt criticized Hoover for not taking more drastic measures to reduce the deficit. Roosevelt wanted government action but he (and his advisors) did not have the concept of the full-employment budget balance to guide their thinking.

Two lessons are to be learned from this example. First, when an actual budget deficit is caused by a fall in GNP, contractionary policies (increasing taxes and reducing expenditures) will cause further decreases in GNP. Second, the actual budget deficit (or surplus) is a poor measure on which to base fiscal policy actions and a poor measure of whether government policies are expansionary or contractionary. Increases in actual budget deficits can either reflect decreases in GNP (as they did during the Great Depression) or expansionary fiscal policies (tax cuts or increases in government spending). Only the full-employment budget balance—which removes any effect of changes in real GNP—can give a clear signal.

_____
* All data in tis example are expressed in nominal terms.

Changes in the federal government's budget balance can be caused by discretionary changes in tax and spending policies. Expansionary fiscal policies tend to increase a budget deficit. Contractionary fiscal policies tend to lower a budget deficit.

Changes in the budget balance may also result from changes in automatic stabilizers—income taxes, unemployment compensation and welfare programs—that respond to changes in GNP. Automatic stabilizers help offset gaps created by changes in aggregate demand.

A decline in GNP reduces income and raises unemployment, decreasing tax receipts and increasing transfer payments, thus increasing the actual budget deficit. An increase in GNP raises income and reduces unemployment, increasing tax receipts and decreasing transfer payments, thus reducing the actual budget deficit.

The full-employment budget measures government receipts and expenditures at the economy's potential GNP level. Changes in the full-employment budget balance reflect changes in fiscal policies.

Crowding-out effect. A decrease in investment and consumption resulting from the increase in interest rates caused by expansionary fiscal policies (holding the money supply constant). This effect is strongest when the economy is close to potential GNP, and it reduces the effect of expansionary fiscal policies.

balance is estimated at potential GNP, it is unaffected by changes in actual GNP, that is, by changes in automatic stabilizers. Thus changes in the full-employment budget are clear signals of discretionary policy changes. *A rise in the full-employment budget surplus means that contractionary fiscal policies have been adopted. A decline in the full-employment budget surplus means that expansionary fiscal policies have been adopted.* By contrast, changes in the actual budget are ambiguous signals. A rising deficit may reflect either expansionary fiscal policies or the effects of automatic stabilizers as the economy slips into a recession.

In addition to providing a way to distinguish discretionary policy changes from the effects of automatic stabilizers, the full-employment budget is important to debates over federal budget deficits. In 1986 the full-employment deficit was estimated to be 4–5 percent of potential GNP, or almost as high as the actual deficit. If this estimate is accurate, automatic stabilizers will not reduce the actual deficit much, even if the economy operates at full employment. Discretionary fiscal policy changes—reducing spending and/or raising taxes—will be necessary to significantly reduce the budget deficits. The effects of these deficits and policies to reduce them are discussed in a policy case in Chapter 31.

Crowding-Out Effect

Another fiscal policy issue is the degree to which expansionary fiscal policy actually raises aggregate demand. There are reasons to believe that the effects of higher government spending may be partially or fully offset by lower private spending. Economists call this result the **crowding-out effect**.

To see why the crowding-out effect occurs, let's consider what happens when government expenditures increase. Recall that in order to increase spending, government must borrow more, raise taxes, or print more money. Because we want to see the effect of fiscal policy alone, we hold the money supply constant.

Effect of borrowing. To borrow more money, the government must sell bonds in the financial market. But doing so increases the supply of bonds, lowering bond prices and increasing real interest rates, as we have already shown. (Put another way, an increase in demand for borrowing will increase the cost of borrowed funds, that is, raise interest rates.) Higher real interest rates cause households and businesses to consume and invest less. Thus higher government purchases are offset to some extent by lower private-sector spending. Because government borrowing effectively *crowds* some private-sector borrowers *out* of financial markets, the effectiveness of expansionary fiscal policies is reduced.

Crowding out is a serious issue in terms of economic growth. To the extent that crowding out slows private investment in new machinery, plants, and technology, it may limit an economy's ability to expand its potential output, that is, to grow. We consider the importance of private-sector investment to growth in more detail in Chapter 30.

Effect of raising taxes. Higher taxes directly reduce private-sector income and thus lower private-sector spending. But, as we noted in Chapter 22, households will reduce consumption by less than the decline in income (because the marginal propensity to consume is less than 1). But to keep spending from falling as much as their incomes, households must either borrow more or sell some of the bonds they own.

(a) Government crowds out private-sector spending

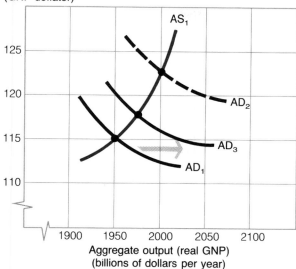

(b) Greater money demand raises interest rates

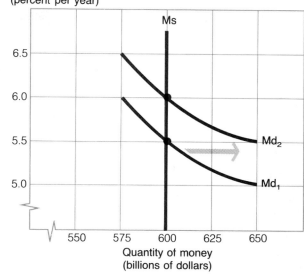

Exhibit 27.4
Crowding-Out Effect of Increased Government Spending
Expansionary fiscal policies increase aggregate demand (to AD_2), ignoring the crowding-out effect. But higher spending also raises demand for money and, consequently, the interest rate, as shown in part (b). As the interest rate rises, investment and interest-sensitive consumption spending fall—crowded out of financial markets—so aggregate demand increases only to AD_3. The difference between AD_2 and AD_3 is an indication of the extent of the crowding-out effect.

Either way, we can expect interest rates to rise and, consequently, private-sector spending will fall. Because private-sector spending is affected by both the decline in income and the crowding-out effect, the expansionary effect of government spending financed by higher taxes is generally quite small. Indeed, *the greater the crowding-out effect, the smaller will be the impact of expansionary fiscal policy*. In fact, if crowding out is large enough, fiscal policy may not raise aggregate demand at all.

Exhibit 27.4 illustrates the crowding-out effect if government raises spending or reduces taxes but the money supply remains unchanged. The direct effect of the expansionary fiscal policy (before considering crowding out) is shown in Exhibit 27.4(a) by the dashed curve AD_2. But with the money supply fixed, higher spending raises the demand for money and therefore the interest rate (to 6 percent), as shown in Exhibit 27.4(b). The higher interest rate lowers investment and interest-sensitive consumption. Taking into account the crowding-out effect, expansionary fiscal policies can be expected to raise aggregate demand only to AD_3. The reduction in aggregate demand from AD_2 to AD_3 reflects the strength of the crowding-out effect.

How strong is the crowding-out effect? Economists do not all agree on the answer to this question. But the evidence suggests that the crowding-out effect is more important when the economy is operating close to its potential GNP level. When there is considerable slack in the economy, expansionary fiscal policies may raise income and consequently the total level of saving. If saving rises enough, public-sector borrowing will not have to crowd out private-sector borrowing. Moreover, an increase in the funds supplied to the U.S. financial market by foreign individuals and businesses may, as it has in recent years, offset the crowding-out effect. But borrowing from the foreign sector has other negative effects, as discussed in Chapter 33.

Rational Expectations: Are Fiscal and Monetary Policies Ineffective?

In addition to the crowding-out effect, some economists believe that the effectiveness of fiscal and monetary policies is reduced because they change expectations. The strongest advocates of this position, the **new classical macroeconomists**, argue that neither fiscal nor monetary policy will affect the economy *if the policy change is fully anticipated.* These economists base their theory on the belief that individuals are rational and have **rational expectations**. That is, individuals can be expected to consider all available information and adjust their expectations to known future events.

Suppose that Congress increases government spending, financing this expansionary fiscal policy by additional borrowing. What effect would this policy have on your expectations? According to rational expectations theory, you would recognize that there is no essential difference between spending financed by borrowing and spending financed by current taxes. Government borrowing today means that higher future taxes will be required to meet interest payments and eventual repayment of the principal. Borrowing does not change the total amount of taxes that will be paid, but it does change the timing. The real wealth of the household sector declines, just as though current taxes were used instead of borrowing. As wealth falls, so does consumption.

In the view of the new classical macroeconomists, the rational response of individuals (less consumption and more saving) makes an increase in borrowing equivalent to an increase in taxes. As we have noted, tax-financed increases in spending have a small effect anyway. If expectations are adjusted, reducing the effect even more, discretionary tax policies may be totally ineffective. The new classical macroeconomists also argue that rational reactions will offset discretionary monetary policies. Suppose that the Fed announces an increase in the money supply. We can expect this action to increase aggregate demand and, consequently, the price level. What kinds of reactions can we expect if the increase in the price level is anticipated?

Anyone lending money will want a higher *nominal* interest rate to cover the anticipated loss in the purchasing power of money. (Instead of falling as the money supply increases, the *real* interest rate may not change at all.) Workers and other resource suppliers will want higher nominal wages and prices to cover the expected price-level increase. As resource prices rise, aggregate supply decreases. If individuals succeed in protecting real wages and real incomes, the drop in aggregate supply will completely offset the higher demand. Although the price level will rise, real GNP will not change.

New classical macroeconomists. Economists who assume that wages and prices are very flexible, a theoretical approach similar to that of classical economists. Their theories suggest that rational responses to anticipated policy actions will make policies completely ineffective.

Rational expectations. An assumption that individuals utilize all available information, including their understanding of the effects of fiscal and monetary policy, in anticipating future economic conditions.

Higher government spending financed by borrowing will raise demand for credit and cause interest rates to rise. Higher interest rates reduce investment and interest-sensitive consumption spending. This crowding-out effect reduces the impact of expansionary fiscal policies.

Government spending financed by taxes directly reduces household income. Consumption falls less than income (because of the marginal propensity to consume) and households must either borrow or sell bonds they hold. Either way, interest rates rise, crowding out private-sector spending. The larger the crowding-out effect, the smaller will be the effect of fiscal policies on aggregate demand.

The new classical macroeconomists argue that fiscal and monetary policies are ineffective in changing real GNP because individuals with rational expectations will take offsetting actions. Expansionary fiscal policies financed with borrowing will lead to expectations of higher taxes and an increase in current saving. Expansionary monetary policy will lead to expectations of a higher price level and higher nominal (not real) interest rates. Aggregate supply decreases, and only the price level (not real output) is affected.

Nonactivists. Economists who believe it unnecessary, undesirable, and impractical to employ discretionary monetary and fiscal policies to stabilize the economy. They recommend stable policies—a constant growth in the money supply and a balanced full-employment budget—and reliance on the economy's automatic adjustment mechanism.

Activists. Economists who believe it necessary, desirable, and practical to use discretionary monetary and fiscal policies to stabilize the economy.

Note, however, that this conclusion applies only to *anticipated* policies. When the economy is surprised by policy actions, short-run output may change. But once the policy action is recognized, the economy should, according to the new classical macroeconomists, adjust immediately.

Not all economists accept this strong conclusion that anticipated policy actions have *no* effect. They observe that it is not enough for individuals to adjust their expectations; they must also adjust their behavior. To the extent that contracts set wages and other resource prices for some specified period of time, for example, the response may be delayed. However, most economists do accept that private-sector responses due to changed expectations may weaken the impact of anticipated policies.

MACROECONOMIC POLICY: ACTIVISM VERSUS NONACTIVISM

Is it necessary to "correct" departures from full employment or price stability with discretionary policies, or will the economy correct itself? Is it practical to use discretionary policies or are there serious problems with them that must be overcome? Should government policy makers be allowed to use their own discretion in setting policies or should they be required to follow fixed rules? Most economists agree that fiscal and monetary policies *can* affect aggregate economic activity. But there is still considerable debate about whether such policies *should* be used to reduce or eliminate swings in the business cycle.

We have observed that government has two alternative policy choices when the economy is not currently operating at its potential output level. It can take no action and rely on the economy's automatic adjustment mechanism. Or it can take discretionary action to shift aggregate demand and close the gap. We can identify proponents of these two policies as **nonactivists** and **activists**, respectively. To a large extent activists are associated with Keynesian beliefs; nonactivists include both monetarists and the new classical macroeconomists.

Franco Modigliani, a Keynesian and a leading proponent of activism, says that activists

> Accept what I regard to be the fundamental practical message of *The General Theory* (of John Maynard Keynes): that a private enterprise economy . . . *needs* to be stabilized, *can* be stabilized, and therefore, *should* be stabilized by appropriate monetary and fiscal policies.[*]

In contrast, Milton Friedman, the founder of modern monetarism, argues that

> We simply do not know enough to be able to recognize minor disturbances when they occur or to be able to predict either what their effects will be with any precision or what monetary policy is required to offset their effects.[†]

These quotations indicate that the disagreement has little to do with whether government policies *can* affect the economy. (The new classical macroeconomists, as we have noted, dispute the effect of policies announced in advance.) The more crucial and controversial question is whether the effects of these policies are

---

[*] Franco Modigliani, "The Monetarist Controversy, or Should We Forsake Stabilization Policies?" *American Economic Review*, March 1977, p. 1.

[†] Milton Friedman, "The Role of Monetary Policy," *American Economic Review*, March 1968, p. 14.

beneficial. Will they actually stabilize the economy? Those who answer *no* to this question stress practical problems in designing and implementing policies, as you will see.

Are Discretionary Policies Necessary?

Activists believe that the economy is inherently unstable. They observe that there are wide swings in two elements of private-sector spending: consumer spending on durable goods and fixed investment. (Durable goods include automobiles, microwave ovens, and other appliances. Fixed investment includes business investment in plant and equipment and residential construction.) Activists also note that demand and supply shocks can create severe economic problems. Certainly, increased spending for national defense during the Vietnam War and the oil-price supply shocks in the 1970s hurt the economy. Activists argue that government fiscal and monetary policies are vital to minimizing instability and the negative effects of such economic upheavals.

Nonactivists counter that durable goods and fixed investment are the two most unstable portions of consumption. They argue that spending on other goods and services is very stable, making total consumption spending more stable. Moreover, nonactivists believe that what appears to be unstable private-sector spending is really a response to unstable government policies. They explain the drop in investment spending in the late 1960s, for example, as a response to the high interest rates caused by tight monetary policy and high government borrowing. They blame the inflationary bias in the economy since World War II on instability in monetary policies.

On balance, the evidence is not conclusive. Some poorly designed and implemented government policies *have* created instability. But the supply shocks of 1973 and 1979 have little to do with macroeconomic policies. (However, they do raise a question of which policy response is best, an issue we address in Chapter 31.) Moreover, the case for government policies depends on more than private-sector instability. Instability would not be a serious problem if the economy's automatic adjustment mechanism were able to restore stability quickly and smoothly.

How Fast Does the Automatic Adjustment Mechanism Work?

Following in the tradition of Keynes, activists believe that wages and prices fall slowly when a contractionary gap opens. Activists note that resource prices are often fixed for substantial periods of time by contracts or by the custom of adjusting wages and salaries annually. Because resource costs do not respond immediately, changes in aggregate demand will have a stronger short-run effect on quantity—both output and unemployment—than on prices. As a result, activists argue that the automatic adjustment mechanism works slowly and that the costs of relying on it are high. Thus the benefits of discretionary policies are also high.

Recent historical data support this view. Wages and prices *have* been slow to respond during nearly every recession since the late 1960s. For example, the rate of inflation continued to rise throughout the 1969–1970 recession. Although price levels rose more slowly in response to the 1981–1982 recession, it was the most severe recession in the last 40 years.

In contrast, nonactivists blame the slow response of wages and prices on government policies. Because workers and businesses expect expansionary policies, they have little reason to reduce wages and prices during a recession. Were it not for the effect of expected government policies, nonactivists believe that workers and businesses would respond rapidly. Any delay would be brief: the time required to get accurate information on which to base price-level expectations.

What Is the Historical Evidence?

As you can see in Exhibit 27.5, the U.S. economy has been more stable in the post–World War II era than in the pre–World War II period. Annual changes in real GNP have been smaller and recessions have been shorter. Activists observe that the postwar period was when the federal government recognized its ability and responsibility to stabilize the economy. They attribute much of the stability to active government policies.

Such reasoning, however, is not proof. Nonactivists attribute the greater stability to other causes. For example, the increasing size of the federal budget increased the importance of automatic stabilizers. Reforms in the banking system—government deposit insurance, for example—helped prevent the financial panics that had characterized the pre–World War II period. In their view, stability is not the result of discretionary government policies.

Exhibit 27.5

Macroeconomic Stability: A Historical View

The graph shows annual percentage changes in real GNP from 1909 to 1986. The shaded areas indicate periods of recession. Note that the fluctuations prior to World War II (1941–1945) are larger and the recessions longer, indicating that the economy has been more stable since the war.

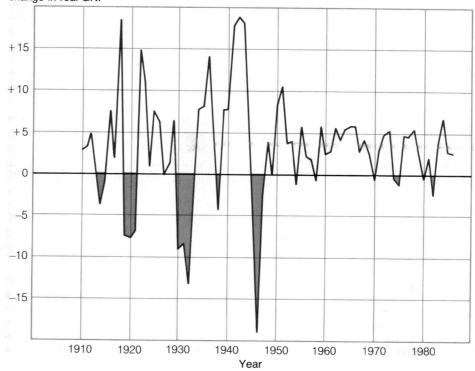

Can we know who is right? Unfortunately, it is difficult to separate cause and effect, so statistical tests have proved inconclusive. However, the debate between activists and nonactivists is not just a dispute over whether discretionary policies are necessary. They also disagree on the question of whether the government can, in fact, make appropriate responses to contractionary and expansionary gaps.

What Information Is Required for Discretionary Policy Action?

Early in this chapter we showed how government policies might shift aggregate demand enough to close any contractionary or expansionary gap that might occur. Making such changes may have appeared easy to do (and they are easy to draw on graphs). But the real world is much more complicated. A large amount of information is required to formulate and implement economic policy. Consider, for example, what you would have to know in order to develop an ideal policy response to a contractionary gap.

Any discretionary fiscal policy requires an estimate of how much aggregate expenditures have to change. In order to make this estimate, we have to know the current level of real GNP and potential GNP. In addition, because it takes time for the full effect of fiscal policies to be felt, we must have some idea of future values of the GNP components. Because fiscal policies have a multiplier effect, we also have to estimate how much total expenditures would rise as a result of an initial policy change. To do so requires that we estimate the effects of crowding out and changes in expectations, as well as the size of the multiplier.

Discretionary monetary policies are also complex to develop. In order to decide how many government securities to buy on the open market, the Fed would have to estimate the deposit expansion multiplier. The Fed would also have to determine how much, if any, excess reserves the banking system might want to hold. Developing a monetary policy is further complicated by the fact that the Fed controls the *money supply*, but the goal of monetary policy is to change *aggregate demand*. The connection between changes in the money supply and short-run changes in aggregate demand are not exact or constant.

The knowledge required for an ideal policy response to cyclical fluctuations is not easy to come by. Economists accept the concept of potential GNP but have no way of directly observing or precisely measuring it. Forecasting future levels of aggregate demand, aggregate supply, and potential GNP is far from an exact science. Nonactivists believe that these difficulties strongly support their position. Activists recognize the information limitations, but they believe that policy makers can know enough to give the economy a push in the right direction.

How Significant and Uncertain Are Policy Lags?

Another practical difficulty in developing discretionary policy is the effect of time lags. Throughout this textbook we have drawn graphs on which aggregate demand shifts from an initial gap to a final equilibrium position. These shifts are not immediate; rather, several time lags, or delays, occur. First, it takes time for policy makers to recognize that a problem exists and additional time to develop a policy response to the problem. In addition, the effects of policy actions are not instantaneous, which creates an additional lag.

Recognition lag. The delay between when a macroeconomic problem occurs and when it is recognized.

Action lag. The delay between when a problem is recognized and when policy actions are taken.

Recognition and action lags. No discretionary policy response can be developed until a problem is recognized. For example, information on GNP is produced only once a quarter, and economists are reluctant to say that a recession exists unless real GNP has declined for two consecutive quarters. Thus the **recognition lag**, the time that passes before a recession can be recognized, might be as long as 4–8 months. Although data on unemployment and prices are available somewhat more frequently, a recognition lag of at least four months for fiscal policies seems a reasonable estimate.*

Monetary policy is also subject to recognition lags, although they are shorter than for fiscal policies. Monetary policy usually aims at intermediate targets, such as interest rates or the supply of money. Data on interest rates are available daily. Money supply figures can be obtained weekly but are subject to such extensive revisions that accurate figures are generally obtainable only monthly. Moreover, economists disagree about which measure of money supply to use and what intermediate target is the best goal for monetary policy.

The recognition lag can be shortened if future events can be forecast with reasonable accuracy. Although forecasts are inexact, activists argue that forecasts do not have to be perfect to be useful. However, some major economic events—such as the oil-price increase in 1979—are not predictable. And some changes are not well understood even after several years. (For example, economists are still unclear about how deregulation of banks and changes in the Fed's operation in the early 1980s affected demand for money.) Forecasts that do not take into account changes in relationships between policy variables and economic activity will be particularly inaccurate and unreliable.

After a problem has been identified, there is an **action lag** while a policy response is being developed and implemented. The action lag is a major obstacle, especially for fiscal policy. To implement a discretionary fiscal policy, Congress must pass and the president approve changes in tax laws or spending programs. Even when there is general agreement that a problem exists, there is apt to be disagreement over the best size and type of fiscal policy response. Which group should be given a tax cut? On which program should more be spent? The short-run economic impact does not depend on the type of government spending. But the political consequences of changing taxes or spending make it difficult for Congress and the president to act swiftly.

In addition, critics observe that fiscal policy tends to be very one-sided. That is, legislators typically are willing to vote for expansionary fiscal measures but not for contractionary fiscal measures. That is, they are willing to spend more and/or tax less (issues of enormous budget deficits aside) but not to cut programs or raise taxes. Indeed, voting for contractionary fiscal measures is often considered to be political suicide.

While monetary policy also is subject to action lags, they are much briefer than for fiscal policy for several reasons. First, the Federal Open Market Committee, the Fed's policy-making group, is small. Thus members can more easily reach consensus. And compared with legislators, board members face less political pressure. Moreover, monetary policy can be implemented quickly when agreement to expand or contract the money supply is reached. The shorter action lag is a

---

*Note also that data on GNP are constantly being revised. Many times the revisions are substantial: as much as 1 or 2 percent, or a potential variation of as much as $70 billion in real GNP. As a result, it is difficult for anyone to know for sure how much change, if any, has occurred until well after the fact.

Impact lag. The delay between when policy actions are taken and when they fully affect aggregate demand.

point in favor of using monetary policy as a stabilizer, assuming that stabilizing policies are desired.

Impact lag. Perhaps even more important is the long and uncertain **impact lag** between the time a policy is implemented and the time its full effect is felt. Fiscal policy changes involve the multiplier effect. Economists estimate that it takes about three months for a round of spending to occur. Thus the economy may not feel most of the multiplier effect for a year or longer. Moreover, the estimated period for a spending round is an average. The actual effect may take more (or less) time, again increasing the uncertainty of the effect. The timing and extent of the crowding-out effect and adjustments in expectations are also uncertain.

Changes in the money supply also suffer from long and variable impact lags. For the Fed's action to have its full effect, banks must receive the new deposits and turn them into new loans. Like the spending multiplier, the deposit expansion process takes time. Most economists believe that this response is quite slow. Because the effect of monetary policy depends on so many other decisions, the impact lag for such policies may run from six months to two years.

Policy implications of lags. Nonactivists note that because of lags, discretionary policies are likely to *destabilize* the economy. Exhibit 27.6 shows potential GNP growing at a constant rate (indicated by the straight line). However, actual GNP at times is below potential GNP (creating a contractionary gap) and at other times is above it (creating an expansionary gap).

Suppose that the economy is initially at point *a*. Actual output is beginning to fall below potential GNP, opening a contractionary gap. If there were no lags, discretionary policies might halt this downward slide. Because of the recognition lag, however, policy makers may not actually recognize the problem until a later time (point *b*). Because of the action lag, the actual policy response may not begin until point *c*. But at that point, the economy's automatic adjustment mechanism has already kicked in, recovery has started, and the contractionary gap has begun to shrink.

Worse still, from the nonactivist's point of view, the discretionary policy may finally have its full effect at point *d*, while the economy is experiencing an expansionary gap. The path of the economy if no policy were implemented is indicated by the smooth line on the graph. The path caused by poorly timed action is shown by the dotted line. Far from stabilizing the economy (reducing the length and depth of the recession), the policy destabilizes the economy (increasing inflation).

Nonactivists' Case for Fixed Rules

Because of the many problems involved in taking action and obtaining expected results, nonactivists have little faith in discretionary policies. Instead, they believe that the private sector is basically stable, that the economy's automatic adjustment mechanism works well, and that automatic stabilizers are a sufficient policy response to cyclical changes in demand. In addition, they believe that policy makers often use discretionary policies for political rather than economic purposes.

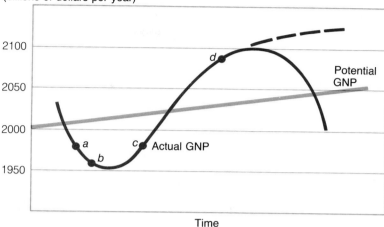

Exhibit 27.6
Discretionary Policy: Lags and Potential Instability
Nonactivists argue that lags may cause discretionary policies to be destabilizing. Suppose that the economy is initially at point *a* where a contractionary gap is beginning to open. If there were no lags, expansionary policy action at this point might prevent further declines. The recognition lag, however, may mean that the problem is not recognized until point *b*, when the gap is nearly at its maximum. The action lag may mean that policy makers do not respond until point *c* when the automatic adjustments have already begun to close the gap. The impact lag may mean that the policy has its full effect on the economy at point *d*. As a result, the policy increases the size of the expansionary gap (following the dashed line), when the automatic adjustment would have been closing the gap.

Instead of leaving policy decisions to politicians, they advocate fixed policy rules that they believe would stabilize the economy. Nonactivists do not all agree on the best rules, but two rules have broad acceptance: (1) a constant rate of growth in the money supply; and (2) a balanced full-employment budget.

Constant growth of the money supply. To stabilize monetary policy, nonactivists favor a rule requiring the Fed to increase the money supply at a constant rate regardless of current economic conditions. In support of this rule they offer several arguments. First, if the money supply grows at a constant rate that is equal to the long-run rate of growth in potential output, the economy could grow *and* prices would be stable. Second, because monetary policy is subject to long and variable impact lags, nonactivists believe it to be impractical to develop and implement short-term policy responses to close GNP gaps. And third, fixed rules would prevent potential mistakes by the Fed.

History is full of such errors by the Fed. In 1958–1959, the Fed cut back the money supply just in time to "help" the economy slide further into recession. In 1968–1969, the Fed increased the money supply even though the economy was already experiencing inflationary pressures. The most serious mistakes occurred during the Great Depression. From 1929 to 1933, the Fed reduced the money supply by 25 percent, adding to contractionary pressures in the middle of the most severe recession in U.S. history. In 1937, as the economy appeared to be struggling toward recovery, the Fed raised the reserve requirements, halting growth in the money supply and extending the Great Depression it had helped to create.

Nonactivists also observe that having the money supply grow at the same rate as long-run real GNP provides an element of automatic stabilization. During a brief recession, the money supply would grow more rapidly than real GNP, helping to close a contractionary gap. And if an increase in aggregate demand opened an expansionary gap, the money supply would grow less rapidly than real GNP, helping to close the gap.

Activists charge that such responses would be inadequate to counterbalance sharp changes in money demand or events such as a major supply shock. Nonactivists, however, believe that demand for money is basically stable and that short-run changes are generally mild and short-lived (and therefore much less of a problem). Individuals would not have to worry about protecting themselves from erratic changes in the money supply, and stable expectations would reduce erratic shifts in aggregate demand. Moreover, nonactivists view the short-run costs of any shift in aggregate demand or aggregate supply as less important than the potential long-run destabilizing effects of discretionary policies.

Balanced full-employment budget. To stabilize fiscal policy, nonactivists generally favor a rule requiring Congress and the president to balance the full-employment budget.* Congress would determine the optimal amount of government spending in terms of allocative efficiency and then adjust tax rates to bring the full-employment budget into balance. The case for this rule is based on arguments similar to those for the constant monetary growth rate. Lags, imperfect knowledge, and opportunity for political judgments to prevail make discretionary fiscal policies unreliable and ineffective in the view of nonactivists.

It is important for you to recognize that we are talking about balancing the full-employment budget, not the actual federal budget. The economy's automatic stabilizers would still function, offsetting instability in private-sector spending to some extent. Thus the actual budget would show a deficit during a recession and a surplus when inflation occurred. But there would be no attempt to adjust the full-employment budget balance to reduce either a contractionary or an expansionary gap. Because the nonactivists believe that the private sector is relatively stable, they also believe that automatic stabilizers are a sufficient policy response to any GNP gaps.

Activists' Case for Discretionary Policies

Activists recognize that imperfect information and lags make it impractical to try to eliminate minor fluctuations in real GNP. They also recognize that policy mistakes in the past have made the economy perform poorly. But they are not

---

* Some nonactivists believe that the government should strive for a full-employment budget surplus. In this way government could pay off some of its outstanding debt, freeing up funds for private-sector investment and thus spurring economic growth. The important point for this discussion is that the full-employment budget balance be constant, not what it is.

When developing discretionary policies, policy makers face the difficulty of measuring actual and potential GNP and predicting the size and timing of the effects of policies.

Discretionary policies are subject to lags. A recognition gap occurs until a problem is recognized. An action gap occurs between recognition of a problem and formulation of a response to it. An impact gap occurs between implementation of a policy and its full effect. Nonactivists argue that lags can cause discretionary policies to further destabilize an economy.

Because of problems in developing and implementing discretionary monetary and fiscal policies, nonactivists propose fixed policy rules: a stable growth of the money supply and a balanced full-employment budget.

Activists recognize the problems of implementing discretionary monetary and fiscal policies, but believe that such policies can give the economy a push in the right direction and prevent major, costly GNP gaps.

ready to abandon the idea of taking action to offset some of the business cycle instability that they believe is inevitable. They believe that discretionary actions should be taken to point the economy in the right direction when problems arise. In their view, the slow response of wages and prices makes reliance on the automatic adjustment mechanism too costly.

No policy approach is perfect, and thus any policy approach is unlikely to provide complete stability. The best approach is the one that will result in the greatest benefits for the least cost. Nonactivists believe that fixed rules are best. Activists believe that moderate actions should be taken. Despite agreement on some important principles, economists continue to be divided over the crucial question of whether discretionary fiscal and monetary policies are necessary, desirable, and practical.

DEFICITS AND DEBT: ISSUES AND OPTIONS

Now that we have considered some of the theoretical and practical problems facing policy makers, we can examine a major policy issue regarding the U.S. economy: the size of federal budget deficits and of the national debt. We noted at the beginning of this chapter that both have grown dramatically in recent years. Moreover, the deficits since 1983 cannot be attributed to war or recession—the traditional causes of deficits. But is the national debt a serious problem? What options do we have for reducing it?

Myths and Realities about the National Debt

Myth and reality are combined in the notion that federal budget deficits and the national debt are cause for concern. In some circumstances moderate deficits and debt may have some desirable effects. But the magnitude of the current deficits and the fact that they largely reflect a deficit in the full-employment budget raise some serious concerns.

Does a growing deficit mean a growing burden? Before we can consider whether they are a burden to the economy, we must put debts and deficits into perspective. That is, we must compare an increase in debt to changes in the ability to service and repay that debt. For example, you may have borrowed to finance your college education. But if your future income rises as a result, your ability to pay the interest and repay the principal also increases. Similarly, comparing federal budget deficits and the size of the national debt to GNP tells us whether the nation is able to pay interest and repay principal and hence how burdensome the debt is.

Exhibit 27.7(a) shows the federal government's budget balance expressed as a percentage of GNP from 1951 to 1986. What do these data suggest? First, budget deficits are certainly not unusual. In fact, deficits occurred in 28 of the last 37 years. The last surplus occurred in 1969.

But deficits in the 1980s have been extraordinarily large. For most of the period shown, federal deficits were about 1–2 percent of GNP. (The primary exception before the 1980s occurred during the major recession in 1975.) By contrast, recent deficits have been over 4.5 percent of GNP and are expected to

(a) Federal budget balance

Percentage of GNP

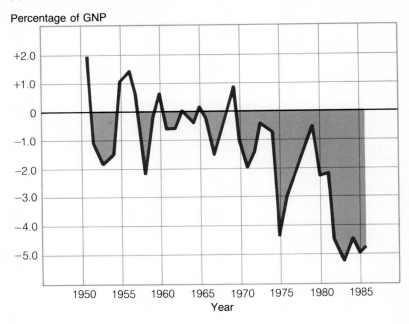

(b) National debt

Percentage of GNP

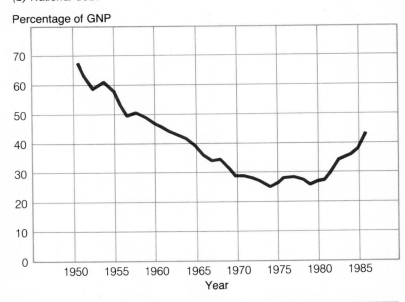

Exhibit 27.7
Deficits and Debt: A Historical View
Part (a) shows the federal budget balance expressed as a percentage of GNP. Areas shaded red correspond to budget deficits. Deficits occurred in 28 of the 37 years shown. For most of the period deficits averaged 1–2 percent of GNP. But since 1980, deficits have run 4–5 percent. Part (b) shows the national debt as a percentage of GNP. From 1951 to 1974, the national debt grew more slowly than GNP, although it increased in absolute terms. Since 1974 the relative size of the debt has increased.

remain almost that large for the rest of the 1980s. To finance a deficit equal to 5 percent of GNP, government borrowing will use up about two-thirds of private saving, which could otherwise be used for business investment or household consumption. As we have stated, such crowding out seriously affects long-run economic growth.

What about the national debt? It has grown in absolute size, increasing by 50 percent between 1951 and 1970. The deficits in the 1970s caused the debt to *double* in a single decade. However, as Exhibit 27.7(b) shows, from 1951 to 1979 the national debt fell from 96 percent of GNP to 34 percent of GNP. That is, the debt grew more slowly than national income, so the nation was better able to afford it. (Just as you can afford to carry more debt—for a bigger house, perhaps—if you earn more.)

However, between 1980 and 1985 the debt doubled once again and the debt grew from one-third of GNP to nearly one-half. Some of that increase was caused by the two recessions between 1980 and 1982. But much of the change and most of the projected increases are the result of fiscal policies that lowered tax receipts while spending continued to increase. This change raises questions about the nation's ability to afford such a debt.

Is debt a future burden?　The current size of the national debt is not necessarily a cause for alarm. But its growth raises questions about whether the debt will seriously burden future generations economically. Those who believe that it will usually argue that the present generation is enjoying the benefits of government spending, while future generations will have to pay taxes to eliminate the debt. In evaluating this argument, we have to recognize that for the most part, we owe the debt to ourselves. This *internal debt* is not really an aggregate burden, although it will redistribute income in the future. That is, future interest payments will transfer income from one group (taxpayers) to another (debt holders).

In contrast, 15 percent of the national debt is *external debt*, held by the foreign sector. Interest and principal payments on the external debt require a transfer of resources from U.S. taxpayers to foreigners. The foreign sector bought more than $90 billion of the new government debt issued from 1980 to 1985. An increase in external debt is not necessarily bad. If the funds allow an increase in productive capacity, the economy may grow fast enough to repay the debt and increase domestic standards of living.

On the other hand, some economists fear that the foreign funds are being used to finance government spending that adds little to future growth. In this case, additional foreign-owned debt *does* represent a future burden, as it does already in Brazil, Argentina, and Mexico. Foreign debt in 1984 represented nearly 50 percent of the GNP in each of those countries, much of it owed to U.S. banks. In seeking to pay off their debts, they are having to make real sacrifices. From 1980 to 1984 the debt burden was partly responsible for a drop in average income in these countries. Although the U.S. debt is not that large a problem now, continued increases in external debt could produce such problems in the future.

Will debt bankrupt the nation?　Even if the debt burden increases, there is no reason for the government to go bankrupt and default on its debt. After all, the U.S. national debt represents a promise to pay U.S. dollars. (The problem is not so simple for Mexico and Brazil because their external debt is owed in dollars.) In other words, the U.S. government could always pay off its debt by printing more money (unless it runs out of paper). It is unlikely to do so, however, because the large increase in the money supply would be highly inflationary. (Moreover, under current law, debt cannot be "monetized" unless the Fed is willing to buy the debt.)

Do deficits cause higher real interest rates?   Deficits financed by borrowing result in increased demand for credit which tends to raise interest rates. But historical evidence suggests that real interest rates and deficits are *not* related. This lack of connection may reflect the fact that, historically, deficits have occurred mostly during recessions. If government borrows during a recession—when overall demand for credit is weak—the borrowing may have little effect on real interest rates. Moreover, prior to 1979 the Fed typically increased the money supply when interest rates began to rise, "monetizing" much of a deficit. In the 1980s, however, the Fed has often declined to finance government debts, forcing government to borrow in the money market, driving up real interest rates.

Do deficits cause inflation?   There is little reason to believe that deficits financed by borrowing cause the price level to rise, especially when deficits occur during recessions. During a recession, aggregate demand is relatively weak. Deficits caused by automatic stabilizers or discretionary fiscal policies add to aggregate demand but have little impact on the price level. Because the crowding-out effect is relatively strong, deficits may have little effect on aggregate demand when the economy is near full employment.

However, there is some evidence that over the long run higher deficits in the United States have been accompanied by more growth in the money supply. Such expansionary monetary policies can result in a higher price level. The exact reason for this relationship is debatable. But some economists believe that it results from the Fed's historical interest in keeping interest rates low. Because the Fed has been willing to allow real interest rates to rise in the 1980s, the rate of inflation has dropped, but deficits have been high.

What are the opportunity costs and the benefits of a deficit?   Federal budget deficits and large and growing national debt that cause higher real interest rates and/or expectations of higher inflation may have serious opportunity costs. Higher real interest rates may reduce private investment, reducing future growth and output—a real cost to future generations. Moreover, if the economy is at full employment, any increase in government spending transfers resources away from the private sector. Conversely, many resources are not utilized by the private sector during recessions. Deficits that stimulate aggregate demand during recessions may enable the economy to avoid the opportunity costs of unused economic resources.

Government spending also can provide benefits. Some spending—to improve roads or education, for example—may increase the economy's potential output. A deficit caused by financing a war or to provide greater national defense may yield present and future benefits. Finally, some deficits result from government policies that also create higher output and employment. As with most economic issues, the important question is whether the extra costs associated with debt or debt reduction are balanced by extra benefits.

Current Situation: What Are the Options?

When we have considered all the positive and negative effects of budget deficits, the national debt, and fiscal and monetary policies, the question still remains: What should government do? Many economists believe that the high current and projected budget deficits will raise real interest rates, crowd out private-sector investment, and reduce future economic growth. They also fear that such high deficits may tempt the Fed to increase the growth of the money supply (and thus cause higher inflation rates) to avoid the crowding-out effect. Finally, the federal budget deficits have caused a heavy inflow of foreign funds, which means that real resources will have to be transferred to the foreign sector in the future.*

Despite these drawbacks, not all economists agree that deficits *should* be reduced, let alone *how* to reduce them. Some express hope that the economy will grow fast enough to eliminate the deficit. As the economy grows, so will income and therefore tax receipts. If the economy grows fast enough, the deficit will automatically be eliminated. This claim was made originally when the 1981 tax cut was passed, but its achievement appears unlikely in the foreseeable future.

Congress apparently agreed with those who believe that the deficit will not decrease without changes in fiscal policies. Passage of the Gramm–Rudman–Hollings bill in 1985 committed Congress (and the president) to reducing the deficit to zero by 1991. A key provision in the original legislation would have *automatically* cut spending as necessary to meet the targeted deficits. Although this provision was declared unconstitutional by the Supreme Court in 1986, Congress has continued to set deficit-reduction targets and work toward meeting them in their budget deliberations.

Some economists are skeptical of the Gramm–Rudman–Hollings law. They note that it fails to distinguish between actual budget deficits and a full-employment budget deficit. Thus it requires contractionary fiscal policies even if the economy is experiencing a contractionary gap—the type of change that makes the budget a destabilizing influence on the economy. The same economists also note that there is nothing necessarily magic about a balanced budget. After all, if the economy grows faster than the debt, the debt burden will decline. Other critics argue that the law is not really macroeconomic policy but a political attempt to reduce the overall size of the federal government.

Many economists, even those skeptical of Gramm–Rudman–Hollings, want to see the deficit reduced but realize that it is no easy task. We noted earlier that the current deficits are structural, that is, full-employment budget deficits. They will not be erased automatically by the elimination of a contractionary gap. To lower such deficits requires either higher taxes or less spending.

Tax increases traditionally meet strong political opposition, especially in election years. Other arguments against tax increases suggest that they have negative effects on work and investment incentives, reducing future growth in potential output. Cutting expenditures is also difficult politically. To some extent, those who favor spending cuts also favor reducing the size of government. Moreover, a large portion of the federal budget appears to be politically immune to spending cuts. Few politicians are willing to cut Social Security, national defense, or Medicare, which together represent over one-half the budget. Another significant portion— nearly 16 percent—is interest payments and veterans' benefits, which represent promised payments. In order to eliminate the budget deficit in 1986, the rest of the budget would have had to be cut by 70 percent. Clearly, there are both costs and benefits to reducing deficits.

---

*The inflow of foreign funds also causes the value of the U.S. dollar to rise. As we discuss in Chapter 33, when the U.S. dollar is stronger than other currencies, U.S. exports are less competitive on world markets, and foreign imports are more attractive to U.S. buyers. Thus U.S. goods and services are "crowded out" of foreign markets and foreign goods "crowd out" U.S. goods and services in the U.S. market.

CONCLUSION

In this chapter we explored both the theory and practice of macroeconomic policy. We showed how such policies could, in theory, be used to close both expansionary and contractionary gaps. But we also showed that discretionary policies have some theoretical and practical limitations and are hotly debated. Although the debate will likely continue, it does not hide the consensus among economists that macroeconomic policies play an important role in the economy.

In Chapters 28 and 29 we continue to discuss macroeconomic policies, looking more specifically at the problems of unemployment and inflation. As you study those chapters, you will see again the debates over the "correct" policy to help society reach its macroeconomic goals of full employment and price stability. A further analysis of the policy options is contained in Chapter 31.

SUMMARY

1. In this chapter we considered the role of government in the macroeconomy and the issues involved in government policies to counteract fluctuations of the business cycle.

2. Government interacts with the private sector, competing for goods, resources, and money. The government's budget balance is the difference between its receipts (taxes and fees) and expenditures (purchases, transfers, and interest paid on national debt). A positive balance is a budget surplus; a negative balance is a budget deficit. The cumulative result of deficits and surpluses over the years is the total national debt.

3. To finance spending, governments can tax and borrow, and the federal government can print money. In the United States, Congress and the president determine the federal government's fiscal policies while the Fed controls monetary policy. Each method of financing government spending has negative effects that must be weighed against the benefits of government spending.

4. Government fiscal and monetary policies are sometimes used to counteract fluctuations in the business cycle. Expansionary policies (more government spending or selling government bonds, for example) can close a contractionary gap. Contractionary policies (higher taxes or reserve requirements, for example) can close an expansionary gap. Another option is for the federal government to take no action, relying on the economy's automatic adjustment mechanism to restore equilibrium. Automatic adjustments may act more slowly than government policies. But contractionary policies tend to lower the price level, and expansionary policies tend to raise the price level while restoring equilibrium.

5. Changes in the budget balance may occur as a result of either discretionary fiscal policies or the actions of automatic stabilizers. The full-employment budget changes only when discretionary fiscal policies change.

6. Effects of discretionary fiscal policies may be limited by the crowding-out effect when the money supply is fixed. Increased government spending or lower taxes raises interest rates, crowding out private investment and consumption. The larger the crowding-out effect, the smaller will be the increase in aggregate demand from expansionary fiscal policies.

7. The new classical macroeconomists argue that anticipated policies are ineffective because rational individuals take offsetting actions. Recognizing that current increases in government borrowing mean higher future taxes, individuals increase saving, offsetting expansionary fiscal policy. Anticipated higher prices lead to decreased aggregate supply, offsetting expansionary monetary policy.

8. Problems confronting policy makers include the difficulty of obtaining accurate measures of economic variables and time lags. Recognition lags occur before problems are recognized. Action lags occur between problem recognition and policy implementation. Impact lags occur between implementation and full effects of a policy.

9. Nonactivists oppose the use of discretionary policies because of measurement problems, time lags, the crowding-out effect, rational expectations, and the political nature of such policy decisions. Instead, they propose that stable policies—constant rate of growth in the money supply and maintaining a balanced full-employment budget—and reliance on the automatic adjustment mechanism be used.

10. Activists view the economy as inherently unstable, that is, subject to unexpected changes in aggregate demand and/or supply. They also believe that the automatic adjustment mechanism closes contractionary gaps slowly. While most activists recognize the problems of developing and implementing effective policies, they remain convinced that discretionary policies are nec-

essary to prevent major GNP gaps and to push the economy in the right direction.

11. Many myths have sprung up regarding the national debt. The growth of the national debt is of concern only to the extent that it grows faster than national income, which it has in recent years. The debt is burdensome only to the extent that it is external (owed to foreigners) and does not fund enough new economic growth to pay the interest costs. The debt cannot bankrupt the nation because it requires payment in U.S. dollars, of which more could always be printed (but at the cost of inflation). Deficits occurring during recessions put little pressure on prices or on real interest rates.

12. Current deficits are large by historical standards and mostly represent deficits in the full-employment budget. They will not fall much even if the economy reaches potential GNP. Future growth should increase tax receipts (as income rises) and help reduce deficits, as long as spending does not also rise. Most economists, however, believe that it will take fiscal actions—either cuts in total spending or increases in taxes—to significantly reduce the deficits.

KEY TERMS

QUESTIONS FOR REVIEW AND DISCUSSION

1. In 1983 and 1984, the best monetary policy for the Fed to follow was subject to much debate. The economy was emerging from a rather severe recession and was growing somewhat. Inflation had dropped significantly but both nominal and real interest rates remained high. Some economists and politicians argued that if the Fed did not boost the rate of growth in the money supply, the recovery would be threatened. Others argued that the Fed should restrain the rate of growth in the money supply to prevent inflation from recurring. How would too little monetary growth threaten to bring on a recession? How would too much growth threaten to cause inflation? How can the Fed decide whether the monetary growth rate is too low or too high?

2. Consider the statement: "One of the difficulties with fiscal policy is the long action lag required for legislative agreement on tax and spending changes. This lag could be reduced significantly if the president were given the authority to change tax rates or spending on certain types of public works projects (highway and building construction, for example)." State whether this proposal would significantly improve the chances that discretionary fiscal policy could stabilize the economy. Explain. Are there other effects that should be considered?

3. In 1983 and 1984, important issues were the nominal rate of interest and the extremely large federal budget deficits projected through the 1980s. What are the possible connections between large budget deficits and nominal interest rates? Under what circumstances will budget deficits also affect real interest rates?

4. Explain how each of the following actions will affect investment. (*Note:* Most affect more than one factor that determines investment.)
   a) Contractionary monetary policy.
   b) An increase in the full-employment budget deficit.
   c) Contractionary monetary policy and expansionary fiscal policy at the same time.
   d) Expansionary monetary policy and contractionary fiscal policy at the same time.

5. In each of the following cases, indicate (a) the type of stabilization policy that activists would favor; and (b) the short-run effects of following the rules approach (constant growth of the money supply and a balanced full-employment budget).
   a) A decrease in velocity, that is, an increase in the quantity of money demanded at each level of nominal GNP.
   b) A drop in autonomous investment spending.

6. From mid-1980 to 1981, nominal interest rates on long-term financial claims (such as 10-year corporate bonds) rose by nearly 4 percent. Why did some economists suggest that an expansion in the money supply would be necessary to lower interest rates? Why did others suggest that a reduction in the growth rate of the money supply would be required? (*Hint:* Recall that nominal interest rates have both a real and an inflation premium component.)

7. Because federal deficits in the mid-1980s were largely full-employment deficits, economists generally believe that it will be necessary to increase taxes or reduce spending to significantly reduce deficits.
   a) Why would the deficits not be reduced by the economy's automatic adjustment mechanism?
   b) How will future economic growth affect the deficits, assuming no changes in spending? What are the effects of large deficits on future economic growth?
   c) What arguments could be used by those who believe that an increase in taxes is better than a decrease in spending. Be sure to note whether these arguments are normative or positive.
   d) What arguments could be used by those who believe that a decrease in spending is better than an increase in taxes. Be sure to note whether these arguments are normative or positive.
   e) Why would economists suggest that a significant reduction in budget deficits be accompanied by faster growth in the money supply (an expansionary monetary policy)?

8. As we noted in this chapter, if the federal government wants to spend more than it receives, it can borrow (sell bonds) or increase the money supply (print money).
   a) What happens to interest rates in either case? Why? (How does your answer depend on price-level expectations?)
   b) Which of the two ways will be more likely to lead to inflation? Why?
   c) Which of the two ways would be politically easier to implement?
   d) In the United States, the agency responsible for the money supply (the Fed) is independent. Is this independence good for the economy? Why or why not?

9. A number of costs are involved in financing a government budget deficit.
   a) How does the cost of a government budget deficit financed by borrowing depend on the strength of the crowding-out effect?
   b) What costs are involved if a government budget deficit is financed by increasing the money supply? (Contrast the effects during periods of relatively full employment and periods of recession.)
   c) What are the costs of eliminating government budget deficits by raising taxes? By reducing government spending? (Contrast the effects during periods of full employment and during periods of recession.)

Unemployment: Some Microeconomic Foundations

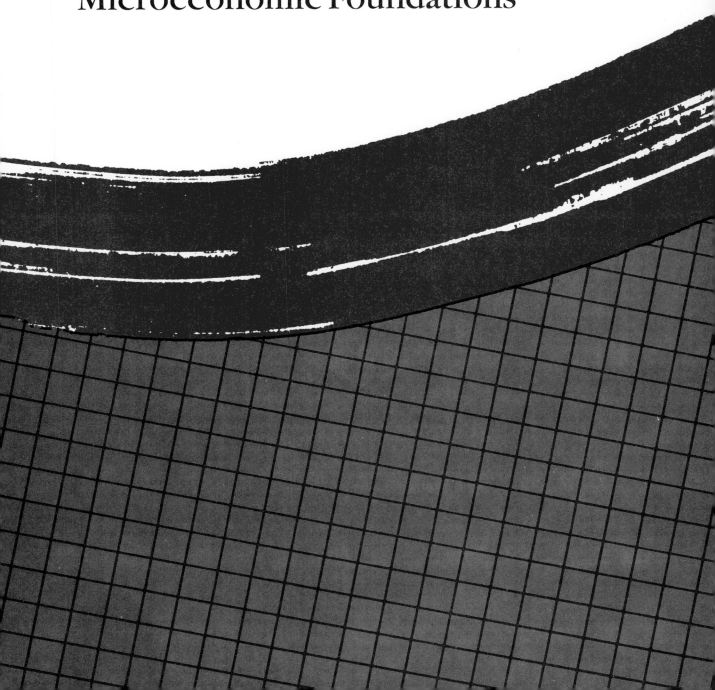

QUESTIONS TO CONSIDER

- [ ] How does the microeconomic view of unemployment differ from the macroeconomic view?
- [ ] Why does job-search theory hold that most unemployment is voluntary?
- [ ] Why does contracts theory hold that most unemployment is involuntary?
- [ ] What factors have caused the natural rate of unemployment to rise in recent years?
- [ ] How do various policy options to reduce unemployment differ?

Achieving full employment is an important economic goal. But economists do not agree on how it can best be accomplished. Will the economy quickly and smoothly adjust to contractionary gaps? Or will the adjustment be slow and costly in terms of unemployment? As you have already learned, these questions are at the heart of economic debates over the proper macroeconomic role for government. In large part the answers depend on the microeconomic behavior of labor markets. In this chapter we explore some of the microeconomic theories developed by economists to explain how labor markets operate. Using different theories, economists have arrived at conflicting conclusions about the speed of the economy's automatic adjustment mechanism.

In drawing these conclusions, economists had to compare actual unemployment rates with some standard. As we noted in Chapter 20, a common but controversial economic measure of unemployment is the natural rate of unemployment, that is, the rate that would exist if the economy were operating at its potential GNP level. But how high (or low) is the natural rate? In this chapter, we explore the microeconomic changes that economists generally believe have caused the natural rate to rise in recent years. Only then can we evaluate macroeconomic policies for lowering the natural rate of unemployment.

LABOR MARKETS: A CLOSER LOOK AT THE UNEMPLOYMENT RATE

Before considering theories about labor markets, however, we should examine the nature of employment and unemployment more closely. Labor-force statistics indicate that at the aggregate level the labor force is reasonably stable. For example, the overall unemployment rate generally changes little from month to month (a 0.2 percent change is often viewed as significant). However, a closer, microeconomic look indicates a great deal of instability. The labor-force status of millions of individuals changes every month. In this section, we explore this apparent instability in order to see the effect of unemployment on the macroeconomy and consider alternative policies to address unemployment.

Flows into and out of Labor Markets

Exhibit 28.1 shows that the labor-market status of a large number of individuals changes in an average month. These data—based on averages for the period 1968–1984—indicate that an average of 4.7 million individuals previously unemployed or out of the labor force found jobs each month. But 4.5 million who had been employed in the previous month became unemployed or dropped out of the labor force (flows 2 and 3). Overall, the flows had little effect on the unemployment rate. But with 8 percent of the population changing status in a typical month, the labor market is clearly dynamic. (In fact, if we count individuals who change jobs without experiencing unemployment, labor-market activity is even higher.) Unfortunately, economists do not fully understand these dynamics, especially flows into and out of the labor force. Thus economists interpret the data differently and suggest a variety of policies to reduce unemployment.

Most economists attribute at least part of the apparent instability to the difficulty in clearly distinguishing between the "unemployed" and those "not in the labor force." Statistics show that nearly one-half of those who withdraw from the labor force in any one month say that they want a job, although they are not actively looking for work. And many of those who withdraw from the labor force reenter it within less than three months. As a result, some economists believe that much of the measured unemployment is largely voluntary. This view suggests that government action to reduce unemployment is unnecessary and probably unworkable.

Exhibit 28.1
Labor-Market Flows, Monthly Averages for the Period 1968–1984
This diagram illustrates the large monthly flows between labor-force categories. In a typical month some 1.6 million individuals who were unemployed the previous month found jobs (flow 1), while another 1.3 million moved from jobs to unemployment (flow 2). A total of 3.1 million moved from being out of the labor force (flow 4) to jobs, while another 1.3 million unsuccessfully searched for work (flow 5). A total of 4.7 million left the labor force (flows 3 and 6). Because the flows in and out of each category are nearly balanced, there is not much monthly change in labor-force status. But beneath that apparent stability is considerable movement.

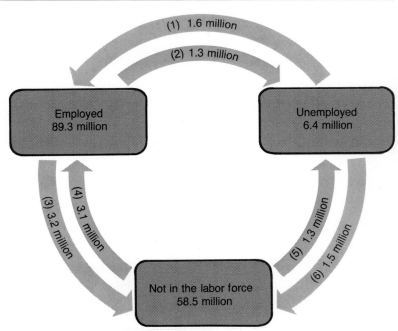

Source: Michael C. Keeley, "Cyclical Unemployment and Employment: Effects of Labor Force Entry and Exit," Federal Reserve Bank of San Francisco, *Economic Review, Number 3,* Summer 1984, p. 10.

Reason	Percentage of the unemployed			Percentage of the total labor force		
	1978 (low unem- ployment)	1983 (high unem- ployment)	1986	1978 (low unem- ployment)	1983 (high unem- ployment)	1986
Job losers	41.7	58.4	49.0	2.5	5.6	3.4
Job leavers	14.1	7.7	12.3	0.9	0.7	0.9
Reentrants	29.9	22.5	26.2	1.8	2.2	1.8
New entrants	14.3	11.4	12.5	0.9	1.1	0.9
Total	100.0	100.0	100.0	6.1	9.6	7.0

**Exhibit 28.2
Unemployment by Reason:
1978, 1983, and 1986**

Source: Employment Report of the President, 1987 (Table B-33).

Other economists believe that the official unemployment rate understates the full extent of unemployment. They note that the official statistics do not include discouraged workers: those who have quit looking for work because they do not believe they can find jobs. This view suggests that government action may be desirable. We cannot hope to resolve this dispute. But the competing theories of unemployment that we discuss later in this chapter partially reflect these different interpretations of the data.

Reasons for Leaving and Entering Labor Markets

Exhibit 28.2 shows some of the reasons why individuals are unemployed. To indicate how important these reasons are across the business cycle, we show data for two years. In 1978 the unemployment rate was 6.1 percent, a figure that some believe was close to the natural rate of unemployment at the time. In 1983 the unemployment rate was 9.6 percent, well above any estimate of the natural rate. Individuals who leave their jobs voluntarily represent a relatively small portion of both the unemployed and the labor force. Even in 1978 when there was little unemployment, such individuals accounted for only 14 percent of the unemployed. Individuals who have lost their jobs make up both the largest portion of the unemployed and the bulk of the cyclically unemployed. Such individuals account for over 80 percent of the increase in unemployment between 1978 and 1983.

In addition, there appears to be a core of unemployed workers in each category in both the best and worst economic circumstances. In the good times of 1978, some 2.5 percent of the labor force still lost a job. In the bad times of 1983, some 3.3 percent were able to enter or reenter the labor force. Many economists suggest that core unemployment reflects frictional unemployment. Others believe that it also includes structural unemployment. And most economists associate core unemployment with the natural rate of unemployment, or the level of unemployment when the economy is producing at its potential GNP level. Thus understanding changes in core unemployment is important to understanding changes in the natural rate of unemployment.

Exhibit 28.2 also shows data for 1986. (You can obtain more recent data from two government publications, the *Monthly Labor Review* or *Employment and Earnings*, if you want to update the table and make your own analysis.) What do these data suggest about the economy? Do the numbers look more like 1978 (a year of low unemployment) or 1983 (a year of high unemployment)? The data reflect the economic recovery that was well under way in 1986. The overall unemployment rate was lower than in 1983, and the relative size of the most cyclically sensitive portion—those who had lost jobs—had fallen. However, that proportion (almost 50 percent) is somewhat higher than it was in 1978. In addition, those who had lost jobs made up a higher proportion of the labor force: 3.4 percent as opposed to 2.5 percent. This analysis is not conclusive, but it does suggest that unemployment in 1986 was somewhat above the natural rate.

Duration of Unemployment

As we noted earlier, one of our main objectives is to understand how quickly and easily the automatic adjustment mechanism operates. In addition, we are concerned with whether the burden of adjusting to equilibrium is widely shared or falls on only a relatively few people. Data on the duration of unemployment are therefore of considerable interest to policy makers. Relatively short-term unemployment is perhaps an acceptable cost for a dynamic economy, especially if this cost is widely shared. But long-term unemployment involves greater personal costs which some economists and politicians believe should be treated with government policies.

Data such as those in Exhibit 28.3 are often used to support the contention that most unemployment is short term and that society should rely on the economy's automatic adjustment mechanism. In 1978 (a relatively good year) nearly one-half the unemployed had been looking for work for 5 weeks or less and less than one-fourth for as long as 15 weeks. Even during the relatively bad year of 1983, one-third of the unemployed had been looking for work for less than five weeks. In fact, on average, 60 percent of the unemployed are out of work for less than one month. Comparing 1983 to 1978, you can see that the long-term unem-

Exhibit 28.3
Unemployment by Duration: 1978, 1983, and 1986

Weeks unemployed	Percentage of the unemployed			Percentage of the total labor force		
	1978 (low unemployment)	1983 (high unemployment)	1986	1978 (low unemployment)	1983 (high unemployment)	1986
Less than 5	46.2	33.3	41.9	2.8	3.2	2.9
5–14	31.0	27.4	31.0	1.9	2.6	2.2
15–26	12.4	15.4	12.7	0.8	1.5	0.9
More than 26	10.4	23.9	14.4	0.6	2.3	1.0
Total	100.0	100.0	100.0	6.1	9.6	7.0

Source: Employment Report of the President, 1987 (Table B-33).

	Percentage of total weeks of unemployment for individuals	
Duration of unemployment	1974	1975
Less than 2 months	31	25
2–3 months	35	30
4–5 months	16	18
6 months or more	18	27
Total	100	100
Aggregate unemployment rate	5.6	8.5

**Exhibit 28.4
Distribution of Total Weeks of
Unemployment: 1974–1975**

Source: Kim B. Clark and Lawrence H. Summers, "Labor Market Dynamics and Unemployment: A Reconsideration," *Brookings Papers on Economic Activity,* 1979:1, Table 1, p. 19.

ployed (26 weeks or more) represent more than twice as large a proportion of the total unemployed when overall unemployment is high. But long-term unemployment accounts for only one-half of the increase in the unemployment rate; a larger percentage of the labor force experiences unemployment in all categories. As we found earlier, 1986 resembles a period of low unemployment, although long-term unemployment was a more serious problem in 1986 than in 1978.

These data suggest that most individuals experience unemployment for only a short period of time. But in some respects the data may be misleading. First, they do not indicate how unemployment for individuals ends. In fact, about one-half of all unemployment ends when an individual withdraws from the labor force. But we noted earlier that many of those who have withdrawn from the labor force (according to the official statistics) still want work and eventually return to work. Thus official statistics may understate the average length of unemployment. In fact, some studies suggest that long-term structural unemployment is the most important aspect of unemployment.

Exhibit 28.4 shows the distribution of those unemployed by total weeks of unemployment based on a study by Clark and Summers.* In these data, individuals who have been unemployed longer (two months or more) are given greater weight in the distribution. The result is very different from that shown in Exhibit 28.3, which emphasized short-term unemployment. The long-term unemployed appear to account for a significant portion of the total weeks of unemployment. In 1974, a year of relatively low unemployment, short-term unemployment (durations of less than two months) accounted for only one-third of all unemployment. Long-term unemployment (durations of four months or longer) accounted for more than one-third of the total. During a recession, such as in 1975, long-term unemployment increases; about 45 percent of all unemployment was long term.

Clark and Summers also demonstrate the significance of long-term unemployment in another way. They estimate that the 1974 unemployment rate would have fallen from 6.0 to 5.75 percent if short-term unemployment (five weeks or

---

*Kim B. Clark and Lawrence H. Summers, "Labor Market Dynamics and Unemployment: A Reconsideration," *Brookings Papers on Economic Activity*, Vol. 1, 1979, p. 16.

less) had been eliminated. However, eliminating long-term unemployment (six months or longer) would have reduced the rate from 6.0 to 3.5 percent.

What can we conclude from this discussion? First, most unemployed individuals experience only a short period of unemployment. Second, the long-term unemployed account for a significant portion of total weeks of unemployment. Third, much of any cyclical rise in unemployment represents an increase in individuals who have lost their jobs and an increase in long spells of unemployment. Fourth, even in the best of times the labor force is much more dynamic than overall unemployment statistics indicate. But what accounts for these facts? How do economists explain labor-market behavior? In the next section we take a close look at two theories that attempt to explain unemployment.

EXPLAINING UNEMPLOYMENT: JOB-SEARCH AND CONTRACTS THEORIES

The overall unemployment rate and dynamics of the labor market reflect, in part, the choices of individuals. For this reason, economists use theories based on microeconomic principles to try to understand and explain the labor market. The two theories we discuss here—the job-search and contracts theories—offer explanations for cyclical changes in unemployment and predictions about the speed of the economy's automatic adjustment mechanism.

Job-Search Theory and Unemployment

The **job-search theory** is an application of the principles of rational choice to unemployment. Unemployed individuals are considered to be engaged in a search for a job that matches what they expect (and want) to find. How long individuals remain unemployed depends on their preferences, expectations about wages and other job characteristics, and overall labor market conditions. Individuals have different skills and job preferences. Some seek part-time or temporary work; others want career jobs. Some have specialized skills; others have very general skills. Some have unrealistic expectations about jobs for which they are qualified. Available jobs offer different wages and other working conditions. To find a match between preferences and jobs, individuals must engage in job search.

Job-search theory identifies both the benefits and the costs of searching for a job. Initially, the major benefit is that you will learn more about available jobs, wages, and working conditions. When you have received a job offer, however, the benefits of continuing your job search depend on the probability of finding another job with higher pay or better working conditions. Likewise, initially the costs of conducting a job search are those connected with search activities. For example, you must scour the newspapers and other ads, call for appointments, travel to interviews, and face the frustration of being rejected. When you have received a job offer, however, the costs of continuing your job search include the opportunity cost of rejecting income that you could have earned by accepting the offer. Following the principles of rational choice, individuals will continue to search for a job (remain unemployed) as long as the expected extra benefits outweigh the extra costs.

Job-search theory. A view of unemployment as a search for information. Unemployed individuals make rational choices, weighing extra benefits of a continued job search (the prospects of finding a better job) against extra costs (accepting a lower paying job).

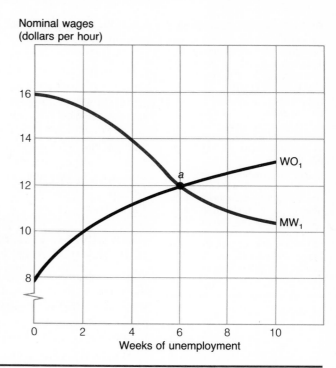

Exhibit 28.5
Job Search and the Duration of Unemployment
The minimum acceptable wage (MW_1) for Anita Braique,
a typical unemployed worker, will decline as she gathers
information about potential jobs and as the cost of continuing to look for a job increases. She encounters
higher and higher job offers, as shown by the wage offer curve (WO_1). The curve shows the rising opportunity
cost of rejecting offers to keep searching for a better
job. Anita will stop searching when she encounters a job
that pays the minimum wage that she is willing to accept. In this case her job search can be expected to last
6 weeks (point a).

Individuals begin their job search with some preconceived notion of how
much they are worth. They know the types of jobs they like, and they have a
perception of current and future prices. These expectations establish the individual's minimal acceptable standards for a job and a nominal wage. Exhibit 28.5
illustrates the job-search process. It shows how the minimally acceptable nominal
wage, MW_1—also called the reservation wage—varies with length of job search
for Anita Braique, an average unemployed individual. If Anita finds a job offering
that wage, she will take the job. (Note that although other aspects of jobs are
certainly important to the employment decision, we use the wage to represent all
benefits. This simplification does not detract from the basic point of the analysis.)
The MW_1 curve slopes downward, indicating that Anita will eventually recognize
the market wage that she can reasonably expect and will, accordingly, revise any
unrealistic expectations.

Exhibit 28.5 also shows the wage offer (WO_1) curve, which indicates the best
offer Anita has received up to that time. Note that this curve slopes upward because
the longer her search continues, the greater is Anita's chance of being offered a
higher wage. At some point, however, Anita's expectations and the reality of labor
market conditions will be the same, and she will take a job. This occurs when
Anita has been unemployed 6 weeks and receives a job offer at $12 per hour
(point a, where WO_1 intersects MW_1). If Anita is a typical unemployed person,
and if these curves represent the normal functioning of the economy, six weeks
of unemployment is associated with the natural rate of unemployment and with
potential GNP. However, any factor that temporarily raises the minimally acceptable
nominal wage (such as anticipation of an increase in prices) will lengthen the
unemployment period. So will any factor that lowers wage offers (such as a drop
in aggregate demand).

Job-search theory and reduced aggregate demand. To understand this last connection, you must know how job-search theory predicts the economy's reaction to a contractionary gap caused by decreased aggregate demand. Job-search theory recognizes that employers respond to a decrease in aggregate demand by lowering product prices and offering correspondingly lower nominal wages. As shown in Exhibit 28.6(a) and (b), the decline in aggregate demand results in a new, lower nominal wage offer curve (WO_2). Unless unemployed workers recognize that product prices are also falling, they will not immediately change their minimally acceptable nominal wage curve (MW_1). Since labor then will be relatively more expensive, employers will reduce the number of workers they hire, increasing unemployment.

In Exhibit 28.6(a), the duration of unemployment rises from six to eight weeks (point *b*, where MW_1 intersects WO_2). This higher level of unemployment is partly normal, or frictional (the six weeks), and partly cyclical (the extra two weeks). The increase in unemployment is also associated with the opening of the contractionary gap in Exhibit 28.6(b). Aggregate output falls and unemployment rises as the economy moves along the initial short-run aggregate supply curve (AS_1) to point *b*. Job-search theory associates this *temporary* rise in unemployment with cyclical unemployment resulting from misperceptions about current and future prices. But as we discussed in Chapter 26, information about actual prices and forecasts of future prices should quickly correct misperceptions and expectations.

As workers revise their expectations to meet reality, the minimally acceptable nominal wage curve falls (to MW_2). Workers accept lower nominal wage offers, recognizing that real income is not affected, since prices have fallen. This downward adjustment in nominal wages causes the short-run aggregate supply curve to increase (to AS_2). This automatic adjustment returns the economy to full employment. The normal job-search process for the individual shown in Exhibit 28.6(a) will again result in six weeks of unemployment (point *c*, where WO_2 intersects MW_2). At that point, the economy again produces at its potential GNP ($2000 billion) and unemployment is again at the natural rate.

By tying search behavior to expectations, job-search theory suggests that cyclical unemployment is only a temporary concern. The automatic adjustment mechanism requires only a revision of expectations about future prices in order to restore equilibrium in the labor market. Because the economy's response to cyclical changes is not instantaneous, some unemployment will result. But if expectations are quickly revised (and the theory assumes that they can be), full employment can be quickly restored.

Job-search theory and characteristics of unemployment. Job-search theory considers unemployment to be the outcome of a rational choice, a weighing by the individual of the benefits and costs of continuing to look for a job. As you have just seen, the theory is consistent with one of the facts about unemployment: For most people unemployment lasts only a short period of time.

The theory also provides a reason why new labor force entrants and reentrants experience higher-than-average unemployment. These individuals are less likely to have much information about what jobs are available. They are also more likely to have incorrect and overly optimistic wage demands. Thus they will end up spending more time trying to find a match between what they feel they are worth and what they are offered in the labor market.

Exhibit 28.6
Job Search: Response to Decreased Aggregate Demand
Initially, Anita Braique will be unemployed for 6 weeks (point a, where WO_1 and MW_1 intersect). We associate this with the natural rate of unemployment and with potential GNP in part (b). If aggregate demand decreases (to AD_2) in part (b), nominal wage offers also decrease (to WO_2) in part (a). The increase in Anita's unemployment period (to 8 weeks, point b) corresponds to the contractionary gap in part (b). As Anita's expectations adjust to the falling price level, her minimum acceptable wage offer decreases (to WO_2), a change reflected in the increase in aggregate supply (to AS_2) in part (b). These adjustments return unemployment to the natural rate and real output to its potential GNP level (point c in both graphs).

(a)

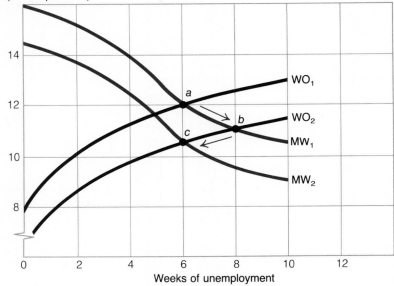

(b)

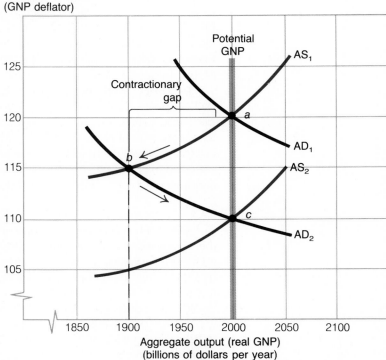

RECAP

Job-search theory views the un-employed as individuals who are gathering information. Unemploy-ment is a rational choice of indi-viduals, who compare the bene-fits of continuing to look for a job (the prospects of finding a better job) to the opportunity costs (re-jecting a current job offer or leav-ing the labor force).

According to job-search theory, a decline in aggregate demand may lead to a temporary rise in unemployment. Individuals may not adjust their wage demands quickly because of inaccurate in-formation or incorrect expecta-tions. When good information is available, however, unemploy-ment should return to the natural rate.

In general, job-search theory offers a plausible explanation for normal fric-tional unemployment. But a complete theory must also provide some explanation for long-term unemployment. As we noted earlier in this chapter, a significant number of individuals remain unemployed for long periods of time even when the economy is booming. However, because it treats unemployment as a rational choice, job-search theory explains long-term unemployment only as a voluntary decision to keep rejecting suitable job offers. Some economists reject this expla-nation and believe that job-search theory, while useful for some purposes, is not a complete theory of labor-market behavior. Moreover, some reject the notion that expectations are the major explanation for temporary unemployment and the cyclical rise in unemployment during recessions. Their alternative, contracts the-ory, is based on the existence of labor contracts.

Contracts Theory and Unemployment

Whereas job-search theory focuses on the relatively short-term unemployment of most individuals, **contracts theory** explains the relative stability of employment for much of the labor force. Proponents of contracts theory divide labor markets into *career* and *casual* markets. In career labor markets, workers and their em-ployers seek a relatively long-lasting employment relationship. This type of rela-tionship describes employment of faculty in colleges and universities, as well as supervisors and production workers in most manufacturing facilities. In casual labor markets, neither employers nor workers necessarily expect the employment relationship to last. Examples of casual labor markets include summer jobs for students.

Career labor markets. Career labor markets are most often characterized by jobs that require highly specialized skills and/or training and education. Because of the difficulty of finding and training suitable workers, employers may be willing to pay a premium to current employees to retain their skills. By offering a long-term relationship, the employer can avoid some of the costs of recruiting, screen-ing, and training new employees. In return, workers in career labor markets receive the benefits of greater job security and opportunities for advancement.

To stabilize employment in career labor markets, employers and employees enter into *contracts* that define their relationships. In unionized organizations, these contracts are usually formal and explicit. Many of the rules covering working conditions are written down and result from formal bargaining between manage-ment and union representatives. Written contracts are not very common in non-union organizations, but informal and implicit contracts are widespread and no less important. Whatever their form, contracts usually restrict managerial options. For example, employers typically agree to promote present workers rather than hire new workers to fill jobs.

Contracts theory. A view of em-ployment based on the existence of explicit or implicit contracts de-fining worker–employer relation-ships. Contracts provide long-term benefits to both workers and em-ployers but fix nominal wages, slowing short-run adjustments in wages.

Career labor markets and reduced aggregate demand. If a decline in aggregate demand reduces demand for a firm's product, an employer may want to lower prices by cutting costs, including employee wages. But contracts typically require employers to maintain nominal wages, at least in the short run. Therefore employers in career labor markets are more likely to lay off some employees temporarily, while maintaining the current nominal wage for those who remain.

Union contracts usually require that those laid off must first be rehired before new employees can be hired. Thus layoffs protect the firm from losing its most experienced and trained workers and give laid-off workers a valuable right to be rehired. Such contract terms not only protect the employer from the greater costs of replacing skilled, experienced workers but also provide workers with a measure of job security. However, the firm is prevented from taking advantage of the increase in aggregate unemployment to hire lower priced workers, at least in the short run. Contracts are not necessarily ideal for either employers or workers, but they represent a compromise between the interests of each and between short-run and long-run considerations. Contracts trade higher short-run costs (higher product costs and more unemployment) for better long-run results (less turnover and greater job security).

Although these aspects of the career labor market benefit both workers and employers, they also slow down the economy's adjustment to a decline in aggregate demand. Because contracts do not allow nominal wages to adjust quickly, the short-run aggregate supply curve will not shift until current contracts expire and can be renegotiated. Eventually, however, new contracts will be written, adjusting wages as necessary to return the economy to full employment. But depending on contract lengths, the adjustment process may be slow.

Contracts theory does not rely on incorrect perceptions about real wages or faulty expectations about future prices by workers to explain the slow response of the automatic adjustment mechanism. Expectations influence the wages that are set when contracts are negotiated. The response to changes in aggregate demand is delayed because nominal wages paid under contracts do not change frequently—and usually not at all in response to temporary changes in demand.

Casual labor markets.   In contrast to those in career labor markets, jobs in casual labor markets require little or no skill. Employers thus have low costs for and little difficulty in hiring new workers. Accordingly, they have little incentive to enter into long-term contracts with workers. Most jobs in casual labor markets offer low pay, poor working conditions, and little job security. The dead-end nature of such jobs also contributes to relatively high turnover. Unemployment for workers is usually short-term, but occurs frequently. As a result, average unemployment rates are higher than average.

Supporters of job-search theory argue that these effects reflect individual preferences (not to obtain more education, for example) and that high turnover contributes to economic efficiency. But advocates of contracts theory see low wages and other unpleasant characteristics of casual labor markets as evidence of structural problems. Employers in career labor markets will incur the costs of hiring and training only for individuals they feel are suitable for a long-term employment relationship. Individuals who lack basic skills and the desire to make a long-term commitment, will be judged unqualified and therefore not suitable for the career labor market.

Some workers may prefer casual markets. But contracts theory argues that other workers are stuck in casual labor markets because they lack—and cannot obtain—the skills required for jobs in career labor markets. The unemployment of such workers is structural, resulting from a mismatch between their skills and the demands of employers in career labor markets. This type of structural unemployment is included in the natural rate of unemployment along with the more "natural" frictional unemployment.

Job-Search and Contracts Theories Compared

Both the job-search and contracts theories offer interesting and helpful views of the operation of labor markets. For example, job-search theory argues that most unemployed workers could find work if they lowered their wage demands to realistic levels. Their refusal to accept offered wages is viewed as a voluntary, rational choice. However, the theory also recognizes that some cyclical unemployment may result from misperceptions of real wages, which is a short-term problem. In either case, it is the failure of real wages to adjust that causes unemployment.

In contrast, contracts theory views much unemployment as involuntary. Because contracts force employers in career labor markets to stop hiring when aggregate demand drops, even those willing to work for less cannot get jobs in those markets. For this reason, proponents of contracts theory suggest that cyclical unemployment may be more accurately viewed as inadequate aggregate demand. Moreover, workers in casual labor markets suffer high unemployment because the jobs offer few incentives for stable work, not because workers are unwilling to work for lower wages. And structural problems prevent many such workers from finding jobs in career labor markets.

These differences between the job-search and contracts theories lead to different attitudes toward unemployment policy. Proponents of job-search theory tend to oppose government attempts to reduce unemployment. They argue that the automatic adjustment mechanism can work both smoothly and quickly if inflationary expectations do not interfere. In contrast, supporters of contracts theory often advocate government policies to reduce unemployment. They believe the automatic adjustments as slow and more unemployment as involuntary. As you will see in Chapter 29, these contrasting theories also lead to different recommendations for policies to fight inflation.

In an important sense, however, neither theory alone offers a complete explanation for unemployment. Neither explains the existence of long-term unemployment very well. And neither provides a convincing explanation of the large-scale monthly fluctuations in the labor market.

On the other hand, both theories add to our understanding of the labor market. Most economists recognize that short-term unemployment responds to the factors included in job-search theory. Policies that lower the cost of looking for a job (such as unemployment compensation) can add to unemployment. Policies that improve information about jobs and reasonable wage offers can lower unemployment. Moreover, job-search theory can help us explore some of the factors responsible for the rise in the natural rate of unemployment. In contrast, contracts theory offers a rationale for some past labor-market behavior—especially the short-term response of unemployment to decreases in aggregate demand. It offers one explanation for why labor markets may fail to adjust quickly, even when information about future prices and government policies is available.

RECAP

According to contracts theory, workers and employers in career labor markets seek a long-term employment relationship. They agree to operate under long-term (formal or informal) contracts, which provide job security for senior employees and lower turnover costs for employers.

Contracts require employers to respond to declining demand by laying off workers, maintaining nominal wage rates, and not hiring new workers. Because nominal wages fall slowly, the economy's automatic adjustment mechanism will operate slowly. According to contracts theory, contract provisions and lack of skills may keep some workers from leaving casual labor markets and finding jobs in career labor markets.

Because job-search theory views most unemployment as short run and voluntary, its supporters oppose government attempts to reduce unemployment. Because contracts theory views unemployment as long run and involuntary, its supporters advocate government attempts to reduce unemployment.

INCREASES IN THE NATURAL RATE OF UNEMPLOYMENT

At the beginning of this chapter we noted that economists generally agree that the natural rate of unemployment has increased during the last 20 years. In this section, we examine the evidence and explanations for this belief. We also discuss some of the policies proposed to reduce the natural rate of unemployment.

Unemployment: Official and Natural Rates

Exhibit 28.7 shows the official unemployment rate and one estimate of the natural unemployment rate for the 1955–1986 period. Note that the official rate has increased in recessions and decreased during recoveries. At the same time, the unemployment rate associated with peaks in the business cycle has increased. In the early 1960s, economists associated this upward drift with a growing GNP gap (shown by the gap between the actual and natural rates of unemployment). But the 1970s were a period of high inflation. If the GNP gap had been growing, there should have been downward, not upward, pressure on prices. (The fact that some of the price-level increases reflect supply shocks complicates the picture.)

Most economists now believe that some part of the increase in official unemployment rates during peaks in the business cycle represents a rise in the

---

Exhibit 28.7
Actual and Natural Rates of Unemployment: 1955–1986
This graph shows both the actual rate of unemployment and one estimate of the natural rate of unemployment. The actual rate rises and falls with the business cycle but also shows an upward trend. (Note that the peaks of the actual unemployment rate coincide with troughs in the business cycle—that is, with recessionary periods shown by the red bands.) The natural rate shows an upward trend, which is associated with demographic changes in the labor market, government programs, structural changes in industrial demand, and international competition.

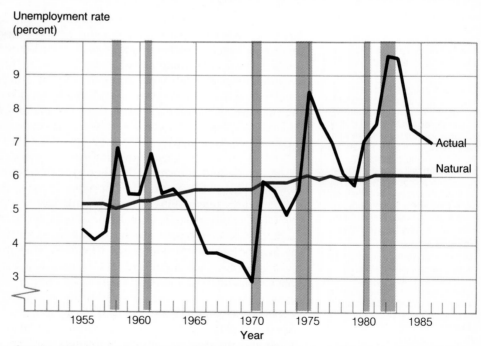

Sources: Actual unemployment rates from *Economic Report of the President, 1987,* Table B-31. Natural rate of unemployment from Robert J. Gordon, *Macroeconomics,* 4th Ed., Table A-1. Copyright © 1987 by Robert J. Gordon. Reprinted by permission of Little, Brown.

natural rate of unemployment. This conclusion is shown in Exhibit 28.7 as the upward-sloping natural rate line. This estimate of the natural rate increases from 5.0 in 1955 to 6.0 percent in 1986. As we have noted before, the natural rate cannot be observed, only estimated. Other estimates of the natural unemployment rate in the early 1980s range from 5 percent to 7 percent.

Factors that Increase the Natural Rate of Unemployment

Whatever the current natural rate of unemployment is, economists generally agree that it did increase in the 1960s and 1970s. Why did it rise? The reasons most often given are demographic changes in the labor force and the use of certain public policies.

Demographic changes. Earlier in this chapter, we showed how job-search theory explains unemployment among workers just entering or reentering the labor market. We noted that such individuals may be unemployed longer because they have unrealistic expectations about available jobs, wages, and working conditions. Thus if new entrants and reentrants become a more important part of the labor force, the natural rate of unemployment will rise.

Two demographic changes increased the proportion of entrants and reentrants in the 1960s and 1970s. First, young workers (below the age of 25) became a larger percentage of the labor force in the 1970s. Since this group contained more than the average proportion of new entrants, this change increased the natural unemployment rate. In addition, many of these young workers sought work in the casual labor market, especially while still in school. (Summer jobs, such as flipping burgers or cleaning up parks are part of the casual labor market.) Casual labor markets, as we have noted, have higher job turnover and more unemployment than career labor markets.

A second demographic change was the increasing proportion of women in the labor force. Statistically, women are more likely to be reentrants or new entrants. Thus their average unemployment rate will be higher than that of men. In addition, married women with a working husband can be more selective about jobs. On average therefore they may spend a longer time looking for a job. To some extent, these factors may become less important over time, since women are increasingly entering the career labor market, seeking the same opportunities as men.

These demographic trends help explain the rise in the natural rate in the 1960s and 1970s. But, as we noted in Chapter 6, those historical trends have largely ended. Teenagers have represented a declining proportion of the labor force since the mid-1970s, a trend expected to continue in the future. And while projections show that the percentage of women in the labor force will continue to increase, future changes will be much smaller than past changes.

Government policies. In addition to demographic changes, economists note that several government policies may have contributed to the rise in the natural unemployment rate. An often cited example is the unemployment compensation program, which provides cash payments to workers who have been laid off or whose jobs have been eliminated. (Note that it is not available to new entrants.) In 1986, government payments for unemployment compensation totaled $14.5 billion.

Most economists recognize three impacts of unemployment compensation on frictional unemployment and hence on the natural rate. First, unemployment payments lower the cost of looking for a job. Thus we can anticipate longer searches, more frictional unemployment, and a higher natural rate. Second, unemployment benefits reduce the costs of layoffs. Thus unions often press for contracts that specify layoffs, rather than nominal wage reductions, as the employers' response to temporary decreases in demand. Finally, the level of benefits provided and the number of the unemployed who were eligible increased during the 1960s and 1970s.

Other economists believe that periodic increases in the minimum wage law have increased the natural rate of unemployment in two ways. First, it has encouraged new entrance into the labor-force. At the same time, it has lowered the number of job openings. Some economists also blame increasing welfare benefits. But in the early and mid-1980s, real benefits (adjusted for price-level rises) fell and some eligibility requirements were stiffened. If these programs did add to the natural rate in the past, they no longer do.

Structural changes and international competition. Structural shifts from manufacturing to services and increased international competition have also been blamed for a rising natural rate of unemployment. These structural shifts have been quite large: Between 1980 and 1986, manufacturing industries lost some 800,000 jobs, while service industries gained some 4 million jobs. Many manufacturing industries resemble the career labor market with steady employment and low job turnover. But many service industries resemble the casual labor market with high rates of job turnover and many part-time or temporary jobs. Thus this shift from manufacturing to service employment may have increased the amount of frictional unemployment, adding to the natural rate.

In addition, international competition, along with the reluctance of workers to accept lower real wages, undoubtedly contributed to the loss of U.S. manufacturing jobs. A number of large plants have closed, eliminating thousands of jobs in local labor markets. Competition may also have caused U.S. firms to change some of the contract rules that formerly provided stable long-term jobs. Thus the major adjustments required of many workers—geographical and occupational mobility and accepting lower real wages—may lead to longer periods of unemployment. Whatever the long-run implications, international competition has probably raised both frictional and structural unemployment and, consequently, the natural rate of unemployment.

Policies to Lower the Natural Rate of Unemployment

As you might expect, economists are divided over whether government policies can—or should—be used to reduce the natural rate of unemployment. Because the natural rate is not likely to be affected by aggregate demand, attempts to lower it have usually involved microeconomic rather than macroeconomic policies. Such policies attempt to reduce the length of the typical job search or to better match the skills of the unemployed with the skills that employers want. In these ways, some economists and politicians hope to lower both the frictional and structural unemployment that are part of the natural rate.

Employment assistance and job training programs. We noted earlier that many women and young people who are first entering or reentering the job market may experience unemployment because they lack accurate information about wages. We also pointed out that some individuals in casual labor markets (including many young workers) usually lack the skills necessary to enter career markets. To the extent that the natural rate of unemployment results from imperfect information or a lack of skills, employment assistance and job training programs may lower the rate. Some information about available jobs, wages, and similar characteristics has been provided for many years through state-run, federally supported employment services. But existing programs have been of only limited help to the unemployed. Many employers inform the state services of openings for only the lowest paying, lowest skilled jobs.

Structural unemployment is the target of job training programs. Modest, federally funded programs were started in the early 1960s. Overall, they succeeded in increasing the skills and job potential of the individuals enrolled. However, they apparently had no effect on the natural rate of unemployment. Many of these programs were cut from the federal budget by the Reagan administration. Some economists argue that the programs failed to provide realistic training and significant job skills. Others suggest that the effort failed because of the modest scale of the programs. It is also possible that job training changed the distribution, but not the level, of unemployment.

Reforming the unemployment insurance program. Because the unemployment compensation program may have contributed to the rise in the natural rate of unemployment, some economists suggest altering this program. They advocate reducing benefits, requiring those eligible for benefits to look harder for jobs, and eliminating payments for those who refuse job offers. These reforms are aimed at increasing efficiency in the economy.

But such efforts are opposed by those who are concerned with equity. Supporters of current programs point out that unemployment compensation may lessen workers' demands for long-term contracts which provide job security. Thus the unemployment program allows producers to respond to shifts in product demand, improving efficiency. Moreover, they argue that by providing time for job searches, the program may allow workers to find more suitable jobs. Workers forced to accept low-wage jobs may soon be unemployed again.

Like all other economic policies, efforts to reduce the natural rate of unemployment require careful consideration of benefits and costs. Because benefits and costs are difficult to measure (especially benefits associated with equity), rational disagreement is inevitable. Moreover, it should be clear from the brief discussion of the causes and possible policies that it is not easy to lower the natural rate of unemployment.

CONCLUSION

In this chapter we explored the nature of unemployment and two theories—the job-search and contracts theories—that economists have developed to help them understand and predict changes in unemployment. While neither theory provides a complete description of unemployment, each offers a view of at least part of the problem. Because their explanations differ, however, economists reach different conclusions about the speed of the automatic adjustment mechanism.

In addition, we noted that while economists generally accept the notion of a natural rate of unemployment, they disagree about appropriate policies to reduce unemployment to this level. Most agree that changes in aggregate demand will affect the actual rate of unemployment in the short run. But aggregate demand policies cannot successfully maintain unemployment below the natural rate over the long run. The effect of attempting to do so, as we discuss in Chapter 29, is inflation.

SUMMARY

1. In this chapter we examined some of the microeconomic foundations of labor markets and their implications for the macroeconomic problem of unemployment.

2. Although the aggregate unemployment rate usually changes slowly, a significant number of people change their labor-force status every month. The largest proportion of the unemployed—those who have lost jobs—are the most cyclically sensitive unemployed. Most unemployment lasts a month or less, but the long-term unemployed account for a significant proportion of total unemployment.

3. Job-search theory views unemployment as a rational choice of individuals, who compare the benefits of continuing to look for a job (the prospects of finding a better job) to the opportunity costs (rejecting a current job offer or leaving the labor force). A decline in aggregate demand may temporarily increase unemployment until individuals can adjust their wage demands to reflect more accurate information and expectations. According to job-search theory, high unemployment rates among teenagers and women reflect the fact that many are new entrants and reentrants who may have unrealistic ideas about wages and working conditions.

4. According to the contracts theory, workers and employers in career labor markets seek a long-term employment relationship and agree to operate under long-term (formal or informal) contracts. Contracts provide job security for senior employees and lower turnover costs for employers. But they require employers to respond to declining demand by laying off workers, maintaining nominal wage rates, and not hiring new workers. Since nominal wages are slow to fall, the economy's automatic adjustment mechanism will operate slowly.

5. Supporters of job-search theory view most unemployment as short run and voluntary; they reject the use of government policies to reduce unemployment. Proponents of contracts theory view a significant part of unemployment as long run and involuntary; they support government attempts to reduce unemployment.

6. Economists generally agree that the natural rate of unemployment has increased in the last 25 years. Demographic factors—the increased proportion of young workers and women—have raised the proportion of unemployed in the new entrant and reentrant categories. In addition, the natural unemployment rate may have been raised by some government programs—such as the unemployment compensation program—that prolong job searches or encourage new entrants.

7. The size of the change in the natural rate of unemployment and the importance of various factors in accounting for it are debatable. Changes in the demographics of the labor force, government policies such as unemployment insurance, structural changes in demand, and international competition have all received attention as possible causes.

8. Proposals to reduce the natural rate of unemployment include job training, employment assistance, and alteration of the unemployment compensation program.

KEY TERMS

Job-search theory, 725
Contracts theory, 729

QUESTIONS FOR REVIEW AND DISCUSSION

1. Using the wage offer and minimum acceptable wage curves shown in this chapter, describe how the actual unemployment rate might be pushed below the natural rate for a short period of time, but how it would adjust to the natural rate in the long run.

2. Why do proponents of job-search theory believe that the automatic adjustment mechanism works quickly and effectively? Why do proponents of contracts theory believe that it operates slowly? According to the contracts theory, can the mechanism be speeded up significantly? Why or why not?

3. Classical economists tended to view unemployment as voluntary, meaning that individuals who wanted to work could find employment if they were willing to accept wages that reflected their value to employers. However, Keynes suggested that in a recession, some unemployment was involuntary. Do you think that public policy should be directed to reducing all unemployment, or simply aimed at involuntary unemployment? Explain how cyclical unemployment can be viewed either as nominal wages that are too high or as aggregate demand that is too low. With which view would you associate activists? Nonactivists?

4. Which of the following individuals would you classify as voluntarily unemployed? Involuntarily unemployed? What criteria makes unemployment voluntary?
   a) A teenager looking for a part-time summer job.
   b) A laid-off worker who draws unemployment compensation and confines her job search to jobs with comparable pay.
   c) An unemployed head of household who refuses to accept a job in the casual labor market.
   d) A person whose spouse is well-paid and who is looking for a "meaningful" job.

5. Some economists favor lowering the minimum wage for teenagers who work during the summer in order to reduce the high unemployment rate for this group. Why would this policy tend to reduce the unemployment rate of teenagers? What are the arguments against this proposal?

6. The closing of a large plant can create a significant amount of local unemployment. What are the costs and benefits of each of the following possible policies?
   a) Subsidizing the company in order to keep the plant open.
   b) Restricting foreign competition that may be responsible for the plant's low profits.
   c) Providing retraining and/or relocating the affected workers.
   d) Doing nothing.

7. What is the relationship between the natural rate of unemployment and potential GNP? Explain the effects of the changing work patterns of women in the 1960s and 1970s on the natural rate and on potential GNP.

Inflation and Unemployment

QUESTIONS TO CONSIDER

☐ How do economists measure inflation?

☐ What causes—and does not cause—inflation?

☐ Why did economists once believe that some increase in inflation could be traded for a reduction in unemployment?

☐ What is the consensus among present-day economists on the trade-off between unemployment and inflation?

☐ How do the expectations and sticky-price views of inflation lead to differing policy proposals?

Those of you who are 20 years old or younger probably do not remember a year when the price level did not increase. In this chapter we want to see why the price level increases (and decreases). Why have we experienced the sustained increases that economists call inflation? To what extent are government monetary and fiscal policies a cause and/or a cure for inflation?

In Chapter 28 we considered explanations and effects of unemployment. In this chapter we do the same for inflation. At times unemployment and inflation appear to be connected: Reducing unemployment may cause prices to rise and reducing inflation may cause unemployment to rise. But why does this trade-off occur, and can macroeconomic policies be used to trade lower unemployment for higher inflation? In this chapter we consider some of the different ways that economists have answered this question. Understanding why economists disagree will help you to understand why the use of aggregate demand policies to fight inflation or to lower unemployment remains controversial.

INFLATION

In Chapter 20 we considered some of the reasons why inflation is usually considered to be undesirable. Inflation harms some people (those on fixed incomes, for example) more than others. Moreover, individuals living in inflationary economies spend a lot of time and energy trying to protect themselves from inflation. Since these conditions threaten both equity and efficiency, why has almost every modern economy experienced inflation? Before you can answer that question, you have to know more about inflation and the economic forces that cause it.

Measuring Inflation

Inflation rate. The annual rate of increase in the price level.

What you usually hear called inflation is actually the **inflation rate**, that is, the annual percentage change in some price-level index. For example, the GNP deflator increased from 111.5 in 1985 to 114.5 in 1986. This is an annual inflation rate of 2.7 percent, calculated as

$$\text{Inflation rate} = \text{Percentage change in GNP deflator}$$

$$= \frac{\text{Deflator, 1986} - \text{Deflator, 1985}}{\text{Deflator, 1985}} \times 100$$

$$= \frac{114.5 - 111.5}{111.5} \times 100$$

$$= 2.7\% \text{ per year}$$

That is, the average price of goods and services as measured by the GNP deflator increased by 2.7 percent in 1986. To check your understanding, verify some of the inflation rates provided in the Appendix at the back of this textbook.

In recent years forecasting the direction of change in prices has been easy. The last annual *decline* in the CPI occurred in 1955, and the GNP deflator has increased every year since 1949. Nevertheless, from time to time and especially in recession periods, there have been monthly declines in the price level. Moreover, there were both large price-level increases and decreases in years prior to the 1940s. The inflation in the U.S. economy, even during periods of recession, actually started after World War II.

Increases in the General Price Level: A Short-Run View

The inflation rate tells us what has happened to prices, but not why. More importantly, the inflation rate for any one year does not indicate whether the increase in prices is temporary or part of a sustained increase. That is, does it represent the effects of a one-time change in economic conditions? Or does it indicate a sustained upward movement in the general price level?

Later in this chapter we consider what economists generally agree is the principal cause of sustained movements in prices: changes in the money supply. First, however, we want to consider the factors that cause short-run changes in the price level. Put simply, *an increase in the price level can be caused by either an increase in aggregate demand or a decrease in aggregate supply.*

Exhibit 29.1 shows changes in actual GNP for the United States. From 1967 to 1968, real GNP (output) rose by more than 4 percent (or faster than the long-run average of 3.2 percent). Exhibit 29.1(a) shows this change as a shift in the aggregate demand curve (from AD_1 to AD_2). As a result, the economy moved along its short-run aggregate supply curve, and the general price level increased from 35.9 to 37.7. That is, the annual inflation rate was 5.0 percent (using the formula previously given), or more than twice the annual rate of the previous five years.

A change in any of the factors that increase aggregate demand will cause the price level to rise. Increases in planned consumption or investment, government spending, the money supply, or net exports can all increase aggregate demand and hence the price level. Thus price-level increases caused by increases in aggregate demand are sometimes referred to as **demand-pull inflation**. Higher aggregate demand is said to be pulling the price level up.

Such was the case in 1967–1968, when government spending, both for the Vietnam War and for President Johnson's War on Poverty, increased dramatically. The large tax cut passed by Congress in 1964 had also helped boost both consumption and investment. And, the Fed increased the money supply in 1968 by 7

Demand-pull inflation. Increases in the price level caused by increases in aggregate demand.

(a) Increase in aggregate demand, 1967–1968

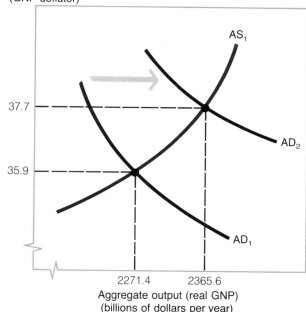

(b) Decrease in aggregate supply, 1973–1974

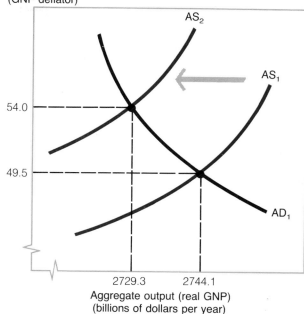

Exhibit 29.1
Increases in the Price Level—Two Causes
An increase in the price level can be caused by either an increase in aggregate demand, as shown in part (a), or by a decrease in aggregate supply, as shown in part (b). Both changes cause excess demand at the old equilibrium price level and thus put upward pressure on prices. They have different effects on real GNP, however. An increase in aggregate demand causes real GNP to rise; a decrease in aggregate supply causes real GNP to fall.

percent, compared to a 4 percent average increase during the preceding five years. All these factors contributed to higher aggregate demand and the consequent increase in both real output (GNP) and prices.

In contrast, between 1973 and 1974, real GNP fell by 0.5 percent. Exhibit 29.1(b) shows this change as a shift in the aggregate supply curve (from AS_1 to AS_2). As a result of this change, the economy moved along its aggregate demand curve, and the price level increased from 49.5 to 54.0. That is, the annual inflation rate was 9.1 percent (using the formula previously given).

We can expect a higher price level to result from an increase in any factor that decreases aggregate supply. Increases in the prices of resources or in expected future price levels will decrease aggregate supply. Thus a rise in the price level that is caused by a decrease in aggregate supply is sometimes called **cost-push inflation**. Higher costs are said to be pushing the price level up.

Such was the case in 1973–1974, when the price of oil—a major resource—increased from $3 to more than $12 a barrel. The increased price of oil raised the cost of production in many industries. In this same period, poor harvests in many parts of the world caused a sharp increase in food prices. Food prices in

Cost-push inflation. Increases in the price level caused by decreases in aggregate supply. Most economists believe that sustained decreases in aggregate supply are unlikely.

the United States increased an average of 12–14 percent. The prices of many other resources and goods also increased because the federal government removed general price ceilings early in 1974.

Faced with higher costs for home heating, transportation, and food, workers demanded higher wages, further increasing costs of production and thus reducing aggregate supply. Finally, businesses and workers became concerned about future inflation and raised their price-level expectations, which also decreased aggregate supply. The overall result was a decrease in real GNP and an increase in prices.

Note that in both 1967–1968 and 1973–1974, the initial change resulted in excess demand (more demanded than supplied) at the old price level. Excess demand drove the price level up as the economy adjusted to a new equilibrium position. But conditions during these two periods also differed in an important respect. When aggregate demand increased, real GNP (in the short run) rose along with prices. But when aggregate supply decreased, real GNP fell as prices rose. By noting how real GNP changes, we can decide whether a particular price-level increase was caused by shifts in aggregate demand or by shifts in aggregate supply.

Inflation: What Does *Not* Cause It

Short-run changes in the price level reinforce the basic macroeconomic principles that have been the focus of our discussion in previous chapters. But short-run changes, such as a single increase in demand or decrease in supply, have only a limited effect on the economy. As we have discussed before, the economy's automatic adjustment mechanism will eventually restore long-run equilibrium. The price level may be higher, but once the economy has fully adjusted, there is no reason for any further increase.

Of far greater importance to economists, politicians, and individuals are the effects of inflation, that is, a sustained upward movement of the price level. Can inflation, like a short-run price-level increase, be caused by shifts in either aggregate demand or supply? In this section we demonstrate why most economists agree that continual increases in aggregate demand are the main cause of inflation. We also show why they believe that there is a long-run connection between inflation and the growth rate of the money supply.

Consider Exhibit 29.2, which shows the price level increasing from 120 to 128 because of two decreases in aggregate supply. Note that each decrease in aggregate supply causes the price level to increase. But to get sustained increases in prices from this source, aggregate supply must continue to decrease. Although such decreases are theoretically possible, they are virtually unheard of. Why? Suppose that the decreases in aggregate supply represent an attempt by oil producers to force oil prices up. An initial decrease in oil supplies will indeed decrease aggregate supply and raise the general price level. But sustained price-level increases require sustained supply shocks. Generally, economists believe that oil producers would not find it in their best interests to continue to reduce the supply of oil.

Once oil prices have risen to their profit-maximizing level, only changes in economic conditions—such as reductions in the supplies of substitutes—would justify further price increases. Moreover, the more oil prices are raised, the faster producers can expect substitutes to develop, reducing the economic power that allowed them to raise prices in the first place. In addition, as you can see in Exhibit 29.2, each decrease in aggregate supply pushes the economy farther away from potential GNP (output). The increase in the size of the contractionary gap increases the downward pressure on wages and prices in general. And, as real

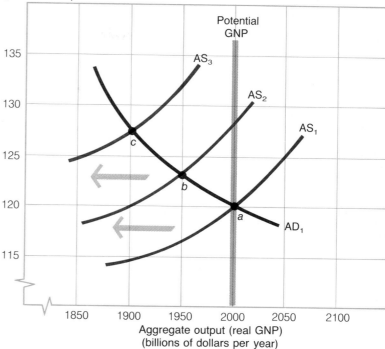

Price-level index
(GNP deflator)

Potential
GNP

Aggregate output (real GNP)
(billions of dollars per year)

Exhibit 29.2
Decreases in Aggregate Supply
The initial equilibrium (point *a*) shows the economy in long-run equilibrium, producing and selling at its potential GNP of $2000 billion. The first "supply shock" decreases aggregate supply (to AS₂), raising the price level and opening a contractionary gap. Actual output at point *b* is $1950 billion, a gap of $50 billion below potential GNP. A second decrease in aggregate supply further increases the price level and further widens the contractionary gap. The widening gap puts downward pressure on prices and tends to make further price increases unprofitable.

GNP falls, so will demand for and sales of the product. Eventually, downward pressures on prices will make further decreases in aggregate supply unprofitable. Thus *decreases in aggregate supply may produce short-run increases in the general price level, but they are unlikely to lead to continuing inflation.*

This sequence of events, in fact, is what occurred in the 1970s with the oil price shocks. The members of the Organization of Petroleum Exporting Countries (OPEC) succeeded in pushing oil prices up in 1973–1974 and again in 1979. Although both events raised the general price level, OPEC did not continually raise oil prices. Actually, the higher oil prices stimulated conservation efforts and the development of substitutes. The fall in oil consumption and decreased demand during the 1981–1982 recession pushed oil prices from more than $35 per barrel in 1980 down to less than $11 per barrel in 1986. Although these supply shocks caused the price level to increase in the mid-1970s and early 1980s, they added only temporary upward pressure on prices.

If decreases in aggregate supply do not cause inflation, what about increases in aggregate demand, the second reason for a short-run increase in the price level? In Exhibit 29.3 we show only changes in potential GNP and aggregate demand because we want to focus on long-run changes in prices. We also assume that the economy moves from one long-run equilibrium position to the next. Both parts (a) and (b) show that potential GNP increases over a period of time, but whether or not the price level increases depends on how much aggregate demand increases.

Exhibit 29.3(a) shows an economy with no inflation. From year to year, aggregate demand and potential GNP both increase at the same rate. The economy

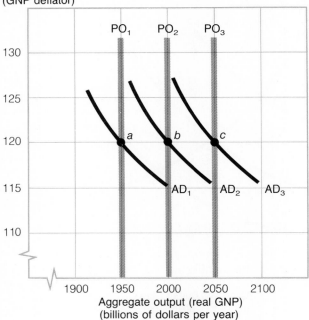

(a) *No inflation: Aggregate demand matches increases in potential GNP.*

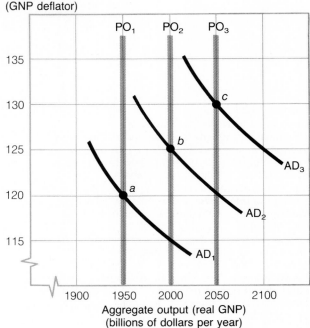

(b) *Inflation: Aggregate demand increases faster than potential GNP.*

Exhibit 29.3
Inflation: A Dynamic View
Both graphs show a growing economy; that is, potential GNP (potential output levels, shown as PO_1, PO_2, and PO_3) increases over time. In part (a) the increases in potential GNP are just matched by increases in aggregate demand as the economy moves from point *a* to point *b* to point *c*. As a result, there is no pressure on the price level and no inflation. In part (b) aggregate demand is growing faster than potential GNP, opening expansionary gaps as the economy moves from point *a* to point *b* to point *c*. (Note that at the price level of 120, AD_2 shows $2050 billion demanded, or more than the new potential GNP (PO_2) of $2000.) This excess demand puts upward pressure on the price level and the result is inflation, or a steady, sustained increase in the price level.

moves from one long-run equilibrium position to the next (from *a* to *b* to *c*) without experiencing excess demand. Thus the economy grows without affecting the price level. In contrast, Exhibit 29.3(b) shows an economy with inflation. Each year, aggregate demand increases faster than potential GNP, opening an expansionary gap at the old price level. Thus each year there is excess demand pressure. Although we do not show the short-run adjustment, as long as aggregate demand continues to grow faster than potential GNP, the price level will continue to increase. That is, the economy will experience inflation.

Implicit in this explanation of inflation is the assumption that aggregate demand grows faster than potential GNP. How can such excess demand be sustained? The factors that can cause excess demand are those that can shift aggregate demand. But with one exception—increases in the money supply—these factors are not likely to cause persistent inflation. For example, an increase in government spending tends to boost aggregate demand and may push prices up temporarily. But can the government continue to increase spending faster than real GNP grows? If the money supply is fixed, higher government spending will crowd out private-sector spending, as you saw in Chapter 27. And, as you have also seen, this crowding-out effect is strongest when, as here, the economy is operating at or near its potential GNP level.

Similarly, other components of real domestic spending are limited by the total amount of GNP available. Thus spontaneous increases in planned spending can be expected to cause only temporary increases in the price level if the money supply is fixed. (How long such "temporary" increases can go on is, however, the subject of much debate.) Moreover, it seems highly unlikely that any spontaneous change in spending could account for a 50 or 200 percent increase in prices in a single year. Long before such a spending change could generate that type of demand pressure, the limits on spending would be reached. Thus if we want to explain large, sustained increases in prices, we must find another explanation.

Inflation: What *Does* Cause It

The limits that apply to other aggregate-demand factors do not apply to increases in the money supply. History has shown that there are few realistic limits to how fast and how long the money supply can be increased. The money supply can easily be doubled in a very short period of time. Large increases in the money supply can last for an extended period of time and, in fact, provide the only reasonable explanation for continuing high rates of inflation. In 1985, Bolivia experienced an inflation rate of 11,750 percent! This inflation was fueled by such large increases in the money supply (almost 8000 percent) that Bolivian currency printed in West Germany and Great Britain was Bolivia's third leading import. (See A Case in Point: Money Supply versus Inflation for more on international links between money and inflation.)

Bolivia obviously is an extreme example, but most economists agree that any large, sustained increase in the price level lasting several years is the result of "too much money chasing too few goods." That is, high inflation rates are caused by excessive growth in the money supply. Milton Friedman wrote that "Inflation is everywhere and always a monetary phenomenon."[*] Most economists agree with Friedman, but some believe that this statement is too strong.

Exhibit 29.4 reinforces this conclusion by showing growth of the money supply (M-1) and annual inflation rates (increases in the GNP deflator) in the United States from 1960 to 1986. As you can see, in the early 1960s low rates of inflation were accompanied by slow growth rates in the money supply. From 1950 to 1964 the money supply grew at an average annual rate of 2.1 percent. During the same period, the annual inflation rate was 2.5 percent. From 1968 to 1973, the money supply grew at an average annual rate of 6.3 percent; the rate of inflation increased to 5.1 percent. During the 1976–1979 period, the inflation rate averaged 7.3 percent, while the money supply grew at an average rate of 7.6 percent.

Exhibit 29.4 shows a clear, but far from perfect, long-run relationship between changes in the money supply and the rate of inflation. But what about the short run? From 1973 to 1976 and from 1980 to 1982, the price level increased faster than the money supply. In those periods, supply shocks had a major effect on the

---

[*] Milton Friedman, *Dollars and Deficits*. Englewood Cliffs, N.J.: Prentice-Hall, 1968, p. 39.

Exhibit 29.4
Changes in the Money Supply and the Price Level: 1960–1986
The graph shows percentage changes in the money supply (measured by M-1) and the price level (measured by the GNP deflator). The two series move together for most of this period. The increases in the growth rates of the money supply from 1960 to 1975 is matched by similar increases in inflation rates. The relationship is not exact. This is particularly true in the 1980s, when money-supply growth was increasing while the inflation rates fell.

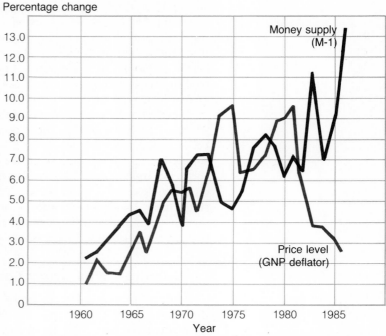

Percentage change

Sources: Money supply from Federal Reserve Bank of Boston; GNP deflator from *Economic Report of the President, 1987.*

price level. What about the 1983–1986 period, when money growth was higher than growth in GNP but inflation fell? Economists disagree about the cause. Some view it as reflecting a major increase in demand for money (M-1) as households reacted to falling interest rates on nonchecking accounts and began to hold more money in NOW accounts, for example.

The important point is that *short-run variations in the rate of inflation can be caused by any factor that shifts aggregate demand or the short-run aggregate supply curve. Long-run trends in the rate of inflation are generally associated with trends in the growth rate of the money supply.* No large, sustained upward movement in the price level can occur without a large, sustained growth in the money supply. A slowly growing money supply will eventually lead to a low rate of inflation.

Lingering Effects of Demand and Supply Shocks

The differences that we have pointed out between temporary and long-run changes in the inflation rate are sometimes difficult to sort out in the real world. We have noted that the effects of a single shift in aggregate supply (a supply shock) or aggregate demand (a demand shock) are temporary. When the effects have run their course, prices will stabilize unless additional shocks occur. But in the real world, the effects of a major demand or supply shock may affect the price level for a substantial period of time.

Consider, for example, the supply shocks that hit the United States in 1973–1974. We noted earlier that increases in oil and food prices decreased aggregate supply and real GNP while the inflation rate nearly doubled in 1974. But the United States experienced further severe inflation in 1975, as the supply shocks of 1973–1974 affected electric rates and transportation costs, driving up product prices. And, as noted, workers raised their price-level expectations and demanded higher wages. These reactions also fueled inflation. The initial boost in oil and food prices occurred in a relatively short period of time. But studies show that it took the economy several years to fully adjust to higher resource prices.

Similarly, we must be careful in interpreting the large drop in inflation in the early and mid-1980s. The economy was again rocked by an oil-price shock in 1979. Inflationary expectations rose again in the face of double-digit inflation rates in 1979 and 1980. But by 1982 the rate of inflation had declined significantly. In part, we can attribute this drop to the Fed's efforts to restrain the growth of the money supply. But part of the decline occurred because the effects of the supply shock had finally ended. The initial shock and its aftereffects left the price index at a much higher level. But once the economy adjusted to the shock, the upward pressure on prices ended. The rate of inflation was high, only temporarily, just as we would have expected from a single supply shock.

A Case in Point
Money Supply versus Inflation:
A Look at International Conditions

The connection between changes in the money supply and the price level becomes obvious when we examine other economies. The table at right shows that those countries in which the growth of the money supply was most rapid—such as Argentina and Brazil—had the highest rates of inflation. Countries with more modest increases in the money supply—Switzerland, for example—had more modest increases in the price level.

But the correlation between the growth of the money supply and inflation is not perfect for any of the countries shown, nor do economists expect it to be. For one thing, monetary growth has no effect on the price level if it simply causes aggregate demand to increase along with potential GNP. For another, demand for money may decline because of the development of substitutes or, in high inflation economies, because of expectations of a rising price level. In such cases, prices may increase faster than money-supply changes indicate. Although other factors also affect the price level, changes in the money supply are one of the most important. When the money supply grows very rapidly over a period of time, inflation can certainly be expected to result.

Country	Period	Average annual percentage change in	
		Money supply	Price level
West Germany	1960–1985	7.7	3.8
Switzerland	1960–1985	6.3	4.1
United States	1960–1985	5.7	5.2
Canada	1960–1985	8.0	5.6
Japan	1960–1985	14.7	6.4
Sweden	1960–1982	8.6	6.9
France	1960–1985	10.5	7.3
India	1960–1985	12.5	7.4
United Kingdom	1960–1985	8.8	8.3
Italy	1960–1984	16.1	9.7
South Korea	1960–1985	25.3	13.5
Mexico	1960–1985	22.6	19.7
Brazil	1960–1984	61.1	72.6
Israel	1975–1985	97.3	129.7
Argentina	1973–1985	218.4	248.8
Bolivia	1960–1985	360.2	528.1

Source: International Monetary Fund, *International Financial Statistics Yearbook,* 1986 (Washington, D.C., 1987).

Change	1964–1971	1972–1980	1981–1984
Demand pressure	+3.28%	−2.44%	−2.76%
Food and energy prices	−0.08	+2.90	−0.81
Import prices	−0.13	+1.59	−0.67
Other	+0.42	+3.92	−0.19
Change in inflation rate	+3.49%	+5.97%	−4.43%

Source: Robert J. Gordon, "Understanding Inflation in the 1980s," *Brookings Papers on Economic Activity,* 1985:1, p. 286.

Exhibit 29.5
Factors Responsible for Changes in Inflation

Disinflation. A decline in the rate of increase of the general price level; the price level continues to rise, but more slowly.

RECAP

It is important to distinguish between a one-time change in the price level and sustained increases in it. After a one-time increase in aggregate demand or decrease in aggregate supply, the economy returns to equilibrium and price stability. Continual increases in aggregate demand create inflation.

Changes in aggregate supply cannot explain inflation because continued decreases in aggregate supply cause contractionary gaps and thus put downward pressure on prices.

Most determinants of aggregate demand cannot explain inflation because they involve spending limits, beyond which the household, business, government, and foreign sectors cannot go to cause continued upward movement of the price level.

Most economists agree that inflation is the result of increases in the money supply that exceed increases in real GNP.

In the real world, it is not always easy to distinguish short-run changes in the price level from inflation because supply shocks and changes in other factors that affect aggregate demand may effect the economy for significant periods of time.

History of Factors that Influence Inflation

We have seen that a change in the price level can be caused by both temporary changes—such as supply shocks—and long-term changes in macroeconomic policies. But which factors have been most significant in terms of the U.S. economy? Exhibit 29.5 shows the results of a study of the influences of various factors on changes in U.S. inflation rates. The last line indicates that the inflation rate (the average annual increase in the price level) was almost 3.5 percent higher in 1971 than in 1964. Almost all of this increase is attributed to excess demand pressures.

From 1972 to 1980 increases in food and energy prices (the supply shocks discussed earlier) combined with increased prices of other imports to raise the inflation rate. At the same time, the macroeconomic policies followed were contractionary, as indicated by the negative sign on the demand pressure variable. (The effect of "other variables"—price level expectations, for example—was also quite significant during this period.)

Finally, you can see that 1981–1984 was a period of **disinflation**. That is, inflation rates decreased. (For more on this topic, see A Case in Point: History of Inflation and Disinflation.) The 1981–1984 disinflation reflects both lower food and energy prices and the Fed's efforts to keep the economy growing slowly. In addition, the increase in the value of the dollar during this period allowed U.S. households and businesses to pay less for foreign imports. For example, a West German product that would have cost $55 in 1980 could have been purchased for $34 in 1984, just because the value of the dollar was higher.

This study supports our conclusion that many factors affect the rate of inflation during any specific period of time. Changes in demand (as in the first and third periods shown) are often the most significant influences. But other factors can have significant short-run effects on the rate of inflation.

UNEMPLOYMENT AND INFLATION: IS THERE A TRADE-OFF?

In the preceding section you saw once again how important it is to distinguish between short-run and long-run views of the economy. This distinction is also very important in determining the connection between unemployment and inflation and whether macroeconomic policies can trade higher prices for lower unemployment.

A Case in Point
History of Inflation and Disinflation

The concepts presented in this chapter help to explain changes in inflation and unemployment rates in the United States and in other countries since 1965. In analyzing the situation, we want to examine evidence on inflation and unemployment and seek explanations for the changes we observe.*

For the United States, Europe, and Japan, the late 1960s were a period of slowly rising but relatively moderate rates of inflation. The annual rate of inflation in the United States in the first half of the 1960s averaged only 1.6 percent. In the last half of that decade, inflation increased to 3.9 percent. Similar increases were felt in many countries.

At least a part of the increase was attributed to increased wage demands. France suffered a general strike in 1968; Italian unions struck often in 1969. But in the United States, much of the increase resulted from expansionary fiscal policies to finance the Vietnam War, and the War on Poverty, and a corresponding expansionary monetary policy. The inflation in the United States soon spread to other countries. Higher prices for U.S. exports raised the cost of living in other countries. Increased U.S. spending on foreign-made goods (imports) increased aggregate demand in other nations and helped push prices up.

Although inflation worsened, the 1960s were good times in terms of unemployment and economic growth. But the moderate (creeping) inflation of the 1960s was replaced by sharply rising (galloping) inflation in the 1970s. In Japan, the rate of inflation in 1974 was 5 times the 1972 rate. In the United States, inflation averaged

over 9 percent in 1974 and 1975. The major causes of these bursts of inflation were the supply shocks caused by higher oil and food prices. But some economists argue that the supply shocks produced inflation (not just short-term price increases) only because overly expansionary macroeconomic policies fueled inflationary expectations.

Following the peak in inflation in 1979–1980, inflation in many countries fell dramatically. Although price levels continued to rise, the rates of increase—the inflation rates—dropped. In contrast to "double-digit" inflation rates in 1980, the United States experienced disinflation in 1983, as the inflation rate fell to less than 4 percent. At least some credit for the slowing of inflation can be given to U.S. antiinflationary monetary policies. However, the United States experienced a severe recession in the early 1980s. As the United States economy slowed, so too did the economies of its trading partners. Less spending by the United States on European and Japanese goods decreased aggregate demand abroad.

In addition, some credit can be given to the absence of any additional momentum from supply shocks. In fact, prices of oil, food, and other important commodities actually fell. The United States also benefitted from the relative increase in the value of the dollar. As the dollar's value in foreign trade rose, the cost to U.S. residents of buying Japanese, European, and other foreign goods fell.

The record on inflation through 1986 looks good, but the important question is whether higher inflation will return. The value of the dollar has fallen, which most economists predict will put upward pressure on U.S. prices. Moreover, the huge federal budget deficits in the United States are a major potential threat to the present economy. The deficits are one reason why some economists are predicting higher inflation in the future.

* The data and analysis are based largely on the work of George A. Kahn, "Inflation and Disinflation: A Comparison Across Countries," *Economic Review*, Federal Reserve Bank of Kansas City, February 1985.

Unemployment and Prices: A Short-Run View

We can easily see a short-run connection between unemployment and the price level. The current unemployment rate reflects the current level of economic activity (real GNP). An increase in real GNP requires an increase in employment (a decrease in unemployment). When aggregate supply is stable, an increase in aggregate demand tends to cause both an increase in the price level and a decrease in unemployment. A decrease in aggregate demand tends to cause a decrease in the price level and an increase in unemployment.

Phillips curve. A plot of the relationship between the rate of inflation and the rate of unemployment. Current theory recognizes an inverse short-run relationship but no long-run relationship.

This inverse relationship between inflation and unemployment is evident in the performance of the U.S. economy. In the 1950s inflation was low, but unemployment was relatively high. In the mid to late 1960s, unemployment fell but inflation rose. In the early 1980s unemployment rose while inflation fell. In each of these cases, changes in aggregate demand (and movement along a short-run aggregate supply curve) appear to explain the facts.

Phillips Curves: Promise and Failure

The connection between inflation and unemployment just described has not always been accepted by economists. Classical economists did not emphasize such a relationship. They believed that employment (and hence unemployment) was determined in labor markets in which wages were flexible. In the classical view, there was only one equilibrium level of employment—that associated with full employment—regardless of the rate of inflation. Aggregate demand determined the inflation rate but had no effect on real wages or on unemployment.

In 1958, however, a New Zealand-born economist, A. W. Phillips, published an article that showed a *long-run* statistical connection between unemployment and inflation. Phillips plotted the rate of change in nominal wages against unemployment on a graph and fitted a curve to the points. Most importantly, he noted that the relationship between inflation and unemployment seemed to be stable for various periods of time. For example, a curve drawn to fit data from 1861 to 1913 also fit data from 1948 to 1957.

Exhibit 29.6(a) shows changes in the general price level (the GNP deflator) and the unemployment rate in the United States for the years 1950–1968. Each point on the graph represents the change in prices and the unemployment rate for a single year. (We show changes in the general price level rather than in wages as Phillips did because we are interested in inflation. However, changes in nominal wages will change product costs and hence change product prices.) As with Phillips's data, most of the points appear to lie on or near the so-called **Phillips curve** shown on the graph.

Although Phillips was not the first economist to notice this relationship, his article popularized the apparent trade-off. Economists and politicians were intrigued by what the Phillips curve suggested. If the relationship was stable (an idea supported by analyses at that time), policy makers might be able to pick a point along the curve that fit their own preferences or biases. Then, by using expansionary macroeconomic policies to increase aggregate demand, they could produce lower unemployment at the expense of a somewhat higher rate of inflation.

For example, the Phillips curve in Exhibit 29.6(a) suggests that an inflation rate of zero could be realized if we accept an unemployment rate of about 6 percent. However, if we are willing to live with a 4 percent inflation rate, the unemployment could be reduced to about 3 percent. In the early and mid 1960s, unemployment averaged 5.5–6 percent. But many economists considered full employment to be a 4 percent unemployment rate. They argued for expansionary policies to stimulate aggregate demand enough to reach this lower unemployment target. Based on the Phillips curve, the cost appeared to be a minimal rise in the inflation rate *as long as aggregate supply remained stable.*

The United States Congress accepted this argument and passed a large tax cut in 1964. This tax cut, complemented by a growth in the money supply, did boost

(a) 1950–1968: A stable relationship (?)

Inflation rate
(annual percentage change in GNP deflator)

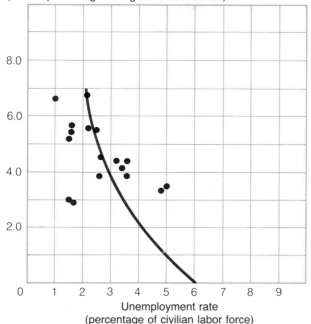

Unemployment rate
(percentage of civilian labor force)

(b) 1969–1986: An unstable relationship

Inflation rate
(annual percentage change in GNP deflator)

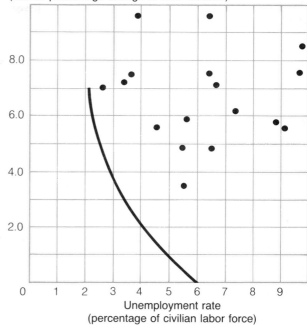

Unemployment rate
(percentage of civilian labor force)

Exhibit 29.6
The Phillips Curve: An Unstable Relationship
The points in part (a) show the unemployment rate and the price level from 1950 to
1968. Most of the points lie on or near the Phillips curve (PC) shown on the graph.
Although the relationship is not perfect, it does suggest a trade-off between unem-
ployment and inflation. The points in part (b) show data for the years 1969 to 1986.
For these years, most of the points lie above the Phillips curve of part (a), suggesting
that there is no stable relationship between inflation and unemployment.

aggregate demand. As the Phillips curve had predicted, unemployment fell to 3.8
percent in 1966 and 1967, while the inflation rate rose to a modest 2.6 percent in
1967. It appeared at the time that macroeconomic policy had achieved a great
triumph: full employment with only mild inflation. Some optimistic economists
actually predicted that it might be possible to use economic policies to end the
business cycle. That is, they hoped to maintain the economy at full employment
while at the same time maintaining reasonable price stability. That prediction
proved premature, partly because the Phillips curve proved to be far from stable.

Problems with the Phillips curve. The expansion of demand in the late
1960s was generally recognized to be excessive, leading to concern about serious
inflation. In response, contractionary policies were implemented in 1969 and 1970.
The Phillips curve predicted that such policies would increase unemployment and
decrease the rate of inflation. The prediction was only half right: between 1969
and 1971, both inflation and unemployment increased.

Exhibit 29.6(b) shows the annual changes in the GNP deflator and rates of unemployment for 1969–1986. Note that these points all lie above the Phillips curve for 1950–1968. Economists recognized that the points for the 1970s could not be on the old Phillips curve. Although the curve had apparently shifted, some economists remained convinced that the relationship was still fairly stable.

However, the points in Exhibit 29.6(b) do not appear to lie along *any* single line or curve. As Arthur Okun put it, "Since 1970, the Phillips curve has been an unidentified flying object and has eluded all efforts to nail it down."* In fact, economists now believe that the original analysis was flawed because Phillips and other economists failed to recognize the importance of inflationary expectations.

The Phillips Curve and Expectations: The Accelerationist Argument

The expectations complication, which fooled most economists in the 1960s, had been predicted by Milton Friedman and Edmund Phelps. As they explained, the basic problem with the analyses was that other economists had confused short-run and long-run relationships. Friedman and Phelps noted that the apparent trade-off of the Phillips curve is only a short-run possibility that corresponds to movement along the short-run aggregate supply curve.

In the long run, output and unemployment are limited by the economy's potential GNP, so no long-run trade-off is possible. To keep the unemployment rate below the natural rate would require continual acceleration (increases) in the money supply. The resulting increases in aggregate demand would result in more and more inflation. The Friedman–Phelps "accelerationist" critique of the trade-off between inflation and unemployment is based on the role that expectations play in determining short-run aggregate supply.

The Phillips curve and aggregate demand. Exhibit 29.7(a) shows aggregate demand and supply in an economy with a potential GNP of $2000. Exhibit 29.7(b) shows a Phillips curve and a vertical line at this economy's natural rate of unemployment (6 percent). The natural rate of unemployment is related directly to potential GNP, since potential GNP is the level of real output the economy will produce if unemployment is at the natural rate. When unemployment is at the natural rate, there is no GNP gap and therefore no tendency for the price level to either rise or fall. Thus point *a* on the Phillips curve—unemployment at the natural rate and no change in prices—corresponds to point *a* in the aggregate demand and supply diagram. In neither case is there any excess demand or supply or any tendency for prices to rise or fall.

But what if aggregate demand increases to AD_2? Aggregate demand has grown too fast, and Exhibit 29.7(a) shows that the economy has been pushed beyond its potential GNP (point *b*). The result is an expansionary GNP gap of $50 billion. At AD_2 higher demand will cause the price level to rise by 8 percent (from 100 to 108). In Exhibit 29.7(b) point *b* is also associated with an 8 percent increase in prices. But unemployment is 5 percent, or below the natural rate, just as actual GNP is above potential GNP in Exhibit 29.7(a). In both diagrams, point *b* does not represent long-run equilibrium. Excess demand will cause higher prices, driving GNP down to its potential level and unemployment up to the natural rate.

---

* Arthur Okun, in Martin S. Feldstein (ed.), *The American Economy in Transition*. Chicago: University of Chicago Press, 1980, p. 166.

(a) Aggregate demand and supply

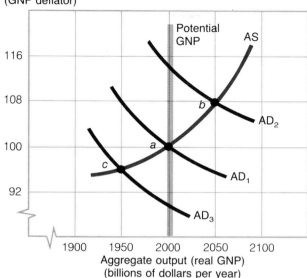

Price-level index
(GNP deflator)

(b) Phillips curve relationship

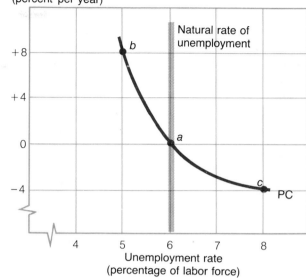

Inflation rate
(percent per year)

Exhibit 29.7
Changes in Aggregate Demand and Movement along a Short-Run Phillips Curve
The two graphs show the link between the aggregate demand and supply diagram
and the Phillips curve. The unemployment rate associated with producing potential
GNP in part (a) is the natural rate of unemployment shown in part (b). In part (a) if
aggregate demand increases to AD_2, an expansionary gap of $50 billion opens and
moves the economy to point *b* on the Phillips curve, or below the natural rate of
unemployment. Thus the higher price level in part (a) means a higher inflation rate in
part (b). A decrease in aggregate demand to AD_3 opens a contractionary gap of $50
billion and moves the economy to point *c* in part (b). Thus the lower price level in part
(a) means a lower inflation rate in part (b).

What if aggregate demand grows more slowly than potential GNP? The result
is a contractionary GNP gap of $50 billion. Exhibit 29.7(a) shows this condition as
point *c*, when aggregate demand is AD_3. Here excess supply has caused the price
level to fall by 4 percent (from 100 to 96). Exhibit 29.7(b) also shows that point
c is associated with a 4 percent decrease in prices. But unemployment is 8 percent,
or above the natural rate, just as actual output is below the potential level in the
aggregate demand and supply diagram. In both diagrams, point *c* does *not* represent long-run equilibrium. Excess supply puts downward pressure on wages
and prices, driving GNP up to its potential level and unemployment down to the
natural rate.

This analysis indicates that the relationship between unemployment and inflation shown by the Phillips curve is only temporary. Higher aggregate demand
tends to temporarily lower unemployment. This trade-off shows as movement
along either the short-run aggregate supply curve or the short-run Phillips curve.
But in the long run the economy will not continue to produce beyond its potential

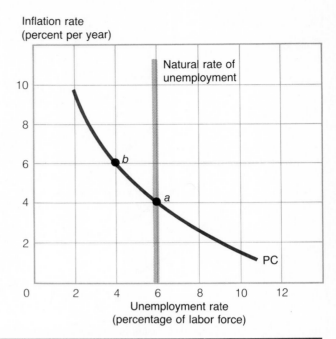

Exhibit 29.8
Short-Run Adjustment along a Phillips Curve
The economy is initially at long-run equilibrium at point
a on the short-run Phillips curve, with unemployment at
a natural rate of 6 percent and the actual and expected
inflation rates at 4 percent per year. If aggregate demand increases too rapidly, an expansionary gap will
open. In the short-run, wages may rise more slowly than
prices, in part because workers are slow to adjust their
inflationary expectations. This movement along the Phillips curve from *a* to *b* reduces unemployment below the
natural rate. (For aggregate demand and supply, the
economy would move along its short-run aggregate
supply curve beyond potential GNP.) But in the long-run,
as prices and expectations adjust, the economy will return to equilibrium with unemployment at the natural
rate.

GNP level. Only the natural rate of unemployment is consistent with long-run
equilibrium. This long-run relationship indicates that any constant and fully anticipated rate of inflation is compatible with long-run equilibrium. There are, as we
have noted elsewhere, significant costs to very high rates of inflation. As a result,
many economists believe that government should adopt fiscal and monetary policies that keep the inflation rate reasonably low. But how low? And should government actually force price-level *decreases*? The answers to these questions are
sharply debated.

Short-run adjustment: Role of expectations. As Friedman and Phelps
noted, the short-run aggregate supply curve and the Phillips curve are stable only
as long as inflationary expectations are constant. A change in inflationary expectations will shift both the aggregate supply curve and the Phillips curve.

We have often observed that demand for and supply of labor are sensitive to
real wages. When workers expect inflation to be 4 percent next year, they want
nominal wages to rise 4 percent. But if both nominal wages and the price level
rise 4 percent, real wages and real product costs will not change. Exhibit 29.8
shows a short-run Phillips curve (PC) intersecting the natural rate of unemployment when the inflation rate is 4 percent (point *a*). We can interpret this curve
to mean that if real wages and prices both rise 4 percent, as expected, the economy
should produce at its potential GNP level and unemployment should be at the
natural rate (6 percent in this case).

Suppose, however, that aggregate demand increases faster than expected, and
actual inflation increases to 6 percent. If actual inflation is not immediately ob-
servable, households and businesses may continue to expect 4 percent inflation.
Businesses may incorrectly view this change as increased demand for their products and seek to increase output. They may even increase nominal wages. If

workers do not immediately perceive the increase in prices, they will interpret higher nominal wages as higher real wages and offer to work more. But if nominal wages rise by 4 percent while prices rise by 6 percent, real wages will actually be falling and businesses will offer more for sale.

Thus incorrect expectations cause the economy to move along its short-run aggregate supply curve. On a Phillips curve, this change shows as movement to the left (to point *b* in Exhibit 29.8). Unemployment falls below the natural rate, which results in greater real GNP than potential GNP. According to the accelerationist argument, unemployment falls below the natural rate only because expected inflation (4 percent) is less than actual inflation (6 percent).

Incorrect inflationary expectations can yield a short-run trade-off between unemployment and inflation, as shown by the Phillips curve. But as Friedman and Phelps note, the trade-off is only temporary. Eventually, producers and workers will realize that actual inflation is higher than they expected. As they revise their expectations, workers will demand nominal wage increases to match the actual inflation rate. But higher nominal wages will raise producers' costs and thus prices, causing short-run aggregate supply to decrease. This process—the automatic adjustment mechanism—results in a return to the potential GNP level, reducing unemployment to the natural rate.

Long-run view. Because there is no long-run trade-off, what we have been calling the Phillips curve is really a short-run Phillips curve. The long-run relationship between unemployment and inflation is simply a vertical line at the natural rate of unemployment. To see why, let's consider the response of an economy if government tries to lower unemployment below the natural rate. In Exhibit 29.9, inflation is initially expected to be 2 percent per year and the natural rate of unemployment is 6 percent. If actual inflation equals expected inflation, the economy will be in long-run equilibrium at point *a*, where PC_1 intersects the natural rate. However, policy makers may decide to use expansionary policies, such as a tax cut or an increase in the money supply, to reduce unemployment. If so, aggregate demand will grow faster than potential GNP and an expansionary gap will open.

In the short run, if actual inflation goes unrecognized, real GNP may rise and unemployment may fall below the natural rate, as we have noted. In Exhibit 29.9 this change shows as movement from point *a* to point *b* along PC_1. This movement corresponds to movement upward and to the right along a short-run aggregate supply curve. In the long run, however, households and businesses will revise their expectations to match the actual inflation rate of 4 percent, shifting the short-run Phillips curve from PC_1 to PC_2. Note that PC_2 intersects the natural rate of unemployment line at point *c*, where actual and expected inflation are 4 percent. Left alone, the economy will adjust to its potential GNP level at the natural rate of unemployment (6 percent).

What if government continues to try to lower unemployment to 4 percent? Aggregate demand once more will increase, causing the economy to move along PC_2 to point *d*, where actual inflation is 6 percent. In the long run, when expectations are revised to account for this higher inflation, the short-run Phillips curve shifts upward once again (to PC_3). As Exhibit 29.9 indicates, expansionary policies cannot maintain unemployment below the natural rate. In the long run, those policies will only increase inflation. Conversely, attempts to lower inflation by decreasing aggregate demand have no long-run effect on unemployment. Thus in the long run the Phillips curve is vertical; there is no long-run trade-off. Only at

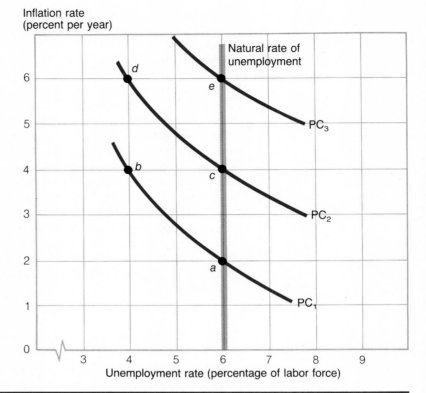

Exhibit 29.9
Long-Run Adjustment to Changes in Demand Pressure
The economy is initially in long-run equilibrium at point *a* on the short-run Phillips curve PC_1, where the actual and expected inflation rates are both 2 percent per year. Attempts to reduce unemployment by using expansionary policies will temporarily push the economy along the Phillips curve to point *b*. If demand pressures are maintained, inflationary expectations will adjust, shifting the Phillips curve (to PC_2). The economy adjusts to point *c* where actual and expected inflation are again equal. Further attempts to lower unemployment below the natural rate cause additional upward shifts in the Phillips curve. In the long-run, unemployment cannot be maintained below the natural rate and there is no long-run trade-off between inflation and unemployment.

the natural rate of unemployment are actual and expected inflation the same; only at this rate will the economy reach long-run equilibrium.

Rational Expectations and the New Classical Macroeconomists

Friedman and Phelps's analysis rests on a particular view of how price-level expectations change. (For more on the effect of expectations, see A Case in Point: Effect of Expections on Inflation and Unemployment Policies.) Their arguments are based on the same kind of analysis we used in Chapter 26 when drawing the short-run aggregate supply curve. That is, we assume that expectations adjust to a change in actual inflation—but always after the change, adapting to historical information. Thus an increase in aggregate demand always causes a temporary expansion in real GNP, since decision makers consistently underestimate price rises. For example, if workers observe that the price level has risen 4 percent per year in the past, they will assume that this trend will continue—until new information suggests that their expectation is wrong.

Some economists criticize the idea that expectations depend largely, if not exclusively, on past events. Would it not be more reasonable, they ask, to assume that individuals utilize all available information when forecasting future price levels? In place of Friedman's *adaptive expectations*, these economists maintain that individuals have *rational expectations*. When forming rational expectations about inflation, individuals do not just look at past inflation rates; they consider any and all information that may affect future price levels. Why, they argue, would individuals make consistent mistakes in forecasting the effects of macroeconomic policies? Why would they always underestimate increases in inflation and overestimate decreases, as they do in Friedman's model? According to the hypothesis of rational expectations, rational individuals would not form their inflationary expectations by looking only at past inflation rates. Rather, they would consider any and all information that may affect future price levels, including the expected effects of announced or anticipated macroeconomic policies.

Note that the hypothesis of rational expectations does not assume that decision makers *always* accurately forecast the rate of inflation or any other significant economic factor. But it does assume that they learn from past events and are as likely to overestimate as underestimate the effects of economic changes. Importantly, the hypothesis suggests that once a policy change is announced or anticipated, expectations will adjust immediately. Many economists currently base their economic models on rational expectations. But the new classical macroeconomists—following the lead of Robert Lucas, Thomas Sargent, and Neil Wallace—also assume (like the classical economists) that wages and prices are very flexible. This assumption, combined with the hypothesis of rational expectations, leads to

A Case in Point
Effect of Expectations on Inflation and Unemployment Policies

Most economists now accept the notion that no long-run trade-off between inflation and unemployment is possible. But why did the Phillips curves drawn for both the United States and England in the 1960s suggest that the relationship was stable in the long run? The answer, according to Milton Friedman, is that there was no consistent expectation of inflation. Prior to the 1960s, government had not tried to increase aggregate demand. Inflation had rarely occurred, so long-run expectations of zero (or at least very low) inflation were reasonable. But the expansionary policies of the 1960s increased not only the price level, but also expectations of inflation.

This analysis also explains why both unemployment and inflation rose in 1969–1971. By 1969 policy-makers recognized that expansionary policies had not only lowered the unemployment rate dramatically but also increased inflation. They expected contractionary policies to raise unemployment and decrease inflation. But when they implemented these policies, they got an unpleasant surprise: Unemployment fell as expected, but inflation continued to rise.

To see why, we must recognize that unemployment in the late 1960s was below the natural rate and that actual inflation was above the expected level. (Not surprising since many economists had been convinced that inflation would not be greatly affected by expansionary policies. They realized that the expansionary actions in the late 1960s were excessive, but they had not considered the role of expectations.) Eventually, expectations caught up with actual inflation, causing the short-run Phillips curve to shift. As the economy adjusted to this new relationship, unemployment rose along with inflation.

But why did inflation continue to rise? Although economists initially rejected Friedman and Phelps's conclusion, most now accept their assessment that workers and producers had come to expect increasing inflation. The private sector expected government to boost aggregate demand in the face of cyclical unemployment. Thus people had every reason to believe that the price level would continue to increase. Increased inflationary expectations decreased short-run aggregate supply (and shifted the short-run Phillips curve). As a result, prices and unemployment continued to increase while GNP decreased.

Observations in the 1960s led many economists to believe in a stable relationship between the rates of unemployment and inflation, as defined by the Phillips curve.

Most economists now believe that there can be a short-run trade-off between unemployment and inflation, since a decline in unemployment to below the natural rate temporarily raises real GNP above its potential level. Short-run trade-offs may be possible because expected inflation does not always match actual inflation.

Economists now believe that there can be no long-run trade-off between unemployment and inflation because expectations adjust to actual inflation. Lowering unemployment below the natural rate increases inflation. Increased inflation causes a revision of expectations and a return to the natural rate of unemployment at which actual and expected inflation are the same.

The hypothesis of rational expectations holds that individuals consider expected future values as well as past history when forecasting inflation. While most economists now accept this position, many reject the assertion of the new classical macroeconomists that responses to changes in aggregate demand are immediate.

a prediction that the economy will quickly and smoothly adjust to any change in demand or supply.

Suppose that the Fed publicly announces that it is increasing the growth rate of the money supply. Most economists would recognize that this announcement will increase aggregate demand. They would predict that there would be a short-run decrease in unemployment until expectations and actual wages and prices change. But they would recognize that faster growth in the money supply (assuming that the growth exceeds that of potential GNP) would lead to higher inflation in the long run.

There is little controversy over the long-run effect of an increase in the growth rate of the money supply. But the new classical macroeconomists would argue that this long-run effect occurs immediately. Because wages and prices are very flexible in their models, they predict immediate shifts in the short-run aggregate supply curve and the short-run Phillips curve. As a result, the announced change in the growth rate of the money supply should raise the price level without affecting real GNP or unemployment. That is, the new classical macroeconomists do not believe that there is even a short-run trade-off between inflation and unemployment when policy changes are known or anticipated. (To see their point, return to Exhibit 29.9 and consider the effect of an increase in aggregate demand that would eventually raise inflation to 4 percent. Note that the economy would move immediately from point a to point c if an increase in expected inflation immediately shifted the Phillips curve from PC_1 to PC_2.) However, many economists are unconvinced that the economy's automatic adjustment mechanism operates as quickly as the new classical economists believe or that short-run trade-offs are impossible.

AGGREGATE DEMAND POLICIES: FIGHTING INFLATION

In our analysis of inflation and unemployment, we have concluded that most economists attribute large, sustained increases in the price level to excessive growth in the money supply. Moreover, most (although, as you just saw, not all) economists believe that there can be short-run trade-offs between unemployment and inflation, but not long-run tradeoffs. However, economists remain divided on how short the short run is. Depending on their view of the short run and how quickly the economy's automatic adjustment mechanism works, they have different views about the appropriateness of policies used to fight inflation. Wage and price controls, which we cover in Chapter 31, are a particularly controversial policy.

The Expectations View and the "Cold Turkey" Approach

Both the new classical macroeconomists and the monetarists (including Milton Friedman) share the view that short-run responses to changes in aggregate demand depend largely on expectations. Most economists agree that, to the degree that short-run responses do depend on expectations, the automatic adjustment mechanism can provide a swift return to full-employment equilibrium. In our society, good information is readily available, making long-term incorrect expectations unlikely.

Their emphasis on expectations leads both monetarists and the new classicists to favor a "cold turkey" approach. That is, they support major, but consistent, reductions in growth of the money supply in order to fight inflation. For example, they would have the Fed announce a new policy of a constant growth rate in the money supply of 3 or 4 percent per year and stick to it. The faster the cycle of inflationary expectations is broken, the sooner the economy can return to full employment and price stability, they argue. As they see it, it is a matter of "pay me now or pay me later." The costs associated with higher current unemployment are, in their opinion, lower than the costs of continued inflation over a longer period of time.

To be effective, policies must be consistent and believable. Otherwise, workers and producers cannot accurately forecast price-level changes. With a consistent policy, households and businesses will quickly adjust their expectations to new, lower rates of inflation. Because this adjustment occurs quickly, the economy would not, in this view, have to suffer a long or deep recession. (The new classical view is similar, but predicts an almost instant adjustment to an announced and believable policy change.)

We noted in Chapter 27 that the monetarists and new classical macroeconomists do not believe that government should intervene to try to offset demand or supply shocks. However, they do advocate using monetary policies to fight inflation. The policy that they propose—slower growth in the money supply—is *not* a discretionary policy for counterbalancing temporary economic fluctuations. Rather, it is a fixed rule meant to bring long-run inflationary pressures under control. If a particular growth rate in the money supply is not enough to bring inflation down to an acceptable level, a slower but still constant rate can be tried.

The "Sticky-Price" View and the Gradual Approach

For the short-run aggregate supply curve to shift, it is not enough for expectations to adjust; actual wages and prices must also adjust. According to economists who hold the expectations view, a change in expectations will cause a shift. But other economists, in the Keynesian tradition, believe that the automatic adjustment mechanism operates slowly because wages and prices are "sticky," not flexible. They generally support the contracts theory we discussed in Chapters 26 and 28, which suggests that many wages are set by explicit or implicit long-run contracts. Thus in the short run, workers cannot respond to changes in aggregate supply by changing wage demands and employers cannot respond by adjusting labor costs.

If actual adjustments are slow, the unemployment costs of large-scale contractionary policies may be high. Economists who believe that the economy adjusts slowly are not against reducing inflation. They agree that lower inflation requires a slower rate of growth in the money supply, but suggest a gradual reduction, not the "cold turkey" approach. A gradual adjustment will take longer to lower inflation, but it may prevent high unemployment and large contractionary gaps.

The Historical Record

The argument of the monetarists and new classical macroeconomists that the automatic adjustment mechanism works swiftly appears to be contradicted by historical evidence. For example, the inflation rate continued to rise during the 1969–1970 recession even though the unemployment rate rose sharply. The recessions in 1974–1975 and again in 1980–1982 also showed the economy's short-run response to reduced aggregate demand included higher unemployment. These recessions—largely traceable to contractionary policies—were the deepest since the 1930s. But the recessions in the early 1980s offer some support for the monetarists' and new classical macroeconomists' point of view. The evidence suggests that the Keynesians underestimated the speed and degree of inflation reduction that occurred. However, the monetarists and new classicists underestimated the resulting amount of unemployment.

As in many real-world situations, both sides claim partial victory and are quick to explain away their faulty predictions. The Keynesians blame their miscalculation on having underestimated the speed with which OPEC would collapse (and thus energy prices would fall). The monetarists and new classicists note that at the time, households and businessses had every reason to expect the government to abandon any inflation-fighting program as soon as unemployment began to rise. At no time since the 1950s had policy makers allowed contractionary policy to run its course and purge the economy of inflationary expectations. Indeed, on some occasions in which contractionary policies were used (1969–1970 and 1974–1975), expansionary policies quickly followed the rise in unemployment.

Historically, policies followed a stop-and-go pattern, with quick and dramatic changes in direction and speed. If we compare managing the economy to driving a car, these policy changes were like alternately flooring the accelerator and slamming on the brakes. Thus in some ways, the economy suffered from the worst of both worlds: Unemployment was consistently high and inflationary expectations were continually fed. Workers and businesses expecting expansionary policies had little reason to settle for lower nominal wage and price increases. A little more restraint at the appropriate time, critics argue, might have broken the inflationary cycle. Antiinflation policies in the 1970s definitely lacked credibility. The monetarists and new classicists note that this historical failure does not mean that the automatic adjustment mechanism would not work quickly if the inflation-fighting policy were believed to be sincere. In fact, they observe that when inflation-fighting policies became believable in the 1980s, the inflation rate fell rapidly.

The Keynesians, however, see the deep recession of 1982 as evidence in support of their position. They credit the rapid fall in inflation to several factors. First, they observe that the effects of earlier supply shocks ended in 1979–1980. Second, they note that oil prices fell in the early 1980s—a sort of "favorable" supply shock. Finally, they point to the decline in the prices of other imports because of the strong relative value of the U.S. dollar. Since that time, there have been no unfavorable supply shocks, and the Fed by its monetary policies has kept the economy operating below its potential GNP level. As a result, the Keynesians argue, it is not surprising that inflation has remained low.

Supply Shocks and Aggregate Demand Policies

So far we have focused on the use of contractionary policies to reduce inflation caused by too much growth in aggregate demand. But what about the price-level increases caused by supply shocks? We explore this issue in more detail in Chapter 31, but the basic dilemma is that supply shocks put upward pressure on price levels while opening contractionary gaps. Their influence on prices is temporary, as we have shown. But what policies are best?

Contractionary policies might prevent an increase in inflationary expectations. But reducing aggregate demand would lead to even higher unemployment. Expansionary policies might reduce the impact on unemployment. But increasing

RECAP

There is general agreement that slower monetary growth will result in lower inflation over the long run.

Some economists believe that the automatic adjustment process can work quickly and favor a "cold turkey" policy of large-scale reduction in growth of the money supply. These economists, including most monetarists and new classicists, stress the importance of expectations in response to changes in aggregate demand.

Other economists, primarily Keynesians, believe that the automatic adjustment process will respond slowly and argue for a more gradual reduction in growth of the money supply.

aggregate demand will lead to even higher prices and a risk of raising inflationary expectations. Doing nothing might be reasonable if the economy's automatic adjustment mechanism operates quickly. But adjustment to a supply shock is more difficult than are adjustments to most contractionary gaps. Because shocks can represent a transfer of real resources out of the country (as was true for higher oil prices), real income has to fall. But who will quickly volunteer to accept lower real wages? There are no easy answers and all policies have considerable costs.

Popularity of Inflationary Policies

We have devoted much of this chapter to showing why excessive growth in the money supply is responsible for inflation. We have emphasized that this effect is widely recognized as the culprit by economists. Why, then, do governments continue to implement inflationary policies? We can offer two explanations for the political popularity of inflationary policies: (1) politicians have a strong preference for high employment; and (2) increasing the rate of growth in the money supply can help finance government spending.

In the United States, the political goal of low unemployment came out of the experience of the Great Depression. The image of a 25% unemployment rate is still vivid, and no elected official can afford to be indifferent to rising unemployment. (Herbert Stein, chairman of the Council of Economic Advisors under President Nixon, said that Nixon was "allergic to unemployment." He had in mind a political allergy, no doubt.) Moreover, the Great Depression introduced the United States to the Keynesian notion that government could do something to reduce unemployment. Later the Phillips curve promised that that "something" would cost nothing (or very little), which economists—but not all voters and politicians—now reject.

In addition, political leaders like to promise government spending on certain programs (ranging from national defense to welfare to local highways). Recall that, unlike the rest of us who must be content with spending what we earn or what we can borrow, national governments have a third option: printing money. Choosing this option is easier politically than raising taxes. Moreover, in countries with underdeveloped financial markets, the ability to borrow substantial funds is limited. In the long run, large-scale monetary expansion will lead to inflation, perhaps even to hyperinflation. But politicians sometimes see these costs as offset by short-run political advantages (especially near election time).

In the United States, monetary growth is under the direct control of the Federal Reserve System. This separation of fiscal and monetary controls is one reason why we have not experienced the hyperinflation that other countries have. But political pressures to minimize unemployment influence both monetary and fiscal policies in this country. As a result, inflation in the United States in the 1970s was greater than that experienced in Japan, for example, where very restrictive macroeconomic policies were used.

CONCLUSION

In this chapter we demonstrated the connection between unemployment and inflation. Economists generally agree that there is no long-run trade-off, but most concede that a short-run trade-off is possible. However, they disagree over the reasons for the relationship and the speed with which the automatic adjustment mechanism operates.

These disagreements are at the heart of the current economic debate over how to fight inflation and respond to future supply shocks. As our discussion of alternative policies clearly indicates, the economic and political dilemmas caused by inflation are serious and have no easy solutions. Inflation was cited as the "number-one enemy" of the economy in the 1970s but has decreased substantially. Has the battle been won? Will inflation remain low? These important questions are as yet unanswered. But by applying the concepts presented in this chapter, you can learn to read the signs of inflation and explain changes in future inflation rates.

So far in our exploration of macroeconomics we have focused largely on the short run and on long-run adjustments to a given level of potential GNP. In Chapter 30 we turn our attention to the long run, to see how potential GNP is determined, how fast it grows, and what policies might increase its rate of growth. Although we must consider the short run, we cannot discuss economic policies intelligently without considering the long run.

SUMMARY

1. In this chapter we examined the causes of inflation, the debate over trade-offs between inflation and unemployment, and the use of macroeconomic policies to reduce either inflation or unemployment.

2. The annual percentage change in the price level is referred to as the inflation rate. But it is important to distinguish between temporary changes and sustained upward movement in the price level. Either an increase in aggregate demand or a decrease in aggregate supply can cause a one-time increase in the price level. But once the economy has adjusted to either change, prices would not continue to rise unless additional shifts in demand or supply occur.

3. Over the long run, inflation is the result of continued excess demand. That is, inflation results from excessive growth of the money supply, causing aggregate demand to grow faster than potential GNP. But any other factor affecting aggregate demand or aggregate supply can change the price level, making it hard to separate the exact causes of a price-level change in the short run.

4. Distinguishing the causes of inflation is further complicated by the length of time that the aftereffects of demand and supply shocks affect the economy.

5. In the early 1960s observations led many economists to believe in a stable relationship between the rate of unemployment and the rate of inflation. Graphs expressing this relationship are known as "Phillips curves," after the economist who popularized the concept. Experience in the 1970s suggested that this relationship was not stable. Economists now generally believe that there is a short-run relationship but that no long-run trade-off is possible.

6. Theoretical support for the lack of a stable long-run trade-off between unemployment and inflation is based on the assumption that expectations adjust to actual inflation. Lowering unemployment below the natural rate causes rising inflation. Increased inflation causes a revision of expectations and a return to the natural rate of unemployment, at which actual and expected inflation are the same.

7. The new classical macroeconomists believe that wages and prices are highly flexible and that households and businesses change their expectations immediately in response to changes in the inflation rate. Thus they maintain that even short-run trade-offs between inflation and unemployment are impossible.

8. There is general agreement among economists that slower monetary growth results in lower inflation over the long run. Some monetarists and new classicists, believing that the automatic adjustment process can work quickly, favor a "cold turkey" policy of large-scale reduction in the growth of the money supply. Keynesians, believing that the automatic adjustment mechanism will respond slowly, argue for a more gradual reduction.

9. The "correct" policy response to a supply shock depends on the resulting trade-off between unemployment and inflation and the speed of the economy's automatic adjustment mechanism. But any policy implemented will have some costs.

10. Despite the inflationary effects of policies that expand the money supply, this "solution" remains a popular political alternative to raising taxes or to high unemployment.

KEY TERMS

Inflation rate, 739
Demand-pull inflation, 740
Cost-push inflation, 741
Disinflation, 748
Phillips curve, 750

QUESTIONS FOR REVIEW AND DISCUSSION

1. Explain how a short-run change in the price level can be caused by either a change in aggregate demand or aggregate supply. Explain why economists tend to agree that sustained increases in the money supply provide the only explanation for high rates of inflation.

2. What short-run change in inflation and unemployment would you expect from each of the following events?
   a) An increase in consumer and business confidence.
   b) A one-time increase in the money supply.
   c) An increase in the rate of growth of the money supply.
   d) An increase in the prices of important resources.
   e) An expectation of a higher rate of inflation.

3. Many economists argue that policy makers created problems for the U.S. economy by the stop-and-go nature of the macroeconomic policies used in the 1960s and 1970s. Some critics argue that the reason is that finding support for contractionary policies to fight inflation is politically more difficult than finding support for expansionary policies to fight recessions and high unemployment. Explain why this belief might be true. (*Hint*: Consider the policies that are required in each case and the effects they have.) Do you think that the political choices made reflect the values of voters, a lack of understanding of economics on the part of voters and politicians, or a basic failure of government?

4. We noted in this chapter that most economists now believe that there is no stable short-run Phillips curve. But the data in Exhibit 29.6(a) suggest there was a stable relationship that existed for many years. Explain why. In particular, consider whether the stability of the observed relationship in Exhibit 29.6(a) might be connected with the absence of government stabilization policies that sought to improve on the economy's au-

tomatic adjustment mechanism. How do supply shocks affect the short-run Phillips curve?

5. In the mid-1980s, the size of projected annual federal budget deficits was an important economic and political issue. Is there necessarily any connection between a budget deficit and inflation? Why were some economists worried that the deficits would be inflationary? What are the Fed's policy options in the face of such deficits? Explain the benefits and costs of each option.

6. Because the short-run Phillips curve suggests that unemployment and inflation are inversely related, some economists have argued that economic theory cannot explain why unemployment and inflation increase together at times. How would you explain increases in both unemployment and inflation? What does your answer mean in terms of the short-run Phillips curve?

7. The long-run Phillips curve indicates that there is no long-run relationship between unemployment and inflation. Explain the reasoning behind the absence of a long-run trade-off. What policies, if any, can you suggest that may shift the position of the Phillips curve?

8. The identity expressed by the equation of exchange $(M \times V = P \times Q)$ indicates that changes in the money supply (M) should be proportional to changes in the price level (P), unless either velocity (V) or real GNP (Q) changes. Using this equation and the graph in Exhibit 29.4, explain the relatively slow growth of the money supply in the early 1960s. The relatively fast growth in the price level from 1975 to 1977 and again from 1980 to 1982? The slowing of inflation in the 1980s?

9. Comment on the statement: "Macroeconomic policies based on the assumption that the automatic adjustment mechanism and expectations are slow to respond to the pressures of a contractionary gap guarantee a slow response."

10. In each case below, explain what change in prices you would expect. (You may find it helpful to explain your answer in terms of the equation of exchange.) State explicitly what variables you must hold constant to reach your conclusions.
    a) The supply of money grows more slowly than real output.
    b) The supply of money grows at the same rate as real output, but the public wants to hold more money.
    c) The supply of money grows, and the public expects this growth to lead to a higher rate of inflation.

CHAPTER 30

Economic Growth:
Increasing Potential GNP

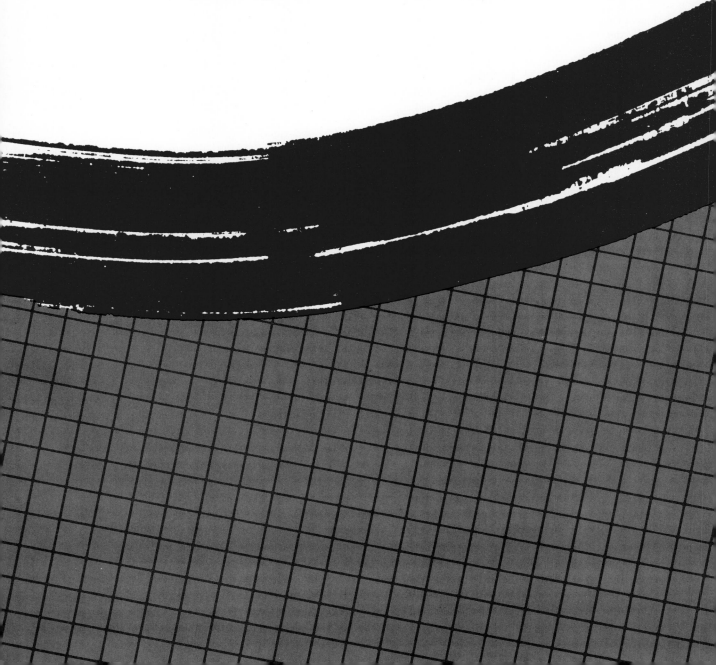

QUESTIONS TO CONSIDER

☐ What is economic growth?

☐ How have economists' views of economic growth changed?

☐ What factors can result in economic growth?

☐ Why has economic growth in many industrialized nations slowed?

☐ What government policies have been used in attempts to stimulate growth?

So far out exploration of macroeconomics has focused on how the economy adjusts to changes in aggregate demand and supply assuming potential GNP remains constant. But in the real world, potential GNP can (and does) increase, resulting in economic growth. Economic growth does not eliminate scarcity. Wants will always exceed an economy's ability to produce. But by increasing its potential GNP, an economy can produce more goods and services and, as a consequence, satisfy more of its wants. We noted the factors that determine potential GNP in Chapter 26. But which of those factors are most important to economic growth? Can economic policies increase the rate of economic growth? These are the questions we address in this chapter.

ECONOMIC GROWTH: DEFINITION AND CAUSES

The most important benefit to a society of economic growth is raising the standard of living by increasing the amount of real goods and services available for consumption. Economists therefore measure economic growth as an increase in **real GNP per capita**, that is, the ratio of real GNP to total population. For example, real GNP in the United States in 1986 was $3674.9 billion, and the total population was 241.5 million. Thus real GNP per capita in 1986 was $15,217, calculated as

$$\text{Real GNP per capita, 1986} = \frac{\text{Real GNP}}{\text{Population}} = \frac{\$3674.9 \text{ billion}}{241.5 \text{ million}} = \$15,217 \text{ per person}$$

Exhibit 30.1 shows percentage changes in real GNP, population, and real GNP per capita for several countries. Note that an increase in real GNP per capita means that the economy has produced more output per person. But we cannot be sure that every person in the economy has more output to consume. Nor can we be sure that every increase in GNP makes us better off. As we noted in Chapter 21, GNP does not take into account costs such as those of air and water pollution. Because GNP includes both consumer and military goods, an economy may show increases in real GNP per capita, but its citizens may not be better off. Nevertheless, most economists equate an increase in real GNP per capita with a higher *average* standard of living.

Real GNP per capita. The average quantity of real output produced per person, calculated by dividing real GNP by total population.

	1965–1973 Percentage changes in			1973–1984 Percentage changes in		
Country	GNP	Population	GNP per capita	GNP	Population	GNP per capita
United States	3.2	1.1	2.1	2.3	1.0	1.3
Japan	9.8	1.2	8.6	4.3	0.9	3.4
UK	2.8	0.4	1.4	1.0	0.0	1.0
Canada	5.2	1.4	3.8	2.5	1.2	1.3
France	5.5	0.8	4.7	2.3	0.5	1.8
West Germany	4.6	0.7	3.9	2.0	−0.1	2.1
China	7.8	2.7	5.1	6.6	1.4	5.2
India	3.9	2.3	1.6	4.1	2.3	1.8
Bolivia	4.4	2.4	2.0	0.8	2.6	−1.8
Brazil	9.8	2.5	7.3	4.4	2.3	2.1
Mexico	7.9	3.3	4.6	5.1	2.9	2.2
Hong Kong	7.9	2.0	5.9	9.1	2.4	6.7
South Korea	10.0	2.2	7.8	7.2	1.5	5.7
Singapore	13.0	1.8	11.3	8.2	1.3	6.9

**Exhibit 30.1
International Growth Rates**

Source: The World Bank, *World Development Report, 1986,* Washington, D.C.: Oxford University Press, 1986, Tables 2 and 25, pp. 182–183 and pp. 228–229.

Growth: Increased Real GNP per Capita

Our definition of growth has three components. Growth represents an *increase;* it is measured in *real* terms; and it is generally expressed on a *per-capita* basis. That growth is an increase is fairly obvious, but why must it be stated in real and per-capita terms?

Real versus nominal GNP. It is relatively easy to see why we measure economic growth as a change in real rather than nominal output. Real GNP is the quantity of economic goods and services available to the economy. But nominal GNP reflects both changes in quantities and changes in the price level. (Remember that nominal GNP is the product of the price level and real GNP.)

For example, per capita nominal GNP in the United States grew by 7.5 percent between 1974 and 1975—from $6887 to $7401. During the same period, the price level increased by 9.8 percent—from 54.0 to 59.3—as measured by the GNP deflator. Thus real GNP per capita actually *declined* by 2.3 percent. *Only if nominal GNP per capita rises faster than the price level will real GNP per capita increase.* And only increases in real GNP enable more wants to be satisfied.

Real GNP per capita versus real GNP. The reasons for defining growth in terms of per capita GNP are also straightforward. Sometimes economists do discuss economic growth in absolute terms. For example, if we wanted to compare the overall influence of the United States and the Soviet Union on the world economy, it might be better to use real GNP, not real GNP per capita. But comparing real GNPs can conceal important differences in average standards of living. For example, in 1984 India's real GNP was $194.8 billion, while Switzerland's was

$104.5 billion. However, India's population was 749 million, while Switzerland's was 6 million. Thus real GNP per capita in India was $260, while in Switzerland it was $16,330. *An economy's average standard of living will increase only if real GNP per capita rises.*

For real GNP per capita to increase, real GNP has to rise faster than population. Many poor countries experience large increases in real GNP, but at the same time they experience large increases in population. As a result, their standards of living improve only slightly or not at all. For example, between 1973 and 1984, real GNP in India increased 4.1 percent, a rate that compares favorably with Japan's 4.3 percent growth rate. However, India's population increased 2.3 percent per year, compared to 0.9 percent per year in Japan. As a result, real output per capita grew only 1.8 percent per year in India, compared to 3.4 percent per year in Japan. Because of this relationship between population and standard of living, many poor nations have tried to improve living standards by reducing birth rates.

When discussing growth, you should recognize that even seemingly small differences in economic growth rates can have tremendous long-run effects on the standard of living. For example, in 1870 real GNP per capita in the United Kingdom was 21 percent higher than in the United States. Between 1870 and 1985 the average annual growth rate in the United States was 1.84 percent per year, apparently not much greater than the 1.24 percent per year in the United Kingdom. However, over the 115-year period, this 0.6 percent difference in growth rates resulted in a real GNP per capita that was 62 percent higher in the United States than in the United Kingdom.*

Another way of expressing the effects of economic growth is by the length of time required for real GNP to double if the growth rate remains constant. A formula called the *rule of 72* is used to calculate the number of years it takes for GNP to double as the ratio of 72 to the annual growth rate. Let's use the U.S. growth rate of 1.8 percent and the British growth rate of 1.2 percent. We can then approximate the length of time required for the U.S. GNP to double as 40 years and that for the United Kingdom as 60 years, calculated as

$$\text{Years to double} = \frac{72}{\text{Annual growth rate}}$$

$$\text{Years to double, U.S.} = \frac{72}{1.8\% \text{ per year}} \quad \text{or} \quad 40 \text{ years}$$

$$\text{Years to double, UK} = \frac{72}{1.2\% \text{ per year}} \quad \text{or} \quad 60 \text{ years}$$

Changes in Real GNP—Short-Run and Long-Run Views

At the beginning of this chapter, we noted that increases in potential GNP can cause economic growth, or increases in real GNP per capita. But must potential GNP increase—that is, must the production possibilities curve shift outward—for an economy to grow? To answer this question we must distinguish short-run changes in real GNP from sustained increases, just as in Chapter 29 we distinguished short-run changes in price levels from inflation.

---

* Based on Robert J. Gordon, *Macroeconomics,* 4th ed. Boston: Little, Brown, 1988, pp. 555–556.

(a) An increase in aggregate demand

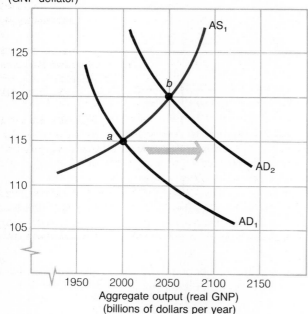

(b) An increase in aggregate supply

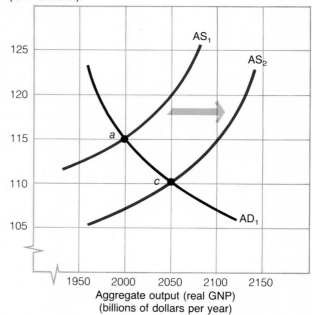

Exhibit 30.2
Short-Run Changes in Real GNP
A short-run increase in real GNP can occur as a result of a change in either aggregate demand or aggregate supply. In part (a) an increase in aggregate demand (from AD_1 to AD_2) increases real output from $2000 billion to $2050 billion. In part (b) an increase in aggregate supply (from AS_1 to AS_2) also increases real GNP from $2000 billion to $2050 billion.

Short-run changes in real GNP. In the short run, real GNP changes in response to changes in either aggregate demand or short-run aggregate supply. Exhibit 30.2(a) shows how an increase in aggregate demand (a shift of the curve from AD_1 to AD_2) increases real GNP. Exhibit 30.2(b) shows how an increase in short-run aggregate supply (a shift of the curve from AS_1 to AS_2) also increases real GNP. Note that because this is a short-run view, we can assume a constant population. Thus higher real GNP means higher real GNP per capita. Real GNP increases from $2000 billion to $2050 billion, an increase of $50 billion (or 2.5 percent), calculated as

$$\text{Growth rate in real GNP} = \frac{GNP_2 - GNP_1}{GNP_1} \times 100 \quad \text{or} \quad \frac{\text{Change in GNP}}{GNP_1} \times 100$$

$$= \frac{\$2050 - \$2000}{\$2000} \times 100$$

$$= \frac{\$50}{\$2000} \times 100 \quad \text{or} \quad 2.5\%$$

Similarly, a decrease in aggregate demand or a decrease in aggregate supply will cause real GNP and/or the growth rate of real GNP to decline from one year to the next.

Short-run changes in real GNP: A historical example. This short-run view of real GNP changes is supported by historic events. For example, from 1962 to 1966, real GNP per capita in the United States increased at an average annual rate of 3.9 percent, or well above the long-run trend of 1.8 percent. Most economists attribute this high growth to increases in aggregate demand, especially increases in government spending. Exhibit 30.3(a) shows changes in aggregate demand, aggregate supply, and potential GNP during this period of time.

Note that actual GNP grew by $409 billion between 1962 and 1966—from $1799 to $2208 billion. (Actual GNP is indicated by the intersection of the aggregate demand and short-run aggregate supply curves.) At the same time, potential GNP grew by $270 billion. How did actual GNP grow by $139 billion more than potential GNP? In 1962 actual GNP ($1799 billion) was below potential GNP ($1826 billion). Part of the increase in real GNP from 1962–1966 reflected the closing of this contractionary gap. In addition, aggregate demand increased fast enough to push actual GNP in 1966 ($2208 billion) above potential GNP ($2096), opening a $112 billion expansionary gap. Economists separate the growth that occurred into two parts: (1) the temporary changes in real GNP resulting from the closing and opening of gaps; and (2) the long-run changes in potential GNP. But long-run economic growth should be measured as increases in potential GNP. To see why, consider what happened in the years after 1966, as shown in Exhibit 30.3(b).

Between 1966 and 1970, real GNP grew by $208 billion (from $2208 billion to $2416 billion). During the same period, potential GNP increased by $320 billion. The slower growth in actual GNP partly reflects the economy's attempt to close the expansionary gap in 1966. Had there been no change in potential GNP, aggregate supply would have decreased. However, because potential GNP increased, aggregate supply continued to increase, although more slowly than before. At the same time, the inflation rate, which averaged only 1.7 percent per year from 1958 to 1964, increased to 3.6 percent in 1966 and to over 5 percent in 1968 and 1969. In addition, real GNP increased at an average annual rate of 2.7 percent from 1966 to 1970. By contrast, potential GNP grew at an average annual rate of 3.7 percent in the same period. As shown in Exhibit 30.3(b), the economy was operating at its potential GNP level in 1970.

Long-run changes in real GNP. The preceding example illustrates an important point about changes in real GNP: *In the short run, real GNP can grow faster or slower than potential GNP. But in the long run, real GNP growth is limited by potential GNP growth.* If real GNP grows faster than potential GNP, an expansionary gap results. If real GNP grows more slowly than potential GNP, a contractionary gap results. In either case, the automatic adjustment mechanism closes the gaps. Thus only increases in potential GNP translate into sustainable increases in real GNP per capita.

If there are two reasons why real GNP might increase, we must distinguish between two basic policy issues: (1) stabilization policy to close GNP gaps; and (2) growth policies to increase potential GNP. If real GNP grows more slowly than potential GNP, a contractionary gap will open. To close the gap, government may use stabilization policies (discretionary fiscal or monetary policies to increase aggregate demand) or allow the economy to stabilize itself. But stabilization

Exhibit 30.3

Changes in Real GNP: 1962–1970

The graphs illustrate changes in real GNP that occurred between 1962 and 1970. Part (a) shows that in 1962 there was a contractionary gap (actual GNP was less than potential GNP). But from 1962 to 1966 aggregate demand grew faster than potential output, causing a significant expansionary gap (actual GNP was larger than potential GNP). While some of the increase in real GNP from 1962 to 1966 represented growth in potential output, another part reflected short-run changes resulting from closing and opening GNP gaps. Part (b) shows that from 1966 to 1970, actual GNP grew more slowly than potential output as the increase in aggregate supply slowed, closing the expansionary gap by 1970.

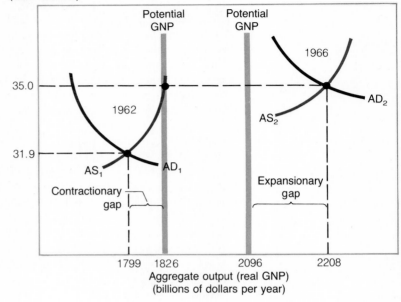

(a) Fast growth from 1962 to 1966

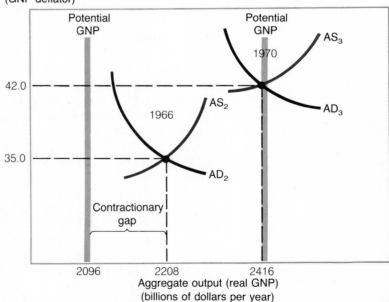

(b) Slower growth from 1966 to 1970

Economic growth is generally measured as an increase in real GNP per capita. It represents an increase in the average standard of living.

The "rule of 72" predicts how long it will take for GNP to double for any constant rate of growth.

Real GNP per capita can increase in the short run due to a closing of a contractionary or opening of an expansionary gap. Over the long run economic growth requires increases in the economy's potential GNP.

policies and the closing of GNP gaps are short-run issues. In this chapter, we want to focus on long-run issues and policies to achieve economic growth, that is, long-run, sustainable increases in potential GNP. Thus we concentrate on factors that help explain the growth rate of potential GNP.

FACTORS IN ECONOMIC GROWTH

Basically, there are two ways of obtaining increases in economic output: putting more resources to work and getting more output from available resources. Thus increased potential GNP requires an increase in the quantity or productivity of one of four factors: (1) supplies of natural resources, such as land, water, and minerals; (2) supplies of labor; (3) supplies of capital resources, such as machinery and buildings; or (4) technology.

Economists currently assume that increases in the availability of virtually all these factors are possible. However, for many centuries economists assumed that only labor supplies could change. The results of these different assumptions help explain why classical economists expected no economic growth, whereas economists now worry about the recent decline in the rate of U.S. economic growth.

Classical Assumptions and Doomsday Predictions

Although modern industrial economies experience regular increases in real GNP per capita, economic growth is relatively recent. Until 1750 or so, neither aggregate economic output nor the population in Western Europe had grown over the long run. Thus it was natural for the classical economists of the eighteenth and nineteenth centuries to search for a theory to explain why economies have a zero growth rate.

Fixed supplies and diminishing returns. Classical economists reached their conclusion about zero growth by assuming that supplies of important resources, especially land, were fixed and that technology changed very slowly, if at all. These were not unreasonable assumptions at the time. Agriculture accounted for most, but not all, economic activity. What manufacturing existed focused largely on processing certain agricultural products, such as cotton or wool. In such an economy land was naturally seen as a major limiting factor.

Moreover, farming was largely labor intensive. There were little capital equipment and few significant scientific advances in farm production. Increases in agricultural output could be achieved only by adding additional labor resources to fixed land supplies. Thus increases in output were limited by the economic **law of diminishing returns**. This law states that less and less extra output can be obtained by adding more and more labor to fixed supplies of land and capital.

To see this effect on a small scale, consider a single farm. A farmer may be able to increase total output by 1000 bushels by hiring a single helper. He may obtain even more output by adding a second and a third helper. But with fixed amounts of land and capital, each additional helper hired will increase output by less and less. As economists are fond of saying, were it not for the law of diminishing returns, we could grow the world's food supply in a flowerpot just by adding enough labor and other resources.

Law of diminishing returns. The proposition that adding labor to a fixed quantity of land and capital will eventually result in smaller and smaller increases in total output if technology is constant.

Thomas Malthus and the "dismal science".   In his famous book, *An Essay on the Principle of Population* (first published in 1798), Thomas Malthus saw a conflict between population growth and what he believed to be a fixed supply of natural resources. He concluded that population tends to grow faster over the long run than the economy's ability to support it.

Malthus recognized that if a country's population is small relative to its land resources, additional workers may increase per capita output. (Even today, labor-intensive agricultural societies view having many children as creating workers who produce more than they eat.) But if population growth continues unchecked, more and more workers are added to the same quantity of land. If capital and technology do not change, the law of diminishing returns means that additional workers eventually will produce less than they consume. At that point, the average standard of living will fall. According to Malthus, population growth will eventually push the average standard of living down to a subsistence level. Beyond that point, starvation, disease, and wars will limit population growth. No wonder economics back then was called the "dismal science"!

Modern Assumptions and Expectations of Economic Growth

Since Malthus's time, the world's population has grown enormously. But its standard of living, especially in the industrialized nations, has also risen dramatically. Modern economists believe Malthus was wrong because he made the wrong assumptions. Since his time, major advances in technology have expanded supplies of capital resources and land for agricultural production. (Note that the world still has the same amount of land as in Malthus's time, but far more of it is now put to agricultural use, particularly in North America.)

Malthus's assumptions were reasonable to him at the time. He had no reason to expect the growth of technology and increase in capital resources to come. Technological change was extremely important to economic growth during the Industrial Revolution in the nineteenth century. And in the United States, technological change may account for as much as 40 percent of the country's economic growth since World War II.

Linked to technological advances are increased supplies of capital resources that have substantially increased **labor productivity**, that is, average output per employed worker. Increases in the *quality* of labor (through education and training) have also contributed to economic growth. As a result, growth in the production of food and other economic goods and services has outstripped population growth, which is not the result Malthus predicted.

However, the world is not completely free from the conditions about which Malthus wrote. As Malthus observed, we cannot view an increase in population as just an increase in labor resources (and thus in aggregate supply). Whenever population grows faster than real output, the average standard of living will decline. As we noted earlier, in poor countries rapid population growth offsets many gains in real output. And some nations with abundant labor resources—the People's Republic of China, for example—have had relatively slow economic growth because of difficulties in putting those resources to effective use.

Moreover, in some African countries such as Ethiopia, the quantity of arable (farm) land has shrunk greatly in recent decades because of severe droughts. In some of these nations, the average standard of living is quite close to or at the subsistence level, and starvation is not a remote possibility but a recurring fact of

Labor productivity. The average output per unit of labor input, most often measured as real output per hour of work.

life. But for most of the world, economic growth is a reality. To understand why and what, if anything, we can do to increase the rate of economic growth, we must consider the factors that contribute to economic growth.

Changes in Natural Resources

Although the world's total supply of any natural resource is fixed, the quantity available for particular purposes may change. Damming rivers can turn water power into electric power and provide energy for economic use. Discoveries of new reserves—oil in the North Sea and in Alaska—or the development of substitutes for natural resources—synthetic rubber—can also add to an economy's potential GNP. Improved transportation systems—the building of the transcontinental railroad in the United States, for example—can make more resources available to the economy.

Changes in the Labor Supply

In Chapter 26, we noted that an increase in the labor supply can raise potential GNP. The increase in the labor supply might occur because of an increase in population. But as we just stated, a larger population not only means more workers, but also more people to feed, house, and clothe. Unless output per worker also increases, real GNP per capita will not increase, although total output may rise. Thus in considering changes in the labor supply, economists now believe that economic growth will occur only if the proportion of the population that contributes to GNP (the employment/population ratio) increases or if labor productivity increases.

The employment/population ratio. An increase in the proportion of the population that is employed—that is, the employment/population ratio—increases the quantity of labor supplied by the same population. Reducing the proportion of the population not in the labor force adds to output just as reducing unemployment does. Thus economists observe that an increase in the employment/population ratio adds to the economy's potential GNP and to real GNP per capita. In the United States, the increasing proportion of women seeking work in the 1960s and 1970s increased both the employment/population ratio and the rate of economic growth. However, changes in the employment/population ratio can have only a limited effect on economic growth. After all, we cannot expect 100 percent of the population to be employed. Moreover, with a few exceptions—efforts to reduce population growth rates or eliminate mandatory retirement programs—little can be done to change this factor.

Changes in the employment/population ratio may reflect changes in the age distribution of the population. In less-developed countries with high birth rates, children account for an increasing proportion of the population. As a result, employment/population ratios are declining, making economic growth more difficult. In the United States, an increasing proportion of the population is reaching age 65 and retiring from the active labor force. This trend may make increases in real GNP per capita more difficult in the future.

Moreover, we can't lose sight of the element of truth in Malthus's gloomy predictions. Without improvements in technology and/or increase in capital resources, the law of diminishing returns would indeed apply. That is, we would expect an increase in labor supply to result in a fall in labor productivity—the average output per employed worker. As a result, the average standard of living would decrease. To achieve significant long-run economic growth, labor productivity must improve.

Quality of labor.   One factor affecting labor productivity is the quality of labor, that is, the skills, training, experience, and mobility of labor. An increase in the quality of labor raises the output per worker and therefore raises real GNP per capita. Although we cannot measure precisely the contribution of this factor, some economists believe that as much as 15–20 percent of the past economic growth in the United States can be attributed to growth in the quality of the labor force.

In any economy, expenditures on education and training can pay off in terms of future economic growth. However, as with all economic decisions, investment in labor quality requires sacrifices. More should be invested only if the extra benefits (higher future growth) are worth the extra costs (less current consumption). However, education, training, and experience of the labor force are just the tip of the labor-quality iceberg. Many economists believe that such intangibles as entrepreneurship, the work ethic, inventiveness, and "Yankee ingenuity" are as or more important. They believe that much of the past economic success of the United States relative to the rest of the world resulted from these unmeasurable but powerful factors.

If these intangibles really are important to economic growth, can an economy somehow foster them? The answer to this question is highly controversial. Some economists suggest that high marginal tax rates in the United States and Western Europe may have stifled innovation. (This argument was offered as a reason for the substantial cuts in the marginal tax rates in both 1981 and 1986.) Others take the same stand on centrally planned economies such as the Soviet Union's. They question whether the U.S.S.R. can continue to grow at its current rate because managers and workers in that system have little incentive to innovate or adopt new technology.

Changes in Capital Resources

In our discussion of Malthus and more recent economic-growth theory, you saw that changes in capital resources—an increased number of machines, for example—can affect economic growth. Such changes actually cause growth indirectly. That is, they increase the productivity of labor, which causes economic growth.

Capital/labor ratio.   Economists measure the effect of changes in capital resources on labor productivity as the **capital/labor ratio**, or the average quantity of capital resources per worker. As this ratio rises, we can anticipate more output per worker because they have more machinery and other capital resources to work with.

A rising capital/labor ratio appears to have played a major role in the economic growth of industrialized nations. For example, the use of more and larger agricultural equipment is credited for much of the tremendous increase in agricultural productivity in the United States. In fact, some economists believe that economic growth requires an increase in capital. That is, it does little good to have a larger and better educated work force if that work force lacks the necessary capital resources to maintain and increase their productivity. Without an increase in

Capital/labor ratio. The average quantity of capital resources per worker, calculated by dividing the stock of capital by the number of employed workers.

Extensive growth. Economic growth achieved by increasing the quantity of economic resources, such as labor and capital resources.

capital, the law of diminishing returns would apply, and output per worker would fall.

Interaction of saving and investment. To increase the capital/labor ratio the economy must increase its investment in capital resources. In fact, investment (over and above the amount necessary to replace worn-out or obsolete capital resources) must grow faster than the labor force. But we said in Chapter 21 that GNP is the sum of consumption, investment, government purchases, and net exports. Thus if the economy is operating at its potential GNP level, an increase in investment requires a decrease in another component of GNP.

For example, a decrease in consumption (that is, an increase in private saving) or a reduction in government purchases would free resources for investment, as would lowering net exports. That is, we could lower the quantity of goods we ship to other countries (exports) and increase the quantity of goods we import. By lowering our exports, we have more potential to produce capital resources domestically. By increasing our imports, we can purchase more capital resources such as machines. Or we can import consumer goods, freeing domestic industries to produce capital resources.

But the foreign sector cannot be relied on indefinitely. For an economy to increase imports faster than exports, it must borrow from other countries. That is, purchases must either be paid for now (with export earnings) or later. But paying later for goods consumed now means borrowing. Inflows of foreign capital can increase output in the short run. Funds supplied by the World Bank, the International Monetary Fund, and by individual countries such as the United States have been important sources of temporary financing in less-developed nations. But, ultimately, economic growth is limited by the amount of internal saving an economy can generate. Eventually nations must trade off current consumption for economic growth and future consumption.

Economists refer to growth caused by an increased supply of capital resources as **extensive growth**. The Soviet Union, which has given a high priority to economic growth, has achieved much of its past growth by allocating a large share of production to capital resources. By fostering extensive growth, central planners in the Soviet Union have managed to increase real output faster than has the U.S. economy in the last 40 years. But extensive growth requires saving, that is, a sacrifice of consumption. Thus while the Soviet Union has grown, it has done so at the expense of satisfying demand for consumer goods.

Keep in mind that in arguing for nations to save today in order to grow tomorrow, we assume that their economies are already producing at the potential GNP level. If there is a contractionary gap, increasing saving or decreasing government spending may reduce aggregate demand unless it is matched by an equal increase in investment. That is, more saving may decrease real GNP in the short run, or what we called the paradox of thrift in Chapter 23. But what happens to demand in the short run can have important effects on long-run supply. If an economy operates at below its potential GNP, it will fail to produce all the goods and services that it can. The result will be less actual saving and investment and thus less growth. Thus maintaining full employment can help an economy grow in the future.

Changes in Technology

Another factor in economic growth—changes in technology—works by increasing the productivity of both labor and other resources. As we noted earlier,

Intensive growth. Economic growth achieved by increasing the productivity of economic resources, that is, by technological progress.

Economies of scale. A situation in which long-run average cost decreases as a firm increases the size (or scale) of its plant and output; implies that larger plants are more technically efficient than small plants if large quantities of goods are produced.

technological changes are credited with a great deal of nineteenth- and twentieth-century economic growth. Economists use the term **intensive growth** to describe growth generated by changes in technology.

We can identify two broad types of technological change that can lead to intensive growth. Some technological changes directly improve methods of production. For example, better soil management, erosion control, and pesticide control have contributed to greater agricultural production throughout the world. Other technological changes take the form of new products such as computers and telecommunications systems. Both types of technological change have been important in the past. Whether they can continue to spur economic growth remains to be seen.

Reallocation of Resources

Finally, increases in productivity and potential GNP may occur if resources are reallocated. As we noted earlier, having more resources is of little direct benefit unless they are effectively organized and used. In many less-developed countries, productivity in the agricultural sector is still relatively low, while individuals are severely underemployed. If surplus labor resources can be moved from the low-productivity agricultural sector to the high-productivity industrial sector, average productivity will increase. The opportunity to make such transfers may be limited, of course, especially if there are few industrial jobs. Moreover, such transfers often require education and training of workers. In addition, transfers may also require increases in capital resources to make workers more productive.

An economy can achieve a limited amount of growth through labor reallocation. The transfer of labor from agricultural to nonagricultural industries was a significant factor in U.S. economic growth in the 1940s and 1950s. And this type of change could still increase economic growth in many less-developed nations. Unfortunately, these countries often do not have many capital resources or the income to invest in labor reallocation.

Reallocating resources may allow countries to employ technology and capital equipment that is productive only when the volume of output is large. Although not every increase in size generates greater productivity, when **economies of scale** do exist, larger firms will be more productive than smaller firms. In such cases, reallocating resources from smaller, less efficient plants to larger, more efficient ones can raise average productivity.

ACCOUNTING FOR ECONOMIC GROWTH

In the preceding discussion we identified the factors responsible for economic growth. In this section we want to explore the actual growth of the U.S. economy. What factors contributed the most to economic growth in the past? How can we explain the growth rate of the U.S. economy relative to two of its main economic rivals, West Germany and Japan? What accounts for the fact that the growth rate of the U.S. economy in the 1970s and early 1980s was far below its historical average?

RECAP

Economic growth can occur because of increases in resources or increases in productivity.

Discovery or development of natural resources can add to the economy's potential GNP.

Labor supplies can increase because of a higher employment/population ratio; population growth; increased skills; or more-efficient work habits and inventiveness.

An increase in the capital/labor ratio resulting from investment in additional capital can increase productivity. Greater investment requires additional saving or an inflow of foreign capital if the economy is operating at full employment. Growth caused by increased capital is called extensive growth.

Technological progress increases productivity, enabling the economy to obtain more output from the same quantity of resources. Such growth is called intensive growth.

Source	1929–1948	1948–1973	1973–1979	1980–1982
Quantity of labor	1.07%	1.21%	1.73%	1.49%
Quality of labor	0.38	0.25	0.17	0.27
Quantity of capital	0.11	0.77	0.76	0.51
Technology	0.49	1.09	0.22	−0.58
Resource allocation	0.53	0.57	0.13	0.07
Other	−0.01	0.00	0.00	0.06
Potential GNP	2.57%	3.89%	3.01%	1.82%
Less: Population growth	0.98	1.48	1.01	1.06
Real GNP per capita	1.59%	2.41%	2.00%	0.76%

Exhibit 30.4
Sources of Economic Growth in the United States: 1929–1982

Source: Edward Denison, *Accounting for Slower Economic Growth.* Washington, D.C.: Brookings Institution, 1985, Table 8-2, p. 112.

Sources of U.S. Economic Growth, 1929–1973

Growth of the U.S. economy from 1929 to 1973 was impressive. Real GNP per capita more than doubled, rising from $5830 in 1929 to $12,950 in 1973. Exhibit 30.4 compares sources of economic growth in potential GNP in four periods. These figures are from a study by economist Edward Denison, who attempted to track and explain U.S. economic growth.*

The first two columns in Exhibit 30.4 show that potential GNP grew faster immediately after World War II than before the war—3.89 percent versus 2.57 percent—and suggests the reasons for it. In both periods, increases in the *quantity* of labor accounted for over 1 percent of growth annually. *Quality* changes in the labor force (rising educational levels and the changing age–gender mix of workers) also contributed significantly to total growth in both periods.

But improved labor quality accounts for less of the growth in the more recent period, which Denison attributes to the rising proportion of young and women workers in the labor force. As Denison points out, these groups were concentrated in low-skilled (and low-paid) occupations, but were not inherently less productive. Thus the faster growth attributed to higher quantities of labor in 1948–1973 was offset by a smaller contribution from improvements in the quality of labor.

Improvements in resource allocation were also responsible for much of the growth. In both the 1929–1948 and 1948–1973 periods, growth occurred because production was transferred to larger plants (economies of scale). Labor transfers—from farm to industrial employment, for example—also resulted in growth. But neither labor nor other resource allocation accounts for the large difference between the two periods. Rather, as Exhibit 30.4 indicates, higher growth after World War II resulted from two factors. First, the quantity of capital contributed more to growth from 1948 to 1973 than from 1929 to 1948. Second, technology—or what Denison calls "advances in knowledge"—added greatly to postwar growth.

---

* In his study Denison actually uses potential national income, not output. As we have noted before, however, national income and aggregate output, although not identical, are very closely related. We can expect that the changes Denison observed in potential national income will apply also to potential GNP. Moreover, Denison, like most economists who have tried to account for growth, does not directly calculate the contribution of technology. Rather, he explains as much of the growth as he can by using other factors. Technology is assumed to account for the rest.

Reasons for the lower rate of capital growth between 1929 and 1948 are obvious. The Great Depression of the 1930s slowed capital investment considerably (which illustrates the importance of high employment to economic growth). Moreover, private investment was postponed during World War II, when the economy concentrated on production of war materiel. The faster growth rate of technology since 1948 may also reflect somewhat the same two events. Expenditures on private research and development during the Great Depression and World War II were small compared to those of the postwar period. Research and development expenditures do not always pay off, but when they do, the result is reflected in economic growth through technological progress. (See A Case in Point: Sources of Growth for a comparison of economic growth in the United States, Japan, and West Germany.)

Slowdown in Economic Growth Since 1973

Since 1973 the rate of economic growth in the United States has slowed considerably. Real GNP per capita grew by only 2.00 percent per year between 1973 and 1979 and by only 0.76 percent per year from 1980 to 1982. The slowdown in real GNP growth reflects economically troubled times. As we noted in Chapter 27, major supply shocks in both 1973–74 and 1979 triggered recessions. The 1981–82 recession in the United States also reflected contractionary policies used to bring down the rate of inflation.

However, our interest in this chapter is not in the temporary changes in GNP that reflect recessions. Rather, we want to know how changes affect the growth rate of potential GNP. Denison's analysis, as shown in Exhibit 30.4, indicates that potential GNP growth has slowed since 1973 in part because of a slight decline in the growth of capital. But the slowdown resulted primarily from less technological progress and the end of resource-allocation contributions to growth.

According to Denison's calculations, technology accounted for a much smaller part of growth in the late 1970s and did not make a positive contribution at all in the early 1980s. In addition, resource allocation, a significant factor in earlier periods, had virtually no effect on the growth rate after 1973. As we suggested earlier, even in the immediate postwar period, the United States had nearly reached the limit of resource allocation as a source of growth. The 1973–1982 period saw other nations reach the limit, too.

Denison believed that labor-productivity growth had fallen—a conclusion confirmed by other data. Since 1890, labor productivity has grown at an average rate of 2 percent per year. From 1950 to 1965 productivity growth was 2.7 percent per year, or well above the long-run trend. Between 1965 and 1973, productivity grew at just under 2 percent per year. Since 1973, however, productivity growth has averaged less than 1 percent per year. Even after the economy rebounded from the recession in 1981–82, productivity growth remained disappointing. In fact, productivity growth averaged less than 1 percent in 1986.

As with many economic variables, productivity growth follows the business cycle. That is, it generally falls during a recession and rises during a recovery. This pattern occurs partly because employers are reluctant to lay off all their most skilled workers for fear of losing them permanently. Thus businesses keep some skilled workers on the payroll, even though there is not enough work to keep

A Case in Point
Sources of Growth:
An International Comparison

Edward Denison also analyzed the high economic-growth rates in West Germany and Japan since World War II. The table below shows that growth in both countries greatly exceeded that of the United States. In all three countries, increases in labor supplies were significant. However, this factor accounts for little of the difference in growth rates.

The biggest difference is the faster increase in capital resources in Japan and West Germany. Some attribute the capital growth to the higher saving rates in Japan

Sources of Economic Growth in the United States, Japan, and West Germany: 1929–1973 (percentage contributions to total growth in national income)

Source	United States 1948–1969	Japan 1953–1971	West Germany 1950–1962
Quantity of labor	0.99%	1.37%	1.22%
Quality of labor	0.31	0.48	0.15
Quantity of capital	0.79	2.10	1.41
Technology	1.19	1.97	0.87
Resource allocation	0.72	2.88	2.52
Other	0.00	0.01	0.10
Potential output	4.00%	8.81%	6.27%

Source: Edward Denison and William Chung, *How Japan's Economy Grew So Fast.* Washington, D.C.: Brookings Institution, 1976, Table 4-8, pp. 42–43.

and West Germany. Because saving and investment are connected, some economists believe that the United States must seek policies to increase saving if growth rates are to increase again. But both Japan and West Germany also received aid from the U.S. economy which helped them modernize and rebuild.

A second important difference is the contribution of resource allocation, including movement out of agriculture and self-employment, and economies of scale. As we noted earlier, the contribution of this factor is limited. The United States simply appears to have reached its limits earlier than the other two countries.

Finally, Denison's calculations indicate that technology is responsible for a relatively large share of the difference in the growth rate between the United States and Japan. These statistics have led some economists to suggest that efforts to increase the rate of technological progress may be necessary to close this gap.

Since 1973, the rate of economic growth in the United States has slowed considerably. Real GNP per capita grew by 2.65 percent per year between 1960 and 1973, but by only 1.46 percent from 1973 to 1985. Because the United States is a major buyer and seller of internationally traded goods, the slowdown in U.S. economic activity was reflected in other countries as well. Growth also slowed in Western Europe and Japan in the latter period, largely as a result of oil-supply shocks. But the economies of both Japan and West Germany experienced greater growth than the U.S. economy.

them fully occupied. In order to see the true impact of productivity on potential GNP, we have to adjust our figures to remove cyclical effects. But even after making these adjustments, we find that productivity growth still averaged only 1 percent per year in the first half of the 1980s, or only one-half the long-run average. Why has productivity growth fallen? We explore some possible explanations in the following sections. Unfortunately, none of them fully explains what happened to productivity.

Declining technological progress. As we noted earlier, Denison attributed part of the decline in real GNP growth to a lower rate of technological progress. Other studies draw similar conclusions. But these studies, like Denison's, measure technological progress as the amount of growth that cannot be explained by other factors. Indirect evidence also indicates that efforts to improve technology may have decreased, however. For example, the percentage of GNP devoted to research and development appears to have fallen.

Declining capital/labor ratio. Recall that an increase in the capital/labor ratio tends to increase labor productivity because workers have more and better machinery with which to work. However, the actual capital/labor ratio in the United States has declined in recent years. Why did it decline? One explanation is that the economy has operated well below the potential GNP level during many of the years since 1973, experiencing three recessions. Recessions tend to slow the rate of capital investment for two reasons: (1) businesses have lower profits with which to finance such spending; and (2) the short-run payoff of new investments is low when business conditions are uncertain and unfavorable.

The rapid increase in energy prices that occurred during this period may also explain part of this change. According to this argument, capital and energy are complements, whereas energy and labor are substitutes. Therefore higher energy costs increase the use of labor and decrease the use of capital, lowering the capital/labor ratio. Higher energy costs—and the consequent decrease in the short-run aggregate supply curve—have also been suggested as causes of the recessions in 1973–1975 and 1980.

Economists generally conclude that the change in the capital/labor ratio accounts for part but not all of the slowdown in productivity. However, many economists still believe that efforts to increase capital growth are a key to increasing labor productivity and, consequently, potential GNP.

Government regulations. Some economists blame part of the productivity slowdown on increased government regulation during the 1970s. Government increasingly regulated the environment, worker health and safety, auto safety, and other areas of social concern during that decade. And these policies did divert some capital resources from investments that could have increased productive capacity or the capital/labor ratio. Moreover, managerial efforts devoted to satisfying government regulations might have been used instead to increase productivity.

But while these policies may have lowered measured productivity, they also offered some benefits. For example, diverting labor and capital resources to pollution control can improve air and water quality and thus the standard of living. Such benefits are not fully measured by GNP, but they may provide a reason not to completely abandon policies that may lower measured growth.

Management problems. Mistakes on the part of managers—and their failure to solve management problems—may also have contributed to lower economic growth. Critics charge that U.S. managers are more interested in short-run results than in long-term gains, leading to too little investment in research and development. Major mistakes may also have made the United States a noncompetitor in some world markets. Certainly, U.S. automakers have paid for responding slowly to changing consumer demands. And the U.S. steel industry has lost sales by failing to invest in modern, cost-cutting technology.

But is this apparent shortsightedness a management problem, or is it related to uncertainties in the economy? Did mistakes by U.S. manufacturers or govern-

RECAP

Studies of economic growth in the United States attribute the growth to an increased supply of labor, a rise in the capital/labor ratio, technological progress, and improved allocation of resources.

The higher growth rate from 1948 to 1973 than from 1929 to 1948 principally reflects an increase in the capital/labor ratio and a higher rate of technological progress.

The slowdown in economic growth in the United States since 1973 has been attributed to a combination of factors, including less technological progress, a declining capital/labor ratio, government regulations, management problems, and misguided macroeconomic policies.

ment regulations divert resources away from investment in capital resources and research and development? To what extent are labor unions also responsible for businesses' shortsightedness and low productivity growth? Unfortunately, we do not have conclusive answers to any of these questions.

Macroeconomic policies. Finally, some critics argue that macroeconomic policies in the 1970s caused high and variable inflation. High inflation, in turn, resulted in less saving and investment because of the tax system. When inflation occurs, individuals receive higher nominal income and pay higher taxes, lowering their real income. If they try to maintain the same real level of consumption, their saving must decline. Similarly, businesses are taxed on inflated profits and will decrease investment. Higher taxes on nominal interest earned also discourages saving.

Advocates of supply-side policies pushed for—and won—some changes in the federal tax system in 1981. (See A Case in Point: Supply-Side Effects of Tax Cuts for more on their views.) Individual tax rates are now indexed (as of 1985), that is, they will be adjusted automatically for changes in the price level. The tax reforms in 1986 lowered tax rates and made the tax rates less progressive. Whether these changes will lead to higher future growth remains to be seen. There is not much evidence that the tax changes in 1981 influenced either saving or growth.

Other economists also blame macroeconomic policies but for different reasons. Keynesians such as James Tobin argue that overly restrictive monetary policies in the 1970s and early 1980s kept the economy operating at below its potential GNP level. When output falls, so does saving and investment, further lowering output. As Tobin observes, maintaining output close to the potential level not only maximizes current production, but also adds to investment and potential GNP growth.

This survey of possible causes has not enabled us to draw any final conclusions about why the U.S. economy's growth has slowed. In fact, most economists believe that the slowdown stems from a combination of the factors we presented and discussed. But because the slowdown seems to have several causes, economists have also suggested a number of possible policies to again speed up the rate of economic growth.

IMPROVING ECONOMIC GROWTH: POLICY OPTIONS

The slowdown in the rate of economic growth that has occurred in recent years is troubling for what it implies, not so much about the present but about the future. For this reason, policies to raise this growth rate are believed to be important. Indeed, the Reagan administration's economic policies have been devoted in large part to this economic goal. As we explore the policies of this and other administrations, keep in mind the following point: *In the long run, economic growth requires an increase in the capital/labor ratio and/or technological progress. Policies to change the rate of economic growth will work if they can affect at least one of these two factors.*

A Case in Point
Supply-Side Effects of Tax Cuts

In most of our discussion of government policy and the macroeconomy, we have stressed the demand side of the economy, especially the demand-side orientation of Keynesian economists. But government policies can also affect the supply side of the economy, that is, aggregate supply and potential GNP. How significant are these effects?

Supply-side economists believe that government policies can make a measurable difference. They advocate government policies to enhance private incentives to work, save, and invest. Most argue for the removal of government regulations, which they believe have stifled economic incentives, and cutting income tax rates.

Lower tax rates increase the rewards of working, thereby increasing the incentive to work. A wage rate of $10 an hour before taxes adds only $4 an hour to after-tax income if the marginal tax rate is 60 percent. But lowering the rate to 25 percent raises the effective wage to $7.50 per hour. As we discussed in Chapter 26, additional work effort on the part of the same population increases aggregate supply and potential GNP.

Lower taxes also increase the incentive to save. A 10 percent interest rate on savings means only a 4 percent after-tax return if the marginal tax rate is 60 percent. Lowering the marginal rate to 20 percent raises the after-tax return on savings to 8 percent. Similarly, lower taxes on business increases the profits that can

be earned on investments in factories and equipment and in research and development of new technologies. As we noted in this chapter, an economy must invest to grow, and to invest it must either save or borrow from foreign economies. Lower taxes may increase both domestic saving and investment and, consequently, increase aggregate supply and potential GNP.

Most economists believe that such policies have relatively small short-run effects on aggregate supply. In fact, supply-side economics is, for the most part, aimed at making small increases in the rate of economic growth. But even small increases add up to significant gains over the long run. However, some ardent supporters of supply-side policies argue that the economy can make a significant short-run response to improved incentives. In supporting the large tax cuts of 1981, for example, they predicted that total tax revenues would actually increase despite lower tax rates.

Actual evidence from the 1981 tax cuts, however, suggests that the effects of tax cuts on aggregate supply are modest at best. Work effort, measured by the labor-force participation rate, has grown more slowly since 1981 than before. The decline in tax revenues was very much as predicted by traditional economic models. While there may be some small long-run effects of tax cuts, the claims of the ardent supply-siders appear to have been exaggerated.

Raising Saving and Investment

The capital/labor ratio can rise only if the growth of capital exceeds that of the labor force. As we noted earlier, in the long run greater investment must be matched by greater saving. Thus policies to improve the capital/labor ratio focus on increasing saving and investment.

Increasing the rate of saving.   The rate of saving is lower in the United States than in other industrialized nations that have had faster growth rates. As a result, some economists (including advisors to the Reagan administration) argue that the United States must increase its rate of saving if it is to again experience greater economic growth.

Policies to increase saving are directed both to personal saving (disposable income minus consumption) and to saving by business (retained earnings). Government can encourage both private and business saving through tax policies. For example, some economists argue for replacing the income tax with a consumption tax. Under such a policy, only the portion of income spent would be taxed, providing a strong incentive for saving. This tax is used in some European countries, but has not yet attracted the attention of many politicians in the United States.

The tax changes passed in 1981 and 1986 included some policies aimed at increasing the rate of saving. Tax rates fell significantly, raising the return on saving. Since income tax rates are now indexed, only changes in real income are taxed. Individuals may no longer deduct interest paid on consumer loans but may continue to deduct interest on home mortgages.

Increasing the rate of investment. As we observed earlier, the objective of growth policies is not higher saving as such but higher investment. Increased saving is important because it raises the supply of funds available for investment. Some economists have also proposed policies to directly increase demand for investment funds. Because investment spending is influenced by the after-tax rate of return, a reduction in taxes stimulates more investment, assuming that all other factors remain the same.

But as you well know by this time, all other things do not always remain unchanged. The 1986 tax changes lowered overall corporate tax rates. But the new tax laws allow much less generous deduction for depreciation. Moreover, a provision that allowed an immediate tax credit for new investment was eliminated. These changes work in opposite directions but appear to be more favorable to service industries (where capital investment is small). They appear to be less favorable to manufacturing industries (where capital investment is large). Some industries that face stiff foreign competition and want to renovate plant and buy new equipment—steel and automobiles, for example—may be harder pressed to make those investments.

Some economists have even argued that corporate taxes should be eliminated entirely. But if receipts from corporate taxes were eliminated, the federal government would either have to find another source of revenue or cut spending significantly. The political battle would be bloody because of existing budget deficits and likely objections that such a change favors affluent stockholders. Moreover, although increased investment in fixed capital is important, some government expenditures also increase potential GNP. Public expenditures on transportation and communication systems, public health, education and training, and research and development are social investments. As with any government spending, there is a short-run trade-off: The more resources the government uses, the fewer are the resources available for the private sector. But some government investments may be as important to long-run growth as additional private investment.

Increasing Technological Change

Another factor that we noted as important, and one that has apparently contributed to the declining growth rate, is technological change. Technological progress cannot be directly controlled, but it can be indirectly stimulated by increasing the resources devoted to research and development of new technologies. Government policies to spur technological progress thus take one of three approaches. First, government spending or subsidies may be targeted to specific projects or ideas. Second, favorable tax treatment of privately funded research and development can provide indirect government encouragement. And third, government can remove potential obstacles to technological growth.

Direct government spending and subsidies. Proponents of direct government subsidies and spending argue that recent declines in technological progress reflect market failures. To the degree that private returns on investment in research fail to capture total social returns, such policies may be warranted. In fact, it is often difficult for a private firm to capture the returns from technological breakthroughs because of the speed with which competitors may imitate them. The best case for direct government subsidies and spending appears to be in the area of basic research, in which the risks of market failure are greatest.

Indirect government support. One form of indirect government support for research and development is the patent system. This system increases the chance that an inventor will be able to capture the returns from innovation by granting a 17-year monopoly on an invention. Another indirect support is the favorable tax treatment of research and development expenditures compared with other forms of investment. Some economists who are concerned about recent declines in technological progress suggest that further support should be given in the form of tax credits. But as we noted earlier, reducing one form of taxes would force government either to cut spending or to find a new source of revenues.

Removing barriers. Other economists believe that government regulations have seriously impeded technological progress. They consider the money and effort that businesses spend to comply with government regulations as diverting resources away from productive uses. Government regulations on pollution, health, and safety appear to have increased both the length of time it takes to turn research into profits and the uncertainty of future returns.

Supporters of deregulation argue that it would have desirable effects on technological progress. They note that current government regulations impose costs on the economy, especially by reducing economic growth. Critics of deregulation acknowledge these costs but argue that regulations also force private decision makers to recognize external costs, thus providing social benefits. The principles of rational choice tell us that only those regulations that add more to social benefits than social costs should be implemented. But the often normative nature of measuring benefits and costs explains why economists rationally disagree about the "correct" policy.

Industrial Policy

Some economists believe that economic growth can be increased by means of a consciously designed and applied **industrial policy**. Actually a set of microeconomic policies, it includes tax rules, research and development grants, direct subsidies, international trade restrictions, and labor-training programs. Supporters of an industrial policy argue that Japan's use of one to redirect resources into industries with growth potential has been a major reason for that nation's high growth rate. They propose that the United States establish a counterpart to Japan's Ministry of International Trade and Industry (MITI) to set industrial priorities. Industries that show promise of growth would be given public support. Workers in other industries would be retrained to improve their mobility.

Supporters of this centralized process note that current industrial policies in the United States are likely contributing to less efficiency and economic growth.

Industrial policy. A set of microeconomic policies designed to affect economic growth; includes tax rules, research and development grants, direct subsidies, international trade restrictions, and labor-training programs.

These policies are a hodgepodge of special favors that have been given to industries having political clout. In many cases industries receiving government support have little growth potential. In contrast, a conscious, centralized process of selecting and supporting growth industries would assist the orderly transfer of resources to them from declining industries. Advocates of changes in U.S. industrial policy include Keynesians, monetarists, new classicists, and supply-siders. Indeed, most economists believe that special favors currently accorded specific industries—such as agriculture, textiles, and steel—are often inefficient.

However, the notion of a centralized, government-set industrial policy has many critics. Some argue that a government agency could not pick winning industries any better than do market forces. Many critics fear that bureaucrats in such an agency would give in to lobbyists, just as they have in the past. A number of the critics, especially some supply-siders, believe that government's role should be limited to assisting the market. They advocate general incentives to saving, investment, and research and development, and elimination of existing barriers to growth. But they believe that the market—not government—should determine where resources can be best utilized.

The issues raised by proponents of industrial policy are important even if their proposed solutions are controversial. Whether the best alternative to the current hodgepodge is a centralized system of specific supports or a decentralized system of general supports will continue to be strongly debated. Policy options to improve international competitiveness of the U.S. economy—including industrial policy—are considered in Chapter 31.

Stabilization Policies and Economic Growth

Economic-growth policies are designed to increase potential GNP. In contrast, stabilization policies are designed to keep the economy operating at close to its potential output (GNP) level while maintaining price stability. Although their aims are different, the two types of policies are closely related.

Supply-side economists note that poor stabilization policies may lead to high and variable rates of inflation. In turn, inflation creates uncertainty and potential distortions through a tax system that discourages saving and investment. Thus poorly designed stabilization policies can lead to slower economic growth. Keynesian economists note that poor stabilization policies may leave the economy operating below its potential output (GNP) level. Because real output is lower, saving and investment will fall, which will also slow economic growth.

Both groups raise valid points. In the long run, the total quantity of saving and investment can be raised only by increasing the proportion of real output that is both saved and invested. In the short run, higher real output associated with lower GNP gaps can raise total saving and investment even if there is no change in the portion of real output saved.

CONCLUSION

Economic growth, like the other economic goals, is not as easy to achieve in the real world as we might wish. Moreover, achieving greater economic growth is not inexpensive. Basically, economists understand how to achieve economic growth, as we have described in this chapter. Indeed, economists disagree less about what causes economic growth than they do about what causes inflation and unemployment. But they do not all agree that government policies have played—or can play—a very positive role in aiding economic growth.

It is not easy to balance the desire for greater economic growth with the desire to achieve other economic objectives. Thus there is no shortage of debate over the "best" policy. Much of this debate centers on the rate of economic growth that can be attained in the short run and the long run and how these rates can be reached. We have become accustomed to economic growth, and political policies intended to support continued growth are likely. But in the final analysis, many growth factors, including technological change, may not be easily manipulated by government policies.

SUMMARY

1. In this chapter we examined the meaning and causes of economic growth, as well as historical growth rates and policies designed to increase economic growth.

2. Economic growth is generally measured as an increase in real GNP per capita and is desired because it represents an increase in the average standard of living. Although real GNP per capita can increase in the short run due to a reduction in the GNP gap, over the long run economic growth requires an increase in the economy's potential GNP.

3. Classical economists, such as Malthus, assumed that land, capital, and technology were fixed. Thus they concluded that long-run economic growth was impossible. They believed that following the law of diminishing returns, increases in the population would eventually cause the standard of living to fall to subsistence levels. Economists now recognize the contribution of increases in land, capital, and technology to economic growth.

4. Growth may occur because of increased availability of natural resources, increased quantity and quality of labor resources, an increase in the capital/labor ratio, improved technology, or improved allocation of resources.

5. Studies of economic growth in the United States attribute this growth to an increase in the quantity and quality of labor resources, an increase in the capital/labor ratio, technological progress, and improved allocation of resources. The higher growth rate from 1948 to 1973 than in 1929 to 1948 principally reflects an increase in the capital/labor ratio and a higher rate of technological progress.

6. The slowdown in economic growth in the United States since 1973 has been attributed to a combination of factors, including a declining capital/labor ratio, government regulations, a lower rate of technological change, management problems, and the failure of stabilization policies.

7. Economists generally agree that in the long run, greater economic growth requires more saving and investment. Some believe that tax incentives to encourage saving and investment can be important. Others argue that the actual effect of tax incentives on saving has been quite small.

8. Technological progress has been important to past economic growth but has apparently slowed in recent years. Some suggest that government policies—direct subsidies and favorable tax treatment—may help to encourage research and development that will lead to technological change.

9. Some economists believe that economic growth can be increased by a centralized government agency coordinating industrial policy. The agency would identify and support industries with the greatest growth potential and encourage transfers of resources away from industries with little growth potential. Critics favor a reliance on market forces, with government's role limited to removing barriers to economic growth.

10. Stabilization and economic-growth policies are closely related. In order to achieve both price stability and economic growth, we must be careful to distinguish short-run problems from long-run problems. Controversies over the length of the short run and the effects of different policies are the focus of continuing economic debate.

KEY TERMS

Real GNP per capita, 765
Law of diminishing returns, 771
Labor productivity, 772
Capital/labor ratio, 774

QUESTIONS FOR
REVIEW AND DISCUSSION

1. Explain how a decline in the supply of an important energy source can slow economic growth.

2. Suppose that a major technological development results in a dramatic increase in the capital/labor ratio in an industry employing a large number of workers. How will this change affect the long-run growth of output in the industry? What are the potential short-run problems? What are the benefits of developing policies to solve these short-run problems? Can you think of any costs?

3. The success of a centralized industrial policy requires selecting and assisting industries that can contribute the most to economic growth. If you were in charge of such a process, what criteria would you use to make the selection? How, if at all, do your criteria differ from those a bank might use to grant a loan?

4. Three important elements of the Reagan administration's economic policies were (a) reducing the size of government, (b) lowering marginal income tax rates, and (c) using restrictive monetary policy to fight inflation. In what way would a supply-side economist argue that each element adds to economic growth? In what way might a Keynesian economist argue that in the short run aggregate demand might be most affected? Does the record of the early 1980s confirm either or both positions?

5. From the standpoint of growth, what are the impacts of each of the following policies? What are their impacts on other economic goals, including allocative efficiency and equity? For each policy develop both a supporting and an adverse argument.
   a) Cutting taxes by lowering rates more for high-income than for low-income taxpayers.
   b) Reducing a full-employment budget deficit by raising taxes.
   c) Reducing a full-employment budget deficit by reducing government spending.
   d) Combining a full-employment budget surplus with an expansionary monetary policy.
   e) Combining a full-employment budget deficit with a contractionary monetary policy.

Economic Encounters
Living With and Curing Hyperinflation

You are probably familiar with the problems caused by inflation. But the inflation most of us have experienced is relatively mild in comparison with that in an economy experiencing *hyperinflation*. In post-World War I Germany, price levels rose by over 100,000,000 percent in just a 14-month period. Although the inflation in Argentina, Bolivia, Brazil, and Israel has not reached these heights (or depths), each has faced hyperinflation in the 1980s.

Runaway Inflation According to the World Bank, the annual rate of inflation in these four countries from 1980 to 1985 ranged from 148 percent in Brazil to 569 percent in Bolivia. Like most averages, these figures hide some periods of even more rapid inflation. In January 1985 Bolivia's price level rose by 80 percent, equivalent to an annual inflation rate of 116,000 percent had prices continued to rise at this rate. But inflation slowed during the rest of the year and rose by *only* 20,000 percent for the year.

Under these conditions money ceases to have much real value at all. People try to spend their money as fast as they get it. Individuals are reluctant to invest in businesses in such an uncertain environment and instead buy real estate, gold, or jewels (items expected to increase in value) or put their savings into foreign economies (where they can expect to receive real returns on their money).

Hyperinflation causes inefficiency; but curing hyperinflation is not painless. Traditional cures for inflation require belt-tightening. Reducing the rate of growth of the money supply—which most economists agree is necessary—slows the economy, increasing unemployment and decreasing output.

Brazil, Bolivia, Argentina, and Israel have experimented in recent years with alternative policies hoping to beat inflation without plunging the ecnomy into a recession. Their plans included direct controls on prices and/or income as well as the more traditional contractionary fiscal and monetary policies. But can hyperinflation be cured without causing an economic slump? So far the results are mixed.

Latin American Woes In 1983, when he became the first democratically elected president of Argentina after years of military rule, Raul Alfonsin hoped to improve the economy. Instead, economic growth was slow and inflation jumped from 250 percent per year to over 2000 percent in 1985. These conditions created an economic and a political crisis for the Argentinian government and led to the announcement in June 1985 of the Austral plan (named for the new currency created to replace the discredited peso.)

The theory behind this new plan was that high inflation rates have a way of sustaining themselves. Workers expecting high inflation continually ask for large wage increases to keep their real incomes from falling. But faced with higher costs, businesses continually raise product prices. The theory suggests that inflation might continue to increase even after monetary growth is reduced as long as individuals expect it to continue. Thus the Austral plan coupled a freeze on wages and prices with restrictive monetary policy. According to the theory, this combination should halt the momentum of inflation without a costly period of unemployment.

The immediate effects of the Austral plan were in line with predictions. As monetary growth slowed, inflation fell dramatically, in part because of the wage and price freeze. However, in April 1986 the government had to take a backward step. Actual prices (as opposed to officially controlled prices) continued to increase. Unions and consumers protested the consequent fall in their real income. The government relaxed the controls for a period of time but reinstituted them in Septem-

Signs of the times: exchange rates posted in San Ysidro, California. (Danuta Otfinowski/Black Star)

ber. By the end of 1986 prices were increasing at an annualized rate of approximately 30 percent—not a low rate but certainly a dramatic improvement in a short period of time. However, inflation surged again in January 1987, and in February a new freeze was imposed. Thus the Austral plan has had

> ## There are no quick and painless solutions to hyperinflation.

only moderate success and is certainly not a blueprint for a painless cure for inflation.

In February 1986 Brazil instituted its anti-inflation program. Modeled on the Austral plan, it attacked the 250 percent annual inflation by freezing prices and wages (after allowing for an 8–15 percent increase in wages) and by creating a new currency—the cruzado. As in Argentina, the Cruzado plan had dramatic and immediate effects on inflation. But within nine months, Brazil's plan was in chaos. Because the money supply growth was not significantly reduced, demand in the economy continued to grow. Inflation was suppressed, not reduced. Consumers faced shortages in regular markets while prices in black markets soared. This failure to control demand was a serious economic mistake, although it did create a short-term political victory for the Brazilian leaders. Once price controls were removed, inflation again shot up and Brazil was engulfed in a quagmire of economic problems.

Bolivia's Black Market Blues   Bolivia had the dubious distinction in 1985 of having the world's highest inflation rate—some 20,000 percent. Under the weight of this staggering hyperinflation the Bolivian currency lost virtually all value, leading to some ludicrous situations. Banks did not bother to count money that customers deposited, either taking their word for the amount or weighing the currency

to get an approximate amount. The 1000 peso bill—the most common denomination—cost more to print than it was worth. Currency printed in West Germany and Britain was Bolivia's third most significant import in 1985. Prices rose so fast that the last people waiting in line at a movie theater paid thousands of pesos more than those at the front of the line. Black-market moneychanging became a full-time occupation for many. The Bolivian economy was on the verge of complete collapse.

The Bolivian government entitled its anti-inflation package the New Economic Policy, but in most respects the plan contained traditional anti-inflation remedies—contractionary monetary and fiscal policies. The budget deficit fell from 28 percent of domestic output in 1984 to 4 percent in 1986 as the government imposed a new wealth tax, froze public-sector wages, and eliminated gasoline subsidies. In contrast to the Austral and Cruzado plans, the Bolivian plan removed controls on prices, interest rates, and goods.

From the perspective of inflation the New Economic Policy was successful. Inflation in Bolivia fell from 20,000 percent in 1985 to only 10 percent in the second half of 1986. But all the economic news was not good. Unemployment rose to almost 20 percent. Real wages of public-sector workers (who account for almost 40 percent of the labor force) fell. Real output fell by 3 percent in 1986.

Not Just a Latin American Problem
In Israel, consumer prices rose by more than 100,000 percent between 1978 and 1985. But most wages and prices were cushioned from this hyperinflation by indexation—automatic increases in wages and interest rates as the price level increases.

By 1985 it was clear that Israel's economy was in trouble. The annual inflation rate surged up to 2000 percent. Israel tackled the problem in a manner closely resembling the Austral plan. Wages and prices were frozen

and indexation of prices and wages was suspended. Steps were taken to reduce the government's budget deficit, which fell from over 10 percent of domestic output in 1985 to around 3 percent in 1986. These policy measures helped to bring inflation down to only 20 percent in 1986, although unemployment increased. Since then inflation has begun to rise, but not yet at the rates of the previous period.

No Quick and Painless Solutions
Economists are generally agreed that hyperinflation is caused by excessive growth in the money supply. In many less-developed economies it is difficult for government to raise money through taxation. At the same time there are tremendous demands for government spending to improve education, social welfare, transportation, and communication services—programs considered important to economic development. Faced with size-

> ## Prices rose so fast that the last people waiting in line at a movie theater paid thousands of pesos more than those at the front.

able deficits, these governments sometimes simply printed money to spend. Such policies, however, are dangerously inflationary. Most economists would agree that curtailing monetary growth is essential to curing rapid inflation, even if the immediate consequences of such policies are somewhat higher unemployment, slower economic growth, and less public-sector support for economic development.

There is some disagreement among economists about whether wage and price controls might be useful in slowing the upward momentum in wages and prices. But price controls create another set of problems. As the experience in Brazil clearly indicates, there is little hope for an end to hyperinflation without monetary restraint.

CHAPTER 31

Macroeconomic Issues and Government Policies

The importance of economics is in the way it helps us to understand the real world and analyze real-world problems and issues. Economic analysis is especially important to an understanding of the effects of economic policies. In this section we consider several particular macroeconomic policy issues. The issues and policies we discover are examples of real situations in which government action has been proposed and used.

By exploring these issues, we seek to learn (1) how to apply economic principles to real-world situations; and (2) how to analyze the effects and effectiveness of alternative economic policies. After studying this introduction and the policy cases that follow, you should better understand the methods of economic analysis. You will also see how lost we would be in explaining or predicting economic outcomes without economic principles to guide our thinking.

Applying the Principles of Rational Choice to Policy Analysis

If we apply the principles of rational choice, which we first introduced in Chapter 2, we can structure the analysis of economic policy in terms of a series of questions.

Why is government action being proposed? It is useful to begin any analysis by considering why government action is being proposed. In other words, is the policy intended to lower unemployment, increase economic growth, or reduce inflation? Implicit in any new policy is a belief that current policies are inadequate. We should ask what supposed failure—either of current policy or of the private sector—suggests that government action is desirable. Before attempting to answer this question, we must establish criteria to judge a policy against.

The macroeconomy is capable of adjusting itself to economic changes. But its speed of adjustment is important to policy decisions. The faster the economy adjusts itself, the weaker the economic arguments for government intervention. Economists who believe that the economy adjusts itself very slowly or incompletely often view government actions as preferable to doing nothing. But government policies can be imperfect. Thus, as Charles Kindleberger has observed, in deciding whether government policies are desirable:

> The trick is to apply the appropriate adage: "If it ain't broke, don't fix it," or "A stitch in time saves nine."[*]

What are the extra benefits and costs of the proposed policy? To decide whether government policies are appropriate, we must apply the principles of rational choice. These principles require that we identify and compare the extra benefits and extra costs of a proposed policy. Thus we do not begin with the normative statement, "In my opinion. . . ." Rather, we must analyze facts and choose only those options for which the extra benefits outweigh the extra costs. In the case of macroeconomic policies, we identify and measure benefits and costs in terms of society's economic goals. These goals include the macroeconomic goals of full employment, price stability, and economic growth, as well as the micro-

---

[*] Charles Kindleberger, "Reversible and Irreversible Processes in Economics," *Challenge*, September/October 1986, pp. 4–10.

economic goals of allocative and technical efficiency, and equity. But in weighing the benefits and costs, you should keep several points in mind.

Economic policies may affect economic behavior. In making choices, individuals and businesses take into account expected government policies. If they expect government to create more jobs in response to a recession, workers will be reluctant to accept wage cuts and managers reluctant to cut prices. As a result, the economy will adjust more slowly than it would otherwise. Similarly, higher taxes may cause households to work and save less. When identifying the benefits and costs of alternative policies, policy makers must be careful to look for potential changes in economic behavior.

Economic policies do not require an all-or-nothing approach. Faced with high unemployment, policy makers do not have to choose to do absolutely nothing or to enact policies that completely eliminate unemployment. Faced with inflation, policy makers do not have to either eliminate all inflation or allow it to continue at the same rate. In these and similar cases, they can use policies that partly address the problem.

Economic policies inevitably involve trade-offs. As the principles of rational choice imply, any decision involves benefits and costs. Government policies to reduce unemployment may raise prices. Waiting for the economy to adjust itself may mean high unemployment for a longer period of time. When considering what policy to pursue, policy makers must be careful to include both benefits (lower unemployment) and costs (price instability).

Economic policies have distributional effects. Macroeconomic policy choices also affect various groups in the economy differently. For example, government policies that create new jobs may also drive prices up. While individuals who gain employment benefit from such a policy, retirees on fixed incomes lose. Just because some individuals gain and others lose under a particular policy is not reason enough to automatically reject it. Few policies—including doing nothing—could pass such a test. But in weighing benefits and costs, policy makers must consider the equity of imposing costs on one group and benefits on another. As we have noted previously, economic analysis cannot determine the equity of policies. But it can help to identify potential winners and losers and the size of gains and losses.

Economic policies that do not work can be eliminated. To be useful, a proposed policy must improve the economy's performance. A policy designed to reduce unemployment is acceptable only if it will, in fact, cause unemployment to fall. That there are *some* benefits to a policy choice is not enough. The extra benefits must *exceed* the extra costs.

Political pressures may affect policy makers. When considering whether policies will work, policy makers may consider political objectives to be as (or more) important than economic objectives. For example, presidents and the Congress often prefer higher inflation to higher unemployment, fearing the wrath of unemployed voters.

Are There Superior Alternative Policies?

In addition to deciding whether the benefits of one policy outweigh its costs, policy makers must also ask whether another policy might be more efficient or equitable. Similarly, rejecting one particular policy does not necessarily mean rejecting government action, if an acceptable alternative policy can be found. But no government action is an alternative that must always be considered. The best policy option—action or doing nothing—is the one that will most improve the economy's performance.

Why Economists Disagree about Government Involvement

It is often said in jest that if you laid all the economists on Earth end to end, they would never reach a conclusion. Economists generally agree that full employment, price stability, and economic growth are the macroeconomic goals against which actual policy performance should be judged. Why, then, do they disagree on the appropriate role of government?

Some disagreements result from inadequate methods of measurement. We cannot directly measure either potential GNP or the natural rate of unemployment, for example. Thus in the mid-1980s, estimates of the natural rate of unemployment ranged from 5 to 8 percent, but the actual unemployment rate was between 6.5 and 8 percent. Economists who accepted the lower natural rate were concerned that the economy was operating at below its potential. Economists who accepted the higher figure feared that faster economic growth would be inflationary.

In addition, some disagreements reflect *normative* economics, or matters of personal values (see Chapter 2). Economic analysis can help us make *positive* statements about predicted effects of a policy. But even when economists can agree on the positive statements, they often suggest different policies because of different values. There is no scientific way to judge normative statements, but economic analysis can help us to avoid answering every economic question with an opinion.

Although economists disagree a lot, they also have a lot in common. They agree on the validity and importance of economic analysis and economic evidence. When economic theories and evidence are conclusive, economists tend to join ranks. For example, most economists agree that sustained, rapid increases in the money supply leads to inflation.

Conclusion

In the following policy cases, we use the analytical framework that we have just discussed. We take a positive approach to policy analysis, concentrating on forecasting potential outcomes rather than advocating particular solutions. Government policies are, in the final analysis, often political judgments. The role of economic analysis is to identify the benefits and costs, and the winners and losers, and to approach the discussion of the issues rationally.

31.1 DEREGULATION OF BANKING: IS THE SYSTEM SAFE?

Banks perform important services for the economy. By offering checking services—a safe and efficient means of payment—they facilitate market exchanges. In addition, they serve as financial intermediaries, moving funds between savers and investors. Banks are also the channel for monetary policy. As we noted in Chapter 24, a safe and stable banking system is important to a smoothly functioning economy. But what government regulations, if any, are desirable?

Why and How Had the Banking System Been Regulated?

Between 1930 and 1933 some 10,000 banks in the United States failed. As a result, many people lost their life savings. Moreover, bank failures resulted in a sharp contraction in the money supply, disrupting the national economy. At the time some economists and politicians believed that excessive competition and fraud were the principal causes of bank failures. Competition for funds, they argued, drove costs up and forced banks to take great risks in order to earn higher returns. By taking large risks, banks became more vulnerable to depositor panics, and the banking system became less stable.

There was also concern that banks had engaged in some activities that were more risky than business loans. Perhaps the riskiest of these activities was the underwriting of new stock issues. Stock underwriters agree to purchase at a certain price a large block of a new stock being issued. They then resell it to their customers—at a profit to themselves, of course. Underwriting created many po-

Anxious customers, eager to withdraw their savings, gather outside the Delaney Street branch of the Bank of the United States on March 4, 1933. Such bank runs were a common occurrence during the Great Depression. To safeguard depositors' funds, the federal government imposed regulations on banks. (UPI/Bettmann Newsphotos)

tential conflicts of interest in banks. In the 1930s, banks were accused of forcing customers, their trust departments, and others to buy securities that they had underwritten. In some cases banks concealed relevant facts, such as the difficulty firms were having repaying loans to the underwriting banks.

A final concern was a fear that large banks would control the financial market. With their greater assets, they were able to offer more services and attract more business than could smaller banks. In addition to threatening the competitive nature of the banking business, the concentration of banking in major metropolitan areas worried some economists and politicians. Local banks had been viewed as supporting local industries. Would farmers and small-town businesses get the same loans from banks in the big cities that they got from their local banks?

As a result of these concerns, three types of regulation emerged from Congress and state legislatures. First, to eliminate competition for deposits, banks were not allowed to pay any interest on checking deposits. In addition, the interest they could pay on savings deposits was limited. Second, to keep them out of risky activities and to limit conflicts of interest, banks were prohibited from offering services such as underwriting securities, selling insurance, and acting as real estate brokers. Finally, to protect local banks and reduce concentration of power, interstate banking was restricted, and in some cases, large metropolitan banks were prevented from operating branches in rural areas. In addition to these regulations, a system of federal deposit insurance was implemented.

Why and How Was Banking Partially Deregulated in the Early 1980s?

From the 1930s to the late 1960s, there were relatively few bank failures. While deposit insurance probably deserves the major credit for reducing bank failure, some economists also believe that the other regulations were helpful. But increased rates of inflation, beginning in the late 1960s and continuing through the 1970s, made continued interest-rate regulations impractical. As inflation rose, new substitutes for checking and savings deposits emerged. Money market mutual funds, for example, paid market interest rates and permitted limited check writing. Unable to offer competitive interest rates, banks began to lose deposits.

In response, banks began to circumvent the regulations. For example, to get around regulations prohibiting them from paying interest on checking accounts, banks invented a new type of account: the automatic transfer service (ATS). Technically these are savings accounts on which banks were allowed to pay interest. But for all practical purposes they are checking accounts, since funds are automatically transferred to a checking account as checks are written.

The new types of financial instruments and services made defining a bank and money more difficult. Because many of the new types of accounts were not subject to reserve requirements, the Fed felt its control of the money supply was inadequate. In response, Congress enacted two reform bills: the Depository Institutions Deregulation and Monetary Control Act of 1980 and the Garn–St. Germain Depository Institutions Act of 1982. These acts essentially legitimized changes that had effectively deregulated the banking industry already.

The new acts eliminated restrictions on interest rates (except for businesses' checking accounts). They also allowed banks of all kinds to offer similar services, make similar types of loans, and subjected all types of banks to similar deposit restrictions. Even so, banking remains a highly regulated industry.

What Are the Benefits and Costs of Deregulation?

Economists generally agree that there are benefits to deregulation. The banking system is more efficient, and individuals can now receive market interest rates on funds held in checking accounts. At the same time, some economists have expressed concern about the safety of banks and the banking system. By removing regulatory barriers, banks are forced to pay more to attract funds. Repeating the argument used in the 1930s, these critics argue that deregulation has led banks to engage in activities that involve more risk but pay higher returns. But have these higher risks compromised the system's stability and soundness? Are these costs of deregulation excessive?

Economists who attribute these costs to deregulation point to the large number of bank failures in the 1980s. During the 1970s fewer than 15 banks failed or were merged out of existence in an average year; fewer than 2 percent were considered to be in danger of failing. In the 1980s, an average of almost 4 banks per week have failed or have been merged out of existence; over 10 percent of all banks are in danger of failing.

But other economists attribute recent problems to regulations that remain, not to deregulation. For example, many banks that have failed were small banks concentrated in geographical areas that were hard hit by problems in the oil industry and agriculture. They argue that regulations restricting banks to small geographical areas increase risk by not allowing banks to diversify. Diversifying lowers risks, as the old economic proverb—"Don't put all your eggs in one basket"—suggests.

Are There Superior Alternatives to Further Deregulation?

Where do we go from here? Any future policy must address two issues: control of the money supply and safety of the banking system. Nearly all economists believe that the Fed must retain the power to set required reserve ratios to control the money supply. Many advocate extending the Fed's power to money market mutual funds and other types of financial institutions in order to control the money supply more completely. But economists have widely different ideas about the desirability of regulating bank safety.

Some economists propose eliminating all regulations regarding bank safety. They argue that the market can best determine the optimal amount of safety and the services that banks and other financial institutions offer. But fears of a return to a time of massive bank failures make use of this option unlikely. At the opposite extreme, other economists argue that we should return to a system of close regulation. To do so, however, regulations would have to extend to all businesses that offer financial services—Sears and Merrill Lynch, for example not just banks. Most economists believe that this option is both impractical and undesirable. The financial marketplace continues to change rapidly. Constant revisions of regulations would be necessary both to accommodate new entrants and to prevent those currently in the industry from exploiting loopholes, as they have in the past.

Fortunately, as we noted in the introduction, policy makers do not have to choose between total regulation and no regulation. They can remove those regulations that seem unjustified and leave others intact. For example, because of the relatively large number of bank failures in the oil and farm belts, economists are increasingly supporting removal of barriers to interstate banking. Such an action might actually reduce risks. But, as we noted above, most also believe that the Fed's control of the money supply should be broadened, not reduced.

There is also strong support among economists for reducing some of the constraints on services provided by banks. Many economists believe that banks can take on such activities as real estate brokerage, stock brokerage, and selling insurance to households without seriously increasing their risks. Government supervision of banks and legal penalties could minimize conflicts of interest without directly prohibiting such otherwise legitimate business activities.

There is less support among economists for banks gaining the right to underwrite securities and to sell commercial risk insurance to businesses. These ventures involve much higher risks and a greater potential for conflicts of interest. But the boundaries between acceptable and unacceptable risks is fuzzy and likely to change. Moreover, banks can and do currently make high-risk loans, such as those made to Latin American governments.

There is strong support among economists for continued government monitoring of bank assets and liabilities. In part, such supervision is a means of providing public information and ensuring some confidence in the banking system. Continued monitoring is also important because most deposits are federally insured. But relaxing regulations somewhat would enable banks to earn greater income without compromising the soundness necessary to an efficient banking system and a stable money supply.

Conclusion

The banking system is an important part of the economy. Because of its special role as a financial intermediary and in the creation of money, banking has been subject to considerable regulation. Changes in the system have resulted from new technology and competition from other financial service institutions and foreign banks. Limits on interest rates and, in some cases, on the types of services that banks can offer have been lifted.

But what type of bank regulatory system—if any—will best serve the U.S. economy in the future? Economists offer different recommendations, but most believe a return to the old style regulation is neither likely nor desirable. Many favor a continued relaxation of restrictions, including allowing interstate banking and a broader range of bank services. There is strong support, however, for continuing the role of regulators in monitoring the quality of bank assets and in setting reserve requirements to assist in monetary control.

QUESTIONS FOR REVIEW AND DISCUSSION

1. Determine whether each of the following statements is true, false, or uncertain and explain why.
   a) A bank that accepts deposits and makes loans within a small geographical area has less risk than one that has loans all over the country and in foreign countries.
   b) A loss of confidence in any one bank will inevitably cause a run on all banks.
   c) When banks must pay higher interest on deposits, they will be tempted to take greater risks.
2. Regulations prohibiting the payment of interest on checking deposits and limiting the interest paid on savings deposits led banks to try other means of attracting customers.
   a) How is offering free checking services like paying interest on deposits? How is it different?

b) If offered a choice, would you prefer free services or actual interest payments on money held in a deposit account? Why?

c) Use your answer to part (b) to explain why free services and other premiums (toasters, television sets, and other products sometimes offered to new depositors) are less efficient than simply paying interest.

3. The historical rationale for regulating banks is based on the special nature of banks compared to other forms of businesses. To have special regulations for banks, it is necessary to distinguish banks from other businesses.

a) What services are provided by banks? How is a bank like a manufacturing company and how is it different? An insurance company? An investment services company, such as Merrill Lynch?

b) Use your answer to (a) to write a definition of a bank that distinguishes it from other businesses.

c) In what ways are banks special (according to your definition)? Do these characteristics provide a rationale for government regulation of banks? Why or why not?

31.2 POLICY RESPONSES TO A SUPPLY SHOCK

Prior to 1973, discussions of macroeconomic policy focused on how best to respond to shifts in aggregate demand. Although some economists believed that powerful unions or producers could raise wages and prices somewhat, most expected aggregate supply to grow slowly over time. However, the experiences of the United States and other countries in 1973–1974 and again in 1979 made it clear that sharp decreases in aggregate supply (supply shocks) were indeed possible.

Poor harvests worldwide in 1972 and 1973 caused the food component of the Consumer Price Index (CPI) to increase by 20 percent in 1973. In addition, the Organization of Petroleum Exporting Countries (OPEC) imposed an oil embargo that resulted in major oil-price increases. As a result, the energy component of the CPI rose by almost 17 percent in 1973 and an additional 22 percent in 1974. Another serious supply shock hit the U.S. economy in 1979, again in the form of higher oil prices, which increased by 45 percent. Thus aggregate supply decreased significantly in both 1973–1974 and 1979.

For the first time, economists and politicians were faced with the question of what government could—and should—do in response to a supply shock. In this policy case we consider their answer, as well as the benefits and costs of alternative macroeconomic policies.

Why and How Might Government Respond to a Supply Shock?

Government intervention was proposed because the supply shocks had a significant effect on the economy. The oil-price increases in 1973-1974 and 1979 had immediate and powerful effects on oil consumers. But oil and other energy supplies are also important resources for almost every sector of the economy. Higher energy prices raised production costs of manufactured goods. Higher

A long line of cars winds through the streets of New York City in February, 1974. Similar lineups occurred throughout the United States after the oil embargo by OPEC. Increased scarcity of gasoline was only one manifestation of the supply shocks during this time. (UPI/Bettmann Newsphotos)

transportation costs further added to retail prices. Even service industries, such as life insurance companies, were affected by increased electricity and heating costs. As a result, the price of almost every product in the economy increased.

Because higher prices reduced real wages, workers demanded higher nominal wages, further increasing costs and causing a secondary decrease in aggregate supply. Secondary effects on real income and nominal wages occur over time and may give the false impression that price increases will be sustained. The Consumer Price Index initially increased rapidly for many months after both the 1973–1974 and 1979 shocks. Almost three-fourths of the CPI's 14.2 percent increase in 1979 was caused by the rise in energy prices. But the CPI also increased by over 11 percent in 1980, although energy prices had leveled off. The continued spiral reflected secondary effects of the supply shock.

Exhibit 31.2.1(a) indicates the two supply-shock problems that macroeconomic policies may attempt to correct. First, a supply shock causes aggregate supply to shift (from AS_1 to AS_2), real GNP to fall, and the price level to increase. In fact, if individuals expect inflation to continue, those expectations may further decrease aggregate supply. Second, a supply shock opens a contractionary gap, and pushes unemployment above the natural rate. The result is higher prices and higher unemployment—the double whammy of stagflation.

In response to an increase in the price level, government might use an *extinguishing policy*. That is, government might use contractionary policies to decrease aggregate demand, thereby extinguishing inflationary pressures, as shown in Exhibit 31.2.1(b). Or, in response to rising unemployment, government might use an *accommodating policy*. That is, it might use expansionary policies to increase aggregate demand, thereby reducing the short-run impact of unemployment, as shown in Exhibit 31.2.1(c). Alternatively, government might do nothing. This *neutral policy* relies exclusively on the economy's automatic adjustment mechanism to restore long-run equilibrium, as shown in Exhibit 31.2.1(d).

(a) Initial effect of a supply shock

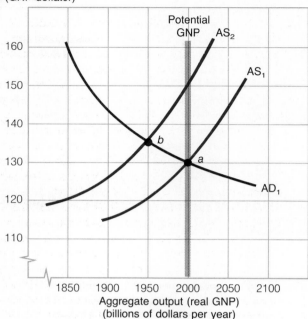

(b) Extinguishing policy

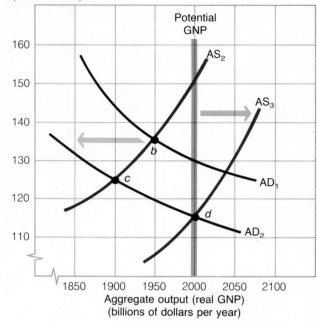

Exhibit 31.2.1
Policy Options for a Supply Shock
A supply shock causes a decrease in aggregate supply (from AS$_1$ to AS$_2$), raising the price level and opening a contractionary gap, as shown in part (a). To reduce high prices brought on by inflationary pressures, policy makers may use an extinguishing policy, decreasing aggregate demand (from AD$_1$ to AD$_2$) as in part (b). While this

What Are the Benefits and Costs of Taking Policy Action?

In deciding which option is best, economists consider two factors: (1) the speed of the automatic adjustment mechanism; and (2) the relative costs of inflation and unemployment.

Accommodating policies.   Some economists believe that the economy's automatic adjustment mechanism is slow to close contractionary gaps. Fearing that supply shocks will cause unacceptably high unemployment and prolonged recessions, these economists therefore recommend accommodating policies. They also note that major supply shocks, such as those of 1973–1974 and 1979 cause a decline in real income for the economy as a whole. Because foreign interests succeeded in imposing higher real costs for imported oil, less real output was available for domestic use. Thus real income had to fall. But workers and businesses sought to maintain real income, which slowed the required adjustments in nominal wages and prices.

If the economy adjusts slowly, as these economists maintain, high unemployment may well be a long-term result, and an accommodating policy may be the

(c) Accommodating policy

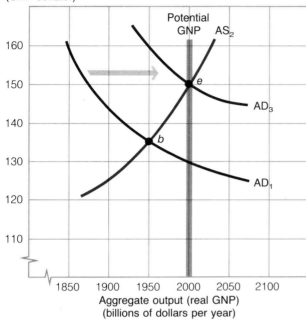

(d) Neutral policy

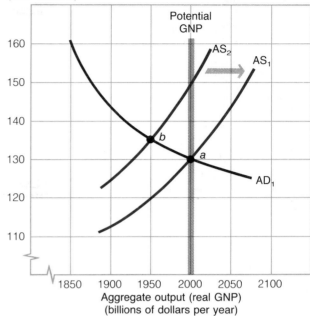

action puts downward pressure on prices, it opens a larger contractionary gap and slows return to full employment. To reduce unemployment, policy makers may turn to an accommodating policy, increasing aggregate demand (from AD_1 to AD_3) as in part (c). However, this action puts additional upward pressure on prices. If no action is taken—a neutral policy—the economy's automatic adjustment mechanism will eventually close the gap as indicated in part (d).

best policy. But in deciding in favor of such a policy, policy makers must be aware that an accommodating increase in aggregate demand will cause larger increases in the price level. And these increases may fuel expectations of continued inflation.

Extinguishing policies. However, some economists reject an accommodating policy response to a supply shock. They believe that an increase in the price level resulting from a supply shock may trigger expectations of continued inflation and thus reduce aggregate supply. In addition, supporters of extinguishing policies argue that use of accommodating policies causes individuals to expect such government action whenever a supply shock occurs. This expectation further slows the economy's automatic adjustment mechanism and raises the cost of future antiinflation efforts. Fearing that increased inflationary expectations may further decrease aggregate supply and delay the return to long-run equilibrium, they recommend extinguishing policies.

By increasing the contractionary gap, such policies may cause somewhat higher unemployment in the short run. But proponents of extinguishing policy believe that the economy's automatic adjustment mechanism operates quickly. A quick response makes the costs of an extinguishing policy—higher unemployment and lost output—relatively small.

Would No Action Be a Better Policy?

As we noted in the introduction, policy makers must always consider the option of a neutral policy, that is, taking no action. Unlike inflation which results from rapid and sustained growth in the money supply, price increases that result from a supply shock cause only a *one-time* increase in the general price level. Eventually, aggregate supply will increase because unemployment forces wages and prices to fall. Given sufficient time to adjust, aggregate supply will fall enough (back to AS_1 in Exhibit 31.2.1a) to restore long-run equilibrium. At that point, the economy will produce at its potential GNP level and unemployment will return to the natural rate.

Is a neutral policy a superior option? Some economists who believe that the automatic adjustment mechanism works reasonably well think so. So do those who believe that policy makers do not have the knowledge or ability to apply any macroeconomic policy accurately. A neutral policy tends to have neutral long-run effects on inflation and unemployment; it makes them neither better nor worse. Unemployment costs with a neutral policy may be higher than with an accommodating policy. But if the automatic adjustment mechanism operates quickly, unemployment may not be a serious problem. The short-run increase in the price level with a neutral policy may be higher than with an extinguishing policy. But if individuals do not raise their price-level expectations, a neutral policy may be the best.

Why Do Economists Disagree about Appropriate Policy Actions?

Now that you understand some of the pros and cons of various policy options, let's consider the historical record and why economists disagree about the decisions that were made. The United States responded to the supply shocks of both 1973–1974 and 1979 with extinguishing policies. That is, contractionary monetary and fiscal policies were used to reduce aggregate demand and dampen inflationary expectations. There is little doubt that these policies resulted in a lower price-level increase than would have occurred with either neutral or accommodating policies. At the same time, those policies helped cause the two most severe recessions since the Great Depression.

Was it worth it? This question is very important, but different economists have answered it differently. Some economists argue that extinguishing actions were unnecessary and undesirable. They note that a supply shock causes only a one-time increase in the general price level, not long-run inflation. The short-run increase in the price level is the unavoidable result of a supply shock, and in the long run no action is needed. Moreover, they point to high unemployment and large contractionary gaps as evidence that the cost of reducing the price level was extremely high.

Some of those who disagree with the actual policy responses would have preferred an accommodating policy response. They would gladly have accepted a somewhat higher increase in the price level in return for lower unemployment and more real GNP. Others who disagree with the actual policies would have preferred a more neutral policy.

But some economists support the government's actions. They note that a short-run rise in unemployment is also an unavoidable result of a supply shock. They blame the prolonged high unemployment rate and major recessions in both 1975 and 1981–1982 in part on individuals' expectations that government would use accommodating policies. This expectation was based on such policy actions in the 1960s and early 1970s. Supporters of extinguishing policies argue that the high economic price paid in 1981–1982 was worthwhile in the long run. They maintain that it established the credibility of policy makers and an unwillingness to tolerate inflation.

Conclusion

Economists do not agree on the best policy reponse to a supply shock, although they do agree that all policies have both costs and benefits. The debate continues because we cannot accurately measure the speed of the automatic adjustment mechanism or the costs of inflation and unemployment. In addition, we do not yet know—nor are we likely to be able to quantify—the long-run costs of various policies' effects on expectations. Finally, economists (and politicians) put different values on the costs of inflation and unemployment.

QUESTIONS FOR REVIEW AND DISCUSSION

1. Japan responded to the 1973–1974 supply shock with extinguishing policies. Great Britain applied accommodating policies. In which of these countries would you expect that the price level increased more? In which would you expect that more output was lost?

2. The following data show some annual economic indicators for an eight-year period.

| | Annual percentage changes in | | | Size of GNP gap |
Year	Nominal GNP	Real GNP	GNP deflator	as a percentage of potential GNP
1	8.6	2.8	5.7	0.6
2	10.0	5.0	4.7	−0.9
3	12.1	5.2	6.5	−2.6
4	8.3	−0.5	9.1	1.3
5	8.5	−1.3	9.8	5.3
6	11.5	4.9	6.4	3.5
7	11.7	4.7	6.7	1.9
8	13.0	5.3	7.3	−0.3

a) In which year(s) do you see evidence of a supply shock? Explain which indicators are significant.
b) What evidence suggests that the effects of a supply shock are temporary but lingering?

3. The following table shows changes in the money supply and the size of the actual and full-employment federal budget balances (see Chapter 27) expressed as a percentage

of potential GNP. (The negative numbers indicate budget deficits.) The years shown correspond to those in the table in Question 2.

Year	Percentage change in money supply (M-1)	Size of federal budget surplus as a percentage of potential GNP	
		Actual	Full employment
1	5.2	−1.5	−2.0
2	6.6	−1.3	−1.4
3	9.2	−1.0	−0.4
4	5.5	−0.6	−0.8
5	4.4	−2.5	−4.1
6	4.9	−1.8	−2.9
7	6.6	−1.7	−1.7
8	8.0	−1.5	−1.3

a) For the year(s) you tied to a supply shock in Question 2, were monetary and fiscal policy neutral, accommodating, or extinguishing? On what evidence in the table of Question 3 do you base your conclusions?

b) What evidence of the effects of these macroeconomic policy actions can you find in the data in Question 2?

4. Some labor-union contracts index members' wages to the Consumer Price Index. As prices rise in response to a supply shock, nominal wages automatically increase.

a) Does indexing protect the real income of workers? Why or why not?

b) How does indexing affect the economy's automatic adjustment mechanism?

c) Suppose that in Charybdis there is no indexation, while in Scyllia the nominal wages of all workers are indexed. Compare the effects of a supply shock (a decrease in aggregate supply) on the two countries. In which will prices rise more? In which will unemployment and lost output be greater? Why?

31.3 REDUCING THE FEDERAL BUDGET DEFICIT

From 1980 to 1986 the portion of the U.S. national debt held by the public increased by more than $1.2 trillion dollars. Debt as a percentage of GNP increased from 27 to 51 percent. This increase was the result of unprecedented peacetime budget deficits. The federal government's budget deficit in 1986 was $204 billion, 4.8 percent of GNP. Moreover, the full-employment budget deficit was over 4 percent, indicating that major reductions in the deficit are unlikely to occur automatically. But what can—and should—government do?

Why and How Should the Deficit Be Reduced?

All deficits are not the same. Because of automatic stabilizers, the federal government tends to have a deficit when the economy is in a recession. These deficits have expansionary short-run effects and may help bring the economy out of recession. But large full-employment budget deficits have created serious economic problems for both the United States and other countries.

A deficit must be financed somehow. If a deficit is financed by increases in the money supply, inflation is a serious concern. (The high rates of inflation experienced in some Latin American countries clearly indicate the dangers.) If a deficit is financed by borrowing, real interest rates tend to rise and investment may fall, thus slowing long-run economic growth.

High U.S. interest rates are also attractive to foreign individuals and businesses. Accordingly, they may choose to buy U.S. businesses, stocks, and government bonds. As we describe in Chapter 33, foreign investments in the U.S. economy drive up the value of the U.S. dollar, which raises the relative price of U.S. goods and services. As a result, U.S. consumers and businesses will buy more foreign-produced goods and services (imports rise). At the same time, U.S. producers have trouble selling their products abroad (exports fall). The high value of the dollar also makes it difficult for countries with large international dollar debts—Mexico, Brazil, and Argentina, for example—to repay those debts. To avoid such problems, then, the United States must reduce future federal budget deficits. In theory, we can reduce deficits in two ways: by either reducing expenditures or increasing tax revenues.

What Are the Benefits and Costs of Taking Policy Action?

Both cutting spending and raising taxes can help to reduce deficits. But both approaches have economic and political costs. (Although a combination of spending cuts and tax hikes is also possible, in this section we explore the benefits and costs of relying mainly on one or the other of the two alternatives.)

Spending cuts. One way to reduce future deficits would be to cut federal government expenditures. As shown in Exhibit 31.3.1, between 1979 and 1986 federal government receipts in the full-employment budget—as a percentage of potential GNP—fell only 0.3 percent, while expenditures increased by 3.1 percent. Thus most of the 3.4 percent increase in the full-employment budget deficit can be attributed to spending increases. However, a major problem with cutting expenditures to reduce deficits is deciding which expenditures to cut. The principles of rational choice tell us that we should eliminate any expenditure that results in more costs than benefits. But there is no economic or political consensus

Exhibit 31.3.1
Changes in the Federal Budget, 1962–1986

	Full-employment federal budget (percentage of potential GNP)			Nominal federal expenditures by type (percentage of actual GNP)				
Year	Receipts	Expenditures	Surplus	National defense	Nondefense purchases	Transfer payments	Net interest	Other
1962	18.7	19.4	−0.7	9.1	2.2	4.9	1.2	2.0
1979	20.1	20.9	−0.8	4.9	2.2	8.4	1.7	3.6
1986	19.7	24.5	−4.8	6.6	2.1	9.5	3.2	3.1

Sources: *Economic Report of the President, 1987;* U.S. Department of Commerce, Bureau of Economic Analysis.

on which expenditures fail to meet this test. Three major targets for cuts—national defense, transfer payments, and interest payments on the national debt—all have supporters and detractors.

Advocates of defense cuts note that expenditures in this category have grown the most since 1979. Opponents counter that such cuts would jeopardize national security and note that spending for national defense is a smaller percentage of GNP than it was in 1962. Some people argue for cuts in transfer payments, since this category accounted for most of the increase in spending between 1962 and 1986. But others believe that transfer payments, such as Social Security, are essential to equity. Net interest on the national debt cannot be directly cut by Congress. Interest payments will fall only if the debt is reduced or interest rates fall.

What about the expenditures that make up the other one-third of the federal budget? Many of these programs also have their advocates. Student-loan programs, improved highways, and basic scientific research, for example, are all supported as public investments that foster long-run economic growth. Moreover, to have eliminated the deficit in 1986, while leaving national defense and transfer and interest payments unchanged, Congress would have had to reduce other expenditures by 90 percent.

Some proponents of large spending cuts want to reduce deficits by eliminating what they see as an unnecessary and undesirable intrusion of the public sector into the private sector. They propose "privatization"—that is, selling off government enterprises such as Conrail or using educational vouchers to ensure access to education without government provision of services. Similarly, they argue for further reducing government regulatory agencies and activities.

Tax increases. National defense, Social Security, and Medicare (which together account for almost one-half of total spending by the federal government) are politically untouchable. And to reduce interest payments the government must first reduce deficits. The seemingly obvious alternative to spending cuts is to raise taxes. But politicians, fearing voter outcry, are slow to adopt this solution.

The political costs of raising taxes are obvious, but what are the economic costs? Some economists argue that incentives to work, save, and invest will be reduced significantly if taxes are increased. Because the U.S. economy already has a very low saving rate and productivity growth, they argue that we cannot afford to reduce incentives. In addition, they worry that tax increases will relieve the pressure on Congress to eliminate unnecessary and wasteful expenditures. Other economists believe that tax increases will have only small effects on incentives. Moreover, they doubt that there is much "fat" in the budget that can be trimmed to reduce the deficit. Some expenditures targeted for cuts—student loans, highways, or scientific research—are, they argue, useful public investments that add to long-run economic growth. They believe that the benefits of reducing the deficit will outweigh the costs of a tax increase.

Would No Action Be a Better Policy?

As we noted in the introduction to this chapter, the likely outcomes of policy actions must be contrasted with those of no action. But most economists view government failure to act on large full-employment deficits as a poor policy choice. Such deficits have high costs to society and can be reduced only through some combination of changes in taxes and expenditures.

Why Do Economists Disagree about the Appropriate Policy Response?

Although they are nearly unanimous in their desire to see deficits reduced, economists disagree sharply about the correct policy action to take. As usual, some of these disagreements are normative—whether cuts in social programs are equitable, for example. In addition, accurately measuring the benefits of many programs and the full costs of higher taxes is impossible. Thus economists also rationally disagree about whether the benefits of spending cuts or raising taxes outweigh the costs.

Despite the political difficulty of agreeing on spending cuts and voting for tax increases, in 1985 Congress voted for the Gramm-Rudman-Hollings Act. This act requires Congress to eliminate the actual deficit by 1991 and to achieve specified deficit-reduction targets for each year until then. If the estimated deficit in the budget passed by Congress does not meet the target, equal cuts in defense and nondefense spending are supposed to be made. (Some nondefense spending, such as Social Security, is exempt from these automatic cuts.) Although a federal court of appeals declared the automatic cuts to be unconstitutional, Congress and President Reagan have continued to try to reduce the deficit. However, the actual budget deficits in fiscal years 1987 and 1988 exceeded the targets, in part because the economy grew more slowly than predicted, and in part because there was no consensus on expenditure cuts or tax increases.

Some economists consider this act to be a political attempt to force necessary consensus. No one really favors cutting expenditures across the board as the act requires. Those who favor spending cuts hope that the act will pressure Congress to agree on some cuts in spending. Others apparently hope that the act may cause some to recognize the necessity of a tax increase.

Conclusion

Economists generally agree that the large full-employment budget deficits experienced in the mid-1980s are costly to the economy and must be reduced. But there is no consensus on the best way to reduce deficits. Some economists argue for expenditure cuts and against tax increases. Typically they stress the negative effects of tax increases on economic incentives and the desirability of cutting unnecessary expenditures to promote economic efficiency. Other economists disagree, pointing out the political difficulties and potential equity problems associated with major spending cuts. In contrast, they view the negative effects of higher taxes on economic incentives as small.

QUESTIONS FOR REVIEW AND DISCUSSION

1. Government can finance spending in three ways: taxing, borrowing, and increasing the money supply.
   a) Explain the effects of each method of financing on the economy.
   b) Assuming that there is general agreement that a certain level of spending is desirable, which method of financing would you recommend? Why?

2. Using the data in Exhibit 31.3.1, explain whether fiscal policy was expansionary or contractionary between 1979 and 1986.

3. One problem that economists see with the recent large federal budget deficits is that they seriously handicap the Fed and monetary policy.
   a) Why would these deficits make the Fed reluctant to increase the rate of growth of the money supply?

b) What are the effects on the economy if the Fed slows the rate of growth of the money supply? (Note the effects on unemployment, growth of real GNP, the price level, and interest rates.) How does this policy affect the actual budget deficit?

c) What are the resulting effects on international capital flows and the exchange rate value of the U.S. dollar if fiscal policy is expansionary and monetary policy contractionary?

4. Keynes argued that under the right circumstances, an actual budget deficit would have favorable effects on the economy. What were the "right circumstances" to which he referred and how is a deficit favorable? Do these circumstances fit the current situation?

31.4 INCOMES POLICIES: A CURE FOR INFLATION?

The traditional policy response to inflation is contractionary policy, especially reducing the rate of growth of the money supply. However, contractionary policy also causes a temporary increase in unemployment. As a result, economists and politicians have looked for less painful methods to lower inflation.

In this example we explore the use of *incomes policies*, which intervene directly in the processes of setting wages and prices. Incomes policies include mandatory and voluntary wage and price controls and tax-based incomes policies (TIP), which offer tax reductions to firms that follow specified wage and price guidelines.

Incomes policies are not a new idea. In fact, an incomes policy was used during the reign of the Roman emperor Diocletion in A.D. 300. (The Romans really tried to enforce it—violators were sentenced to death—but still were unable to get full compliance.) But are such policies effective? Can they reduce the costs of reducing inflation? Are they a substitute for traditional policies?

Why and How Might Government Impose Incomes Policies?

Incomes policies are based on a belief that some wage and price increases are not "justified" by economic forces. That is, they do not represent a response to fundamental demand and supply conditions. Rather, they are unwarranted attempts by strong unions and/or strong businesses to exercise economic power by forcing wages and/or prices up. Some proponents argue that incomes policies would prevent such wage and price increases from occurring, or at least slow wage and price increases. In either event, upward pressure on the price level would diminish.

Some economists also propose incomes policies as a way to speed up the economy's adjustment when contractionary policies are utilized to lower inflation. They believe that wages and prices are heavily influenced by past inflation rates and thus are slow to adjust as necessary to close contractionary gaps. By forcing wage and price adjustments, incomes policies may decrease inflationary expectations. As a result, incomes policies may help reduce the unemployment costs of contractionary policies.

Incomes policies can take a variety of forms. The mildest form is *jawboning*, or what some call an "open-mouth" policy. Jawboning is an attempt to talk unions and businesses out of planned or announced wage and price increases. For example, in 1962 President Kennedy publicly chastised U.S. steel companies for announcing a large price increase. Coupled with threats to cancel outstanding defense contracts, jawboning worked; the steel companies rescinded the announced price increase. Presidents Johnson, Nixon, and Carter also employed jawboning in their struggles with inflation.

A more formal approach to incomes policies is the use of *wage and price controls*. Wage and price "guideposts" or "voluntary" controls, were used in 1962–1967 and in 1978–1979. More formal, "mandatory" wage and price controls with legal penalties were first used in the United States during World War II. They were also enacted during the Korean War and most recently in 1971–1974. Wage and price controls have also been used in Brazil, Argentina, Israel, and Bolivia as part of their fights against inflation rates that averaged several hundred percent per year.

Wage and price controls pressure workers and businesses to hold down costs and prices. One alternative, *tax-based incomes policies (TIP)*, instead provides tax incentives for complying with wage and price controls. Under TIP, government sets an aggregate wage target—perhaps a 5 percent average increase in wages. Employers who give larger average wage increases are required to pay higher taxes. Those who give smaller wage increases can earn tax reductions. By holding wages down, TIP seeks to hold down product costs and thus reduce pressures for higher prices.

What Are the Benefits and Costs of Incomes Policies?

Inflation clearly imposes costs on an economy. Price stability—an economic goal—is sacrificed. Moreover, wages and/or prices that exceed market rates cause allocative inefficiency. If inflation becomes a way of life, individuals expect more inflation and make their economic plans accordingly. They may change their expectations only slowly, even if government begins using contractionary policies. As a result, unemployment and lost output may be high for a long time. But incomes policies can slow actual wage and price increases. Thus such policies may speed the economy's adjustment, reducing the duration of unemployment and restoring long-run equilibrium.

Incomes policies can also impose significant costs on the economy. In the first place, there is no sure way to determine a reasonable or acceptable wage or price increase. To remedy this problem, some economists suggest limiting wage increases to gains in productivity, or output per worker. When wage increases match productivity gains, product costs are unaffected. But productivity is very difficult to measure in service industries. (How would you measure the output of your economics professor? By the number of students that passed economics? By the grade-point average in economics classes?) Moreover, productivity standards make no allowance for changes in wages and prices that may be warranted by changes in demand.

As we noted in Chapter 5, unless the *relative* prices of products and resources adjust, the economy cannot operate efficiently. General wage and price controls inevitably distort price signals. The results of distorted price signals are shortages and surpluses and a tendency for *actual* and *official* prices to differ. In Chapter 3, you learned that a price ceiling in a single market creates a shortage. Although prices cannot legally rise above a ceiling, actual prices often do. Illegal or black markets commonly develop when legal markets cannot adjust.

Members of the Price Commission named by President Nixon are sworn into office in October, 1971. This commission was charged with implementation of general wage and price controls in the period from 1971 to early 1974. (UPI/Bettmann Newsphotos)

Are incomes policies effective? In the introduction to this chapter, we noted that policies are judged in part by whether they meet their objectives. Incomes policies have both succeeded and failed. As utilized in the early 1960s, they appeared to work well, but more recent outcomes have been less satisfactory. Overall, incomes policies do not appear to be effective when there is excess aggregate demand. The apparent success of such policies in the early 1960s, for example, may have resulted from the lack of excess demand pressures at the time. When such pressures were present in 1966–1967, however, incomes policies were unsuccessful.

Price controls imposed in 1971–1974 likewise failed. At the time, the Nixon administration wanted to reduce inflation and unemployment. A general freeze on wages and prices was followed by a series of formally administered controls. The freeze and the controls did reduce the price level while they were in operation. But when the controls were lifted in 1974, prices rose to the level they probably would have reached if the controls had never been enacted.

Wage and price controls imposed by Brazil and Argentina during the mid-1980s also failed. Although they caused a spectacular drop in inflation when imposed, they were not accompanied by controls on growth of the money supply; high rates of inflation returned when controls were removed.

Is There a Better Alternative?

As we noted in Chapter 26, most economists consider inflation to be the result of excess growth in the money supply. Accordingly, they believe that reducing the rate of money-supply growth is vital to slowing inflation. Even those who believe that incomes policies may be useful suggest them only as a complement to—not a substitute for—policies that slow money-supply growth.

Israel was successful in bringing inflation down from 1000 to 20 percent in a very short period of time, using a combination of limited money-supply growth and wage and price controls. But not all of its success can be attributed to incomes policies. And when incomes policies are used instead of the more painful limits on the money-supply's growth—as in Brazil—the result has been still worse inflation when the incomes policies are ended.

Why Do Economists Disagree about Incomes Policies?

As is so often the case, disputes about incomes policies revolve around the speed with which the economy adjusts on its own and on the costs of inflation and unemployment. Proponents of incomes policies believe that they speed up an otherwise sluggish adjustment. And a slow adjustment implies long periods of inflation—the high cost of taking no action.

In contrast, some opponents of incomes policies argue that they are at best unnecessary. These economists believe that the economy adjusts rapidly to changes. Because they believe that high price levels will last only a short time, they see the cost of allowing the economy to adjust on its own as low. Conversely, they view the cost of incomes policies as high because such policies distort prices, causing resources to be inefficiently utilized. In addition, these economists argue that incomes policies—by fueling expectations that policies to limit the growth of the money supply will not be used—may in fact slow the economy's adjustment.

Conclusion

Incomes policies have been proposed as one tool in the fight against inflation. If they are successful in holding wages and prices to levels justified by demand and supply conditions, they may reduce inflationary pressures without serious effects on efficiency. By forcing actual wages and prices down, they may complement money-supply controls. But there is widespread agreement among economists that incomes policies are ineffective if there are significant excess demand pressures in the economy. Opinion is more mixed about their use under other circumstances. Many economists remain quite skeptical. They tend to believe that incomes policies are impractical and potentially expensive, even when combined with credible money-supply controls.

QUESTIONS FOR REVIEW AND DISCUSSION

1. The economic czar of Fortunia wants to ensure that wage and price increases throughout the economy put no upward pressure on the price level.
    a) Workers producing plastic dinner plates have increased their output from 100 to 110 plates per hour. Can the czar give them a wage increase from $10 to $11 per hour without increasing product costs and prices?
    b) Is there any legitimate reason for wages in any industry to rise faster than productivity? Why or why not?
    c) Can strong businesses and unions create sustained increases in the price level by continually raising prices and wages? Why or why not?
2. Proponents of the new classical macroeconomics (see Chapter 27) argue that incomes policies are unnecessary. Other economists disagree.
    a) In an economy in which wages and prices are very flexible, why could limiting the growth of the money supply end inflation at very little cost?
    b) What arguments would the new classical macroeconomists use to explain why the Fed's tight money controls during the early 1980s successfully reduced inflation but, at the same time, caused a serious recession?
    c) If wages and prices are slow to adjust and if individuals' expectations are heavily influenced by past inflation, explain how wage and price controls might be useful.

3. Economists generally agree that incomes policies can only temporarily suppress inflation, if there is continued excess demand pressure.
   a) Why is suppressing inflation temporarily not the same as reducing it more permanently?
   b) What long-run effects would you anticipate if wage and price controls suppress inflation while excess demand pressures continue?

31.5 THE TRADE DEFICIT AND GLOBAL COMPETITIVENESS

Since 1980, the United States has experienced an extremely large trade deficit. In 1986, exports were almost $150 billion less than imports in real terms. By historical standards this trade deficit is unprecedented. Trade deficits and surpluses of 1–2 percent of GNP are quite common, but the 1986 trade deficit was over 4 percent of real GNP. The deterioration in the trade balance has raised concern that U.S. industries have lost their "global competitiveness," that is,

> The degree to which a nation can, under free and fair market conditions, produce goods and services that meet the test of international markets while simultaneously maintaining or expanding the real incomes of its citizens.*

As we have noted throughout this textbook, competitiveness is highly desirable in and among market economies. But what can and should government do to improve competitiveness?

Why and How Might Government Policies Improve Competitiveness?

Economists generally agree that the size of the current trade deficit is a cause for concern. Trade deficits must be financed by borrowing from foreigners, and eventually such borrowing must be repaid—with interest. The higher that debt is, the less domestic production can be used to satisfy domestic wants. Some forecasters believe that the United States may soon owe foreigners as much as $1 trillion. If large trade deficits continue, the United States will have to devote a significant portion of its domestic production to paying interest on its foreign debt, a problem that already plagues the Mexican, Brazilian, and Argentinian economies.

Fiscal and monetary policies.   Any policy to reduce the trade deficit requires an analysis of the cause(s) of that deficit. There is little question that fiscal and monetary policies are an important part of the problem. In the early 1980s the federal government borrowed heavily to finance its large budget deficits. At the same time, the Fed limited the growth of the money supply in order to lower inflation. In combination, these policies resulted in high real interest rates in the United States, which attracted large capital inflows. Capital inflows increased demand for the dollar and caused the U.S. dollar to rise in value.

This rise in the value of the dollar reduced the competitiveness of U.S. businesses by increasing the relative price of U.S. goods and services. The "strong

---

* *Global Competition: The New Reality*, The President's Commission on Industrial Competitiveness, 1985, p. 6.

dollar" made it more difficult for U.S. exporters to sell abroad and easier for foreign producers to sell in the United States. Although the value of the U.S. dollar began to fall in 1985, some economists believe that its value will have to continue to fall well below 1980 levels to recapture the market for U.S. goods and services.

To the extent that the decline in U.S. competitiveness stems from fiscal and monetary policies, the solution must involve those policies. Reducing the federal budget deficit would help to lower real interest rates, as would a more expansionary monetary policy (unless matched by a similar policy abroad). Similarly, fiscal policy changes in other countries—lowering tax rates or otherwise stimulating investment—would raise real returns on investment there. Although changes in fiscal and monetary policies may not be the only policy response necessary, they are part of nearly all proposed solutions to the trade deficit.

But is competitiveness strictly a macroeconomic issue? Some economists believe that the problem is at least partly the result of a microeconomic problem: declining productivity. Growth in productivity has averaged less than 1 percent in the United States since 1973, which is well below the average rate in the 1950s and 1960s and far below the rates of our major trading partners. Slow productivity growth means rising labor costs and downward pressure on real wages. It also creates a danger that more and more U.S. industries will be underpriced by foreign competitors.

Industrial policy. One proposed solution to this microeconomic problem is the so-called *industrial-policy* approach. Government would take an active role in directing and fostering improved U.S. competitiveness. Advocates view the recent loss of competitiveness as stemming in part from ineffective and inefficient private-sector responses. They argue that managers focus on short-run results to satisfy impatient shareholders.

Proponents of an industrial policy for the United States often suggest a co-operative relationship among industry, labor, and government, with the initiative and much of the funding coming from the private sector. A national development bank and a planning council would help identify and support "sunrise" industries—those industries considered important for future U.S. competitiveness. Firms in sunrise industries would develop plans for improved competitiveness and would be rewarded with some public financing to help them develop new products and improve production processes. The planning council would also provide retraining and relocation assistance to help move resources out of "sunset" industries—those industries in which the United States has lost its comparative advantage.

Free-market policies. In contrast, *free-market policies* would decrease the role of government. Advocates view the decline in U.S. competitiveness as the result of excessive government regulation and poorly designed tax policies. They suggest reducing government regulation of pollution control, health and safety, and pensions. Such regulation, they argue, creates barriers to firms entering and exiting industries and thus causes allocative inefficiency. If antitrust laws permitted more mergers and allowed firms to engage in joint research and development projects, U.S. firms would be stronger competitors. Lifting trade restrictions that now shelter U.S. firms would force them to become more competitive worldwide. Lower tax rates and greater tax incentives for research and development would increase investment and encourage more product development.

Fair-trade policies. Finally, many economists and politicians favor a *fair-trade approach*. They believe that the lack of U.S. competitiveness is partly caused by "unfair trading practices." Dumping—that is, selling goods below cost—is an issue, as are direct and indirect government subsidies to producers. Import restrictions—tariffs, quotas, and other nontariff restrictions—are a special target. Some of the countries with the largest trade surpluses—Japan, South Korea, and Taiwan—are those in which U.S. firms have had great difficulty penetrating trade barriers. Reducing or eliminating these barriers would, according to proponents, allow U.S. businesses to compete on a "level playing field."

What Are the Benefits and Costs of Trade-Deficit Policies?

As always, in choosing the "best" policy, policy makers must weigh the benefits and costs of different approaches and select the one for which benefits most outweigh its costs. (Note that although we discuss each policy approach separately, many economists believe that a *combination* of policies should be followed.)

Fiscal and monetary policies. As we discussed more fully in the policy case on federal budget deficits, reducing these deficits means raising taxes or cutting spending. Both actions have political and economic costs. Tax increases direct resources toward the public sector and may stifle saving and work effort. Reducing "unnecessary" government expenditures is universally accepted, but there is much disagreement over which expenditures are unnecessary. Moreover, reducing expenditures and raising taxes are both contractionary policies. But if government eases monetary policy to reduce this contractionary effect, inflation may result.

Industrial policy. Advocates of an industrial-policy approach argue that this is a more systematic, rational way of reducing the trade deficit. In a way, the United States already has an implicit industrial policy of sorts. Tax policies, direct and indirect subsidies, and various trade restrictions already enacted into law provide support (and discouragement) of industrial development. But Congress passes a lot of legislation to satisfy domestic special interest groups rather than to specifically improve global competitiveness.

Supporters of industrial policy point to agricultural policies as an example of the benefits of a cohesive industrial policy. In the 1930s U.S. agriculture was a dying industry. With the help of government research funds, cooperative marketing arrangements, and government help in promoting exports, agriculture became a highly technical, highly productive industry. Agriculture currently accounts for almost 20 percent of the nation's exports and enjoys a comparative advantage in international trade.

But industrial policies also involve costs. One potential cost is that government planners may be less capable than the marketplace in picking individual winners and losers. And an agency responsible for industrial policy would be subject to the same political pressures that affect any government agency.

Free-market policies. The free-market approach also involves both benefits and costs. Relaxing regulations lowers production costs; lowering taxes raises profitability; and allowing more mergers increases financial strength and market position. Although each of these policies may increase the global competitiveness of U.S. firms, there are costs to be considered. Relaxing regulations may increase pollution and reduce worker safety; lower taxes may increase the federal budget deficit; and mergers may reduce competition among U.S. firms.

Fair-trade policies.   Economists generally favor lower trade barriers because free trade allows each country to produce efficiently and to satisfy more wants. Proponents of fair-trade policies argue that the United States should take action to pressure other countries to lower tariffs, remove quotas, and eliminate subsidies and other restrictions. But the United States sometimes uses the same policies it opposes: subsidizing exports of grain and imposing tariffs and quotas to restrict imports of steel, textiles, and automobiles. Almost all economists support negotiations to eliminate restrictions. But some argue for retaliation when negotiations fail. In early 1987, threats of retaliation by the United States caused some European countries to drop plans to restrict U.S. grain imports. The United States also imposed retaliatory tariffs when Japanese manufacturers of semiconductor chips were accused of violating an antidumping agreement. But retaliation is a risky strategy because it may only escalate protectionism.

Would No Action Be a Better Policy?

The problem of a trade imbalance is, according to economic theory, likely to correct itself over time. The ability of the United States to import more than it exports depends on the willingness of foreigners to continue to loan us money. But eventually they will want to be repaid. When foreigners are unwilling to loan us more, demand for U.S. dollars will fall and the dollar will depreciate. If it falls far enough (and remains low long enough), the trade imbalance will correct itself.

However, few economists recommend waiting for this self-correction. In the first place, it will likely take some time to occur. In the meantime, the United States will run up a sizable debt to foreigners, and just financing this debt will be very expensive. Although there is no consensus on the policies that should be used, most economists suggest that efforts be made to decrease the trade deficit now.

Japanese cars on the dock await shipment to United States markets. Increased imports of foreign automobiles during the 1980s were a visible symbol of decreased international competitiveness of U.S. manufacturers. (UPI/ Bettmann Newsphotos)

Why Do Economists Disagree about Trade-Deficit Policies?

Economists generally agree that the high value of the dollar helped to cause very large U.S. trade deficits in the early 1980s. Most believe that lowering the federal budget deficit and, consequently, interest rates is essential to improving competitiveness. There is also widespread agreement among economists on the desirability of removing trade barriers both by the United States and by other countries.

Economists do not agree, however, on whether government should take any other steps to improve the competitiveness of U.S. businesses. Some economists recommend no additional government action. Others recommend active support of emerging industries and steps to ease the transition from dying industries. Others suggest removing what they see as government obstacles to competitiveness. These disagreements stem in part from subjective, normative elements in the debate and in part from the difficulty of assessing the degree to which various proposals would increase competitiveness.

Conclusion

The U.S. trade deficit has grown tremendously in recent years. Even though some of the blame may lie with federal budget deficits, the decline in competitiveness of U.S. industries also appears to be an important factor. A wide variety of solutions have been proposed, ranging from removing the influence of government to adding new government programs. But the difficulty of getting political and international agreement makes a quick end to the debate unlikely.

QUESTIONS FOR REVIEW AND DISCUSSION

1. Many economists argued that U.S. firms faced competitive disadvantages in the early 1980s as the value of the U.S. dollar increased significantly.
   a) Explain how a sufficiently large reduction in the value of the U.S. dollar would give U.S. businesses a competitive advantage in international markets.
   b) What are the disadvantages of allowing the dollar's value to fall? (Note who bears the costs of this fall.)

2. In 1987 President Reagan imposed tariffs on some Japanese products because Japanese manufacturers of semiconductor chips (used in computers) were accused of unfairly "dumping" the chips below cost.
   a) What are the benefits (and who receives them) if chips are "dumped" in the United States?
   b) What are the costs (and who pays them) if "dumping" occurs?
   c) How would you determine whether chips (or any other product) were being sold "below cost"? (That is, what costs would you consider? How does the principle of opportunity cost apply?)

3. The industrial-policy approach suggests the use of direct subsidies and other means to support selected industries.
   a) What criteria would you use to determine which industries to support?
   b) Would the criteria you use be like or different from those used by private financial firms (such as banks)?
   c) Explain how critics of the industrial-policy approach argue that the real criteria used are more likely to be political rather than economic.

PART NINE

International Economics

International Trade

QUESTIONS TO CONSIDER

☐ How important is international trade to the U.S. economy?

☐ Why do nations engage in international trade?

☐ What are the benefits and costs of international trade?

☐ Why do nations sometimes impose restrictions on international trade?

☐ What alternatives to trade restrictions do economists recommend and why?

Economic news in the United States increasingly concerns international trade and finance. International trade accounts for a smaller part of goods and services produced and consumed in the United States than in most other noncommunist countries. Nevertheless, some $331 billion worth of U.S. goods and services were sold to other countries in 1986, and U.S. residents bought almost $496 billion worth of goods and services produced abroad that year.

Why do countries trade? You would probably find life very different without Italian shoes, French wines, German automobiles, and Japanese electronic products. But international trade involves costs as well as benefits. For example, U.S. shoemakers, vintners, car companies, and stereo producers often lose the battle for consumers' dollars to foreign producers. In this chapter we present the benefits and costs of trade in more detail and show why some producers, workers, and politicians support trade restrictions—and why most economists don't.

INTERNATIONAL TRADE AND THE UNITED STATES

Trade is the very essence of market transactions. Every time you go to work or to the grocery store you are engaging in trade; that is, you are trading your services for income and the income for food. As you will see, the principles governing international trade and the reasons why trade is beneficial are the same whether we are considering nations within the world economy or individuals within a nation's economy. First, however, we must consider the extent of international trade.

International trade is big business. As Exhibit 32.1 indicates, about $1.8 trillion worth of goods flowed among countries in 1985. But the importance of international trade varies by country. Some 7 percent of all U.S. goods and services produced are sold in other countries. As we noted in Chapter 6, these products are considered to be exports by the U.S. economy and imports by the countries that buy them. A number of other countries export a much larger percentage of their total production. West Germany, for example, exported about one-third of its total production. In the Netherlands, exports accounted for nearly 65 percent of all goods and services produced, and in Belgium they represented 76 percent.

Country	Exports of goods (billions of U.S. dollars)	Imports of goods (billions of U.S. dollars)	Exports as a percentage of domestic GNP
United States	213.1	361.6	7.0
Japan	177.2	130.5	16.4
United Kingdom	101.2	109.0	29.3
Canada	90.6	81.1	29.8
West Germany	183.9	158.5	36.7
Netherlands	68.3	65.2	64.5
Belgium	53.7	56.2	75.7*
Total World	1782.9	1879.0	

* Figure is for 1984.

Source: International Monetary Fund, *International Financial Statistics, 1986 Yearbook.*

Exhibit 32.1
Volume of International Trade, 1985

However, the importance of international trade to the United States is much greater than the relatively small amount of total production that is exported. The U.S. economy depends heavily on imports of natural resources, such as oil. And as we have already noted, imported goods such as shoes, steel, and automobiles are important competitors for products made in the United States.

Volume of U.S. International Trade

Another important aspect of international trade is the balance (or imbalance) of imports and exports of goods and services. As Exhibit 32.2 shows, in 1986 the United States exported $221.7 billion worth of goods (excluding services) but imported $369.5 billion worth. Thus the **trade balance (balance on merchandise trade)**—the difference between the values of goods exported and imported—for 1986 was −$147.7 billion. That is, the United States had a $147.7 billion **trade deficit**. However, the U.S. trade balance has not always been negative. Indeed, for many years, exports exceeded imports, giving the nation a **trade surplus**.

Trade balance (balance on merchandise trade). The difference between the values of exports and imports of goods only (excludes imports and exports of services).

Trade deficit. A negative trade balance; occurs when the value of imports exceeds the value of exports.

Trade surplus. A positive trade balance; occurs when the value of exports exceeds the value of imports.

Exhibit 32.2
U.S. International Trade, 1986 (in billions of U.S. dollars)

Exports of goods	221.7
Less: Imports of goods	369.5
Trade balance	−147.7
Exports of goods and services	370.7
Less: Imports of goods and services	496.1
Balance on goods and services	−125.4

Source: U.S. Department of Commerce, *Survey of Current Business,* March 1987, Table 1-2, p. 44.

Category	Exports of goods (billions of U.S. dollars)	Imports of goods (billions of U.S. dollars)	Net exports (billions of U.S. dollars)
Foods and feeds	22.6	24.0	−1.4
Industrial supplies	63.4	103.1	−39.7
Energy products	8.2	38.1	−29.9
Capital goods	79.2	75.7	3.5
Automobiles	23.9	78.1	−54.2
Consumer goods	14.5	78.0	−63.5
Other goods	18.2	10.6	7.6
Total merchandise trade	221.8	369.5	−147.7
Services	148.9	126.6	22.3
Trade of goods and services	370.7	496.1	−125.4

Source: U.S. Department of Commerce, *Survey of Current Business,* March 1987, Tables 2 and 3.

Exhibit 32.3
U.S. International Trade by Category, 1986

Balance on goods and services. The difference between the value of exports and imports of both goods and services.

In addition to trading goods, countries also import and export services. As a resident of the United States, if you travel to Europe on British Airways, for example, you are buying a service made in Great Britain. Your expenditure is counted as an import in the United States and an export in Great Britain. Services traded internationally include not only expenditures for travel and transportation, but also international investments. In 1986, the U.S. **balance on goods and services**, including imports and exports of both goods and services, showed a $125.4 billion deficit.*

Exhibit 32.3 shows exports and imports by category. As you can see, the United States is a net exporter of both agricultural products and capital resources. It is a net importer of industrial supplies and consumer goods. Indeed, net imports of petroleum products alone were $29.9 billion in 1986. Exhibit 32.3 also indicates that the United States had a significant surplus of trade in services.

The volume of international trade has increased significantly over the past 25 years. In 1960, total trade in the United States (exports plus imports) was $200 billion, equivalent to 12 percent of all goods and services produced.† The volume in 1986 ($892 billion) was equal to 24 percent of total U.S. production. The rising volume and relative importance of international trade is an important trend. It means that U.S. businesses face increasing competition for the dollars spent by U.S. households and businesses. In addition, U.S. businesses are increasingly looking to foreign markets for sales.

---

* If you have studied macroeconomics, you may find it useful to remember that the balance on goods and services is roughly equal to net exports as used in accounting for national income and gross national product.

† If you have studied macroeconomics, you may be interested in knowing that the data in this paragraph are stated in real terms; that is, the effect of inflation have been removed.

Changing Pattern of U.S. International Trade

The pattern of U.S. international trade in goods has changed substantially over the past 10 years as shown in Exhibit 32.4. Europe and Canada remain our largest trading partners and account for virtually the same proportion of total trade at the beginning and end of the period. But U.S. trade with Japan and the developing Asian countries, including Hong Kong, Singapore, and South Korea, has increased dramatically. Total volume of trade with these countries quadrupled between 1975 and 1985.

As a result, trade with the major oil-exporting nations of the Middle East (from the U.S. perspective, mostly imports of oil) became relatively less important. In 1975 trade with these nations represented 14 percent of all U.S. trade; in 1985 it was only 6 percent. Imports from these countries increased dramatically in 1980, reflecting the large oil-price increases that occurred in 1979–1980. But the dollar volume of trade with these nations declined as oil prices dropped and the United States imported more oil from other countries, such as Mexico.

Another significant change in the U.S. trade pattern is the nation's rising trade deficit. In 1986 the U.S. trade deficit represented over 4 percent of the nation's total production of goods and services. In the 25 years prior to 1980, the largest deficit—equal to 1.9 percent of the nation's total production—occurred in 1972.

Why are the deficits so large? As Exhibit 32.4 indicates, the value of U.S. exports has grown more slowly than that of its imports. Average annual growth in exports between 1975 and 1985 was 7 percent. Over the same period, imports increased at a rate of 13 percent per year. This pattern held for nearly all the world regions shown, but was strongest in U.S. trade with Japan and the developing Asian countries. Exports to this region increased by 9 percent, but imports increased by 19 percent. We consider other reasons for U.S. trade deficits and possible solutions in Chapter 33. (This topic is also explored in Chapter 31.)

Exhibit 32.4
Shifting Pattern of U.S. Trade (billions of U.S. dollars, nominal terms)

Region	Total trade (imports + exports)		Exports from United States		Imports into United States		Trade deficits	
	1975	1985	1975	1985	1975	1985	1975	1985
Europe	49.7	135.5	28.2	53.6	21.5	81.9	6.6	−28.3
Canada	44.5	116.7	21.7	47.3	22.8	69.4	−1.0	−22.2
Oil exporters	30.3	33.6	10.4	12.0	19.9	21.6	−9.5	−9.6
Latin America	34.3	80.1	17.1	31.0	17.2	49.1	0.1	−18.1
USSR and Eastern Europe	3.1	3.8	2.5	2.9	0.6	0.9	1.9	2.0
Developing Asia	22.7	90.2	11.0	29.0	11.7	61.2	−0.7	−32.2
Japan	21.9	95.0	9.6	22.6	12.3	72.4	−2.8	−49.8

Source: Joseph A. Whitt, Jr., Paul Kuch, and Jeffrey Rosenweig, "The Dollar and Prices: An Empirical Analysis," *Economic Review,* Federal Reserve Bank of Atlanta, October 1986.

GAINS FROM INTERNATIONAL TRADE

Clearly, international trade is an important part of the U.S. economy—and that of most nations. But why? We can summarize the reasons for trade as follows: *Countries trade with each other because each country can benefit*. This principle is basic to understanding why economists generally agree that trade restrictions are usually not in a nation's best long-run interest. Trade can be beneficial when two countries possess different natural and/or capital resources. It can be beneficial when they have different preferences. And it can be beneficial when the efficiency with which they produce a given set of goods differs. Studying the benefits of trade can help you identify the factors that determine which goods a country will import and which it will export.

Differences in Resources

Countries are often motivated to trade because they have different natural resources. The United States, for example, has an abundant quantity of fertile land. In 1986 we exported $27 billion worth of agricultural products. Saudi Arabia, on the other hand, has few natural resources other than sand and oil. The Saudis rely heavily on exports of petroleum products.

Similarly, the capital/labor ratio—which measures the value of capital resources such as machinery and equipment per worker—helps to predict trade flows. For example, the United States has a high capital/labor ratio compared to India, meaning that the United States has more abundant capital resources. Thus we would expect the United States to export goods for which capital resources are relatively important but India to export goods that require relatively more labor.

We trade with Brazil to get coffee and with Honduras to get bananas, neither of which grow in North America. We travel to the Caribbean, trading for sunshine, beautiful beaches, and warm water. Citizens of many countries attend U.S. colleges and universities, trading for educational services.

Differences in Preferences

Trade would also tend to occur even if all countries had identical resources because countries have different preferences. The British, for example, prefer tea to coffee; Americans have the opposite preference. Even if each country had the same quantities of tea and coffee, trade would be beneficial. By trading coffee for tea, the British would be sacrificing something of less value to them (coffee) for an item they value more (tea). At the same time, Americans would also gain. Even though the total quantity of goods would be the same, both countries would have increased their satisfaction by trading.

Differences in Productivity: Absolute Advantage

Differences in resources and preferences create opportunities for gains through trade and explain some trade patterns. Even more significant, however, trade offers an opportunity for countries to specialize—to produce the goods that they can produce most efficiently. Thus trade allows countries to escape the limits imposed by their own production possibilities. As a result, trade enables the world

Absolute advantage. The ability to produce a good or service with fewer resources; refers only to relative productivity.

to satisfy more wants because it allows resources to be used more efficiently. A country that is more productive in making a certain good—that can produce the good with fewer resources—has an **absolute advantage** in producing that good. Thus, because of its climate, Brazil has an absolute advantage in growing coffee beans.

Assume for the moment that there are only two countries in the world: the United States and Tradesia. Assume also that only two products are produced: computers and applesauce and that both nations can produce both products. Exhibit 32.5 indicates that U.S. workers can produce more applesauce in a week than workers in Tradesia (100 cases per week compared to 50 cases). Greater productivity gives the United States an absolute advantage in producing applesauce. On the other hand, Tradesia has an absolute advantage in producing computers because its workers produce more computers per week (25 compared to 10).

This simple example shows why absolute advantage means that trade will increase efficiency. If one U.S. worker switches from producing computers to producing applesauce, the United States will produce 100 more cases of applesauce and 10 fewer computers per week. If one Tradesian worker stops producing

Exhibit 32.5
Gains from Trade: Absolute Advantage

(a) Labor productivity

	Quantity produced by one worker in one week	
Product	*in the United States*	*in Tradesia*
Applesauce	100 cases	50 cases
Computers	10 computers	25 computers

(b) Opportunity cost

	Opportunity cost per unit produced	
Product	*in the United States*	*in Tradesia*
Applesauce	0.10 computer	0.50 computer
Computers	10 cases of applesauce	2 cases of applesauce

(c) Gains from trade

	Cases of applesauce		
Country	*Changes in output*	*Goods traded*	*Final result*
United States	+100 cases	−60 cases	+40 cases
Tradesia	− 50	+60	+10
Net effect	+ 50 cases	0 cases	+50 cases

	Number of computers		
Country	*Changes in output*	*Goods traded*	*Final result*
United States	−10 computers	+12 computers	+ 2 computers
Tradesia	+25	−12	+13
Net effect	+15 computers	0 computers	+15 computers

applesauce and starts producing computers, that country will have 50 fewer cases of applesauce and 25 more computers. From a worldwide perspective (in this two-country world), this change results in a net increase in production of both goods: 50 more cases of applesauce and 15 more computers. Because more goods have been produced using the same amount of resources, using absolute advantages has increased efficiency.

The world has benefited, but what about the United States and Tradesia? Suppose that Tradesia agrees to ship 12 computers to the United States in exchange for 60 cases of applesauce. Compared to the position before switching resources and trading, the United States is better off. It has 40 more cases of applesauce—100 more were produced but 60 traded—and 2 more computers—10 were not made, but 12 were received in trade. Tradesia is also better off. It has 10 more cases of applesauce—it sacrificed making 50 cases but received 60 U.S. cases—and 13 more computers—it made 25 more but traded 12 to the United States. *When each country specializes in what it can produce most efficiently, trading can result in greater worldwide output and can benefit all countries involved.*

Gains from specialization reflect different opportunity costs of production in the United States and Tradesia. A U.S. worker can produce *either* 100 cases of applesauce or 10 computers in a week. Thus in the United States each computer has an opportunity cost of 10 cases of applesauce (100 cases of applesauce ÷ 10 computers). In Tradesia the opportunity cost is 2 cases of applesauce per computer (50 cases of applesauce ÷ 25 computers). Thus it is more efficient to produce computers in Tradesia, where the opportunity cost is lower.

Similarly, the U.S. opportunity cost of producing applesauce is 0.10 computer compared to 0.50 computer in Tradesia. Thus the United States can produce applesauce more efficiently than Tradesia. As this example indicates, if each country produces with its efficiency advantage (lower opportunity cost), more goods can be produced from the same amount of resources. Because the size of the "pie" for the world is larger as a result of this specialization, each country can have a bigger "slice."

Differences in Opportunity Cost: Comparative Advantage

It is not difficult to see that trading can be beneficial when each country has an absolute advantage in one commodity. (If you are better in economics and your friend is better in biology, you can both make better grades by helping each other study.) However, you may be surprised to learn that *both countries can gain from trade even if one country has an absolute advantage in producing both goods.*

Suppose, for example, that a U.S. worker can produce more computers or more applesauce in a week than a Tradesian worker, as Exhibit 32.6 shows. The key word in that sentence is the word *or.* A worker cannot produce both a week's worth of applesauce and a week's worth of computers in a single week. To produce a week's worth of applesauce, a week's worth of computer production must be sacrificed. The opportunity cost of producing applesauce is thus the quantity of computers that must be sacrificed.

If we measure efficiency in terms of opportunity cost, we see that the U.S. opportunity cost of a case of applesauce is 0.10 computer. The Tradesian opportunity cost is 0.40 computer per case. Thus the United States is more efficient in producing applesauce. But Tradesia has a lower opportunity cost of producing

(a) Labor productivity

	Quantity produced by one worker in one week	
Product	*in the United States*	*in Tradesia*
Applesauce	100 cases	20 cases
Computers	10 computers	8 computers

(b) Opportunity cost

	Opportunity cost per unit produced	
Product	*in the United States*	*in Tradesia*
Applesauce	0.10 computer	0.40 computer
Computers	10 cases of applesauce	2.5 cases of applesauce

(c) Gains from trade

	Cases of applesauce		
Country	*Changes in output*	*Goods traded*	*Final result*
United States	+100 cases	−60 cases	+40 cases
Tradesia	− 40	+60	+20
Net effect	+ 60 cases	0 cases	+60 cases

	Number of computers		
Country	*Changes in output*	*Goods traded*	*Final result*
United States	−10 computers	+12 computers	+2 computers
Tradesia	+16	−12	+4
Net effect	+ 6 computers	0 computers	+6 computers

Exhibit 32.6
Gains from Trade: Comparative Advantage

---

computers: 2.5 cases of applesauce per computer compared with 10 cases per computer in the United States.

In other words, although the United States has an absolute advantage in producing both applesauce and computers, Tradesia has a **comparative advantage** in producing computers. A country has a comparative advantage when it can produce a good for a lower opportunity cost. Workers in Tradesia produce fewer computers in a week than workers in the United States, but the opportunity cost is lower. Put another way, a U.S. worker can produce 5 times as many cases of applesauce but only 25 percent more computers. Relatively speaking, U.S. workers are better—have a comparative advantage—at producing applesauce but are at a relative disadvantage when producing computers.

When countries use the principle of comparative advantage to select which goods to produce and trade internationally, more goods are produced worldwide. To see why, look again at Exhibit 32.6. If one U.S. worker stops producing computers and starts producing applesauce, the United States will produce 10 fewer

Comparative advantage. The ability to produce a good or service at a smaller opportunity cost; refers to relative efficiency.

computers but 100 more cases of applesauce. At the same time, if two Tradesian workers quit producing applesauce and begin making computers, Tradesia will produce 16 more computers and 40 fewer cases of applesauce. The result is increased efficiency because 6 more computers and 60 more cases of applesauce are produced from the same resources. *When countries specialize in producing products for which they have a comparative advantage, efficiency improves worldwide.*

Again, both the world and the two nations benefit from trade. Suppose that Tradesia agrees to trade 12 computers to the United States for 60 cases of applesauce. Compared to its initial position, Tradesia has 4 more computers (16 were made but 12 traded away) and 20 more cases of applesauce. The U.S. has 40 more cases of applesauce and 2 more computers.

Absolute versus comparative advantage. Although both absolute advantage and comparative advantage support the idea that trade benefits both nations, comparative advantage is the more reliable guide to decision making. Absolute advantage shows only the benefits obtained from producing. To make decisions about what goods to produce, the extra costs must also be considered.

As in our two-country example, a country's resources may be more productive (have an absolute advantage) in two tasks. But they cannot be more efficient (have a comparative advantage) at both tasks because using resources to produce one good requires the sacrifice of another good. The more productive resources are, the greater is the sacrifice or opportunity cost involved. That is, the better a country is at producing any good, the greater the sacrifice required to produce another good.

This important conclusion does not depend on the particular numbers we used in the example. No country can have a comparative advantage in producing all goods. There is always some comparative advantage and hence gains to be made from specializing and trading. These gains are a major reason why economists generally agree that trade is beneficial and that trade restrictions are not in a country's best economic interests.

Terms of Trade

As you have just seen, specialization along the lines of comparative advantage means greater worldwide efficiency and production. As a result, countries can gain through trade. But how much will each country gain? In the last part of our example, we assumed that the United States exchanged 60 cases of applesauce for 12 computers. This means that the **terms of trade**—the relative price expressed in terms of physical commodities—were 5 cases of applesauce per computer. But what, if anything, can we say about the terms of trade in the real world?

In our simple example, suppose that the terms of trade were set at 15 cases of applesauce per computer. Would the United States be willing to trade applesauce for computers with Tradesia on these terms? The answer is *no*. To see why, let's suppose that the United States traded for 10 computers. To do so, it would have to make 150 cases of applesauce to export (10 computers × 15 cases of applesauce). To produce 150 cases of applesauce, however, the United States would have to sacrifice making 15 computers (because every 10 cases of applesauce means that one less computer can be made). In other words, after trading, the United States would have the same amount of applesauce but 5 fewer computers.

Terms of trade. The relative prices of goods and services involved in international trade expressed in physical terms (for example, 5 cases of applesauce per computer).

Because it would be worse off, the United States would not be willing to trade. The terms of trade are too high to make trading profitable for the United States.

Why are the terms of trade too high? Because the United States *can* make computers, it attains an economic gain by trading only if computers can be imported more cheaply than they can be made. That is, the terms of trade—the price of imports—must be more favorable than the domestic opportunity cost. In our example, it costs the United States 15 cases of applesauce to trade for one computer. But it costs only 10 cases of applesauce to make one computer.

The terms of trade can also be too low to tempt nations to produce goods for export. Tradesia will gain economically by exporting computers only if it can make a profit, that is, if the terms of trade exceed the opportunity cost of production. (Nations also may or may not trade with certain countries for political reasons, as is the case in U.S. trade relations with the Soviet Union, Eastern Europe, and Cuba. Economic analysis cannot easily predict the direction of political actions, but it can identify the economic costs of restricting trade.)

These principles allow us to calculate the maximum and minimum terms of trade for the example given in Exhibit 32.6. The maximum terms of trade are 10 cases of applesauce for one computer, or the opportunity cost of making a computer in the United States. Unless the terms of trade (price of a computer) are less than 10 cases of applesauce, it will not be economically profitable for the United States to import computers. The minimum terms of trade are 2.5 cases of applesauce per computer, or the opportunity cost of making a computer in Tradesia. If the terms of trade are lower, it would not be economically profitable for Tradesia to export computers. To check your understanding, express the minimum and maximum terms of trade in number of computers. (Your answers should be a maximum price of 0.40 computer per case and a minimum price of 0.10 computer per case.)

The closer the terms of trade are to the maximum, the greater are the gains received by Tradesia. The closer the terms are to the minimum, the greater are the gains received by the United States. In the example in Exhibit 32.6, the terms are 5 cases of applesauce per computer. *Because these terms fall between the minimum and maximum levels, both nations find trade profitable.* To check your understanding, calculate the gains to each nation if the terms of trade are 3 cases per computer and 12 computers are traded. (Because the price of computers declines relative to applesauce, the United States, the importer, gains more. Tradesia, the exporter, gains less.)

Demand and Supply: International Equilibrium

Minimum and maximum terms of trade are linked to costs. But we cannot predict whether actual terms will be closer to the maximum or minimum values by looking only at relative costs. To understand how the terms of trade are determined, we must also consider demand and supply conditions in each country. As we first noted in Chapter 3, demand and supply determine the price of a product in a market economy. Exhibit 32.7 shows domestic demand and supply of applesauce in the United States and Tradesia. We can compare the price and quantity of applesauce produced and consumed both with and without trade.

If there is no trade, the applesauce market in Tradesia, shown in Exhibit 32.7(a), will reach equilibrium at a price of $5 per case (where D_T and S_T intersect).

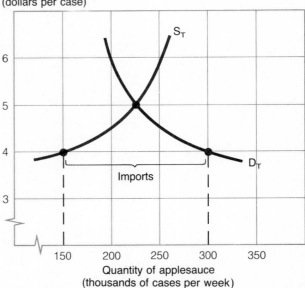

(a) Market for applesauce in Tradesia

Price of applesauce
(dollars per case)

Exhibit 32.7
World Market for Applesauce
Part (a) shows that with no trade the market for applesauce in Tradesia will reach equilibrium at a price of $5 per case. Part (b) shows that the U.S. market will achieve equilibrium at a price of $3 per case. If international trade is allowed, applesauce will be exported from the United States, where it can be produced more cheaply. When demand for and supply of applesauce in both countries are combined, worldwide equilibrium occurs at a price of $4 per case, as part (c) indicates. At that price, exports from the United States equal imports into Tradesia.

At this price, 225,000 cases will be bought and sold. Similarly, Exhibit 32.7(b) indicates that the equilibrium price of applesauce in the United States will be $3 per case if there is no trade.* Because the price in Tradesia is higher than the price in the United States, however, worldwide equilibrium is not achieved. If trading between the countries is not restricted, a firm can earn a profit simply by buying U.S. applesauce and selling it in Tradesia (if shipping costs do not eliminate profits). Such trading gains would be possible as long as there is a difference in price.

When international trade is allowed, there are two conditions for equilibrium. First, the price in both countries must be the same (except for transportation costs). And second, quantity supplied worldwide must equal quantity demanded worldwide. That is, the quantity exported from the United States must equal the quantity imported by Tradesia and bought by Tradesian residents.

The first condition is not met when there is no trade because the price of applesauce is higher in Tradesia than in the United States. But examining the world market in Exhibit 32.7(c), you can see that both conditions are met when the world price (and the price in each country) is $4 per case. Not only are the prices the same (condition 1) but the quantity demanded and supplied worldwide are both 550,000 cases (condition 2).

---

* In this example, prices in both countries are expressed in dollars. In the real world, countries use different currencies. However, because our interest here is in the relative price of applesauce in the two countries, we have translated the foreign prices into dollar prices. In Chapter 33 we discuss how the relative "prices" of currencies of two countries are determined.

(b) Market for applesauce in the United States

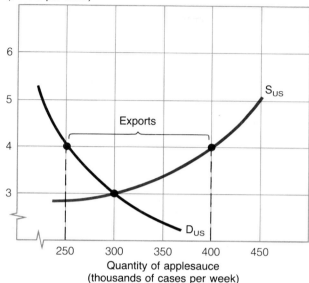

(c) World market for applesauce

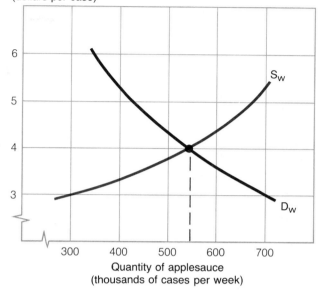

Note that equilibrium does not mean that the quantity produced in each country is equal to the quantity bought. Tradesia produces only 150,000 cases but consumes 300,000. Imports from the United States are part of the available supply in Tradesia. They make up the difference between quantity produced domestically and quantity consumed. Similarly, in the United States, total demand represents demand by U.S. residents (D_{US}) together with demand by Tradesians (D_T) for U.S. exports.

How do the U.S. and Tradesian markets adjust to reach this price and level of production? Adding demand by Tradesian residents to that of U.S. residents causes U.S. applesauce prices to rise from $3 to $4 per case. In response, U.S. applesauce producers increase quantity offered for sale from 300,000 to 400,000 cases per week. Although U.S. customers buy less applesauce as the price rises, U.S. producers export 150,000 cases to Tradesia. In Tradesia, the market price of applesauce falls from $5 to $4 per case when the supply from the United States is added to the domestic supply. Although Tradesian applesauce producers offer less for sale, imports from the U.S. allow Tradesian residents to increase the quantity of applesauce consumed from 225,000 to 300,000 cases per week.

This example illustrates several important points. First, when there is international trade, we cannot predict prices or quantities exchanged simply by looking at domestic demand and supply. The available supply in any country depends on quantities supplied by both domestic and foreign producers. Likewise, demand by foreign residents must be added to demand by domestic residents. Second, as you saw in this example, international trade does not mean complete specialization. The Tradesian demand for applesauce is met partly by Tradesian firms and partly by imports from the United States. This situation—where foreign producers compete against domestic producers in the same markets—is typical. The lack of complete specialization partly reflects preferences; some U.S. residents, for example, prefer Fords and Chevrolets to Toyotas and Volvos.

INTERNATIONAL TRADE: GAINS AND LOSSES

So far we have indicated how it is possible for countries to gain through international trade. We have also shown how demand and supply determine a worldwide equilibrium price for a single product. But our references to gains are from the perspective of the country as a whole. Not all individuals in a country stand to gain from trade. And of those who do gain, some gain more than others. Like most other economic activities, international trade involves both benefits and costs. In this section, we examine these benefits and costs, paying special attention to which groups in the economy tend to benefit and which tend to lose. This distinction is important because those who stand to lose often argue for trade restrictions, seeking to avoid the costs associated with trade.

Higher Prices for Exported Goods

Looking at the price of applesauce in the United States, we can see one of the costs of trade. Before trade, the price was $3 per case, based on domestic demand and supply. After trade, it is $4 per case. In general, a price increase accompanies most goods that are exported. Demand for U.S. applesauce is higher when both the domestic and foreign demand are combined. Higher demand drives prices up, causing U.S. consumers to pay more and buy less applesauce.

Thus it appears that U.S. residents lose by trading internationally. But trade is not a one-way street. At the same time, Tradesian suppliers are offering computers to U.S. buyers at lower prices than before. Overall, as you saw earlier, more is available and consumers in both countries gain as a group. Those who consume more applesauce than computers, however, may be worse off as individuals.

Decreased Demand in Import-Competing Industries

Another major cost of trade is the decline in Tradesian applesauce production from 225,000 cases before trade to 150,000 cases after trade. In other words, trade means that less applesauce will be produced in Tradesia (and sold at a lower price). Thus profits of Tradesian applesauce firms are lower, wages paid Tradesian applesauce workers are lower, and fewer Tradesian workers will be employed in this industry. From the standpoint of producers and workers in the Tradesian applesauce industry, then, imports are a threat. In response, they may seek government protection from imported applesauce. In the United States, efforts to restrict imports of automobiles, steel, shoes, and textiles have been supported both by producers and unions representing workers in those industries.

Lower Prices for Imports and Greater Demand for Exports

However, trade involves benefits as well as costs. Although prices of exported goods are higher because of trade, prices of imports are lower. Thus consumers of imported goods gain. Although trade reduces demand for goods and labor in import-competing industries, demand in export industries rises, resulting in higher profits, increased employment, and higher wages in such industries. In addition, we must not forget the first lesson of trade: By increasing efficiency worldwide, total production and consumption are greater in the world (and in each country) than without trade. These benefits must be compared to costs to estimate the net gain to an entire country. Economists generally believe that the extra benefits of trade are greater than the extra costs.

Distributional Effects of Trade

The greater efficiency associated with trade means greater output worldwide. Moreover, countries are willing to trade only when the terms of trade benefit each, improving their overall economic positions. On the other hand, not every firm or individual is better off. That is, trade has distributional effects. Those who consume above-average amounts of imported goods gain more because of lower prices. Those who consume above-average amounts of exported goods lose more because of higher prices. Moreover, producers and workers in export industries gain, whereas producers and workers in import-competing industries lose. These distributional effects are a major reason why some individuals seek restrictions on trade.

Concentrated costs. Note, however, that the distributional effects of trade have several important characteristics. First, *the costs of trade are often more highly concentrated and more directly visible than the benefits.* For example, a growing percentage of shoes sold in the United States is imported. We gain from lower shoe prices as a result. But our individual gains are small, even if the total gain is large. On the other hand, many U.S. shoemakers have suffered substantially lower profits. As a result, many have closed factories and laid off workers.

The concentration of costs and the diffusion of benefits are important for two reasons. They help explain why politicians often seek to restrict trade. Moreover, they suggest a possible way of dealing with the distributional problem without resorting to trade restrictions. A part of the gains from trade could be used to compensate those who lose, by subsidizing job training or job relocation for displaced workers, for example. If the net gain from trade were shared, support for free trade might be easier to win.

Costs and mobility. Second, *the costs of trade are smaller when labor and capital are highly mobile and greater when mobility is restricted.* As we have noted, some losers under unrestricted trade are workers and producers in import-competing industries, such as shoes. Their losses reflect the decrease in demand which suggests that resources be reallocated—away from import-competing industries to other industries—in the interest of efficiency. If workers in shoe factories can quickly and easily find other employment, the unemployment costs related to free trade will be small.

But if workers left unemployed by free trade lack the skills to move to other jobs, or if other jobs require a move across country, the costs are significant, at least to unemployed shoeworkers. This cost may justify distributional aid. However, it also suggests that such aid might best take the form of programs to increase labor mobility, including retraining and/or relocation assistance, rather than restricting trade. Such programs would help society to improve the allocation of resources (efficiency), while reducing the distributional costs (equity) of free trade. As we discuss later in this chapter, such programs have been a part of U.S. economic policy for many years.

Long run versus short run. And third, *benefits tend to be greater and costs lower when considered over the long run; the opposite is true for the short run*. In some respects, this point is much like the second one. Given enough time, workers will find other employment even if it means some retraining or relocation. Thus in a long-run analysis, the benefits of greater efficiency worldwide outweigh the costs. Bear in mind, however, that a meaningful economic analysis must recognize both the short-run costs and the long-run benefits. If, as most economists believe, the long-run benefits outweigh the short-run costs, trade should be encouraged. However, it is still reasonable to suggest, as many do, that short-run costs should be shared by those who benefit from trade.

TRADE RESTRICTIONS AND ALTERNATIVE TRADE POLICIES

Most economists agree that free trade—that is, unrestricted trade—is beneficial to an economy overall. They also recognize that trade restrictions are common in the real world. In this section we consider several questions: What are the effects of trade restrictions? Are there legitimate reasons for proposing restrictions? What are the alternatives?

Import Tariffs

A common form of trade restriction is an **import tariff**, which is a tax on imported goods. You can see the results of an import tariff by returning to our example of demand for and supply of applesauce in Tradesia. Like Exhibit 32.7(c), Exhibit 32.8 shows that in the absence of trade restrictions, applesauce will sell for $4 per case. Tradesians will buy 300,000 cases per week, including 150,000 cases imported from foreign countries.

What if Tradesian applesauce producers and workers successfully lobby their legislators for an import tariff of $0.50 per case? Tradesian applesauce producers and workers will then gain at the expense of Tradesian consumers and foreign producers. The tariff will raise the price of foreign applesauce in Tradesia to $4.50 per case. Even if they charge the same price as foreign producers will have to charge, Tradesian producers can increase their sales from 150,000 to 200,000 cases per week, as shown in Exhibit 32.8. Sales, profits, and employment in the applesauce industry will increase. Tradesian applesauce producers and their employees will be better off.

Import tariff. A tax placed on imported goods.

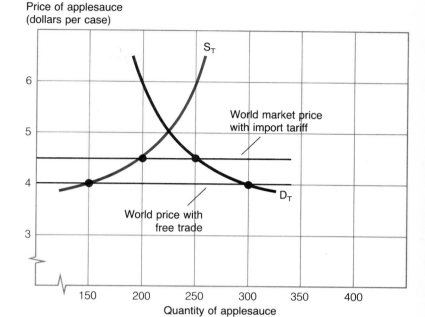

Price of applesauce
(dollars per case)

Exhibit 32.8
Effects of Import Tariffs on Market for Applesauce in Tradesia
With free trade, the world price of applesauce will be $4 per case. At that price, Tradesia will import 150,000 cases per week (the difference between quantity demanded and quantity supplied). But Tradesian applesauce producers and their workers may argue for a protective tariff. If a tariff of $0.50 per case is imposed, the market price in Tradesia will increase to $4.50 per case, and the quantity of imports will fall to 50,000 cases per week. Tradesian producers will sell more, but Tradesian consumers will pay more for fewer cases of applesauce. The Tradesian government will collect $25,000 per week from the tariff ($0.50 × 50,000 cases imported).

In addition, imports fall from 150,000 cases (the difference between quantity demanded and domestic supply at a price of $4 per case) to 50,000 cases. Thus part of the gain to Tradesian producers and workers is paid by foreign producers and workers. The tariff also gives the Tradesian government additional receipts. With a $0.50 per case tariff on imported applesauce, the Tradesian government collects $25,000 per week (50,000 cases × $0.50 per case).

However, the Tradesian consumer would have to pay more for less. The price of applesauce rises by $0.50 per case and quantity consumed falls by 50,000 cases. Thus part of the gain to Tradesian producers and workers will come at the expense of Tradesian consumers. Other Tradesian producers and workers also stand to lose. Tradesian bakers making applesauce cakes and restaurants serving applesauce will pay more for applesauce, and their profits will fall. Moreover, if many products are subject to tariffs, workers in many industries may seek higher wages in an effort to maintain their standard of living in the face of rising prices.

Tariffs also damage efficiency. Protected industries produce more than they would in the absence of tariffs. Thus they use more resources (such as labor) than they would otherwise. As a result, nonprotected industries will be forced to pay higher prices for resources. Some economists also note that industries may be somewhat less efficient producers when they are protected against the efficiency-stimulating effects of greater competition. Nobody benefits from goods not produced because of inefficiency.

Restrictions on trade also harm efficiency indirectly. Because foreign countries can sell fewer of their goods to Tradesia, they have less to spend on Tradesian goods. Hence quantities of goods demanded and supplied internationally will fall.

Import quota. A limit on the quantity of a particular good that can be imported.

These effects are often multiplied as one nation retaliates for another's tariffs by establishing its own tariff system. For example, the United States might respond to a Tradesian tariff on applesauce by placing a tariff on Tradesian computers. In general, economists believe that the domestic economy suffers a net loss as a result of an import tariff. That is, a few gain but not as much as the rest of the economy loses. However, the short-run costs and distributional effects can be significant.

To illustrate, let's consider the U.S. shoe industry, which responded to a significant loss in profits because of foreign competition by pressuring Congress to impose a tariff on foreign-made shoes. Domestic shoe manufacturers and their employees have benefited from higher production, profits, wages, and employment. But consumers have paid higher prices for shoes, foreign producers have sold fewer shoes, and China has restricted imports of U.S. agricultural products, hurting U.S. farmers. Moreover, U.S. resource allocation has suffered since resources that could be more efficiently utilized elsewhere remain in the shoe industry. There may very well be legitimate concerns about the short-run costs to U.S. shoeworkers who lose their jobs and producers who lose profits. However, tariffs and other protectionist measures are not efficient policy responses to this concern because they result in a net loss to the economy as a whole.

Import Quotas

Another common form of trade restriction is an **import quota**, which is a limit on the quantity of a particular good that may be imported. In some ways the effects of quotas and tariffs are alike. In fact, Exhibit 32.8 also shows what would happen if Tradesia limited imports of applesauce to 50,000 cases per week. The quota causes imports to fall from 150,000 to 50,000 cases per week, and like a tariff, it also causes prices to rise. Tradesian consumers again pay more for less. In fact, consumers may actually lose more from quotas than from tariffs, since quotas also restrict consumer choice.

Tradesian producers and workers benefit from increased demand for domestic applesauce. Tradesian companies benefit from reduced competition and, as a result, may actually be able to charge more and produce less. The lack of competition may also harm technical efficiency, as Tradesian producers have less incentive to use the best technology. And allocative efficiency will suffer if quotas enable Tradesian applesauce producers to ignore or delay responding to changing consumer tastes.

A major difference between quotas and tariffs is that a quota does not increase Tradesian government receipts. Moreover, foreign producers may gain as a result. Although they can sell fewer cases of applesauce, the price per case is higher. There is some evidence, for example, that Japanese car manufacturers have increased their profits while complying with U.S. import quotas by selling more expensive models at higher prices.

"Voluntary" quotas. In recent years, certain U.S. industries especially hard hit by foreign imports—shoes, steel, autos, and textiles—have put increased pressure on the government for protection. In some cases, the U.S. government has negotiated "voluntary" quotas. For example, Japan agreed to voluntarily restrict exports of automobiles to the United States in return for a U.S. agreement not to raise the import tariff on imported automobiles. Voluntary quotas, however, yield the same results as mandatory quotas: fewer imports, higher import prices, and

protection of the domestic industry. And, like other restrictions, they invite retaliation, further increasing restrictions on trade worldwide and further reducing potential gains. One study estimated that voluntary quotas on Japanese automobiles cost U.S. consumers $4.3 billion in 1983, not counting any loss caused by restrictions on choice. That is, each job saved by the quota cost $160,000. It seems that another policy approach would surely be more desirable.

Other Nontariff Barriers

In addition to tariffs and quotas, imports are sometimes restricted by other nontariff barriers. For example, automobiles imported into the United States are required to meet standards for safety and pollution control. Imported drugs must meet standards of safety and effectiveness imposed by the U.S. Food and Drug Administration. For the most part, the United States has imposed these restrictions on imports to force them to meet standards that apply to U.S. products. These restrictions are not strictly intended to reduce foreign competition. However, U.S. automakers and other U.S. producers complain that Japan imposes restrictions on imports that are not required of Japanese producers. To the extent that these barriers are selectively applied to imports, they are trade restrictions with effects similar to those of tariffs and quotas.

Arguments for Trade Restrictions

Despite the problems with trade restrictions, they remain politically popular. In fact, the political pressures for the United States to increase trade restrictions have been particularly strong recently. In this section, we consider some of the arguments used to justify trade restrictions and the reasons why economists reject some of these arguments.

Promoting national security. In some cases, proponents of trade restrictions argue that such measures are necessary to protect an industry vital to national security, regardless of the effects on efficiency. What do the principles of rational choice tell us about this argument? As always, we must consider not only the benefits but the costs of a particular policy. The United States once restricted oil imports on the grounds that it was important to national security to encourage domestic exploration and production of oil. The limits on oil imports into the United States actually resulted in faster use of domestic oil reserves and higher oil prices at the same time. The national security argument has also been used to prohibit or restrict exports. The United States limits trade in some technologically advanced products—such as some computer technology—and in certain military goods. The reasons for such restrictions are political, not economic, although they impose economic costs as do all other restrictions.

The U.S. steel industry, which has been hard hit by foreign imports, has argued that steel production is essential to national security. While this may be true, some economists are skeptical that steel producers protected from competition will again become strong and efficient. The critics argue that U.S. steel producers did not use the opportunity granted by protection in the past to do so.

Protecting infant industries. Comparative advantage suggests that it is in the long-run interest of a country to import items that can be produced more efficiently abroad. But what about the short run? Supporters of the "infant-industry" argument note that sometimes it is difficult for a new industry to compete initially with established foreign companies. They argue that short-run protection will allow the industry to develop to the point where it can compete.

Economists have several problems with this approach. First, they note that it is often difficult to identify industries capable of long-run survival that would not survive without protection. Many question the notion that an industry could be profitable in the long run but unable to survive short-run losses without *government* assistance. They observe that private financing is normally sufficient to cover short-run losses in successful industries. And if government assistance is necessary, direct subsidies may be better than trade restrictions. Finally, they argue that assistance to infant industries must be short term, but government policies often fail to set reasonable end dates for assistance.

Supporting domestic industries. The "buy American" argument has been popularized in TV ads, by politicians, and on bumper stickers. Supporters argue that "If we buy from abroad, we get goods but foreigners get our money. If we buy at home, we get both goods and money." This argument, however, fails to recognize that the objective of economic activity is to satisfy the greatest quantity of society's wants. Money by itself satisfies no significant wants. Only economic goods can satisfy wants.

Whether foreigners have more of our money or not is irrelevant to the issue for several reasons. First, foreigners as a group have little else to do with our money (and no reason to seek it) except to use it to buy goods in exchange. If we could convince foreigners to continually accept money in exchange for real economic goods, we could exchange something that costs little to produce for something of significant value. This type of exchange is unlikely, however, because foreigners also want goods, not money. Ultimately, trade involves the exchange of goods for goods, a notion we explore in more detail in Chapter 33.

Retaliating for other nations' restrictions. There is actually some economic support for the notion that trade restrictions may be necessary to protect the U.S. economic position in the face of other nations' restrictions. Proponents argue that only in this manner can we limit the actions of other nations who gain at our expense by imposing trade restrictions on U.S. exports. Economists generally agree that an absence of all trade barriers would be preferable. If retaliatory measures succeed in reducing trade restrictions they may be a useful tactic. But retaliation is also risky, and may only lead to further retaliation.

In 1986, for example, the United States imposed a 35 percent tariff on Canadian cedar shingles. Canada responded with "compensating tariffs" on U.S. computer parts, novels, and oatmeal. The United States then slapped tariffs on oil-well piping. The immediate effects of such trade wars are reduced trade and inefficiency. But supporters of such get-tough policies argue that such tariffs are necessary to force reluctant countries to lower their own barriers. They point to the success of U.S. threats in 1987 that forced some European countries to relax restrictions on U.S. grain exports.

Protecting domestic workers from cheap foreign-labor competition. Some who favor trade restrictions argue that, without protection, U.S. workers would be forced to accept the same low wages as workers in less-developed nations. This argument fails in two respects. First, the level of wages paid to foreign labor does not, by itself, establish whether the products they make are cheaper. To make this calculation, we must compare both the relative wages and the relative productivities of workers in the two countries. To the extent that higher paid U.S. workers are more productive than their foreign counterparts, they are also more efficient and can compete without accepting lower wages.

And second, even if U.S. workers cannot compete with foreign labor in one industry, they probably have a comparative advantage in another industry. As our earlier discussion shows, it is impossible for even "cheap" foreign labor to have a comparative advantage in the production of all goods. Thus economists argue that trade restrictions cause inefficiency by keeping labor resources from their best use. The industries hit hardest by foreign imports—shoes, textiles, steel, and autos—appear to be industries in which other countries have a competitive advantage, in part because wages and living standards are low. In fact, the United States may *not* be able to effectively compete in those areas. But it does seem to have a comparative advantage in producing chemicals, industrial machinery, and scientific instruments.

Preventing high unemployment. There is an element of truth in the argument that free trade can cause unemployment, at least in the short run. Trade will reduce demand for some domestic products and hence lower employment in those industries. However, as we have pointed out elsewhere, unutilized resources are not without value as long as we live in a world of scarcity. In the absence of trade restrictions, export industries will demand more labor, which should offset the lower demand in import-competing industries. In other words, to the extent that unemployment results from free trade, it should be only a short-run problem of labor resources moving from import to export industries. And as you will see in the next section, economists believe that policies other than trade restrictions can more efficiently address the short-run unemployment problem.

Alternatives to Trade Restrictions

In proposing alternatives to trade restrictions, economists focus on policies that offer greater benefits than costs. As a result, some economists support direct subsidies as opposed to trade restrictions, when legitimate reasons exist to support domestic industries.

Subsidies and efficiency. These economists believe that direct subsidies do not raise product prices. Thus consumers do not experience high costs directly. Domestic industries that use imported products do not experience higher costs. (Subsidies do impose indirect costs in the form of higher taxes, however.) Economic studies suggest that direct subsidies impose smaller costs than do trade restrictions. Although economists view direct subsidies as being more efficient than trade restrictions, they do not argue for direct subsidies whenever free trade decreases profits and employment in an industry. They recognize that subsidies can raise the profits of firms that are not efficient enough to compete on their own. But the benefits of direct subsidies must be balanced against the costs before they can be justified.

Subsidies and equity. As we noted earlier, some economists also favor subsidies to help retrain or relocate workers in import-competing industries. That is, rather than trying to save jobs in a particular industry, they favor helping workers make a smooth and equitable transition from one job to another. In this way, both equity and efficiency can be addressed.

Until recently, workers displaced because of reductions in trade barriers were given additional unemployment insurance payments under the Trade Adjustment Assistance (TAA) Program. Most studies of this particular program have concluded that it met its equity goals, despite the difficulty of determining whether specific workers were displaced because import policies changed. However, the program appeared to be inefficient. Critics argue that it spent too much on cash grants that were not tied to adjustment efforts. Rather than increase mobility, the grants tended to slow it. Many economists believe that future legislation should put greater emphasis on educational and relocation programs that provide efficiency gains, as well as help to the displaced.

Economists disagree over the extent to which such help is desirable, however. Some argue that most workers who lose their jobs find new ones without government help and that special assistance for those affected by import policies is unnecessary. Others argue that workers in the industries most affected—shoes, textiles, steel, and autos—will be hard pressed to find new jobs, especially if adjustments involve closing large plants.

Reasons for the Popularity of Trade Restrictions

Despite these problems, economists generally agree that subsidies are a more efficient solution than are trade restrictions. Why, then, do trade restrictions remain the most common policy? One reason is that a direct subsidy appears to be a handout. Some firms and individuals are reluctant to accept such direct help, and policy makers are often reluctant to give it.

By contrast, trade restrictions most visibly and directly harm foreign producers and workers; they most visibly and directly benefit domestic producers and workers. Foreign producers and workers do not vote, whereas domestic producers and workers vote and lobby their legislators. Consumers and producers in other industries are often unaware of the extra costs they pay. Indeed, they may view rising prices and falling demand as the result of "unfair" foreign competition, not a shift in comparative advantage.

U.S. Trade Policy

As we noted earlier, one serious problem with trade restrictions is that countries tend to counterattack with their own restrictions. That is, a Japanese tariff on U.S. products is likely to be followed by a U.S. tariff on Japanese goods. As a result, trade wars may develop and the resulting loss in efficiency worldwide may be great.

Tariff barriers have generally declined since the 1930s, a time in which trade wars reached epidemic proportions. (Some economists believe that the trade restrictions were an important factor in the Great Depression of the 1930s.) In 1930, goods imported into the United States paid an average tariff of 53 percent. By 1967, the average tariff was only 8.3 percent. Much of this reduction resulted from negotiations between countries, which were spurred by the General Agreement on Tariffs and Trade (GATT) signed by the United States and 23 other countries in 1947. The most recent conference, the "Tokyo Round," led to an agreement in 1979 to reduce tariffs by nearly one-third and eliminated a large number of nontariff barriers. In 1986, trading nations began negotiations in Ponte del Este, Argentina, which may produce even lower trade barriers.

Despite the trend toward freer trade, however, restrictions continue to play an important role in trade. Moreover, Congress continues to debate (and sometimes to pass) trade restrictions. Serious discussions about limiting trade on shoes, textiles, steel, and autos continue. When countries such as Japan continue to impose import restrictions on U.S. products, Congress is more tempted to erect competing barriers to trade.

On taking office, President Reagan clearly stated his policy objective: to reduce trade barriers. He vetoed legislation that would have imposed additional restrictions on shoe and textile imports and prevented additional controls on imported steel and automobiles. But Reagan was not immune to the retaliatory argument. He encouraged the 1986 retaliatory tariffs against Canadian cedar shingles. In early 1987, he threatened to impose a 200 percent tariff on brandy, white wine, and soft cheese exported by European countries unless they reduced some of the trade barriers he blamed for falling grain sales. And he imposed tariffs on some Japanese products when the Japanese were accused of selling semiconductor chips below costs.

Moreover, you should recognize that the United States has many policies that restrict trade. Some—such as import controls on certain agricultural products—support domestic price controls. In other cases—such as with textiles and automobiles—a wide range of policies from tariffs and quotas are used to restrict trade. The United States and other nations have been reluctant to reduce or abolish restrictions by themselves, despite generally favoring free trade.

CONCLUSION

Economists generally believe that the benefits of free trade outweigh the costs and problems it creates. Although the adjustments required by free trade involve some costs, the country as a whole benefits from greater efficiency and satisfies more of its wants. Thus economists generally recommend a minimum of trade restrictions. Instead, they favor direct subsidies if problems arise that require government assistance.

The flow of goods and services has important consequences for the international economy, but so does the flow of funds. In Chapter 33 we consider the reasons for and implications of financial flows: the flow of funds from the United States to foreign financial markets and of foreign funds into U.S. financial markets. In addition, we look at how the relative prices of currencies are determined. Why did the value of the U.S. dollar increase dramatically in the early 1980s, and plunge in the mid-1980s? To completely understand the foreign sector of the economy, you must understand the effects of these financial flows.

SUMMARY _____

1. In this chapter we examined the reasons for and the benefits and costs of international trade, as well as the reasons for and arguments against trade restrictions.

2. International trade occurs because both countries involved in trade can gain from the exchange. Gains are

possible because of differences in resources, preferences, and, most important, relative efficiency.

3. Comparative advantage—the ability to produce a good at a lower opportunity cost—not absolute advantage—the ability to produce a good using fewer resources—

determines which country can produce a certain good most efficiently. Because every use of resources has an opportunity cost (other goods not produced), a country will always have a comparative advantage in producing at least one good. If countries specialize in producing goods for which they have a comparative advantage and then engage in trade, total world output can be increased, enabling all nations to gain from trade.

4. The terms of trade express in physical terms the relative prices of traded goods. For a country to gain from trade, the terms of trade must be favorable relative to domestic opportunity costs. That is, a product will be imported only if the quantity of products that must be sacrificed is less than the opportunity cost of producing them domestically. A product will be exported only if the quantity of products received in trade is greater than the opportunity cost of production.

5. The world price of a traded good depends on demand and supply in all trading countries. The price of an imported product will be lower than the price of a domestic product (if there were no trade) because imports increase supply. The price of an exported product will be higher than the price of a domestic product (without trade) because exports increase demand.

6. The costs of trade include higher prices for exported goods, as well as decreased demand and lower employment in import-competing industries. The benefits from trade include lower prices for imported goods, greater demand and employment in export industries, and increased total production.

7. Trade has distributional effects, benefiting some workers and industries and increasing costs to others. Import-competing industries and workers with lower short-run mobility are the most adversely affected. Because costs are highly concentrated and visible, politicians often support trade restrictions.

8. Common forms of trade restrictions include import tariffs, import quotas (both mandatory and "voluntary"), and nontariff barriers, such as required standards of safety and/or pollution control.

9. Rationales for trade restrictions include protecting national security interests, allowing "infant industries" to become established, supporting domestic industry, retaliating for other nations' restrictions, protecting U.S. wage rates, and maintaining high employment. Economists generally reject these arguments, favoring direct subsidies if problems arise from free trade.

KEY TERMS

Trade balance (balance on merchandise trade), 821
Trade deficit, 821
Trade surplus, 821
Balance on goods and services, 822
Absolute advantage, 825
Comparative advantage, 827
Terms of trade, 828
Import tariff, 834
Import quota, 836

QUESTIONS FOR REVIEW AND DISCUSSION

1. Some early economists (known as the mercantilists) called a trade surplus a "favorable balance of trade," implying that a country with a trade surplus was better off than one with a trade deficit.
   a) Based on the mercantilists' reasoning, what types of trade policy do you think they favored?
   b) Adam Smith argued in his book, *The Wealth of Nations*, that the wealth of a nation was greater when free trade was encouraged. In what way does free trade increase total wealth? What are the costs of free trade?
   c) Does the U.S. economy gain more from exporting $1 million worth of goods or from importing $1 million worth of goods? Explain.

2. Consider the statement: "A U.S. worker who produces goods exported to West Germany makes a product that helps the United States import West German steel. Thus in a fundamental way, we can say that the U.S. worker is producing steel for the U.S. economy."
   a) Does this statement express a fundamental truth or a fallacy?
   b) What difference does it make to the U.S. economy whether steel is produced by U.S. workers in the steel industry or obtained by trading U.S. exports for foreign steel?
   c) Does this difference help explain why politicians from steel-producing areas tend to support restrictions on imported steel?

3. The following data show the relative productivity with which beer and TV sets can be produced in Tropicola and Temperania.

| Product | Quantity produced per worker per day in | |
	Tropicola	Temperania
Beer	200 barrels	400 barrels
TV sets	5 sets	8 sets

a) For which product(s) does Temperania have an absolute advantage?
b) What is the opportunity cost of a TV set in each country?

c) For which product(s) does Tropicola have a comparative advantage?

d) Would both countries benefit from trade if the terms of trade were 45 barrels of beer per TV set? What terms would make trade unprofitable for Temperania? For Tropicola?

e) What factors might explain why Temperanian workers can produce more TV sets per day?

4. Explain how each of the following situations would likely affect the relative price of beer and TV sets (or the terms of trade) in Tropicola and Temperania.

a) Improved technology that allows Tropicolan workers to produce more TV sets per day than before.

b) A switch in Tropicolans' preferences from local fruit juices to imported beer.

c) An increase in the price of Temperanian beer.

d) A decrease in the quality of TV programs in Tropicola.

e) An import tariff on imported TV sets in Tropicola.

f) In each case, the terms of trade will worsen for one of the two countries. In which cases will the residents of Tropicola be worse off after the change than before?

5. A U.S. manufacturer makes the following argument: "Our industry has difficulty competing with foreign producers not because we are less productive but because of the maze of government regulations governing worker safety and pollution. If these were eliminated, we could expand our business and provide many more jobs for U.S. workers."

a) Explain why government regulations such as those mentioned would place a U.S. manufacturer in a less competitive position.

b) Would the U.S. economy be better off if such regulations were eliminated? Be sure to consider both private and social benefits from and costs of the regulations in your answer.

6. The United States currently imposes a tariff on imported automobiles. If the tariff were eliminated, what would you expect to happen to

a) prices of automobiles in the United States?

b) prices of automobiles in Japan?

c) profits of U.S. automakers?

d) employment in the U.S. auto industry?

e) demand for U.S. exports?

7. Discuss the statement: "Trade restrictions are necessary to protect the wages of U.S. workers. Without protection, the standard of living of U.S. workers would fall to the low levels of workers in other countries."

CHAPTER 33

International Finance

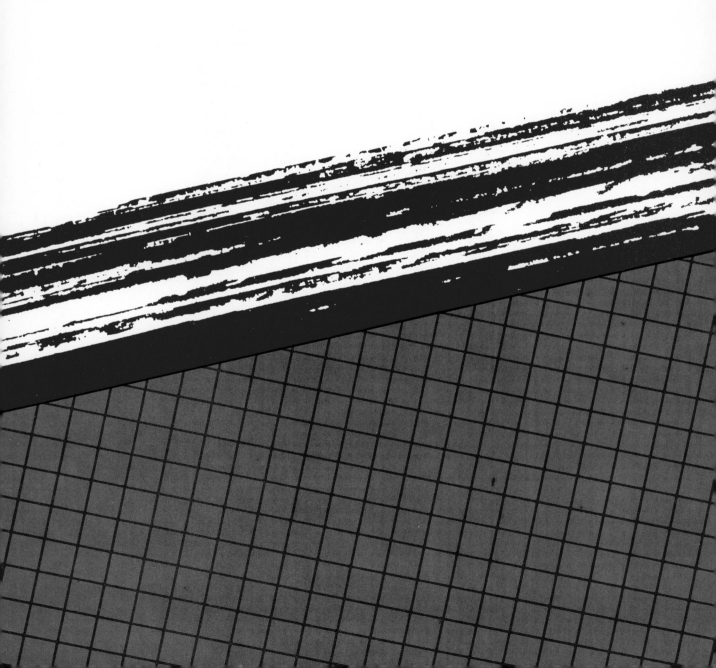

QUESTIONS TO CONSIDER

☐ How do exchange rates affect international trade?

☐ Why do individuals and businesses in one nation demand the currency of another nation?

☐ What factors affect international monetary flows?

☐ How does a gold standard operate and why did the United States go off the gold standard?

☐ What were the restrictions of the Bretton Woods system and why does the United States now allow the dollar to "float"?

In Chapter 32 we discussed the flow of goods and services from one country to another. But not all international transactions are trades of goods or services. Japanese and French businesses buy U.S. companies and build factories in the United States. Egyptians and Argentinians buy stock in U.S. firms and U.S. government bonds. Many U.S. corporations, such as IBM, Coca-Cola, and Exxon, operate throughout the world. Sometimes they produce goods and services in the United States for export to other countries. But they also build or buy plants and other facilities in foreign countries. (There seems to be a McDonald's in every major city in Europe, for example.) In this chapter we show how these international transactions, along with trade in goods and services, affect the U.S. economy.

In addition, you must recognize that international transactions involve more than one currency. For example, prices are stated in marks in West Germany and in pounds in Great Britain. When international transactions occur, the flow of goods and services (or financial claims such as stocks and bonds) in one direction is matched by a flow of currency in the opposite direction. When U.S. residents buy Japanese cars, for example, dollars flow out of the United States to Japan. But Japanese car manufacturers want yen to pay their workers. Someone—either the U.S. buyer or the Japanese seller—will have to exchange dollars for yen. In this chapter you will see how international currency exchanges determine the relative values of two currencies. You will also learn something about systems that have been used to set currency values.

EXCHANGE RATES AND INTERNATIONAL TRADE

International trade is in many respects like the trade that occurs entirely within a country. Buyers and sellers agree on a price and exchange currency for goods and services. But international trade often involves more than one language and more than one set of legal, cultural, and institutional factors. In addition, because each country uses a different monetary unit, international trade involves the exchange of two currencies.

		Exchange rate	
Country	Currency	Dollars per unit of foreign currency	Units of foreign currency per dollar
Australia	Dollar	0.6864	1.4569
Belgium	Franc	0.0263	37.9600
Canada	Dollar	0.7646	1.3079
France	Franc	0.1642	6.0910
India	Rupee	0.0776	12.8900
Italy	Lira	0.0007	1300.5000
Japan	Yen	0.006605	151.4000
Mexico	Peso	0.000912	1097.0000
Netherlands	Guilder	0.4833	2.0690
Portugal	Escudo	0.007107	140.7000
Sweden	Krona	0.1564	6.3940
Switzerland	Franc	0.6527	1.5320
United Kingdom	Pound	1.6040	0.6234
West Germany	Mark	0.5469	1.8285

**Exhibit 33.1
Foreign Currency Exchange
Rates, March 1987**

Exhibit 33.1 shows the monetary units used by a number of countries. Many give their currency a unique name—the rupee in India, the yen in Japan, the krona in Sweden, for example. Currencies of different countries may have the same name but are really different currencies with different values. For example, the monetary unit in both the United States and Canada is the dollar. But the U.S. dollar and the Canadian dollar are different currencies and can have very different values. Similarly, the Swiss franc and the French franc are different currencies having different values, even though they have the same name.

Currencies are not usually exchanged on a one-for-one basis. The rate at which one currency trades for another—the number of yen received in exchange for one French franc, for example—is what economists call an **exchange rate**. Exchange rates between the dollar and various other currencies are also shown in Exhibit 33.1. An exchange rate between two currencies can be stated in terms of either currency. For example, the exchange rate between the Indian rupee and the U.S. dollar is shown as 12.89 rupees per dollar (fourth column), and as $0.0776 per rupee (third column). Note that these are not two different rates, only two way of expressing the same rate.

Exchange rates also reflect relative prices. Let's say that you are visiting in France and see a bottle of wine you like selling for 45.68 francs. If you can buy the same wine in the United States for $9 per bottle, would it be cheaper to buy it in France or wait until you get home? Using the data in Exhibit 33.1, you can convert francs into dollars (or dollars into francs). With an exchange rate of 6.091 francs per dollar, the French price is equivalent to $7.50 U.S. dollars. You can save money by buying the wine in France. To check your understanding, determine the price in francs that would be equivalent to the $9 price in dollars. (Your answer should be 54.82 francs.)

In the current international monetary system, exchange rates are not fixed, and when they change, they make products in one country more or less expensive.

Exchange rate. The price of one currency in terms of another; the quantity of one currency that must be given up to obtain a unit of another currency (for example, 150 yen per dollar).

Currency appreciation. An increase in the exchange rate for the domestic currency (for example, from 150 to 160 yen per dollar); each unit of the domestic currency buys more units of the foreign currency; makes imports from foreign countries less expensive to domestic residents but exports to foreign countries more expensive to foreign residents.

Currency depreciation. A decline in the exchange rate for the domestic currency (for example, from 150 to 140 yen per dollar); each unit of the domestic currency buys fewer units of the foreign currency; makes imports from foreign countries more expensive to domestic residents but exports to foreign countries less expensive to foreign residents.

For example, if the value of the French franc falls relative to the U.S. dollar, it will be even less expensive to buy the French wine in France instead of in the United States. Conversely, if the value of the dollar falls, there may be no price differential, or it may be relatively cheaper to wait and buy the wine when you get home. To check your understanding, determine whether it is cheaper to buy the wine in France or the United States if the exchange rate is 4.5 francs per dollar. (You should find that the U.S. price is equivalent to 40.5 francs, and therefore it is cheaper to buy in the United States.)

Economists refer to changes in the relative value of currencies as **currency appreciation** (when the exchange rate rises) and **currency depreciation** (when the exchange rate decreases). For example, between 1975 and 1980 the U.S. dollar depreciated against the West German mark, falling from 2.46 marks per dollar to 1.82 marks per dollar. From 1980 to 1985, however, the dollar appreciated, rising from 1.82 marks per dollar to 2.92 marks per dollar. *When the dollar appreciates, foreign goods become less expensive to U.S. residents.* You may think that having the U.S. dollar appreciate would be wonderful and having it depreciate would be terrible. But there are pluses and minuses to changes in both directions. As the U.S. dollar appreciates, U.S. residents will buy more foreign-made goods because they are less expensive than before. But because other currencies must have depreciated at the same time, foreign residents will buy fewer U.S.-made goods. Thus *appreciation of the U.S. dollar decreases exports and increases imports to this country and thus can worsen a trade deficit; depreciation has the opposite effects.*

FOREIGN-EXCHANGE MARKETS

As you have seen, exchange rates affect the relative prices of imports and exports. But what determines exchange rates and what causes them to change? Economists find it useful to treat the exchange rate as a price: the price of one currency in terms of another. In this way they can consider how the price is determined by the interaction of demand and supply of currency in foreign-exchange markets. But why would anyone demand marks or yen or dollars? As we show in this section, currencies are demanded and supplied every time there is an international exchange of goods, services, or financial claims.

International Exchanges and the Flow of Dollars

The circular-flow model in Exhibit 33.2 shows the types of international exchanges that can occur and how they are connected to exchanges of foreign currencies. At the top are the elements of international trade: exports and imports. At the bottom are international capital flows: financial investment in physical and financial assets such as factories, stocks, and bonds. Connected with each international exchange is a flow of dollars into or out of the United States.

Note that the flow of exports is matched by a flow of dollars into the United States. That is, if IBM sells computers to a firm in France, the French firm must pay IBM in dollars. To obtain these dollars, the French firm must exchange francs for dollars. The French firm will therefore demand dollars from (and supply francs to) the foreign-exchange market. Thus *U.S. exports will be matched by demand for U.S. dollars in foreign-exchange markets.*

Conversely, the flow of imports is matched by a flow of dollars out of the United States. That is, if you buy a Japanese car from a U.S. car dealer, you pay for the car in dollars. But the car dealer had to pay its Japanese supplier in yen. To obtain these yen, the car dealer had to exchange dollars for yen. The dealer will therefore demand yen from (and supply dollars to) the foreign-exchange market. Thus *U.S. imports will be matched by supply of U.S. dollars in foreign-exchange markets.*

The same principles apply in international capital markets. When a U.S. firm purchases a foreign company or builds a plant in another country, it is demanding foreign physical assets. (Economists refer to these purchases as direct foreign investment.) And U.S. residents and businesses may also buy financial claims—stock in foreign firms or the bonds of foreign governments, for example. To purchase foreign assets, U.S. firms and residents must exchange dollars for foreign currency. And when foreign firms buy U.S. companies, factories, stocks, or bonds, they must exchange foreign currencies for dollars. Thus, *demand by foreign residents for U.S. physical and financial assets leads to a demand for U.S. dollars. Demand by U.S. residents for foreign investments leads to a supply of U.S. dollars.*

Exhibit 33.2
The Flows of International Exchanges
This exhibit shows the international economic exchanges between the United States and the rest of the world. The top part of the exhibit shows trade flows; exports and imports of goods and services are matched by an equal but opposite flow of dollars. The bottom part shows international financial or capital flows, representing financial investments in foreign assets by U.S. residents and financial investments by foreigners in U.S. assets.

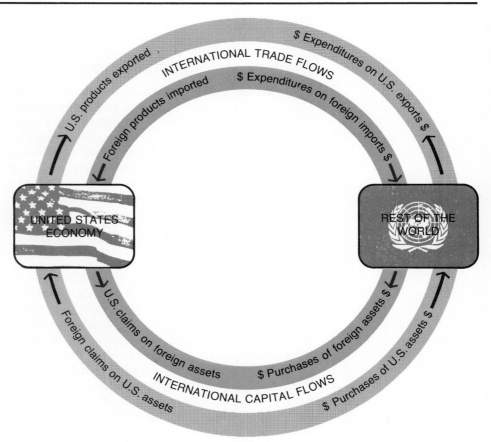

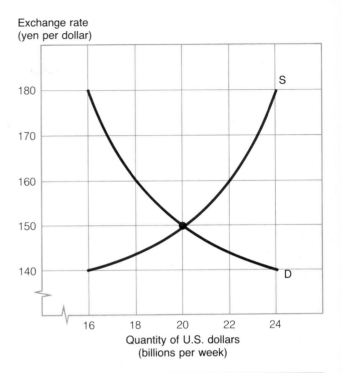

Exhibit 33.3
Demand for and Supply of U.S. Dollars in
Foreign-Exchange Markets
International economic exchanges between the United
States and the rest of the world result in demand for
and supply of dollars in foreign-exchange markets.
When U.S. residents purchase foreign imports or make
financial investments in foreign countries, they supply
U.S. dollars in exchange for foreign currencies to purchase foreign imports or make financial investments in
foreign countries. Foreign residents demand dollars in
exchange for foreign currencies to purchase U.S. exports or to make financial investments in U.S. assets. In
this graph, the exchange rate of the U.S. dollar is expressed in terms of yen (the currency of Japan). Equilibrium occurs at an exchange rate of 150 yen per dollar, with $20 billion exchanged per week.

Demand for and Supply of Foreign Exchange

As you just saw, trade and capital flows lead to demand for and supply of
dollars to be used for international exchanges. In Chapter 3, we introduced the
idea that the forces of demand and supply determine price in a market economy.
In the international economy, demand for and supply of different currencies
determines an exchange rate, that is, the price of one currency in terms of another.

For simplicity let's initially assume that exchange rates are determined only
by demand and supply. That is, as economists put it, we assume that the system is
one of **flexible (or freely floating) exchange rates**, which, for the most part,
characterizes the current international monetary system. (Later in this chapter, we
consider systems in which rates cannot freely adjust to market conditions.) Exhibit
33.3 shows how demand for and supply of foreign currencies interact in a foreign-
exchange market.* The horizontal axis shows the quantity of dollars. The vertical
axis indicates the price of a dollar, or its exchange rate—in this case the exchange
rate between the dollar and the Japanese yen. As in other markets, the foreign-
exchange market determines an equilibrium price (exchange rate)—in this case
150 yen per dollar. At any higher rate, there is a surplus. At any lower rate, there
is a shortage.

Flexible (or freely floating)
exchange rates. A system in
which exchange rates are determined by demand and supply
without government intervention
in foreign-exchange markets.

* For those who have studied macroeconomics, note that this market is not the same as the demand
for and supply of money, although they are closely related. The demand for and supply of dollars here
are related to international exchanges. Thus the demand for dollars does not reflect the demand by
U.S. residents to hold cash in a bank, but rather the demand by foreign residents to obtain dollars,
which they can use to buy U.S. goods and services or to invest in U.S. assets.

Since this market is free to adjust, the exchange rate will always move to equilibrium, eliminating any shortage or surplus. In general, foreign-exchange markets work like other markets. An increase in demand increases the price (or exchange rate). An increase in supply causes the exchange rate to fall. Note that *as the exchange rate (yen per dollar) rises, the dollar appreciates in value and the yen depreciates.*

Shapes of demand and supply curves. A decline in the exchange rate (yen per dollar) means that foreigners can buy dollars more cheaply. A specific quantity of yen buys more dollars and hence more U.S. products. That is, depreciation of the dollar reduces the prices of U.S. exports to Japanese residents and should cause U.S. exports to increase. As exports increase, more dollars will be demanded in the foreign-exchange market. Thus the demand for dollars curve slopes downward, as do most demand curves, because changes in the exchange rate affect relative prices.

At the same time, a decrease in the exchange rate reduces the value of the dollar and makes Japanese products more expensive to U.S. residents. Because of the effect on relative prices, U.S. consumers (and businesses) will demand fewer Japanese goods and will supply smaller quantities of U.S. dollars as the exchange rate falls. Thus the supply of dollars curve slopes upward, as do most supply curves.*

Factors that change imports and exports. Clearly, demand for and supply of currencies in foreign-exchange markets reflect international transactions: exports, imports, and foreign investments. But what changes the willingness of U.S. and foreign firms and individuals to make such transactions? Why would U.S. residents buy more Japanese or French products? Why would U.S. firms buy more raw materials from African countries or more products from Brazil? What would cause Canadian residents or British firms to buy more goods and services from U.S. firms? The same factors that influence demand for any good affect demand for imports and exports: (1) tastes and preferences; (2) income; and (3) relative prices.

Changes in tastes and preferences, including those stimulated by changes in product quality, increase or decrease demand for exports and imports. Thus they change demand for and supply of U.S. dollars in foreign-exchange markets and hence exchange rates. Tastes and preferences partly account for increased U.S. demand for Japanese products in recent years. In particular, U.S. buyers have liked the quality and performance of Japanese automobiles. At the same time, other nations have a strong preference for U.S. capital resources, especially those involving advanced technology.

Similarly, a change in the income of U.S. residents will cause increased or decreased demand for goods and services. If income rises, demand increases not only for goods produced by U.S. firms, but also for foreign goods and services—Swedish automobiles and travel in Asia, for example. More imports will increase the supply of dollars. And lower income in foreign countries will lessen demand for U.S. exports and thus demand for dollars. By affecting demand and supply of dollars, changes in income can affect exchange rates.

---

* Technically, the slope of the supply curve is positive only if the demand by U.S. residents for foreign goods is price elastic (see Chapter 4). We assume for simplicity—and reflecting reality—that the supply curve has its usual positive slope.

In addition, the relative prices of domestic and foreign goods are important factors in international trade. If U.S. computer makers improve their production methods, for example, the price of U.S. computers will fall relative to computers made abroad. This change—reflecting a new comparative advantage—will increase the quantity of computers exported and demand for U.S. dollars. In fact, we expect the price of identical goods traded internationally to be the same in all trading nations, as we noted in Chapter 32. This principle, known as *purchasing power parity*, means that exchange rates should adjust so that equivalent goods are equivalently priced throughout the world.

Suppose that the price of wheat is $3 per bushel in the United States and 12 marks in West Germany. If the exchange rate is 3 marks per dollar, wheat will cost the equivalent of $4 per bushel in West Germany. Because the U.S. price is lower, U.S. exports will rise and imports will decline. Greater U.S. exports increase demand for dollars. Reduced imports decrease supply of dollars. As a result, the price (exchange rate) of a dollar will increase. If the exchange rate rises to 4 marks per dollar, purchasing power parity is restored, so that wheat costs the equivalent of $3 per bushel in both the United States and West Germany. In the real world, of course, U.S. prices would also change, and the adjustment of exchange rates would thus be less. But the basic principle holds true regardless.

Purchasing power parity also suggests that exchange rates adjust to eliminate the effects of different inflation rates—increases in the average price of goods and services—in two nations. If the inflation rate is higher in Japan than in the United States, the prices of Japanese goods will rise relative to U.S. goods. As a result, Japanese exports will fall and foreign imports into Japan will rise. These changes in trade flows mean an increased supply of and a decreased demand for Japanese yen. Consequently, the yen will depreciate. But depreciation of the yen lowers the price of Japanese exports and raises the price of foreign goods to Japanese residents. According to purchasing power parity, the yen will continue to depreciate until the effects of higher inflation have been eliminated.

We want to emphasize several important points about purchasing power parity and the importance of trade flow in determining exchange rates. First, purchasing power parity applies only to the average prices of goods and services traded internationally. Tariffs and other restrictions on trade can prevent parity from being achieved. Second, parity prices change when tastes and preferences or comparative advantage change. And third, the rule of purchasing power parity predicts only general movements in exchange rates over the long run, largely in response to sustained differences in overall prices or inflation rates. To understand short-run changes in exchange rates, you have to consider changes in international capital flows.

Factors that change international capital flows. Foreign investment in the United States and U.S. investment in foreign economies depend largely on real interest rates. Individuals and firms will invest in another country only if they expect to earn more profit than they could by investing the same amount in their own country. Thus if real interest rates in France are 12 percent while U.S. rates are 8 percent, more U.S. businesses will invest in France. To invest they will have to exchange dollars for francs, increasing the supply of dollars in foreign-exchange markets. As a result, the value of the dollar will fall relative to the franc. That is, *when a country's real interest rate is high relative to interest rates in the rest of the world, its currency's value will appreciate.*

RECAP

Under a system of floating exchange rates, the equilibrium exchange rate is determined by demand for and supply of foreign exchange.

If demand for dollars increases, the exchange rate increases, representing an appreciation of the dollar's value. If supply of dollars increases, the exchange rate decreases, representing a depreciation of the dollar's value.

In the long run, changes in tastes and preferences, income, and relative prices affect demand for and supply of imports and exports and thus demand and supply of currencies.

In the short run, interest rates affect demand for and supply of other nations' financial assets and thus demand for and supply of currencies.

Evidence indicates that as much as $200 billion held by banks, multinational corporations, and wealthy individuals is continually in search of the highest possible short-run return. Because of this so-called "hot money," a change in relative interest rates can result in a substantial change in the international flow of funds. Economists generally believe that international capital flows are the cause of most short-run fluctuations in exchange rates. Thus short-run changes in trade flows (exports and imports) are strongly influenced by changes in exchange rates caused by changes in relative interest rates. For example, many economists believe that high real interest rates in the United States are the reason for the very large trade deficits experienced in the 1980s.

When evaluating potential investments, investors also consider risk. The greater the risk, the higher is the interest rate required by investors. Some economists believe that demand for U.S. financial assets has been relatively strong in recent years because the U.S. government is relatively stable compared to the governments of many nations. There is little risk that a change in the U.S. government will cause the seizure of private firms or property, for example, as has happened in some Third-World nations.

Finally, the return that an investor can expect to receive also depends on expectations of future exchange rates. For example, suppose that investors can choose between a one-year U.S. government bond paying 12 percent interest and a one-year West German government bond paying 5 percent. If investors expect the exchange rate between the two countries to remain steady, funds will flow out of West Germany and into the United States.

But what if the exchange rate is expected to change from an initial value of 4 marks per dollar to 3.75 marks per dollar at the end of one year? If you buy a $1000 bond in the United States, you will have $1120 after one year—your original $1000 plus $120 of interest. Alternatively, you could exchange your $1000 for 4000 marks at the initial exchange rate and buy a West German bond for 4000 marks. In one year, you will have 4200 marks. At the expected exchange rate at that time—3.75 marks per dollar—this amount equals $1120 (4200 marks ÷ 3.75 marks per dollar).

Although the West German bond pays a lower interest rate, each mark that you receive will have increased in value. Part of the return expected from buying the West German bond is the anticipated appreciation of the mark relative to the dollar. Under the current and expected exchange rates, a 5 percent real interest rate in West Germany is equal to a 12 percent interest rate in the United States. Because these interest rates are equivalent, we would not expect any additional capital flows.

Changes in the dollar's value: Historical examples. Recent fluctuations in the value of the dollar show that it has responded to changes in demand and supply. For example, we noted that differences in inflation from nation to nation affect demand for a nation's goods. In 1975–1976, inflation rates were generally lower in the United States than in other countries. As a result, the dollar appreciated in value. From 1977–1979, U.S. inflation rates were relatively high and the value of the dollar depreciated.

Inflation rates are not the only factors that affect demand and supply and thus the value of the dollar. Interest rates are also important. From 1980–1985, U.S. real interest rates were high relative to those in most of the world. The result was a large net capital inflow and appreciation of the dollar. But in 1986–1987, U.S.

interest rates moved closer to those of other countries, in part because of increased belief that the U.S. federal budget deficit would be reduced. As a result, the value of the dollar depreciated again.

Balance of Payments Accounting

To trace the components of the demand for and supply of foreign exchange, economists have developed a system of accounts corresponding to different types of international transactions. Each international transaction leads to a payment either to or by U.S. residents. Thus U.S. imports are matched by payments from U.S. residents. Foreign investments in the United States are matched by payments to U.S. residents. Balances between payments to and from U.S. residents for different types of transactions are the basis for international accounting systems. Thus the accounts are referred to as *balance of payments accounts*.

Balance on current account. The top part of Exhibit 33.4 shows the calculations leading to the **balance on current account** figure. The first line shows exports and imports of economic goods. The difference between exports and imports, shown on the right, is the trade balance. To obtain the balance on goods and services, we also add exports and imports of various services, including transportation and travel. Note that dollars spent by U.S. residents for food and hotels in foreign nations or travel on foreign airlines is counted as an import of foreign services. Just like imports of foreign goods, these transactions result in a supply of dollars to foreign-exchange markets. Even if you pay for your foreign travel with U.S. dollars or traveler's checks, the hotel or restaurant will exchange the dollars into foreign currency.

Another substantial component of current account is income earned on foreign investments. Interest payments that you receive on a bond issued by a French firm and the income Coca-Cola receives from a plant it owns in West Germany are treated as payments for services exported. Both result in a flow of dollars into the United States, just as exported goods do. When Egyptian residents receive interest on U.S. government bonds they hold and when Toyota or Volvo receive income from factories they own in the United States, dollars are supplied to foreign-exchange markets, just as when goods are imported.

The final item in the balance on current account is transfers, including gifts, grants, and foreign aid. Exhibit 33.4 indicates that the United States had a substantial negative trade balance of $147.7 billion in 1986. To some extent this deficit was offset by a surplus of trade in services. But the final balance on current account was still a deficit of over $140 billion.

Note that in balance of payment accounts, transactions that result in a flow of dollars into the U.S. economy (such as exports of goods and services) are shown with a positive sign. Transactions with a negative sign represent flows of dollars out of the economy (such as imports). In terms of demand for and supply of foreign exchange, inflows (positive exchanges) represent demand for dollars by the foreign sector. Outflows (negative exchanges) indicate a supply of dollars by the domestic sector.

Balance on capital account. The bottom part of Exhibit 33.4 shows the calculations leading to the **balance on capital account** figure. Foreign investments in U.S. physical assets—Honda's building of an automobile plant in the United States, for example—are direct foreign investment. These investments,

Balance on current account. Net exports of goods and services less net transfers (gifts and foreign aid) to foreign residents and foreign governments; a negative balance indicates that imports plus transfers to domestic residents exceed exports plus transfers to foreign residents.

Balance on capital account. The net flow of funds used to purchase physical and financial assets; a positive balance indicates that purchases of domestic assets by foreigners exceed purchases of foreign assets by domestic residents.

	Demand for U.S. dollars	Supply of U.S. dollars	Balances
Current account transactions:			
Exports of goods	221.8		
Imports of goods		−369.5	
Trade balance			−147.7
Exports of transportation and travel services	31.0		
Imports of transportation and travel services		−41.1	
Income from U.S. investments abroad and other services	117.9		
Income from foreign investments in the U.S. and other services		−85.5	
Balance on goods and services			−125.4
Private and public transfers, net		−15.2	
Balance on current account			−140.6
Capital account transactions:			
Direct foreign investment in U.S.	25.6		
Direct U.S. investment abroad		−31.9	
Foreign financial investment in U.S.	154.3		
U.S. financial investment abroad		−68.2	
Balance on capital account			79.8
Official asset transactions:			
Change in assets of foreign governments	33.4		
Change in assets of U.S. government	0.3		
Balance on official transactions			33.7
Statistical discrepancy			27.1
Balance of payments			0.0

Exhibit 33.4
Balance of Payments Accounts, 1986 (in billions of U.S. dollars)

Source: U.S. Department of Commerce, *Survey of Current Business,* March 1987 (Table 1-2, p. 44).

along with purchases of U.S. financial assets (such as stocks and bonds), result in an inflow of dollars. They represent a demand for dollars by the foreign sector. Similarly, U.S. investments in foreign physical and financial assets result in an outflow of dollars. Thus they represent a supply of dollars by the domestic sector.

Official asset transactions. Balance of payments accounts also include transactions by U.S. and foreign governments. In 1986 both U.S. and foreign governments added to the demand for dollars. We have more to say about these transactions later in the chapter, since they are more significant under a system in which exchange rates do not adjust freely.

Statistical discrepancies. Under a system of freely floating exchange rates, the market for foreign exchange tends to be in equilibrium. That is, quantity of dollars demanded equals quantity of dollars supplied. From an accounting standpoint, then, the positive and negative totals should always be identical, so the final balance of payments should always be zero. Any one balance—on current account or capital account, for example—may not be zero, but when all are considered together, equilibrium requires that the balance be zero.

Why then do the numbers in Exhibit 33.4 not balance? In the real world, international transactions are difficult to measure precisely. Thus the balance of payments accounts include a final category: the *statistical discrepancy*. This number is simply the amount required to make the quantity of dollars demanded and supplied equal. In this case the statistical discrepancy is shown as a surplus of $27.1 billion, the amount necessary to make the final balance zero.

Note, however, that *equilibrium in the market for dollars does not mean that there will be a balance between exports and imports or between inflows or outflows of capital flows. It does mean that any trade deficit will be offset by a net inflow of investment funds, and that any trade surplus will be matched by a net outflow of investment funds.* Thus, if a nation experiences a net inflow of investment funds, this will be offset by a rising trade deficit—more imports and fewer exports.

Indeed most economists believe that the U.S. trade deficits in the 1980s have been the result of very large inflows of foreign capital attracted by relatively high real interest rates in the United States. The large capital inflow increased demand for U.S. dollars and the value of the dollar. Foreign goods accordingly became relatively inexpensive to U.S. residents and U.S. goods relatively expensive to foreign residents. Thus while an imbalance in current accounts did occur, it was the result of capital flows.

FIXED EXCHANGE-RATE SYSTEMS

So far we have focused on foreign-exchange markets in which exchange rates float freely. In this system, demand and supply are the only forces that determine exchange rates. Indeed, the current international finance system is based largely on floating exchange rates. However, foreign-exchange systems that rely on **fixed (or pegged) exchange rates** have existed in the past and have supporters who suggest their return. In this section, we consider the benefits and costs of two systems that have been used in the past—the gold standard and the Bretton Woods system.

Fixed Rates under the Gold Standard

Fixed (or pegged) exchange rates. A system in which exchange rates are not allowed to adjust in response to changes in demand for and supply of currency.

When nations agree to use a gold standard to fix exchange rates, they must follow three basic rules. First, each country must define its currency in terms of a certain quantity of gold. Second, each country must be willing to buy and sell gold at the fixed price. Third, each country must maintain a fixed ratio between its domestic money supply and its stock of gold. When these three rules are agreed upon and followed, the gold system provides an automatic mechanism for establishing an equilibrium in balance of payments.

(a) Initial equilibrium

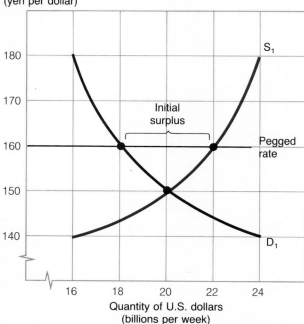

(b) Adjustment to equilibrium

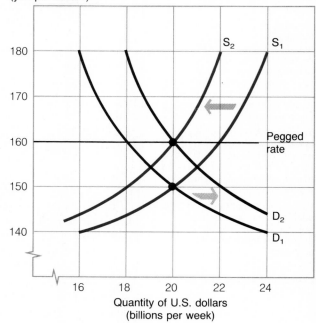

Exhibit 33.5
Equilibrium Adjustments under a Gold Standard
Under a gold standard, every currency exchanges for a fixed quantity of gold. Thus the exchange rate of every currency is fixed or pegged. Part (a) shows the U.S. dollar pegged at 160 yen per dollar, or higher than the equilibrium rate. By the rules of the gold standard, the U.S. government would have to sell $4 billion of gold (equal to the surplus) and, because it owns less gold, reduce the domestic money supply. As the money supply declines, U.S. interest rates rise, spending by U.S. residents falls, and U.S. prices fall. These changes will decrease imports and financial investments in foreign countries, decreasing supply of U.S. dollars (from S_1 to S_2). In addition, exports increase and financial investment in the United States rises, increasing the demand for U.S. dollars (from D_1 to D_2). As a result of these adjustments, a new equilibrium is achieved at the pegged rate of 160 yen per dollar.

Disequilibrium and adjustment under a gold standard. We illustrate the operation of a gold standard in Exhibit 33.5(a). In this market, the equilibrium exchange rate (where D_1 intersects S_1) is 150 yen per dollar. However, the fixed (pegged) rate is 160 yen per dollar. If the United States follows the established rules, it must be willing to buy and sell gold at the pegged price. To eliminate the surplus, the U.S. government will have to sell $4 billion of gold. By selling gold for dollars, the U.S. government will "demand" enough dollars to satisfy quantity supplied at the pegged rate. (In the balance of payments account this would show as part of the official asset transactions of the U.S. government.)

But selling gold is only the first stage in the gold standard's automatic adjustment mechanism. According to the rules, the United States must maintain a fixed ratio between its domestic money supply and its stock of gold. Because it had to sell some gold to cover the surplus of dollars in the foreign-exchange market, the U.S. government must reduce the domestic money supply. With less money available, U.S. residents will demand and consume fewer goods, including imports. Prices of all goods, including exports, will fall. The decrease in the money supply will also cause interest rates to rise, at least temporarily. (Interest rates rise because a decrease in the money supply reduces the supply of loanable funds.)

With more foreign funds flowing into the U.S. economy as foreign residents buy U.S. exports, stocks, and bonds, demand for U.S. dollars rises (to D_2 in Exhibit 33.5b). At the same time, lower imports and smaller outflows of investment funds reduce the supply of dollars (to S_2). Following these changes, the equilibrium exchange rate equals the *pegged rate*, and no further adjustments are necessary. Note that this adjustment mechanism works only if all three rules for a gold standard are followed. The willingness to buy and sell gold at the agreed-on price keeps exchange rates fixed. The strict relationship between the domestic money supply and the quantity of gold held allows the system to adjust to equilibrium. As you will see later in this chapter, when the gold standard was actually used, countries often violated these rules, blocking the automatic adjustment mechanism.

Both floating-rate and gold-standard systems have automatic adjustment mechanisms. In a floating-rate system, exchange rates provide an automatic adjustment mechanism. Under the gold standard, adjustments depend on changes in the domestic money supply, which requires government policy changes.

Advantages and disadvantages of a gold standard.   Proponents of a gold standard point to several advantages. First, when they are uncertain about future exchange rates, businesses face an additional risk (an exchange-rate risk) when engaged in international trade. For example, suppose that a U.S. company contracts to buy steel from a Japanese manufacturer at a price of 420 million yen, with the steel to be delivered and paid for in yen in six months. But what if the exchange rate between the Japanese yen and the U.S. dollar falls from 150 to 140 yen per dollar? The U.S. company, which agreed to the transaction when the price was equivalent to $2.8 million, must now pay $3.0 million for the steel. Because of increased risk, businesses may be less willing to engage in international trade. But exchange-rate risk can be avoided when exchange rates are fixed.

Second, the rules of a gold-standard system automatically restore equilibrium in the foreign-exchange market. Gold-standard proponents argue that, while floating-rate systems also create equilibrium, they do so by allowing currency values to change. Finally, supporters of the gold standard note that fixed rates prevent governments from constantly increasing the money supply. Rapid growth in the money supply will raise the prices of all goods and services; that is, it will cause inflation. Limiting the growth of the money supply can prevent inflation. Any inflation that does occur would not last long, since exports would fall and imports would rise. As a result, the government would have to buy dollars, reducing the money supply and lowering inflation.

Since it has these advantages, why did the trading nations agree to abolish the gold standard? Some critics charge that fixed rates, by limiting money supply, limit a country's ability to stimulate spending in response to economic downturns (recessions). Since increased spending causes increased production and hiring of workers, limits on the money supply may interfere with the macroeconomic goals of economic growth and full employment.

Some opponents of a gold standard also fear that the quantity of gold mined in the world is not enough to allow the money supply to grow in proportion to production. If so, a gold standard would force economies to deflate their currency, that is, to lower overall prices. But this type of adjustment can be slow and requires some unemployment, making the adjustment painful and expensive. The reliance on a single physical resource is another weakness of the gold standard, since a major new discovery of gold would create economic turmoil. Indeed, in the sixteenth century European prices rose dramatically when the Spanish began importing gold from the New World. Other opponents of a gold standard are concerned about the potential economic power that it would give to South Africa and the Soviet Union, the major producers of gold.

The Gold Standard in Practice

Critics of the gold standard find other support in the historical record. Certainly, the last attempt at a gold standard was less than an outstanding success. It began in 1879, when the United States and other major trading nations adopted it. But in 1914, World War I broke out. Nations promptly abandoned the rules for the gold standard, expanding their money supplies in excess of their gold supplies in order to finance the war effort.

Even during its relatively brief existence, the gold standard suffered from a lack of international agreement on acceptable fixed rates. England, for example, wanted a rate for the pound that was too high, that is, likely to cause a continual surplus in the foreign-exchange market. Any attempt to reinstitute a gold standard today would face similar problems. Countries with major international debts favor relatively high prices for their currency, which allows them to repay debts with appreciated currency. Countries to which the debts are owed favor the opposite.

In the years after World War I, some countries (including the United States) continued to follow the rules selectively. Many countries sought to gain a competitive edge in international trade by reducing the price of their currency and by erecting tariff and other trade barriers. The result was international uncertainty and a failure of the automatic mechanism to bring foreign-exchange markets into equilibrium. By the time the Great Depression struck most of the world in the 1930s, the international monetary system was a shambles.

Fixed Exchange Rates under the Bretton Woods System

Near the end of World War II, many nations began planning for the reestablishment of economic order. In 1944, representatives of most of the countries that were heavily involved in international trade met in Bretton Woods, New Hampshire, to establish a new international monetary system based on fixed exchange rates. That system went into effect in 1946 and prevailed until the early 1970s.

Fixed rates and exchange-rate policies. Like the gold standard, the Bretton Woods system established exchange rates in terms of the price of an ounce of gold. The price of gold was set at 12.5 British pounds or 35 U.S. dollars per ounce, implying an exchange rate of 2.80 U.S. dollars per British pound ($35 ÷ £12.5). Under the Bretton Woods system, each country was supposed to set a value for its currency as close to a long-run equilibrium level as possible. If each country's exchange rate remained at or very near this equilibrium rate, the system functioned as intended. A country might run deficits in one period but would run offsetting surpluses in another.

Adjustment to temporary disequilibrium.

The Bretton Woods system, like any fixed-rate system, required a mechanism to respond to changes in demand for and supply of currencies. In a floating-rate system, the exchange rate adjusts. In a gold system, the domestic money supply adjusts. Under the Bretton Woods system, a government was supposed to buy and sell enough of its currency to eliminate any shortages or surpluses that arose. As you learned from the discussion of balance of payments accounting, such official asset transactions can either add to demand or to supply. The Bretton Woods system was based on the assumption that most disequilibriums were only small, temporary deviations from equilibrium. Thus the nations that created the system did not consider making adjustments in the money supply or allowing fluctuations in the exchange rate to be necessary.

Adjustments to "fundamental disequilibrium."

But what happens if a country's currency is pegged above the long-run equilibrium rate? The result will be a continual surplus of currency. A country could not continue to buy its own currency because it would run out of gold or supplies of some other currency with which to buy. (Continuing to respond to a shortage of foreign exchange would not be difficult, of course, unless the supply of paper used to print more money became scarce.)

A country that experienced a long-run surplus or shortage position in the market for its currency was faced with what the Bretton Woods system called a *fundamental imbalance.* That is, demand for and supply of currency were apt to be continually unbalanced. A country facing a long-run surplus (a balance of payments deficit) had three basic options. First, it could impose tariffs, quotas, or other trade restrictions. By reducing imports, the surplus in the foreign-exchange market would fall. However, trade restrictions violated one of the principal objectives of the Bretton Woods agreement: to expand and encourage trade.

A second option for a nation facing a long-run surplus was to decrease its domestic money supply until prices fell and interest rates rose, as under the gold standard. Falling prices increase exports and reduce imports. Higher interest rates attract capital inflows. Demand for the currency will rise, supply will fall, and equilibrium will be restored. However, this type of adjustment sometimes interfered with a nation's domestic economic and political goals. For example, in the 1950s, the United States adhered to the Bretton Woods rules by slowing the growth rate of the money supply in order to keep the surplus of dollars in the foreign-exchange market from worsening. But in doing so, the government restricted the nation's ability to expand its production and caused higher unemployment.

As a last resort, a nation with a continuing currency surplus might choose **devaluation**, or a reduction of its fixed exchange rate. (Do not confuse devaluation with depreciation. Devaluation is a deliberate, planned reduction in a fixed rate. Depreciation is the natural result of adjustments in a floating-rate system.) Under the Bretton Woods system, devaluation was generally forced by high inflation caused by a government's failure to control its domestic money supply.

Advantages and disadvantages of the Bretton Woods system.

Many of the arguments for and against the Bretton Woods system are like those for and against the gold standard. In theory, both are fixed-rate systems. And if countries adjust their macroeconomic policies when there is a fundamental disequilibrium,

Devaluation. A deliberate, planned reduction in the exchange rate under a system of fixed exchange rates.

Exchange rates are fixed (at least in theory) under both a gold standard and the Bretton Woods system.

Under a gold standard, if a country has a surplus in the foreign-exchange market, that country must sell gold (and demand its currency) and reduce its money supply. A nation's money supply must be maintained at a fixed ratio to its supply of gold.

Under a gold standard, a change in the money supply causes a change in domestic prices and interest rates. The resulting change in trade and capital flows help to restore foreign-exchange markets to equilibrium.

Under the Bretton Woods system, if the foreign-exchange market is not in equilibrium, a country must buy or sell its currency.

Under the Bretton Woods system, if disequilibrium persists, a country can either change the fixed rate or adjust domestic macroeconomic policies. Many countries chose to change the fixed rate.

both systems can reduce the likelihood of inflation. But when official rates are out of line, there are incentives to create black markets. In Brazil and Argentina, the black market is so well established that the "unofficial" black-market exchange rate is published in the newspapers.

Moreover, as with the gold standard, participating nations often broke the rules of the Bretton Woods system when it served their domestic economic or political purposes. As a result, exchange rates were not really fixed and speculation about future devaluations often created major problems. For example, in the early 1970s, persistent surpluses indicated that the U.S. exchange rate was too high for long-run equilibrium. Those who expected the United States to devalue the dollar because of this problem began to sell large amounts of dollars in foreign-exchange markets. This increase in the supply of dollars pushed the market into a greater surplus position. Such speculation worsened the problem and eventually caused the system to collapse.

President Nixon twice devalued the dollar, first in 1971 and again in 1973, but these actions did not solve the problem. This failure by one of the major trading nations led to the breakdown of the Bretton Woods system. By 1973 several countries had abandoned the attempt to maintain a fixed rate for their currency, preferring instead to allow the currencies to float. The system ended because it was not possible to maintain a system of fixed exchange rates when the foreign-exchange markets were very unstable. The required adjustments in macroeconomic policies were considered politically, if not economically, undesirable.

The Current International Monetary System

After the devaluation of 1973, the Nixon administration decided to allow the dollar to float, and many other nations followed suit. However, the current system is not totally a freely floating system. First, some countries, notably some Third-World nations, still maintain fixed exchange rates in terms of the dollar or some other currency. Second, the United States, Japan, the United Kingdom, West Germany, and France have agreed to let governments intervene in foreign-exchange markets to smooth out minor changes in demand or supply. As a result, the current system is often termed a *managed-float system*.

In fact, balance of payments data indicate that governments intervene extensively in foreign-exchange markets, buying and selling currencies. In 1985, representatives of the United States, France, West Germany, Japan, and the United Kingdom agreed to encourage depreciation in the value of the dollar. These countries subsequently intervened in foreign-exchange markets, selling dollars and buying other currencies to accomplish this task. In the short run, this intervention did cause the dollar to depreciate. However, many economists suggest that intervention is not effective in the long run and cannot substitute for changes in basic economic policies.

Some supporters of the Bretton Woods system were concerned that a floating-rate system would stifle trade, but these fears proved to be groundless. Exchange rates have fluctuated more under this system than they did when rates were pegged. And the rise of oil prices in the late 1970s did cause some uncertainty in the foreign-exchange market. But international trade has generally increased since the floating-rate system was adopted. The seeming success of the current system has won the support of most economists although some still fear that fluctuations may be excessive. Most of the controversy now centers on whether a fixed exchange-rate system—a gold standard, for example—might be a useful way to control money supply growth and hence inflation. But support for this position is not widespread among economists, and few politicians will concede national control of the money supply.

CONCLUSION

In this chapter we considered various ways of determining exchange rates and noted the changing attitudes toward fixed-rate and floating-rate systems. But not all countries are part of the current floating-rate system. Those who manage planned economies—such as that of the Soviet Union—have vastly different views on exchange rates. And, as noted, some Third-World nations continue to use fixed rates.

In Chapter 34 we consider some of the distinctive features of planned economies and less-developed nations. These economies not only provide an interesting contrast to the developed market economies on which we have focused thus far, but they also have a major effect on the U.S. economy.

SUMMARY

1. In this chapter we considered the meaning and determination of exchange rates in both floating-rate and fixed-rate systems. We also explored some of the advantages and drawbacks of these approaches.

2. An exchange rate expresses the price of one currency in terms of another. A change in the exchange rate also results in a change in the relative prices of goods and services in the two countries. If the exchange rate of one currency rises relative to another currency, the rising currency is said to appreciate and the other currency to depreciate. When a nation's currency appreciates, we can expect its exports to fall and its imports to rise. When its currency depreciates, we can expect its exports to rise and its imports to fall.

3. Every international exchange leads to demand for or supply of currency in foreign-exchange markets. To pay for U.S. exports, foreigners demand dollars. To pay for foreign imports, U.S. residents supply dollars. When foreigners buy U.S. physical or financial assets, they demand dollars. When U.S. residents buy foreign physical or financial assets, they supply dollars.

4. Under a system of floating exchange rates, the interaction of demand and supply determines the rate. Foreign residents seeking to buy U.S. goods and services or U.S. physical or financial assets demand dollars while supplying foreign currencies. And U.S. residents seeking to buy foreign goods and services or foreign physical or financial assets supply dollars while demanding foreign currencies. Demand and supply forces will automatically eliminate currency surpluses and shortages.

5. Changes in tastes and preferences, income, and relative prices of goods and services affect international trade and thus demand and supply of currencies in the long run. Relative real interest rates affect financial capital flows and hence short-run demand and supply of currencies.

6. Balance of payments accounting reflects demand for and supply of foreign exchange. The trade balance is the difference between dollars demanded to purchase U.S. exports and dollars supplied to purchase foreign imports. The balance on capital account is the difference between dollars demanded to purchase U.S. physical and financial assets and dollars supplied to purchase foreign assets. When government asset transactions are also considered, the *net* balance should be zero (except for any statistical discrepancy) because we expect the foreign-exchange market to reach equilibrium.

7. A gold standard is an international monetary system in which three rules are followed: (a) each country fixes the price of gold in terms of its currency; (b) each country is willing to buy or sell gold at the fixed price; and (c) each country maintains a fixed ratio between the domestic supply of money and its stock of gold. Shortages and surpluses in the market for foreign exchange force a government to adjust its domestic money supply, which restores equilibrium at the fixed rate.

8. The Bretton Woods system also involved fixed rates but had no automatic adjustment mechanism. Temporary shortages and surpluses were to be offset with official government purchases or sale of currency. Long-term

shortages and surpluses were to be offset with changes in domestic money supplies. Instead, many countries chose to devalue their currency rather than change fiscal and monetary policies when faced with long-run "fundamental disequilibrium."

9. Proponents of fixed-rate systems believe that international trade is stimulated as uncertainty about future exchange rates is reduced. They also believe that fixed rates reduce the chance of inflation. The gold system also has an automatic adjustment mechanism. Floating-rate proponents point to difficulties in establishing and maintaining fixed rates, especially when the system requires governments to control their domestic money supplies. They observe that, in practice, rates do not remain fixed for very long and that even a gold standard requires government action, while the automatic adjustment mechanism in a floating-rate system does not.

KEY TERMS

Exchange rate, 846
Currency appreciation, 847
Currency depreciation, 847
Flexible (or freely floating) exchange rates, 849
Balance on current account, 853
Balance on capital account, 853
Fixed (or pegged) exchange rates, 855
Devaluation, 859

QUESTIONS FOR REVIEW AND DISCUSSION

1. The early economists (known as mercantilists) believed that a nation's wealth would be increased if it held more gold.
   a) What trade policies do you believe the mercantilists would recommend (recognizing that during their time, a nation that imported more than it exported had to pay out gold to cover the difference)?
   b) Why are present-day economists critical of the mercantilists?
   c) Under a system of floating exchange rates, what happens when a country exports more than it imports (including the "export" of financial capital used to purchase foreign assets)?

2. Answer the following questions to show your understanding of exchange rates.
   a) If the exchange rate between the Japanese yen and the U.S. dollar is 200 yen per dollar, what is the exchange rate between the dollar and the yen?
   b) If the exchange rate between the U.S. dollar and the Swedish krona is $0.12 per krona, how much will a

U.S. resident have to pay for a Volvo priced at 150,000 krona? How much will a Swedish firm have to pay (in krona) for a U.S. machine priced at $27,000?
   c) If a case of French wine costs either $75.00 or 525 francs, what is the exchange rate between the franc and the dollar (expressed as francs per dollar)?

3. The following table shows the approximate exchange rate of the U.S. dollar in terms of the West German mark for four years.

Year	Marks per dollar	Dollars per mark
1968	4.0	
1978	2.0	
1983	2.5	
1987	1.8	

   a) Calculate the exchange rate of the mark in terms of the dollar for each year.
   b) In which period(s) did the dollar depreciate? What happened to the mark at the same time?
   c) How much would a West German automobile priced at 30,000 marks cost in dollars in each year? How much would a U.S. automobile priced at $15,000 cost in marks in each year?
   d) What might explain the change in the exchange rate from 1968 to 1978? From 1978 to 1983? From 1983 to 1987?
   e) In any issue of the Wall Street Journal you can find the current exchange rate of the mark. Look up the most recent rate you can find. Has the mark appreciated or depreciated since 1987? What might explain why?

4. Perhaps you have heard someone refer to the existence of a balance of payments "problem." In the context of a system of fixed rates, what do you suppose this means? What meaning, if any, could it have under a system of floating rates?

5. Suppose that you could set the exchange rate of the U.S. dollar against other foreign currencies at any level you wanted to.
   a) What are the advantages and disadvantages of a higher rate? Of a lower rate?
   b) Could you determine a "best" rate? Why or why not?
   c) What changes occur as a country's currency depreciates?

6. What effect would each of the following changes have on the exchange rate of the U.S. dollar, that is, its price in terms of the Japanese yen? (Express each as a change in demand for and/or supply of currency.)
   a) Improved quality of U.S. consumer goods.
   b) Higher real interest rates in Japan.
   c) Reducing the growth rate of the U.S. money supply.

d) Increased foreign aid on the part of the U.S. government (included as part of net transfers).

e) An increase in the number of Japanese tourists to the United States.

7. Explain how each change in Question 6 would affect (a) the balance on current account and (b) the balance on capital account.

8. In the early 1980s the U.S. dollar appreciated against the Japanese yen and other major currencies.

a) What reasons might account for this change? (Check them against facts that you can find in a recent *Employment Report of the President.*)

b) Why were some analysts concerned about the effects of the "strong" dollar on the U.S. economy?

c) What options would the U.S. government have for dealing with this "problem"?

d) What ramifications did the U.S. dollar's appreciation have for Latin American countries (such as Argentina and Brazil) with large foreign debts that had to be paid in U.S. dollars?

e) What factors could have caused the dollar to depreciate since 1985? (Check your answers against facts that you can find in a recent *Employment Report of the President.*)

9. In recent years several Asian economies—Taiwan, South Korea, and Hong Kong—have closely tied their currencies to the U.S. dollar, in effect, fixing the exchange rate.

a) What are the advantages to those countries of fixing the exchange rate relative to the dollar?

b) Would they be better off fixing the value of their currency at a high or low value relative to the dollar? Why?

c) What are the disadvantages of fixing rates? (Note especially the effects on the economy of having a rate that is too high and one that is too low.)

10. Large U.S. trade deficits in the 1980s coincided with large capital inflows into the U.S. economy.

a) What are the major causes of the inflows of foreign capital? (Economists do not agree, so you should give several possible explanations, indicating the logic supporting each.)

b) Why do many observers believe that inflows of foreign capital are a potential problem for the U.S. economy? (Explain what problems may arise and why.)

c) The United States also received a large quantity of foreign capital in the nineteenth century. In contrast to the current situation, however, inflows of foreign capital in the nineteenth century were seen as useful, not as a problem. What is different about current inflows and those in the last century?

Economic Encounters
Third-World Debt: Can It Ever Be Repaid?

Less-developed countries (LDCs) of the Third World are up to their necks in foreign debt—by some estimates as much as $1 trillion worth. About half of this debt is owed by Latin American countries—especially Brazil, Mexico, Argentina, and Venezuela—and much of the foreign debt is owed to banks in the United States. Not only have these countries not reduced their debt, many have had to resort to additional borrowing just to meet scheduled interest payments. Just how did these countries get into this mess, and where will the debt crisis lead?

increased relative to the currencies of the LDCs. Together, these events raised the real burden of the LDC debt.

At the same time, the ability to service the debt fell. The growth rate of the LDCs fell in the early 1980s. Moreover, slow growth in the industrialized countries and the worldwide recession in 1982 also dramatically reduced the demand for LDCs' exports. Exports of the large Latin American

Why So Much Debt? Foreign borrowing is helpful to less-developed countries (LDCs) if used to finance projects that add to the economy's potential output. The consequent growth in income allows the debt to be repaid and the standard of living increased. But the buildup of debt to large-scale proportions in the 1970s was largely attributable to the oil price shocks that hit the world in 1973 and 1979. Oil-importing LDCs (Brazil, for example) increased their debt from $4 billion in 1973 to $15 billion in 1974. The second shock in 1979 raised their debt to the $50-billion level. Higher oil prices encouraged some oil-exporting LDCs (Mexico, for example) to borrow. Initially, such borrowing was used to finance the development of oil production. However, some LDCs also borrowed against expected future oil receipts to diversify and broaden their industrial base.

This initial borrowing did significantly increased the debt of these countries but did not create a debt crisis. Indeed, most of the heavy borrowers also were experiencing substantial economic growth—an average of 4.7 percent per year for LDCs compared with 2.5 percent for industrial countries over the 1973 to 1982 period. Moreover, exports in Brazil, Argentina, Mexico, and Venezuela grew by 17.5 percent per year between 1973 and

IMF restrictions angered Brazilian workers, who took to the streets to protest stiff wage cuts. (Abril Editoria/Gamma-Liaison)

1982. With rapid economic growth and relatively low interest rates, the ability of the LDCs to repay was growing faster than the increase in debt payments. But changes in the economic environment in the early 1980s highlighted the inherent risks of the debt both to the lenders and the LDCs.

The Debt Crisis Emerges Much of the LDC debt—and a very large percentage of the debt of Mexico, Argentina, and Brazil—is owed to U.S. banks and is tied to U.S. interest rates. Between the end of 1977 and the end of 1980, U.S. interest rates rose from just over 6 percent to almost 15 percent. Moreover, the value of the U.S. dollar

borrowers—Brazil, Argentina, Mexico, and Venezuela—fell by almost 12 percent in 1982. Mexico and Venezuela, both of which rely heavily on oil exports, experienced a severe shock as oil prices dropped sharply in the mid-1980s.

Although an important part of the debt crisis can be blamed on external factors, poor internal economic policies in the LDCs also contributed to the problems. Inflationary macroeconomic policies and artificially high exchange rates strongly encouraged imports while reducing the quantity of exports. Moreover, high inflation and an uncertain economic environment discouraged both local and foreign investment and encouraged "capital flight." That is, individuals with savings preferred to store their wealth in foreign banks and buy stocks of foreign businesses. Finally, in some cases the funds borrowed were squandered—used to finance poorly designed projects, make political payoffs, or subsidize inefficient government enterprises.

What Can Be Done? The LDCs appear to be increasingly frustrated by the burdens of debt and the consequences of that debt on their economies. Most of the largest borrowers have at one time or another threatened to default. In 1985 Peru announced that it would not limit debt payments to 10 percent of its export revenues. In 1987 Brazil announced that it would suspend all payments until a more acceptable debt package was negotiated. But is default the only way out?

The ideal solution to the debt crisis is fast growth in the LDCs. But the LDCs cannot grow unless they can sell more exports, especially to the industrialized economies. Thus macroeconomic and trade policies in the industrialized economies are important. If the industrialized economies grow slowly or impose trade barriers, the debt crisis will likely continue. Moreover, restrictive monetary policies in the industrialized economies also keep real interest rates high, thereby adding to the burden of existing debt.

Many observers note that LDCs will require additional foreign financing to enable them to make the investments in plant and equipment—and in

---

Much of the LDC debt is owed to U.S. banks and is tied to U.S. interest rates.

---

education and training—that are essential to growth. This new financing need not create a new concern as long as the exports grow fast enough to enable the LDCs to service and eventually repay both the old and the new debt.

But to stand eventually on their own, the LDCs must be able to gener-

ate funds for investment without relying as heavily on foreign borrowing. This will require the discipline to adopt appropriate macroeconomic policies to set a climate for profitable investment, thereby reducing capital flight and encouraging direct foreign investment.

To some extent, LDCs have made attempts to restore order to their economies—with mixed results. Virtually all the debtor nations have, at one time or another, tried the traditional austerity measures suggested by the International Monetary Fund (IMF). The largest Latin American borrowers cut imports by an average of 50 percent from 1981–1983. Some made bold attempts to reduce the size of government budget deficits and to cut monetary growth rates to slow inflation.

But these traditional remedies are often painful. Imports of capital resources were significantly reduced as were public investments in education and training. In 1986 investment in Brazil was 30 percent lower than in 1981; in Argentina it was 50 percent less. While there may be useful short-run policies, they may also jeopardize future economic growth. Moreover, the traditional remedies are contractionary, causing higher unemployment and lower real wages. Such measures often result in large-scale political protests.

Many economists argue that additional foreign funds are needed to generate economic growth in the LDCs. But they also recognize that it is desirable for much of this financing to come from direct foreign investment, not more borrowing. To attract this investment and to reverse capital flight, the LDCs will have to use appropriate macroeconomic policies, avoiding rapid inflation and economic instability.

The debt burden could also be lowered through so-called "debt-equity swaps." Under these schemes, a private business buys LDC debt from a bank and exchanges it for local currency, which it uses to acquire a factory and equipment in the LDC. As a result, the LDC gets new foreign investment and reduces its outstanding loans. Al-

though these swaps have benefits, they are not without costs. Unless the foreign business actually constructs a new factory, there is no net addition to the LDC's capital resources, but merely a

---

The ideal solution to the debt crisis is fast growth in the LDCs.

---

new owner. If the government simply prints new money to buy back its loan, the increase in the money supply will be inflationary. Moreover, as some LDCs note, the net result of these swaps is that foreign businesses acquire a larger stake in their economies.

Should the debt simply be forgiven? After all, at least a part of the buildup can be attributed to policies in the industrialized countries, and much of the debt will not be repaid, anyway. Critics of this policy argue that it creates a bad precedent. If all LDCs decided they wanted forgiveness, the transfer of wealth would be substantial. Moreover, the LDCs will continue to depend on foreign financing. What country or private bank would want to make future loans if there was a high probability that such ventures would turn out to be worthless?

Muddling Through the Crisis Outside of the worst cases (largely confined to some of the African nations), the LDC debtors have managed to continue to pay at least a part of the required interest payments on their debt. Some economists are optimistic that the LDCs will be able to muddle through this crisis if they are given the necessary temporary financing and if they make the necessary policy adjustments to strengthen their economies. These economists believe that future growth in the LDCs will eventually enable repayment of most of the debt. In the meantime, these countries remain highly vulnerable to events, many of which are not under their control. Muddling through may eventually work, but the potential for continued crises continues.

CHAPTER 34

Comparative Economic Systems and Economic Development

QUESTIONS TO CONSIDER

☐ What features distinguish a market capitalist economic system from a planned socialist economic system?

☐ Which system is superior?

☐ How well has the planned socialist system worked for the Soviet Union?

☐ What features characterize the economies of the less-developed countries?

☐ How might these nations improve the economic well-being of their citizens?

T hroughout this textbook we have concentrated on the economy of the United States. Most of what you have learned directly applies to the economies of Western Europe and Japan. But the economies of the Soviet Union, China, and Eastern Europe—representing about one-third of the world's population—are vastly different. As we noted in Chapter 1, these are planned socialist economies, not the market capitalist economies with which you are now familiar. In the first part of this chapter we explore the differences between these two types of economic systems in more detail and the operation of the Soviet Union's economy specifically.

In addition, nearly three-fourths of the world's population lives in countries with significantly less industry and lower standards of living than either the United States or the Soviet Union. As you will see in the second part of this chapter, these nations share certain common problems that have caused them to be less developed. A wide variety of economic strategies have been proposed to strengthen the economies of these countries.

MARKET CAPITALISM VERSUS PLANNED SOCIALISM

In Chapter 1 we noted that in market capitalist economies, most resources are privately owned. In planned socialist economies, most resources are owned by the government. As you have seen throughout this textbook, the interaction of demand and supply determines how resources are allocated in market economies. In planned socialist economies, central government agencies make allocation and distribution decisions. That is, the "invisible hand" of markets is replaced by the "visible hand" of government planning.

In this section, we describe "pure" models of market capitalism and planned socialism. In the real world, of course, no economy fits either model perfectly. However, as Exhibit 34.1 shows, the economy of Hong Kong is very close to pure market capitalism and that of Albania is very close to pure socialism. Although the U.S. economy is close to pure market capitalism, the role of government is very

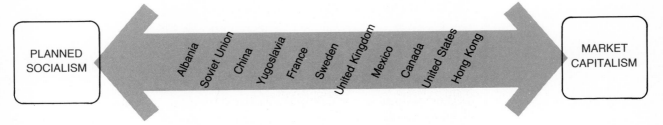

Exhibit 34.1
Range of Economic Systems
Real-world economies utilize a mixture of capitalism and socialism, of market opera-
tions and planning. This exhibit indicates that the economies of Hong Kong and the
United States closely resemble market capitalism. At the other extreme, the econo-
mies of Albania, the Soviet Union, and China closely resemble planned socialism.
France, Sweden, and the United Kingdom utilize more planning and government own-
ership than does the United States, but less than do China and the Soviet Union.

significant. But planning and state ownership are much more important in France
and the United Kingdom. However, recent sales of some state-owned enterprises
in both countries have moved those economies closer to market capitalism.

The economies of both the Soviet Union and China are close to pure planned
socialism. But recent changes in both countries have increased the importance of
the private sector and quantity of goods sold in markets. Not all countries fit neatly
into these categories. For example, Yugoslavia actually combines heavy reliance
on markets with government ownership. Nevertheless, most nations fit one of the
two patterns closely enough for economists to make some useful predictions
based on these models.

Moreover, you should bear in mind that the pure forms of these economic
systems reflect the ideals held by the nations that utilize them. For example,
although the economy of the United States may fall short of being a pure market
capitalist economy, many economists and politicians in this country believe that
system to be the ideal. They argue for minimal government intervention in the
economy and for limiting government activities to those that help markets to
function better. In the Soviet Union, the situation is reversed. Although that country's economy has some capitalistic elements, they are considered to be less
desirable economic options than is a centralized, planned approach.

Market Capitalism and Planned
Socialism: A Comparison

Exhibit 34.2 shows the basic characteristics of market capitalism and planned
socialism. These systems represent two very different methods of answering the
fundamental economic questions of what, how, and for whom to produce. In this
section, we consider three additional questions: Who sets an economy's goals?
Who decides how to meet those goals? And what incentives do individuals have
to make the system work?

Setting goals. The basic goal of any economic system is to satisfy society's
wants. We have defined this goal as allocative efficiency: producing the mix of
goods and services that yields the greatest satisfaction. In a market economy,

however, the goal is often more specifically stated as satisfying *individual* wants. Markets can aid in achieving this goal by providing the goods and services most in demand (within the limits of technology and resource supplies).

In planned socialist economies, collective wants are deemed more important than individual wants, although they could be the same. Central government planners decide what the economy will produce, even though that may not be the mix of goods and services that satisfies the most individual wants. Preferences are established by central planners, with no specific reference to the preferences of individuals.

Every economic system, whatever its goals, must have good information on which to base activities to achieve those goals. Decision makers must know the relative availability of resources and the relative wants of society. In market capitalism, decision makers rely on prices to signal changes in the relative scarcity of resources and changes in relative wants. Businesses do not have to collect information about total demand or supply—prices tell them what and how to produce. However, when market failures occur—external benefits and costs, for example—prices may not be completely satisfactory guides.

When government planners set goals with little regard for individual wants, they do not require information on consumer demand. They must, however, determine the resources they have for meeting the goals they have set. Thus to plan for the economy as a whole, government officials must know a great deal about the quantities of resources available and the capacities of plants and farms. Central planners must collect this information from the thousands of factories and farms in that country. They must then consolidate the information and analyze it.

Meeting goals. Every economy has limited resources and must decide how to allocate resources to produce the goods and services desired. In a market capitalist economy, resource ownership is largely private. Thus most decisions about what and how to produce and how much to invest are made by private businesses. But profit-seeking businesses are guided by market demand which reflects the preferences of households. And individuals have a lot of freedom to decide where and how much to work. As a result, economic decision making is highly decentralized in a market economy. Although government regulations influence these decisions, ultimately individuals decide what will be produced.

In planned socialist economies, government owns most of the nonhuman resources. Government planners allocate those resources and set goals for the managers of production facilities. Individual choice about where and how much

**Exhibit 34.2
Characteristics of
Economic Systems**

Type of economic system	Who owns most resources?	Who makes most economic decisions?	How is information acquired?
Market capitalism	Households	Households and business managers	Prices signal changes in wants and resource scarcity
Planned socialism	Government	Government planners	Planners determine preferences and collect information on available resources

to work is often severely limited. Thus there is little room for individual consumer wants to influence basic decisions about what is produced.

Incentives to meet economic goals. Regardless of the economic system, many decisions will be made by individuals, either as business managers or workers. Even in a centrally planned economy, workers must decide how hard to work, and managers must translate centrally established goals and plans into goods and services produced. For an economic system to work, individuals must have some incentive to make it work.

In market capitalism, incentives are basically material. Individual choices about where to work, how much to work, and what occupations to choose are heavily influenced by expected incomes. Profits provide the incentives for producers to satisfy consumer demand in the most technically efficient manner possible. Workers and managers in planned socialism are also influenced to some extent by material rewards. But those who control most planned economies attempt to minimize income differentials. As a result, they reduce material incentives to some extent. In the real world, most such economies have experienced severe shortages of consumer goods. The incentive to earn greater income is less when individuals have few ways to use income to improve their standard of living.

How Well Do the Two Systems Work?

In the preceding discussion, we highlighted how the two systems might operate in theory. In practice, neither system operates without problems. Market capitalist economies have experienced high unemployment and unstable prices. Planned socialist economies have had more stable prices and employment, but have often lacked innovation and efficiency.

In short, there is no simple answer to which system is better. It may be fairest to say that each system has advantages in meeting its own goals. History has shown that market economies are better able to meet individuals' demand for goods and services. But some planned economies—most notably that of the U.S.S.R.—have been successful in meeting their goal of high economic growth. However, by allocating a high percentage of resources to capital resources, they have not met as many demands for consumer goods and services. And many Third-World nations that have chosen planned socialism have not experienced the hoped-for growth. Indeed, the failures of planned socialist economies outnumber the successes.

A comparison of real economies is very complicated. The type of economic system is only one of many factors that determine economic outcomes. A nation's supplies of natural resources, labor, and capital also influence the goals it can set and meet. For example, China and the Soviet Union have lower GNP per capita than the United States. But to what extent is a lower GNP per capita the result of different economic systems? Perhaps the best way to discuss the issues involved is to consider the pros and cons of each system from the perspective of their proponents.

Views of proponents of market capitalism. Proponents of market capitalism see the difficulty of gathering accurate information on an entire economy's resources (and wants, if consumer goods and services are to be produced) as a great weakness of planned socialism. As a result, they argue, planners may not respond appropriately to changes in relative scarcity and wants. In contrast,

RECAP

In market capitalism most resources are privately owned and markets are the principal mechanism that determine resource allocation.

In planned socialism most resources are collectively owned and central plans are the principal mechanism that determine resource allocation.

Proponents of market capitalism believe that markets are the most efficient way of providing information; that profits and income create the best incentives; and that decentralized economic power leads to the greatest amount of individual freedom.

Proponents of planned socialism believe that capitalism concentrates economic power; that the drive for maximum profits creates inequities; and that central planning can reduce unemployment and increase economic growth.

prices determined in smoothly functioning markets communicate nearly all the information necessary to ensure efficient responses.

Similarly, they argue that planned economies provide few incentives for individuals to help the economy reach its goals, let alone to innovate. Market economies—through higher incomes and profits—provide these incentives. Thus market economies automatically promote allocative and technical efficiency. Finally, supporters of market capitalism argue that it is the economic system most consistent with political and economic freedom. Concentrating power in the hands of central government planners, on the other hand, is more consistent with authoritarian control. Thus market capitalism promotes equity.

Views of proponents of planned socialism. Proponents of planned socialism believe that market capitalism often concentrates economic power in the hands of a few wealthy individuals. As a result, they argue, it creates major inequalities and inequities that can be only partially remedied through public redistribution policies. In their quest for maximum profits, businesses tend to create undesirable working conditions. Socialism eliminates unequal ownership of property and can put worker safety ahead of profits. Thus planned socialism promotes equity.

Further, they charge that because wealth and income are unequally distributed in market economies, resources are not used to meet society's most important wants. Price instability and high unemployment cause economic waste (as well as human hardship). By focusing on fulfilling the wants of the broader society (not individual desires for more chrome on their cars, for example) and avoiding unemployment and price fluctuations, central planners make better use of a country's resources. Thus planned socialism promotes allocative and technical efficiency.

In summary, the proponents of each system conclude that theirs is more efficient and equitable. Their conclusions, however, involve many value judgments, especially in the argument over equity. Because of the normative aspects of these positions, economists will always disagree about which system is "best." However, other disagreements arise when a theoretical model of one system is compared with real-world examples of the other. In such a contest, the model wins every time. After all, theoretical models are designed to describe the operation of an ideal system. If you are to make valid comparisons of economic systems, you should learn something about the operation of a real planned economy. Thus in the next section, we consider how the Soviet Union's economy functions.

ECONOMY OF THE SOVIET UNION

In the Soviet Union, as in any centrally planned socialist economy, the government owns and controls most resources and the vast majority of output is produced by public enterprises.* Most economic activity is directed according to a centrally determined and administered plan. As a real-world economy (not a model), it has had both failures and successes. Moreover, the Soviet system is a product of its

---

* Although the Soviet Union is often called a communist country, it does not meet the definition of Communism set down by Karl Marx: "From each according to ability, to each according to need." Rather, it fits the socialist definition: "From each according to ability, to each according to contribution." While some socialists argue that socialism requires a free discussion of public wants—which is not characteristic of Soviet life—most economists describe the economy of the U.S.S.R. as socialist.

history. In many ways, it still operates as it did in the 1930s. To try to understand it, we have to examine its historical roots. Then we can consider the centralized planning function as it now operates and some of the problems the system has encountered. Finally, we will attempt to draw some basic conclusions about the Soviet economy.

Early History of the Soviet Economy

In 1917 when the communists seized control of the Russian government, the economy was a disaster. Russia lagged behind most of Western Europe in industrialization and had a very inefficient system of agriculture. World War I and the revolution brought further economic chaos. The country's new rulers abolished much of the old economic order. But preoccupied with eliminating political opposition to their government, they did not replace it with a new economic system until 1928. At that time the Soviet government issued its first Five Year Plan but with little idea of how a planned socialist economy might operate. Nevertheless, they plunged ahead, developing the theory and practice as they went along.

The first economic plan called for nationalization of industry and agriculture, both of which were to be controlled by a central plan. Moreover, in line with the priorities of communist leader Joseph Stalin, the plan called for a massive transfer of resources from agriculture to heavy industry. Stalin believed that industrialization was necessary both for economic development and increased military strength. The plan called for the Soviet economy to become as independent and self-sufficient as possible. At that time the Soviets had the only socialist economy in the world and felt (correctly, no doubt) that they had few allies on which to depend.

The essential objectives of this first economic plan remain a part of Soviet planning even today. First priority is given to industry, both to increase economic capacity and to provide military goods. Agriculture is valued, but has been a consistent problem. Expansion of farming into marginal lands in the 1950s and 1960s was designed to boost total output, but production has been erratic, with massive crop failures in some years. While these failures may be good news to U.S. farmers (because of increased exports), they have caused difficulties for the Soviet economy. Finally, consumer goods receive the lowest priority. In Stalin's earliest years, per capita consumption actually fell. Even now, consumer goods are scarcer than in many market economies.

Because of its emphasis on investment in heavy industry, however, the Soviet economy achieved very high rates of growth from 1928 until World War II broke out in 1939. According to official Soviet statistics, the annual growth rate averaged nearly 15 percent. Western observers calculate the growth more conservatively: somewhere in the range of 5–12 percent per year. But even 5 percent per year growth is remarkable. Few countries ever achieve that rate of growth over such an extended period of time. (By contrast, the U.S. growth rate in the 1960s—considered to be a strong growth period—was less than 4 percent per year.) In addition, the Soviet Union's rapid economic growth was achieved while the rest of the world was experiencing the Great Depression.

Developing the Economic Plan

Neither the overall Soviet economic priorities nor the basic structure of the Soviet economy has changed much over the years. Since the 1930s, it has been

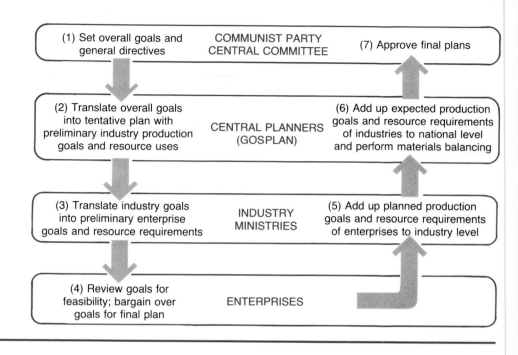

**Exhibit 34.3
Economic Planning
Process in the
Soviet Union**

tightly controlled by a central plan. Exhibit 34.3 provides a simplified version of the Soviet economic planning process.* Overall economic goals are set by the Communist Party's Central Committee (the top officials in the Communist Party). The goals specify how much to allocate to production of consumption goods, how much to invest in capital goods, and which industries to expand and which to reduce. At this level, however, few details are provided.

The next step of the process involves the central planning bureaucracy, in particular the agency known as Gosplan. This group is responsible for converting the goals into operational plans. It establishes preliminary production quotas, or targets, and allocates resources by industry. The size of the planning task is enormous. The Soviet economy produces an estimated 20 million different products. The central plan actually covers *only* a few thousand items. Even so, most planning at this level is done by product groups—molded plastic or shoes, for example. Many different products are included in each group, but centralized planning on a more detailed level would be impossible.

The preliminary central plan is submitted to the Industrial Ministries—a group of planning agencies—each of which is responsible for a particular industry. (In some cases, Regional Ministries rather than Industrial Ministries are involved because production of certain items—such as consumer goods and housing—is organized geographically. The principles remain the same, however.) Ministry planners translate industry goals into plans or production targets for each "enterprise"—the Soviet equivalent of a firm. Enterprise managers review the plans, noting whether all necessary supplies have been allocated.

---

*An organizational chart that accurately displayed all elements in just the central planning system would fill a large wall poster. See, for example, Paul K. Cook, "The Political Setting," in *Soviet Economy in the 1980s: Problems and Prospects.* Washington, D.C.: U.S. Government Printing Office, 1983, selected papers submitted to the Joint Economic Committee, 97th Congress, 2nd session, part 1, pp. 18–21.

Although managers do not have any ultimate authority, their influence can be significant. Because they are evaluated on whether they meet the targets assigned to them in the plan, managers and ministers alike try to obtain more supplies and lower production quotas. Central planners in the Soviet Union, however, tend to drive hard bargains and planning is generally tight. The final plan is then submitted to political authorities for approval, ending the planning process.

Materials balancing. The central plan establishes targets for production, investment, and costs. But the critical element is the plan for *materials balancing*: allocating resources so as to achieve the desired level of output. In the Soviet Union, Gosplan is responsible for ensuring that resources required by industries to meet their planned output goals are available to them. There are three sources of resources: (1) existing supplies; (2) supplies produced during the period; and (3) imports.

As the final plan begins to take shape, Gosplan calculates the total sources and uses of each resource. It is possible that they will balance, but usually, Gosplan must adjust sources and/or uses. Because the Soviets aim for maximum growth and full employment, Gosplan typically must either increase sources or reduce uses. For example, if total uses for steel exceeds the planned sources, Gosplan could order steel factories to increase production. But increasing steel production will require more coal, iron ore, electricity, and other resources. In fact, a change in the amount of any one good produced will have far-reaching effects on resources. The Soviet goal of self-sufficiency also limits Gosplan's use of imported resources and products.

As a result, materials balancing in the Soviet Union often means reducing uses of resources. To reduce uses, Gosplan can either cut back on the resources given to factories (or force them to use substitutes) or it can reduce production of consumer goods. In the past, Gosplan has used both options, but most often it has reduced consumer goods, reflecting Soviet economic priorities.

Implementing the Plan

Actual implementation of the central plan falls to managers of Soviet enterprises. These managers are responsible for operating industrial plants, state-run agricultural farms, and retail establishments. Each manager is given a plan, which amounts to a quota, and an indication of the resources they will receive. Managers are charged with carrying out the plan—not with developing alternatives—but generally they are not told how to operate their enterprises.

As an incentive to make the plans work, enterprise managers are rewarded with large bonuses—amounting to 25 to 50 percent of their salaries if they meet their assigned goals. But their options and controls are limited. For example, Gosplan and the ministries not only determine what supplies an enterprise receives, but also matches up suppliers and customers. The managers of the two enterprises must then determine grade of product, delivery date, and other important but unplanned specifics. Since neither supplier nor customer has an option, supplying managers have little incentive to satisfy customer managers. But they do have major incentives to meet the quantitive goals of the plan in any way possible.

Two characteristics of the planning and implementation process create problems for the Soviet economy. First, the planners operate on the principle that managers will be more efficient if planned targets are difficult (but not impossible) to achieve. Second, managers receive large bonuses for reaching their targets but none if they do not. To understand the problems that can arise as a result, try to imagine how you might act if you were a manager trying to meet a production target.

First, you would probably try to build some slack into the plan. Thus you might underreport the resources you have on hand (ensuring enough to meet the production goal). Or you might understate your factory's capacity (to keep the production goal low). Once you begin implementing the plan, you might refuse to slow down or halt production to try new technology or new ideas to improve productivity. Moreover, since your "customers" have no choice but to accept whatever you produce, you can reduce quality, use inferior materials, or change the grade of a product if necessary to meet the quantity target.

You can also manipulate the target. If the plan calls for producing 1 million cans of shaving cream, for example, you might order each can filled one-fourth of an ounce less full. If the goal is to produce $1 million worth of dresses, you might choose to make them out of silk instead of cotton. Finally, you might decide to employ people who specialize in obtaining supplies on quick notice—even though they may use threats, bribes, or other such means. Although these actions may help you achieve your production goals, each of these responses creates a problem for the economy.

The "Second Economy"

The preceding description of the planning and implementation process describes most—but by no means all—economic activity in the Soviet Union. A complete picture of the Soviet economy must include the *second economy,* a combination of legal and illegal economic activities. The most important and best known legal part of the second economy is private agricultural production. Workers on state and collective farms are allowed to farm relatively small plots (usually one acre or less) and to sell what they produce. Although such plots account for only 3 percent of all agricultural land, they produce nearly one-fourth of all agricultural commodities. Such plots are especially important for livestock and vegetable production.

Other parts of the legal private sector include certain personal services, such as physicians and teachers who are allowed to sell their after-work services. Although these and other legal private activities are tolerated, they are not completely accepted. In fact, they violate the principles of the Soviet economy because they are unplanned. Moreover, it is sometimes difficult to clearly distinguish between legal and illegal activities. For example, farm workers may "divert" supplies from the collective farm for use on the private plot, or they may "borrow" equipment. Although private farming is permitted, the use of state-owned equipment and supplies is not. But there is little doubt such use occurs.

Some activities are clearly illegal, such as producing goods for sale on the black market. Severe shortages, lack of variety, and relatively poor quality of the consumer goods provided by the state leave ample room for a black market to function. Smuggling and stealing from warehouses is also an important industry. Of course, similar activities occur in the United States and all other countries, where the underground economy is a place for illegal activities (such as drug trafficking) and tax evasion.

In fact, some illegal aspects of the Soviet "second economy" appear to be tolerated by the authorities. Certainly, the second economy helps to provide some of the consumer goods that make wage and other material incentives effective. Moreover, the ability to acquire supplies on the black market—by hook or crook or both—helps to overcome poor resource allocation. But such activities undoubtedly channel resources and efforts away from the targets of the official economic plan. In addition, the existence of the second economy is, at least in part, an indication of system failure.

Success and Failure

Drawing firm conclusions about the Soviet economy is somewhat difficult because impartial and accurate information is scarce. Moreover, the goals of the Soviet Union's economic system are different from those of the U.S. and other market economies. Still, observers of the Soviet system have reached several general conclusions.

Economic-growth rate has been high. We noted earlier the high growth rate of the Soviet economy prior to World War II. Since the war, the rate of growth has continued to be high. Between 1950 and 1979, the Soviet economy grew at just under 5 percent annually, according to Western calculations (Soviet figures put it higher still). In contrast, the U.S. economy grew only about 3.5 percent annually. Over this period, only the growth rate of the Japanese economy exceeds that of the Soviet Union's.

The high rate of Soviet economic growth has several explanations. First, by severely restricting the production of consumer goods, central planners have forced a high rate of capital growth. Then by maintaining almost zero unemployment, they have further increased production. In addition, Russia started at a lower level of economic development, making high percentage increases in production easier to attain. Finally, the Soviet economy grew in part by importing or imitating technology developed in other parts of the world.

Despite its past record, however, some economists question whether the Soviet economy can continue to grow at the same rate. In fact, the economy has slowed considerably in the late 1970s and 1980s, and several problems seem to have emerged. First, much of the growth in the past was the result of increased supplies of labor and capital. However, population growth has slowed, and central planners have begun to give more priority to consumer goods. Moreover, future Soviet economic growth appears to depend heavily on technology, as in most developed economies. But the Soviets lag in adopting the most advanced technology: information processing, computers, and similar technological areas. Limited incentives for innovation at the plant level may not only have contributed to the slowdown in growth, but may pose a major obstacle to future growth.

Degree of equity is unclear. Proponents of socialism argue that it produces a more equal distribution of income. Comparative data are scarce but there appears to be little difference between income-distribution patterns in the Soviet Union and in many market economies. Top Soviet political officials are a privileged class. They receive finer houses, shop in special stores, have access to better educational institutions for their children, and enjoy many other privileges not available to others in Soviet society.

Labor income—wages and salaries—seems to be distributed about as unequally in the Soviet Union as in the United States, probably because wages and bonuses are important incentives in both countries. Moreover, Soviet citizens do not have other sources of income, such as rent and interest. Thus, overall, income distribution in the United States is more unequal. However, many goods and services—health care, education, and housing—are provided at no direct cost or at low cost in the Soviet Union. The standard of living of the lowest income groups in the Soviet Union is therefore somewhat higher than indicated by income distribution.

Innovation and quality have suffered. In discussing implementation of the central plan, we noted several problem areas: managers misrepresenting resources or capacity and producing low-quality products. There are strong incentives to "beat the system," but few incentives to produce more high-quality products at less cost. Indeed, managers who succeed in raising productivity often find their reward to be a higher quota in subsequent periods.

Managers in many market economies—especially in the United States—have also been criticized for focusing on meeting short-term goals and failing to make the best long-run decisions. (Some economists have suggested that this behavior occurs because large corporations are controlled by corporate plans and, like planned economies, have difficulty developing appropriate incentives for managers.) But the problem appears to be particularly pronounced in planned socialist economies.

Full employment and price stability may be myths. The Soviets point proudly to full employment and stable prices. However, some Western observers believe that these claims are exaggerated. In their opinion, many workers are underemployed even though few individuals are without a job. Managers hold on to workers who are not busy full time in order to ensure that they will meet their production quotas. Government allocation of resources—including labor—may also result in some individuals working in jobs for which they are overqualified. And although official statistics show little or no inflation, they disregard prices on the black market, a major force in the Soviet economy. Moreover, rubles (the Soviet currency) are not the only way of measuring prices. The hours spent waiting in line to purchase the few consumer goods available also has an economic cost.

RECAP

Until recently, the Soviet economy had experienced rapid economic growth. A high rate of population growth, transfer of resources from agricultural to industrial production, high rates of capital investment, and imported technology were the source of past growth.

Slower population growth, limited technological progress, and the lack of incentives to develop and implement new technology have been cited as reasons for a slower growth rate more recently.

Is there a bottom line? Ultimately the evaluation of a system becomes a matter of personal judgment and preference. Is the price that the Soviets pay for full employment too high? Has it been worth the sacrifice of consumer goods to build up industrial and military strength? Nearly everyone has an opinion on these and other aspects of the Soviet system.

Those who study comparative economics are cautious about comparisons, but they do agree on two points. Either type of economic system can be made to operate and both have experienced successes and failures. Whether the Soviet Union can make the necessary reforms to continue its economic progress is debatable. Other planned socialist economies—especially those of Hungary and China—have introduced more decentralized decision making, placed more emphasis on markets, and improved efficiency as a result. But the Soviet Union believes that such changes would violate the very premise of its economic system and therefore resists them.

ECONOMIC DEVELOPMENT AND THE THIRD WORLD

The United States and the Soviet Union have quite different economic systems, as you have seen. But in some respects they are alike. Each has the characteristics of a **developed economy**. Both are highly industrialized, have average standards of living far above subsistence levels, and maintain sophisticated institutions (government, education, transportation, and communication). Economists often refer to the developed market capitalist economies—the United States, Canada, Western Europe, Japan, and Australia—as the economic "First World." And they often refer to the developed planned socialist economies—the Soviet Union and Eastern Europe—as the economic "Second World."

In contrast, **less-developed countries (LDCs)**—Ethiopia, Sudan, Zaire, Sri Lanka, and Bolivia, to name only a few—are often called "Third-World" nations. Unlike the developed nations, they have little industry and very limited educational and communication systems. Poverty is not an isolated phenomena but the typical way of life, encompassing the majority of the population and persisting from year to year, generation to generation.

There is no neat dividing line between the developed and less-developed countries. Moreover, like all classifications, there is much diversity within the Third World—from the near-destitute situation in Ethiopia to moderate success in South Korea. (For more on some of the newly industrialized economies, see A Case in Point: The Dragons Are Coming!) But less-developed countries do face similar problems that justify grouping them together. As you will see, however, there are no simple ways to relieve their absolute and relative poverty.

Dimensions of Poverty

Exhibit 34.4 shows the relative and absolute poverty of Third-World nations. Following the classification scheme of the World Bank, less-developed countries are divided into two groups: low-income and middle-income. Middle-income countries are more developed in important ways than are low-income countries. But they are still less developed than the industrial market economies. (Centrally planned economies other than China are not included because of the lack of comparable data.)

Low output per capita. The extent of poverty in Third-World economies is evident from the low levels of output per capita in the low-income countries. Output per capita in 1984 ranged from a low of $110 per year in Ethiopia to a high of $360 per year in Sudan. You probably cannot imagine trying to exist for a year on $200–$400 of income. Indeed, in 1984, four-person families with incomes below $10,609—over ten times the average income in many LDCs—were officially classified as poor in the United States. Although GNP statistics may not accurately reflect actual standards of living, they do reflect *relative* standards of living.

Moreover, as we noted earlier, in most Third-World nations nearly everyone is poor. The situation is better in some of the middle-income countries, especially Israel and Hong Kong, but these are exceptional cases. The poorest countries also suffer from income inequalities. Most have a successful upper class, but almost no middle class and little chance for upward mobility.

Developed economy. An economy that is industrialized, has relatively high standards of living, and has sophisticated institutions (government, education, transportation, and communication).

Less-developed countries (LDCs). Nations that have relatively low standards of living, limited industrialization, and minimal education, transportation, and communication systems; collectively known as the Third World.

Country	GNP per capita (dollars per year)	Average life expectancy (years)	Daily calorie supply (percent of required)	Population per physician
Low income				
Ethiopia	110	44	93	81,120
Bangledesh	130	50	81	9,010
Zaire	140	51	96	13,940*
Tanzania	210	52	98	17,740*
India	260	56	96	2,610
China	310	69	111	1,730
Sri Lanka	360	70	106	7,620
Sudan	360	48	90	9,070
Middle income				
Bolivia	540	53	82	1,950
Nigeria	730	50	86	10,540
Thailand	860	64	105	5,020
Turkey	1,160	64	123	1,500
Colombia	1,390	65	110	1,700*
Chile	1,700	70	105	950
Brazil	1,720	64	106	1,200
South Korea	2,110	68	118	1,440
Mexico	2,040	66	126	1,140
Hungary	2,100	70	135	320
Yugoslavia	2,120	69	141	670
Greece	3,770	75	144	390
Israel	5,060	75	121	400
Hong Kong	6,330	76	122	1,260
Industrial market				
Italy	6,420	77	140	750
United Kingdom	8,570	74	128	680
Austria	9,140	73	132	580
Japan	10,630	77	113	740
France	9,760	77	139	460
West Germany	11,130	75	130	420
Canada	13,280	76	130	510
Sweden	11,860	77	116	410
United States	15,390	76	137	500
Switzerland	16,330	77	129	390

**Exhibit 34.4
Indicators of Economic
Status**

* These numbers are from The World Bank, *World Development Report, 1985.*
Source: The World Bank, *World Development Report, 1986.*

High birth and death rates. With a few exceptions, life expectancy in
the less-developed countries is below that in the developed countries. Poverty is
a major reason: The daily calorie supply per person is *on average* below the
subsistence level in some countries and only just above it in others. And health
care, as indicated by the number of persons per physician, is far below the standard

A Case in Point
The Dragons Are Coming!

In Oriental tradition China is known as the *big dragon*. Economists have nicknamed the fast-growing economies of South Korea, Taiwan, Singapore, and Hong Kong the *little dragons*. Using a strategy of export promotion, these areas have increased the output of their economies by an average of 9 percent per year over the past two decades. Although they all experienced slower growth in 1985—an average of only 2.3 percent—they are expected to grow at a 6–8 percent pace within the next few years. They have become a force to be reckoned with in international product markets, including textiles, electronics, and automobiles.

In the past the little dragons have relied on low-cost labor to attract foreign investment and foreign sales. Taiwan's exports to the United States are largely labor-intensive goods produced directly for U.S. firms. General Motors was attracted to South Korea by labor costs of $2.16 per hour, compared to $24.40 in the United States. Two Japanese companies—Matsushita and Sanyo—have recently built new plants in Singapore to take advantage of cheap labor.

A symbol of the growing economic strength of the little dragons, however, is their decision to invest in foreign economies and to undertake joint ventures with foreign companies. A Singapore electronics company, Singatronics, bought a U.S. company in order to acquire its brand name and its distribution network. Uaewoo, a South Korean firm, has entered into several joint ventures with General Motors, including manufacturing a new model Pontiac to be sold in the United States.

Much of this past growth has been virtually invisible in the United States. For the most part the little dragons have acted as subcontractors, manufacturing goods for U.S. and, more recently, Japanese firms. The vast majority of their exports to the United States have been sold under U.S. or Japanese labels. But South Korea, the strongest of the little dragons, is seeking to do to the Japanese what the Japanese did to U.S. firms in the 1960s: take over the low-cost end of many markets. Hyundai is successfully battling the Japanese in the subcompact auto market with its Excel. While South Korea sold only 65 cars to the United States in 1985, in 1986 this figure was more like 140,000. Projected sales for 1987 should top 300,000. Uaewoo, another South Korean conglomerate, manufactures Leading Edge computers, a successful IBM look-alike. South Korean firms have captured as much as 10 percent of the market for VCRs, a figure that is expected to increase.

Although they have not yet earned full status as First-World economies, the little dragons can no longer be counted among the less-developed countries. In fact, these "newly industrialized countries" hope to make the transition from developing to developed economies. If they don't succeed—and many economists believe that they will—it won't be for lack of trying. As U.S. firms seek to regain some of the international competitiveness lost over the last few years, they had better keep a sharp eye on the Far East. The dragons are coming!

of the developed countries. At the same time, population growth in many Third-World nations is rapid. There is no simple correlation between population growth and poverty, but most economists believe that rapid population growth makes it difficult to improve standards of living.

Economic Growth versus Economic Development

A low standard of living is clearly one of the most significant problems in less-developed countries. In order to raise their standards of living, Third-World nations must increase their total production of goods and services. That is, economic growth is perhaps their most important economic goal. But achieving economic growth is not a simple matter, especially in nations with poor transportation and education systems and unstable or outmoded social and political sys-

Economic development. The process of changing economic, social, and political systems in order to sustain economic growth and overcome mass poverty.

tems. These features are both products of nations' less-developed status and obstacles to their progress.

To achieve economic growth, an economy must increase resources supplied—especially capital resources—and/or improve technology. But many economists believe that **economic development** in Third-World nations will also require changes in social, political, and institutional systems. As you will see, the failure of some proposed solutions can be attributed to failure to address these fundamental—and essential—aspects of development.

Dimensions of Economic Development

We can identify the systems that must be changed by considering how Third-World nations differ from First-World and Second-World countries. As Exhibit 34.5 shows, the typical less-developed country is more dependent on agriculture, is more rural, has lower educational achievement, and is more dependent on primary exports, such as largely unprocessed minerals and agricultural products. In addition, these nations have had a history of political and economic instability.

Heavy concentration in agriculture. In many Third-World countries, 75 percent of the population is engaged in agriculture, much of it subsistence farming. (Among the industrialized market economies, only Japan and Italy have as much as 10 percent of the population in agriculture.) In some ways agriculture is a key industry for less-developed countries. Improvements in agricultural technology can increase yields per acre dramatically and raise the standard of living. By reducing the demand for farm labor, this step can also free workers for industrial production.

Low degree of urbanization. In the more advanced industrialized countries, most of the population lives in urban areas. In the less-developed countries, most of the population still lives in rural areas. Rural life, of course, reflects the concentration in agriculture. In developed countries, urbanization reflects industrialization and a large number of service jobs. However, urbanization can create problems in a less-developed country. In many Third-World nations, people have been attracted to urban areas faster than new industrial jobs have been created. Not only has this shift caused declines in agricultural output, but it has also resulted in heavy unemployment in urban areas and even greater poverty.

Low educational attainment. Educational services are poor in many less-developed countries. Teachers are scarce, and relatively few of the population attain even a high school diploma, much less attend college. Although workers without high school diplomas can perform most industrial jobs, education and training are related. Most Third-World economies have too few trained individuals. One result is low labor productivity (units produced per worker).

Dependency on primary exports. Most less-developed countries are too small to ever be totally self-sufficient. Indeed, the economics of comparative advantage discussed in Chapter 32 suggest that all nations are better off when they trade. For Third-World nations, successful trade can provide income not only to buy manufactured products, but also to finance investment in capital resources and thus increase their capacity to produce.

Country	Agricultural output as percent of total	Percent of labor force in agriculture	Urban population as percent of total	Percent of age group in secondary school	Primary commodities as percent of merchandise exports
Low income					
Ethiopia	48	80	15	13	99
Bangledesh	48	75	18	19	39
Zaire	36*	72	39	23*	—
Tanzania	52*	86	14	3	87*
India	35	70	25	34	47
China	36	69	22	35	43
Sri Lanka	28	53	21	56	70
Sudan	33	71	21	18	98*
Middle income					
Bolivia	25	46	43	35	—
Nigeria	27	68	30	16*	—
Thailand	20	70	18	29	68
Turkey	19	58	46	38	54
Colombia	20	34	67	49	81
Chile	6	16	83	65	92*
Brazil	13	31	72	42	59
South Korea	14	36	64	89	9
Mexico	9	37	69	55	73
Hungary	20	18	55	74	37
Yugoslavia	15	32	46	82	24
Greece	18	31	65	82	50
Israel	5	6	90	78	19
Hong Kong	1	2	93	68	8
Industrial market					
Italy	6	12	71	75	15
United Kingdom	2	3	92	85	35
Austria	4	9	56	74	15
Japan	4	11	76	94	3
France	—	9	81	89	26
West Germany	2	6	86	50	13
Canada	3	5	75	101	45
Sweden	3	6	86	85	22
United States	2	4	74	97*	30
Switzerland	—	6	60	—	7

* These numbers are from The World Bank, *World Development Report, 1985.*
Source: The World Bank, *World Development Report, 1986.*

**Exhibit 34.5
Indicators of Economic Development**

But to succeed in trade, a nation must be able to compete and to diversify. Many less-developed nations instead depend on the export of minerals and agricultural products—called *primary exports*. When a country is very heavily dependent on the export of one or two main products, it is highly vulnerable to changes in demand and supply that occur frequently in international markets. And when a nation exports many of its raw materials, it loses the opportunity to gain income by processing those materials and selling more finished goods.

Inadequate transportation and communication systems. Economic development, as we indicated, requires an economic system with adequate transportation and communication systems. We tend to take them for granted in the United States, but in many Third-World nations, it is difficult and expensive to transport goods from one part of the country to another. Inadequate transportation and communication systems hamper industrial growth, reduce efficiency, and virtually isolate some members of an economy.

Political and economic instability. Economists generally agree that less-developed countries have a history of economic and political instability. Economic instability is most visible as high unemployment and highly unstable prices. Political instability is observed as turnover of governments and radical changes in economic goals.

Political and economic instability hamper economic development. Private individuals and firms worry about not recovering their investments. Indeed, in many countries businesses have lost some or all of their investments as a result of political decisions. Price instability makes individuals reluctant to put their savings to work in domestic financial markets, which also lowers private investment. Many of these problems and symptoms are related, presenting a major challenge for the less-developed countries. But what is required and what strategies are useful for economic development? We address these questions in the next several sections.

Conditions for Economic Development

Economic development is a process that is complicated and has many dimensions. A high priority for Third-World nations seeking economic growth is to increase their investment in capital resources—that is, machines and factories. Not only can such investment spur industrial growth but it can also help increase agricultural productivity. Moreover, even though many jobs in modern industries require few skills, almost every industry requires some skilled labor. In addition, management and entrepreneurial skills are required. In order to grow, then, less-developed nations must improve the education and training of their work forces.

Similarly, Third-World nations must increase agricultural and industrial productivity if their economies are to grow. Adopting improved technologies would increase productivity, lowering the cost of goods and making them more competitive in world markets. Unfortunately, not all technology used in the United States and other developed economies can be instantly adopted by less-developed nations. Some modern equipment is extremely expensive; some modern techniques require a highly skilled labor force. In addition to investing in new machines, technology, and worker training, less-developed nations must invest in transportation, communication, health, and education. As we noted, these aspects of what economists call the *social infrastructure* are underdeveloped in most Third-World nations.

All these investments, of course, cost money. Unfortunately, the low incomes of the less-developed countries limit the possibility of generating substantial investment funds from domestic saving. And political and economic instability tends

RECAP

Less-developed countries have some serious structural problems: high poverty, heavy concentration on agriculture, low urbanization, poor education, limited industrialization, heavy dependence on the export of primary products, inadequate transportation and communication systems, and political and economic instability. These structural problems make economic progress difficult and complex.

In order to develop, the less-developed countries must invest in capital and human resources. Funds for these investments may be earned through exports, borrowed from foreign banks or governments, or obtained as gifts from foreign governments. High poverty and low rates of saving make financing much growth without foreign help difficult.

to cause any private saving to be put into gold, jewelry, or foreign bank accounts where they are available to finance new investment. Thus Third-World nations must raise investment funds in one of four other ways: (1) running a trade surplus; (2) attracting foreign investment; (3) borrowing from foreign financial institutions or governments; or (4) obtaining grants from foreign governments. The most successful less-developed nations have used a combination of these sources. But none is easy or without potential problems.

Strategies for Economic Development

Because of the many problems and complexity of economic development, there is no single or easy way to make it happen. Moreover, most economists argue that a country should pursue several options at the same time to reduce the risk of failure. In searching for a strategy, less-developed countries must address some of the questions that follow.

Import substitution or export promotion? Successful trade is essential for most Third-World nations, as it is for the more industrialized countries. Most developing economies have to import at least some, if not all, of the capital resources they require. International trade can generate funds to pay for capital resources, but only if the nation can run a trade surplus on noncapital goods.

To create a surplus, a nation may choose import substitution or export promotion. *Import substitution* is the domestic production of some goods that were previously imported. If successful, it will free export earnings to pay for capital resources. Import substitution has been a popular strategy for many less-developed countries, who see it both as a way to develop domestic industries and to become more self-sufficient. Efforts to improve productivity in local industries—including agricultural production—can increase total production and raise the standard of living.

Nevertheless, import substitution as normally practiced has not always been a success. Some Third-World nations have tried to produce locally what they can more cheaply buy abroad. (The relatively large number of inefficiently operated steel mills in less-developed countries is an example.) And some poorer nations have imposed trade restrictions to protect domestic industries from foreign competition. As we noted in Chapter 32, economists believe that free trade offers greater benefits than trade restrictions.

In contrast, *export promotion* requires that a nation make its goods more attractive to foreign buyers. Revenues from greater exports can then be used to pay for imported capital resources. South Korea, Hong Kong, Taiwan, and Japan all used this strategy successfully. Economists generally consider export promotion to be consistent with the principle of comparative advantage and increased worldwide trade. They suggest that less-developed economies should try to find some niche in the world marketplace. Ideally, this niche should not be just the production of raw materials, but one that will allow the country to process raw materials to some degree and thus increase its income. Moreover, they reject as shortsighted the strategies of some nations, notably Japan, that combine export promotion with trade restrictions.

Industry or agriculture? Noting the difference in focus on agriculture between developed and less-developed nations, many Third-World nations tried shifting most of their attention to industrialization. Although industrialization is important, an exclusive focus on it can cause agricultural output to fall and urban unemployment to rise at the same time.

Economists now suggest that less-developed nations also increase their efforts to develop agriculture. As we noted earlier, greater agricultural productivity will improve the food supply, making the economy less dependent on imported food and improving the standard of living. It will also free workers for jobs in industry. A more balanced policy toward the two sectors, and more efforts to provide industrial jobs in rural areas are seen as crucial to sound economic growth and development.

Private foreign investment? Less-developed countries must also decide whether to encourage private foreign investment. Foreigners can provide funds for capital purchases and help a nation industrialize, modernize, and provide training for its workers. Foreign-owned businesses may also provide a market for domestic raw materials and intermediate goods (such as steel).

Many Third-World nations are reluctant to allow foreign investment, however. They view foreign investors as exploiters of local labor and contributors of little of their profits to the domestic economy. Countries that have allowed foreign investment have often required local ownership of a substantial percentage of the company and limited the transfer of profits out of the country. In some cases governments have taken over private businesses. Needless to say, such restrictions and uncertainty limit foreign investments. The challenge for less-developed nations, then, is to find a way to encourage foreign investment, while at the same time ensuring that they receive the benefits from it.

Foreign loans? Although foreign loans can be used to finance economic development, this strategy can be dangerous. A number of less-developed countries, especially in Latin America, are heavily in debt. They borrowed substantial sums of money, much of it from U.S. banks. But they currently find it virtually impossible to pay interest charges, much less repay any of the principal owed. In some cases, this debt crisis may reflect poor investment decisions or the use of borrowed funds to finance consumption rather than investment. But the worldwide recessions in the 1980s followed by slow economic growth have made it difficult for Third-World countries to increase their exports. Third-World countries also claim that trade restrictions in First-World countries have further limited their ability to export goods profitably. In addition, rising interest rates and falling prices of major exports have increased the less-developed nations' burden of debt. And both the rise and fall of oil prices in the 1980s hurt debtor nations. Increased oil prices in the early 1980s hurt oil importers, such as Brazil; the decline in oil prices in the mid-1980s hurt oil exporters, such as Mexico.

Foreign aid? Another possible source of funds—foreign aid—also has costs as well as benefits. Is accepting foreign aid a useful way to begin economic development, or does it create a dependency and stifle self-reliance? As usual, the answer depends on the situation. In some countries, most notably Tanzania, foreign aid has been badly used, resulting in overly ambitious plans and acquisition of complex machinery that the country has been unable to maintain. But examples of successful aid can be found and are, in fact, more numerous. The issue is less whether aid is granted but how it is used and for what purposes. If aid is used to fund poorly designed projects or to build palaces for the ruling elite, success cannot be expected. On the other hand, well-chosen and well-designed projects can be highly successful.

Free markets or centralized planning? Finally, the governments of developing countries have to choose a type of economic system. Should they opt for a centrally planned economy? Or should they allow markets to make economic decisions? Some economies, including those of the Ivory Coast, Singapore, and Hong Kong, have stressed international trade, private investment, and market capitalism. Others—Cuba, Vietnam, and North Korea, for example—have adopted planned socialist economies. Most, however, have followed a mixed strategy, although many utilize centralized economic planning more than do most developed nonsocialist economies.

For example, governments in most developing nations have chosen to intervene to improve the social infrastructure, that is, transportation and communication systems, schools, hospitals. Many economists accept this type of intervention as useful for economic development. But many are skeptical of other government activities. There are numerous examples of government mistakes, such as large-scale projects—dams or steel mills—that remain incomplete, and examples of state-operated enterprises that are highly inefficient.

In addition, the role of government in Third-World trade policies remains controversial. Some of the success of Hong Kong and South Korea may have resulted from policies that violate the principles of free trade. Other countries—Brazil and Chile, for example—have burdened their economies with trade restrictions. The problems arising from poor government decisions underscore the importance of developing flexible and efficient political and social institutions as a part of economic development.

What Will the Future Bring?

As you have seen, Third-World economies face many problems. Can they succeed with so many handicaps? Can development strategies help them? The experience of the past 30 years is inconclusive. Some economies are no better off now than then. But the growth record of many less-developed countries is good—exceeding that of the developed economies.

A few economies have almost made it over the hump—South Korea and Hong Kong, for example. Others, including Brazil, Mexico, China, and Argentina have made great strides, although progress has not been sure and steady. But economists have learned a great deal about obstacles and options from the experiences of these economies. The evidence is ample that the future is far from hopeless. Whether it is bright remains a point of contention among economists.

Most economists believe the Third-World nations will continue to require the help of industrialized economies. Some of this help may be in the form of foreign aid or private investments, but equally, if not more importantly, the industrialized economies can help by keeping their economies healthy, growing, and free of trade restrictions. In this way, the Third-World countries can earn the funds required to import capital goods, improving economic growth and standards of living.

Finally, even under the best of circumstances, economic development does not happen quickly. The developed economies have a tremendous head start and, despite problems, they continue to grow. Thus even remarkable progress in raising per capita output levels—such as in South Korea and Hong Kong—will not close the gap. Less-developed countries appear likely to lag behind in relative terms for a long time to come.

CONCLUSION

We end as we began, noting that all economies face the fundamental problem of scarcity. But you have learned that not all take the same approach to allocating society's scarce resources and goods. The approaches that different nations have taken have produced radically different outcomes. What system is best and what system less-developed countries should use to improve their standards of living remain controversial. But whatever path Third-World nations choose, it seems likely that they will require the help of the First-World and Second-World nations if they are to raise significantly their standards of living. And in watching the progress of less-developed countries, it may be that the more developed countries will also find a key to continued growth.

SUMMARY

1. In this chapter we compared planned socialist and market capitalist economies, discussed the economy of the Soviet Union, and explored the problems of less-developed countries.

2. In market capitalism, most resources are privately owned and most allocation decisions are directed by market forces. In planned socialism, most resources are owned by the government and most allocation decisions are directed by government plan.

3. In market capitalism, the economy seeks to satisfy individual wants, as expressed by market demand. Although government policies and regulations are influential, the market is the preferred mechanism for answering the fundamental economic questions of what to produce, how to produce, and to whom to distribute. In planned socialism, satisfying collective wants, as defined by central planners, is the primary goal. Although markets are sometimes permitted, the plan is the preferred mechanism for answering the fundamental economic questions.

4. Proponents of market capitalism believe that markets are a more efficient way to obtain information about demand and resource scarcity; that private property rights and the connection between income and consumption provide the best incentives to utilize resources efficiently; and that decentralized economic and political power make market capitalism most consistent with personal freedom.

5. Proponents of planned socialism believe that market capitalism often results in concentrated economic and

political power; that the drive for maximum profits creates inequity and inattention to important social wants; that inflation and unemployment significantly reduce the efficiency of market economies; and that planning leads to more economic growth.

6. The Soviet Union is a centrally planned socialist economy. In 1928, the Soviets launched their first Five Year Plan, emphasizing industrialization and the production of military and capital resources. This emphasis on industrial and military goods as opposed to consumer goods remains true today.

7. The top economic goals for the Soviet economy are determined by the leaders of the Communist party. Gosplan, the central planning bureau, is responsible for developing an economic plan to achieve these goals. In cooperation with industry planning bureaus and enterprise managers, Gosplan develops the plan and allocates resources and other materials. Actual implementation of the plan is the responsibility of enterprise managers.

8. In addition to planned activities, there is a "second economy" in the Soviet Union: a combination of legal and illegal activities. Some private-enterprise activities are permitted, although generally they are not encouraged.

9. The Soviet economy has historically achieved a very high rate of growth. High population growth, large-scale transfer of resources from agricultural to industrial production, high rates of capital investment, and imported technology have been the source of past

growth. Slow population growth, limited technological progress, and the lack of incentives to develop and implement new technology have been cited as reasons for slower growth rates more recently.

10. Some of the less-developed countries have serious structural problems: high poverty, heavy concentration on agriculture, low urbanization, poor education, limited industrialization, heavy dependence on the export of primary products, inadequate transportation and communication systems, and political and economic instability. These structural problems make economic progress difficult and complex.

11. In order to develop, less-developed countries must invest in capital and human resources. Funds for these investments may be earned through exports, borrowed from foreign banks or governments, or obtained as gifts from foreign governments.

12. Less-developed countries must decide whether to promote exports or to produce goods that substitute for foreign imports, whether to emphasize agriculture instead of developing industry, whether to encourage or limit foreign investment, whether to rely heavily on foreign aid and foreign loans, and whether to utilize a free-market or planned-socialist economy.

KEY TERMS

Developed economy, 878
Less-developed countries (LDCs), 878
Economic development, 881

QUESTIONS FOR REVIEW AND DISCUSSION

1. Suppose that you were an enterprise manager in the Soviet Union. You are promoted and receive a bonus based only on meeting the quota you negotiate with the industry ministry.
   a) Explain the steps you would take to ensure your promotion and bonus.
   b) How important are the following to decisions you make? Producing a quality product. Satisfying the demands of firms and individuals who use your product. Making sure that your plant uses the most efficient technology.
   c) What are the long-run implications of such an incentive system?
   d) What changes in the evaluation system can you suggest that would improve efficiency?

2. Some critics of U.S. business argue that managers focus too much on short-run goals. In many large firms, managers can expect to stay in any particular job for less than two years. They are evaluated on the basis of profits that they can generate during that period of time.
   a) Explain how this system of evaluation may lead to a purely short-run focus.
   b) Explain how short-run profits may be affected by reducing expenditures for training employees, maintaining equipment, and buying new machinery. What are the long-run implications of these actions?
   c) What changes in the evaluation system can you suggest that would improve efficiency?

3. Every economy faces similar issues, although different economic systems address them differently. Compare and contrast the economies of the United States and the Soviet Union by explaining how each system would approach the following issues. When answering, consider the mechanisms used, the relative importance of various economic goals, and the ease with which reasonably satisfactory results can be obtained.
   a) Maintaining full employment.
   b) Achieving a high rate of saving and investment.
   c) Determining the quantities of automobiles, heavy machinery, housing, and clothing to produce.
   d) Setting the wages of college professors, farmers, and factory workers.

4. In the early nineteenth century the United States had some of the same characteristics that we now associate with less-developed countries. How were the problems faced by the United States at that time similar to those of today's LDCs? How were they different?

5. Some LDCs have placed significant constraints on businesses operated by foreigners. What are some of the benefits of foreign manufacturing facilities? What are some of the potential costs?

6. Some LDCs are heavily dependent on exports of one commodity—copper in Chile and oil in Mexico and Nigeria, for example.
   a) What problems are caused by such dependency?
   b) What are the advantages and disadvantages of using trade restrictions to develop local industry?
   c) What are the advantages and disadvantages of trying to develop substitutes for foreign imports?
   d) What are the advantages and disadvantages of trying to develop export industries?
   e) If you were in charge of selecting the best new industry to develop, what factors would influence your choice?

A P P E N D I X

AGGREGATE OUTPUT AND NATIONAL INCOME: 1929–1986

Year	Nominal Gross National Product (current dollars)	Real Gross National Product (1982 dollars)	Net National Product (1982 dollars)	National income (1982 dollars)	Real GNP per capita (1982 dollars)	Annual change in real GNP per capita (1982 dollars)
1929	103.9	709.6	622.8	574.0	5828.0	—
1930	91.1	642.8	554.1	517.7	5243.0	−10.0
1931	76.4	588.1	499.1	454.4	4735.0	−9.7
1932	58.5	509.2	420.9	381.7	4111.0	−13.2
1933	56.0	498.5	412.0	369.0	3952.0	−3.9
1934	65.6	536.7	451.5	409.1	4276.0	8.2
1935	72.8	580.2	496.1	455.8	4632.0	8.3
1936	83.1	662.2	578.3	524.2	5216.0	12.6
1937	91.3	695.3	611.0	564.2	5481.0	5.1
1938	85.4	664.2	579.5	530.0	5164.0	−5.8
1939	91.3	716.6	632.2	575.1	5554.0	7.6
1940	100.4	772.9	687.9	630.7	5850.0	5.3
1941	125.5	909.4	823.1	766.5	6817.0	16.5
1942	159.0	1080.3	993.4	952.8	8011.0	17.5
1943	192.7	1276.2	1190.5	1162.3	9333.0	16.5
1944	211.4	1380.6	1295.7	1242.9	9976.0	6.9
1945	213.4	1354.8	1269.4	1204.9	9682.0	−2.9
1946	212.4	1096.9	1008.9	947.4	7758.0	−19.9
1947	235.2	1066.7	975.0	904.7	7401.0	−4.6
1948	261.6	1108.7	1011.9	950.0	7561.0	2.2
1949	260.4	1109.0	1007.3	933.2	7434.0	−1.7
1950	288.3	1203.7	1097.1	1015.0	7905.0	6.3
1951	333.4	1328.2	1216.4	1123.4	8576.0	8.5
1952	351.6	1380.0	1263.0	1169.0	8759.0	2.1
1953	371.6	1435.3	1313.2	1211.2	8960.0	2.3
1954	372.5	1416.2	1288.8	1183.0	8687.0	−3.0
1955	405.9	1494.9	1362.3	1251.5	9009.0	3.7
1956	428.2	1525.6	1387.3	1284.6	9032.0	0.3
1957	451.0	1551.1	1407.7	1298.7	9019.0	−0.1
1958	456.8	1539.2	1391.5	1276.2	8801.0	−2.4
1959	495.8	1629.1	1477.2	1358.8	9161.0	4.1
1960	515.3	1665.3	1508.9	1390.5	9217.0	0.6
1961	533.8	1708.7	1548.1	1421.8	9302.0	0.9
1962	574.6	1799.4	1634.3	1497.3	9646.0	3.7
1963	606.9	1873.3	1703.0	1561.9	9899.0	2.6
1964	649.8	1973.3	1797.0	1650.2	10284.0	3.9
1965	705.1	2087.6	1903.9	1746.9	10744.0	4.5
1966	772.0	2208.3	2016.1	1840.6	11235.0	4.6
1967	816.4	2271.4	2070.3	1896.2	11431.0	1.7
1968	892.7	2365.6	2155.8	1972.9	11786.0	3.1
1969	963.9	2423.3	2203.4	2019.1	11956.0	1.4
1970	1015.5	2416.2	2186.4	1989.0	11783.0	−1.4
1971	1102.7	2484.8	2245.3	2032.5	11966.0	1.6
1972	1212.8	2608.5	2355.2	2137.3	12428.0	3.9
1973	1359.3	2744.1	2480.5	2255.0	12949.0	4.2
1974	1472.8	2729.3	2453.2	2227.6	12762.0	−1.4
1975	1598.4	2695.0	2408.0	2172.0	12478.0	−2.2
1976	1782.8	2826.7	2529.4	2278.9	12964.0	3.9
1977	1990.5	2958.6	2649.0	2393.3	13434.0	3.6
1978	2249.7	3115.2	2791.5	2526.7	13996.0	4.2
1979	2508.2	3192.4	2851.1	2582.3	14185.0	1.4
1980	2732.0	3187.1	2831.0	2562.6	13995.0	−1.3
1981	3052.6	3248.8	2879.1	2610.4	14123.0	0.9
1982	3166.0	3166.0	2782.8	2518.5	13626.0	−3.5
1983	3405.7	3279.1	2884.7	2603.7	13975.0	2.6
1984	3765.0	3489.9	3082.8	2794.8	14754.0	5.6
1985	3998.1	3585.2	3159.6	2866.8	14963.0	1.4
1986	4206.1	3674.9	3233.9	2917.5	15218.0	1.7

Sources: U.S. Department of Commerce, *The National Income and Product Accounts of the United States, 1929–1982; Survey of Current Business* (various issues).

AGGREGATE EXPENDITURES: 1929–1986

Year	Consumption (1982 dollars)	Investment (1982 dollars)	Government purchases (1982 dollars)	Net exports (1982 dollars)
1929	471.4	139.2	94.2	4.7
1930	439.7	97.5	103.3	2.3
1931	422.1	60.2	106.8	−1.0
1932	384.9	22.6	102.2	−0.5
1933	378.7	22.7	98.5	−1.4
1934	390.5	35.3	110.7	0.1
1935	412.1	60.9	113.0	−5.9
1936	451.6	82.1	132.5	−4.2
1937	467.9	99.9	127.8	−0.3
1938	457.1	63.1	137.9	6.0
1939	480.5	86.0	144.1	6.1
1940	502.6	111.8	150.2	8.2
1941	531.1	138.8	235.6	3.9
1942	527.6	76.7	483.7	−7.7
1943	539.9	50.4	708.9	−23.0
1944	557.1	56.4	790.8	−23.8
1945	592.7	76.6	704.5	−18.9
1946	655.0	178.1	236.9	27.0
1947	666.6	177.9	179.8	42.4
1948	681.8	208.2	199.5	19.2
1949	695.4	168.8	226.0	18.8
1950	733.2	234.9	230.8	4.7
1951	748.7	235.2	329.7	14.6
1952	771.4	211.8	389.9	6.9
1953	802.5	216.6	419.0	−2.7
1954	822.7	212.6	378.4	2.5
1955	873.8	259.8	361.3	0.0
1956	899.8	257.8	363.7	4.3
1957	919.7	243.4	381.1	7.0
1958	932.9	221.4	395.3	−10.3
1959	979.4	270.3	397.7	−18.2
1960	1005.1	260.5	403.7	−4.0
1961	1025.2	259.1	427.1	−2.7
1962	1069.0	288.6	449.4	−7.5
1963	1108.4	307.1	459.8	−1.9
1964	1170.6	325.9	470.8	5.9
1965	1236.4	367.0	487.0	−2.7
1966	1298.9	390.5	532.6	−13.7
1967	1337.7	374.4	576.2	−16.9
1968	1405.9	391.8	597.6	−29.7
1969	1456.7	410.3	591.2	−34.9
1970	1492.0	381.5	572.6	−30.0
1971	1538.8	419.3	566.5	−39.8
1972	1621.9	465.4	570.7	−49.4
1973	1689.6	520.8	565.3	−31.5
1974	1674.0	481.3	573.2	0.8
1975	1711.9	383.3	580.9	18.9
1976	1803.9	453.5	580.3	−11.0
1977	1883.8	521.3	589.1	−35.5
1978	1961.0	576.9	604.1	−26.8
1979	2004.4	575.2	609.1	3.6
1980	2000.4	509.3	620.5	57.0
1981	2024.2	545.5	629.7	49.4
1982	2050.7	447.3	641.7	26.3
1983	2146.0	504.0	649.0	−19.9
1984	2246.3	652.0	675.2	−83.6
1985	2324.5	647.7	721.2	−108.2
1986	2418.7	657.2	746.8	−147.8

Sources: U.S. Department of Commerce, *The National Income and Product Accounts of the United States, 1929–1982; Survey of Current Business* (various issues).

POTENTIAL GNP AND GNP GAP: 1955–1986

Year	Potential GNP (billions of 1982 dollars)	GNP gap	
		(Billions of 1982 dollars)	(Percent of potential GNP)
1929	—	—	—
1930	—	—	—
1931	—	—	—
1932	—	—	—
1933	—	—	—
1934	—	—	—
1935	—	—	—
1936	—	—	—
1937	—	—	—
1938	—	—	—
1939	—	—	—
1940	—	—	—
1941	—	—	—
1942	—	—	—
1943	—	—	—
1944	—	—	—
1945	—	—	—
1946	—	—	—
1947	—	—	—
1948	—	—	—
1949	—	—	—
1950	—	—	—
1951	—	—	—
1952	—	—	—
1953	—	—	—
1954	—	—	—
1955	1465.7	−29.2	−2.0
1956	1510.1	−15.5	1.0
1957	1556.0	4.9	0.3
1958	1606.0	66.8	4.2
1959	1658.3	29.2	1.8
1960	1712.2	46.9	2.7
1961	1768.0	59.3	3.4
1962	1825.6	26.2	1.4
1963	1885.4	12.1	0.6
1964	1925.5	−47.8	−2.5
1965	2023.2	−64.4	−3.2
1966	2096.5	−111.8	−5.3
1967	2172.5	−98.9	−4.6
1968	2251.2	−114.4	−5.1
1969	2332.8	−90.5	−3.9
1970	2416.5	0.3	0.0
1971	2500.0	15.2	0.6
1972	2586.0	−22.5	−0.9
1973	2675.0	−69.1	−2.6
1974	2764.4	35.1	1.3
1975	2846.5	151.5	5.3
1976	2930.1	103.4	3.5
1977	3016.2	57.6	1.9
1978	3104.7	−10.5	−0.3
1979	3195.3	2.9	0.1
1980	3281.3	94.2	2.9
1981	3367.7	118.9	3.5
1982	3456.4	290.4	8.4
1983	3547.5	268.4	7.6
1984	3640.9	151.0	4.1
1985	3736.8	151.6	4.1
1986	3835.2	160.3	4.2

Sources: Potential GNP data based on Robert J. Gordon, *Macroeconomics*, 4th ed., Table A-1. Copyright © 1987 by Robert J. Gordon. Reprinted by permission of Little, Brown and Company. Updated by author. Real GNP used to calculate GNP gap from *Economic Report of the President, 1987*, Table B-2, and *Survey of Current Business* (various issues).

INDUSTRIAL PRODUCTION: 1929–1986

Year	Index of Industrial Production (1967 = 100)
1929	—
1930	—
1931	—
1932	—
1933	—
1934	—
1935	—
1936	—
1937	—
1938	—
1939	16.0
1940	18.4
1941	23.3
1942	26.7
1943	32.4
1944	34.9
1945	29.9
1946	25.8
1947	29.0
1948	30.2
1949	28.6
1950	33.1
1951	35.9
1952	37.2
1953	40.4
1954	38.2
1955	43.0
1956	44.9
1957	45.5
1958	42.6
1959	47.7
1960	48.8
1961	49.1
1962	53.2
1963	56.3
1964	60.1
1965	66.1
1966	72.0
1967	73.5
1968	77.6
1969	81.2
1970	78.5
1971	79.6
1972	87.3
1973	94.4
1974	93.0
1975	84.8
1976	92.6
1977	100.0
1978	106.5
1979	110.7
1980	108.6
1981	111.0
1982	103.1
1983	109.2
1984	121.4
1985	123.8
1986	125.1

Source: Economic Report of the President, 1987 (Table B-45).

PRICE INDEXES: 1929–1986

Year	GNP deflator (1982 = 100)	Annual changes in GNP deflator (percent per year)	Consumer Price Index (1967 = 100)	Annual changes in CPI (percent per year)	Misery Index (change in CPI plus unemployment rate)
1929	14.6	—	51.3	—	—
1930	14.2	−2.7	50.0	−2.5	0.7
1931	13.0	−8.5	45.6	−8.8	−0.1
1932	11.5	−11.5	40.9	−10.3	5.6
1933	11.2	−2.6	38.8	−5.1	18.5
1934	12.2	8.9	40.1	3.4	28.3
1935	12.5	2.5	41.1	2.5	24.2
1936	12.5	0.0	41.5	1.0	21.1
1937	13.1	4.8	43.0	3.6	20.5
1938	12.9	−1.5	42.2	−1.9	12.4
1939	12.7	−1.6	41.6	−1.4	17.6
1940	13.0	2.4	42.0	1.0	18.2
1941	13.8	6.2	44.1	5.0	19.6
1942	14.7	6.5	48.8	10.7	20.6
1943	15.1	2.7	51.8	6.1	10.8
1944	15.3	1.3	52.7	1.7	3.6
1945	15.7	2.6	53.9	2.3	3.5
1946	19.4	23.6	58.5	8.5	10.4
1947	22.1	13.9	66.9	14.4	18.3
1948	23.6	6.8	72.1	7.8	11.6
1949	23.5	−0.4	71.4	−1.0	4.9
1950	23.9	1.7	72.1	1.0	6.3
1951	25.1	5.0	77.8	7.9	11.2
1952	25.5	1.6	79.5	2.2	5.2
1953	25.9	1.6	80.1	0.8	3.7
1954	26.3	1.5	80.5	0.5	6.0
1955	27.2	3.4	80.2	−0.4	4.0
1956	28.1	3.3	81.4	1.5	5.6
1957	29.1	3.6	84.3	3.6	7.9
1958	29.7	2.1	86.6	2.7	9.5
1959	30.4	2.4	87.3	0.8	6.3
1960	30.9	1.6	88.7	1.6	7.1
1961	31.2	1.0	89.6	1.0	7.7
1962	31.9	2.2	90.6	1.1	6.6
1963	32.4	1.6	91.7	1.2	6.9
1964	32.9	1.5	92.9	1.3	6.5
1965	33.8	2.7	94.5	1.7	6.2
1966	35.0	3.6	97.2	2.9	6.7
1967	35.9	2.6	100.0	2.9	6.7
1968	37.7	5.0	104.2	4.2	7.8
1969	39.8	5.6	109.8	5.4	8.9
1970	42.0	5.5	116.3	5.9	10.8
1971	44.4	5.7	121.3	4.3	10.2
1972	46.5	4.7	125.3	3.3	8.9
1973	49.5	6.5	133.1	6.2	11.1
1974	54.0	9.1	147.7	11.0	16.6
1975	59.3	9.8	161.2	9.1	17.6
1976	63.1	6.4	170.5	5.8	13.5
1977	67.3	6.7	181.5	6.5	13.6
1978	72.2	7.3	195.4	7.7	13.8
1979	78.6	8.9	217.4	11.3	17.1
1980	85.7	9.0	246.8	13.5	20.6
1981	94.0	9.7	272.4	10.4	18.0
1982	100.0	6.4	289.1	6.1	15.8
1983	103.9	3.9	298.4	3.2	12.8
1984	107.9	3.8	311.1	4.3	11.8
1985	111.5	3.3	322.2	3.6	10.8
1986	114.5	2.7	328.4	1.9	8.9

Sources: *Economic Report of the President, 1987* and *Survey of Current Business* (various issues) for GNP deflator; Bureau of Labor Statistics for Consumer Price Index.

MONEY SUPPLY AND VELOCITY: 1929–1986

Year	M-1 Billions of dollars	M-1 Percentage change	M-1 Velocity (% of nominal GNP)	M-2 Billions of dollars	M-2 Percentage change	M-2 Velocity (% of nominal GNP)
1929	26.6	—	3.9	46.6	—	2.2
1930	25.8	−3.0	3.5	45.7	−1.9	2.0
1931	24.1	−6.6	3.2	42.7	−6.6	1.8
1932	21.1	−12.4	2.8	36.0	−15.7	1.6
1933	19.9	−5.7	2.8	32.2	−10.6	1.7
1934	21.9	10.0	3.0	34.4	6.8	1.9
1935	25.9	18.3	2.8	39.1	13.7	1.9
1936	29.5	13.9	2.8	43.5	11.2	1.9
1937	30.9	4.8	3.0	45.7	5.1	2.0
1938	30.5	−1.3	2.8	45.5	−0.4	1.9
1939	34.2	12.1	2.7	49.3	8.4	1.9
1940	39.7	16.1	2.5	55.2	12.0	1.8
1941	46.5	17.1	2.7	62.5	13.2	2.0
1942	55.4	19.1	2.9	71.2	13.9	2.2
1943	72.2	30.3	2.7	89.9	26.3	2.1
1944	85.3	18.1	2.5	106.8	18.8	2.0
1945	99.2	16.3	2.2	126.6	18.5	1.7
1946	106.5	7.4	2.0	138.7	9.6	1.5
1947	111.8	5.0	2.1	146.0	5.3	1.6
1948	112.3	0.4	2.3	148.1	1.4	1.8
1949	111.2	−1.0	2.3	147.5	−0.4	1.8
1950	114.1	2.6	2.5	150.8	2.2	1.9
1951	119.2	4.5	2.8	156.5	3.8	2.1
1952	125.2	5.0	2.8	164.9	5.4	2.1
1953	128.2	2.5	2.9	171.2	3.8	2.2
1954	130.3	1.6	2.9	177.2	3.5	2.1
1955	134.5	3.2	3.0	183.7	3.7	2.2
1956	136.0	1.1	3.1	186.9	1.7	2.3
1957	136.8	0.6	3.3	191.8	2.6	2.4
1958	138.4	1.2	3.3	201.1	4.8	2.3
1959	141.4	3.6	3.4	293.3	4.7	1.6
1960	141.4	0.0	3.6	304.3	3.8	1.7
1961	144.3	2.1	3.7	324.9	6.8	1.6
1962	147.9	2.5	3.9	350.2	7.8	1.6
1963	152.4	3.1	4.0	379.7	8.4	1.6
1964	158.3	3.9	4.1	409.4	7.8	1.6
1965	165.1	4.2	4.3	442.6	8.1	1.6
1966	172.7	4.6	4.5	471.5	6.5	1.6
1967	179.6	4.0	4.5	503.7	6.8	1.6
1968	192.1	7.0	4.6	545.4	8.3	1.6
1969	203.5	5.9	4.7	579.1	6.2	1.7
1970	211.2	3.8	4.8	603.2	4.2	1.7
1971	225.2	6.8	4.9	676.4	12.1	1.6
1972	241.6	7.1	5.0	760.9	12.5	1.6
1973	259.2	7.3	5.2	836.2	9.9	1.6
1974	272.2	5.0	5.4	887.2	6.1	1.7
1975	285.0	4.7	5.6	970.1	9.3	1.6
1976	301.0	5.6	5.9	1095.7	12.9	1.6
1977	324.0	7.6	6.1	1234.4	12.7	1.6
1978	350.5	8.2	6.4	1339.6	8.5	1.7
1979	377.6	7.7	6.6	1450.2	8.3	1.7
1980	401.1	6.2	6.8	1566.7	8.0	1.7
1981	429.5	7.1	7.1	1714.6	9.4	1.8
1982	457.6	6.6	6.9	1874.5	9.3	1.7
1983	508.9	11.2	6.7	2109.3	12.5	1.6
1984	544.5	7.0	6.9	2277.9	8.0	1.7
1985	593.9	9.1	6.7	2484.6	9.1	1.6
1986	672.5	13.2	6.3	2683.2	8.0	1.6

Sources: Data from 1929 to 1958 from U.S. Department of Commerce, *Historical Statistics of the United States: Colonial Times to 1970;* data from 1959 to 1986 from Federal Reserve Bank of Boston.

FEDERAL GOVERNMENT BUDGET: 1929–1986

| | Actual federal government budget | | | | |
| | (in billions of 1982 dollars) | | | (as % of real GNP) | |
Year	Receipts	Expenditures	Budget surplus	Expenditures	Budget surplus
1929	26.0	18.5	7.5	2.6	1.1
1930	21.8	19.7	2.1	3.1	0.3
1931	16.2	32.3	−16.2	5.5	−2.7
1932	15.7	27.8	−12.2	5.5	−2.4
1933	24.1	35.7	−11.6	7.2	−2.3
1934	29.5	52.5	−23.0	9.8	−4.3
1935	32.0	52.8	−20.8	9.1	−3.6
1936	40.8	69.6	−28.8	10.5	−4.3
1937	54.2	57.3	−3.1	8.2	−0.4
1938	50.4	67.4	−17.1	10.2	−2.6
1939	53.5	70.9	−17.3	9.9	−2.4
1940	66.9	76.9	−10.0	10.0	−1.3
1941	112.3	148.6	−36.2	16.3	−4.0
1942	156.5	381.6	−225.2	35.3	−20.8
1943	260.3	568.9	−308.6	44.6	−24.2
1944	268.6	624.8	−356.2	45.3	−25.8
1945	272.0	539.5	−267.5	39.8	−19.7
1946	209.8	191.8	18.0	17.5	1.6
1947	199.5	139.4	60.2	13.1	5.7
1948	186.0	150.4	35.6	13.6	3.2
1949	167.7	178.7	−11.1	16.1	−1.0
1950	210.9	172.4	38.5	14.3	3.2
1951	257.4	231.5	25.9	17.4	1.9
1952	265.5	280.0	−14.5	20.3	−1.1
1953	271.8	299.6	−27.8	20.9	−1.9
1954	244.1	267.3	−23.2	18.9	−1.6
1955	268.8	252.2	16.5	16.9	1.1
1956	279.4	258.0	21.4	16.9	1.4
1957	283.5	275.6	7.9	17.8	0.5
1958	267.0	301.7	−34.7	19.6	−2.3
1959	298.0	301.6	−3.6	18.5	−0.2
1960	313.6	303.9	9.7	18.2	0.6
1961	317.3	329.8	−12.5	19.3	−0.7
1962	336.1	349.2	−13.2	19.4	−0.7
1963	356.8	355.9	0.9	19.0	0.0
1964	353.2	363.2	−10.0	18.4	−0.5
1965	372.2	370.7	1.5	17.8	0.1
1966	410.0	415.1	−5.1	18.8	−0.2
1967	425.1	461.8	−36.8	20.3	−1.6
1968	469.2	485.1	−15.9	20.5	−0.7
1969	501.8	480.7	21.1	19.8	0.9
1970	465.2	494.8	−29.5	20.5	−1.2
1971	456.5	506.3	−49.8	20.4	−2.0
1972	499.4	535.5	−36.1	20.5	−1.4
1973	532.7	544.0	−11.3	19.8	−0.4
1974	544.3	565.7	−21.5	20.7	−0.8
1975	497.3	614.2	−116.9	22.8	−4.3
1976	539.0	623.9	−84.9	22.1	−3.0
1977	570.7	639.1	−68.4	21.6	−2.3
1978	611.4	651.9	−40.6	20.9	−1.3
1979	642.5	663.0	−20.5	20.8	−0.6
1980	646.2	717.7	−71.5	22.5	−2.2
1981	680.3	748.2	−67.9	23.0	−2.1
1982	635.3	781.2	−145.9	24.7	−4.6
1983	635.1	804.5	−169.4	24.5	−5.2
1984	673.3	830.9	−157.6	23.8	−4.5
1985	705.7	883.3	−177.7	24.6	−5.0
1986	722.1	899.8	−177.7	24.5	−4.8

Budget figures were deflated using the GNP deflator.

Sources: U.S. Department of Commerce, *The National Income and Product Accounts of the United States, 1929–1982; Survey of Current Business* (various issues).

FEDERAL GOVERNMENT BUDGET: 1929–1986

Year	Full-employment budget (in billions of 1982 dollars)			(as % of potential GNP)	
	Receipts	Expenditures	Budget surplus	Expenditures	Budget surplus
1929	—	—	—	—	—
1930	—	—	—	—	—
1931	—	—	—	—	—
1932	—	—	—	—	—
1933	—	—	—	—	—
1934	—	—	—	—	—
1935	—	—	—	—	—
1936	—	—	—	—	—
1937	—	—	—	—	—
1938	—	—	—	—	—
1939	—	—	—	—	—
1940	—	—	—	—	—
1941	—	—	—	—	—
1942	—	—	—	—	—
1943	—	—	—	—	—
1944	—	—	—	—	—
1945	—	—	—	—	—
1946	—	—	—	—	—
1947	—	—	—	—	—
1948	—	—	—	—	—
1949	—	—	—	—	—
1950	—	—	—	—	—
1951	—	—	—	—	—
1952	—	—	—	—	—
1953	—	—	—	—	—
1954	—	—	—	—	—
1955	259.9	251.5	8.4	17.2	0.6
1956	274.5	258.0	16.5	17.1	1.1
1957	284.5	276.3	8.2	17.8	0.5
1958	285.1	297.3	−12.2	18.5	−0.8
1959	298.4	301.0	−2.6	18.2	−0.2
1960	319.1	303.6	15.5	17.7	0.9
1961	326.3	326.9	−0.6	18.5	0.0
1962	336.7	349.5	−12.9	19.1	−0.7
1963	355.2	356.2	−0.9	18.9	0.0
1964	344.7	364.7	−20.1	18.9	−1.0
1965	353.8	374.3	−20.4	18.5	−1.0
1966	380.0	421.1	−41.1	20.1	−2.0
1967	399.7	468.0	−68.2	21.5	−3.1
1968	439.3	492.8	−53.6	21.9	−2.4
1969	478.9	488.9	−10.1	21.0	−0.4
1970	470.2	496.0	−25.7	20.5	−1.1
1971	467.3	505.2	−37.8	20.2	−1.5
1972	502.2	535.5	−33.3	20.7	−1.3
1973	518.4	545.7	−27.3	20.4	−1.0
1974	550.4	567.0	−16.7	20.5	−0.6
1975	531.4	603.7	−72.3	21.2	−2.5
1976	562.9	616.0	−53.1	21.0	−1.8
1977	582.5	634.0	−51.6	21.0	−1.7
1978	604.8	651.1	−46.3	21.0	−1.5
1979	638.2	663.0	−24.8	20.7	−0.8
1980	668.0	711.7	−43.6	21.7	−1.3
1981	710.0	739.3	−29.3	22.0	−0.9
1982	705.2	764.7	−59.5	22.1	−1.7
1983	697.9	791.3	−93.5	22.3	−2.6
1984	700.0	825.9	−125.9	22.7	−3.5
1985	726.7	879.8	−153.1	23.5	−4.1
1986	740.6	897.5	−156.9	23.4	−4.1

Sources: Potential GNP and full-employment budget from Robert J. Gordon, *Macroeconomics*, 4th ed., Table A-1. Copyright © 1987 by Robert J. Gordon. Reprinted by permission of Little, Brown and Company. Updated by author. Real GNP and actual expenditures from *Economic Report of the President, 1987* and U.S. Department of Commerce, *Survey of Current Business* (various issues).

STATE AND LOCAL GOVERNMENT BUDGET: 1929–1986

	Actual state and local government budget (in billions of 1982 dollars)			(as % of real GNP)	
Year	Receipts	Expenditures	Budget surplus	Expenditures	Budget surplus
1929	52.1	53.4	−1.4	7.5	−0.2
1930	54.9	59.2	−4.2	9.2	−0.7
1931	59.2	65.4	−6.2	11.1	−1.0
1932	63.5	66.1	−2.6	13.0	−0.5
1933	64.3	64.3	0.0	12.9	0.0
1934	70.5	66.4	4.1	12.4	0.8
1935	72.8	68.8	4.0	11.9	0.7
1936	68.8	64.8	4.0	9.8	0.6
1937	69.5	64.1	5.3	9.2	0.8
1938	72.1	69.8	2.3	10.5	0.4
1939	75.6	75.6	0.0	10.5	0.0
1940	76.9	71.5	5.4	9.3	0.7
1941	75.4	65.9	9.4	7.3	1.0
1942	72.1	59.9	12.2	5.5	1.1
1943	72.2	55.6	16.6	4.4	1.3
1944	72.5	55.6	17.0	4.0	1.2
1945	73.9	57.3	16.6	4.2	1.2
1946	67.0	57.2	9.8	5.2	0.9
1947	69.7	65.2	4.5	6.1	0.4
1948	75.0	74.6	0.4	6.7	0.0
1949	83.0	86.0	−3.0	7.8	−0.3
1950	89.1	94.1	−5.0	7.8	−0.4
1951	93.2	95.2	−2.0	7.2	−0.1
1952	99.6	100.0	−0.4	7.2	0.0
1953	105.8	105.4	0.4	7.3	0.0
1954	110.3	114.8	−4.6	8.1	−0.3
1955	116.5	121.0	−4.4	8.1	−0.3
1956	124.6	127.8	−3.2	8.4	−0.2
1957	132.3	136.8	−4.5	8.8	−0.3
1958	141.4	149.5	−8.1	9.7	−0.5
1959	153.3	154.6	−1.3	9.5	−0.1
1960	161.8	161.5	0.3	9.7	0.0
1961	173.4	174.7	−1.3	10.2	−0.1
1962	183.7	182.4	1.3	10.1	0.1
1963	195.7	194.1	1.5	10.4	0.1
1964	212.2	209.1	3.0	10.6	0.2
1965	223.4	223.4	0.0	10.7	0.0
1966	243.4	242.0	1.4	11.0	0.1
1967	262.1	265.2	−3.1	11.7	−0.1
1968	286.2	285.9	0.3	12.1	0.0
1969	303.5	299.7	3.8	12.4	0.2
1970	323.3	319.0	4.3	13.2	0.2
1971	345.9	340.1	5.9	13.7	0.2
1972	385.6	356.6	29.0	13.7	1.1
1973	396.8	369.5	27.3	13.5	1.0
1974	394.6	381.3	13.3	14.0	0.5
1975	404.0	396.6	7.4	14.7	0.3
1976	428.1	404.0	24.1	14.3	0.9
1977	445.9	405.9	40.0	13.7	1.4
1978	457.5	417.2	40.3	13.4	1.3
1979	452.0	416.9	35.1	13.1	1.1
1980	455.1	423.8	31.3	13.3	1.0
1981	452.8	416.4	36.4	12.8	1.1
1982	449.4	414.3	35.1	13.1	1.1
1983	469.4	423.7	45.7	12.9	1.4
1984	501.2	437.8	63.4	12.5	1.8
1985	517.9	471.6	46.4	13.2	1.3
1986	542.3	487.2	55.0	13.3	1.5

Budget figures were deflated using the GNP deflator.

Sources: U.S. Department of Commerce, The National Income and Product Accounts of the United States, 1929–1982 and *Survey of Current Business* (various issues).

CIVILIAN POPULATION AND LABOR FORCE: 1929–1986

Year	Civilian noninstitutional population aged 16 and over (millions)	Civilian labor force (millions)	Civilian employment/ population ratio (percent)	Civilian unemployment rate (percent)
1929	85.6	49.2	55.6	3.2
1930	87.1	49.8	52.2	8.7
1931	88.2	50.4	48.1	15.9
1932	89.3	51.0	43.6	23.6
1933	90.5	51.6	42.8	24.9
1934	91.7	52.2	44.6	21.7
1935	92.9	52.9	45.5	20.1
1936	94.1	53.4	47.2	16.9
1937	95.2	54.0	48.6	14.3
1938	96.5	54.6	45.8	19.0
1939	97.8	55.2	46.8	17.2
1940	100.4	55.6	47.6	14.6
1941	101.5	55.9	50.4	9.9
1942	102.6	56.4	54.5	4.7
1943	103.7	55.5	57.6	1.9
1944	104.6	54.6	57.9	1.2
1945	105.6	53.9	56.1	1.9
1946	106.5	57.5	53.6	3.9
1947	101.8	59.4	56.0	3.9
1948	103.1	60.6	56.6	3.8
1949	104.0	61.3	55.4	5.9
1950	105.0	62.2	56.1	5.3
1951	104.6	62.0	57.3	3.3
1952	105.2	62.1	57.3	3.0
1953	107.1	63.0	57.1	2.9
1954	108.3	63.6	55.5	5.5
1955	109.7	65.0	56.7	4.4
1956	111.0	66.6	57.5	4.1
1957	112.3	66.9	57.1	4.3
1958	113.7	67.6	55.4	6.8
1959	115.3	68.4	56.0	5.5
1960	117.2	69.6	56.1	5.5
1961	118.8	70.5	55.4	6.7
1962	120.1	70.6	55.5	5.5
1963	122.4	71.8	55.4	5.7
1964	124.5	73.1	55.7	5.2
1965	126.5	74.5	56.2	4.5
1966	128.1	75.8	56.9	3.8
1967	129.9	77.3	57.3	3.8
1968	132.0	78.7	57.5	3.6
1969	134.3	80.7	58.0	3.5
1970	137.1	82.8	57.4	4.9
1971	140.2	84.4	56.6	5.9
1972	144.1	87.0	57.0	5.6
1973	147.1	89.4	57.8	4.9
1974	150.1	91.9	57.8	5.6
1975	153.2	93.8	56.1	8.5
1976	156.2	96.2	56.8	7.7
1977	159.0	99.0	57.9	7.1
1978	161.9	102.3	59.3	6.1
1979	164.9	105.0	59.9	5.8
1980	167.7	106.9	59.2	7.1
1981	170.1	108.7	59.0	7.6
1982	172.2	110.2	57.8	9.7
1983	174.2	111.6	57.9	9.6
1984	176.4	113.5	59.5	7.5
1985	178.2	115.5	60.1	7.2
1986	180.6	117.8	60.7	7.0

Data from 1929–1946 are for persons 14 years of age and over; data from 1947 to 1986 are for persons 16 years of age and over.
Source: U.S. Department of Labor, *Employment and Earnings* (various issues).

G L O S S A R Y

A

Ability-to-pay principle. A theory of taxation that states that individuals should be taxed in proportion to their income or some other measure of ability to pay.

Absolute advantage. The ability to produce a good or service with fewer resources; refers only to relative productivity.

Absolute poverty approach. Poverty defined by an income below the level necessary to maintain a minimum standard of living.

Accounting identities. Relationships between macroeconomic variables that are always true by definition.

Accounting profit. The difference between revenues and explicit costs, ignoring implicit costs.

Action lag. The delay between when a problem is recognized and when policy actions are taken.

Activists. Economists who believe it necessary, desirable, and practical to use discretionary monetary and fiscal policies to stabilize the economy.

Affirmative action programs. Government requirements that employers adopt programs and make extraordinary efforts to recruit, hire, and promote individuals from specific groups, such as women, blacks, and Hispanics, that have been subjected to past economic or institutional discrimination.

Aggregate demand (AD). Demand for all goods and services in the economy; relationship between total quantity of goods and services demanded and general price level.

Aggregate expenditures (AE). Total expenditures on final goods by all sectors of the economy during a particular period of time.

Aggregate output. The total quantity of all goods and services produced in the economy in a given period of time.

Aggregate supply (AS). Supply of all goods and services in the economy; relationship between total quantity of goods and services supplied and general price level.

Allocative efficiency. Producing the combination of goods and services that satisfies society's wants to the greatest degree.

"All-other-things-unchanged" assumption. The assumption commonly made in demand-and-supply analysis that all determinants of quantity demanded and quantity supplied, except price, are held constant.

Antitrust policy. Government actions that attempt to control market power and monopolistic behavior and to foster competitive behavior.

Arbitration. The settlement of differences between two parties (such as a union and management) by an impartial third party, the arbitrator, whose decision is legally binding on the other two parties.

Assets. Items of value.

Automatic stabilizers. Taxes and expenditures that automatically change when economic activity changes. Stabilizers cause a decrease in the actual budget balance when GNP falls and an increase when GNP rises. These changes reduce cyclical changes in aggregate demand. Important stabilizers are income taxes, unemployment compensation, and welfare.

Autonomous consumption. The portion of consumption that is independent of the level of income. A change in a factor other than income causes a change in autonomous consumption and results in a shift in a consumption line.

Average-cost pricing. A price-setting option for rate regulation whereby price is set equal to average total cost (P = ATC), including an allowance for normal profit; the most commonly used price-setting mechanism.

Average fixed cost (AFC). Total fixed costs divided by the quantity of goods or services produced (total product). Mathematically, AFC = TFC ÷ Q.

Average product (AP). The ratio of total quantity produced (total product) to units of variable resources used to produce those goods. Mathematically, AP = Q ÷ Units of variable resources.

Average propensity to consume (APC). The ratio of consumption to income at some specified level of income; indicates the proportion of a specified level of income that will be spent on consumption.

Average tax rate. The proportion of income paid in taxes; the ratio of taxes paid to taxable income.

Average total cost (ATC). Also called *unit cost*; calculated as total costs divided by the quantity of goods or services produced (total product). Mathematically, ATC = TC ÷ Q or ATC = AVC + AFC.

Average variable cost (AVC). Also called *unit variable cost*; calculated as total variable costs divided by the quantity of goods or services produced (total product). Mathematically, AVC = TVC ÷ Q.

B

Balance on capital account. The net flow of funds used to purchase physical and financial assets; a positive balance indicates that purchases of domestic assets by foreigners exceed purchases of foreign assets by domestic residents.

Balance on current account. Net exports of goods and services less net transfers (gifts and foreign aid) to foreign residents and foreign governments; a negative balance indicates that imports plus transfers to domestic residents exceed exports plus transfers to foreign residents.

Balance on goods and services. The difference between the values of exports and imports of both goods and services.

Barriers to entry. Legal, technological, or economic factors that make it impossible or very difficult for a new firm to enter a particular market; examples include control of key resources, economies of scale, and government patents or licenses.

Barter. An exchange of one product or service for another; an exchange not involving money.

Benefits-received principle. A theory of taxation that states that individuals should be taxed in proportion to the benefits they receive from government goods and services.

Bilateral monopoly. A model of a labor market in which market power exists on both sides of the market; a union with control over the supply of labor and an employer with market power demanding labor.

Bonds. IOUs of a business or government representing a promise to pay a specified sum of interest at regular intervals (usually every four or six months) for a specified period of time. At the end of the loan period, the borrower is obligated to repay the original amount loaned.

Budget balance. The difference between government receipts (taxes and fees) and expenditures (purchases, transfers, and interest payments on national debt).

Budget constraint. In indifference-curve analysis, a line indicating the combinations of two goods that a buyer can purchase, given the price of each good and the buyer's income.

Budget deficit. A negative budget balance, when expenditures exceed receipts.

Budget surplus. A positive budget balance, when receipts exceed expenditures.

Business cycle. The recurring but irregular swings in aggregate economic activity. A complete cycle has four phases: recession, trough, recovery, and peak.

Business firm. An organization that produces goods and services for sale.

C

Capital/labor ratio. The average quantity of capital resources per worker, calculated by dividing the stock of capital by the number of employed workers.

Capital resources. The buildings, machinery, roads, transportation equipment, and other long-lasting items that can be used to produce goods and services. Also called *capital goods*.

Cartel. A form of oligopoly in which firms formally agree to establish a common price, in effect acting as a monopoly.

Causation. The presumption that a change in one factor causes a change in another factor with which it is statistically correlated.

Ceiling price. A legal maximum price established by government for a specific market.

Checking deposits. Funds held in checking accounts by banks; may be transferred by writing a check; included in the M-1 definition of money.

Circular-flow model. A model of a market economy that shows the interaction of households and businesses in product and resource markets.

Classical economic theory. Macroeconomic theories of economists in the late 1800s and early 1900s who assumed that interest rates, wages, and prices were flexible; this theory predicts that the economy will tend to operate at full employment.

Classical quantity theory. The proposition of the classical economists that changes in the money supply cause proportional changes in the price level; based on the equation of exchange (M × V = P × Q) assuming velocity (V) is constant and real GNP (Q) equals potential GNP.

Closed shop. A workplace in which the employer is obligated to hire only union members; severely limited by the Taft–Hartley Act.

Collective bargaining. The process by which a union and management negotiate a mutually acceptable contract and define the meanings of contract terms.

Commodity money. An item used as a medium of exchange that also has significant value for other uses.

Comparative advantage. The ability to produce a good or service at a smaller opportunity cost; refers to relative efficiency.

Competitive resource market. A resource market in which no individual buyer or seller has any market power, resources move freely, and buyers and sellers have perfect information on available alternatives.

Complements. Goods that can be used with other goods, such as hot dogs and hot-dog rolls. When two goods are complements, an increase in the price of one leads to a decrease in demand for the other.

Conglomerate merger. A merger between firms that otherwise have no economic relationship; a merger that is neither horizontal nor vertical.

Constant-cost industry. An industry in which entry and exit of firms has no effect on product costs; characterized by a horizontal long-run supply curve.

Constant returns to scale. A situation in which long-run average cost is constant; implies that large and small plants have equal technical efficiency.

Consumer price index (CPI). A price index reflecting changes in the prices of consumer goods; involves the use of a constant market-basket approach.

Consumer products. Goods such as autos, food, appliances, and movies, and services such as health care that directly satisfy consumer wants.

Consumer surplus. The difference between the total benefits buyers receive and the total expenditures they make for all units of a product they consume.

Consumption expenditures (C). Expenditures of households on final goods during a particular period of time.

Consumption schedule. A table showing the level of consumption expenditures at various levels of disposable income.

Contestable market. A market with costless and unrestricted entry and exit.

Contractionary gap. When potential GNP exceeds actual GNP; a positive GNP gap. When the actual unemployment rate is greater than the natural rate of unemployment.

Contractionary policies. Changes in fiscal and/or monetary policies that decrease aggregate demand. Higher taxes and lower spending are contractionary fiscal policies; raising the required reserve ratio and selling government securities are contractionary monetary policies.

Contracts theory. A view of employment based on the existence of explicit or implicit contracts defining worker–employer relationships. Contracts provide long-term benefits to both workers and employers but fix nominal wages, slowing short-run adjustments in wages.

Corporation. A firm created as a legal entity separate from the persons who established it. It is usually owned by many individuals, whose liability is limited to their investment in the firm.

Correlation. The statistical relationship between two factors and the extent to which changes in one factor are accompanied by changes in the other.

Cost-push inflation. Increases in the price level caused by decreases in aggregate supply. Most economists believe that sustained decreases in aggregate supply are unlikely.

Craft union. A union of workers sharing a common skill, trade, or profession.

Cross elasticity of demand. A measure of the responsiveness of quantity demanded for one product to a change in the price of another product, usually expressed as the percentage change in quantity demanded for one product divided by the percentage change in the price of another product.

Crowding-out effect. A decrease in investment and consumption resulting from the increase in interest rates caused by expansionary fiscal policies (holding the money supply constant). This effect is strongest when the economy is close to potential GNP, and it reduces the effect of expansionary fiscal policies.

Currency appreciation. An increase in the exchange rate for the domestic currency (for example, from 150 to 160 yen per dollar); each unit of the domestic currency buys more units of the foreign currency; makes imports from foreign countries less expensive to domestic residents but exports to foreign countries more expensive to foreign residents.

Currency depreciation. A decline in the exchange rate for the domestic currency (for example, from 150 to 140 yen per dollar); each unit of the domestic currency buys fewer units of the foreign currency; makes imports from foreign countries more expensive to domestic residents but exports to foreign countries less expensive to foreign residents.

Cyclical unemployment. Unemployment resulting from decreases in aggregate economic output. Cyclical unemployment increases during recessions and decreases during recoveries.

D

Demand. All the quantities of a product that individuals are both willing and able to buy at every possible price during a specified period of time.

Demand curve. A graphic representation of the demand schedule; the demand curve always slopes downward and to the right.

Demand function. An algebraic expression showing how quantity demanded is affected by market price and other factors influencing demand.

Demand-pull inflation. Increases in the price level caused by increases in aggregate demand.

Demand schedule. A table showing quantities of a product that consumers are willing and able to buy at various prices during a specified period of time.

Dependent variable. In any given relationship, an element that is affected by a change in the value of an independent variable.

Deposit multiplier. The ultimate change in checking deposits (bank money) caused by a $1 initial change in bank reserves; in a simple banking system, equal to 1 ÷ Required reserve ratio.

Depreciation (capital consumption allowance). An estimate of that part of the original cost of capital goods, such as machinery and buildings, that has been used up or worn out during a specific period of time. A business cost representing the value of capital resources used to produce goods; the fractional cost charged each year over the life of the resource to reflect both physical wear and tear and obsolescence. Unlike other costs, no payment is made for depreciation.

Devaluation. A deliberate, planned reduction in the exchange rate under a system of fixed exchange rates.

Developed economy. An economy that is industrialized, has relatively high standards of living, and has sophisticated institutions (government, education, transportation, and communication).

Diminishing marginal returns. A situation in which each additional unit of a variable resource has a smaller marginal product than the previous unit; total product increases, but at a decreasing rate.

Discouraged workers. Individuals who are out of work and who currently are not looking for work because they believe that they cannot find it. They are not officially classified as unemployed.

Discretionary fiscal policy. Deliberate changes made in elements of the federal government's budget—taxes, transfer payments, and/or government purchases of goods and services—to affect the level of aggregate demand. The aim of such policies is to achieve macroeconomic stabilization— full employment and stable prices.

Discretionary policies. Deliberate changes in monetary and/or fiscal policies to counteract cyclical changes in economic activity, that is, to reduce or eliminate expansionary and contractionary gaps. Also called countercyclical policies.

Diseconomies of scale. A situation in which long-run average cost increases as a firm increases the size (or scale) of its plant and output; implies that larger plants are less technically efficient than smaller plants.

Disinflation. A decline in the rate of increase of the general price level; the price level continues to rise, but more slowly.

Disposable income (DI). Income received by households in a particular period of time and available to be spent or saved; household income after taxes have been deducted and transfer payments have been added.

Dividends. The portion of a corporation's profits paid out to its shareholders.

E

Economic development. The process of changing economic, social, and political systems in order to sustain economic growth and overcome mass poverty.

Economic discrimination. Income inequality caused by hiring, firing, promoting, or paying a wage differential on the basis of some factor, such as race, sex, or age, that has no direct relationship to marginal productivity.

Economic growth. An increase in society's production possibilities.

Economic model. A simplified verbal, tabular, graphic, or mathematical representation of a real economy that is used to analyze and predict how the economy would work under the specified conditions.

Economic profit. The difference between revenues and the full opportunity costs of all resources used, including both explicit and implicit costs.

Economic rent. Payment for a resource in excess of the real opportunity cost of that resource.

Economics. The study of how individuals and societies, faced with the problem of scarcity, choose how to produce, exchange, and consume goods and services.

Economic system. The institutions and mechanisms used to determine what and how to produce and who will receive the goods and services produced.

Economies of scale. A situation in which long-run average cost decreases as a firm increases the size (or scale) of its plant and output; implies that larger plants are more technically efficient than small plants if large quantities of goods are produced.

Equation of exchange. The identity of total spending and nominal GNP, or $Ms \times V = P \times Q$.

Equilibrium price. The price at which quantity supplied equals quantity demanded; graphically, the point of intersection of the demand and supply curves.

Equimarginal principle. The principle that for equilibrium to exist, the ratio of extra benefits to extra costs for each product (or resource) must be equal. For consumer choice it means that for each product consumed, buyers will receive the same marginal utility per dollar. Mathematically,

$$\frac{\text{Marginal utility of product A}}{\text{Price of product A}} = \frac{\text{Marginal utility of product B}}{\text{Price of product B}}$$

Equity. Distributing goods and services in a manner considered by society to be fair.

Exchange rate. The price of one currency in terms of another; the quantity of one currency that must be given up to obtain a unit of another currency (for example, 150 yen per dollar).

Expansionary gap. When actual GNP exceeds potential GNP; a negative GNP gap. When actual unemployment is below the natural rate of unemployment.

Expansionary policies. Changes in fiscal and/or monetary policies that increase aggregate demand. Lower taxes and higher spending are expansionary fiscal policies; reducing the required reserve ratio and buying government securities are expansionary monetary policies.

Explicit costs. Costs involving direct payment for resources used by a firm. The only costs considered in calculating accounting profit.

Exports (X). Expenditures made by foreign households, businesses, and governments for goods produced domestically. Exports must be added to aggregate domestic expenditures when measuring GNP; they represent spending to purchase domestically produced goods.

Extensive growth. Economic growth achieved by increasing the quantity of economic resources, such as labor and capital resources.

External benefits. Benefits from a product received by individuals other than those who demand and supply it.

External costs. Costs of a product that are borne by individuals other than those who demand and supply it.

Externalities. Benefits and costs from any product that affect individuals other than those who demand and supply the product.

F

Fallacy of composition. Incorrectly concluding that what is true of the part is also true of the whole.

Fallacy of division. Incorrectly concluding that what is true of the whole is also true of every part.

Final goods. Products and services that are (or will be) sold to their ultimate user. GNP is a measure of the value of final goods produced.

Financial markets. Markets for funds used to make investments and to finance consumption. Markets in which lenders supply and borrowers demand loanable funds. In these markets, dollars saved become dollars invested.

Fixed costs. Costs associated with fixed resources; they are constant in the short run. Examples include rental payments on buildings, interest paid on debt, and property taxes.

Fixed (or pegged) exchange rates. A system in which exchange rates are not allowed to adjust in response to changes in demand for and supply of currency.

Fixed investment. Expenditures by businesses for capital resources, such as new plants, equipment, or commercial buildings, and by households for residential construction during a particular period of time.

Fixed resources. Resources that in the short run do not vary directly with output; that is, output can be increased (within limits) without using more fixed resources. Typical examples are buildings and machinery.

Flexible (or freely floating) exchange rates. A system in which exchange rates are determined by demand and supply without government intervention in foreign-exchange markets.

Flow. A quantity or activity measured over a period of time, such as the gross national product produced in a particular year or the amount of income earned in a specific month. (*See* Shock.)

Foreign sector. The part of a nation's economy made up of foreign individuals, businesses, and governments that participate in the nation's product, resource, and financial markets.

Fractional reserve banking system. A system in which banks hold reserves that are only a fraction of their deposits.

Frictional unemployment. Unemployment resulting from normal job-search activities, or from imperfect knowl-

edge and imperfect mobility. Although a permanent feature of a dynamic economy, frictional unemployment is temporary for any individual.

Full-employment budget. Government receipts and expenditures that would occur under existing fiscal policies if the economy were producing at its potential GNP level. Changes in the full-employment budget reflect discretionary changes in fiscal policies.

Future value (FV). A sum of money to be received or paid at a future time.

G

General price level. The average price of all goods and services in the economy.

GNP deflator. The ratio of nominal GNP to real GNP expressed as a percentage; a measure of the general price level.

GNP gap. The difference between real GNP and potential GNP for a specific period of time. When positive, it measures the output lost as a result of unemployment.

Government purchases (G). Expenditures by the government sector to purchase final goods; a part of aggregate expenditures.

Gross national product (GNP). A measure of the total market value of all final goods and services produced in the economy during a given period of time.

H

Horizontal equity. A principle of taxation that suggests that individuals in equal economic circumstances should pay an equal amount of taxes.

Horizontal merger. A merger between firms that produce substitute products and that would otherwise be competitors.

Household. Any person or group of people living together and functioning as a single economic unit.

Household theory of labor supply. A theory suggesting that labor supply decisions are made within households, based on considerations of taste and preferences, market wages, nonmarket productivity, and other family resources.

Human capital. The skills, education, training, and experience of individuals.

Human resources. The strength, skills, training, and talents of society's population that can be used to produce goods and services.

I

Impact lag. The delay between when policy actions are taken and when they fully affect aggregate demand.

Imperfect competition. Any market structure that does not have the characteristics of pure competition; monopoly, oligopoly, and monopolistic competition are imperfect competition market structures.

Implicit costs. Opportunity costs for resources that a firm owns and uses; benefits not received from the next best use of the resource. Costs considered in calculating economic profit but not in calculating accounting profit.

Import quota. A limit on the quantity of a particular good that can be imported.

Imports (M). Expenditures by U.S. households, businesses, and governments for goods and services produced in other countries. These expenditures must be deducted from aggregate expenditures in order to measure GNP; they represent aggregate spending that is not used to purchase domestically produced goods.

Import tariff. A tax placed on imported goods.

Incidence of poverty. The percentage of the population that falls into the poverty group by official standards.

Income effect. The change in quantity demanded resulting from a change in real income caused by a change in price.

Income elasticity of demand. A measure of responsiveness of quantity demanded to a change in income; usually expressed as percentage change in quantity demanded divided by percentage change in income.

Increasing-cost industry. An industry in which entry of new firms raises the price of resources and product costs; characterized by an upward sloping long-run supply curve.

Increasing marginal returns. A situation in which each additional unit of a variable resource has a greater marginal product than the previous unit; total product increases at an increasing rate.

Independent variable. In any given relationship, an element that is subject to independent change. A change in the value of an independent variable affects the value of the dependent variable.

Indexation. Adjusting the nominal values of wages, transfer payments, income tax brackets, or other economic variables in direct proportion to changes in the general price level.

Indifference curve. A graphic representation of the indifference set.

Indifference map. A graph displaying several indifference curves representing different levels of satisfaction, or total utility.

Indifference set. A table showing several combinations of goods and services that would give a buyer the same total utility.

Induced consumption. A change in consumption in response to a change in income (holding other factors constant); results in a movement along a consumption line.

Industrial policy. A set of microeconomic policies designed to affect economic growth; includes tax rules, research and development grants, direct subsidies, international trade restrictions, and labor-training programs.

Industrial union. A union of workers sharing a common employer; workers may or may not share a common skill or trade.

Industry. A group of firms producing the same or similar products.

Inferior goods. Goods for which demand varies inversely with income, decreasing as income rises and increasing as income falls—for example, margarine.

Inflation. A sustained upward movement in the general level of prices.

Inflation rate. The annual rate of increase in the price level.

Injunction. A court order prohibiting a defendant, such as a labor union, from engaging in certain practices, such as striking.

In-kind transfers. Noncash government transfers, such as Food Stamps, subsidized housing, and medical care.

Institutional discrimination. Any practices in social institutions that result in differential and inequitable treatment of individuals on the basis of race, sex, age, or some other characteristic not related to economic productivity.

Intangible capital. Technological knowledge and legal rights such as patents and trademarks.

Intensive growth. Economic growth achieved by increasing the productivity of economic resources, that is, by technological progress.

Intercept. The point at which a line on a graph touches one of the axes.

Interest rate. The ratio of the dollars paid in interest charges to total dollars borrowed; usually stated as an annual percentage rate.

Intermediate goods. Products and services that are used to produce other goods and services or are purchased for resale. The value of intermediate goods is excluded from GNP.

Inventory investment. The value of final goods produced in a particular period of time but not sold. The unsold goods are considered to have been "bought" by the businesses that produced them, and thus are counted as part of business investment expenditures.

Investment (I). Expenditures for fixed investment and inventory investment.

Isocost. A curve showing combinations of two resources that result in the same total costs; the slope of an isocost is the ratio of the prices of the two resources.

Isoquant. A curve showing combinations of two resources that will produce the same level of output.

J

Job-search theory. A view of unemployment as a search for information. Unemployed individuals make rational choices, weighing extra benefits of a continued job search (the prospects of finding a better job) against extra costs (accepting a lower paying job).

K

Keynesian theory. The economic propositions of John Maynard Keynes, including the belief that fluctuations in aggregate output are generally caused by changes in private-sector demand. Keynesian economists generally recommend government policies to boost aggregate demand during recessions.

L

Labor federation. An organization composed of several unions that provides services to member unions and seeks through political action to improve the status of its workers.

Labor force. The total number of individuals classified by government statistics as either employed or unemployed.

Labor productivity. The average output per unit of labor input, most often measured as real output per hour of work.

Law of demand. The principle that as the price of any product decreases (increases), the quantity of the product demanded will increase (decrease).

Law of diminishing marginal returns. The principle that beyond a certain point, additional variable resources added to a constant quantity of fixed resources will result in smaller and smaller increases in total product.

Law of diminishing marginal utility. The principle that beyond a certain point, the marginal utility of the last unit declines as more is consumed.

Law of diminishing returns. The proposition that adding labor to a fixed quantity of land and capital will eventually result in smaller and smaller increases in total output if technology is constant.

Law of supply. The principle that as the selling price of any product increases (decreases), the quantity of the product supplied also increases (decreases).

Legal reserves. Reserves held by banks to satisfy legal minimums imposed by the Fed. They include currency held in bank vaults and banks' deposits held at the Fed.

Less-developed countries (LDCs). Nations that have relatively low standards of living, limited industrialization, and minimal education, transportation, and communication systems; collectively known as the Third World.

Liabilities. Claims on assets.

Liquidity. How quickly and inexpensively an asset may be turned into money without risk or loss of value. Money has perfect liquidity; other assets, less liquidity.

Long run. A period of time in which a firm can alter all its resources. In the long run, a firm can change all resources.

Long-run average cost (LRAC). The minimum average total cost for each level of output when a firm can change all its resources.

Long-run equilibrium. A position in which quantity of aggregate output demanded at the current price level equals the economy's potential output: graphically, when the aggregate demand and short-run aggregate supply curves intersect at the potential output level. The position the economy will achieve if wages and prices fully adjust to aggregate demand.

Long-run marginal cost (LRMC). The extra cost for an extra unit of output when all resources can be changed.

Long-run supply curve (LRS). The long-run relationship between price and quantity supplied by all firms.

Lorenz curve. A graphic representation of the actual income distribution obtained by plotting the cumulative percentage of income received against the cumulative percentage of families or individuals. The greater the deviation of the actual Lorenz curve from a diagonal straight line, the greater is the degree of inequality.

Lump-sum tax. A tax, such as the property tax, that is unaffected by the level of aggregate output.

M

M-1. The narrow official definition of money, which includes only currency held by the public and checking deposits.

M-2. A broader official definition of money, including not only currency held by the public and checking deposits (M-1 money) but also savings deposits, small time deposits, money market mutual fund shares, and money market deposit accounts.

Macroeconomics. That level of economic analysis concerned with the activity of the entire economy and the interactions between large sectors of it.

Marginal. A term used by economists to denote *extra* or *additional*.

Marginal cost (MC). The additional cost associated with producing one additional unit of output; calculated as change in total costs divided by change in quantity of goods or services produced (change in total product). Mathematically, MC = Change in TC ÷ Change in Q.

Marginal-cost pricing. A price-setting option for rate regulation whereby price is set where demand equals marginal cost (P = MC). As a result, MSB = MSC, but the price may be too low to allow a normal profit.

Marginal factor cost (MFC). The change in total cost that results from the use of one additional unit of a variable resource.

Marginal product (MP). The extra quantity of goods produced (change in total product) per unit of variable resource added. Mathematically, MP = Change in Q ÷ Change in variable resources.

Marginal propensity to consume (MPC). The ratio of changes in consumption to changes in income; indicates the proportion of any additional income that will be spent on consumption.

Marginal propensity to save (MPS). The ratio of changes in saving to changes in disposable income; shows the proportion of any additional disposable income that will be saved.

Marginal rate of substitution. The quantity of one product that may be sacrificed to obtain one unit of another product for the same total utility; the slope of an indifference curve, or mathematically,

$$\frac{\text{Marginal utility of product A}}{\text{Marginal utility of product B}}$$

Marginal rate of technical substitution. The ratio of marginal products of two substitute resources; the slope of an isoquant measures the marginal rate of technical substitution.

Marginal revenue (MR). The extra revenue obtained from the sale of one extra unit, calculated as

$$\text{Marginal revenue} = \frac{\text{Change in total revenue}}{\text{Change in total product}}$$

Marginal revenue product (MRP). The change in total revenue that results from the use of one additional unit of a variable resource.

Marginal social benefit (MSB). The extra benefit society receives from one additional unit of some good.

Marginal social cost (MSC). The extra cost to society of producing one more unit of some good.

Marginal tax rate. The percentage of additional income that must be paid in taxes; the ratio of additional tax owed to additional income.

Marginal utility (MU). The additional satisfaction derived from consuming one additional unit of a good or service; the increase in total utility associated with a one-unit increase in quantity.

Market. The interaction of buyers (market demand) and sellers (market supply) which determines a price and quantity exchanged.

Market capitalism. An economic system in which most resources are privately owned by individuals and most economic interactions occur in markets.

Market economy. An economy in which households and businesses interact in markets to determine prices and thus answer the fundamental economic questions of what and how much to produce, how to produce it, and to whom to distribute goods and services.

Market equilibrium. A state in which neither buyers nor sellers have any reason to change quantity demanded or supplied; the market in balance, with quantity demanded equal to quantity supplied at the existing market price.

Market failure. Inability of a market to achieve allocative efficiency, technical efficiency, or equity; for example, poorly defined property rights or lack of competition.

Market power. The ability to influence market price.

Market structure. The characteristics of an industry, including number of buyers and sellers, uniqueness of goods and services produced, and ease of entry and exit.

Mature oligopoly. A form of oligopoly in which there is little or no price competition, little or no entry or exit of existing firms, reliance on nonprice competition, predictable responses to economic changes, and mutual tolerance and acceptance among existing rival firms.

Merger. The combining of two or more firms under the control of one firm.

Microeconomics. That level of economic analysis concerned with the activity of individual units of the economy and their interrelationships.

Monetarists. Economists who believe that fluctuations in aggregate output are generally caused by changes in the money supply.

Monetary assets. Bonds or other debt obligations that promise the holders future payments that are fixed in nominal terms.

Monetary policy. Federal Reserve System actions taken to influence the size or growth rate of the money supply.

Money. Items such as coins, paper bills, and checking account deposits that are widely accepted in market exchanges. Any item used as a medium of exchange.

Money supply. The total quantity of money in circulation at any time.

Monopolistic competition. A market structure in which a relatively large number of relatively small firms each produces a somewhat distinctive or differentiated product. Barriers to entry and exit usually are small. The distinctive nature of the products gives each firm a small amount of market power.

Multiplier. The amount that equilibrium GNP will change as a result of a change in autonomous expenditures. Measured as the ratio of the change in equilibrium GNP to the change in autonomous expenditures. The simple multiplier effect, assuming a constant price level, can also be calculated as $1 \div (1 - \text{MPC})$.

N

National debt. The total amount owed by the federal government; the cumulative effect of past budget deficits and surpluses.

National income (NI). Total income earned by the household sector; the sum of wages, rent, interest, and profits. It represents payment for resources used to produce final goods during a particular period of time.

Natural monopoly. An industry in which a single producer, operating the most technically efficient plant, can supply the entire market demand; a result of economies of scale.

Natural rate of unemployment. The unemployment rate achieved when the economy has eliminated all cyclical unemployment; sometimes referred to as the *full-employment* unemployment rate.

Natural resources. The land, water, minerals, climate, and other products of nature that can be used to produce goods and services.

Negative income tax. A system that guarantees a minimum income to the poor through government income transfers, the amount of which depends on how far below the poverty threshold a family's income is.

Net national product (NNP). Gross national product minus depreciation (capital consumption allowance).

New classical macroeconomists. Economists who assume that wages and prices are very flexible, a theoretical approach similar to that of classical economists. Their theories suggest that rational responses to anticipated policy actions will make policies completely ineffective.

Nominal. A term used to identify economic variables measured in terms of current prices.

Nominal GNP. The value of the gross national product measured by current quantities and current prices.

Nominal income. The actual number of dollars of income earned, expressed in terms of current dollars unadjusted for changes in the general price level.

Nominal interest rate. The actual rate of interest in a financial market; includes a premium reflecting the expected rate of inflation. The actual or market interest rate charged for borrowed funds; determines how many dollars must be paid in interest.

Nonactivists. Economists who believe it unnecessary, undesirable, and impractical to employ discretionary monetary and fiscal policies to stabilize the economy. They recommend stable policies—a constant growth in the money supply and a balanced full-employment budget—and reliance on the economy's automatic adjustment mechanism.

Nonprice competition. Competing with other firms using approaches such as advertising and product differentiation instead of changing price.

Normal goods. Goods for which demand varies directly with income, rising as income rises and decreasing as income decreases—for example, steak.

Normal profit. Opportunity cost of owner investment, the minimum level of profit necessary to justify a decision to produce in the long run, or an economic profit of zero; considered an implicit cost when calculating economic profit but ignored when calculating accounting profit.

Normative statement. A statement involving value judgments of what ought to be.

O

Oligopoly. A market structure in which a relatively small number of relatively large firms each produces goods or services that are close substitutes or are somewhat differentiated. Barriers to entry are typically high. Firms must consider the actions and reactions of competitors when making decisions.

Open-market operations. The buying and selling of government securities by the Fed; used to change the quantity of bank reserves and hence the supply of money.

Opportunity cost. The value of the next best option that must be sacrificed when a choice is made.

Opportunity cost of capital. The cost of funds used by a firm for investment, expressed as an annual percentage rate; reflects market interest rates, with allowance for future inflation and the risk involved in the investment.

Origin. The point on a graph representing a zero value for both variables; the intersection of the horizontal and vertical axes, generally the lower left corner of a graph.

P

Partnership. A form of business organization in which two or more individuals share the ownership, profits, and liabilities of the firm.

Patent. The legal right to produce a specified product or to use a specified process exclusively; granted for 17 years in the United States.

Peak. The end of the recovery phase; the point at which real aggregate output reaches its highest level.

Personal income. The total amount of income, before taxes, received by all households from all sources.

Phillips curve. A plot of the relationship between the rate of inflation and the rate of unemployment. Current theory recognizes an inverse short-run relationship but no long-run relationship.

Physical capital. Long-lasting capital resources, such as buildings and machinery, that yield benefits both in the present and in the future.

Planned socialism. An economic system in which most resources are owned by government and their use is controlled by a government plan.

Positive statement. A statement limited to a factual description of what is or what will be.

Potential GNP. The aggregate output that could be produced with the available technology if labor and other economic resources were fully employed.

Poverty threshold. A sliding income scale, adjusted according to family characteristics and the general level of prices, below which poverty is officially considered to exist.

Precautionary motive. Holding money to meet unexpected expenditures; related to money's function as a liquid store of value.

Present value (PV). The current value of money to be received or paid in a future period; the number of dollars that must be invested today at a specified interest rate in order to have a certain sum of money at a particular future time.

Price. The amount of one item that an individual will sacrifice in order to obtain another item and often stated in terms of the quantity of money that must be sacrificed.

Price discrimination. Selling identical goods and services at different prices to different groups of buyers.

Price elastic. A situation in which the percentage change in quantity is larger than the percentage change in price, giving an elasticity coefficient greater than 1 (ignoring the sign).

Price-elasticity coefficient. The number obtained by using the price elasticity formula. When its absolute value (ignoring the sign) is greater than 1, the demand (or supply) is price elastic; when it is less than 1, the demand (or supply) is price inelastic; when it equals 1, the demand (or supply) has unitary elasticity.

Price elasticity of demand. A measure of the response of buyers to a change in price, usually expressed as the percentage change in quantity demanded, divided by the percentage change in price.

Price elasticity of supply. A measure of the response of sellers to a change in price, usually expressed as the percentage change in quantity supplied, divided by the percentage change in price.

Price fixing. Formal agreement among firms in an oligopoly to maintain artificially high prices or to restrict market supply.

Price index. A measure of price level in a given year as a percentage of the price level in some specified base, or reference, year.

Price inelastic. A situation in which the percentage change in quantity is smaller than the percentage change in price, giving an elasticity coefficient less than 1 (ignoring the sign).

Price leadership. A form of oligopoly in which one firm—the leader—initially sets prices and other firms follow with matching increases or decreases. A tacit understanding rather than a formal agreement binds the firms.

Price searcher. Any firm that is not a price taker; a firm that can influence price and must search for the price that maximizes profits.

Price taker. A firm in a purely competitive market; a firm facing a horizontal (perfectly price elastic) demand curve; a firm that can sell all it wants to at the market price but nothing at any higher price. A price taker has zero market power.

Private goods. Goods and services that benefit only those people who purchase them. People who are unwilling or unable to pay for them can be prevented from receiving their benefits.

Private sector. The part of a nation's economy made up of households and businesses.

Product differentiation. The strategy of making a product appear to be different from similar products, regardless of whether it actually is. It may be achieved by varying product design, features and service, or through advertising.

Production function. The relationship between the quantity of resources used and the quantity of goods produced; the maximum amount of goods that can be produced using various combinations of resources and the best available technology.

Production possibilities curve. A curve showing the various combinations of output that an economy can produce with its existing resources when operating at maximum technical efficiency.

Productivity. The relationship between the quantity of goods or services produced and the quantity of a variable resource used.

Product markets. Markets in which businesses sell and households buy goods and services.

Profits. The difference between the total of all revenues received from the sales of goods and the total of all costs of producing those goods.

Progressive tax. A tax for which the average tax rate increases as income increases.

Proportional tax. A tax for which the average tax rate is constant for all income levels.

Proprietorship. A firm in which one person owns all the productive property, receives all the profits, and is personally responsible for all the liabilities.

Public choice theory. An economic theory based on rational choice principles that attempts to explain how choices are made in the public (government) sector.

Public finance. The size and distribution of government spending and taxation at the federal, state, and local levels.

Public goods. Goods and services that cannot benefit one person without benefiting all. People who cannot or will not pay for them cannot be prevented from receiving their benefits.

Public sector. The part of a nation's economy made up of federal, state, and local governments.

Pure competition. A model of a market with a very large number of firms, each producing virtually identical products. Perfect information exists and entry and exit are unrestricted.

Pure monopoly. A market structure in which a single firm produces a product for which there are no close substitutes; entry and exit are very restricted; model used to predict behavior of a firm with significant market power.

Q

Quantity demanded. The amount of a product that consumers are both willing and able to buy at a specified price.

Quantity supplied. The quantity of a product that suppliers are both willing and able to offer for sale at a specified price.

R

Rate base. Term used by rate regulators to refer to a firm's total investment. In average-cost pricing, price is set to allow the firm to earn a normal rate of return on the rate base.

Rate of return. The ratio of profits earned from an investment to total dollars invested.

Rate regulation. Government actions to set prices in markets as an alternative to antitrust action; may take the form of marginal-cost pricing or average-cost pricing.

Rational choice. Selecting among economic alternatives by comparing extra benefits expected to be received with extra costs expected to be incurred; an economic model used to explain the choices made by individuals, businesses, and government.

Rational expectations. An assumption that individuals utilize all available information, including their understanding of the effects of fiscal and monetary policy, in anticipating future economic conditions.

Real. A term used to identify economic variables measured in terms of constant prices of some base year.

Real GNP. The value of the gross national product measured by current quantities and constant prices.

Real GNP per capita. The average quantity of real output produced per person, calculated by dividing real GNP by total population.

Real income. Income expressed in terms of its purchasing power; nominal income adjusted to remove the effects of changes in the general price level.

Real interest rate. The nominal, or actual, rate of interest less the expected rate of inflation. The cost of borrowed funds stated in real terms; reflects the amount of real purchasing power a borrower can expect to pay in interest.

Recession. The phase of the business cycle in which real aggregate output of the economy is decreasing.

Recognition lag. The delay between when a macroeconomic problem occurs and when it is recognized.

Recovery. The phase of the business cycle in which real aggregate output of the economy is increasing.

Regressive tax. A tax for which the average tax rate decreases as income increases.

Relative poverty approach. Poverty defined by an income below some fraction of the average income; focuses on inequality of income.

Relative price. The price of one good in comparison to the prices of other goods.

Required reserve ratio. The minimum portion of deposits that must be legally held as reserves, as set by the Fed.

Reserves. Funds held by banks in order to meet the demands of their depositors and the legal requirements of the Federal Reserve System.

Resource markets. Markets in which households sell and businesses buy resources used to produce goods and services.

Resources. The human, capital, and natural resources that can be used to produce goods and services.

Retained earnings. The portion of a corporation's profits not paid out to its shareholders but retained by the corporation to finance future production.

Right-to-work laws. State laws that prohibit unions from negotiating union-shop provisions in labor–management contracts. The power to enact such laws was granted to the states by the Taft–Hartley Act (1947).

Rule of reason. A legal standard under which the prosecutor must prove not only that an offense has occurred but also that the social welfare will be enhanced by prohibiting, modifying, or punishing the act.

S

Saving (S). The portion of income received by households during a particular period of time that is not spent on final goods.

Saving schedule. A table showing the level of saving for various levels of disposable income.

Say's law. The proposition, popularized by nineteenth-century French economist Jean Baptiste Say, that supply creates its own demand.

Scarcity. The fundamental conflict between unlimited human desires and limited availability of resources.

Shortage. A situation in which quantity demanded exceeds quantity supplied at the existing market price; excess demand.

Short run. A period of time in which a firm cannot alter all its resources. In the short run, a firm can change only variable, not fixed, resources.

Short-run equilibrium. A position in which quantity of aggregate output demanded at the current price level equals quantity supplied; graphically, where the aggregate demand and short-run aggregate supply curves intersect.

Slope. The ratio of the change in the vertical direction to the change in the horizontal direction between two points along a graph of a straight line.

Social benefits. Benefits measured from the perspective of society; include both private benefits and external benefits.

Social costs. Costs measured from the perspective of society; include both private costs and external costs.

Social regulation. Government regulation aimed at correcting for externalities and imperfect information; concerned with safety and quality of goods, accuracy and completeness of available information, and external benefits and costs.

Stagflation. A period of time during which the total output of the economy falls, while the levels of general prices and unemployment rise.

Standard of living. The quantity of wants that can be satisfied, or the quantity of goods and services that can be purchased, with current income.

Stock. (1) Shares of ownership in a corporation. (2) A quantity existing at some moment in time, such as the stock of capital resources or the stock of inventory possessed by the business sector on December 31 of any year. (*See* Flow.)

Structural unemployment. Unemployment resulting from a mismatch in the labor market between the location and skills of unemployed workers, the location and skill requirements of available jobs; may also reflect discrimination. Unlike with frictional unemployment, unemployment for individuals may be prolonged.

Substitutes. Goods that satisfy similar desires and therefore compete for the consumer's dollar. When two goods are substitutes, an increase in the price of one leads to an increase in demand for the other.

Substitution effect. The change in quantity demanded resulting from a change in the price of a product relative to the price of substitute products.

Sunk cost. Cost incurred as a result of a past decision; historical cost that cannot be recovered and that is irrelevant to economic decisions.

Supply. All the quantities of a product that suppliers are both willing and able to offer for sale at every possible price during a specified period of time.

Supply curve. A graphic representation of the supply schedule; the typical supply curve slopes upward and to the right.

Supply function. An algebraic expression showing how quantity supplied is affected by market price and other factors influencing supply.

Supply schedule. A table showing quantities of a product that suppliers are willing and able to offer for sale at various prices during a specified period of time.

Supply shocks. Sharp declines in aggregate supply caused by a decrease in the supply of key resources; may cause a decline in potential output.

Support price. A legal minimum price established by government for a specific market.

Surplus. A situation in which quantity supplied exceeds quantity demanded at the existing market price; excess supply.

T

Tacit collusion. Informal agreement among firms in an oligopoly not to engage in price competition.

Technical efficiency. Producing goods and services for the least possible cost while maintaining full utilization of resources.

Terms of trade. The relative prices of goods and services involved in international trade expressed in physical terms (for example, 5 cases of applesauce per computer).

Time value of money. The difference between the present and future value of money, expressed as an annual percentage rate.

Total costs (TC). The sum of total variable costs and total fixed costs. Mathematically, TC = TVC + TFC.

Total fixed costs (TFC). The sum of all costs associated with a particular quantity of fixed resources; they are typically constant over a given range of total product in the short run.

Total product (TP or Q). The total quantity of goods that can be produced with a given quantity of resources in a specific period of time.

Total revenue (TR). The total number of dollars received from sales, calculated as the product of price and quantity sold, or TR = P × Q.

Total utility. The total amount of satisfaction obtained from all units of a good or service consumed.

Total variable costs (TVC). The sum of all costs for the quantity of variable resources used; they increase as total product increases.

Trade balance (balance on merchandise trade). The difference between the values of exports and imports of goods only (excludes imports and exports of services).

Trade deficit. A negative trade balance; occurs when the value of imports exceeds the value of exports.

Trade surplus. A positive trade balance; occurs when the value of exports exceeds the value of imports.

Transaction cost. The time, effort, and other costs of arranging and negotiating an exchange.

Transactions motive. The desire to hold money in order to make economic transactions, that is, to buy resources and products in economic markets. This motive is related to money's function as a medium of exchange.

Transfer payments. Payments, usually made by government, to individuals for the purpose of redistributing income.

Trough. The end of the recession phase; the point at which real aggregate output reaches its lowest level.

U

Underemployed. Individuals who have jobs but either work part-time when they would prefer full-time work or work at jobs below their capabilities and skills.

Unemployment rate. The number of individuals unemployed, expressed as a percentage of the labor force.

Union. An organization of employees that seeks primarily through collective bargaining with management to secure for its members improvements in wages, hours, and other working conditions.

Union shop. A workplace in which all employees must become members of a labor union within a specified period of time after being hired. Contract provisions establishing a union shop are illegal in states that have right-to-work laws.

Unitary price elasticity. A situation in which the percentage change in quantity demanded (or supplied) equals the percentage change in price or income; the absolute value of the elasticity coefficient is 1.

Utility. A measure of the satisfaction obtained from consuming a good or service.

V

Value of the marginal product (VMP). The value to society of using one additional unit of a variable resource; calculated as the marginal product of the additional unit of resource multiplied by the price of the final product it helps to create; equals the marginal revenue product when the firm sells in a competitive product market.

Variable costs. Costs associated with variable resources; they increase directly with total product in the short run. Examples include costs of labor and materials.

Variable resources. Resources that vary directly with output; that is, any increase in output requires greater use of variable resources. Typical examples are labor and raw materials.

Velocity (V). The average number of times each dollar in the money supply is spent during a specific period of time; calculated as the ratio of nominal GNP to the money supply, that is, V = (P × Q) ÷ Ms.

Vertical equity. A principle of taxation that suggests that individuals in unequal economic circumstances should pay an unequal amount of taxes.

Vertical merger. A merger between firms that would otherwise have a buyer–seller relationship.

Y

Yellow-dog contract. A contract in which employees stipulated that they were not and would not become a member of a labor union; outlawed in the United States by the Norris–LaGuardia Act (1932).

Yield. The interest rate (return) received from the purchase of a financial claim; varies inversely with the price of the financial claim. Market interest rates are yields.

I N D E X

The boldfaced numbers indicate the
pages on which key terms are defined
in the margins.

A

V

Value:
    economic, 535
    market, 533–534
    of money, 511
    social, 539–541
Variables, dependent and independent, 18–19
Velocity (of money), **650**–653
Vertical axis, 19
Vietnam War, 704, 740–741, 749
Voluntary quotas, 836–837
Voluntary unemployment, 564

W

Wage and price controls, 788, 808–810

Wage contracts, 681
Wages. *See also* Income
    in aggregate supply, 669–671
    and contractionary gaps, 584
    and inflation, 749, 788
    during recessions, 704–705
    in Soviet Union, 877
    types of:
        minimum, 66, 734
        nominal (reservation), 671, 680–681, 726–727
        real, 561–565, 671–672, 680
Wallace, Neil, 757
Wants, satisfying. *See* Utility
War on Poverty, 679, 695, 740–741, 749
Wars, national debt during, 693. *See also* Korean War; Vietnam War; World War I; World War II

Wealth, 570, 571, 871. *See also* Income
    real, 664
    stored as money, 619
Wealth of Nations, The (Smith), 102
Weighted averages, 528
Welfare programs, 698
West German economic growth, 779
Whitt, Joseph A., Jr., 823
Work and economic growth, 35. *See also* Employment *entries*
Workers, discouraged, 504
World Bank, 775
World War I, 858
World War II, 571, 693, 777, 778, 809

Y

Yields (returns), **648**